lonely planet

Prague
& the Czech Republic

Prague
p32

Bohemia
p173

Moravia
p225

Mark Baker, Neil Wilson

PLAN YOUR TRIP

Welcome to Prague & the Czech Republic ... 4

Prague & the Czech Republic Map..... 6

Prague & the Czech Republic's Top 12 8

Need to Know 14

First Time the Czech Republic 16

What's New 18

If You Like.... 19

Month by Month....... 21

Itineraries 23

Travel with Children.... 25

Eat & Drink Like a Local........... 27

Regions at a Glance.... 30

MASOPUST CARNIVAL P21

WRANGEL/GETTY IMAGES ©

ON THE ROAD

PRAGUE............ 32

Neighbourhoods at a Glance 34

Sights.................. 44

Activities 101

Tours.................. 103

Festival & Events 109

Sleeping............... 109

Eating................. 121

Drinking & Nightlife..... 142

Entertainment.......... 157

Shopping.............. 163

BOHEMIA...........173

Top Sights........... 174

Kutná Hora 179

Terezín 182

České Budějovice..... 185

Český Krumlov 192

Třeboň 198

Tábor................ 201

Plzeň................205

Karlovy Vary 211

Mariánské Lázně...... 219

JORISVO/SHUTTERSTOCK ©

Contents

MORAVIA......... 225
Brno 227
Telč 235
Třebíč 237
Mikulov 238
Valtice-Lednice 244
Znojmo 246
Olomouc 248
Kroměříž 254

UNDERSTAND

Prague & the Czech Republic Today 258
History 260
Czech Life 269
Arts in the Czech Republic 273
Architecture 278
The Czech Republic on Page & Screen 282
A Nation of Beer Lovers 286

ST. VITUS CATHEDRAL P42

SURVIVAL GUIDE

Directory A–Z 290
Transport 297
Language 304
Index 311
Map Legend 319

TOP SIGHTS

Prague Castle 36
St Vitus Cathedral 42
Charles Bridge 54
Prague Jewish Museum 66
Old Town Hall & Astronomical Clock 68
Vyšehrad Citadel 104
Karlštejn Castle 174
Konopiště Chateau 176

Welcome to Prague & the Czech Republic

Since the fall of communism in 1989, the Czech Republic – and its capital in particular – has evolved into one of Europe's most popular travel destinations.

Prague, Cradle of Culture

Everyone who visits the Czech Republic starts with Prague, the cradle of Czech culture and one of Europe's most fascinating cities. Prague offers a near-intact medieval core of Gothic architecture that can transport you back 500 years – the 14th-century Charles Bridge, connecting two historic neighbourhoods across the Vltava River, with the castle ramparts and the spires of St Vitus Cathedral rising above, is one of the classic sights of world travel. But the city is not just about history; it's a vital urban centre with a rich array of cultural offerings, and a newly emerging foodie scene.

Castles & Chateaux

The Czech Republic's location at the heart of the former Austro-Hungarian Empire has seen a long history of raiding tribes, conquering armies and triumphant dynasties. This turbulent past has left a legacy of hundreds of castles – everywhere you look there seems to be a turreted fortress perched above a town, or a summer palace lazing peacefully amid manicured parkland. The number and variety of castles is simply awe-inspiring – everything from grim Gothic ruins clinging to a dizzy pinnacle of rock, to majestic, baroque mansions filled with the finest furniture that Europe's artisans could provide.

Folklore & Tradition

The Czech Republic may be a modern, forward-thinking nation riding into the future on the back of the EU and NATO, but it is also a country rich in tradition. This is most apparent in South Bohemia and Moravia, where a still-thriving folk culture sparks into life during the summer festival season. During this time, communities from Český Krumlov to Telč to Mikulov don traditional garb, pick up their musical instruments – and wine glasses – and sing and dance themselves silly, animating ancient traditions in one of the best examples of 'living history' in the Czech Republic.

Where Beer Is God

The best beer in the world just got better. Since the invention of Pilsner Urquell in 1842, the Czechs have been famous for producing some of the world's finest brews. But the internationally famous brand names – Urquell, Staropramen and Budvar – have been equalled, and even surpassed, by a bunch of regional Czech beers and microbreweries that are catering to a renewed interest in traditional brewing. Never before have Czech pubs offered such a wide range of ales – names you'll now have to get your head around include Kout na Šumavě, Svijanský Rytíř and Velkopopovický Kozel.

Why I Love Prague & the Czech Republic

By Neil Wilson, Writer

Well, there's the beer. Not only did the Czechs invent the best beer in the world, they've been reinventing it over the last decade with a wave of innovative new microbreweries. And the history. If you want to learn about European history, you'll find it all here compressed into an easily digested package – from Good King Wenceslas and the Defenestration of Prague to the Habsburg empire, two world wars, the Cold War and the Velvet Revolution. Then there's cubist architecture, weird art and the Czechs' deliciously dark sense of humour. And did I mention the beer?

For more about our writers, see p320

Above: Old Town Square (p68), Prague

Prague & the Czech Republic

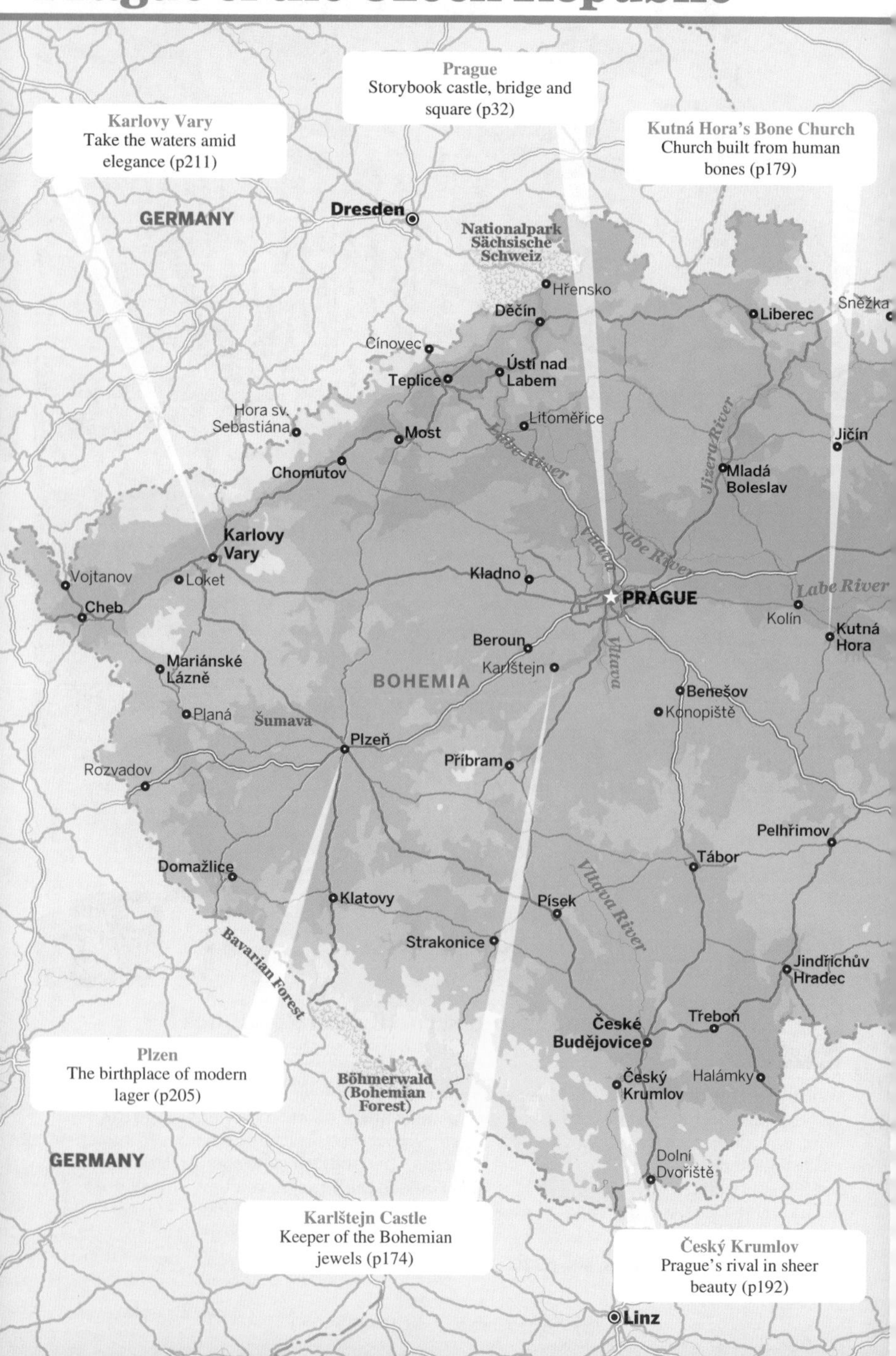

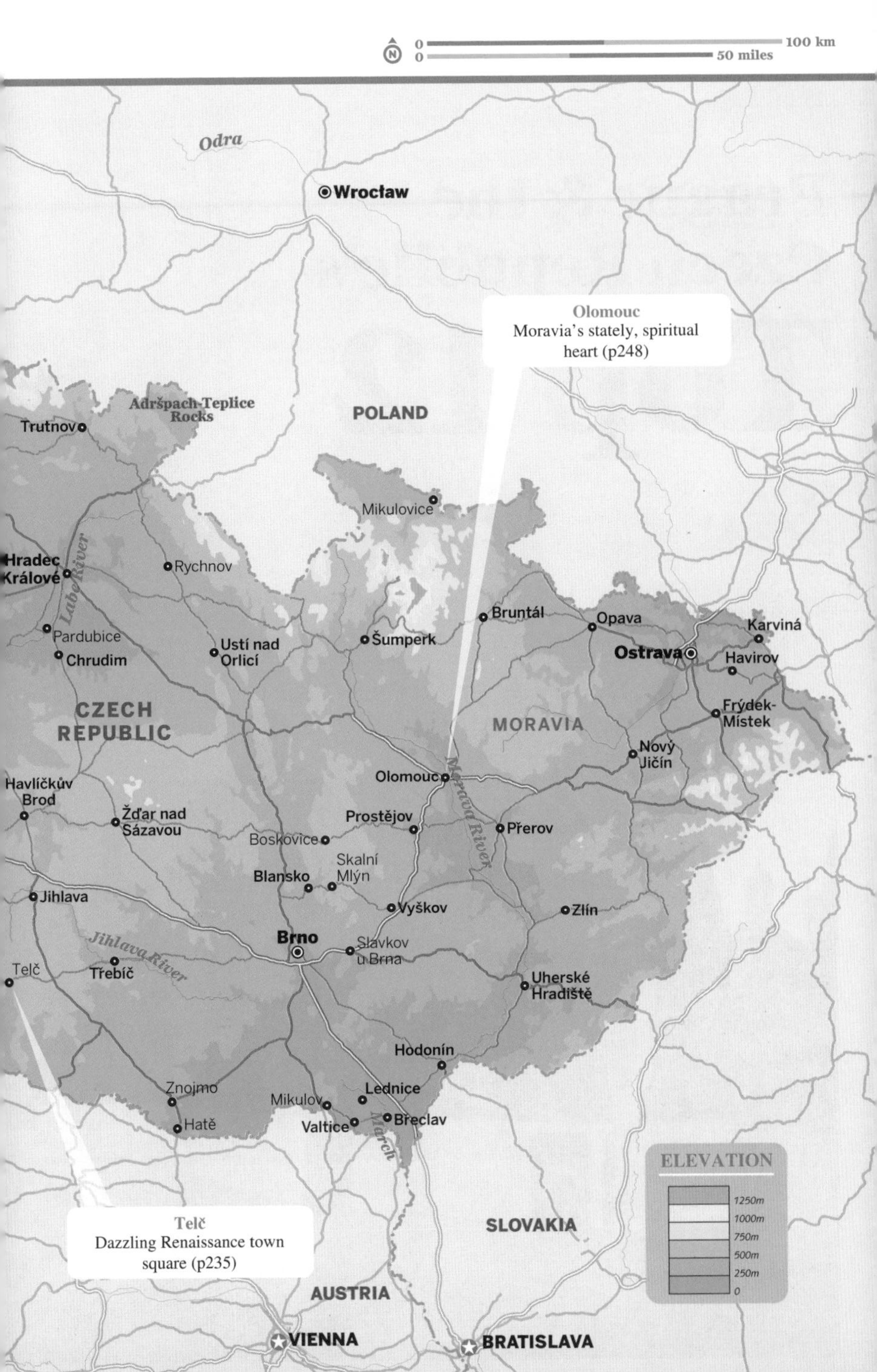

0
100 km
0
50 miles
Odra
Wrocław
Olomouc
Moravia's stately, spiritual heart (p248)
Adršpach-Teplice Rocks
POLAND
Trutnov
Mikulovice
Hradec Králové
Labe River
Rychnov
Bruntál
Opava
Karviná
Pardubice
Ustí nad Orlicí
Šumperk
Ostrava
Havirov
Chrudim
Frýdek-Místek
CZECH REPUBLIC
MORAVIA
Nový Jičín
Olomouc
Morava River
Havlíčkův Brod
Žďar nad Sázavou
Prostějov
Přerov
Boskovice
Skalní Mlýn
Blansko
Jihlava
Vyškov
Zlín
Jihlava River
Brno
Slavkov u Brna
Telč
Třebíč
Uherské Hradiště
Hodonín
Znojmo
Lednice
Mikulov
Hatě
Valtice
Břeclav
March
ELEVATION
1250m
1000m
750m
500m
250m
0
SLOVAKIA
Telč
Dazzling Renaissance town square (p235)
AUSTRIA
VIENNA
BRATISLAVA

Prague & the Czech Republic's Top 12

1

Counting Statues on Charles Bridge

1 Whether you visit alone in the early morning mist or shoulder your way through the afternoon crowds, crossing Charles Bridge (p54) is the quintessential Prague experience. Built in 1357, its 16 elegant arches withstood wheeled traffic for 500-odd years – thanks, legend claims, to eggs mixed into the mortar – until it was made pedestrian-only after WWII. By day, the famous baroque statues stare down with stony indifference on a fascinating parade of buskers, jazz bands and postcard sellers; at dawn, they regain something of the mystery and magic their creators sought to capture.

Gawking at Prague Castle

2 A thousand years of history is cradled within the walls of Prague's hilltop castle (p36), a complex of churches, towers, halls and palaces that is almost a village in its own right. This is the cultural and historical heart of the Czech Republic, comprising not only collections of physical treasures such as the golden reliquaries of St Vitus Treasury and the Bohemian crown jewels, but also the sites of great historic events such as the murder of St Wenceslas and the Second Defenestration of Prague.

LIANEM/SHUTTERSTOCK ©

2

MINIKHAN/SHUTTERSTOCK ©

Prague's Old Town Square

3 Despite the swarms of tourists, crowded pavement cafes and over-the-top commercialism, it's impossible not to enjoy the spectacle of Prague's premier public space (p68): tour leaders thrusting through the crowds gathered to watch the Astronomical Clock; students handing out flyers for a drama production; middle-aged couples in rain jackets and sensible shoes, frowning at pink-haired, leather-clad punks; and a bored-looking guy with a placard advertising a museum of torture instruments. Verily, all of human life is here.

Renaissance Splendour of Český Krumlov

4 This sleepy, southern Bohemian town (p192) is arguably the Czech Republic's only other world-class, must-see sight aside from Prague. None other than *National Geographic* has dubbed this former medieval stronghold one of the 'world's greatest places', and once you catch a glimpse of the rocky, rambling Renaissance castle with its mesmerising multicoloured tower, you'll feel the appeal. Yes, this really is that fairy-tale town the tourist brochures promised.

3

4

TEQUIERO/SHUTTERSTOCK ©

TICHR/SHUTTERSTOCK ©

Kutná Hora's Bone Church

5 In the 14th century Kutná Hora (p179) rivalled Prague as the most important town in Bohemia, growing rich on the veins of silver ore that laced the rocks beneath it. Today it's an attractive town with several fascinating and unusual historical attractions. Get an insight into the life of a medieval miner on a tour of a former silver mine, or marvel at the ingenuity of the man who created art out of human remains at the grimly fascinating 'bone church' of Sedlec. Sedlec Ossuary (p179)

Fairy-Tale Karlštejn Castle

6 Karlštejn Castle (p174) was born of a grand pedigree, starting life in 1348 as a hideaway for the crown jewels and treasury of the Holy Roman Emperor, Charles IV. Perched high on a crag overlooking the Berounka River, this cluster of turrets, sheer walls and looming towers is as immaculately maintained as it is powerfully evocative. The brightest star among the constellation of castles that lie scattered across Bohemia, Karlštejn will fulfil even your wildest expectations as to what a Central European fairy-tale castle should look like.

Modern Art at Veletržní Palác

7 In 1996 the huge, grimly functionalist Veletržní Palác (p94), built in 1928 to house international trade fairs, became the new home of the National Gallery's museum of 20th- and 21st-century art. This vast, ocean-liner-like building can now lay claim to being one of Prague's best (and biggest) galleries, including works by Van Gogh, Picasso, Klimt, Mucha and the impressionists, as well as masterpieces by Czech expressionist, cubist and surrealist artists, notably the stunning 1930s paintings of Prague by Austrian artist Oskar Kokoschka.

EURASIA/ROBERTHARDING/GETTY IMAGES ©

JUSTINAS GALINIS/SHUTTERSTOCK ©

Telč

8 Telč (p235) is a quiet and pretty town, a good place to relax by the waterside with a book and a glass of wine. The old town, ringed by medieval fish ponds and unspoilt by modern buildings, is a Unesco World Heritage Site with a sprawling, cobble-stoned town square where you can stroll along Gothic arcades and admire elegant Renaissance facades. In the soft light of a summer evening, when the tour groups have gone, it's a peaceful, magical place where photographers and artists find endless inspiration.

Czech Beer

9 'Where beer is brewed, life is good', according to an old Czech proverb. Which means that life in the Czech Republic must be very good indeed, as the country is awash in breweries both large and small. Czech beer has been famous for its quality and flavour since the invention of Pilsner Urquell (p207) in 1842, but in recent years there has been a renaissance of microbreweries and craft beers, and you can now enjoy everything from classic *ležák* (pale lager) to *kvasnicové* (yeast beer) and *kávové pivo* (coffee-flavoured beer).

Underrated Olomouc

10 Olomouc (p248), set in a broad, fertile stretch of the Morava River basin, is one of the Czech Republic's most underrated cities. Legend says it was founded by Julius Caesar. Today it is a youthful, laid-back university town, friendly and cheap, with cobbled streets and the largest trove of historical architecture outside Prague – and hardly a tourist in sight. Despite a somewhat bedraggled, sooty outskirts, its historical centre is certainly northern Moravia's most beautiful town. Don't forget to try the cheese, *Olomoucký sýr,* reputedly the smelliest in the country.

Prague's Jewish Museum

11 The slice of Staré Město bounded by Kaprova, Dlouhá and Kozí streets is home to the remains of the once-thriving mini-town of Josefov, Prague's former Jewish ghetto. The museum (p66) encompasses half a dozen ancient synagogues, a ceremonial hall and former mortuary, and the powerful and melancholic Old Jewish Cemetery. These exhibits tell the often tragic and moving story of Prague's Jewish community, from the 16th-century creator of the Golem, Rabbi Loew, to the horrors of Nazi persecution.

Karlovy Vary

12 Karlovy Vary (p211) is the oldest of the Bohemian spas, and probably the third-most popular tourist city in the Czech Republic. It's also the most beautiful of the 'big three' spas – most of the present buildings date from the late 19th and early 20th centuries, a visual feast of 'neo' styles and art nouveau. The various spa treatments are not for drop-in visitors, but you're free to sample the sulphurous spring waters till your teeth float. Many locals attribute any sense of well-being to the so-called '13th spring', the local Becherovka herb liqueur.

11

12

Need to Know

For more information, see Survival Guide (p289)

Currency

Czech crown (Koruna česká; Kč)

Language

Czech

Visas

Generally not needed for stays of up to 90 days.

Money

The currency is the Czech crown (*Koruna česká*, or Kč). Euros do not circulate. ATMs are widely available, and credit cards are accepted almost everywhere.

Mobile Phones

The Czech Republic uses the GSM 900/1800 system, the same system used around Europe, though not compatible with most mobile phones in North America or Japan (though many mobiles have multiband phones that will work).

Time

Central European Time (GMT/UTC plus one hour)

When to Go

Apr-May

➡ Trees begin to bud the first week of April and by May, towns and cities are in full bloom. The Prague Spring Festival begins in mid-May, so buy tickets and book hotel rooms well in advance. Easter weekend can bring glorious sunshine but also troves of travellers.

Sep-Oct

➡ Prague comes back to life after the summer break and the concert season resumes in earnest. There's still plenty of light and sun to get in a full day of sightseeing. The weather is particularly lovely for strolling in West Bohemia's spa towns.

Dec

➡ The holiday season kicks off on the 5th of the month, the eve of St Nicholas Day (Sv Mikuláš), when kids dress up as angel, devil or St Nick himself. Enjoy a cup of svařák (mulled wine) at Christmas markets in town squares across the country.

Daily Budget

Budget: less than €70

- Dorm bed: €12
- Self-catering and lunch specials: €12
- Admission to major tourist attractions: €10

Midrange: €70–180

- Double room: €100–140
- Three-course dinner in casual restaurant: €25
- Concert ticket: €10–30

Top End: more than €170

- Double room in luxury hotel: €230
- Seven-course tasting menu in top restaurant: €90
- Private guided tour of Prague with driver: €200

Advance Planning

Three months before Book accommodation if visiting in high season. Check the Prague Spring or Dvořák Festival programs and book tickets.

One month before Reserve tables at top-end restaurants, and buy tickets online for weekend visits to Karlštejn Castle.

One week before Make Friday- or Saturday-night reservations for any restaurants you don't want to miss. Check website programs for art galleries, jazz clubs and music venues.

Useful Websites

Living Prague (www.livingprague.com) Insider guide to the city by a British expat.

Lonely Planet (www.lonelyplanet.com/prague) Destination information, hotel bookings, traveller forum and more.

Prague Events Calendar (www.pragueeventscalendar.com) Covers music, entertainment, culture, sport etc.

Prague City Tourism (www.prague.eu) Official tourist information website.

CzechTourism (www.czechtourism.com) Official tourist information for the Czech Republic.

IDOS (http://jizdnirady.idnes.cz) Train and bus timetables, and fares for the Czech Republic.

Arriving in the Czech Republic

Václav Havel Airport Prague (p297) Buses to metro stops Nádraží Veleslavín (No 119) and Zličín (No 100) depart every 10 minutes from stops outside the arrivals terminal (32Kč). A taxi to the centre costs 500Kč.

Praha hlavní nádraží (p299) Prague's main train station is in the centre, a short walk from Wenceslas Square, and accessible by metro line C (red).

Florenc bus station (p298) International buses arrive here, just east of Prague centre, with metro and tram links to the rest of the city.

Car The Czech Republic is surrounded by EU Schengen countries; there are no passport checks on the border. Prague is an easy drive from many major cities.

Getting Around

The Czech Republic has a comprehensive network of buses and trains, though a car is the easiest way to cover ground quickly. For getting around Prague, the centre is easily managed on foot (though be sure to wear comfortable shoes).

Walking Central Prague is compact, and individual neighbourhoods are easily explored on foot.

Tram Extensive network; best way to get around shorter distances between neighbourhoods.

Metro Fast and frequent, good for visiting outlying areas or covering longer distances.

Bus Not much use in the city centre, except when travelling to/from the airport; operates in areas not covered by tram or metro.

Taxi Relatively cheap but prone to rip-off drivers.

Sleeping

Gone are the days when Prague was a cheap destination. The Czech capital now ranks alongside most Western European cities when it comes to the quality, range and price of hotels. Accommodation ranges from cosy, romantic hotels set in historic townhouses to the new generation of funky design hotels and hostels. Book as far in advance as possible (especially during festival season in May, and at Easter and Christmas/New Year).

Useful Websites

Mary's Travel & Tourist Service (p290) Friendly, efficient agency offering private rooms, apartments and hotels in Prague.

Prague Apartments (p290) Online service with comfortable, Ikea-furnished flats.

Stop City (p290) Specialises in apartments, private rooms and pensions in the city centre, Vinohrady and Žižkov areas.

For much more on **getting around**, see p300

First Time the Czech Republic

For more information, see Survival Guide (p289)

Checklist

- Make sure your passport is valid for at least six months after your arrival date.
- Inform your debit-/credit-card company of your intended travel dates and destination.
- Arrange for appropriate travel insurance.
- Contact your mobile (cell) phone provider to inquire about roaming charges or getting an international plan.

What to Pack

- European two-pin electrical adapter.
- When there, consider buying a cheap extension cord with multiple sockets – lots of tourist accommodation is sadly lacking in electrical outlets.
- Comfortable walking shoes – Czech cities are best appreciated on foot.
- Umbrella and/or packable waterproof jacket.
- A small day-pack (the smaller the better to avoid having to check it when visiting museums).

Top Tips for Your Trip

- Parking can be a pain in many Czech towns – follow signs to main tourist car parks and walk into the centre rather than risk cruising narrow one-way streets in the hope of finding a space.
- Make your first stop in town the tourist office, and ask for a street map. It's the easiest way to make sense of the often random medieval layouts of many Czech towns.
- Try to visit popular sights – especially ones that are day-trip destinations from Prague – early or late in the day to avoid the worst of the crowds.
- Most castles and chateaux are only accessible by guided tour. Tours in English are more expensive and less frequent than Czech tours – consider taking the latter and asking for an *anglický text* (a printed script in English).

What to Wear

Most Czechs are pretty style-conscious and take pleasure in looking good. Folk here still dress up for dinner, and as for going to the opera in anything but your best, well, you must be a tourist.

Pack layers of clothing – Czech weather can be fickle, with thunderstorms and cool spells even in summer. In spring and autumn, a light trench jacket and a small umbrella will mean you're prepared for the odd shower. In winter, bring a warm coat, hat and gloves to ward off the subzero temperatures, and footwear that can cope with snow and ice.

Sleeping

Accommodation in the Czech Republic runs the gamut from summer campsites to family pensions to hotels at all price levels. Places that pull in international tourists – Prague, Karlovy Vary and Český Krumlov – are the most expensive and beds can be hard to find during peak periods, but there's rarely any problem finding a place to stay in smaller towns.

Money

ATMs are everywhere, and will generally accept Visa, MasterCard and other major debit and credit cards. There is nearly always a cash withdrawal fee (around 2%) for foreign cards. Many Prague ATMs dispense 2000Kč notes, which are hard to change in shops or pubs.

Most hotels accept credit cards, but a fair number of restaurants, shops and other businesses do not. Some businesses will have a minimum purchase requirement (usually around 200Kč) before they will accept a card payment.

To exchange cash, it's best to use a bank. Avoid the private exchange booths *(směnárna)*, which often involve incurring costly, hidden fees. Never change money on the black market. It is always a scam.

Bargaining

Bargaining is rare in all instances except perhaps at a junk or flea market. Normally you're expected to pay the stated price.

Tipping

Not a traditional tipping culture, though service workers in contact with foreign visitors will expect something.

➡ **Hotels** Tip the bellman at top-end hotels 20Kč to 50Kč per large bag for assistance; gratuity for cleaning staff is at your discretion.

➡ **Pubs** Not expected, though you can round up to the nearest 10Kč if the service is good.

➡ **Restaurants** For decent service 10%.

➡ **Taxis** Not expected, though you can round up to the nearest 10Kč for good service.

Language

English is mandatory in schools and widely understood. Most important signage (eg on public transport) is bilingual. That said, older people, especially outside of tourist areas, may only have German or Russian as a second language. Generally speaking, however, it's possible to enjoy a visit without knowing a word of Czech, but learning a few basic phrases, if only hello, goodbye, please and thank you, will ensure a warmer reception in restaurants and pubs.

Etiquette

➡ **Greetings** It's customary to say *dobrý den* (good day) when entering a shop, cafe or pub, and to say *na shledanou* (goodbye) when you leave. When meeting people for the first time, a firm handshake, for both men and women, is the norm.

➡ **Visiting** If you're invited to someone's home, bring flowers or a small gift for your host, and remove your shoes when you enter the house.

➡ **Manners** On the tram and metro, it's good manners to give up a seat for an elderly or infirm passenger.

➡ **Beer** Never pour the dregs of your previous glass of beer into a newly served one. This is considered to be the behaviour of barbarians.

MATT MUNRO/LONELY PLANET ©

Klášterní Pivovar Strahov (p142), Prague

What's New

Prague's Karlín

Devastated by the floods of 2002, Prague's Karlín district has been slowly regenerating ever since, but in the last couple of years it has really begun to blossom into a desirable neighbourhood, with its combination of old art-nouveau apartment blocks, leafy squares and new wave of modern restaurants and wine bars.

Castle Security Checks

Security checks involving bag searches and body scans were introduced at entrances to the Prague Castle complex in summer 2016, resulting in queues of up to an hour at busy times. Don't forget to factor this in when you visit. (p36)

Food Paradise on Dlouhá Street

Prague's conversion to the foodie cult is epitomised by the new Gurmet Pasáž Dlouhá, which is lined with artisan food shops, cafes and restaurants. (p163)

Shrine to Apple Cult

The new Stáre Město Apple Museum claims to be the world's biggest private collection of Apple computers and other hardware. Devotees, and there are many, will want to make the pilgrimage. (p75)

More & More Microbrews

Look out Pilsner Urquell – in the last five years the number of microbreweries in the Czech Republic has increased exponentially, and the quota in Prague has more than doubled.

Karlštejn Bike Adventure

The popularity of Biko Adventures cycling tours to Karlštejn has led to the creation of this excellent day trip for noncyclists. (p300)

David Černý's 'K'

The shiny Quadrio shopping mall that has taken shape above Národní třída metro station conceals the newest of David Černý's public artworks, K – an ever-changing stack of rotating metal discs that form and reform the head of quintessential Prague writer Franz Kafka. (p83)

Prague Metro Extended

The expansion of Prague's metro system continues with the opening of a new stretch of line A (green on the maps), extending west from Dejvice to Nemocnice Motol. The No 119 airport bus now terminates at Nádraží Veleslavín station.

For more recommendations and reviews, see lonelyplanet.com/czech-republic

If You Like...

Castles & Chateaux

Prague Castle The world's biggest ancient castle, and the cradle of Czech culture. (p36)

Archbishop's Chateau Kroměříž's Unesco World Heritage Site is a superbly preserved example of an 18th-century princely residence. (p255)

Hluboká Chateau An over-the-top confection of neo-Gothic frivolity modelled on England's Windsor Castle. (p189)

Český Krumlov State Castle An almost impossibly picturesque castle and its frescoed tower perched high above a medieval streetscape. (p194)

Telč Chateau A sumptuous Renaissance residence lodged amid beautiful tended gardens. (p235)

Karlštejn Castle The archetypal fairy-tale castle straight out of Hans Christian Andersen's imagination. (p174)

Lednice Chateau A massive neo-Gothic chateau with splendid interiors and extensive gardens. (p244)

Food & Wine

Taste of Prague Fantastic food tour of Prague's finest eating places, with a side of Czech history. (p107)

Mikulov Wine Trail Hop on a bike and explore the wineries of South Moravia on this waymarked and educational trail. (p240)

Třeboň's fish restaurants Třeboň is famous for its freshwater fish restaurants, where you can sample carp, pike, eel and other species. (p200)

Olomouc This provincial North Moravia town has an underrated restaurant scene and is famous for its smelly local cheese. (p252)

National Wine Centre The cellars of Valtice Chateau offer excellent wine-tasting sessions where you can learn all about Czech wines. (p245)

Museums

National Technical Museum This fascinating collection of planes, trains and automobiles is a dazzling presentation of the country's industrial heritage. (p94)

Czech Silver Museum Don a hard hat and overalls and join a guided tour of the old silver mines that lie beneath Kutná Hora's streets. (p179)

Museum of Romani Culture Artefacts, videos and musical recordings showcase the underappreciated culture of the Roma community. (p230)

Techmania Science Centre A former factory houses this family-friendly interactive science centre. (p208)

Marionette Museum The age-old Bohemian tradition of puppetry is lovingly documented in this museum in Český Krumlov. (p194)

South Bohemian Motorcycle Museum The former Czechoslovakia was famous for its Jawa motorbikes and there are plenty of vintage models on display here. (p185)

Beer

Pilsner Urquell Brewery This is the one that everyone wants to see, the place where pilsner-style lager was invented in 1842. (p207)

Staropramen Brewery Prague's only surviving large-scale brewery offers a tour that covers the century-old history of brewing on this site. (p111)

Brewery Museum Plzeň's brewery museum tells the tale of beer-making in Bohemia in the days before Pilsner Urquell was a thing. (p207)

Budweiser Budvar Brewery Fountainhead of the original Budweiser beer, and still wrangling over the name. (p185)

GRAPHIA/SHUTTERSTOCK ©

Lednice Chateau (p244), Lednice

Chodovar Brewery Are they taking things too far? Not only can you sample the beer here, but you can soak away your aches and pains in a 'beer spa'. (p222)

Regent Brewery Visit the birthplace of South Bohemia's second-favourite beer (p199; after Budvar).

Jewish Interest

Prague Jewish Museum This cluster of six monuments, plus a 13th-century synagogue, is a poignant monument to Prague's Jewish community. (p66)

New Jewish Cemetery This vast graveyard in Prague is most famous as the last resting place of writer Franz Kafka. (p91)

Terezín Former WWII concentration camp, and a sobering memorial to the horrors of the Holocaust. (p182)

Třebíč A Unesco World Heritage Site, Třebíč's old towns contain the best-preserved Jewish ghetto in Europe. (p237)

Great Synagogue Plzeň's great synagogue is the third-largest in the world, after Jerusalem and Budapest. (p207)

Mikulov Better known as the centre of Moravian wine country, Mikulov once had an important Jewish community. (p238)

Offbeat Attractions

Sedlec Ossuary One of the Czech Republic's best-known attractions, a church crypt housing artwork fashioned from thousands of human bones. (p179)

Znojmo Underground Explore parts of the 27km of manmade tunnels beneath the town, in places crawling on hands and knees. (p246)

Singing Fountain Coloured lights and orchestrated water spouts dance along to Celine Dion in Mariánské Lázně. (p219)

Underground Plzeň Once used for storing beer, these hand-excavated tunnels and chambers date back to the 14th century. (p207)

Graphite Mine A clanking electric train carries you deep into the subterranean world where pencil leads come from. (p194)

Capuchin Monastery The highlights of Brno's monastery tour are the desiccated corpses of 18th-century monks and abbots. (p229)

Month by Month

TOP EVENTS

Easter Monday, March or April

Prague Spring, May

Karlovy Vary Film Festival, July

Český Krumlov International Music Festival, July

Dvořák Prague International Music Festival, September

January

Days are short – the sun sets around 4.30pm in mid-January – but post–New Year accommodation prices are the cheapest you'll find, ideal for that romantic getaway in a cosy hotel with an open fireplace.

Three Kings' Day (Svátek Tří králů)

On 6 January, Three Kings' Day (also known as Twelfth Night) marks the formal end of the Christmas season. The Czechs celebrate with carol-singing, bell-ringing and gifts to the poor.

February

The frost can be cruel in February, with temperatures below -10°C, so wrap up well. But the Czech countryside looks mighty pretty in the snow.

Masopust

Once banned by the communists, street parties, fireworks, concerts and revelry mark the Czech version of carnival. Celebrations start on the Friday before Shrove Tuesday (aka Mardi Gras), and end with a masked parade through the town or village.

March

The first buds of spring begin to green the countryside, and the Easter holidays bring Easter markets, hand-painted Easter eggs, and the first tourist influx of the year.

Easter Monday (Pondělí velikonoční)

Mirthful spring! Czech boys chase girls and swat them on the legs with willow switches decked with ribbons, the girls respond with gifts of hand-painted eggs, then everyone parties. The culmination of several days of spring-cleaning, cooking and visiting family and friends.

Febiofest

This festival (www.febiofest.cz) of film, TV and video features new works by international film-makers. It kicks off in Prague then continues throughout the rest of the Czech Republic.

April

The weather transforms from shivers to sunshine. By the end of the month town squares are covered with outdoor cafe tables, and peak tourist season begins.

Burning of the Witches (Pálení čarodějnic)

This Central European, pre-Christian festival (known as *Walpurgisnacht* in German) features the burning of bonfires, especially on hilltops, all over the country. It's held on the night of 30 April.

May

May is Prague's busiest and most beautiful month, with trees and gardens in full blossom, and a string of major festivals. Book accommodation well in advance, and expect to pay top dollar.

☆ Prague Spring (Pražské jaro)

Running from 12 May to 3 June, this international music festival is Prague's most prestigious event, with classical music concerts held in theatres, churches and historic buildings. (p108)

June

Something of a shoulder season, June promises great weather for beer gardens and river cruises without the May festival crowds or the hordes of student backpackers who arrive in Prague and Český Krumlov in July and August.

☆ Prague Fringe Festival

This nine-day festival of international theatre, dance, comedy and music, inspired by the innovative Edinburgh Fringe, takes place in late May/early June. Hugely popular with visitors and now pulling in more and more locals. (p109)

Festival of Songs, Olomouc

A four-day international festival (www.festamusicale.com) of choral music, held at the beginning of June.

July

Most of the country swelters in summer, so pack some lightweight clothes and opt for accommodation with air-conditioning.

☆ Karlovy Vary International Film Festival

The Czech Republic's top film festival usually attracts a handful of film stars, and the town's hotels are full to the brim. (p216)

☆ Český Krumlov International Music Festival

Krumlov's most important cultural event is this month-long celebration of classical music, with a nod to other genres such as folk, pop and jazz. (p197)

August

Hot and sticky weather continues. Many Praguers leave the city for holidays, and hotel rates fall.

☆ Czech Motorcycle Grand Prix

Brno's autodrome buzzes with excitement as international motorcycling stars line up for this major event (www.automotodrombrno.cz/grand-prix). The city is mobbed for the weekend.

September

The hot and humid summer weather mellows out as September approaches, and the hordes of visiting backpackers, students and school groups thin out, making this a great month to visit.

☆ Dvořák Prague International Music Festival

Two weeks in September are given over to Prague's second-most-popular music festival (www.dvorakovapraha.cz) after Prague Spring, a celebration of the works of the Czech Republic's most famous classical composer, with a program of performances by the world's top orchestras, chamber ensembles and soloists.

Znojmo Wine Festival

Moravia's biggest annual festival is dedicated to wine. In addition to wine tastings, there are musical performances, parades and general merriment scattered all around town. (p247)

December

Cold and dark it may be, but a warming glass of *svařák* (mulled wine) will set you up to enjoy the Christmas markets and New Year celebrations in cities across the Czech Republic. Expect peak season hotel prices in Prague.

Mikuláš (St Nicholas Day)

On the night of 5 December, all over the country, you'll see families dressed up as Mikuláš, Anděl a Čert (St Nicholas, the Angel and the Devil), dishing out treats to children who have been good (bad children get potatoes or coal!), marking the start of the Christmas season.

Itineraries

Prague in Four Days

For the first day, wander through the courtyards of **Prague Castle**, then spend the morning visiting **St Vitus Cathedral** and the castle grounds. Descend from the castle to Malá Strana along Nerudova street, and stop to admire the baroque beauty of **St Nicholas Church**. As day fades, stroll across Charles Bridge in the evening light. Start the second day in the **Old Town Square**; after seeing the **Astronomical Clock**, climb to the top of the **Old Town Hall Tower** for a great view of the square. Dedicate the afternoon to visiting the half-dozen monuments that comprise the **Prague Jewish Museum**.

On day three, take a metro ride out to Vyšehrad and explore Prague's other castle, the **Vyšehrad Citadel**, with its gorgeous views along the Vltava River. Don't miss the impressive tombs of composers Dvořák and Smetana and other famous Czechs in the **Vyšehrad Cemetery**. For the last day, take time to escape the city: take a boat trip along the Vltava to the rural suburb of Troja and visit the suburban delights of **Prague Zoo** and **Troja Chateau**.

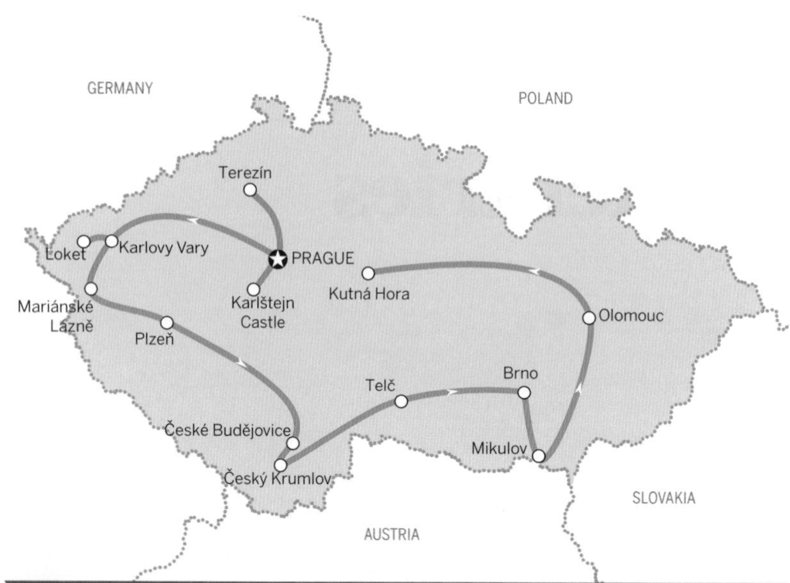

Essential Czech Republic

Begin in **Prague** and take your time enjoying one of Europe's most beautiful cities. Three nights is the minimum, but allow five so you can make a couple of day trips – one to the photogenic cluster of turrets at **Karlštejn Castle**, and one to evocative and heart-rending **Terezín**, a former concentration camp for European Jews during the Holocaust.

Now, head west to the gorgeous spa town of **Karlovy Vary** to sample the sulphurous spring waters and stroll among its elegant colonnades. Plan on a day trip from here to picture-postcard **Loket** with its riverside castle. Allow a morning to explore the smaller but arguably prettier spa town of **Mariánské Lázně** before continuing southeast to **Plzeň**. The capital of West Bohemia deserves an overnight stop followed by a tour of the famous brewery where Pilsner Urquell is made.

Continue the beer theme at **České Budějovice**, home of the Budvar brewery and also one of Central Europe's largest and most attractive town squares. From here, it's an easy 50-minute drive to the Unesco-recognised beauty of **Český Krumlov**; spend one day wandering around its picturesque streets and castle, and a second taking a boat trip along the Vltava River.

Now you enter Moravia and arrive in the gorgeous Renaissance town of **Telč**, where you can stroll over narrow bridges spanning ancient fish ponds and tour the ornate chateau before settling into a sidewalk cafe for the evening. Move on to **Brno**, the buzzing capital of Moravia and the country's second city, and spend a day exploring its museums and cafe culture before continuing to **Mikulov**, in the heart of South Moravian wine country. Allow a day here to visit a local winery, and rent a bicycle to explore the surrounding hills.

Afterwards, move on to **Olomouc**, one of the Czech Republic's most underrated destinations. It has a lovely old town square, some good museums, several microbreweries and lots of good places to eat. From here it's a straight cut east back towards Prague, but allow one more full day to visit the medieval town of **Kutná Hora**. The magnificent cathedral of St Barbara here is almost a match for Prague's St Vitus, and the weird 'bone church' at Sedlec ossuary is one of the Czech Republic's oddest sights.

Plan Your Trip

Travel with Children

Czechs are family-oriented, and there are plenty of activities around the city for children. An increasing number of restaurants in Prague and around the country cater specifically for children, with play areas and so on, and many offer a children's menu (*dětský jídelníček*).

Prague & the Czech Republic for Kids

While most traditional tourist sights in the Czech Republic – castles and museums – are geared towards adult travellers, there are plenty of ways younger visitors can stay busy. There's lots of green space, and many large cities have family-friendly parks and zoos. Judging by the number of mothers with prams on the streets, the country appears to be in the midst of a mini-baby boom, bringing with it a new generation of family-friendly museums and attractions.

Outdoor Fun

A handful of large cities, including Prague, Brno and Plzeň, have excellent zoos that are bound to please younger visitors. The Prague Zoo (p97) is located along a northern bank of the Vltava, which means getting to the zoo can be paired with a boat trip with Prague Steamboat Co (p300) or a stroll through lovely Stromovka (p98) park. Once there, you'll find a children's zoo (petting allowed), a miniature cable car, a huge kids' play area and, of course, the animals.

There are safe, well-designed playgrounds all over the country. In Prague,

Best Regions for Kids

Prague

The classic outdoor play area in central Prague, Petřín (p60) has a whole range of diversions, from a lookout tower and observatory to a mirror maze.

Bohemia

The beer-making metropolis of Plzeň is surprisingly good for kids as well. The Techmania Science Centre (p208), filled with gizmos, will appeal to teenage geeks. DinoPark (p208), a dinosaur park, will enthrall younger ones.

Moravia

Brno's Labyrinth under the Cabbage Market (p229) is a cool underground trek for kids. The Znojmo Underground (p246), in southern Moravia, offers high-adrenaline adventure tours for older teens.

several of these can be found on islands in the Vltava. At the southern end of Malá Strana, traffic-free Children's Island (p60) is equipped with playground equipment, rope swings, a mini football pitch, a skateboarding area and a cafe-bar where parents can sip a coffee or beer. There's an extensive list of play areas at www.living prague.com/kids.htm.

Once on the river, in summer (generally April to October) you can hire rowing boats and pedalos from several jetties dotted around **Slav Island** (Slovanský ostrov; Map p78; Masarykovo nábřeží; 5, 17) and splash around on the Vltava. If that sounds too energetic, there are lots of organised boat trips on offer.

Rainy-Day Fun

Children's theatre is a long-standing Czech tradition, and towns and cities across the country will have puppet shows and kid-friendly dramatic performances. The Spejbl & Hurvínek Theatre (p62) puts on puppet shows, while Minor Theatre (p160) stages live children's theatre.

Budding astronomers will want to take in shows at the Prague Planetarium (p100) or the Brno Observatory & Planetarium (p230). Consult the websites during your visit, but both offer at least a handful of English-friendly presentations. Shark tanks and touch pools are among the attractions at Mořský Svět (p100), Prague's only aquarium. A branch of the Moravian Museum (p229) in Brno, the Bishop's Court (p229), houses the largest freshwater aquarium in the country, with plenty of info on Moravian wildlife.

Child-Friendly Museums & Galleries

With a growing number of kids to entertain, more museums have geared their collections to be more appealing to younger audiences, adding video and 3D effects and making the exhibits more 'hands on'. Prague's National Technical Museum (p94) has a huge room stuffed with vintage trains, planes, cars and buses, and interactive exhibits in the photography and printing-industry sections. Plzeň's Techmania Science Centre (p208) lets kids get close-up to the exhibits, and the Brno **Technical Museum** (Technické muzeum vs Brně; 541 421 411; www.technical-museum.cz; Purkyňova 105; adult/concession 130/70Kč; 9am-5pm Tue-Fri, 10am-6pm Sat & Sun; 12) is stuffed with old-school gadgetry.

At Prague's Art Gallery for Children (p70), the kids not only get to look at art, but make it, add to it and alter it. There are paints and materials to play with, and even workshops for five- to 12-year-olds (only in Czech at present, though staff speak English). The Lego Museum (p77) in Prague is Europe's largest private collection of Lego models, with a play area at the end where kids can build stuff from Lego themselves.

PLANNING

- **Admission costs** The maximum age for child discounts on admission fees varies from 12 to 18; children under six often get in for free.
- **Transport** Children under six years of age travel free on public transport, but be sure to carry proof of age.
- **Kids in Prague** (www.kidsin prague.com) has loads of useful information on places to go and things to do.
- **Babysitting** Most top-end hotels provide a babysitting service. **Domestica** (257 322 363; www.domestica.cz; Lidická 7; per hr from 150Kč; 4, 5, 7, 10, 16, 21) is an agency that provides English-speaking babysitters.

PHOTO BY HANNEKE LUIJTING/GETTY IMAGES ©

Plan Your Trip

Eat & Drink Like a Local

Traditional Czech cuisine is classic meat-and-potato fare, which can be immensely satisfying when prepared well and stodgy if done poorly. A new wave of restaurants is transforming the Czech dining scene with a focus on fresh, locally grown produce and an innovative approach.

The Year in Food

Each year fruit and veg markets follow the annual procession from early-season offerings like strawberries and cherries to late arrivals like tomatoes and squash. Weekend farmers markets are a staple of many Prague neighbourhoods.

Winter (Dec–Feb)

Don't expect much in the way of fresh fruits and vegetables, but housewives are keen canners, so there's no shortage of preserved beets, pickles and tomatoes. Carnival season *(Masopust)*, in February, usually involves a pig slaughter, with heaps of pork and sausage.

Spring (Mar–May)

The growing season gets off to a slow start, but things start rolling at Easter, with coloured eggs, baked meats, and loaves of various cakes and breads. *Mazanec* is a sweet holiday bread made with raisins and almonds, while *beránek* is a cake baked in the shape of a lamb.

Summer (Jun–Aug)

The first fruits of the season, strawberries and wild cherries, are soon followed by plums, apricots, pears and watermelon. It's high grilling season, so look out for cookouts featuring pork, chicken and sausages, inevitably knocked back by a beer or three.

Autumn (Sep–Nov)

Mushroom pickers head to the woods in early autumn. Wine festivals take place throughout September and October. St Martin's Day, 11 November, is celebrated with young wine and roast goose.

Food Experiences

Meals of a Lifetime

➡ **Field** (p127) Prague Michelin-starred restaurant that features traditional recipes and home-grown ingredients.

➡ **U Kroka** (p142) Away from the centre of Prague, but worth the trip for authentic roast pork and dumplings.

➡ **Šupina & Šupinka** (p201) The lowly carp gets royal treatment, harvested fresh from nearby fish ponds.

➡ **Svatováclavský Pivovar** (p252) A proper beer house serving home-brewed beer and authentic Moravian cooking.

➡ **Pavillon** (p232) Wild boar, fresh lamb or whatever is in season served in an elegant functionalist dining room.

Beer Snacks

Most pubs have a *'K vašemu pivu'* ('with your beer') section of the menu, devoted to snacky treats. These include spicy pork or beef sausages *(klobásy)*, fried or boiled, served with mustard on rye bread or a roll; frankfurters *(párky)*; a Hungarian snack of fried pastry coated with garlic, cheese, butter or jam *(langoše)*; a patty made from strips of raw potato and garlic *(bramborák)*; and chips or French fries *(hranolky)* or fried sliced potatoes *(brambůrky)*. Beer cheese – cheese marinated in garlic, spices and oil – is a great accompaniment for a couple of cold lagers. Look for the word *syr* (cheese) in the 'with your beer' section of the menu.

Local Specialities

Soups & Stews

The first course of a traditional Czech meal is usually a hearty *polévka* (soup) – often *bramboračka* (potato soup), *houbová polévka* (mushroom soup) or *hovězí vývar* (beef broth). Ones worth looking out for are *cibulačka* (onion soup), a delicious, creamy concoction of caramelised onions and herbs, and *česnečka* (garlic soup), a powerfully pungent broth that is curiously addictive.

Roast Pork & Dumplings

What roast beef and Yorkshire pudding is to the English, *pečené vepřové koleno s knedlíky a kyselé zelí* (roast pork with bread dumplings and sauerkraut) is to the Czechs; it's a dish so ubiquitous that it is often abbreviated to *'vepřo-knedlo-zelo'*. The pork is rubbed with salt and caraway seeds, and roasted long and slow – good

Jablkový závin (apple strudel)

roast pork should fall apart, meltingly tender, at the first touch of a fork or finger.

The dumplings should be light and fluffy – *houskové knedlíky* (bread dumplings) are made from flour, yeast, egg yolk and milk, and are left to rise like bread before being cooked in boiling water and then sliced.

Other 'Musts' on the Menu

Other staples of Czech restaurant menus include *svíčková na smetaně* (slices of marinated roast beef served with a sour-cream sauce garnished with lemon and cranberries); *guláš* (a casserole of beef or pork in a tomato, onion and paprika gravy); and *vepřový řízek* (Wienerschnitzel; a thin fillet of pork coated in breadcrumbs and fried, served with potato salad or *hranolky* – French fries).

Sweets

The classic Czech dessert is *ovocné knedlíky* (fruit dumplings), but the best are to be found at domestic dinner tables rather than in restaurants. Large, round dumplings made with sweetened, flour-based dough are stuffed with berries, plums or apricots, and served drizzled with melted butter and a sprinkle of sugar.

More common desserts in restaurants consist of *zmrzlina* (ice cream), *palačinky* or *lívance* (pancakes) and *jablkový závin* (apple strudel).

FOOD BLOGS

Local bloggers are passionate about their pursuits and a great way to stay abreast of shifting food trends. The best blogs in English include:

➡ **Czech Please** (www.twitter.com/czechplease)

➡ **Bohemian Bites** (http://bohemianbites.wordpress.com)

➡ **Eating Prague** (http://eatingpraguetours.com/blog)

➡ **Pivní Filosof** (www.pivni-filosof.com)

➡ **Taste of Prague** (www.tasteofprague.com/pragueblog)

Regions at a Glance

Prague

History
Culture
Food & Drink

Czech Capital

Prague Castle has always been the seat of Czech power, and its host of museums and historic buildings help you chart the course of the country's history for more than a millennium.

Art, Music & Literature

The Czech capital has long been a draw for artists, writers and musicians, from Mozart and Mucha to Kafka and Kokoschka, and their influences on and interactions with the city are recorded in a plethora of museums and art galleries.

Prague's Restaurant Scene

The last few years have seen Prague aspiring to join the premier league of gastronomic destinations, and the latest crop of innovative restaurants, friendly wine bars and fascinating food tours have seen it nudge closer to its goal.

p32

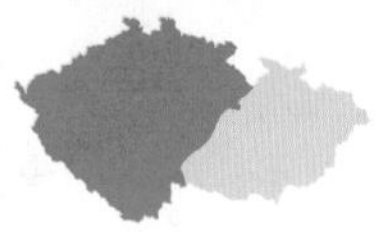

Bohemia

Food
Castles
Beer

Třeboň Carp

South Bohemia has been famous for fish farms since the 16th century, and is still the country's main source of carp, a Czech delicacy. Třeboň's restaurants are an ideal place to try it out.

Český Krumlov Castle

There are enough castles in the Bohemian countryside to keep an enthusiast busy for a lifetime, ranging from Gothic ruins to baroque beauties. But when it's floodlit at night, Český Krumlov is almost certainly the most picturesque castle in the country.

Pilsner Urquell Brewery

'Where beer is brewed, life is good' goes the old Czech saying, and it doesn't get much better than in Bohemia, where you can visit world-famous breweries like Pilsner Urquell.

p173

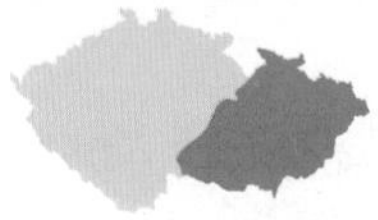

Moravia

Food & Drink
Culture
Architecture

Moravian Wine Country

The southern part of Moravia, near the Austrian border, produces the country's finest wines, and taking a tour of the wineries here is a highlight of any visit.

Olomouc

Little known outside the Czech Republic, this university town is steeped in Moravian culture and tradition, from its gorgeous Gothic and Renaissance architecture, to its many museums and galleries, and an international festival of choral music.

Brno

Prague gets all the plaudits for it gorgeous architecture, but the Czech Republic's second city was a hotbed of functionalist and Bauhaus design in the 1920s, a legacy lovingly embodied in the stunning Villa Tugendhat.

p225

On the Road

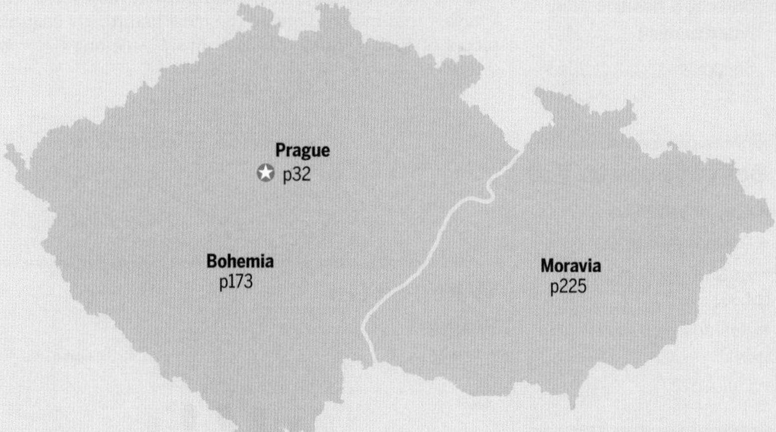

Prague p32

Bohemia p173

Moravia p225

Prague

POP 1.3 MILLION

Includes ➡

Sights 44
Activities 101
Tours 103
Festivals & Events 109
Sleeping 109
Eating 121
Drinking & Nightlife 142
Entertainment 157
Shopping 163

Best Places to Eat

- ➡ Sansho (p129)
- ➡ Café Lounge (p122)
- ➡ La Bottega Bistroteka (p126)
- ➡ Restaurace U Veverky (p140)
- ➡ Field (p127)

Best Places to Sleep

- ➡ Fusion Hotel (p114)
- ➡ Savic Hotel (p113)
- ➡ Icon Hotel (p115)
- ➡ Mosaic House (p114)
- ➡ Brix Hostel (p118)
- ➡ Czech Inn (p115)

Why Go?

The 1989 Velvet Revolution that freed the Czechs from communism bequeathed to Europe a gem of a city to stand beside stalwarts such as Rome, Amsterdam and London. Not surprisingly, visitors from around the world have come in droves, and on a hot summer's day it can feel like you're sharing Charles Bridge with half of humanity. But even the crowds can't take away from the spectacle of a 14th-century stone bridge, a hilltop castle and a lovely, lazy river – the Vltava – that inspired one of the most hauntingly beautiful pieces of 19th-century classical music, Smetana's *Moldau* symphony.

When to Go

Prague

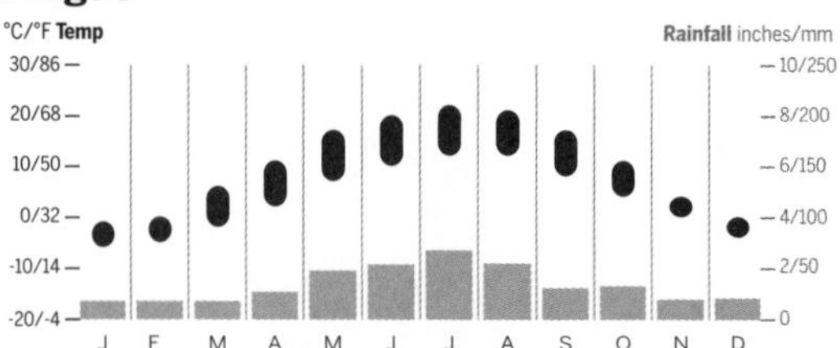

Apr Trees and flowers bud in spectacular fashion, though Easter can get very crowded.

Jul & Aug High summer brings hot days but lots of sunshine and great walking and cycling weather.

Sep & Oct Still plenty of light for daytime walks; cultural calendar resumes at entertainment venues.

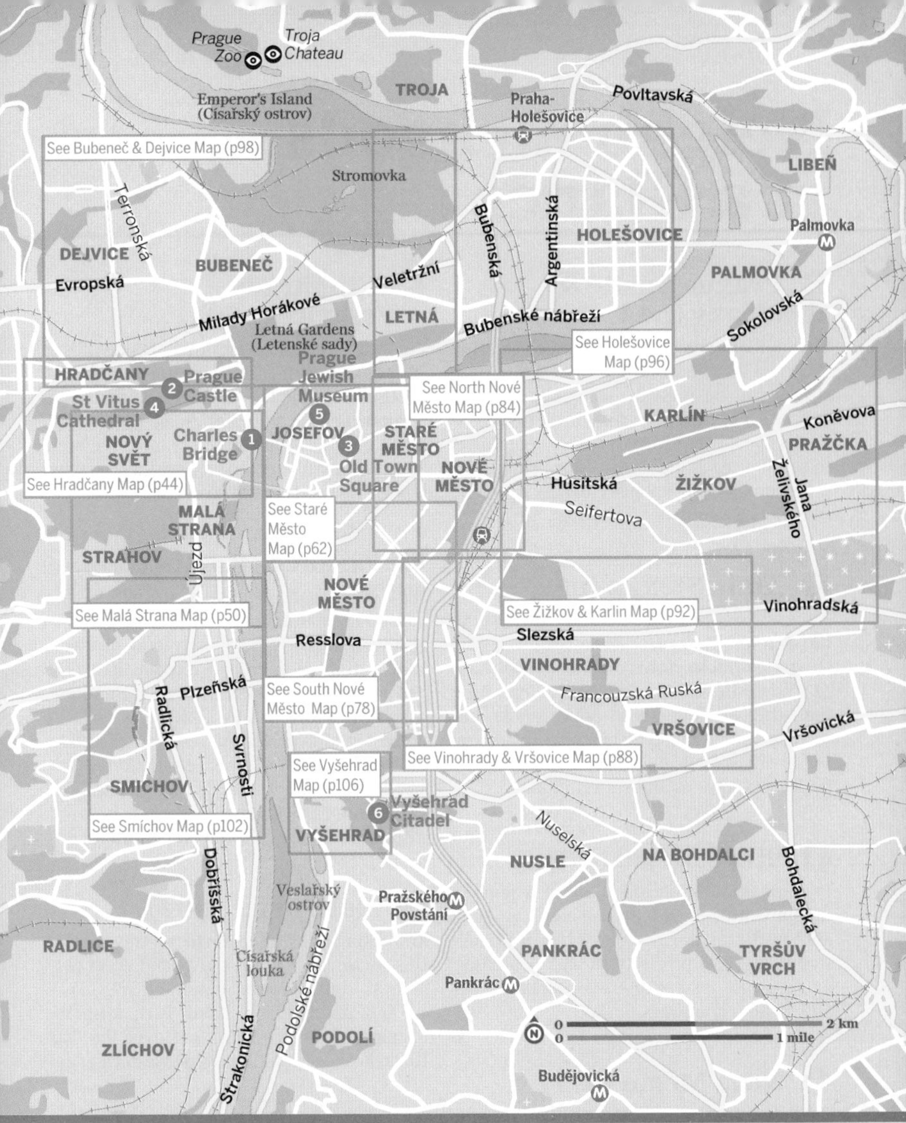

Prague Highlights

❶ **Charles Bridge** (p54)
Crossing this 14th-century bridge, is the quintessential Prague experience.

❷ **Prague Castle** (p36)
Ambling through the cultural and historical heart of the old Bohemian kingdom and the modern Czech state.

❸ **Old Town Square** (p68)
Enjoying the daily spectacle of Prague's premier public space, a market square for more than 1000 years.

❹ **St Vitus Cathedral** (p42)
Experiencing the sense of awe as you enter the soaring Gothic nave, lit by gorgeous stained glass.

❺ **Prague Jewish Museum** (p66) Visiting a half a dozen ancient synagogues, a ceremonial hall and former mortuary, and the melancholic Old Jewish Cemetery.

❻ **Vyšehrad Citadel** (p104)
Strolling the ruins of this abandoned hilltop fortress, the summit where legend says the city was founded.

Neighbourhoods at a Glance

❶ Prague Castle & Hradčany (p44)

This hilltop neighbourhood encompassing the Prague Castle complex and surrounding streets can be packed during the day but empties out by night because few Prague residents live up here. There are plenty of things to see, but fewer places to eat or drink. It's a pretty but impractical place to stay, as public transport is spotty in these parts.

❷ Malá Strana (p52)

Almost too picturesque for its own good, the baroque district of Malá Strana (Little Quarter) tumbles down the hillside between Prague Castle and the river. It's quieter here than the Old Town, with fewer sights and nightspots, but any deficiency on that score is more than made up for by the many pretty parks and gardens and stately palaces.

❸ Staré Město (p61)

Prague's Staré Město (Old Town) is famous for its Gothic spires, Jewish heritage sites and medieval town square, but its backstreets are also prime territory for seeking out gourmet restaurants, cool cocktail bars and fashion boutiques.

❹ Nové Město (p77)

The name translates as 'New Town', though the buildings and street plan here go back some seven centuries. It's a sprawling area, bordering the Old Town on all sides. While Nové Město has its share of museums and sights, it's best known as the city's commercial heart, seen best along sweeping Wenceslas Square. It's a good choice for hotels, given the proximity to the centre and excellent transport.

❺ Vinohrady & Vršovice (p88)

Vinohrady (literally 'vineyards') is one of the city's most sought-after residential neighbourhoods, known for its excellent restaurants and fashionable bars and cafes. Adjacent Vršovice is not quite as sophisticated, though the area along Krymská street has a pleasingly shabby hipster vibe and several good bars.

❻ Žižkov & Karlín (p89)

Hilly Žižkov is the polar opposite of its neighbour to the south, Vinohrady. It's a traditionally working-class neighbourhood of steep streets that are lined, more often than not, by raucous pubs. There are two sights here worth the effort: the TV Tower and the National Monument. Karlín, just north of Žižkov, has undergone a massive rebuilding project since the tragic 2002 flood and has blossomed into a desirable residential quarter, with an emerging cafe and restaurant scene.

❼ Holešovice (p94)

A working-class area north of the centre, Holešovice is short on sights and good restaurants, but has some emerging art galleries and trendy clubs. Letná Park, with its Instagram-worthy images out over the Old Town, is on the area's extreme western edge.

❽ Bubeneč & Dejvice (p98)

Bubeneč & Dejvice are adjoining residential neighbourhoods north of the Old Town. Considered the city's most prestigious address, Bubeneč has nice hotels and a few good restaurants scattered about. Within its boundaries is the central city's largest park, Stromovka.

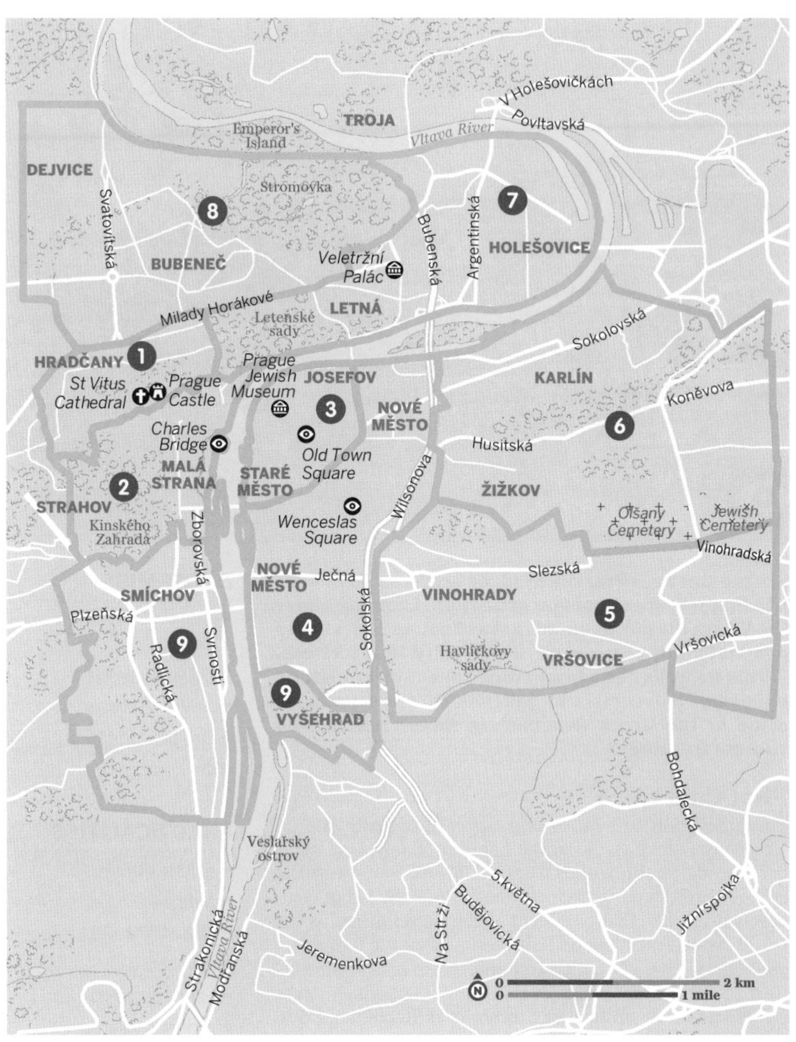

❾ Smíchov & Vyšehrad (p101)

Smíchov, south of Malá Strana, is a former industrial area that has seen a recent boom in office and luxury hotel construction. The area has few sights but lots of pubs. Vyšehrad, south of Nové Město, is a leafy residential area, dominated by the ruins of an ancient castle said to be where Prague was founded.

MATT MUNRO/LONELY PLANET ©

TOP SIGHT
PRAGUE CASTLE

Prague Castle – Pražský hrad, or just *hrad* to Czechs – is Prague's most popular attraction. Looming above the Vltava River, its serried ranks of spires and palaces dominate the city centre like a fairy-tale fortress. Within its walls lies a fascinating collection of historic buildings, museums and galleries that are home to some of the Czech Republic's greatest artistic and cultural treasures.

First Courtyard

The First Courtyard lies within the castle's main gate on Hradčany Square (Hradčanské náměstí), flanked by huge, baroque statues of battling Titans (1767–70) that dwarf the castle guards standing beneath them. After the fall of communism in 1989, then-president Václav Havel hired his old pal Theodor Pistek, the costume designer on the film *Amadeus* (1984), to replace their communist-era khaki uniforms with the stylish pale-blue kit they now wear, which harks back to the army of the first Czechoslovak Republic of 1918 to 1938.

The changing of the guard takes place every hour on the hour, but the longest and most impressive display is at noon, when banners are exchanged while a brass band plays a fanfare from the windows of the Plečnik Hall, which overlooks the First Courtyard.

DON'T MISS

- Story of Prague Castle
- Lobkowicz Palace
- St Vitus Treasury
- Basilica of St George
- Golden Lane

PRACTICALITIES

- Pražský hrad
- Map p44
- ☎ 224 372 423
- www.hrad.cz
- Hradčanské náměstí 1
- grounds free, sights adult/concession Tour A & C 350/175Kc, Tour B 250/125Kc
- ⏲ grounds 6am-11pm year-round, gardens 10am-6pm Apr-Oct, closed Nov-Mar, historic bldg 9am-5pm Apr-Oct, to 4pm Nov-Mar
- Ⓜ Malostranská, j22

Second Courtyard

Beyond the Matthias Gate lies the Second Courtyard, centred on a baroque fountain and a 17th-century well with lovely Renaissance latticework.

St Vitus Treasury

On the right of the Second Courtyard, the Chapel of the Holy Cross (1763) houses the St Vitus Treasury (Svatovítský poklad; Map p44; 224 373 442; www.hrad.cz; nádvoří II, Pražský hrad; adult/child 300/150Kč, admission incl with Prague Castle Tour C ticket; 10am-6pm Apr-Oct, to 5pm Nov-Mar; 22), a spectacular collection of ecclesiastical bling that was founded by Charles IV in the 14th century. Gold and silver reliquaries crusted in diamonds, emeralds and rubies contain saintly relics ranging from fragments of the True Cross to the withered hand of a Holy Innocent. The oldest items include a reliquary arm of St Vitus dating from the early 10th century, while the most impressive treasures include a gold coronation cross of Charles IV (1370) and a diamond-studded baroque monstrance from 1708.

Royal Garden

A gate on the northern side of the Second Courtyard leads to Powder Bridge (Prašný most; 1540), which spans the Stag Moat and leads to the Royal Garden (Královská zahrada; Map p44; 10am-6pm Apr-Oct, closed Nov-Mar; 22) FREE, which started life as a Renaissance garden built by Ferdinand I in 1534. It is graced by several gorgeous Renaissance structures.

The most beautiful of the garden's buildings is the 1569 Ball-Game House (Míčovna; Royal Gardens; Map p5) FREE, a masterpiece of Renaissance sgraffito where the Habsburgs once played a primitive version of badminton. To the east is the Summer Palace (Letohrádek; Map p45), or Belvedere (1538–60), the most authentic Italian Renaissance building outside Italy; to the west is the 1695 former Riding School (Jízdárna; Map p44; admission varies; 10am-6pm). All three are used as venues for temporary exhibitions.

Prague Castle Picture Gallery

The Swedish army that looted the famous bronzes in the Wallenstein Garden (p56) in 1648 also nicked Rudolf II's art treasures. This gallery (Map p44; adult/child 100/50Kč, admission incl with Prague Castle Tour C ticket; 9am-5pm Apr-Oct, to 4pm Nov-Mar; 22) in the castle's beautiful Renaissance stables houses an exhibition of 16th- to 18th-century European art, based on the Habsburg collection that was begun in 1650 to replace the lost paintings; it includes works by Cranach, Holbein, Rubens, Tintoretto and Titian.

SECURITY CHECKS

Security checks were introduced at all entrances to the Prague Castle complex (including the Royal Gardens, South Gardens and Stag Moat) in summer 2016. This has resulted in long queues (up to one hour) to enter the castle at busy times, especially at the most popular entrance on Hradčany Square.

According to the *Guinness World Records,* Prague Castle is the largest ancient castle in the world – 570m long, an average of 128m wide and occupying 7.28 hectares.

SOUTH GARDENS

At the castle's eastern gate, you can either descend the Old Castle Steps to Malostranská metro station or take a sharp right and wander back to Hradčany Square through the South Gardens (Zahrada na valech; Map p44; 10am-6pm Apr-Oct, closed Nov-Mar) FREE. The terrace garden offers superb views across the rooftops of Malá Strana and permits a peek into the back garden of the British embassy.

Third Courtyard

As you pass through the passage on the eastern side of the Second Courtyard, the huge western facade of St Vitus Cathedral soars directly above you; to its south (to the right as you enter) lies the Third Courtyard. At its entrance you'll see a 16m-tall granite monolith (Map p44) dedicated to the victims of WWI, designed by Jože Plečnik in 1928, and a copy of a 14th-century bronze figure of St George (Map p44) slaying the dragon; the original is on display in the Story of Prague Castle exhibition.

The courtyard is dominated by the southern facade of St Vitus Cathedral, with its grand centrepiece, the Golden Gate.

Old Royal Palace

The Old Royal Palace (Starý královský palác; Map p44; admission with Prague Castle tour A & B tickets; ⏲9am-5pm Apr-Oct, to 4pm Nov-Mar; 🚊22) at the courtyard's eastern end is one of the oldest parts of the castle, dating from 1135. It was originally used only by Czech princesses, but from the 13th to the 16th centuries it was the king's own palace.

The Vladislav Hall (Vladislavský sál) is famous for its beautiful, late-Gothic vaulted ceiling (1493–1502) designed by Benedikt Rejt. Though more than 500 years old, the flowing, interwoven lines of the vaults have an almost art-nouveau feel, in contrast to the rectilinear form of the Renaissance windows. The vast hall was used for banquets, councils and coronations, and for indoor jousting tournaments – hence the Riders' Staircase (Jezdecké schody), through an arch on the northern side, designed to admit a knight on horseback. All the presidents of the republic have been sworn in here.

A door in the hall's southwestern corner leads to the former offices of the Bohemian Chancellery (České kanceláře). On 23 May 1618, in the second room, Protestant nobles rebelling against the Bohemian Estates and the Habsburg emperor threw two of his councillors and their secretary out of the window. They survived, as their fall was broken by the dung-filled moat, but this Second Defenestration of Prague sparked off the Thirty Years' War.

At the eastern end of the Vladislav Hall a door to the right leads to a terrace with great views of the city. To the right of the Riders' Staircase you'll spot an unusual Renaissance doorway framed by twisted columns, which leads to the Diet (Sněmovna), or Assembly Hall, which displays another beautifully vaulted ceiling.

PRAGUE CASTLE TICKETS

There are three kinds of tickets for Prague Castle (each valid for two days), which allow entry to different combinations of sights:

Tour A (adult/child/family 350/175/700Kč) Includes St Vitus Cathedral, Old Royal Palace, Story of Prague Castle, Basilica of St George, Powder Tower, Golden Lane, Daliborka and Rosenberg Palace.

Tour B (adult/child/family 250/125/500Kč) Includes St Vitus Cathedral, Old Royal Palace, Basilica of St George, Golden Lane and Daliborka.

Tour C (adult/child/family 350/175/700Kč) Includes St Vitus Treasury and Prague Castle Picture Gallery.

You can buy tickets at either of two information centres in the Second (Map p44; ☎224 372 423; www.hrad.cz; ⏲9am-5pm Apr-Oct, to 4pm Nov-Mar) and Third Courtyards (Map p44; ☎224 372 434; www.hrad.cz; ⏲9am-5pm Apr-Oct, to 4pm Nov-Mar), or from ticket offices at the entrances to all the main sights.

Basilica of St George

Story of Prague Castle

Housed in the Gothic vaults beneath the Old Royal Palace, this huge and impressive museum (Map p44; www.hrad.cz; adult/child 140/70Kč, admission incl with Prague Castle Tour A ticket; ⌚9am-5pm Apr-Oct, to 4pm Nov-Mar; 🚊22) ranks alongside the Lobkowicz Palace as one of the most interesting collections of artefacts in the castle. It traces 1000 years of the castle's history, from the building of the first wooden palisade to the present day, illustrated by models of the site at various stages in its development.

The exhibits include the grave of a 9th-century warrior discovered in the castle grounds, the helmet and chain mail worn by St Wenceslas, and a replica of the gold crown of St Wenceslas, which was made for Charles IV in 1346. Anyone with a serious interest in Prague Castle should visit here first.

St George Square

St George Sq (Jiřské náměstí), the plaza to the east of St Vitus Cathedral, lies at the heart of the castle complex.

Basilica of St George

The striking, brick-red, early-baroque facade that dominates the square conceals the Czech Republic's best-preserved Romanesque basilica (Bazilika sv Jiří; Map p44; www.hrad.cz; Jiřské náměstí; admission incl with Prague Castle tour A & B tickets; ⌚9am-5pm Apr-Oct, to 4pm Nov-Mar), established in the 10th century by

ROYAL CROWN OF BOHEMIA

The royal crown of Bohemia was created for Charles IV in 1346 using gold from the ducal coronet once worn by St Wenceslas. It is studded with 18 sapphires, 15 rubies, 25 emeralds and 20 pearls; some of the stones are 7cm to 10cm across and weigh 60 to 80 carats. The cross on top is said to contain a thorn from Christ's crown of thorns – it bears the inscription 'Hic est spina de corona Domini' (Here is a thorn from the Lord's crown). The crown, along with the rest of the crown jewels, is kept locked away in the Coronation Chamber above the Chapel of St Wenceslas in St Vitus Cathedral, but a copy can be seen in the Story of Prague Castle (p39) exhibition.

In the 1920s President Masaryk hired a Slovene architect, Jože Plečnik, to renovate the castle; his changes created some of its most memorable features and made the complex more tourist-friendly.

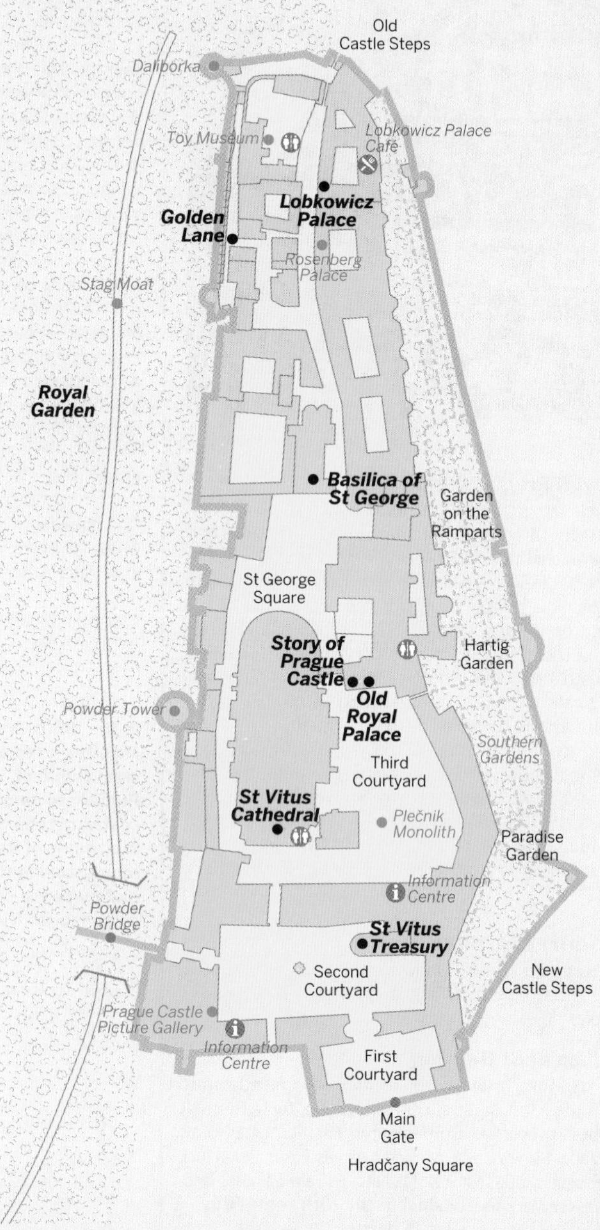
PRAGUE CASTLE
Old Castle Steps
Daliborka
Toy Museum
Lobkowicz Palace Café
Lobkowicz Palace
Golden Lane
Rosenberg Palace
Stag Moat
Royal Garden
Basilica of St George
Garden on the Ramparts
St George Square
Story of Prague Castle
Hartig Garden
Old Royal Palace
Powder Tower
Southern Gardens
Third Courtyard
St Vitus Cathedral
Plečnik Monolith
Paradise Garden
Information Centre
Powder Bridge
St Vitus Treasury
Second Courtyard
New Castle Steps
Prague Castle Picture Gallery
Information Centre
First Courtyard
Main Gate
Hradčany Square

Vratislav I (the father of St Wenceslas). What you see today is mostly the result of restorations made between 1887 and 1908.

The austerity of the Romanesque nave is relieved by a baroque double staircase leading to the apse, where fragments of 12th-century frescoes survive. In front of the stairs lie the tombs of Prince Boleslav II (d 997; on the left) and Prince Vratislav I (d 921), the church's founder. The arch beneath the stairs allows a glimpse of the 12th-century crypt; Přemysl kings are buried here and in the nave.

On the right side of the crypt is a gruesome statue of a decomposing corpse, complete with a snake coiled in its abdominal cavity. Dating from the 16th century, it is an allegory of Vanity, although it is known as Brigita after a Prague legend. An Italian sculptor murdered his girlfriend, a local girl named Brigita, but when her buried body was discovered he was driven by remorse to create this sculpture of her decaying corpse.

Powder Tower

A passage to the north of St Vitus Cathedral leads to the Powder Tower (Prašná Věž; Map p44; adult/concession 70/40Kč, admission incl with Prague Castle Tour A ticket; ⏲9am-5pm Apr-Oct, to 4pm Nov-Mar), also called Mihulka, which was built in the 15th century as part of the castle's defences. Later it became the workshop of cannon- and bell-maker Tomáš Jaroš, who cast the bells for St Vitus Cathedral. Today it houses an exhibition on the history of the Castle Guard.

George Street

George Street (Jiřská) runs from the Basilica of St George to the castle's eastern gate.

Golden Lane

The picturesque alley known as Golden Lane (Zlatá ulička; Map p44; admission incl with Prague Castle tour A & B tickets; ⏲9am-5pm Apr-Oct, to 4pm Nov-Mar; 🚋22) runs along the northern wall of the castle. Its tiny, colourful cottages were built in the 16th century for the sharpshooters of the castle guard, but were later used by goldsmiths. In the 19th and early 20th centuries they were occupied by artists, including the writer Franz Kafka (who frequently visited his sister's house at No 22 from 1916 to 1917).

A footpath on the western side of the Powder Bridge leads down to the Stag Moat (Jelení příkop; open April to October), and doubles back through a modern red-brick tunnel beneath the bridge. If you continue east along the moat you can follow the path uphill to the left to reach the Summer Palace. A gate on the outer wall of the castle, overlooking the moat, leads to a nuclear shelter started by the communists in the 1950s but never completed; its tunnels run beneath most of the castle.

TOP SIGHT
ST VITUS CATHEDRAL

PETR BONEK/SHUTTERSTOCK ©

Built over a time span of almost 600 years, St Vitus is one of the most richly endowed cathedrals in Central Europe. It is pivotal to the religious and cultural life of the Czech Republic, housing treasures that range from the 14th-century Bohemian crown jewels to glowing art-nouveau stained glass, and the tombs of Bohemian saints and rulers from St Wenceslas to Charles IV.

The Nave

The foundation stone of the cathedral was laid in 1344 by Emperor Charles IV, on the site of a 10th-century Romanesque rotunda dedicated to St Wenceslas. The architect, Matthias of Arras, began work on the choir in the French Gothic style, but died eight years later. His German successor, Peter Parler – a veteran of Cologne's cathedral – built most of the eastern part, but it remained unfinished. It was only in 1861 that a concerted effort was made to complete the project – everything between the western door and the crossing was built during the late 19th and early 20th centuries, and it was finally consecrated in 1929.

Inside, the nave is flooded with colour from stained-glass windows created by eminent Czech artists of the early 20th century – note the one by Alfons Mucha in the third chapel on the northern side, which depicts the lives of Sts Cyril and Methodius (1909). Nearby is a wooden sculpture of the crucifixion (1899) by František Bílek.

Walk up to the crossing, where the nave and transept meet, which is dominated by the huge and colourful south window (1938) by Max Švabinský, depicting the Last Judgment – note the fires of Hell burning brightly in the lower

DON'T MISS

- Stained-glass window by Alfons Mucha
- South window
- Tomb of St John of Nepomuk
- Chapel of St Wenceslas
- Golden Gate

PRACTICALITIES

- Katedrála sv Víta
- Map p44
- 257 531 622
- www.katedralasvatehovita.cz
- Third Courtyard, Prague Castle
- admission incl with Prague Castle Tour A & B tickets
- 9am-5pm Mon-Sat, noon-5pm Sun Apr-Oct, to 4pm Nov-Mar
- 22

right-hand corner. In the north transept, beneath the baroque organ, are three carved wooden doors decorated with reliefs of Bohemian saints, with smaller panels beneath each saint depicting their martyrdom – look on the lower left side of the left-hand door for St Vitus being tortured in a cauldron of boiling oil. Next to him is the martyrdom of St Wenceslas; he is down on one knee, clinging to a lion's-head door handle, while his treacherous brother Boleslav drives a spear into his back. You can see that very door handle on the other side of the church, on the door to the Chapel of St Wenceslas.

The Ambulatory

The eastern end of the cathedral is capped with graceful late-Gothic vaulting dating from the 14th century, and ringed by side chapels. In the centre, opposite the pulpit, lies the ornate Royal Mausoleum (1571–89) with its cold marble effigies of Ferdinand I, his wife Anna Jagellonská and their son Maximilián II.

As you round the far end of the ambulatory you pass the tomb of St Vitus – as well as being a patron saint of Bohemia, Vitus is a patron of actors, entertainers and dancers. Further round is the spectacular, baroque silver tomb of St John of Nepomuk, its draped canopy supported by a squadron of silver angels (the tomb contains 2 tonnes of silver in all).

The nearby Wallenstein Chapel contains the worn grave slabs of cathedral architects Matthias of Arras and Peter Parler. Beyond is the ornate, late-Gothic Royal Oratory, a fancy balcony with ribbed vaulting carved to look like tree branches. The biggest and most beautiful of the cathedral's numerous side chapels is Parler's Chapel of St Wenceslas. Its walls are adorned with gilded panels containing polished slabs of semiprecious stones. Wall paintings from the early 16th century depict scenes from the life of the Czechs' patron saint, while even older frescoes show scenes from the life of Christ.

Great South Tower of St Vitus Cathedral

The cathedral's bell tower (Map p44; admission 150Kč; ⏲10am-6pm Apr-Oct, to 5pm Nov-Mar; 🚋22) was left unfinished in the 15th century; its soaring Gothic lines are capped by a Renaissance gallery added in the late 16th century, and a bulging spire that dates from the 1770s. You can climb the 297 steps to the top for excellent views; the entrance is outside the cathedral in Prague Castle's Third Courtyard (admission not included with Prague Castle tour ticket). You also get a close look at the clockworks, dating from 1597. The tower's Sigismund Bell, made by Tomáš Jaroš in 1549, is the largest bell in the Czech Republic.

GOLDEN GATE

The cathedral's south entrance is known as the Golden Gate (Zlatá brána), an elegant, triple-arched Gothic porch designed by Peter Parler. Above it is a mosaic of the Last Judgment (1370–71) – on the left, the godly are raised into Heaven by angels; on the right, sinners are cast down into Hell by demons; and in the centre, Christ reigns in glory with saints Procopius, Sigismund, Vitus, Wenceslas, Ludmila and Adalbert below. Beneath them Charles IV and his wife kneel in prayer.

The cathedral crypt (no longer open to the public) contains sarcophagi with the remains of Czech rulers including Charles IV, Wenceslas IV, George of Poděbrady and Rudolf II. You can see it in the Virtual Tour on the cathedral's website.

CROWN JEWELS

On the southern side of the Chapel of St Wenceslas, a small door, sealed with seven locks, hides a staircase leading up to the Crown Chamber, where the Bohemian crown jewels are kept. You can see replicas in the Old Royal Palace (p38).

Sights

The Vltava River winds through the middle of Prague like a giant question mark, with the city centre straddling its lower half. There is little method in Prague's haphazard sprawl – it's a city that has grown organically from its medieval roots, snagging villages and swallowing suburbs as it spread out into the wooded hills of Central Bohemia.

The oldest parts of the city cluster tightly just south of the river bend – Hradčany, the medieval castle district, and Malá Strana (Little Quarter) on the western bank; Stáre Město (Old Town), Nové Město (New Town) and the ancient Vyšehrad citadel on the eastern bank.

Beyond the centre lie the mostly 19th- and 20th-century suburbs, just a 10-minute tram ride away – elegant Vinohrady, grungy Žižkov and up-and-coming Karlín to the east, Holešovice, Bubeneč and Dejvice to the north and northwest, and formerly industrial Smíchov to the south.

Prague Castle & Hradčany

Prague Castle is the big sight here, of course. Other attractions include the cluster of art galleries around Hradčany Square, the religious relics of the Loreta, and the gorgeous

Hradčany

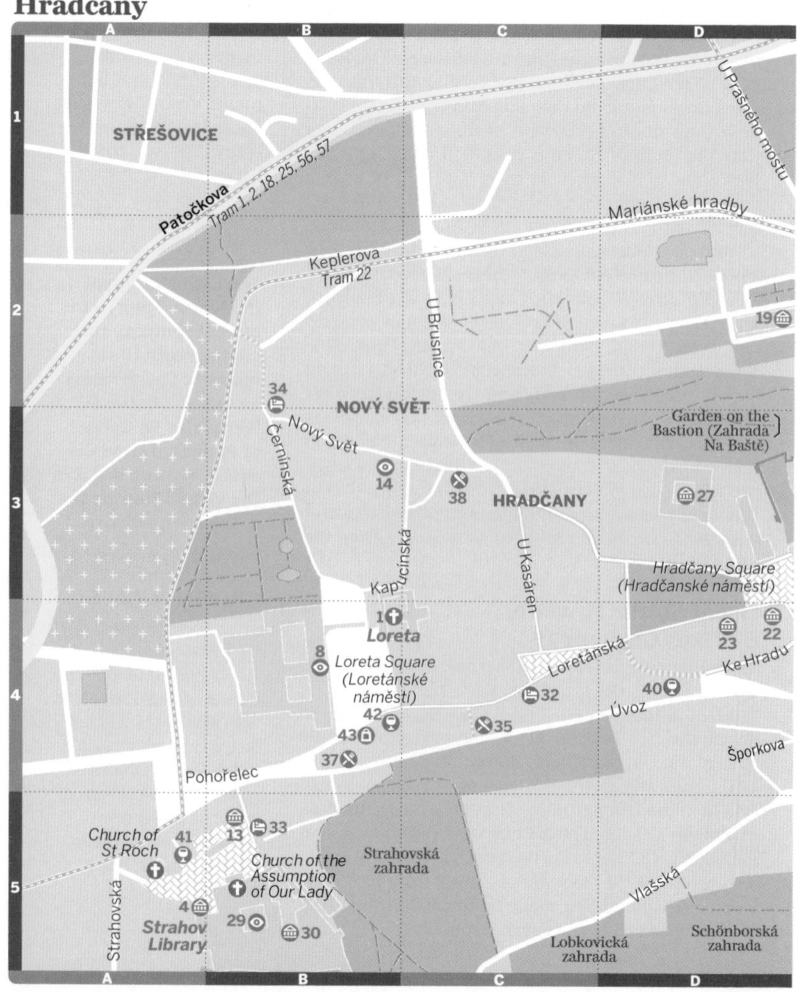

baroque library of Strahov Monastery. All are within easy walking distance of each other.

★Prague Castle CASTLE
See p36.

★St Vitus Cathedral CHURCH
See p42.

Within the Castle Complex

Lobkowicz Palace MUSEUM
(Lobkovický palác; Map p44; ☎233 312 925; www.lobkowicz.com; Jiřská 3; adult/concession/family 275/200/690Kč; ⏲10am-6pm; 🚊22) This 16th-century palace houses a private museum known as the Princely Collections, which includes priceless paintings, furniture and musical memorabilia. Your tour includes an audio guide dictated by owner William Lobkowicz and his family – this personal connection really brings the displays to life, and makes the palace one of the castle's most interesting attractions.

Built in the 16th century, the palace has been home to the aristocratic Lobkowicz family for around 400 years. Confiscated by the Nazis in WWII, and again by the communists in 1948, the palace was finally returned in 2002 to William Lobkowicz, an American property developer and grandson

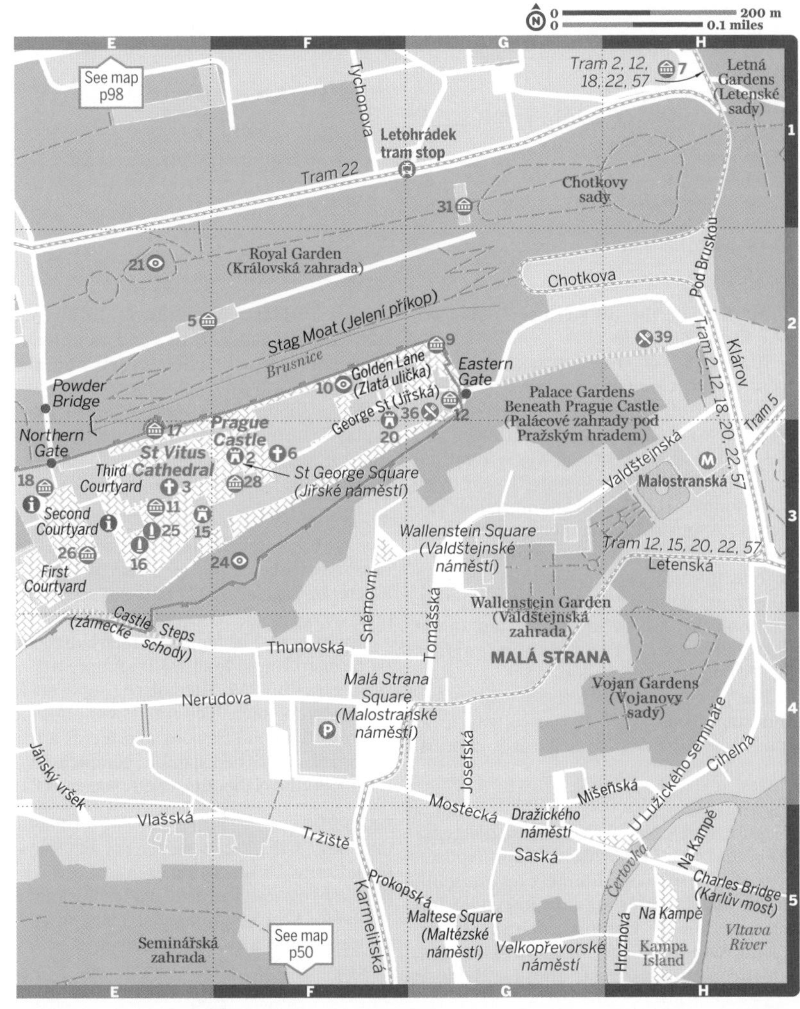

Hradčany

Top Sights
1 Loreta ... B4
2 Prague Castle ... F3
3 St Vitus Cathedral ... E3
4 Strahov Library ... A5

Sights
5 Ball-Game House ... E2
6 Basilica of St George ... F3
7 Bílek Villa ... H1
8 Černín Palace ... B4
9 Daliborka ... G2
10 Golden Lane ... F2
11 Great South Tower of St Vitus Cathedral ... E3
12 Lobkowicz Palace ... G2
13 Miniature Museum ... B5
14 Nový Svět Quarter ... B3
15 Old Royal Palace ... E3
16 Plečník Monolith ... E3
17 Powder Tower ... E3
18 Prague Castle Picture Gallery ... E3
19 Riding School ... D2
20 Rosenberg Palace ... F2
21 Royal Garden ... E2
22 Salm Palace ... D4
23 Schwarzenberg Palace ... D4
24 South Gardens ... F3
25 St George Slaying the Dragon ... E3
26 St Vitus Treasury ... E3
27 Šternberg Palace ... D3
28 Story of Prague Castle ... F3
29 Strahov Monastery ... B5
30 Strahov Picture Gallery ... B5
31 Summer Palace ... G1

Sleeping
32 Domus Henrici ... C4
33 Hotel Monastery ... B5
34 Romantik Hotel U Raka ... B2

Eating
35 Host ... C4
36 Lobkowicz Palace Café ... G2
37 Malý Buddha ... B4
38 U Zlaté Hrušky ... C3
39 Villa Richter ... H2

Drinking & Nightlife
40 Kafe U zelených kamen ... D4
41 Klášterní pivovar Strahov ... A5
42 Pivnice U Černého Vola ... B4

Shopping
43 Houpací Kůň ... B4

of Maximilian, the 10th Prince Lobkowicz, who fled to the US in 1939.

Highlights of the museum include paintings by Cranach, Breughel the Elder, Canaletto and Piranesi; original musical scores annotated by Mozart, Beethoven and Haydn (the seventh prince was a great patron of music – Beethoven dedicated three symphonies to him); and an impressive collection of musical instruments. But it's the personal touches that make an impression, such as the 16th-century portrait of a Lobkowicz ancestor wearing a ring that William's mother still wears today, and an old photo album with a picture of a favourite family dog smoking a pipe.

The palace has an excellent cafe (p122), and stages concerts of classical music at 1pm each day (www.prague-castle-concert.cz; 340Kč to 490Kč).

Toy Museum MUSEUM

(Muzeum Hraček; Map p62; ☎224 372 294; Husova 20; adult/child/family 70/50/200Kč; ⏲10am-6pm; 🚊22) The second-largest toy museum in the world houses an amazing collection put together by film-maker Ivan Steiger. It's an Aladdin's Cave for adult collectors, but it can be a bit frustrating for the kids as most displays are hands-off. Toys range from Märklin model trains and Steiff teddy bears to Victorian dolls, Action Men and the definitive Barbie collection.

The exhibition has moved to the Clam Gallas Palace in the Old Town for the duration of 2017 while the building undergoes renovations.

Rosenberg Palace PALACE

(Rožmberský palác; Map p44; Jiřská 1; admission incl with Prague Castle Tour A ticket; ⏲9am-5pm Apr-Oct, to 4pm Nov-Mar; 🚊22) This Renaissance palace once served as the 'Institute of Noblewomen' – effectively a home for aristocratic ladies fallen on hard times, founded by Empress Maria Theresa in 1755. The palace chapel soars three storeys high, decorated with trompe l'œil paintings and frescoes, and there's a recreation of a lady's bedchamber, complete with commode and elaborate period mousetrap!

Daliborka MUSEUM

(Map p44; Zlatá ulička; admission incl with Prague Castle tour A & B tickets; ⏲9am-5pm Apr-Oct, to 4pm Nov-Mar) This tower is named after the knight Dalibor of Kozojedy, imprisoned here in 1498 for supporting a peasant rebellion, and later executed. According to legend, he played a violin that could be heard throughout the castle; composer Bedřich Smetana based his 1868 opera *Dalibor* on the tale. You can peer into the bottle dungeon, and see a small display of torture instruments.

Around Hradčany

Strahov Monastery MONASTERY

(Strahovský klášter; Map p44; ☎233 107 711, guided tours 602 190 297; www.strahovskyklaster.cz; Strahovské nádvoří 1; 🚋22) In 1140 Vladislav II founded Strahov Monastery for the Premonstratensian order. The present monastery buildings, completed in the 17th and 18th centuries, functioned until the communist government closed them down and imprisoned most of the monks; they returned in 1990. The main attraction here is the magnificent Strahov Library.

Inside the main gate is the 1612 **Church of St Roch** (kostel sv Rocha), which is now an art gallery, and the **Church of the Assumption of Our Lady** (kostel Nanebevzetí Panny Marie), built in 1143 and heavily decorated in the 18th century in the baroque style; Mozart is said to have played the organ here.

★ **Strahov Library** HISTORIC BUILDING

(Strahovská knihovna; Map p44; ☎233 107 718; www.strahovskyklaster.cz; Strahovské nádvoří 1; adult/child 100/50Kč; ⏱9am-noon & 1-5pm; 🚋22) Strahov Library is the largest monastic library in the country, with two magnificent baroque halls dating from the 17th and 18th centuries. You can peek through the doors but, sadly, you can't go into the halls themselves – it was found that fluctuations in humidity caused by visitors' breath was endangering the frescoes. There's also a display of historical curiosities.

The stunning interior of the two-storey-high **Philosophy Hall** (Filozofický sál; 1780–97) was built to fit around the carved and gilded, floor-to-ceiling walnut shelving that was rescued from another monastery in South Bohemia (access to the upper gallery is via spiral staircases concealed in the corners). The feeling of height here is accentuated by a grandiose ceiling fresco, *Mankind's Quest for True Wisdom* – the figure of Divine Providence is enthroned in the centre amid a burst of golden light, while around the edges are figures ranging from Adam and Eve to the Greek philosophers.

The lobby outside the hall contains an 18th-century **Cabinet of Curiosities**, displaying the grotesquely shrivelled remains of sharks, skates, turtles and other sea creatures; these flayed and splayed corpses were prepared by sailors, who passed them off to credulous landlubbers as 'sea monsters'. Lying on a table to the right of the entrance, along with a narwhal tusk, are two long, brown, leathery things. The prudish attendant may tell you they're elephants' trunks, but they're actually preserved whales' penises.

Another case (beside the door to the corridor) contains historical items, including a miniature coffee service made for the Habsburg empress Marie Louise in 1813, which fits into four false books. Opposite it is the **Xyloteka** (1825), a set of booklike boxes, each one bound in the wood and bark of the tree it describes, with samples of leaves, roots, flowers and fruits inside. As you enter the corridor, look to the left to find a facsimile of the library's most prized possession, the **Strahov Evangeliary**, a 9th-century codex in a gem-studded 12th-century binding.

The corridor leads to the older but even more beautiful **Theology Hall** (Teologiský sál; 1679). The low, curved ceiling is thickly encrusted in ornate baroque stuccowork, and decorated with painted cartouches depicting the theme of 'True Wisdom', which was acquired, of course, through piety; one of the mottoes that adorns the ceiling is *initio sapientiae timor domini:* 'the beginning of wisdom is the fear of God'.

Strahov Picture Gallery GALLERY

(Strahovská Obrazárna; Map p44; ☎220 517 278; www.strahovskyklaster.cz; Strahovské nádvoří II; adult/child 120/60Kč; ⏱9.30-11.30am & noon-5pm; 🚋22) In Strahov Monastery's second courtyard is the Strahov Picture Gallery, with a valuable collection of Gothic, baroque, rococo and romantic art on the 1st floor, and temporary exhibits on the ground floor. Some of the medieval works are extraordinary – don't miss the very modern-looking 14th-century Jihlava Crucifix. You can also wander around the monastery's cloister, refectory and chapter house.

★ **Loreta** CHURCH

(Map p44; ☎220 516 740; www.loreta.cz; Loretánské náměstí 7; adult/child/family 150/80/310Kč, photography permit 100Kč; ⏱9am-5pm Apr-Oct, 9.30am-4pm Nov-Mar; 🚋22) The Loreta is a baroque place of pilgrimage founded by Benigna Kateřina Lobkowicz in 1626, designed as a replica of the supposed Santa Casa (Sacred House; the home of the Virgin Mary) in the Holy Land. Legend says that the original Santa Casa was carried by angels to the Italian town of Loreto as the Turks were advancing on Nazareth.

The duplicate **Santa Casa** is in the centre of a courtyard complex, surrounded by cloistered arcades, churches and chapels. The interior is adorned with 17th-century frescoes and reliefs depicting the life of the Virgin Mary, and an ornate silver altar with a wooden effigy of Our Lady of Loreto. Above the entrance to the courtyard 27 bells, made in Amsterdam in the 17th century, play 'We Greet Thee a Thousand Times' on the hour.

Behind the Santa Casa is the **Church of the Nativity of Our Lord** (kostel Narození Páně), built in 1737 to a design by Kristof Dientzenhofer. The claustrophobic interior includes two skeletons of the Spanish saints Felicissima and Marcia, dressed in aristocratic clothing with wax masks concealing their skulls.

At the corner of the courtyard is the unusual **Chapel of Our Lady of Sorrows** (kaple Panny Marie Bolestné), featuring a crucified bearded lady. She was St Starosta, pious daughter of a Portuguese king who promised her to the king of Sicily against her wishes. After a night of tearful prayers she awoke with a beard, the wedding was called off, and her father had her crucified. She was later made patron saint of the needy and the godforsaken.

The church's **treasury** (1st floor) has been ransacked several times over the centuries, but it remains a bastion of over-the-top religious bling centred on the 90cm-tall Prague Sun (Pražské slunce), made of solid silver and gold and studded with 6222 diamonds.

Šternberg Palace — GALLERY

(Šternberský palác; Map p44; ☎233 090 570; www.ngprague.cz; Hradčanské náměstí 15; incl admission to all National Gallery venues; adult/child 300/150Kč; ⌚10am-6pm Tue-Sun; 🚋22) The baroque Šternberg Palace is home to the National Gallery's collection of European art from ancient Greece and Rome up to the 18th century, including works by Goya and Rembrandt. Fans of medieval altarpieces will be in heaven; there are also several Rubens, some Brueghels, and a large collection of Bohemian miniatures.

Pride of the gallery is the glowing *Feast of the Rosary* by Albrecht Dürer, an artist better known for his engravings. Painted in Venice in 1505 as an altarpiece for the church of San Bartolomeo, it was brought to Prague by Rudolf II; in the background, beneath the tree on the right, is the figure of the artist himself. For a bit of grotesque, snot-nosed realism, it's worth a trip to the back of the 1st floor to see the 16th-century Dutch painting *The Tearful Bride*.

Tickets are valid for seven days, and give admission to all six of the National Gallery's permanent exhibitions: Kinský Palace, Convent of St Agnes, Veletržní Palác, Šternberg Palace, Schwarzenberg Palace and Salm Palace.

Miniature Museum — MUSEUM

(Muzeum Miniatur; Map p44; ☎233 352 371; www.muzeumminiatur.cz; Strahovské nádvoří II; adult/child 100/50Kč; ⌚10am-5pm; 🚋22) Siberian technician Anatoly Konyenko once manufactured tools for microsurgery, but in his spare time he spent 7½ years crafting a pair of golden horseshoes for a flea. See those, as well as the Lord's Prayer inscribed on a single human hair, a grasshopper clutching a violin, and a camel caravan silhouetted in the eye of a needle. Weird but fascinating.

Nový Svět Quarter — AREA

(Map p44; 🚋22) In the 16th century, houses were built for castle staff in an enclave of curving cobblestone streets down the slope north of the Loreta. Today these diminutive cottages have been restored and painted in pastel shades, making the 'New World' quarter a perfect alternative to the castle's crowded Golden Lane. Danish astronomer Tycho Brahe once lived at Nový Svět 1.

Bílek Villa — GALLERY

(Bílkova Vila; Map p44; ☎233 323 631; http://en.ghmp.cz/frantisek-bileks-studio; Mickiewiczova 1; adult/child 120/60Kč; ⌚10am-6pm Tue-Sun; 🚋18, 22) This striking art-nouveau villa, designed by sculptor František Bílek in 1911, now houses a museum of his unconventional works. Bílek's distinctive sculptures, mostly in wood, take inspiration from his religious beliefs. Dramatic compositions such as *The Fall* show Adam and Eve cowering in fear of God's wrath, while *Wonderment* expresses the feeling of awe at God's presence.

Bílek's most famous work is a wooden relief of *The Crucifixion*, on display in St Vitus Cathedral (p42) – you can see a charcoal preliminary sketch of it among the artist's drawings in the 1st-floor gallery. The villa served not only as a studio but also as the artist's home, and there are several rooms with handmade art-nouveau furniture designed by Bílek, all rich in symbolism. Be sure to ask for an English text at the ticket desk – it will provide some much-needed context.

PRAGUE FOR FREE

Once a famously inexpensive destination, Prague is no longer cheap; there's not much on offer without a price attached. Parks and gardens, some museums and galleries, and gazing at the glorious architecture are all free, as is the street entertainment on Charles Bridge.

Without having to buy a ticket, you can wander through the courtyards and gardens of **Prague Castle** (p36), watch the changing of the guard ceremony and visit the western end of the nave of **St Vitus Cathedral** (p42). Nearby **Charles Bridge** (p54), with its array of jazz bands, buskers, caricature artists and postcard sellers, is a smorgasbord of free entertainment.

Over in Old Town Square, the hourly performance by the **Astronomical Clock** (p68) is a classic tick without a ticket, as is the baroque glory of the nearby **Church of St Nicholas** (p70). Although you'll have to pay for a guided tour of the **Municipal House** (p72), you can wander through the glorious art-nouveau cafe, the lobby and to the downstairs American Bar without paying for admission.

Visits to most churches in Prague (except St Nicholas Church in Malá Strana) are free, as are the beautiful **Wallenstein Garden** (p56) and imposing **Vyšehrad Citadel** (p104).

Salm Palace GALLERY

(Salmovský Palác; Map p44; ☎233 081 713; www.ngprague.cz; Hradčanské náměstí 1; adult/child 300/150Kč incl admission to all National Gallery venues; ⏰10am-6pm Tue-Sun; 🚋22) Overlooking the entrance to Prague Castle, the austerely neoclassical Salm Palace – built in 1810 as a luxury aristocratic residence – provides hanging space for the National Gallery's temporary exhibitions (see website for latest program), and houses the NG's collection of 19th-century Czech art. Tickets can be bought in the glass-fronted information office between the Salm and Schwarzenberg Palaces.

Tickets are valid for seven days, and give admission to all six of the National Gallery's permanent exhibitions: Kinský Palace, Convent of St Agnes, Veletržní Palác, Šternberg Palace, Schwarzenberg Palace and Salm Palace.

Schwarzenberg Palace GALLERY

(Schwarzenberský palác; Map p44; ☎224 810 758; www.ngprague.cz; Hradčanské náměstí 2; adult/child 300/150Kč incl admission to all National Gallery venues; ⏰10am-6pm Tue-Sun; 🚋22) Sporting a beautifully preserved facade of black-and-white Renaissance sgraffito, the Schwarzenberg Palace houses the National Gallery's collection of baroque art. Sadly, a lot of the paintings are poorly lit and suffer from reflections from nearby windows – a shame, as the inside of the palace itself is less impressive than the outside, and the collection is really only of interest to aficionados.

The ground floor is given over to two masters of baroque sculpture, Matthias Braun and Maximilian Brokof, whose overwrought figures appear to have been caught in a hurricane, such is the liveliness of their billowing robes. The highlights of the 1st floor are the moody 16th-century portraits by Petr Brandl and Jan Kupecký, while the top floor boasts a display of engravings by Albrecht Dürer.

Tickets are valid for seven days, and give admission to all six of the National Gallery's permanent exhibitions: Kinský Palace, Convent of St Agnes, Veletržní Palác, Šternberg Palace, Schwarzenberg Palace and Salm Palace.

Černín Palace ARCHITECTURE

(Černínský Palác; Map p44; Loretánské náměstí; ⏰closed to the public; 🚋22) The late-17th-century early-baroque palace opposite the Loreta boasts Prague's largest monumental facade. This imposing building has housed the foreign ministry since the creation of Czechoslovakia in 1918, except during WWII when it served as the headquarters of the Nazi Reichsprotektor; this is where the documents that dissolved the Warsaw Pact were signed in 1991.

In 1948, Jan Masaryk – son of the Czechoslovak Republic's founding father, Tomáš Garrigue *Masaryk*, and the only noncommunist in the new Soviet-backed government – fell to his death from one of the upper windows. Did he fall, or was he pushed? A new movie, Masaryk (released in 2017) by Czech director Julius Sevcík, examines this murky episode in Prague's history.

Malá Strana

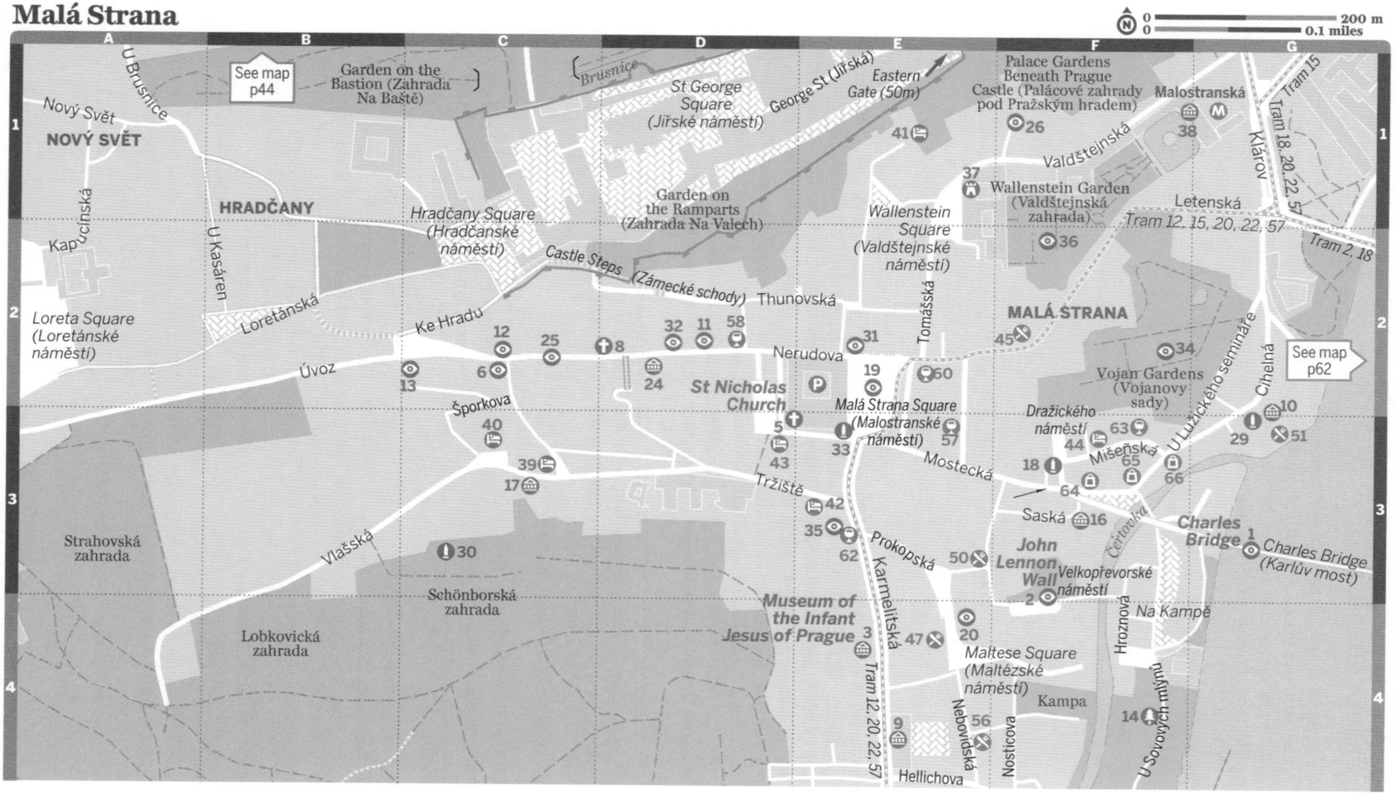
0 200 m
0 0.1 miles
A
B
C
D
E
F
G
1
2
3
4
See map p44
See map p62
Garden on the Bastion (Zahrada Na Baště)
Brusnice
St George Square (Jiřské náměstí)
George St (Jiřská)
Eastern Gate (50m)
Palace Gardens Beneath Prague Castle (Palácové zahrady pod Pražským hradem)
Malostranská
Tram 15
Tram 18, 20, 22, 57
Klárov
U Brusnice
Nový Svět
NOVÝ SVĚT
Kapucínská
HRADČANY
U Kasáren
Hradčany Square (Hradčanské náměstí)
Garden on the Ramparts (Zahrada Na Valech)
Castle Steps (Zámecké schody)
Thunovská
Valdštejnská
Wallenstein Garden (Valdštejnská zahrada)
Letenská
Tram 12, 15, 20, 22, 57
Tram 2, 18
Wallenstein Square (Valdštejnské náměstí)
Tomášská
MALÁ STRANA
Loreta Square (Loretánské náměstí)
Loretánská
Ke Hradu
Nerudova
Úvoz
St Nicholas Church
Malá Strana Square (Malostranské náměstí)
Vojan Gardens (Vojanovy sady)
U Lužického semináře
Cihelná
Šporkova
Dražického náměstí
Mišeňská
Mostecká
Tržiště
Saská
Čertovka
Charles Bridge
Charles Bridge (Karlův most)
Strahovská zahrada
Vlašská
Schönborská zahrada
Lobkovická zahrada
Prokopská
Karmelitská
John Lennon Wall
Velkopřevorské náměstí
Na Kampě
Hroznová
Museum of the Infant Jesus of Prague
Maltese Square (Maltézské náměstí)
Kampa
Tram 12, 20, 22, 57
Nebovidská
Nosticova
U Sovových mlýnů
Hellichova
1
2
3
5
6
8
9
10
11
12
13
14
16
17
18
19
20
24
25
26
29
30
31
32
33
34
35
36
37
38
39
40
41
42
43
44
45
47
50
51
56
57
58
60
62
63
64
65
66

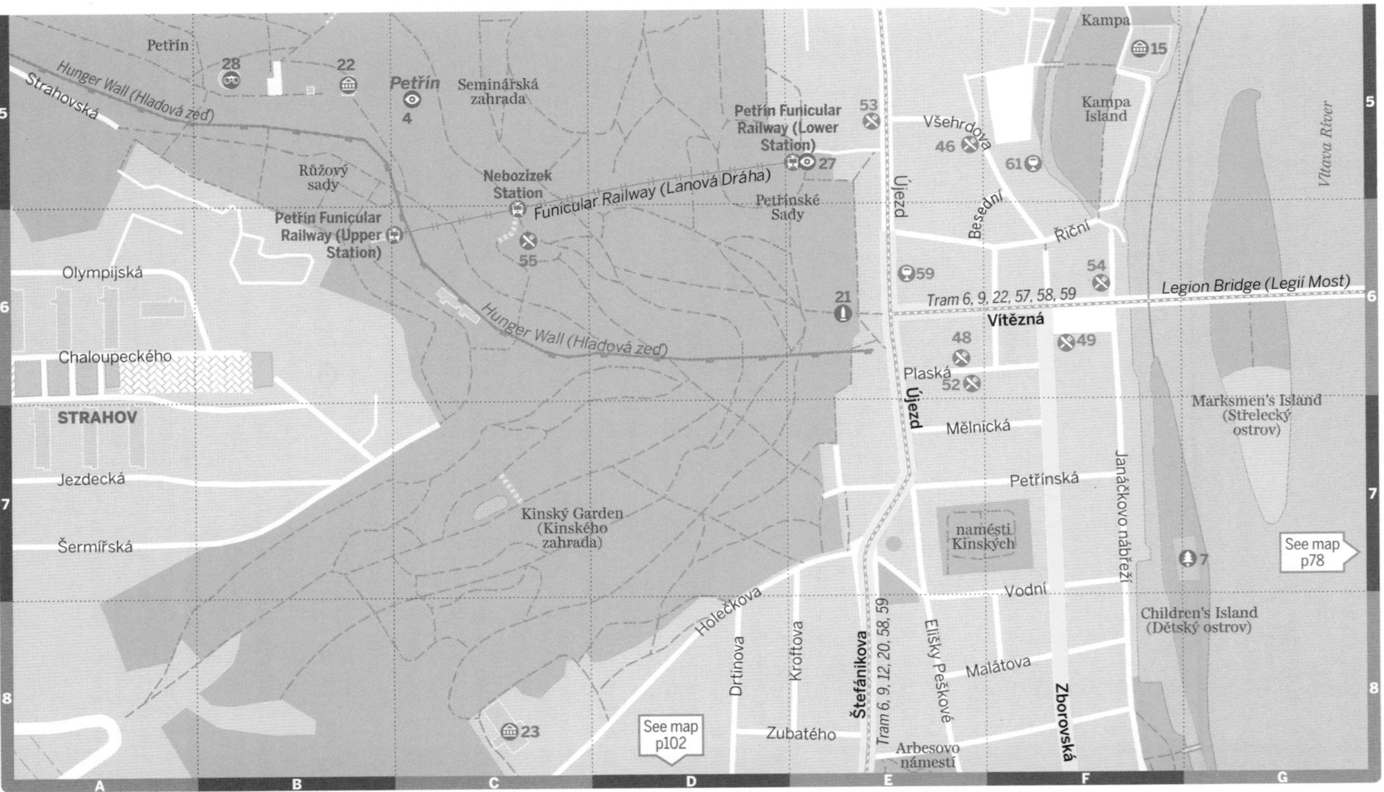
Petřín
Hunger Wall (Hladová zeď)
Strahovská
28
22
Petřín
4
Seminářská zahrada
Petřín Funicular Railway (Lower Station)
53
27
Všehrdova
46
61
Kampa
15
Kampa Island
Vltava River
Růžový sady
Nebozízek Station
Funicular Railway (Lanová Dráha)
Petřínské Sady
Petřín Funicular Railway (Upper Station)
55
Újezd
Besední
Říční
54
59
Olympijská
Tram 6, 9, 22, 57, 58, 59
Legion Bridge (Legií Most)
21
Vítězná
48
49
Chaloupeckého
Hunger Wall (Hladová zeď)
Plaská
52
STRAHOV
Újezd
Mělnická
Marksmen's Island (Střelecký ostrov)
Jezdecká
Petřínská
Janáčkovo nábřeží
Kinský Garden (Kinského zahrada)
náměstí Kinských
Šermířská
See map p78
7
Vodní
Holečkova
Children's Island (Dětský ostrov)
Drtinova
Kroftova
Štefánikova
Tram 6, 9, 12, 20, 58, 59
Elišky Peškové
Malátova
Zborovská
23
See map p102
Zubatého
Arbesovo náměstí
A
B
C
D
E
F
G
5
6
7
8

Malá Strana

Top Sights

1 Charles Bridge ... G3
2 John Lennon Wall ... F3
3 Museum of the Infant Jesus of Prague ... E4
4 Petřín ... C5
5 St Nicholas Church ... D3

Sights

6 Bretfeld Palace ... C2
7 Children's Island ... G7
8 Church of Our Lady of Unceasing Succour ... D2
9 Czech Museum of Music ... E4
10 Franz Kafka Museum ... G2
11 House at the Three Fiddles ... D2
12 House of the Golden Horseshoe ... C2
13 House of the Two Suns ... C2
14 Kampa ... F4
15 Kampa Museum ... F5
16 Karel Zeman Museum ... F3
17 KGB Museum ... C3
18 Malá Strana Bridge Tower ... F3
19 Malostranské náměstí ... E2
20 Maltese Square ... E4
21 Memorial to the Victims of Communism ... E6
22 Mirror Maze ... B5
23 Musaion ... C8
24 Museum Montanelli ... D2
25 Nerudova ... C2
26 Palace Gardens Beneath Prague Castle ... F1
27 Petřín Funicular Railway ... E5
28 Petřín Lookout Tower ... B5
29 Proudy (David Černý Sculpture) ... G3
30 Quo Vadis (David Černý Sculpture) ... C3
31 Smiřický Palace ... E2
32 St John of Nepomuk House ... D2
33 St Nicholas Church Bell Tower ... E3
34 Vojan Gardens ... F2
35 Vrtbov Garden ... E3
36 Wallenstein Garden ... F2
37 Wallenstein Palace ... E1
38 Wallenstein Riding School ... F1

Sleeping

39 Design Hotel Sax ... C3
40 Dům u velké boty ... C3
41 Golden Well Hotel ... E1
42 Hotel Aria ... E3
Hunger Wall Residence ... (see 48)
Little Quarter Hostel ... (see 25)
43 Little Town Budget Hotel ... D3
44 Lokál Inn ... F3

Eating

45 Augustine ... F2
46 Bar Bar ... E5
47 Café de Paris ... E4
48 Café Lounge ... E6
49 Café Savoy ... F6
50 Cukrkávalimonáda ... E3
51 Hergetova Cihelna ... G3
52 Ichnusa Botega Bistro ... E6
53 Noi ... E5
54 Pastař ... F6
55 Restaurant Nebozízek ... C6
Terasa U Zlaté studně ... (see 41)
56 U Modré Kachničky ... E4

Drinking & Nightlife

57 Blue Light ... E3
58 Hostinec U Kocoura ... D2
59 Klub Újezd ... E6
60 Malostranská beseda ... E2
61 Mlýnská Kavárna ... F5
62 U Malého Glena ... E3
63 Vinograf ... F3

Shopping

64 Artěl ... F3
65 Chemistry ... F3
Marionety Truhlář ... (see 64)
66 Shakespeare & Sons ... F3

Malá Strana

Malá Strana's sights are a great mixture of historic buildings, baroque churches and offbeat museums, anchored by the ultimate Prague experience of strolling across medieval Charles Bridge. The main sights are within walking distance of the bridge, but you might want to hop on a tram to visit the southern part of the neighbourhood, or take the funicular to the top of Petřín Hill.

Prague Castle to Charles Bridge

★Charles Bridge BRIDGE

See p54.

★St Nicholas Church CHURCH

(Kostel sv Mikuláše; Map p50; ☎257 534 215; www.stnicholas.cz; Malostranské náměstí 38; adult/child 70/50Kč; ⏰9am-5pm Mar-Oct, to 4pm Nov-Feb; 🚋12, 15, 20, 22) Malá Strana is dominated by the huge green cupola of St Nicholas Church, one of Central Europe's finest baroque buildings. (Don't confuse it with the other Church of St Nicholas on Old Town Square.) On the ceiling, Johann Kracker's 1770 *Apotheosis of St Nicholas* is Europe's largest fresco (clever trompe l'oeil techniques have made the painting merge almost seamlessly with the architecture).

The building was begun by famed baroque architect Kristof Dientzenhofer; his son Kilian continued the work and Anselmo Lurago finished the job in 1755. Mozart himself tickled the ivories on the 2500-pipe organ in 1787, and was honoured with a requiem Mass here (14 December 1791). Take the stairs up to the gallery to see Karel Škréta's gloomy 17th-century Passion Cycle paintings and the scratchings of bored 1820s tourists and wannabe Franz Kafkas on the balustrade. See the website for the church's program of classical music concerts.

You can climb the church's bell tower via a separate entrance on the corner of Malostranské náměstí and Mostecká. During the communist era, the tower was used to spy on the nearby American embassy – on the way up you can still see a small, white cast-iron urinal that was installed for the use of the watchers

St Nicholas Church Bell Tower TOWER

(Map p50; http://en.muzeumprahy.cz/prague-towers; Malostranské náměstí; adult/child 90/65Kč; ⏲10am-10pm Apr-Sep, to 8pm Mar & Oct, to 6pm Nov-Feb; 🚊12, 15, 20, 22) During the communist era, the bell tower of St Nicholas Church was used to spy on the nearby American embassy – on the way up you can still see a small, white cast-iron urinal that was installed for the use of the watchers. Today it provides visitors with a grand view over Malá Strana and Charles Bridge.

Malostranské Náměstí SQUARE

(Map p50; 🚊12, 15, 20, 22) Malostranské náměstí, Malá Strana's main square, is divided into an upper and lower part by St Nicholas Church, the district's most distinctive landmark. The square has been the hub of Malá Strana since the 10th century, though it lost some of its character when Karmelitská street was widened early in the 20th century, and a little more when Prague's first Starbucks opened here in 2008.

Today it's a mixture of official buildings and touristy restaurants, with a tram line running through the middle of the lower square. The nightclub and bar at No 21, Malostranská beseda (p143), was once the old town hall. It was here in 1575 that non-Catholic nobles wrote the so-called České Konfese (Czech Confession), a pioneering demand for religious tolerance addressed to the Habsburg emperor that was eventually passed into Czech law by Rudolf II in 1609. On 22 May 1618, Czech nobles gathered at the **Smiřický Palace** (Map p50; Malostranské náměstí 18; 🚊12, 15, 20, 22) to plot a rebellion against the Habsburg rulers – the next day they flung two Habsburg councillors out of a window at Prague Castle.

Karel Zeman Museum MUSEUM

(Museum of Film Special Effects; Map p50; ☎724 341 091; www.muzeumkarlazemana.cz; Saský dvůr, Saská 3; adult/child 200/140Kč; ⏲10am-7pm, last admission 6pm; 🚊12, 15, 20, 22) Bohemia-born director Karel Zeman (1910–89) was a pioneer of movie special effects whose work is little known outside the Czech Republic. This fascinating museum, established by his daughter, reveals the many tricks and techniques he perfected, and even allows visitors a bit of hands-on interaction – you can film yourself on your smartphone against painted backgrounds and 3D models.

Zeman's inventive use of animation and matte paintings combined with live action – seen in films such as *Cesta do pravěku* (Journey to the Beginning of Time; 1955) and *Baron Prášil* (The Fabulous Baron Munchausen; 1961) – influenced more famous directors including George Lucas, Tim Burton and Terry Gilliam (who remade *The Adventures of Baron Munchausen* in 1988).

Nerudova STREET

(Map p50; 🚊12, 15, 20, 22) Following the tourist crowds downhill from the castle via Ke Hradu, you will arrive at Nerudova, architecturally the most important street in Malá Strana; most of its old Renaissance facades were 'baroquefied' in the 18th century. It's named after the Czech poet Jan Neruda (famous for his short stories, *Tales of Malá Strana*), who lived at the **House of the Two Suns** (dům U dvou slunců; Map p50; Nerudova 47; 🚊12, 15, 20, 22) from 1845 to 1857.

The **House of the Golden Horseshoe** (dům U zlaté podkovy; Map p50; Nerudova 34; 🚊12, 15, 20, 22) is named after the relief of St Wenceslas above the doorway – his horse was said to be shod with gold. From 1765 Josef of Bretfeld made his **Bretfeld Palace** (Map p50; Nerudova 33; 🚊12, 15, 20, 22) a social hotspot, entertaining Mozart and Casanova. The baroque **Church of Our Lady of Unceasing Succour**

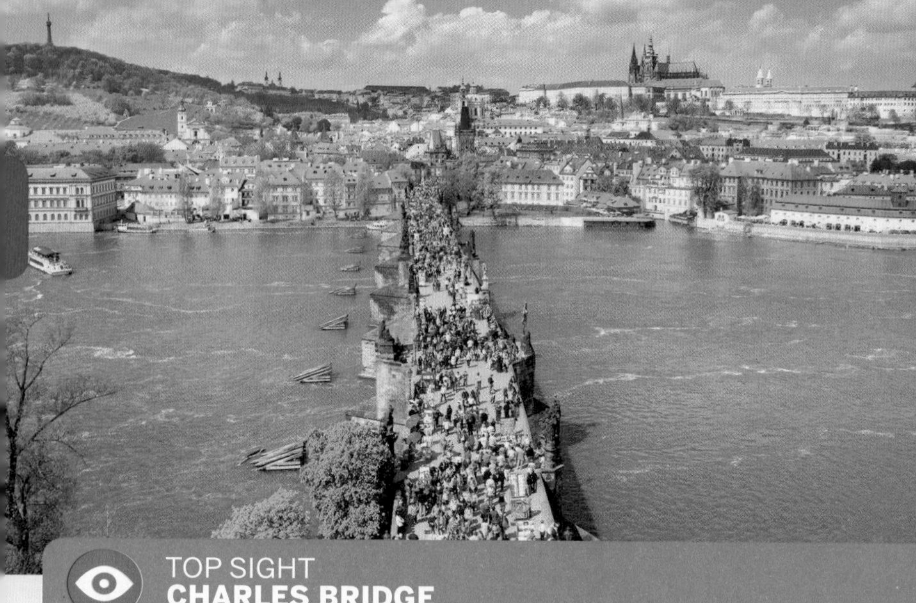

TOP SIGHT
CHARLES BRIDGE

KAPRIK/SHUTTERSTOCK ©

Strolling across Charles Bridge is everybody's favourite Prague activity, browsing the stalls of hawkers and caricaturists and listening to buskers beneath the impassive gaze of the baroque statues that line the parapets. Don't forget to look at the bridge itself (the bridge towers have great views) and the grand vistas up and down the river.

History

In 1357 Charles IV commissioned Peter Parler (the architect of St Vitus Cathedral) to replace the 12th-century Judith Bridge, which had been washed away by floods in 1342. (You can see the only surviving arch of the Judith Bridge by taking a boat trip with Prague Venice (p108).

The new bridge was completed in 1390, and took Charles's name only in the 19th century – before that it was known simply as Kamenný most (Stone Bridge). Despite occasional flood damage, it withstood wheeled traffic for 500-odd years – thanks, legend says, to eggs mixed into the mortar (though recent investigations have disproved this myth) – until it was made pedestrian-only after WWII.

DON'T MISS

- The view from the Old Town Bridge Tower
- St John of Nepomuk Statue
- Busking jazz musicians

PRACTICALITIES

- Karlův most
- Map p50
- 24hr
- 2, 17, 18 to Karlovy lázně, 12, 15, 20, 22 to Malostranské náměstí

The Bridge Towers

Perched at the eastern end of Charles Bridge in Staré Město, the elegant late-14th-century Old Town Bridge Tower (Staroměstská mostecká věž; Map p62; 224 220 569; http://en.muzeumprahy.cz/prague-towers; Charles Bridge; adult/child 90/65Kč; 10am-10pm Apr-Sep, to 8pm Mar & Oct, to 6pm Nov-Feb; 17, 18) was built not only as a fortification but also as a triumphal arch marking the entrance to the Old Town. Here, at the end of the Thirty Years' War, an invading Swedish army was finally repulsed by a band of students and

Jewish ghetto residents. Like the bridge itself, the tower was designed by Peter Parler and incorporates many symbolic elements.

The tower houses an exhibition about the design and construction of Charles Bridge and the bridge towers, and displays of historical artefacts retrieved by archaeologists from the bed of the river. The main justification for paying the admission fee, however, is the amazing view from the top of the tower.

There are actually two towers at the Malá Strana end of Charles Bridge. The lower one was originally part of the long-gone 12th-century Judith Bridge, while the taller one was built in the mid-15th century in imitation of the Staré Město tower. The taller Malá Strana Bridge Tower (Map p50; http://en.muzeumprahy.cz/prague-towers; Mostecká; adult/child 90/65Kč; ⏲10am-10pm Apr-Sep, to 8pm Mar & Oct, to 6pm Nov-Feb; 🚊12, 15, 20, 22) is open to the public and houses a small exhibit on the tower's history but, like its Staré Město counterpart, the main attraction is the view from the top.

The Statues

The first monument erected on the bridge was the crucifix near the eastern end, in 1657. The first statue – the Jesuits' 1683 tribute to St John of Nepomuk – inspired other Catholic orders, and over the next 30 years a score more went up, like ecclesiastical billboards. New ones were added in the mid-19th century, and one (plus replacements for some lost to floods) in the 20th century.

The most famous figure is the monument to St John of Nepomuk. According to the legend on the base of the statue, Wenceslas IV had him trussed up in armour and thrown off the bridge in 1393 for refusing to divulge the queen's confessions (he was her priest), though the real reason had to do with the bitter conflict between church and state; the stars in his halo allegedly followed his corpse down the river. Tradition says that if you rub the bronze plaque, you will one day return to Prague. A bronze cross set in the parapet between statues 17 and 19 marks the point where he was thrown off.

BRADÁČ

At the Staré Město end of the bridge, look over the downstream parapet at the retaining wall on the right and you'll see a carved stone head known as Bradáč (Bearded Man). When the river level rose above this medieval marker, Praguers knew it was time to head for the hills. A blue line on the modern flood gauge nearby shows the level of the 2002 flood, no less than 2m above Bradáč!

Although the bridge has survived for more than 600 years, it was badly damaged in the floods of 1890 when three of the arches collapsed. You can see photographs of the damage and repair work in the Charles Bridge Museum (p76).

STATUES

As most of the statues on the bridge were carved from soft sandstone, several weathered originals have been replaced with copies. Some originals are housed in the Casemates at Vyšehrad (p104); others are in the Lapidárium (p100) in Holešovice.

LOCAL KNOWLEDGE

LOCAL LIFE IN MALÁ STRANA

➡ **Parks** Picturesque it may be, but Malá Strana is also a place of work for many Praguers, filled as it is with government offices, embassies and consulates. Favourite parks where locals relax during lunch breaks include **Vojan Gardens** (p58) and **Kampa park** (p59).

➡ **Hang-outs** A popular venue for after-work drinks among local artists, journalists and politicians is **Mlýnská Kavárna** (p143).

➡ **Petřín** Summer or winter, **Petřín** (p60) is every bit as popular with local families as it is with tourists. On the weekend, the hill's lookout tower and Mirror Maze are thronging with excited kids.

(kostel Panny Marie ustavičné pomoci; Map p50; Nerudova 24; 🚋12, 15, 20, 22) was a theatre from 1834 to 1837, and staged Czech plays during the Czech National Revival.

Built in 1566, **St John of Nepomuk House** (Map p50; Nerudova 18; 🚋12, 15, 20, 22) is adorned with the image of one of Bohemia's patron saints, while the **House at the Three Fiddles** (dům U tří houslíček; Map p50; Nerudova 12; 🚋12, 15, 20, 22), a Gothic building rebuilt in Renaissance-style during the 17th century, once belonged to a family of violin makers.

Most of the buildings bear house signs.

Museum Montanelli GALLERY

(Map p50; ☎257 531 220; www.muzeummontanelli.com; Nerudova 13; adult/child 50Kč/free; ⏲2-6pm Tue-Fri, 1-6pm Sat & Sun; 🚋12, 15, 20, 22) Tourists, drawn in by an attractive cafe and bookshop, rub shoulders with connoisseurs of the Czech art world in this private gallery. Having rapidly become a focus for contemporary art in Prague, it provides a showcase for up-and-coming artists from Central and Eastern Europe, as well as staging exhibitions by more established international names.

Northern Malá Strana

Wallenstein Garden GARDENS

(Valdštejnská zahrada; Map p50; www.senat.cz; Letenská 10; ⏲7.30am-6pm Mon-Fri, 10am-6pm Sat & Sun Mar-Oct, to 7pm daily Jun-Sep; Ⓜ Malostranská, 🚋12, 15, 20, 22) FREE This huge, baroque garden is an oasis of peace amid the bustle of Malá Strana's streets. Created for Duke Albrecht of Wallenstein in the 17th century, its finest feature is the huge loggia decorated with scenes from the Trojan Wars, flanked on one side by an enormous fake stalactite grotto – see how many hidden animals and grotesque faces you can spot.

The **bronze statues** of Greek gods lining the avenue opposite the loggia are copies – the originals were carted away by marauding Swedes in 1648 and now stand outside the royal palace of Drottningholm near Stockholm. At the eastern end of the garden is an **ornamental pond**, home to some seriously large carp, and the **Wallenstein Riding School** (Valdštejnská jízdárna; Map p50; ☎257 073 136; www.ngprague.cz; Valdštejnská 3; adult/child 150/80Kč; ⏲10am-6pm Tue-Sun; Ⓜ Malostranská), which hosts temporary exhibitions. Enter the garden via a gate beside Malostranská metro station, the main entrance on Letenská, or through the Wallenstein Palace.

Wallenstein Palace PALACE

(Valdštejnský palác; Map p50; ☎257 075 707; www.senat.cz; Valdštejnské náměstí 4; ⏲10am-5pm Sat & Sun Apr-Oct, 1st weekend of the month Nov-Mar; Ⓜ Malostranská, 🚋12, 15, 20, 22) FREE Valdštejnské náměstí, a small square northeast of Malostranské náměstí, is dominated by the monumental 1630 palace of Albrecht of Wallenstein, general of the Habsburg armies, who financed its construction with properties confiscated from Protestant nobles he defeated at the Battle of Bílá Hora in 1620. It now houses the Senate of the Czech Republic, with limited public access.

Enter via the Senate Information Centre in the first courtyard – the self-guided tour takes in the more spectacularly decorated parts of the palace. The ceiling fresco in the Baroque Hall shows Wallenstein as a warrior at the reins of a chariot, while the unusual oval Audience Hall has a fresco of Vulcan at work in his forge.

Palace Gardens Beneath Prague Castle GARDENS

(Palácové zahrady pod Pražským hradem; Map p50; ☎257 010 401; www.palacove-zahrady.cz; Valdštejnská 12-14; adult/child 90/60Kč; ⏲10am-7pm May-Sep, to 6pm Apr & Oct; Ⓜ Malostranská, 🚋12, 15, 20, 22) The beautiful, terraced gardens on the steep southern slopes below the castle date from the 17th and 18th centuries, when they were created for the owners of the adjoining palaces. They were restored in the 1990s and contain a Renaissance loggia with frescoes of Pompeii and a baroque portal with sundial

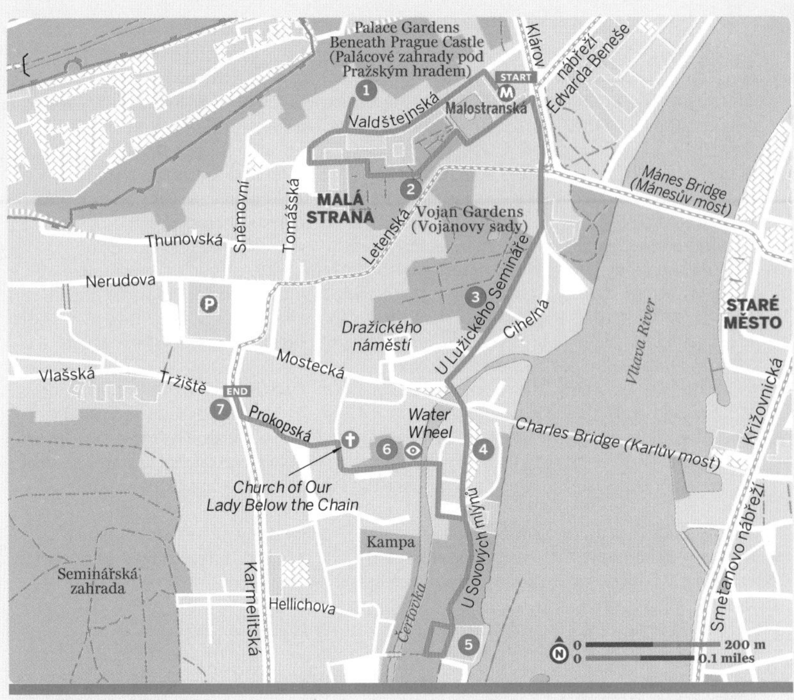

City Walk
Malá Strana Gardens

START MALOSTRANSKÁ METRO
END PETŘÍN HILL
LENGTH 2.5KM; 1½ HOURS

Except for Vojan, the gardens are open April to October only, but the walk is still worth doing in winter.

From Malostranská metro station head west along Valdštejnská to find the entrance to the 1 **Palace Gardens beneath Prague Castle** (p56). After exploring the gardens, return to Valdštejnská and turn right, then left into the Wallenstein Palace and through the courtyard to the 2 **Wallenstein Garden** (p56). Head for the northeastern corner and leave through the gate beside Malostranská metro station. Turn right on Klárov and continue along U Lužického semináře. A gate on the right leads to the 3 **Vojan Gardens**, a peaceful corner where local folk sit in the sun on the park benches.

Continue along U Lužického semináře and bear left across the little bridge over the Čertovka. Pass under Charles Bridge and through the picturesque square of 4 **Na Kampě** into the leafy riverside park known as Kampa, one of the city's favourite chill-out zones and home to the modern art collections of the 5 **Kampa Museum** (p59).

Retrace your steps and bear left along Hroznová, which leads to a bridge over the Čertovka beside a water wheel. The bridge is covered with padlocks placed there by couples as a sign of enduring love.

The bridge leads to a tiny cobbled square with the 6 **John Lennon Wall** (p59) on one side and the baroque palace that houses the French embassy on the other. The far end of the square curves right, past the severe Gothic towers of the Church of Our Lady Below the Chain. Turn left opposite the church and bear right along Prokopská; cross busy Karmelitská and turn right.

Just past the bar called U Malého Glena is an alley on your left that leads to the 7 **Vrtbov Garden** (p60), one of Malá Strana's least visited, but most beautiful, gardens.

THE ROYAL WAY

The Royal Way (Královská cesta) was the ancient processional route followed by Czech kings on their way to St Vitus Cathedral for coronation. The route leads from the **Powder Gate** (p75) along Celetná, through Old Town Sq and Little Square (Malé náměstí), along Karlova (Charles St) and across **Charles Bridge** to Malá Strana Sq (Malostranské náměstí), before climbing up Nerudova to the castle. The only procession that makes its way along these streets today is the daily crush of tourists shouldering their way past a gauntlet of souvenir shops and leaflet touts.

Celetná, leading from the Powder Gate to Old Town Square, is an open-air museum of pastel-painted baroque facades covering Gothic frames resting on Romanesque foundations, deliberately buried to raise Staré Město above the floods of the Vltava River. But the most interesting building – Josef Gočár's delightful **House of the Black Madonna** (dům U černé Matky Boží) – dates only from 1912.

Little Square, the southwestern extension of Old Town Square, has a Renaissance fountain with a 16th-century wrought-iron grill. Here, several fine baroque and neo-Renaissance exteriors adorn some of Staré Město's oldest structures. The most colourful is the 1890 **VJ Rott Building** (Map p62; Malé náměstí; M Staroměstská), decorated with wall paintings by Mikuláš Aleš, which now houses the Prague incarnation of the Hard Rock Cafe.

A dog-leg from the southwestern corner of the square leads to narrow, cobbled **Karlova**, which continues as far as Charles Bridge – this section is often choked with tourist crowds. On the corner of Liliová is the house called **At the Golden Snake**, the site of Prague's first coffee house, opened in 1708 by an Armenian named Deomatus Damajan.

Karlova sidles along the massive southern wall of the **Klementinum** (p75) before emerging at the riverside on Křížovnické náměstí. On the northern side of the square is the 17th-century **Church of St Francis Seraphinus** (kostel sv Františka Serafinského; Map p62; www.krizovnici.eu; Karlova), its dome decorated with a fresco of the Last Judgment. It belongs to the Order of the Knights of the Cross with the Red Star, the only Bohemian order of Crusaders still in existence.

Just south of Charles Bridge, at the site of the former Old Town mill, is **Novotného lávka**, a riverside terrace full of sunny, overpriced *vinárny* (wine bars) with great views of the bridge and castle. Its far end is dominated by a statue of composer Bedřich Smetana.

that cleverly catches the sunlight reflected off the water in a Triton fountain.

From the entrance on Valdštejnská, there are lots of steps to climb to reach the top of the gardens, but your reward is plenty of pleasant spots to sit and read, or just take in the view.

Franz Kafka Museum MUSEUM

(Muzeum Franzy Kafky; Map p50; ☎257 535 373; www.kafkamuseum.cz; Cihelná 2b; adult/child 200/120Kč; ⏰10am-6pm; M Malostranská, 🚊12, 15, 20, 22) This much-hyped exhibition on the life and work of Prague's most famous literary son, entitled 'City of K', explores the intimate relationship between the writer and the city that shaped him, through the use of original letters, photographs, quotations, period newspapers and publications, and video and sound installations.

Does it vividly portray the claustrophobic bureaucracy and atmosphere of brooding menace that characterised Kafka's world? Or is it a load of pretentious bollocks? You decide.

Proudy (David Černý Sculpture) PUBLIC ART

(Currents; Map p50; www.davidcerny.cz; Hergetova Cihelná; M Malostranská) Sounds of laughter and clicking cameras greet *Proudy* (2004) by David Černý, a saucy animatronic sculpture of two guys pissing in a puddle shaped like the Czech Republic. The microchip-controlled sculptures are writing out famous quotations from Czech literature with their 'pee'.

Vojan Gardens GARDENS

(Vojanovy sady; Map p50; U Lužického semináře; ⏰8am-dusk; M Malostranská) FREE While less manicured than most of Malá Strana's parks, Vojan Gardens is a popular spot with locals who like to come here to take a breather with the kids, sit in the sun or even hold summer parties.

Southern Malá Strana

★Museum of the Infant Jesus of Prague MUSEUM

(Muzeum Pražského Jezulátka; Map p50; ☎257 533 646; www.pragjesu.cz; Karmelitská 9; ⏲church 8.30am-7pm Mon-Sat, to 8pm Sun, museum 9.30am-5.30pm Mon-Sat, 1-6pm Sun, closed 1 Jan, 25 & 26 Dec & Easter Mon; 🚋12, 15, 20, 22) FREE The Church of Our Lady Victorious (kostel Panny Marie Vítězné), built in 1613, has on its central altar a 47cm-tall waxwork figure of the baby Jesus, brought from Spain in 1628 and known as the Infant Jesus of Prague (Pražské Jezulátko). At the back of the church is a museum, displaying a selection of the frocks used to dress the Infant.

The Infant is said to have protected Prague from the plague and from the destruction of the Thirty Years' War. An 18th-century German prior, ES Stephano, wrote about the miracles, kicking off what eventually became a worldwide cult; today the statue is visited by a steady stream of pilgrims, especially from Italy, Spain and Latin America. It was traditional to dress the figure in beautiful robes, and over the years various benefactors donated richly embroidered dresses. Today the Infant's wardrobe consists of more than 70 costumes donated from all over the world; these are changed regularly in accordance with a religious calendar.

★John Lennon Wall HISTORIC SITE

(Map p50; Velkopřevorské náměstí; 🚋12, 15, 20, 22) After his murder on 8 December 1980, John Lennon became a pacifist hero for many young Czechs. An image of Lennon was painted on a wall in a secluded square opposite the French embassy (there is a niche on the wall that looks like a tombstone), along with political graffiti and Beatles lyrics.

Despite repeated coats of whitewash, the secret police never managed to keep it clean for long, and the Lennon Wall became a political focus for Prague youth (a lot of Western pop music was banned by the communists, and some Czech musicians were even jailed for playing it).

Post-1989 weathering and lightweight graffiti ate away at the political messages and images, until little remained of Lennon but his eyes, but visiting tourists began making their own contributions. The wall is the property of the Knights of Malta, and they have repainted it several times, but it soon gets covered with more Lennon images, peace messages and inconsequential tourist graffiti. In recent years the Knights have bowed to the inevitable and don't bother to whitewash it any more.

Kampa PARK

(Map p50; 🚋12, 15, 20, 22) Kampa – an 'island' bounded by the Vltava and Čertovka (the Devil's Stream) – is the most peaceful and picturesque part of Malá Strana. It was once farmland (the name Kampa comes from *campus,* Latin for 'field'), but in the 13th century Prague's first mill, the **Sovovský mlýn** (now Kampa Museum, was built here, and other mills followed.

The north part of the island was settled in the 16th century after being raised above flood level. (In 1939 the river was so low that it was again joined to the mainland, and coins and jewellery were found in the dry channel.) Houses and restaurants are clustered around a picturesque little square called **Na Kampě**; at its northern end, at about waist height on the wall to the left of the little gallery under the stairs leading up to Charles Bridge, is a small **memorial plaque** that reads *Výska vody 4.září 1890* (height of waters, 4 September 1890), marking the level reached by the floodwaters of 1890. Directly above it – above head height – is another marking the height of the 2002 floods.

The area where the Čertovka passes under Charles Bridge is sometimes called **Prague's Venice** – the channel is often crowded with dinky tour boats.

Kampa Museum GALLERY

(Muzeum Kampa; Map p50; ☎257 286 147; www.museumkampa.cz; U Sovových mlýnů 2; adult/concession 240/120Kč; ⏲10am-6pm; 🚋12, 15, 20, 22) Housed in a renovated mill building, this gallery is devoted to 20th-century and contemporary art from Central Europe. The highlights of the permanent exhibition are extensive collections of bronzes by cubist sculptor Otto Gutfreund and paintings by František Kupka; the most impressive canvas is Kupka's *Cathedral,* a pleated mass of blue and red diagonals. Outside you can get a close-up look at some of David Černý's famous crawling babies (the ones that swarm over the TV Tower (p91) in Žižkov).

Czech Museum of Music MUSEUM
(České muzeum hudby; Map p50; ☎257 257 777; www.nm.cz; Karmelitská 2/4; adult/concession 120/80Kč; ⏰10am-6pm Wed-Mon; 🚋12, 15, 20, 22) A 17th-century baroque monastery building with an impressive central atrium makes a beautiful setting for Prague's Museum of Music. The museum's permanent exhibition, entitled 'Man-Instrument-Music', explores the relationship between human beings and musical instruments through the ages, and showcases an incredible collection of violins, guitars, lutes, trumpets, flutes and harmonicas.

Highlights include a grand piano once played by Mozart in 1787, and the Rožmberk Court Ensemble of 16th-century woodwind instruments. The exhibits are brought to life by recordings of music played using the actual instruments on display.

Vrtbov Garden GARDENS
(Vrtbovská zahrada; Map p50; ☎257 531 480; www.vrtbovska.cz; Karmelitská 25; adult/concession 65/55Kč; ⏰10am-6pm Apr-Oct; 🚋12, 15, 20, 22) This 'secret garden', hidden along an alley at the corner of Tržiště and Karmelitská, was built in 1720 for the Earl of Vrtba, the senior chancellor of Prague Castle. It's a formal baroque garden, climbing steeply up the hillside to a terrace graced with baroque statues of Roman mythological figures by Matthias Braun – see if you can spot Vulcan, Diana and Mars.

Below the terrace (on the right, looking down) is a tiny studio once used by Czech painter Mikuláš Aleš, and above is a little lookout with good views of Prague Castle and Malá Strana.

KGB Museum MUSEUM
(Map p50; http://kgbmuseum.com; Vlašská 13; 350Kč; ⏰10am-5pm Tue-Sun; 🚋12, 15, 20, 22) The enthusiastic Russian collector of KGB memorabilia who established this small museum will insist on showing you around his treasure trove of spy cameras, concealed pistols, weapons (including an original garotte, known as 'Stalin's scarf') and sinister electrical 'interrogation equipment' (read: torture). There are also rare photographs of Prague taken in 1968 by a KGB officer, with ordinary citizens strangely absent from the street scenes.

Quo Vadis (David Černý Sculpture) MONUMENT
(Where Are You Going; Map p50; www.davidcerny.cz; Vlašská 19; 🚋12, 15, 20, 22) This golden Trabant (an East German car) on four human legs is a David Černý tribute to the 4000 East Germans who occupied the garden of the then West German embassy in 1989, before being granted political asylum and leaving their Trabants behind. You can see the sculpture through the fence behind the German embassy. Head uphill along Vlašská, turn left into a children's park, and left again to find it.

Maltese Square SQUARE
(Maltézské náměstí; Map p50; 🚋12, 15, 20, 22) References to the Knights of Malta around Malá Strana hark back to 1169, when the military order established a monastery in the Church of Our Lady Beneath the Chain on the square. Disbanded by the communists, the Knights have regained much property under post-1989 restitution laws, including the John Lennon Wall (p59).

Children's Island PARK
(Dětský ostrov; Map p50; access from Nábřežní; ⏰24hr; Ⓜ Anděl) FREE Prague's smallest island offers a leafy respite from the hustle and bustle of the city, with a selection of swings, slides, climbing frames and sandpits to keep the kids busy, as well as a rope swing, skateboard ramp, mini football pitch, netball court, and lots of open space for older siblings to run wild.

There are plenty of benches to take the strain off weary parental legs, and a decent bar and restaurant at the southern end.

Petřín

★Petřín HILL
(Map p50; 🚋Nebozízek, Petřín) This 318m-high hill is one of Prague's largest green spaces. It's great for quiet, tree-shaded walks and fine views over the 'City of a Hundred Spires'. Most of the attractions atop the hill, including a lookout tower and mirror maze, were built in the late 19th to early 20th century, lending the place an old-fashioned, fun-fair atmosphere.

Once upon a time the hill was draped with vineyards, and you can still see the quarry that provided stone for most of Prague's Romanesque and Gothic buildings. The huge stone fortifications that run from Újezd to Strahov, cutting across Petřín's peak, are called the **Hunger Wall**. It was built in 1362 under Charles IV, constructed by the city's poor in return for food under an early job-creation scheme.

In the peaceful **Kinský Garden** (Kinského zahrada), on the southern side of Petřín, is the

18th-century wooden **Church of St Michael** (kostel sv Michala), transferred here, log by log, from the village of Medveďov in Ukraine. Such structures are rare in Bohemia, though still common in Ukraine and northeastern Slovakia.

Petřín is easily accessible on foot from Strahov Monastery, or you can ride the funicular railway from Újezd up to the top. You can also get off two-thirds of the way up at Nebozízek.

Petřín Funicular Railway FUNICULAR
(Lanová draha na Petřín; Map p50; ☎800 191 817; www.dpp.cz; Újezd; adult/child 32/16Kč; ⏲9am-11.30pm; 9, 12, 15, 20, 22) First opened in 1891, Prague's funicular railway now uses modern coaches that trundle back and forth on 510m of track, saving visitors a climb up Petřín. It runs every 10 minutes (every 15 minutes November to March) from Újezd to the Petřín Lookout Tower, with a stop at Nebozízek. A full-price ticket or day-pass is required to ride.

Memorial to the Victims of Communism MONUMENT
(Památník obětem komunismu; Map p50; cnr Újezd & Vítězná; 9, 12, 15, 20, 22) This striking sculptural group consists of several ragged human figures (controversially, all are male) in progressive stages of disintegration, descending a staggered slope. A bronze strip inlaid into the ground in front of them records the terrible human toll of the communist era – 205,486 arrested; 170,938 driven into exile; 248 executed; 4500 who died in prison; and 327 shot while trying to escape across the border.

Petřín Lookout Tower VIEWPOINT
(Petřínská rozhledna; Map p50; ☎257 320 112; www.petrinska-rozhledna.cz; Petřínské sady; adult/child 120/65Kč; ⏲10am-10pm Apr-Sep, to 8pm Mar & Oct, to 6pm Nov-Feb; Petřín) The summit of Petřín is topped with this 62m-tall Eiffel Tower lookalike built in 1891 for the Prague Exposition. You can climb its 299 steps (or take the lift) for some of the best views in the city – on clear days you can see the forests of Central Bohemia to the southwest.

Mirror Maze HISTORIC BUILDING
(Zrcadlové bludiště; Map p50; www.petrinska-rozhledna.cz; Petřínské sady; adult/child 75/55Kč; ⏲10am-10pm Apr-Sep, to 8pm Mar & Oct, to 6pm Nov-Feb; Petřín) Below the Petřín Lookout Tower (p61) is the Mirror Maze, built for the 1891 Prague Exposition. As well as the maze of distorting mirrors, which was based on the Prater in Vienna, there's a diorama of the 1648 battle between Praguers and Swedes on Charles Bridge.

Opposite is the **Church of St Lawrence** (kostel sv Vavřince), which contains a ceiling fresco depicting the founding of the church in 991 at a pagan site with a sacred flame.

Musaion MUSEUM
(Ethnographical Museum; Map p50; ☎257 214 806; www.nm.cz; Kinského zahrada 98; adult/child 70/40Kč; ⏲10am-6pm Tue-Sun; 9, 12, 15, 20) This renovated summer palace houses the National Museum's ethnographic collection, with exhibits covering traditional Czech folk culture and art, including music, costume, farming methods and handicrafts. There are regular folk concerts and workshops demonstrating traditional crafts such as blacksmithing and woodcarving; in the summer months there's a garden cafe.

Staré Město

Old Town Square & Around

★Old Town Square SQUARE
See p68.

★Prague Jewish Museum MUSEUM
See p66.

★Church of Our Lady Before Týn CHURCH
(Kostel Panny Marie před Týnem; Map p62; ☎222 318 186; www.tyn.cz; Staroměstské náměstí; suggested donation 25Kč; ⏲10am-1pm & 3-5pm Tue-Sat, 10am-noon Sun Mar-Dec; M Staroměstská) Its distinctive twin Gothic spires make the Týn Church an unmistakable Old Town landmark. Like something out of a 15th-century – and probably slightly cruel – fairy tale, they loom over Old Town Square, decorated with a golden image of the Virgin Mary made in the 1620s from the melted-down Hussite chalice that previously adorned the church.

It takes some imagination to visualise the original church in its entirety because it's partly hidden behind the four-storey **Týn School** (not a Habsburg plot to obscure this former Hussite stronghold, but almost contemporaneous with it). The church's name originates from the Týn Courtyard (p64) located behind it.

Though impressively Gothic on the outside, the church's interior is smothered in heavy baroque. Two of the most interesting features

Staré Město

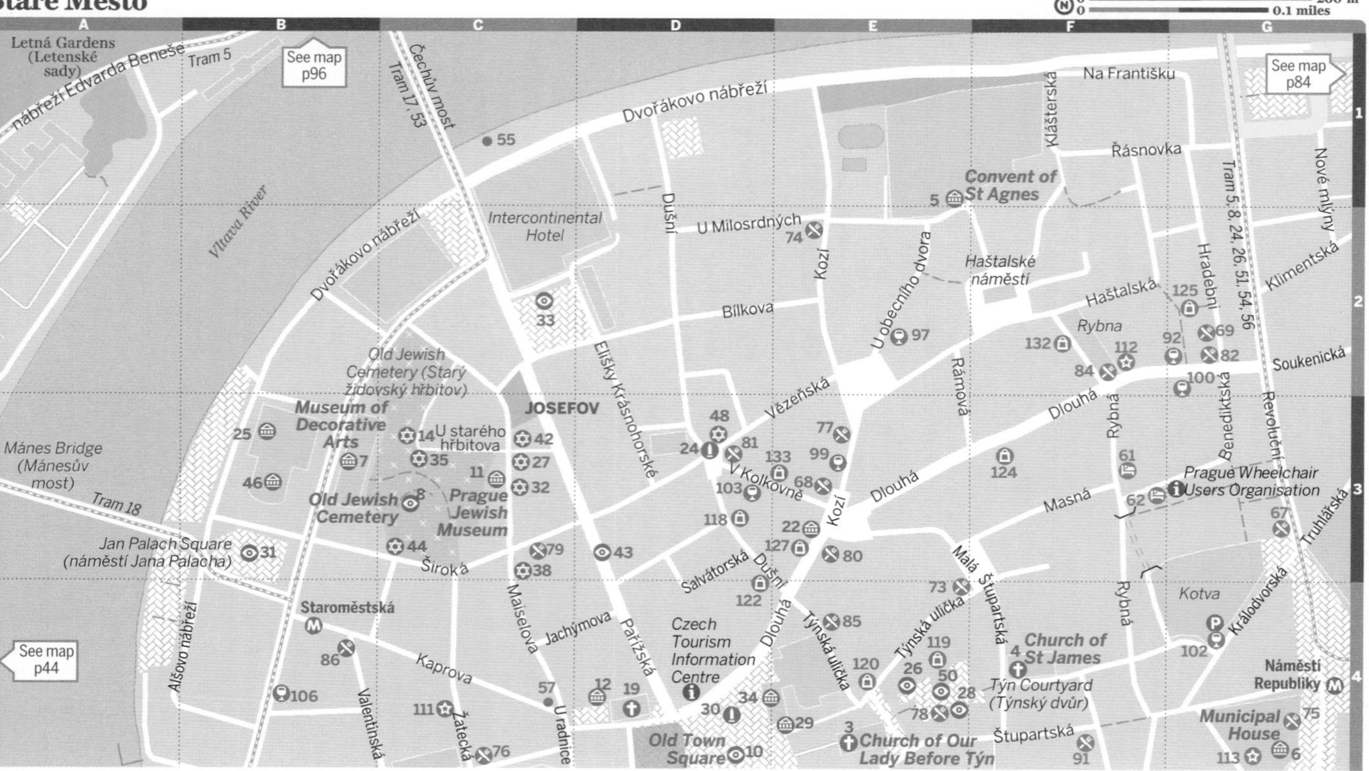
Letná Gardens (Letenské sady)
nábřeží Edvarda Beneše
Tram 5
See map p96
Čechův most
Tram 17, 53
55
Dvořákovo nábřeží
Na Františku
See map p84
Klášterská
Řásnovka
Nové mlýny
Tram 5, 8, 24, 26, 51, 54, 56
Vltava River
Intercontinental Hotel
Dušní
U Milosrdných
74
Kozí
5
Convent of St Agnes
Haštalské náměstí
Hradební
Klimentská
Haštalská
125
Bílkova
33
U obecního dvora
97
Rybna
132
112
92
69
82
Soukenická
84
100
Old Jewish Cemetery (Starý židovský hřbitov)
JOSEFOV
Elišky Krásnohorské
Vězeňská
Rámová
Dlouhá
Rybná
Benediktská
Revoluční
48
77
Museum of Decorative Arts
25
14
U starého hřbitova
42
24
81
7
35
27
133
99
61
124
Mánes Bridge (Mánesův most)
46
11
32
V Kolkovně
68
Prague Wheelchair Users Organisation
Old Jewish Cemetery
8
Prague Jewish Museum
103
Dlouhá
Masná
62
Tram 18
118
22
Kozí
67
Truhlářská
Jan Palach Square (náměstí Jana Palacha)
31
44
79
43
127
80
Široká
38
Salvátorská
Dušní
Malá Štupartská
Kotva
122
73
Staroměstská
Maiselova
Jachymova
Pařížská
Czech Tourism Information Centre
Dlouhá
Týnská ulička
85
Týnská ulička
119
Church of St James
Králodvorská
See map p44
86
Kaprova
4
102
Alšovo nábřeží
120
26
50
Náměstí Republiky
106
Valentinská
57
12
19
34
28
Týn Courtyard (Týnský dvůr)
111
Žatecká
U radnice
30
78
Municipal House
75
3
29
Old Town Square
10
Church of Our Lady Before Týn
Štupartská
76
91
113
6
200 m
0.1 miles

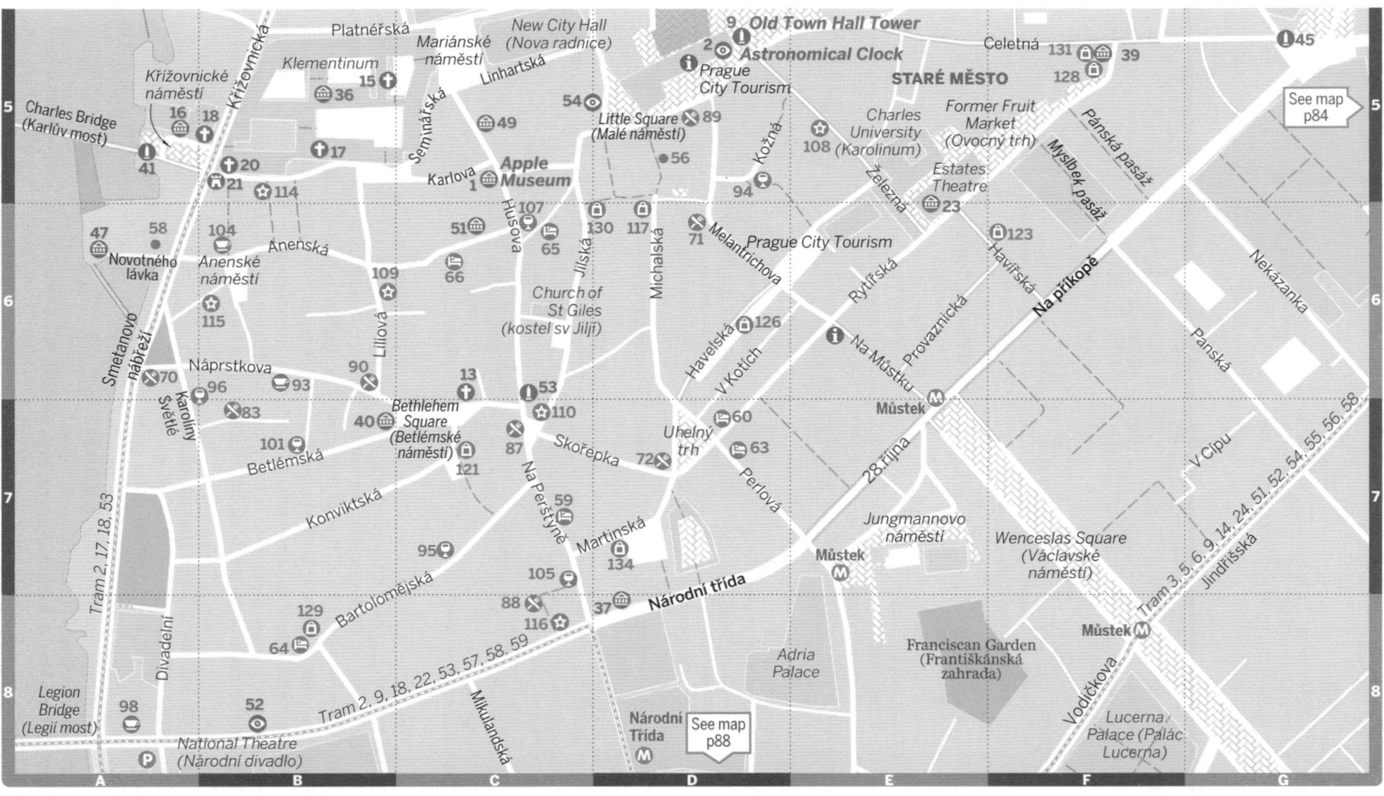

Old Town Hall Tower
Astronomical Clock
Prague City Tourism
New City Hall (Nova radnice)
Mariánské náměstí
Platnéřská
Klementinum
Křižovnické náměstí
Křižovnická
Charles Bridge (Karlův most)
Linhartská
Seminářská
Karlova
Apple Museum
Little Square (Malé náměstí)
Kožná
Celetná
STARÉ MĚSTO
Charles University (Karolinum)
Former Fruit Market (Ovocný trh)
Estates Theatre
Železná
Pánská pasáž
Myslbek pasáž
See map p84
Husova
Jilská
Michalská
Melantrichova
Prague City Tourism
Havířská
Na příkopě
Nekázanka
Novotného lávka
Anenská
Anenské náměstí
Church of St Giles (kostel sv Jiljí)
Rytířská
Havelská
V Kotích
Na Můstku
Provaznická
Panská
Smetanovo nábřeží
Liliová
Náprstkova
Karolíny Světlé
Můstek
Bethlehem Square (Betlémské náměstí)
Skořepka
Uhelný trh
Betlémská
28.října
V Cípu
Perlová
Konviktská
Na Perštýně
Martinská
Jungmannovo náměstí
Wenceslas Square (Václavské náměstí)
Tram 3, 5, 6, 9, 14, 24, 51, 52, 54, 55, 56, 58
Jindřišská
Tram 2, 17, 18, 53
Bartolomějská
Národní třída
Divadelní
Tram 2, 9, 18, 22, 53, 57, 58, 59
Adria Palace
Franciscan Garden (Františkánská zahrada)
Vodičkova
Legion Bridge (Legií most)
National Theatre (Národní divadlo)
Mikulandská
Národní Třída
See map p88
Lucerna Palace (Palác Lucerna)

Staré Město

Top Sights
1 Apple Museum C5
2 Astronomical Clock D5
3 Church of Our Lady Before Týn E4
4 Church of St James F4
5 Convent of St Agnes E1
6 Municipal House G4
7 Museum of Decorative Arts B3
8 Old Jewish Cemetery C3
9 Old Town Hall Tower D5
10 Old Town Square D4
11 Prague Jewish Museum C3

Sights
12 Art Gallery for Children D4
13 Bethlehem Chapel C6
14 Ceremonial Hall C3
15 Chapel of Mirrors B5
16 Charles Bridge Museum A5
17 Church of St Clement B5
18 Church of St Francis Seraphinus B5
19 Church of St Nicholas D4
20 Church of the Holy Saviour B5
21 Colloredo-Mansfeld Palace B5
22 Dvorak Sec Contemporary E3
23 Estates Theatre E6
24 Franz Kafka Monument D3
25 Galerie Rudolfinum B3
26 Granovsky Palace E4
27 High Synagogue C3
28 House at the Black Bear E4
29 House at the Stone Bell E4
30 Jan Hus Statue D4
31 Jan Palach Square B3
32 Jewish Town Hall C3
33 Josefov C2
34 Kinský Palace D4
35 Klaus Synagogue C3
36 Klementinum B5
37 Lego Museum D8
38 Maisel Synagogue C3
39 Museum of Czech Cubism F5
40 Náprstek Museum B7
41 Old Town Bridge Tower A5
42 Old-New Synagogue C3
43 Pařížská D3
44 Pinkas Synagogue C3
45 Powder Gate G5
46 Rudolfinum B3
47 Smetana Museum A6
48 Spanish Synagogue D3
49 Toy Museum C5
50 Týn Courtyard E4
51 Václav Havel Library C6
52 Viola Building B8
53 Viselec (David Černý Sculpture) C6
54 VJ Rott Building C5

Activities, Courses & Tours
55 Prague Boats C1
56 Prague Special Tours D5
Prague Venice (see 16)
57 Precious Legacy Tours C4
58 Wittmann Tours A6

Sleeping
59 Ahoy! Hostel C7
60 Design Hotel Jewel D7
61 Design Hotel Josef F3
62 Old Prague Hostel F3
63 Perla Hotel D7
64 Residence Karolina B8
65 Savic Hotel C6
66 U Zeleného Věnce C6

Eating
67 Ambiente Pizza Nuova G3
68 Bakeshop Praha E3
69 Banh Mi Makers G2
70 Bellevue A6
71 Country Life D6
72 Culinaria D7
73 Divinis E4

are the huge rococo **altar** on the northern wall and the **tomb of Tycho Brahe**, the Danish astronomer who was one of Rudolf II's most illustrious court scientists (he died in 1601 of a burst bladder following a royal piss-up – he was too polite to leave the table to relieve himself). On the inside of the southern wall of the church are two small windows – they are now blocked off, but once opened into the church from rooms in the neighbouring house at **Celetná 3**, where the teenage Franz Kafka once lived (from 1896 to 1907).

As for the exterior of the church, the north portal overlooking Týnská ulička is topped by a remarkable **14th-century tympanum** that shows the Crucifixion and was carved by the workshop of Charles IV's favourite architect, Peter Parler. Note that this is a copy; the original is in the Lapidárium (p100).

The entrance to the church is along a passage from the square, through the third (from the left) of the Týn School's four arches. The Týn Church is an occasional concert venue and has a very grand-sounding pipe organ.

Týn Courtyard SQUARE

(Týnský dvůr; Map p62; entrances on Malá Štupartská & Týnská ulička; Ⓜ Náměstí Republiky) This picturesque courtyard tucked behind the Church of Our Lady Before Týn (p61) was originally a sort of medieval caravanserai – a fortified hotel, trading centre and customs

74 Field ... E2
75 Francouzská Restaurace ... G4
76 George Prime Steak ... C4
77 Home Kitchen ... E3
78 Indian Jewel ... E4
79 Kafka Snob Food ... C3
80 Kalina ... E3
81 Kolkovna ... D3
82 La Bottega Bistroteka ... G2
83 Lehká Hlava ... B7
84 Lokál ... F2
85 Maitrea ... E4
86 Mistral Café ... B4
87 Monarch Gastrobar ... C7
Naše maso ... (see 82)
88 Pho Viet ... C8
89 U Prince ... D5
90 V zátiší ... B6
91 Vino di Vino ... F4

Drinking & Nightlife
Black Angel's Bar ... (see 89)
92 Bokovka ... G2
93 Café Kampus ... B6
94 Čili Bar ... D5
Duende ... (see 96)
95 Friends ... C7
Grand Cafe Orient ... (see 128)
96 Hemingway Bar ... B6
97 James Joyce ... E2
Kavárna Obecní dům ... (see 6)
98 Kavárna Slavia ... A8
99 Kozička ... E3
Literární Kavárna Řetězová ... (see 66)
100 Prague Beer Museum ... G2
101 Red Pif ... B7
102 T-Anker ... G4
103 Tretter's New York Bar ... D3
104 Tricafe ... B6
105 U Medvídků ... C7
106 U Rudolfina ... B4
107 U Tří růží ... C6
U Zlatého Tygra ... (see 1)

Entertainment
108 AghaRTA Jazz Centrum ... E5
109 Blues Sklep ... B6
Dvořák Hall ... (see 46)
Estates Theatre ... (see 23)
110 Jazz Republic ... C7
111 National Marionette Theatre ... C4
Prague Spring Box Office ... (see 46)
112 Roxy ... F2
113 Smetana Hall ... G4
114 Ta Fantastika ... B5
115 Theatre on the Balustrade ... B6
116 Vagon ... C8

Shopping
117 Art Deco Galerie ... D6
118 Bohème ... D3
119 Botanicus ... E4
120 Bric A Brac ... E4
121 Denim Heads ... C7
122 Dušní 3 ... D4
123 Frey Wille ... F6
124 Granát Turnov ... F3
125 Gurmet Pasáž Dlouhá ... G2
126 Havelská Market ... D6
127 Klara Nademlýnská ... E3
128 Kubista ... F5
Le Patio Lifestyle ... (see 118)
129 Leeda ... B8
Manufaktura ... (see 71)
Material ... (see 119)
130 Maximum Underground ... D6
Modernista ... (see 6)
131 Pohádka ... F5
St Vol ... (see 86)
132 Talacko ... F2
133 TEG1 ... E3
134 TEG2 ... D7

office for visiting foreign merchants. Now attractively renovated, the courtyard houses shops, restaurants and hotels. The courtyard is still often referred to by its German name, Ungelt (meaning 'customs duty').

Established as long ago as the 11th century, it was busiest and most prosperous during the reign of Charles IV. In the northwest corner is the 16th-century **Granovsky Palace** (Dům Granovských; Map p62; Týnský dvůr; M Náměstí Republiky), with an elegant Renaissance loggia, and sgraffito and painted decoration depicting biblical and mythological scenes. Across the yard, to the right of the V Ungeltu shop, is the **House at the Black Bear** (dům U černého medvěda; Map p62; Týnský dvůr; M Náměstí Republiky), whose baroque facade is adorned with a statue of St John of Nepomuk above the door and a bear in chains on the corner, a reminder of the kind of 'entertainment' that once took place here.

Kinský Palace GALLERY
(Palác Kinských; Map p62; 224 810 758; www.ngprague.cz; Staroměstské náměstí 12; incl admission to all National Gallery venues; adult/child 300/150Kč; 10am-6pm Tue-Sun; P; M Staroměstská) The late-baroque Kinský Palace sports Prague's finest rococo facade, completed in 1765 by the redoubtable Kilian Dientzenhofer. Today the palace is home to a branch of the National Gallery, housing its

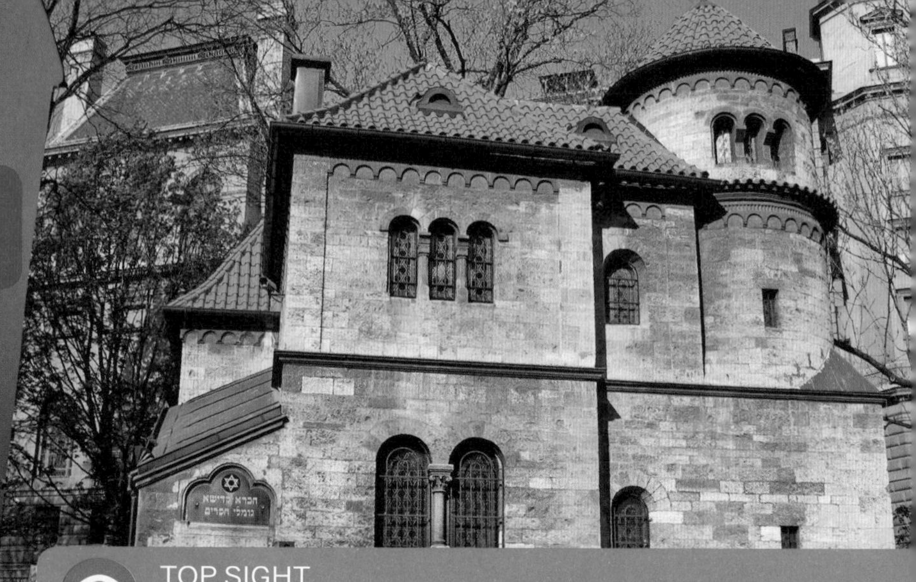

ANASTAZZO/SHUTTERSTOCK ©

TOP SIGHT
PRAGUE JEWISH MUSEUM

Six Jewish monuments clustered together in Josefov now constitute the Prague Jewish Museum, holding what is probably the world's biggest collection of sacred Jewish artefacts, many of them rescued from demolished Bohemian synagogues: the Maisel, Pinkas, Spanish and Klaus synagogues; the Ceremonial Hall; and the Old Jewish Cemetery. There is also the Old-New Synagogue, one of Prague's oldest buildings.

Pinkas Synagogue

The handsome Pinkas Synagogue (Pinkasova synagóga; Map p62; www.jewishmuseum.cz; Široká 3; incl in admission to Prague Jewish Museum; 9am-6pm Sun-Fri Apr-Oct, to 4.30pm Nov-Mar; M Staroměstská) was built in 1535 and used for worship until 1941. After WWII it was converted into a memorial, with wall after wall inscribed with the names, birth dates, and dates of disappearance of the 77,297 Czech victims of the Nazis. It also has a collection of paintings and drawings by children held in the Terezín concentration camp during WWII.

Old Jewish Cemetery

The Pinkas Synagogue contains the entrance to the Old Jewish Cemetery (Starý židovský hřbitov; Map p62; www.jewishmuseum.cz; Pinkas Synagogue, Široká 3; incl in admission to Prague Jewish Museum; 9am-6pm Apr-Oct, to 4.30pm Nov-Mar; M Staroměstská), Europe's oldest surviving Jewish graveyard. Founded in the early 15th century, it has a palpable atmosphere of mourning even after two centuries of disuse (it was closed in 1787); however, this is one of Prague's most popular sights, so if you're hoping to have a moment of quiet contemplation you'll probably be

DON'T MISS

- Old-New Synagogue
- Old Jewish Cemetery
- Spanish Synagogue

PRACTICALITIES

- Židovské muzeum Praha
- Map p62
- 222 749 211
- www.jewishmuseum.cz
- Reservation Centre, Maiselova 15
- ordinary ticket adult/child 300/200Kč, combined ticket incl entry to Old-New Synagogue 480/320Kč
- 9am-6pm Sun-Fri Apr-Oct, to 4.30pm Nov-Mar
- M Staroměstská

disappointed. Around 12,000 crumbling stones (some brought from other, long-gone cemeteries) are heaped together, but beneath them are perhaps 100,000 graves, piled in layers because of the lack of space.

The most prominent graves, marked by pairs of marble tablets with a 'roof' between them, are near the main gate; they include those of Mordechai Maisel and Rabbi Loew. The oldest stone (now replaced by a replica) is that of Avigdor Karo, a chief rabbi and court poet to Wenceslas IV, who died in 1439. Most stones bear the name of the deceased and his or her father, the date of death (and sometimes of burial), and poetic texts. Elaborate markers from the 17th and 18th centuries are carved with symbols representing the deceased's name or occupation, eg hands (giving a blessing) for a Cohen (Cohens are descended from temple priests), a violin for a musician.

Since the cemetery was closed, Jewish burials have taken place at the Jewish Cemetery in Žižkov. There are remnants of another old Jewish burial ground at the foot of the TV Tower in Žižkov.

You exit the cemetery through a gate between the Klaus Synagogue and the Ceremonial Hall.

Old-New Synagogue

Completed around 1270, the Old-New Synagogue (Staronová synagóga; Map p62; www.jewishmuseum.cz; Červená 2; adult/child 200/140Kč; 9am-6pm Sun-Fri Apr-Oct, to 4.30pm Nov-Mar; 17) is Europe's oldest working synagogue and one of Prague's earliest Gothic buildings. You step down into it because it predates the raising of Staré Město's street level in medieval times to guard against floods. Men must cover their heads (bring a hat or take one of the paper yarmulkes handed out at the entrance). Note that entry is not included with a Prague Jewish Museum ordinary ticket.

Around the central chamber are an entry hall, a winter prayer hall and the room from which women watch the men-only services. The interior, with a pulpit surrounded by a 15th-century wrought-iron grill, looks much as it would have 500 years ago. The 17th-century scriptures on the walls were recovered from beneath a later 'restoration'. On the eastern wall is the Holy Ark that holds the Torah scrolls. In a glass case at the rear, little light bulbs beside the names of the prominent deceased are lit on their death days.

Across the narrow street is the 16th-century High Synagogue, so-called because its prayer hall (closed to the public) is upstairs. Around the corner is the Jewish Town Hall (Židovská radnice; closed to the public; M Staroměstská), built by Mordechai Maisel in 1586 and given its rococo facade in the 18th century. It has a clock tower with one Hebrew face where the hands, like the Hebrew script, run 'backwards'.

BUYING TICKETS

You can buy tickets at the Information & Reservation Centre at Maiselova 15, the Pinkas Synagogue, the Klaus Synagogue and the Spanish Synagogue. You can also buy tickets online, but they must be printed out before use – digital copies are not accepted.

One of the oldest gravestones in the Old Jewish Cemetery is that of Rabbi Judah Loew ben Bezalel, chief rabbi of Prague in the late 16th century. Rabbi Loew is famously associated with the legend of the Golem, a supernatural being created from the mud of the Vltava. Loew breathed life into the creature by using secret incantations, and bid it to protect the Jews of Prague from harm.

MORDECHAI MAISEL

Mordechai Maisel (1528–1601), a contemporary of Rabbi Loew, was one of Prague's wealthiest men. He was known for his philanthropy, paying for the paving of the ghetto streets, providing for Jewish widows and orphans, and building and bequeathing the beautiful Maisel Synagogue.

CATARINA BELOVA/SHUTTERSTOCK ©

TOP SIGHT
OLD TOWN HALL & ASTRONOMICAL CLOCK

Prague's Old Town Hall, founded in 1338, is a hotchpotch of medieval buildings presided over by a tall Gothic tower with a splendid Astronomical Clock. The town hall has several historic attractions, and hosts art exhibitions on the ground floor and the 2nd floor.

Astronomical Clock

Every hour, on the hour, crowds gather beneath the Old Town Hall Tower (Věž radnice; Map p62; ☎236 002 629; www.staromestskaradnicepraha.cz; Staroměstské náměstí 1; adult/child 130/80Kč, incl Old Town Hall tour 180Kč; ⏰11am-10pm Mon, 9am-10pm Tue-Sun; MStaroměstská) to watch the Astronomical Clock (Map p62; Staroměstské náměstí; ⏰chimes on the hour 9am-9pm; MStaroměstská) in action. Despite a slightly underwhelming performance that takes only 45 seconds, the clock is one of Europe's best-known tourist attractions, and a 'must-see' for visitors to Prague. After all, it's historic, photogenic and – if you take time to study it – rich in intriguing symbolism.

Four figures beside the clock represent the deepest civic anxieties of 15th-century Praguers: Vanity (with a mirror), Greed (with his money bag; originally a Jewish moneylender, but cosmetically altered after WWII), Death (the skeleton) and Pagan Invasion (represented by a Turk). The four figures below these are the Chronicler, Angel, Astronomer and Philosopher.

On the hour, Death rings a bell and inverts his hourglass, and the 12 Apostles parade past the windows above the clock, nodding to the crowd. On the left-hand side are Paul (with a sword and a book), Thomas (lance), Jude (book), Simon (saw), Bartholomew (book) and Barnabas (parchment); on the right-hand side are Peter (with a key), Matthew (axe), John

DON'T MISS

- The parade of Apostles during the hourly chiming of the Astronomical Clock
- The view from the top of the tower
- The guided tour, where you can see the inner workings of the 12 Apostles

PRACTICALITIES

- Staroměstské náměstí
- Map p62
- MStaroměstská

(snake), Andrew (cross), Philip (cross) and James (mallet). At the end, a cock crows and the hour is rung.

The clock is scheduled to be out of action from spring 2017 to summer 2018 while the clock tower undergoes renovations.

Exterior

The Old Town Hall's best feature is the view across the Old Town Square from its 60m-tall clock tower. It's well worth the climb up the modern, beautifully designed steel spiral staircase; there's also a lift.

A plaque on the building's eastern face lists the 27 Protestant nobles who were beheaded here in 1621 after the Battle of Bílá Hora; white crosses on the ground mark where the deed was done. If you look at the neo-Gothic eastern gable, you can see that its right-hand edge is ragged – the wing that once extended north from here was blown up by the Nazis in 1945, on the day before the Soviet army marched into the city.

Guided Tour

The guided tour of the town hall takes you through the council chamber and assembly room, with beautiful mosaics dating from the 1930s, before visiting the Gothic chapel and taking a look at the inner workings of the 12 Apostles who parade above the Astronomical Clock every hour. The tour is rounded off with a trip through the Romanesque and Gothic cellars beneath the building.

THE CLOCK FACE

On the upper face, the disc in the middle of the fixed part depicts the world known at the time – with Prague at the centre, of course. The gold sun traces a circle through the blue zone of day, the brown zone of dusk in the west, the black disc of night, and dawn in the east. From this the hours of sunrise and sunset can be read.

The Old Town Hall's original clock of 1410 was improved in 1490 by Master Hanuš, producing the mechanical marvel you see today. Legend has it that Hanuš was blinded afterwards so he could not duplicate his work elsewhere.

THE CALENDAR WHEEL

The calendar wheel beneath the clock's astronomical wizardry, with 12 seasonal scenes celebrating rural Bohemian life, is a duplicate of one painted in 1866 by the Czech Revivalist Josef Mánes. You can have a close look at the beautiful original in the Prague City Museum (p83). Most of the dates around the calendar wheel are marked with the names of their associated saints; 6 July honours Jan Hus.

OLD TOWN ORIGINS

The origins of Staré Město (Old Town) date back to the 10th century, when a marketplace and settlement grew up on the east bank of the river. In the 12th century this was linked to the castle district by Judith Bridge, the forerunner of Charles Bridge, and in 1231 Wenceslas I honoured it with a town charter and the beginnings of a fortification.

The town walls are long gone, but their line can still be traced along the streets of Národní třída, Na příkopě (which means 'on the moat') and Revoluční, and the Old Town's main gate – the **Powder Gate** (p75) – still survives.

collection of ancient and oriental art, ranging from ancient Egyptian tomb treasures and Greek Apulian pottery (4th century BC) to Chinese and Japanese decorative art and calligraphy.

Alfred Nobel, the Swedish inventor of dynamite, once stayed in the palace; his crush on pacifist Bertha von Suttner (née Kinský) may have influenced him to establish the Nobel Peace Prize (she was the first woman laureate in 1905). Many older Praguers have a darker memory of the place, for it was from its balcony in February 1948 that Klement Gottwald proclaimed communist rule in Czechoslovakia. There are Kafka connections here too – young Franz once attended a school around the back of the building, and his father ran a shop in the premises next to the House at the Stone Bell, now occupied by the Kafka Bookshop.

Tickets are valid for seven days, and give admission to all six of the National Gallery's permanent exhibitions: Kinský Palace, Convent of St Agnes, Trade Fair Palace, Šternberg Palace, Schwarzenberg Palace and Salm Palace.

House at the Stone Bell — GALLERY

(Dům U kamenného zvonu; Map p62; ☎224 828 245; www.ghmp.cz; Staroměstské náměstí 13; adult/child 120/60Kč; ⏲10am-8pm Tue-Sun; Ⓜ Staroměstská) During restoration in the 1980s a baroque stucco facade was stripped away from this elegant medieval building to reveal the original 14th-century Gothic stonework; the eponymous stone bell is on the building's corner. Inside, two restored Gothic chapels now serve as branches of the Prague City Gallery (with changing exhibits of contemporary art) and as chamber-concert venues.

Church of St Nicholas — CHURCH

(Kostel sv Mikuláše; Map p62; www.svmikulas.cz; Staroměstské náměstí; ⏲10am-4pm Mon-Sat, noon-4pm Sun; Ⓜ Staroměstská) FREE The baroque wedding cake in the northwestern corner of Old Town Square is the Church of St Nicholas, built in the 1730s by Kilian Dientzenhofer (not to be confused with the Dientzenhofers' masterpiece in Malá Strana). Considerable grandeur has been worked into a very tight space; originally the church was wedged behind the Old Town Hall's northern wing (destroyed in 1945).

Chamber concerts are often held beneath its stucco decorations, a visually splendid (though acoustically mediocre) setting.

★ Church of St James — CHURCH

(Kostel sv Jakuba; Map p62; http://praha.minorite.cz; Malá Štupartská 6; ⏲9.30am-noon & 2-4pm Tue-Sat, 2-4pm Sun; Ⓜ Náměstí Republiky) FREE The great Gothic mass of the Church of St James began in the 14th century as a Minorite monastery church, and was given a beautiful baroque facelift in the early 18th century. But in the midst of the gilt and stucco is a grisly memento: on the inside of the western wall (look up to the right as you enter) hangs a shrivelled human arm.

Legend claims that when a thief tried to steal the jewels from the statue of the Virgin around the year 1400, the Virgin grabbed his wrist in such an iron grip that his arm had to be lopped off. (The truth may not be far behind: the church was a favourite of the guild of butchers, who may have administered their own justice.)

Pride of place inside goes to the over-the-top tomb of Count Jan Vratislav of Mitrovice, an 18th-century lord chancellor of Bohemia, found in the northern aisle. It's well worth a visit to enjoy St James's splendid pipe organ and famous acoustics. Recitals – free at 10.30am or 11am after Sunday Mass – and occasional concerts are not always advertised by ticket agencies, so check the noticeboard outside.

Art Gallery for Children — GALLERY

(Galerie umění pro děti; Map p62; ☎732 513 559; www.galeriegud.cz; Náměstí Franze Kafky 3; adult & child 170Kč, family 270Kč, child aged 2 & under free; ⏲2-6pm Wed-Fri, 10am-6pm Sat & Sun; Ⓜ Staroměstská) The clue is in the name: at the Art Gallery for Children the kids not only get to look at art, but make it, add to it and alter it. There are paints and materials to play with, and even workshops for five- to 12-year-olds (only in Czech at present, though staff speak English).

Dvorak Sec Contemporary GALLERY
(Map p62; ☎607 262 617; www.dvoraksec.com; Dlouhá 5; ⏰1-7pm Mon-Sat; Ⓜ Staroměstská) FREE One of Prague's leading independent art galleries, the Dvorak Sec specialises in promoting modern art of international importance from the United States, Britain, Germany and the Czech Republic. Past exhibitions have included the likes of Julian Opie, Jiří David, Paul Brainard, Dana Bell, David Černý and Roman Týc.

Colloredo-Mansfeld Palace PALACE
(Colloredo-Mansfeldský palác; Map p62; ☎222 232 053; www.ghmp.cz; Karlova 2; adult/child 60/30Kč; ⏰10am-6pm Tue-Sun; 🚊2, 17, 18) The shabby halls of this decaying 18th-century aristocratic palace are in the process of being restored as an information centre and exhibition space for the City of Prague Gallery. Meanwhile you can wander its baroque corridors and visit the grand ballroom – which appeared in Miloš Forman's 1984 film *Amadeus* – with ceiling frescoes untouched since the 1760s.

Václav Havel Library GALLERY
(Knihovna Václava Havla; Map p62; ☎222 220 112; www.vaclavhavel-library.org; Řetězová 7, Galerie Montmartre; ⏰noon-5pm Tue-Sun; 🚊2, 17, 18) FREE This small gallery, supported by the foundation that protects the legacy of the Czech Republic's late playwright-president, houses a permanent exhibition on the life and work of Václav Havel, and a series of temporary exhibitions of art on related themes such as human rights, *samizdat* (underground) publishing, and the struggle for freedom and democracy.

Josefov

Josefov AREA
(Jewish Quarter; Map p62) The slice of Staré Město bounded by Kaprova, Dlouhá and Kozí contains the remains of the once-thriving quarter of Josefov, Prague's former Jewish ghetto, where half-a-dozen old synagogues and the town hall survive along with the powerfully melancholy Old Jewish Cemetery. All are now part of the Prague Jewish Museum (p66).

★ **Museum of Decorative Arts** MUSEUM
(Umělecko-průmyslové muzeum; Map p62; ☎251 093 111; www.upm.cz; 17.listopadu 2; adult/child 120/70Kč; ⏰10am-7pm Tue, to 6pm Wed-Sun; 🚊2, 17, 18) This museum opened in 1900 as part of a European movement to encourage a return to the aesthetic values sacrificed to the Industrial Revolution. Its four halls are a feast for the eyes, full of 16th- to 19th-century artefacts such as furniture, tapestries, porcelain and a fabulous collection of glasswork. At the time of research it was closed due to extensive renovations taking place; it was scheduled to reopen in 2017 with double the amount of space for its permanent exhibitions.

★ **Convent of St Agnes** GALLERY
(Klášter sv Anežky; Map p62; ☎224 810 628; www.ngprague.cz; U Milosrdných 17; incl admission to all National Gallery venues; adult/child 300/150Kč; ⏰10am-6pm Tue-Sun; 🚊6, 8, 15, 26) In the northeastern corner of Staré Město is the former Convent of St Agnes, Prague's oldest surviving Gothic building. The 1st-floor rooms hold the National Gallery's permanent collection of medieval and early Renaissance art (1200–1550) from Bohemia and Central Europe, a treasure house of glowing Gothic altar paintings and polychrome religious sculptures.

In 1234 the Franciscan Order of the Poor Clares was founded by Přemysl king Wenceslas I, who made his sister Anežka (Agnes) the first abbess of the convent. Agnes was beatified in the 19th century and, with hardly accidental timing, Pope John Paul II canonised her as St Agnes of Bohemia just weeks before the revolutionary events of November 1989.

In the 16th century the convent was handed over to the Dominicans, and after Joseph II dissolved the monasteries it became a squatters' paradise. It is only since the 1980s that the complex has been restored and renovated. In addition to the art gallery and the 13th-century cloister, you can visit the French Gothic **Church of the Holy Saviour**, which contains the tombs of St Agnes and Wenceslas I's Queen Cunegund. Alongside this is the smaller **Church of St Francis**, where Wenceslas I is buried; part of its ruined nave now serves as a chilly concert hall.

The gallery is fully wheelchair-accessible, and the ground-floor cloister has a tactile presentation of 12 casts of medieval sculptures with explanatory text in Braille.

Tickets are valid for seven days, and give admission to all six of the National Gallery's permanent exhibitions: Kinský

Palace, Convent of St Agnes, Trade Fair Palace, Šternberg Palace, Schwarzenberg Palace and Salm Palace.

Pařížská STREET

(Map p62; Ⓜ Staroměstská) When the Josefov ghetto was cleared at the turn of the 20th century, the broad boulevard of Pařížská třída (Paris Ave) was driven in a straight line through the heart of the old slums. This was a time of widespread infatuation with the French art-nouveau style, and the avenue is lined with elegant apartment buildings adorned with stained glass and sculptural flourishes.

In the last decade Pařížská has become a glitzy shopping strand, studded with expensive brand names such as Dior, Louis Vuitton and Fabergé.

Franz Kafka Monument MONUMENT

(Map p62; cnr Vězeňská & Dušní; Ⓜ Staroměstská) Commissioned by Prague's Franz Kafka Society in 2003, Jaroslav Róna's unusual sculpture of a mini-Kafka riding on the shoulders of a giant empty suit was based on the writer's story *Description of a Struggle,* in which the author explores a fantasy landscape from the shoulders of 'an acquaintance' (who may be another aspect of the author's personality).

Jan Palach Square SQUARE

(náměstí Jana Palacha; Map p62; 🚋 17, 18) Jan Palach Sq is named after the young Charles University student who in January 1969 set himself alight in Wenceslas Square in protest against the Soviet invasion. On the eastern side of the square, beside the entrance to the philosophy faculty building where Palach was a student, is a bronze memorial plaque with a ghostly death mask.

Palach is buried in the **Olšany Cemetery** (Map p92; 🚋 5, 10, 11, 13, 16).

Rudolfinum HISTORIC BUILDING

(Map p62; ☎ 227 059 270; www.ceskafilharmonie.cz; Alšovo nábřeží 12; 🚋 2, 17, 18) Presiding over Jan Palach Sq is the Rudolfinum, home to the Czech Philharmonic Orchestra. This and the National Theatre, both designed by architects Josef Schulz and Josef Zítek, are considered Prague's finest neo-Renaissance buildings. Completed in 1884, the Rudolfinum served as the seat of the Czechoslovak Parliament between the wars, and as the administrative offices of the occupying Nazis during WWII.

The impressive Dvořák Hall (p158), its stage dominated by a vast organ, is one of the main concert venues for the Prague Spring festival. The northern part of the complex houses the **Galerie Rudolfinum** (Map p62; ☎ 227 059 205; www.galerierudolfinum.cz; Alšovo nábřeží 12; adult/child 140/90Kč; ⏲ 10am-6pm Tue, Wed & Fri-Sun, to 8pm Thu; 🚋 2, 17, 18). There's also a cafe with tables ranged amid the Corinthian pillars of the Column Hall.

Along the Royal Way

★ Municipal House HISTORIC BUILDING

(Obecní dům; Map p62; ☎ 222 002 101; www.obecnidum.cz; náměstí Republiky 5; guided tour adult/concession/child under 10yr 290/240Kč/free; ⏲ public areas 7.30am-11pm, information centre 10am-8pm; Ⓜ Náměstí Republiky, 🚋 6, 8, 15, 26) Restored in the 1990s after decades of neglect, Prague's most exuberantly art-nouveau building is a labour of love, every detail of its design and decoration carefully considered, every painting and sculpture loaded with symbolism. The restaurant (p128) and cafe (p147) here are like walk-in museums of art-nouveau design, while upstairs there are half a dozen sumptuously decorated halls that you can visit by guided tour.

The Municipal House stands on the site of the Royal Court, seat of Bohemia's kings from 1383 to 1483 (when Vladislav II moved to Prague Castle), which was demolished at the end of the 19th century. Between 1906 and 1912 this magnificent art-nouveau edifice was built in its place – a lavish joint effort by around 30 leading artists of the day, creating a cultural centre that was the architectural climax of the Czech National Revival.

The mosaic above the entrance, **Homage to Prague**, is set between sculptures representing the oppression and rebirth of the Czech people; other sculptures ranged along the top of the facade represent history, literature, painting, music and architecture. You pass beneath a wrought-iron and stained-glass canopy into an interior that is art nouveau down to the doorknobs (you can look around the lobby and the downstairs bar for free, or book a guided tour in the information centre).

First stop on the guided tour is Smetana Hall (p157), Prague's biggest concert hall, with seating for 1200 beneath an art-nouveau glass dome. The stage is framed by sculptures representing the Vyšehrad legend (to the right) and Slavonic dances (to the left). On 28 October 1918 an independent Czechoslovak Republic was declared in Smetana Hall, and in November 1989 meetings took

THE MISSING MONUMENTS

Prague witnessed several profound changes of political regime during the 20th century: from Habsburg empire to independent Czechoslovak Republic in 1918; to Nazi Protectorate from 1938 to 1945; to communist state in 1948; and back to democratic republic in 1989.

Each change was accompanied by widespread renaming of city streets and squares to reflect the heroes of the new regime. The square in front of the Rudolfinum, for example, has been known variously as Smetanovo náměstí (Smetana Sq; 1919–42 and 1945–52); Mozartplatz (Mozart Square; 1942–45); náměstí Krasnoarmějců (Red Army Sq; 1952–90); and náměstí Jana Palacha (Jan Palach Sq; 1990–present).

This renaming was often followed by the removal of monuments erected by the previous regime. Here are three of Prague's most prominent 'missing monuments'.

The Missing Virgin

If you look at the ground in **Old Town Square** (Staroměstské náměstí) about 50m south of the Jan Hus statue, you'll see a circular stone slab set among the cobblestones at the far end of the brass strip marking the Prague Meridian. This was the site of a Marian column (a pillar bearing a statue of the Virgin Mary), erected in 1650 in celebration of the Habsburg victory over the Swedes in 1648. It was surrounded by figures of angels crushing and beating down demons – a rather unsubtle symbol of a resurgent Catholic Church defeating the Protestant Reformation.

The column was toppled by a mob – who saw it as a symbol of Habsburg repression – on 3 November 1918, five days after the declaration of Czechoslovak independence. Its remains can be seen in the **Lapidárium** (p100).

The Missing Dictator

If you stand in the northwest corner of Old Town Square and look north along the arrow-straight avenue of Pařížská you will see, on a huge terrace at the far side of Čechův most, a giant metronome. If the monumental setting seems out of scale that's because the terrace was designed to accommodate the world's biggest statue of Stalin. Unveiled in 1955 – two years after Stalin's death – the 30m-high, 14,000-tonne colossus showed Uncle Joe at the head of two lines of communist heroes, Czech on one side, Soviet on the other. Cynical Praguers accustomed to constant food shortages quickly nicknamed it *fronta na maso* (the queue for meat).

The monument was dynamited in 1962, in deference to Khrushchev's attempt to airbrush Stalin out of history. The demolition crew was instructed to get rid of it quickly, quietly and without an audience. The **Museum of Communism** (p82) has a superb photo of the monument – and of its destruction.

The Missing Tank

At the southern edge of Malá Strana, **Náměstí Kinských** was until 1989 known as *náměstí Sovětských tankistů* (Soviet Tank Crews Square), named in memory of the Soviet soldiers who 'liberated' Prague on 9 May 1945. For many years a Soviet T-34 tank – allegedly the first to enter the city (in fact, it was a later Soviet 'gift') – squatted menacingly atop a pedestal here.

In 1991 artist David Černý decided that the tank was an inappropriate monument to the Soviet soldiers and painted it bright pink. The authorities had it painted green again, and charged Černý with a crime against the state. This infuriated many parliamentarians, 12 of whom repainted the tank pink. Their parliamentary immunity saved them from arrest and secured Černý's release.

After complaints from the Soviet Union the tank was removed. Its former setting is now occupied by a circular fountain surrounded by park benches; the vast granite slab in the centre is split by a jagged fracture, perhaps symbolic of a break with the past. The tank still exists, and is still pink – it's at the Military Museum in Lešany, near Týnec nad Sázavou, 30km south of Prague.

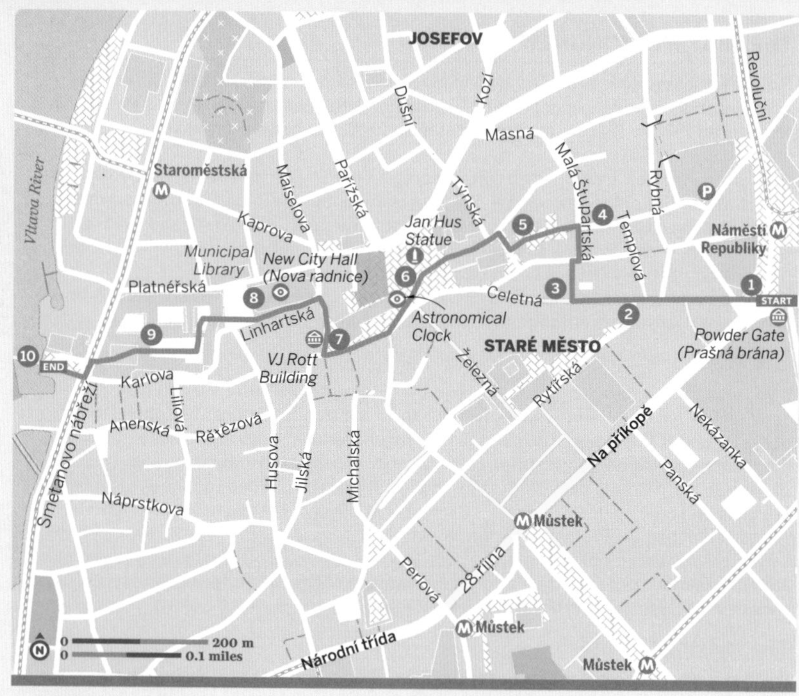

City Walk
Old Town Off the Beaten Track

START REPUBLIC SQ (NÁMĚSTÍ REPUBLIKY)
END CHARLES BRIDGE
LENGTH 1.5KM, 45 MINUTES

From **1 Republic Square** head towards the Gothic extravaganza of the Powder Gate and set off along Celetná, which is lined with interesting buildings, including the **2 House of the Black Madonna**, a fine example of cubist architecture.

Turn right into the passage at Celetná 17, which leads through a courtyard housing the **3 Celetna Theatre**, whose facade, foyer and cafe sport a mixture of medieval, baroque and modern design motifs, then go straight along Malá Štupartská for a look at the baroque sculptures of the **4 Church of St James** (p70). The cobbled passage opposite the church leads to **5 Týn Courtyard** (p64), a lovely square with a Renaissance loggia. Exit at the far end and go along the alley to the right of the Church of Our Lady Before Týn.

You emerge into **6 Old Town Square** (p68), dominated by the brooding statue of Jan Hus and the Gothic tower of the Old Town Hall. Continue past the clock to reach **7 Little Square**, which is dominated by the gorgeously decorated facade of the VJ Rott building. From here, bear right and then left into Linhartská.

This leads to the quieter **8 Mariánské náměstí** (Virgin Mary Sq) and New City Hall, seat of Prague's city council. Nip into the lobby of the Municipal Library (on the northern side of the square) for a peek at the interesting book tower sculpture by Matej Kren.

Facing New City Hall is the main gate of the **9 Klementinum** (p75). Go through the gate and turn left; on your right is the Chapel of Mirrors, where classical concerts are held daily. Continue through the triple arch, then turn right to pass through quiet courtyards (look up to your right to spot a modern sculpture of a child with a paper plane, perched on a ledge).

At the far end of the Klementinum you emerge into the bustling crowds of Křížovnické náměstí. End your walk by climbing up the **10 Old Town Bridge Tower** (p54) for a view over Charles Bridge.

place here between the Civic Forum and the Jakeš regime. The Prague Spring (Pražské jaro) music festival always opens on 12 May, the anniversary of Smetana's death, with a procession from Vyšehrad to the Municipal House followed by a gala performance of his symphonic cycle *Má vlast* (My Country) in Smetana Hall.

Several impressive **official apartments** follow, but the highlight of the tour is the octagonal **Lord Mayor's Hall** (Primatorský sál), whose windows overlook the main entrance. Every aspect of its decoration was designed by Alfons Mucha, who also painted the superbly moody murals that adorn the walls and ceiling. Above you is an allegory of Slavic Concord, with intertwined figures representing the various Slavic peoples watched over by the Czech eagle. Figures from Czech history and mythology, representing the civic virtues, occupy the spaces between the eight arches, including Jan Hus as Spravedlnost (justice), Jan Žižka as Bojovnost (military prowess) and the Chodové (medieval Bohemian border guards) as beady-eyed Ostražitost (vigilance).

Powder Gate TOWER

(Prašná brána; Map p62; http://en.muzeumprahy.cz/prague-towers; Na příkopě; adult/child 90/65Kč; ⏲10am-10pm Apr-Sep, to 8pm Oct & Mar, to 6pm Nov-Feb; Ⓜ Náměstí Republiky) Construction of the 65m-tall Powder Gate was begun in 1475 on the site of one of Staré Město's 13 original city gates. The exterior is a froth of Gothic decoration, while the interior houses little more than a few information panels about the tower's construction – the main attraction is the view from the top.

The gate was built during the reign of King Vladislav II Jagiello as a ceremonial entrance to the city, but was left unfinished after the king moved from the neighbouring Royal Court to Prague Castle in 1483. The name comes from its use as a gunpowder magazine in the 18th century. Josef Mocker rebuilt and decorated it and put up a steeple between 1875 and 1886, giving it its neo-Gothic icing.

Museum of Czech Cubism GALLERY

(Map p62; ☎778 543 901; www.czkubismus.cz; House at the Black Madonna, Ovocný trh 19; adult/child 150/80Kč; ⏲10am-6pm Tue-Sun; Ⓜ Náměstí Republiky) Though dating from 1912, Josef Gočár's House of the Black Madonna (Dům U černé Matky Boží) – Prague's first and finest example of cubist architecture – still looks modern and dynamic. It now houses an exhibition of the Museum of Decorative Arts' collection of cubist furniture, ceramics and glassware, as well as displays on Prague's unique cubist architecture.

Estates Theatre HISTORIC BUILDING

(Stavovské divadlo; Map p62; ☎224 902 231; www.narodni-divadlo.cz; Ovocný trh 1; Ⓜ Můstek) Prague's oldest theatre and finest neoclassical building, the Estates Theatre is where the premiere of Mozart's *Don Giovanni* was performed on 29 October 1787, with the maestro himself conducting. Opened in 1783 as the Nostitz Theatre (after its founder, Count Anton von Nostitz-Rieneck), it was patronised by upper-class German citizens and thus came to be called the Estates Theatre – the Estates being the traditional nobility.

After WWII it was renamed the Tylovo divadlo (Tyl Theatre) in honour of the 19th-century Czech playwright Josef Kajetán Tyl. One of his claims to fame is the Czech national anthem, *Kde domov můj?* (Where is My Home?), which came from one of his plays. In the early 1990s the theatre's name reverted to Estates Theatre. To see the interior you can attend a performance (p158) – the program is on the website – or phone to arrange a guided tour (per person 200Kč).

★ Apple Museum MUSEUM

(Map p62; ☎774 414 775; www.applemuseum.com; Husova 21; adult/child 300/140Kč; ⏲10am-10pm; Ⓜ Staroměstská) This shrine to all things Apple claims to be the world's biggest collection of Apple products, with at least one of everything made by the company between 1976 and 2012. Sleek white galleries showcase row upon row of beautifully displayed computers, laptops, iPods and iPhones like sacred reliquaries; highlights include the earliest Apple I and Apple II computers, an iPod 'family tree' and Steve Jobs's business cards.

Klementinum HISTORIC BUILDING

(Map p62; ☎606 100 293; www.klementinum.com; entrances on Křížovnická, Karlova & Mariánské náměstí; guided tour adult/child 220/140Kč; ⏲10am-5pm Apr-Oct, to 4pm Nov, Dec & Mar; Ⓜ Staroměstská, 🚋2, 17, 18) The Klementinum is a vast complex of beautiful baroque and rococo halls, now mostly occupied by the Czech National Library. Most of the buildings are closed to the public, but you can walk freely through the courtyards, or take a 50-minute **guided tour** of the baroque Library Hall, the Meridian Hall, the Astronomical Tower and (if no events are taking place) the Chapel of Mirrors.

When the Habsburg emperor Ferdinand I invited the Jesuits to Prague in 1556, to boost the power of the Roman Catholic Church in Bohemia, they selected one of the city's choicest pieces of real estate and in 1587 set to work on the **Church of the Holy Saviour** (kostel Nejsvětějšího Spasitele; Map p62; www.farnostsalvator.cz; Křížovnické náměstí; open for religious services) FREE, Prague's flagship of the Counter-Reformation. Its western facade faces Charles Bridge, its sooty stone saints glaring down at the traffic jam of trams and tourists on Křížovnické náměstí.

After gradually buying up most of the adjacent neighbourhood, the Jesuits started building their college, the Klementinum, in 1653. By the time of its completion a century later it was the largest building in the city after Prague Castle. When the Jesuits fell out with the pope in 1773, it became part of Charles University.

The baroque **Library Hall** (1727), magnificently decorated with ornate gilded carvings and a ceiling fresco depicting the Temple of Wisdom, houses thousands of theological volumes dating back to 1600. The **Meridian Hall** was used to determine the exact time of noon, using a beam of sunlight cast through a hole in one of the walls.

Also dating from the 1720s, the Astronomical Tower is capped with a huge bronze of Atlas and was used as an observatory until the 1930s; it houses a display of 18th-century astronomical instruments.

The **Chapel of Mirrors** (Zrcadlová kaple; Map p62; 222 220 879; www.klementinum.com; adult/child incl Astronomical Tower & Baroque Library 220/140Kč; 10am-7pm, tours hourly Mon-Thu, every 30min Fri-Sun; 2, 17, 18) also dates from the 1720s and is an ornate confection of gilded stucco, marbled columns, fancy frescoes and ceiling mirrors – think baroque on steroids. Concerts of classical music are held here daily (tickets are available at most ticket agencies).

There are two other interesting churches in the Klementinum. The **Church of St Clement** (kostel sv Klimenta; Map p62; www.exarchat.cz; Karlova; services 8.30am & 10am Sun), lavishly redecorated in the baroque style from 1711 to 1715 to plans by Kilian Dientzenhofer, is now a Greek Catholic chapel. Conservatively dressed visitors are welcome to attend the services. And then there's the elliptical Chapel of the Assumption of the Virgin Mary, built in 1600 for the Italian artisans who worked on the Klementinum (it's still technically the property of the Italian Government).

Charles Bridge Museum MUSEUM

(Muzeum Karlova Mostu; Map p62; 776 776 779; www.charlesbridgemuseum.com; Křížovnické náměstí 3; adult/concession 170/70Kč; 10am-6pm; 2, 17, 18) Founded in the 13th century, the Order of the Knights of the Cross with the Red Star were the guardians of Judith Bridge (and its successor Charles Bridge), with their 'mother house' at the Church of St Francis Seraphinus on Křížovnické náměstí. This museum, housed in the order's headquarters, covers the history of Prague's most famous landmark.

There are displays on ancient bridge-building techniques, masonry and carpentry, and models of both the Judith and Charles Bridges. In Room 16 you can descend into the foundations of the building to see some of the original stonework of Judith Bridge (dating from 1172), but perhaps the most impressive exhibits are the old photographs of flood damage to Charles Bridge in 1890, when three arches collapsed and were swept away.

Smetana Museum MUSEUM

(Muzeum Bedřicha Smetany; Map p62; 222 220 082; www.nm.cz; Novotného lávka 1; adult/child 50/30Kč; 10am-noon & 12.30-5pm Wed-Mon; 2, 17, 18) This small museum is devoted to Bedřich Smetana, Bohemia's favourite composer. It isn't that interesting unless you're a Smetana fan, and has only limited labelling in English, but there's a good exhibit on popular culture's feverish response to Smetana's opera *The Bartered Bride* – it seems Smetana was the Andrew Lloyd Webber of his day.

Southwestern Staré Město

Bethlehem Chapel CHURCH

(Betlémská kaple; Map p62; 224 248 595; www.bethlehemchapel.eu; Betlémské náměstí 3; adult/child 60/30Kč; 10am-6pm; 2, 9, 18, 22) The Bethlehem Chapel is a national cultural monument, being the birthplace of the Hussite cause. Jan Hus preached here from 1402 to 1412, marking the emergence of the Reform movement from the sanctuary of the Karolinum (where he was rector). Every year on the night of 5 July, the eve of Hus's burning at the stake in 1415, a memorial is held here with speeches and bell-ringing.

In 1391, Reformist Praguers won permission to build a church where services could be held in Czech instead of Latin, and proceeded to construct the biggest chapel Bohemia had ever seen, able to hold 3000 worshippers.

In the 18th century the chapel was torn down. Remnants were discovered around 1920, and from 1948 to 1954 – because Hussitism had official blessing as an ancient form of communism – the whole thing was painstakingly reconstructed in its original form, based on old drawings, descriptions and traces of the original work. Architecturally, it was a radical departure, with a simple square hall focused on the pulpit rather than the altar.

An explanatory text in English is available at the chapel entrance. Only the southern wall of the chapel is brand new, and you can still see some original parts in the eastern wall: the pulpit door, several windows and the door to the preacher's quarters. These quarters, including the rooms used by Hus and others, are also original; they are now used for exhibits. The wall paintings are modern, and are based on old Hussite tracts. The indoor well predates the chapel.

Náprstek Museum MUSEUM

(Náprstkovo muzeum; Map p62; ☎224 497 500; www.nm.cz; Betlémské náměstí 1; adult/child 100/70Kč; ⏲10am-6pm Tue & Thu-Sun, 9am-6pm Wed; 🐾; 🚋2, 9, 18, 22) The small Náprstek Museum houses an ethnographical collection of Asian, African and American cultures, founded by Vojta Náprstek, a 19th-century industrialist with a passion for both anthropology and modern technology – his technology exhibits are now part of the National Technical Museum (p94) in Holešovice.

Lego Museum MUSEUM

(Muzeum Lega; Map p62; ☎775 446 677; www.muzeumlega.cz; Národní 31; adult/child/family 200/50/520Kč; ⏲10am-8pm; Ⓜ Národní Třída, 🚋2, 9, 18, 22) The Lego Museum is Europe's largest private collection of Lego models, with a play area at the end where kids can build stuff from Lego.

Viselec (David Černý Sculpture) SCULPTURE

(Hanging Out; Map p62; www.davidcerny.cz; Husova; 🚋2, 9, 18, 22) Here's some more inspired madness from artist David Černý: look up as you walk along Husova street and you'll see a bearded, bespectacled chap not unlike Sigmund Freud casually dangling by one hand from a pole way above the ground.

Nové Město

Nové Město means 'New Town', although this crescent-shaped district to the east and south of Staré Město was new only when it was founded by Charles IV in 1348. It extends eastwards from Revoluční and Na Příkopě to Wilsonova and the main train line, and south from Národní třída to Vyšehrad. The main sights – mostly museums and historic buildings – are concentrated in and around Wenceslas Square, and many of the surrounding blocks are honeycombed with pedestrian-only arcades – Prague's famous *pasážy* (passages) – lined with shops, cafes, cinemas and theatres.

Wenceslas Square & Around

★Wenceslas Square SQUARE

(Václavské náměstí; Map p78; Ⓜ Můstek, Muzeum) More a broad boulevard than a typical city square, Wenceslas Square has witnessed a great deal of Czech history – a giant Mass was held here during the revolutionary upheavals of 1848; in 1918 the creation of the new Czechoslovak Republic was celebrated here; and it was here in 1989 that the fall of communism was announced. Originally a medieval horse market, the square was named after Bohemia's patron saint during the nationalist revival of the mid-19th century.

At the southern end of the square is Josef Myslbek's muscular equestrian **statue of St Wenceslas** (sv Václav; Map p78; Václavské náměstí; Ⓜ Muzeum), the 10th-century pacifist Duke of Bohemia and the 'Good King Wenceslas' of Christmas carol fame. Flanked by other patron saints of Bohemia – Prokop, Adalbert, Agnes and Ludmila – he has been plastered with posters and bunting at every one of the square's historical moments.

Near the statue, a small **memorial** to the victims of communism bears photographs and handwritten epitaphs to anticommunist rebels Jan Palach and Jan Zajíc. In contrast to the solemnity of this shrine, the square around it has become a monument to capitalism, a gaudy gallery of fast-food outlets and expensive shops.

Following a police attack on a student demonstration on 17 November 1989, angry citizens gathered in Wenceslas Square by the thousands night after night. A week later, in a stunning mirror image of Klement Gottwald's 1948 proclamation of communist rule in Old Town Square, Alexander Dubček and Václav

South Nové Město

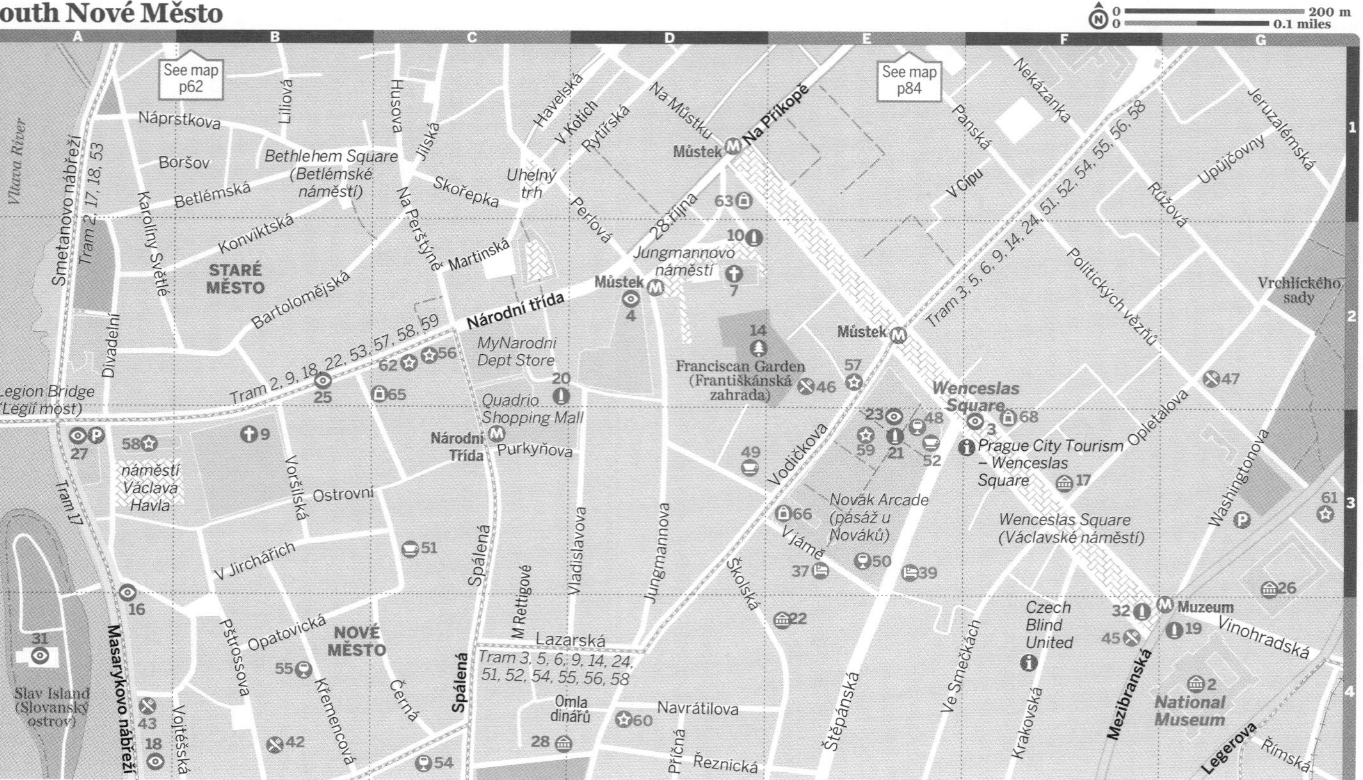

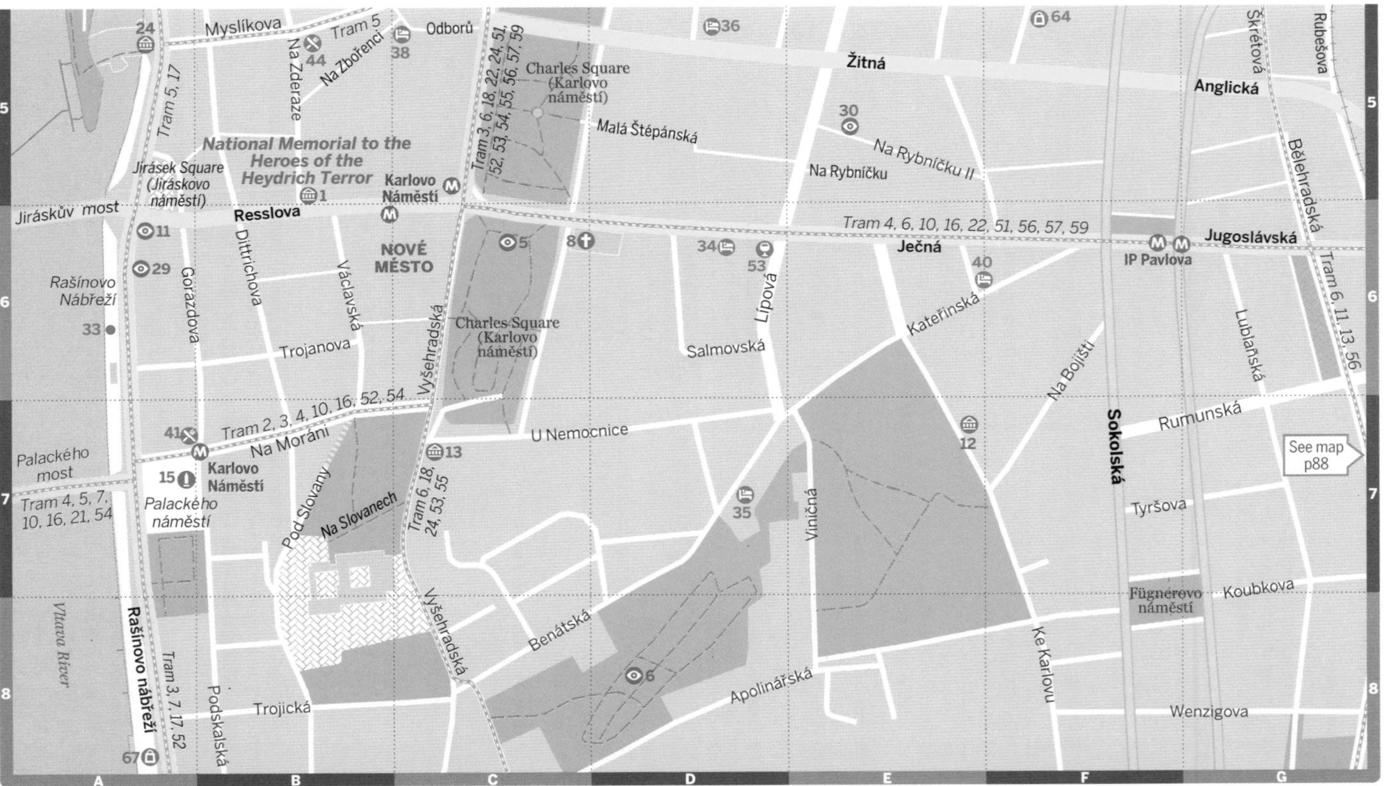
Myslíkova
Tram 5
Odborů
Na Zderaze
Na Zbořenci
Žitná
Anglická
Škrétová
Rubešova
Tram 5, 17
Tram 3, 6, 18, 22, 24, 51, 52, 53, 54, 55, 56, 57, 59
Charles Square (Karlovo náměstí)
Malá Štěpánská
Na Rybníčku II
Na Rybníčku
Bělehradská
National Memorial to the Heroes of the Heydrich Terror
Jirásek Square (Jiráskovo náměstí)
Karlovo Náměstí
Jiráskův most
Resslova
Tram 4, 6, 10, 16, 22, 51, 56, 57, 59
Ječná
Jugoslávská
IP Pavlova
Tram 6, 11, 13, 56
Rašínovo Nábřeží
Gorazdova
Dittrichova
Václavská
NOVÉ MĚSTO
Vyšehradská
Charles Square (Karlovo náměstí)
Lípová
Salmovská
Kateřinská
Lublaňská
Trojanova
Na Bojišti
Sokolská
Rumunská
Tram 2, 3, 4, 10, 16, 52, 54
Na Moráni
U Nemocnice
See map p88
Palackého most
Karlovo Náměstí
Palackého náměstí
Tram 4, 5, 7, 10, 16, 21, 54
Pod Slovany
Na Slovanech
Tram 6, 18, 24, 53, 55
Viničná
Tyršova
Fügnerovo náměstí
Koubkova
Vltava River
Rašínovo nábřeží
Tram 3, 7, 17, 52
Podskalská
Trojická
Benátská
Apolinářská
Ke Karlovu
Wenzigova
A
B
C
D
E
F
G
5
6
7
8

South Nové Město

Top Sights
1 National Memorial to the Heroes of the Heydrich Terror ... B5
2 National Museum ... G4
3 Wenceslas Square ... F3

Sights
4 Adria Palace ... D2
5 Charles Square ... C6
6 Charles University Botanical Garden ... D8
7 Church of Our Lady of the Snows ... D2
8 Church of St Ignatius ... C6
9 Convent of St Ursula ... B3
10 Cubist Lamp Post ... D2
11 Dancing House ... A6
12 Dvořák Museum ... E7
13 Faust House ... C7
14 Franciscan Garden ... D2
15 František Palacký Memorial ... A7
16 Goethe Institute ... A4
17 Hotel Jalta Nuclear Bunker ... F3
18 House of the Hlahol Choir ... A4
19 Jan Palach Memorial ... G4
20 K (David Černý Sculpture) ... C2
21 Kun (David Černý Sculpture) ... E3
22 Leica Gallery ... E4
23 Lucerna Palace ... E3
24 Mánes Gallery ... A5
25 Národní Třída ... B2
26 National Museum New Building ... G3
27 National Theatre ... A3
28 New Town Hall ... C4
29 Rašínovo nábřeží 78 ... A6
30 Rotunda of St Longinus ... E5
31 Slav Island ... A4
32 Wenceslas Statue ... F4

Activities, Courses & Tours
33 Prague Steamboat Co ... A6

Sleeping
34 ArtHarmony ... D6
Dancing House Hotel ... (see 11)
35 Hotel 16 ... D7
36 Hotel Suite Home ... D5
37 Icon Hotel ... E3
38 Mosaic House ... C5
39 Radisson Blu Alcron Hotel ... E3
40 Sophie's Hostel ... E6

Eating
41 Black Dog Cantina ... A7
Ginger & Fred ... (see 11)
42 Globe Bookstore & Café ... B4
43 Klub Cestovatelů ... A4
44 Lemon Leaf ... B5
45 Mangal ... F4
Room ... (see 37)
46 Styl & Interier ... E2
47 U Ferdinanda ... G2

Drinking & Nightlife
Cafe Louvre ... (see 56)
48 Cellarius ... E3
49 Friends Coffee House ... D3
50 Jáma ... E3
Kavárna Lucerna ... (see 23)
51 Kavárna Velryba ... C3
52 Kávovarna ... E3
53 Pivovarský Dům ... D6
54 Red Room ... C4
55 U Fleků ... B4

Entertainment
56 Image Theatre ... C2
57 Kino Světozor ... E2
58 Laterna Magika ... A3
59 Lucerna Music Bar ... E3
60 Minor Theatre ... D4
National Theatre ... (see 27)
61 Prague State Opera ... G3
62 Reduta Jazz Club ... C2
Rock Café ... (see 62)
Wonderful Dvořák ... (see 12)

Shopping
63 Baťa ... D1
64 Bazar ... F5
65 Belda Jewellery ... C2
Globe Bookstore & Café ... (see 42)
66 Jan Pazdera ... E3
67 Náplavka Farmers Market ... A8
68 Palác Knih Neo Luxor ... F3

Havel stepped onto the balcony of the Melantrich Building to a thunderous and tearful ovation, and proclaimed the end of communism in Czechoslovakia.

★**National Museum** MUSEUM
(Národní muzeum; Map p78; ☎224 497 111; www.nm.cz; Václavské náměstí 68; Ⓜ Muzeum) Looming above Wenceslas Square is the neo-Renaissance bulk of the National Museum, designed in the 1880s by Josef Schulz as an architectural symbol of the Czech National Revival. Its magnificent interior is a shrine to the cultural, intellectual and scientific history of the Czech Republic. The museum's main building is closed until 2018 for a major overhaul that will extend exhibition spaces, and create covered courtyards and a museum shop and cafe.

National Museum New Building MUSEUM
(Map p78; ☎224 497 111; www.nm.cz; Vinohradská 1; adult/child 200/140Kč; ⌚10am-6pm; Ⓜ Muzeum) In 2009 the National Museum expanded into the old Radio Free

Europe/Radio Liberty building next door. This so-called New Building now hosts changing exhibitions on various historical, scientific and technological themes.

Jan Palach Memorial MONUMENT

(Map p78; Václavské náměstí 68; 24hr; Muzeum) In January 1969 university student Jan Palach set fire to himself in front of the National Museum to protest against the Soviet-led invasion of Czechoslovakia the preceding August. Palach later died from his burns and became a national hero. The memorial sits at the exact spot where Palach fell, marked by a cross in the pavement just below the steps to the museum's entrance.

Hotel Jalta Nuclear Bunker HISTORIC BUILDING

(Map p78; 222 822 111; www.hoteljalta.com; Václavské náměstí 45; adult/child 120/60Kč; tours in English 2-7pm Fri-Sun; Můstek, Muzeum) Hidden beneath the 1950s Hotel Jalta on Wenceslas Square lies a communist-era nuclear shelter that was opened to the public in 2013. The tour, led by a guide in period security police uniform, takes in a series of secret chambers; the highlight is the comms room, where wiretaps in the bedrooms of important guests were monitored.

★ **Mucha Museum** GALLERY

(Muchovo muzeum; Map p84; 221 451 333; www.mucha.cz; Panská 7; adult/child 240/160Kč; 10am-6pm; 3, 5, 6, 9, 14, 24) This fascinating (and busy) museum features the sensuous art-nouveau posters, paintings and decorative panels of Alfons Mucha (1860–1939), as well as many sketches, photographs and other memorabilia. The exhibits include countless artworks showing Mucha's trademark Slavic maidens with flowing hair and piercing blue eyes, bearing symbolic garlands and linden boughs.

There are also photos of the artist's Paris studio, one of which shows a trouserless **Gaugin** playing the harmonium; a powerful canvas entitled *Old Woman in Winter;* and the original of the 1894 poster of actress **Sarah Bernhardt** as Giselda, which shot him to international fame. In 1910 Mucha was invited to design the Lord Mayor's Hall in Prague's Municipal House, and following the creation of Czechoslovakia in 1918, he designed the new nation's banknotes and postage stamps.

His crowning achievement, however, was the *Slav Epic,* a series of huge, historical paintings, which has been on show in the city's Veletržní Palác since 2012. It embarks on a world tour in 2017 and 2018, and it is not certain where (or even if) it will be displayed on its return.

The fascinating video documentary about Mucha's life is well worth watching, and helps put his achievements in perspective.

Lucerna Palace ARCHITECTURE

(Palác Lucerna; Map p78; www.lucerna.cz; Vodičkova 36; 3, 5, 6, 9, 14, 24) The most elegant of Nové Město's many shopping arcades runs through the art-nouveau Lucerna Palace (1920), between Štěpánská and Vodičkova streets. The complex was designed by Václav Havel (grandfather of the former president), and is still partially owned by the family. It includes theatres, a cinema, shops, a rock club and several cafes and restaurants.

In the marbled atrium hangs artist David Černý's sculpture **Kun** (Horse; Map p78; www.davidcerny.cz; Vodičkova 36; 24hr), a wryly amusing counterpart to the equestrian statue of St Wenceslas in Wenceslas Square. Here St Wenceslas sits astride a horse that is decidedly dead; it's safe to assume this is a reference to Václav Klaus, president of the Czech Republic from 2003 to 2013.

The neighbouring **Novák Arcade**, connected to the Lucerna and riddled by a maze of passages, has one of Prague's finest art-nouveau facades (overlooking Vodičkova), complete with mosaics of country life.

Leica Gallery GALLERY

(Map p78; 222 211 567; www.lgp.cz; Školská 28; adult/child 70/40Kč; 10am-9pm Mon-Fri, 2-8pm Sat & Sun; 3, 5, 6, 9, 14, 24) The Leica Gallery stages exhibitions of 20th-century and contemporary photography by both Czech and international photographers; past exhibitions have featured the work of Helmut Newton, Leni Riefenstahl, and Magnum Photo Agency photographer Elliott Erwitt. There's also a comfortable cafe and bookshop.

Franciscan Garden PARK

(Františkánská zahrada; Map p78; entrances from Jungmannovo náměstí, Vodičkova & Václavské náměstí; 7am-10pm Apr-Sep, to 7pm Oct-Mar; 3, 5, 6, 9, 14, 24) FREE This hidden oasis of peace and greenery lies just west of the bustle of Wenceslas Square. There are entrances from the end of the Světovor arcade off Vodičkova, the Alfa arcade off Wenceslas Square, and on Jungmannovo náměstí.

Na Příkopě STREET

(Map p84; Můstek) Na Příkopě (On the Moat) –along with Revoluční (Revolution),

28.října (28 October 1918; Czechoslovak Independence Day) and Národní třída (National Ave) – follows the line of the moat that once ran along the foot of Staré Město's city walls (the moat was filled in at the end of the 18th century).

Na Příkopě meets Wenceslas Square at Na Můstku (On the Little Bridge). A small stone bridge once crossed the moat here – you can still see a remaining arch in the underground entrance to Můstek metro station, on the left just past the ticket machines.

In the 19th century, this fashionable street was the haunt of Prague's German cafe society. Today it is (along with Wenceslas Square and Pařížská) the city's main upmarket shopping precinct, lined with banks, shopping malls and tourist cafes.

Museum of Communism MUSEUM

(Muzeum Komunismu; Map p84; ☎224 212 966; www.muzeumkomunismu.cz; Na příkopě 10; adult/child under 10yr 190Kč/free; ⏲9am-9pm; Ⓜ Můstek) It's difficult to think of a more ironic site for a museum of communism – in an 18th-century aristocrat's palace, between a casino on one side and a McDonald's on the other. Put together by an American expat and his Czech partner, the museum tells the story of Czechoslovakia's years behind the Iron Curtain in photos, words and a fascinating and varied collection of...well, stuff.

The empty shops, corruption, fear and double-speak of life in socialist Czechoslovakia are well conveyed, and there are rare photos of the Stalin monument that once stood on Letná terrace – and its spectacular destruction. Be sure to watch the video about protests leading up to the Velvet Revolution: you'll never think of it as a pushover again.

Church of Our Lady of the Snows CHURCH

(Kostel Panny Marie Sněžné; Map p78; www.pms.ofm.cz; Jungmannovo náměstí 18; Ⓜ Můstek) This Gothic church at the northern end of Wenceslas Square was begun in the 14th century by Charles IV, but only the chancel was ever completed, which accounts for its proportions – seemingly taller than it is long. Charles had intended it to be the grandest church in Prague; the nave is higher than that of St Vitus Cathedral, and the altar is the city's tallest.

It was a Hussite stronghold, ringing with the sermons of Jan Želivský, who led the 1419 defenestration that touched off the Hussite Wars. The church is approached through an arch in the Austrian Cultural Institute on Jungmannovo náměstí, but you can get a good view of the exterior from the neighbouring Franciscan Garden (p81). Beside the church is the Chapel of the Pasov Virgin, now a venue for temporary art exhibitions.

Cubist Lamp Post PUBLIC ART

(Map p78; Jungmannovo náměstí; Ⓜ Můstek) Angular but slightly chunky, made from striated concrete – the world's only cubist lamp post would be worth going out of the way to see. So it's a happy bonus that this novelty is just around the corner from Wenceslas Square.

Národní Třída STREET

(National Ave; Map p78; 🚋2, 9, 18, 22) Národní třída is central Prague's 'high street', a stately row of midrange shops and grand public buildings, notably the National Theatre at the Vltava River end.

THE HEYDRICH ASSASSINATION

In 1941, in response to a series of crippling strikes and sabotage operations by the Czech resistance movement, the German government appointed SS general Reinhard Heydrich, an antisubversion specialist, as Reichsprotektor of Bohemia and Moravia. Heydrich immediately cracked down on resistance activities with a vengeance.

In a move designed to support the resistance and boost Czech morale, Britain secretly trained a team of Czechoslovak paratroopers to assassinate Heydrich. The daring mission was code-named Operation Anthropoid and, against all odds, it succeeded. On 27 May 1942, two paratroopers, Jan Kubiš and Jozef Gabčík, attacked Heydrich as he rode in his official car through the city's Libeň district – he later died from the wounds. The assassins and five co-conspirators fled but were betrayed in their hiding place in the **Church of Sts Cyril & Methodius** (p86); all seven died in the ensuing siege.

The Nazis reacted with a frenzied wave of terror, which included the annihilation of two entire Czech villages, Ležáky and Lidice, and the shattering of the underground movement.

Fronting Jungmannovo náměstí, at the eastern end, is an imitation Venetian palace known as the **Adria Palace** (Map p78; Národní třída 36; M Můstek). Its distinctive, chunky architectural style, dating from the 1920s, is known as 'rondocubism'. Note how the alternating angular and rounded window pediments echo similar features in neoclassical baroque buildings such as the Černín Palace.

Beneath it is the **Adria Theatre**, birthplace of Laterna Magika and meeting place of the Civic Forum in the heady days of the Velvet Revolution. From here, Dubček and Havel walked to the Lucerna Palace and their 24 November 1989 appearance on the balcony of the Melantrich Building. Wander through the arcade for a look at the lovely marble, glass and brass decoration; the main atrium has a 24-hour clock from the 1920s, flanked by sculptures depicting the signs of the zodiac. It was once the entrance to the offices of the Adriatica insurance company (hence the building's name).

Along the street, inside the arcade near No 16, is the **1989 students' memorial** – a bronze plaque on the wall with a cluster of hands making the peace sign and the date '17.11.89', in memory of students beaten up by police on that date.

West of Voršilská, the lemon-yellow walls of the **Convent of St Ursula** (klášter sv Voršila; Map p78; Národní třída 10; 2, 9, 18, 22) frame a pink church, which has a lush baroque interior that includes a battalion of Apostle statues. Out front is the figure of St John of Nepomuk, and in the facade's lower-right niche is a statue of St Agatha holding her severed breasts – one of the more gruesome images in Catholic hagiography.

Across the road is the art-nouveau facade (by Osvald Polívka) of the **Viola Building** (Map p62; Národní třída 7; 2, 9, 18, 22), former home of the Prague Insurance Co, with the huge letters 'PRAHA' entwined around five circular windows, and mosaics spelling out *život, kapitál, důchod, věno* and *pojišťuje* (life, capital, income, dowry and insurance). The building next door, a former publishing house, is also a Polívka design.

On the southern side at No 4, looking like it has been built out of huge glass blocks, is the **Nová Scéna** (1983), the 'New National Theatre' building, now home of Laterna Magika (p160).

Finally, facing the Vltava near Smetanovo nábřeží is the magnificent National Theatre. Across from the theatre is the Kavárna Slavia (p147), known for its art-deco interior and river views, and once the place to be seen or to grab an after-theatre meal. Now renovated, it's once again the place to be seen – though mainly by other tourists.

K (David Černý Sculpture) PUBLIC ART

(Statue of Kafka; Map p78; www.davidcerny.cz; Spálená 22; M Národní Třída) FREE Located in the courtyard of the Quadrio shopping centre above Národní třída metro station, David Černý's giant rotating bust of Franz Kafka is formed from some 39 tonnes of mirrored stainless steel. It's a mesmerising show as Kafka's face rhythmically dissolves and re-emerges, possibly playing on notions of the author's ever-changing personality and sense of self-doubt.

National Theatre ARCHITECTURE

(Národní divadlo; Map p78; tour bookings 221 714 161; www.narodni-divadlo.cz; Ostrovní 1, main entrance on Národní třída; tour in English per person 200Kč; tours 8.30-11am Sat & Sun; 2, 9, 18, 22) The National Theatre is the neo-Renaissance architectural flagship of the Czech National Revival, and one of Prague's most impressive buildings. Funded entirely by private donations and decorated inside and out by a roll-call of prominent Czech artists, architect Josef Zítek's masterpiece burned down within weeks of its 1881 opening but, incredibly, was funded again and restored in less than two years.

Individual visitors can book a guided tour of the building on weekend mornings only.

Northern Nové Město

★ Prague City Museum MUSEUM

(Muzeum hlavního města Prahy; Map p84; 224 816 773; www.muzeumprahy.cz; Na Poříčí 52; adult/child 120/50Kč; 9am-6pm Tue-Sun; M Florenc) This excellent museum, opened in 1898, is devoted to the history of Prague from prehistoric times to the 20th century (labels are in English as well as Czech). Among the many intriguing exhibits are an astonishing scale model of Prague, and the Astronomical Clock's original 1866 calendar wheel with Josef Mánes's beautiful painted panels representing the months – that's January at the top, toasting his toes by the fire, and August near the bottom, sickle in hand, harvesting the corn.

The medieval and renaissance galleries display lots of fascinating household artefacts, including a reliquary made of carved bone, plus more valuable items such as a 16th-century

North Nové Město

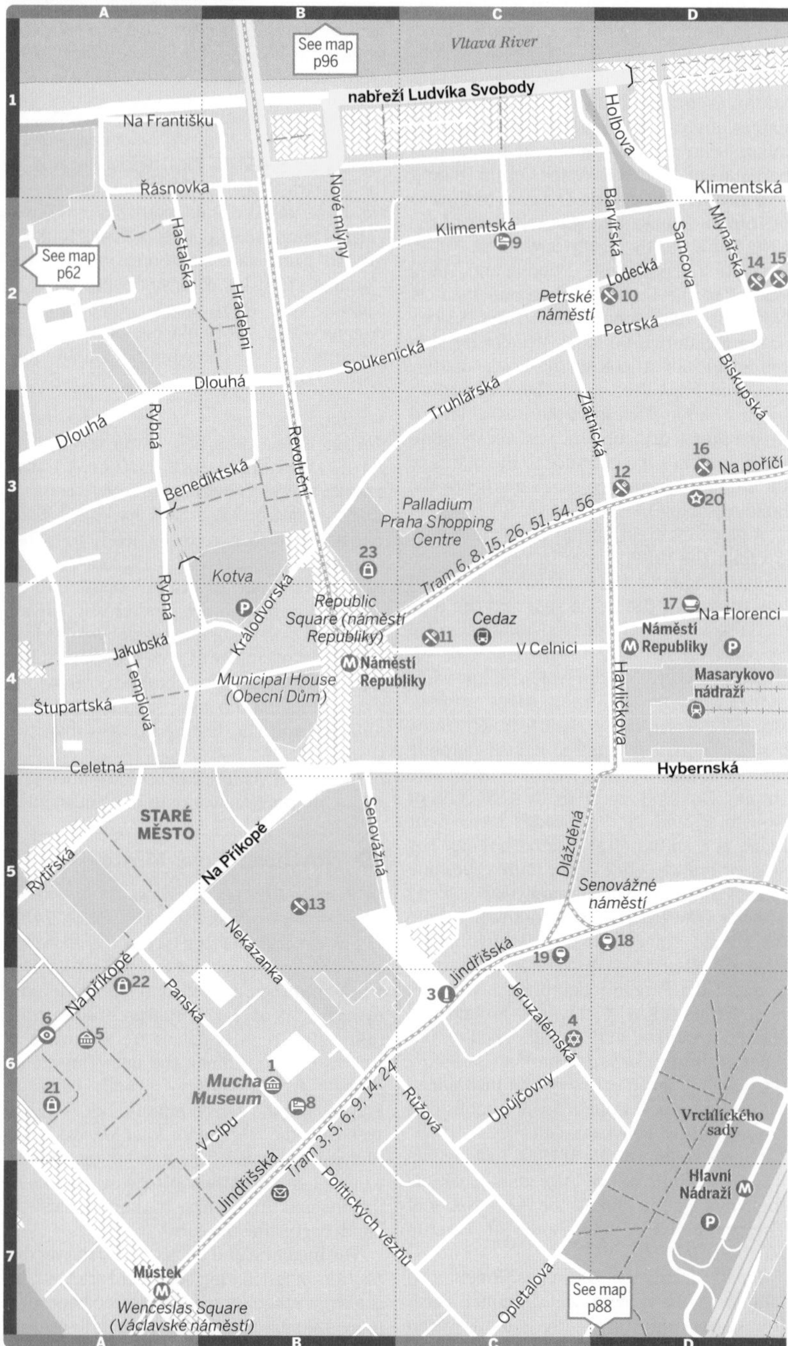

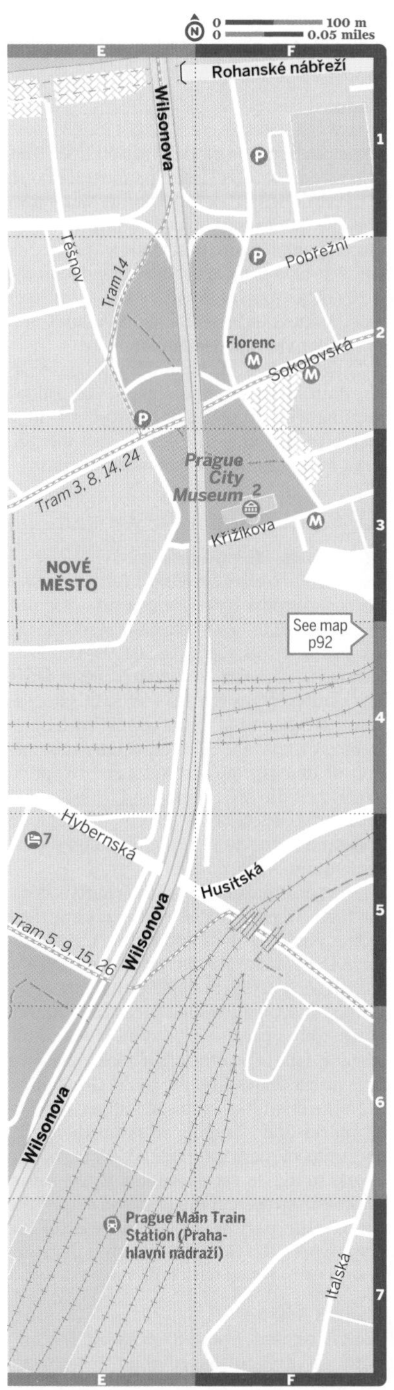

North Nové Město

Top Sights
1 Mucha Museum....B6
2 Prague City Museum....F3

Sights
3 Jindřišská Tower....C6
4 Jubilee Synagogue....C6
5 Museum of Communism....A6
6 Na Příkopě....A6

Sleeping
7 Alfa Tourist Service....E5
8 Fusion Hotel....B6
9 Moods Hotel....C2

Eating
10 Al Forno....D2
11 Brasserie La Gare....C4
12 Café Imperial....D3
13 Kogo....B5
14 Maso a kobliha....D2
15 Sansho....D2
16 Siam Orchid....D3

Drinking & Nightlife
17 EMA Espresso Bar....D4
18 Hoffa....D5
19 Vinograf....C5

Entertainment
20 Archa Theatre....D3

Shopping
21 Bontonland....A6
22 Moser....A6
23 Palladium Praha Shopping Centre....B3

bronze figure of Hercules which was perhaps created for the Wallenstein Palace (it was found in a private house in the Old Town in 1905).

But what everybody comes to see is Antonín Langweil's 1:480 **scale model of Prague** as it looked between 1826 and 1834. The display is most rewarding after you get to know Prague a bit, as you can spot the changes – look at St Vitus Cathedral, for example, still only half-finished. The model has been digitised, and you can view a six-minute 'fly-through' of Langweil's Prague in a cinema in the museum basement (screenings every half-hour; admission 30Kč).

Jindřišská Tower TOWER

(Jindřišská věž; Map p84; 224 232 429; www.jindrisskavez.cz; Jindřišská 1; adult/child 120/50Kč; 10am-7pm Apr-Sep, to 6pm Oct-Mar; 3, 5, 6, 9, 14, 24) This bell tower, dating from the 15th century but rebuilt in Gothic style in the 1870s,

VINOHRADY'S VINEYARDS

Prague is generally known for beer, not wine. And that's probably for good reason. It may come as a surprise, then, that several centuries ago vineyards in Prague produced a substantial amount of wine, and the centre of this activity was Vinohrady (which means 'vineyards'). Vinohrady, so the story goes, got its start in winemaking back in the 14th century, when Emperor Charles IV ordered the first grapes to be planted. The vineyards lasted around 400 years before the area was given over mostly to farms and eventually the luxury townhouses you see today. A small section of the vineyards survives to this day around the area of the **Viniční Altán** (p151) open-air wine garden.

dominates the end of Jindřišská, a busy street running northeast from Wenceslas Square. Having stood idle for decades, the tower was renovated and reopened in 2002 as a tourist attraction, complete with exhibition space, whisky bar, cafe and restaurant, and a lookout gallery on the 10th floor.

Jubilee Synagogue SYNAGOGUE
(Jubilejní synagóga; Map p84; ☎222 319 002; www.synagogue.cz; Jeruzalémská 7; adult/child 80/50Kč; ⏲11am-5pm Sun-Fri Apr-Oct, closed on Jewish holidays; M Hlavní Nádraží) The colourful Moorish facade of the Jubilee Synagogue, also called the Velká synagóga (Great Synagogue), dates from 1906; note the names of the donors on the stained-glass windows, and the grand organ above the entrance. It houses an exhibition of artefacts, photographs and films charting the post-WWII history of Prague's Jewish community.

Along the River

Dancing House ARCHITECTURE
(Tančící dům; Map p78; http://tadu.cz; Rašínovo nábřeží 80; 🚊5, 17) The Dancing House was built in 1996 by architects Vlado Milunić and Frank Gehry. The curved lines of the narrow-waisted glass tower clutched against its more upright and formal partner led to it being christened the 'Fred & Ginger' building, after legendary dancing duo Fred Astaire and Ginger Rogers. It's surprising how well it fits in with its ageing neighbours.

The building houses offices, a ground-floor gallery, a rooftop restaurant and, since 2016, a luxury hotel.

Mánes Gallery GALLERY
(Výstavní síň Mánes; Map p78; ☎224 932 938; www.galeriemanes.com; Masarykovo nábřeží 1; ⏲10am-8pm Tue-Sun; 🚊5, 17) FREE Spanning a branch of the river beneath a 15th-century water tower is the Mánes Building (1927–30), a masterpiece of architecture designed by Otakar Novotný. It houses an art gallery founded in the 1920s by a group of artists headed by painter Josef Mánes, and is still one of Prague's best venues for viewing contemporary art.

However, half of the building is leased as a restaurant (p129) and office space, following financial problems that arose during a major renovation in 2012–14, and the gallery's long-term future remains uncertain.

Charles Square & Around

★**National Memorial to the Heroes of the Heydrich Terror** MUSEUM
(Národní památník hrdinů Heydrichiády; Map p78; ☎224 916 100; www.pamatnik-heydrichiady.cz; Resslova 9; ⏲9am-5pm Tue-Sun Mar-Oct, 9am-5pm Tue-Sat Nov-Feb; M Karlovo Náměstí) FREE The Church of Sts Cyril & Methodius houses a moving memorial to the seven Czech paratroopers who were involved in the assassination of Reichsprotektor Reinhard Heydrich in 1942, with an exhibit and video about Nazi persecution of the Czechs. The church appeared in the 2016 movie based on the assassination, *Anthropoid*.

The paratroopers hid in the church's crypt for three weeks after the killing, until their hiding place was betrayed by the Czech traitor Karel Čurda. The Germans besieged the church, first trying to smoke the paratroopers out and then flooding the crypt with fire hoses. Three paratroopers were killed in the ensuing fight; the other four took their own lives rather than surrender to the Germans.

In the crypt itself you can still see the bullet marks and shrapnel scars on the walls, and signs of the paratroopers' last desperate efforts to dig an escape tunnel to the sewer under the street. On the Resslova side of the church, the narrow gap in the wall of the crypt where the Germans inserted their fire hoses is still pitted with bullet marks.

Charles Square SQUARE
(Karlovo náměstí; Map p78; M Karlovo Náměstí) With an area of more than 7 hectares,

Charles Square is Prague's biggest square; it's more like a small park, really, and was originally the city's cattle market. Presiding over it is the **Church of St Ignatius** (kostel sv Ignáce; Map p78; Ječná 2; Ⓜ Karlovo Náměstí), a 1660s baroque tour de force designed for the Jesuits by Carlo Lurago.

The baroque palace at the southern end of the square belongs to Charles University. It's known as **Faust House** (Faustův dům; Map p78; Karlovo náměstí 40; Ⓜ Karlovo Náměstí) because, according to a popular German legend, this was where Mephistopheles took Dr Faust away to hell through a hole in the ceiling. The building also has associations with Rudolf II's English court alchemist, Edward Kelley, who toiled here in the 16th century trying to convert lead into gold.

Dvořák Museum MUSEUM

(Muzeum Antonína Dvořáka; Map p78; ☎ 224 923 363; www.nm.cz; Ke Karlovu 20, Vila Amerika; adult/child 50/30Kč; ⏱ 10am-1.30pm & 2-5pm Tue-Sun; Ⓜ IP Pavlova) The most striking building in the drab neighbourhood south of Ječná is the energetically baroque Vila Amerika, a 1720s, French-style summer house designed by Kilian Dientzenhofer. It's one of the city's finest baroque buildings and now houses a museum dedicated to the composer Antonín Dvořák. Special concerts (p159) of Dvořák's music are staged here from May to October.

New Town Hall HISTORIC BUILDING

(Novoměstská radnice; Map p78; ☎ 224 948 229; www.nrpraha.cz; Karlovo náměstí 23; adult/child 60/40Kč; ⏱ 10am-6pm Tue-Sun Apr-Sep; Ⓜ Karlovo Náměstí) The New Town Hall was built in the late 14th century, when the New Town was still new. From the window of the main hall (the tower was not built until 1456), two of Wenceslas IV's Catholic councillors were flung to their deaths in 1419 by followers of the Hussite preacher Jan Želivský, sparking the Hussite Wars.

This event gave 'defenestration' (throwing out of a window) a lasting political meaning, and a similar scenario was repeated at Prague Castle in 1618. You can visit the Gothic Hall of Justice, which was the site of the defenestration, and climb the 221 steps to the tower top.

Rotunda of St Longinus ARCHITECTURE

(Map p78; Na Rybničku II) This rotunda is one of the few surviving examples of circular Romanesque churches in the city.

RIVERFRONT ARCHITECTURE

The Nové Město riverfront, stretching south from the National Theatre to Vyšehrad, is lined with some of Prague's grandest 19th- and early-20th-century architecture. It's a great place for an evening stroll, when the setting sun gilds the facades with a beautiful golden light.

Masarykovo nábřeží (Masaryk Embankment) sports a series of stunning art-nouveau buildings. At No 32 is the **Goethe Institute** (Map p78; Masarykovo nábřeží 32; 🚋 17), once the East German embassy. No 26 is a beautiful apartment building with owls perched in the decorative foliage that twines around the door, dogs peeking from the balconies on the 5th floor, and birds perched atop the balustrade.

No 16 is the **House of the Hlahol Choir** (Map p78; Masarykovo nábřeží 16; 🚋 5, 17), built in 1906 by Josef Fanta for a patriotic choral society associated with the Czech National Revival. It's decorated with elaborate musical motifs and topped by a giant mosaic depicting Music – the motto beneath translates as 'Let the song reach the heart; let the heart reach the homeland'.

At the next bridge is **Jirásek Square** (Jiráskovo náměstí), dedicated to writer Alois Jirásek (1851–1930), author of *Old Czech Legends* (studied by all Czech schoolchildren) and an influential figure in the drive towards Czechoslovak independence. His statue is overlooked by the famous **Dancing House** (p86).

A little further along the riverbank is **Rašínovo nábřeží 78** (Map p78; 🚋 5, 17), an apartment building designed by the grandfather of the late president Václav Havel – this was where Havel first chose to live (in preference to Prague Castle) after being elected as president in December 1989, surely the world's least pompous presidential residence.

Two blocks south, sitting on Palackého náměstí, is Stanislav Sucharda's extraordinary art-nouveau **František Palacký Memorial** (Map p78; Palackého náměstí; Ⓜ Karlovo Náměstí); a swarm of haunted bronze figures (allegories of the writer's imagination) swirling around a stodgy statue of the 19th-century historian and giant of the Czech National Revival.

Charles University Botanical Garden GARDENS

(Botanická zahrada Univerzity Karlovy; Map p78; ☎221 951 879; www.bz-uk.cz; Viničná 7, main entrance on Na Slupi; garden free, glasshouses adult/child 55/30Kč; ⏱10am-7.30pm Apr-Aug, to 6pm Sep-Feb; 🚋14, 18, 24) Just south of Karlovo náměstí is Charles University's botanical garden. Founded in 1775 and moved from Smíchov to its present site in 1898, it's the country's oldest botanical garden. The steep, hillside garden concentrates on Central European flora and is especially pretty in spring.

Vinohrady & Vršovice

There are only a couple of 'sights' in the traditional sense. Don't miss a walk through Vinohrady's pretty park, Riegrovy sady, with beautiful vistas out over the Old Town and Prague Castle.

Riegrovy Sady GARDENS

(Rieger Gardens; Map p88; entrance on Chopinova, across from Na Švíhance, Vinohrady; ⏱24hr; Ⓜ Jiřího z Poděbrad) Vinohrady's largest and prettiest park was designed as a classic English garden in the 19th century, and it's still a good place to put down a blanket and chill out.

Vinohrady & Vršovice

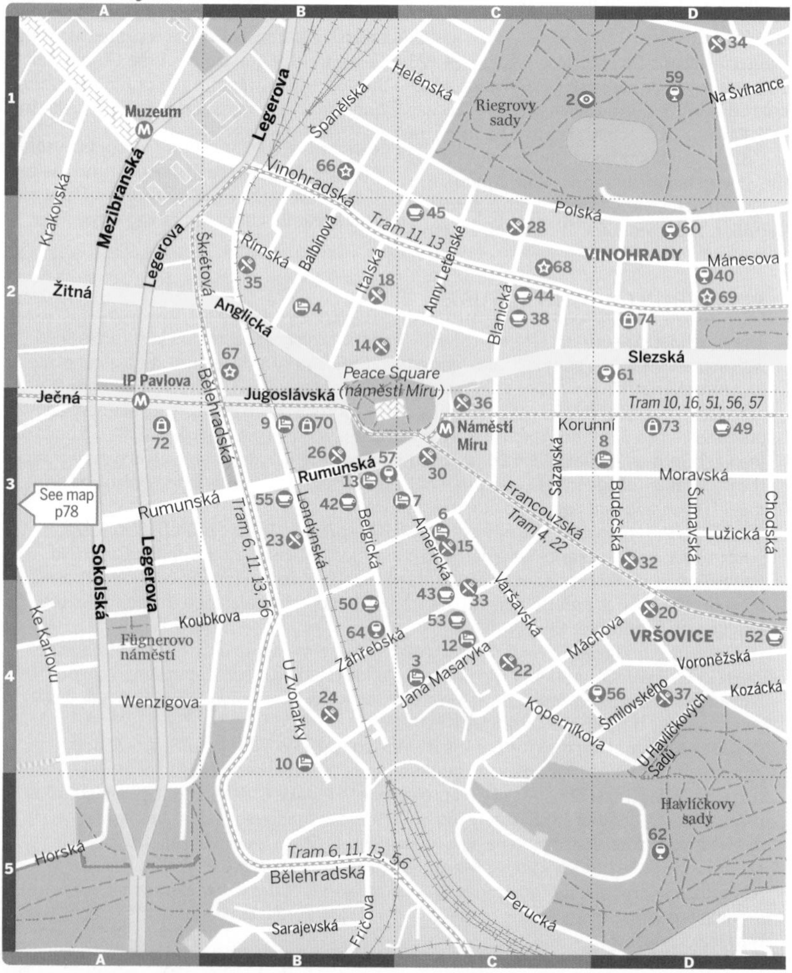

The bluff towards the back of the park affords photo-op-worthy shots of Prague Castle. In summer, the park's open-air beer garden (p150) is the place to be.

Church of the Most Sacred Heart of Our Lord CHURCH
(Kostel Nejsvětějšího Srdce Páně; Map p88; ☎222 727 713; www.srdcepane.cz; náměstí Jiřího z Poděbrad 19, Vinohrady; ⏲services 8am & 6pm Mon-Sat, 9am, 11am & 6pm Sun; Ⓜ Jiřího z Poděbrad) This church from 1932 is one of Prague's most original pieces of 20th-century architecture. It's the work of Jože Plečnik, a Slovenian architect who also worked on Prague Castle. The church is inspired by Egyptian temples and early Christian basilicas. It's usually only open to the public during mass.

Žižkov & Karlín

One of Prague's earliest industrial suburbs, Žižkov has long had a reputation as a rough-and-ready neighbourhood, and was full of left-wing revolutionary fervour well before the communist takeover of 1948. There are a couple of major sights which could be covered in an afternoon, but the main attraction here is the bars.

The mostly residential suburb of Karlín is one of Prague's hottest up-and-coming

Vinohrady & Vršovice

Sights

1 Church of the Most Sacred Heart of Our Lord ... E2
2 Riegrovy sady ... C1

Sleeping

3 Ametyst ... C4
4 Arkada ... B2
5 Czech Inn ... E4
6 Happy House Rentals ... C3
7 Holiday Home ... C3
8 Hotel Anna ... D3
9 Hotel Luník ... B3
10 Le Palais Hotel ... B4
11 Louren Hotel ... F2
12 Orion ... C4
13 Stop City ... B3

Eating

14 Aromi ... B2
15 Bad Jeff's ... C3
Café FX ... (see 67)
16 Cafe Jen ... F4
17 Cafe Sladkovský ... E4
18 Dish ... B2
19 Ha Noi ... F2
20 Javánka & Co ... D4
21 Kofein ... E2
22 Las Adelitas ... C4
23 Loving Hut ... B3
24 Madame Lyn ... B4
25 Mozaika Burger & Co ... E2
26 Originál 1869 ... B3
27 Osteria Da Clara ... G4
28 Pastička ... C2
29 Pho Vietnam Tuan & Lan ... E2
30 Pizzeria Grosseto ... C3
31 Plevel ... E4
32 Restaurace U Bulínů ... D3
33 Ristorante Sapori ... C4
34 The Tavern ... D1
35 U Bilé Krávy ... B2
36 Vinohradský Parlament ... C3
37 Zelená Zahrada ... D4

Drinking & Nightlife

38 Al Cafetero ... C2
39 Bad Flash Bar ... E4
40 Bar & Books Mánesova ... D2
41 Beer Geek ... E2
42 Bio Zahrada ... B3
43 Blatouch ... C4
44 Café Celebrity ... C2
45 Café Kaaba ... C2
46 Cafe V Lese ... E4
47 Cafe Zenit ... E4
48 Coffee Source ... E4
49 Dobrá Trafika ... D3
50 Galerie Kavárna Róza K ... B4
51 Hospůdka Obyčejný Svět ... F3
52 Kavárna Šlágr ... D4
53 Kavárna Zanzibar ... C4
54 Le Caveau ... E2
55 Mama Coffee ... B3
56 Oliveira ... D4
57 Prague Beer Museum ... B3
58 Ráno Kavu Večer Víno ... E4
59 Riegrovy Sady Beer Garden ... D1
60 Saints ... D2
61 Sokolovna ... D2
62 Viniční Altán ... D5
63 Vinohradský Pivovar ... G3
64 Žlutá Pumpa ... B4

Entertainment

65 Infinity ... H2
66 Le Clan ... B1
67 Radost FX ... B2
68 Techtle Mechtle ... C2
69 Termix ... D2

Shopping

70 Dům Porcelánu ... B3
71 Jiřího z Poděbrad Farmers Market ... E2
72 Karel Vávra ... A3
73 Obchod s Uměním ... D3
74 Vinohradský Pavilon ... D2

neighbourhoods, with lovely art-nouveau buildings – Lýčkovo náměstí is one of the prettiest squares in the city – and lots of good restaurants, cafes and wine bars.

★ National Monument MUSEUM

(Národní Památník na Vítkově; Map p92; ☎224 497 600; www.nm.cz; U Památníku 1900, Žižkov; exhibition only adult/child 80/60Kč, roof terrace 80/50Kč, combined ticket 120/80Kč; ⏰10am-6pm Wed-Sun Apr-Oct, Thu-Sun Nov-Mar; 🚌133, 175, 207) While this monument's massive functionalist structure has all the elegance of a nuclear power station, the interior is a spectacular extravaganza of polished art-deco marble, gilt and mosaics, and is home to a fascinating museum of 20th-century Czechoslovak history.

Although, strictly speaking, not a legacy of the communist era – it was completed in the 1930s – the huge monument atop Žižkov Hill is, in the minds of most Praguers over a certain age, inextricably linked with the Communist Party of Czechoslovakia, and in particular with Klement Gottwald, the country's first 'worker-president'.

The monument's central hall – home to a dozen marble sarcophagi that once bore the remains of communist luminaries – houses a moving **war memorial** with sculptures by Jan Sturša. There are exhibits recording the founding of the Czechoslovak Republic in 1918, WWII, the 1948 coup, the Soviet invasion of 1968 – poignant newsreel footage and a handful of personal possessions record the tragic story of Jan Palach, who set himself on fire to protest the Soviet invasion – and the Velvet Revolution of 1989. Upstairs you can visit the Ceremonial Hall and the Presidential Lounge.

But the most grimly fascinating part of the museum is the Frankenstein-like **laboratory** beneath the Liberation Hall, where scientists once battled to prevent Gottwald's corpse from decomposing. On display in a glass-walled sarcophagus by day, his body was lowered into this white-tiled crypt every night for another frantic round of maintenance and repair. In the corner is the refrigerated chamber where Gottwald spent his nights (now occupied by the shattered remains of his sarcophagus), and in the adjoining room is a phalanx of 1950s control panels, switches and instruments that once monitored the great leader's temperature and humidity.

Jan Žižka Statue MONUMENT

(Map p92; 133, 175, 207) A colossal statue of Jan Žižka, a 15th-century Hussite general and hero of Czech history, was erected on top of Vítkov Hill in 1950, commanding superb views across Stáre Město to Prague Castle. It's said to be the biggest equestrian statue in the world.

It was commissioned in 1931 from the Prague sculptor Bohumil Kafka (no relation to Franz), who had a huge studio specially constructed for the project and worked on the statue until his death in 1941, by which time he had succeeded only in creating a full-size plaster version. The statue was eventually cast in bronze – 16.5 tonnes of it – in 1950 and unveiled on 14 July of that year, the anniversary of the Battle of Vítkov Hill.

TV Tower TOWER

(Televizní Vysílač; Map p92; 210 320 081; www.towerpark.cz; Mahlerovy sady 1, Žižkov; adult/child/family 200/120/490Kč; observation decks 8am-midnight; M Jiřího z Poděbrad) Prague's tallest landmark – and depending on your tastes, either its ugliest or its most futuristic feature – is the 216m-tall TV Tower, erected between 1985 and 1992. But more bizarre than its architecture are the 10 giant crawling babies that appear to be exploring the outside of the tower – an installation called **Miminka** (Mummy; Map p92; www.davidcerny.cz), by artist David Černý.

Completely renovated in 2013, the 93m-high observation decks are fitted out with comfortable sofas and futuristic hanging armchairs, with screens showing film clips of the tower's construction. There's also a cafe, cocktail bar and restaurant at the 66m level, and even a luxury one-room 'hotel' (all clearly aimed at the 'oligarch' market).

Olšany Cemetery CEMETERY

(Olšanské Hřbitovy; Map p92; www.hrbitovy.cz; Vinohradská 153, Žižkov; 8am-7pm May-Sep, to 6pm Mar, Apr & Oct, to 5pm Nov-Feb; 5, 10, 11, 13, 15, 16) FREE Huge and atmospheric, Prague's main burial ground was founded in 1680 to handle the increased deaths during a plague epidemic. Jan Palach (p72), the student who set himself on fire in January 1969 to protest the Soviet invasion, is buried here. To find his grave, enter the main gate (flanked by flower shops) on Vinohradská and turn right – it's about 50m along on the left of the path.

The oldest gravestones can be found in the northwestern corner of the cemetery, near the 17th-century **Chapel of St Roch** (kaple sv Rocha; Map p92), but the most flamboyant art-nouveau memorials and mausoleums are concentrated around the main entrance and along the main path leading north. The cemetery's most elaborate monument, the **Hrdličkova family tomb**, lies just inside the main entrance and shows the deceased soldier Hans appearing to his mother in a dream, while she is comforted by Emperor Franz Josef I.

There are several entrances to the cemetery running along Vinohradská, east of Flora metro station, and also beside the chapel on Olšanská.

New Jewish Cemetery CEMETERY

(Nový židovské hřbitov; Map p92; 226 235 216; www.kehilaprag.cz; Izraelská 1, Žižkov; 9am-5pm Sun-Thu, to 2pm Fri Apr-Oct, 9am-4pm Sun-Thu, to 2pm Fri Nov-Mar, closed on Jewish holidays; M Želivského) FREE Franz Kafka is buried in this cemetery, which opened around 1890 when the older Jewish cemetery – at the foot of the TV Tower – was closed. To find **Kafka's grave** (Map p92; M Želivského), follow the main avenue east (signposted), turn right at row 21, then left at the wall; it's at the end of the 'block'. Fans make a pilgrimage on 3 June, the anniversary of his death.

The entrance is beside Želivského metro station; men should cover their heads

Žižkov & Karlin

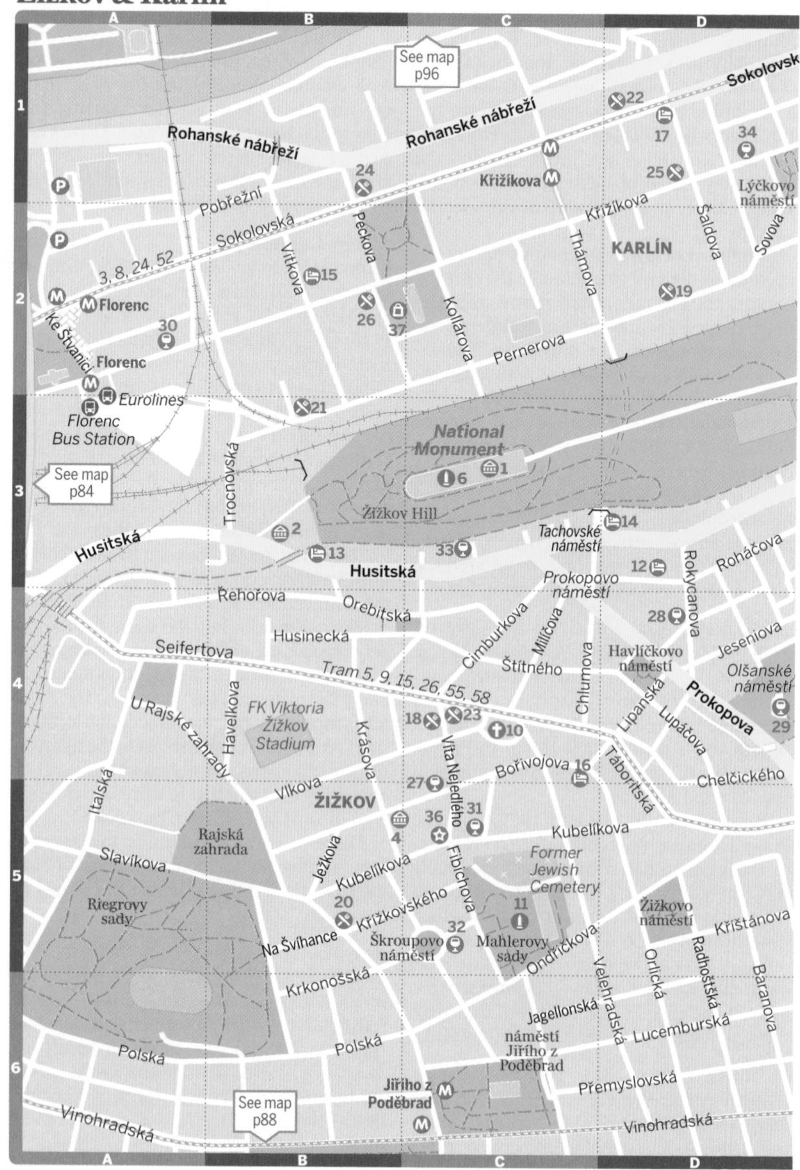

(yarmulkes are available at the gate). Last admission is 30 minutes before closing.

Hunt Kastner GALLERY

(Map p92; ☎603 525 294; www.huntkastner.com; Bořivojova 85, Žižkov; ⏰1-6pm Tue-Fri, 2-6pm Sat; 🚋5, 9, 15, 26) **FREE** This small gallery highlights some of the best up-and-coming Czech artists working in the visual arts, including painting, photography and video. The owners are enthusiastic and happy to talk about local art with walk-ins.

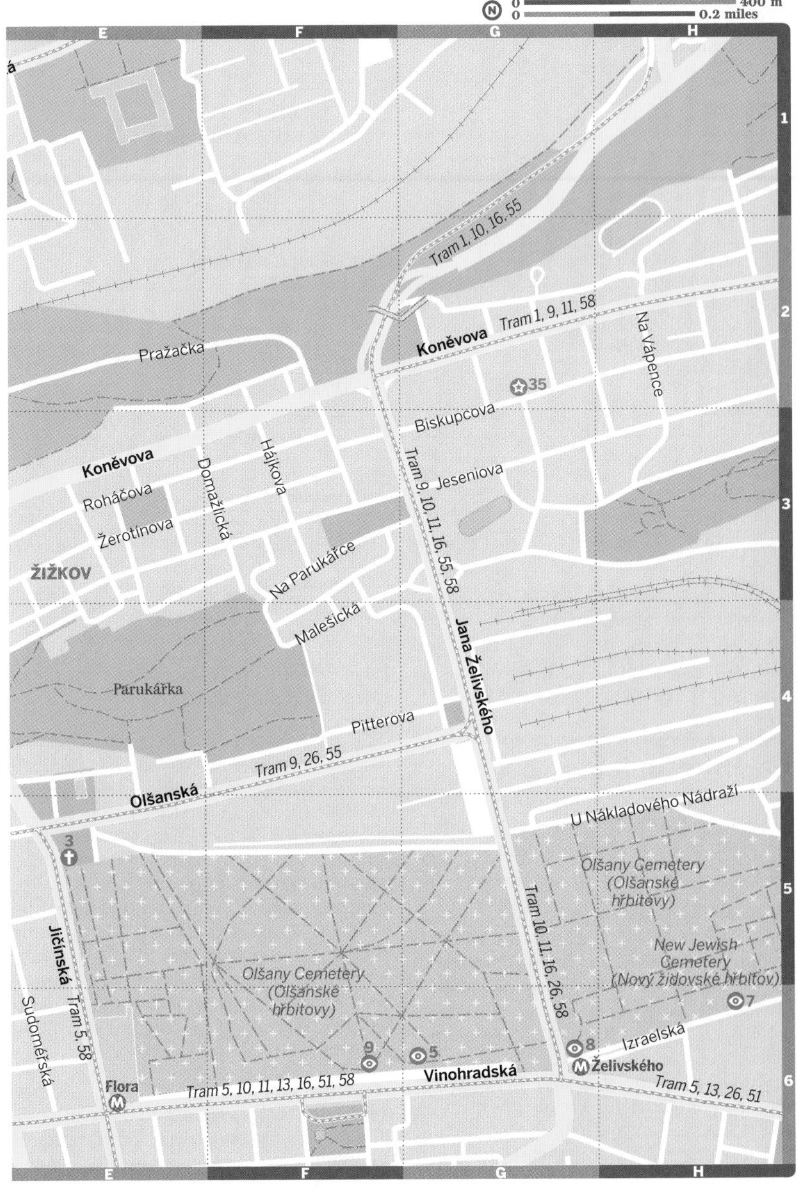

Army Museum MUSEUM

(Armádní muzeum Žižkov; Map p92; ☎973 204 900; www.vhu.cz; U památníku 2, Žižkov; ⏲10am-6pm Tue-Sun; 🚌133, 175, 207) FREE On the way up Žižkov Hill you will find this grim-looking barracks of a museum, with a rusting T34 tank parked outside. It's for military enthusiasts only, with exhibits on the history of the Czechoslovak Army and resistance movement from 1918 to 1945, including a small display of personal effects of one of the paratroopers who took part in

Žižkov & Karlin

Top Sights
1 National Monument....C3

Sights
2 Army Museum....B3
3 Chapel of St Roch....E5
4 Hunt Kastner....B5
5 Jan Palach's Grave....G6
6 Jan Žižka Statue....C3
7 Kafka's Grave....H6
Miminka (David Černý Sculpture)....(see 11)
8 New Jewish Cemetery....G6
9 Olšany Cemetery....F6
10 St Procopius' Basilica....C4
11 TV Tower....C5

Sleeping
12 Brix Hostel....D3
13 Hostel Elf....B3
14 Hostel Lípa....D3
15 Hotel Alwyn....B2
16 Hotel Theatrino....C4
17 Pentahotel Prague....D1

Eating
18 Café Pavlač....C4
19 Eska....D2
20 Hanil....B5
21 Indian by Nature....B3
22 Krystal Bistro....D1
23 Kuře V Hodinkách....C4
24 Lokál Hamburk....B1
25 Můj šálek kávy....D1
26 Nejen Bistro....B2
Restaurace Akropolis....(see 36)

Drinking & Nightlife
27 Bukowski's....C5
28 Fatal Music Club....D4
29 Hospoda Parukářka....D4
30 Pivovarský Klub....A2
31 U Kurelů....C5
32 U Sadu....C5
U Slovanské Lípy....(see 14)
33 U Vystřeleného oka....C3
34 Veltlin....D1

Entertainment
35 Kino Aero....G2
36 Palác Akropolis....C5

Shopping
37 Karlín Farmers Market....B2

the 1942 assassination of Reichsprotektor Reinhard Heydrich.

Holešovice

Holešovice is divided into distinct western and eastern halves, with most of the important sights in the western part near Veletržní Palác.

★Veletržní Palác — MUSEUM

(Trade Fair Palace; Map p96; 224 301 111; www.ngprague.cz; Dukelských hrdinů 47; incl admission to all National Gallery venues; adult/child 300/150Kč; 10am-6pm Tue-Sun; M Vltavská, 1, 6, 8, 12, 17, 25, 26) The National Gallery's collection of 'Art of the 19th, 20th and 21st Centuries' is spread over four floors and is a strong contender for Prague's best museum. It has an unexpectedly rich collection of world masters, including works from Van Gogh, Picasso, Schiele, Klimt and on and on, but the holdings of Czech interwar abstract, surrealist and cubist art are worth the trip alone.

Tickets are valid for seven days, and give admission to all six of the National Gallery's permanent exhibitions: Kinský Palace, Convent of St Agnes, Trade Fair Palace, Šternberg Palace, Schwarzenberg Palace and Salm Palace.

★National Technical Museum — MUSEUM

(Národní Technické Muzeum; Map p96; 220 399 111; www.ntm.cz; Kostelní 42; adult/concession 190/90Kč; 9am-5.30pm Tue-Fri, 10am-6pm Sat & Sun; ; 1, 8, 12, 25, 26 to Letenské náměstí) Prague's most family-friendly museum got a high-tech renovation in 2012 and is a dazzling presentation of the country's industrial heritage. If that sounds dull, it's anything but. Start in the main hall, filled to the rafters with historic planes, trains and automobiles. There are separate halls devoted to exhibits on astronomy, photography, printing and architecture.

Letná Gardens — PARK

(Letenské sady; Map p96; 24hr; ; 1, 8, 12, 25, 26 to Letenské náměstí) Lovely Letná Gardens occupies a bluff over the Vltava River, north of the Old Town, and has postcard-perfect views out over the city, river and bridges. It's ideal for walking, jogging and beer-drinking at a popular beer garden (p153) at the eastern end of the park. From the Old Town, find the entrance up a steep staircase at the northern end of Pařížská ulice. Alternatively,

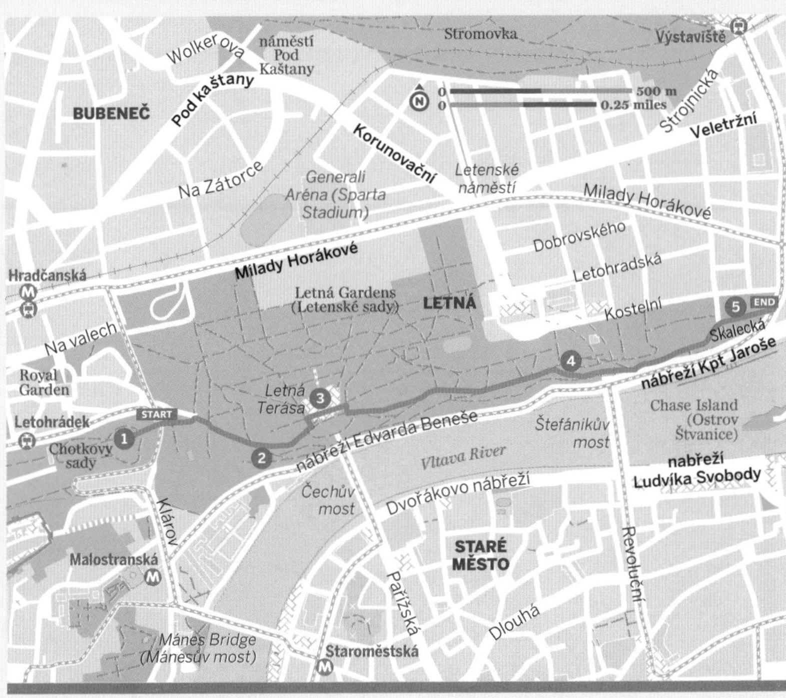

City Walk
Lovely Letná Gardens

START CHOTKOVY SADY TRAM STOP
END EXPO '58 RESTAURANT
LENGTH 2KM; ONE HOUR

Catch tram 2, 12, 18 or 20 to the Chotkovy sady stop, find a green footbridge and cross it towards the west (in the direction of Prague Castle); here you'll find a 1 **stone grotto** dedicated to the novelist Josef Zeyer. There's a park bench nearby, with the first of several photo-op spots, offering superb views out over Malá Strana and up to Prague Castle.

Cross the footbridge again, this time heading east towards Letná Gardens. From here, follow the main path, which bears right from the park entrance, then detour further right to visit the 2 **Hanavský pavilón**, where you can enjoy another eye-opening panorama and, perhaps, a little lunch.

The path continues along the top of a bluff above the Vltava, with great views over the river and the eastern and southern parts of the city, before arriving at a monumental stepped terrace topped by a giant, creaking 3 **metronome** that sits on a spot once occupied by a giant statue of Stalin.

Continue east along the path, zigging and zagging but basically hugging the ridge, to arrive at one of the city's most popular summertime watering holes, the 4 **Letná Beer Garden** (p153). Line up at the beer kiosk to buy a Gambrinus in a plastic cup (45Kč) and take a seat at one of the picnic tables. If you're hungry, there's a small terrace here serving pizza and a fancier, tablecloth place, Letenský zámeček, nearby.

Letná Gardens extends another 300m eastward, before sloping into Holešovice proper. About 100m from the beer garden stands an architectural curiosity, the retro-futuristic 5 **Expo '58 Restaurant**. Built for the Brussels World Exposition of 1958, the restaurant was later re-erected here and eventually renovated. It's no longer a restaurant, but instead houses an advertising agency. From here you can head back to the beer garden or walk down the hill to Holešovice.

Holešovice

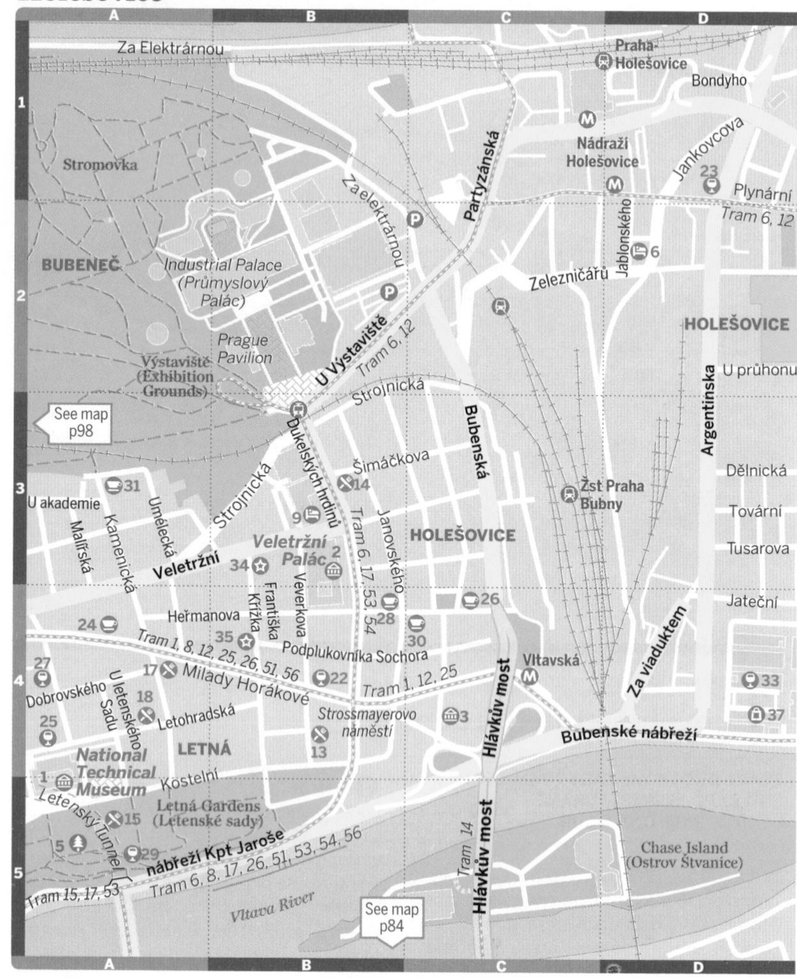

take the tram to Letenské náměstí and walk south for about 10 minutes.

DOX Centre for Contemporary Art ARTS CENTRE

(Map p96; ☎295 568 123; www.dox.cz; Poupětova 1; adult/concession 180/90Kč; ⊙10am-6pm Mon, 11am-7pm Wed & Fri, 11am-9pm Thu, 10am-6pm Sat & Sun, closed Tue; 🚋6, 12 to Ortenovo náměstí) This noncommercial art gallery and exhibition space forms the nucleus of Holešovice's expanding reputation as one of the city's more hip districts. The exhibitions highlight a wide range of media, including video, sculpture, photography and painting. You'll find a cafe and an excellent bookstore (heavy on art and architecture) on the upper level.

Chemistry Gallery GALLERY

(Map p96; ☎606 649 170; www.thechemistry.cz; Bubenská 1; ⊙11am-7pm Tue-Sat; Ⓜ Vltavská) Edgy gallery dedicated to showing the works of young Czech and international artists working in contemporary urban art, street art and graffiti. Artists include Pasta Oner, arguably the best-known Czech street artist.

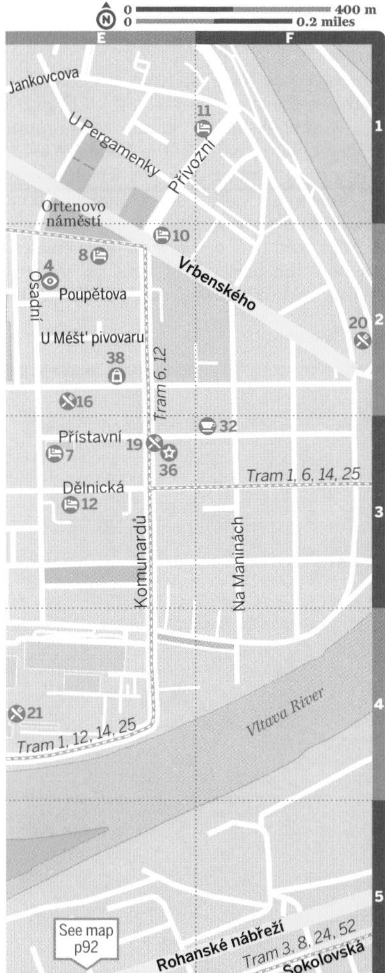

Holešovice

Top Sights
1 National Technical Museum ... A5
2 Veletržní Palác ... B3

Sights
3 Chemistry Gallery ... C4
4 DOX Centre for Contemporary Art ... E2
5 Letná Gardens ... A5

Sleeping
6 Absolutum Hotel ... D2
7 Hotel Extol Inn ... E3
8 Hotel Leon ... E2
9 Parkhotel Praha ... B3
10 Plaza Alta Hotel ... E2
11 Plus Prague Hostel ... F1
12 Sir Toby's Hostel ... E3

Eating
13 Bistro 8 ... B4
14 Bohemia Bagel ... B3
15 Letenský zámeček ... A5
16 Molo 22 ... E2
17 Mr Hot Dog ... A4
18 Peperoncino ... A4
19 Phill's Corner ... E3
20 Pivovar Marina ... F2
Sasazu ... (see 33)
21 Tràng An Restaurace ... E4

Drinking & Nightlife
Café Jedna ... (see 2)
22 Cobra ... B4
23 Cross Club ... D1
24 Erhartova Cukrárna ... A4
25 Hells Bells ... A4
26 Kavárna Liberál ... C4
27 Klášterní Pivnice ... A4
28 Kumbal ... B4
29 Letná Beer Garden ... A5
30 Ouky Douky ... C4
31 Park Cafe & Bar ... A3
32 Phill's Twenty7 ... F3
33 Sasazu ... D4

Entertainment
34 Alfred Ve Dvoře ... B3
35 Bio Oko ... B4
36 La Fabrika ... E3

Shopping
BENDOX ... (see 4)
37 Holešovická tržnice ... D4
38 Pivní Galerie ... E2

The setting is a gritty, 1930s functionalist building that once housed the city's electric works and is now home to a community of small businesses, artists and creative types.

Prague Zoo ZOO

(Zoo Praha; ☎296 112 230; www.zoopraha.cz; U Trojského zámku 120, Troja; adult/concession/family 200/150/600Kč; ⏰9am-7pm Jun-Aug, to 6pm Apr, May, Sep & Oct, to 5pm Mar, to 4pm Nov-Feb; 👪; 🚌112, Ⓜ Nádraží Holešovice) Prague's attractive zoo is set in 60 hectares of wooded grounds on the banks of the Vltava. It makes for a great outing for kids. There are sizeable collections of giraffes and gorillas, but pride of place goes to a herd of rare horses. Attractions include a miniature cable car and a big play area.

Bubeneč & Dejvice

There are only a handful of traditional tourist sights in the area, and most of these are grouped around the Výstaviště exhibition grounds and adjoining Stromovka park. Divoká Šárka (p109) is a wild patch of rock and green space, situated in the western end of Dejvice that gets very little attention from visitors but is a true nature escape.

Bubeneč

Stromovka PARK

(Královská obora; Map p98; entry at Výstaviště or Nad Královskou oborou 21; 24hr; 1, 8, 12, 25, 26)

Just west of Výstaviště, Stromovka is central Prague's largest park. In the Middle Ages it was a royal hunting preserve, which is why it's sometimes called the Královská obora (Royal Hunting Ground). Rudolph II had rare trees planted here and several lakes created. It's now the preserve of strollers, joggers, cyclists and in-line skaters. Enter from the

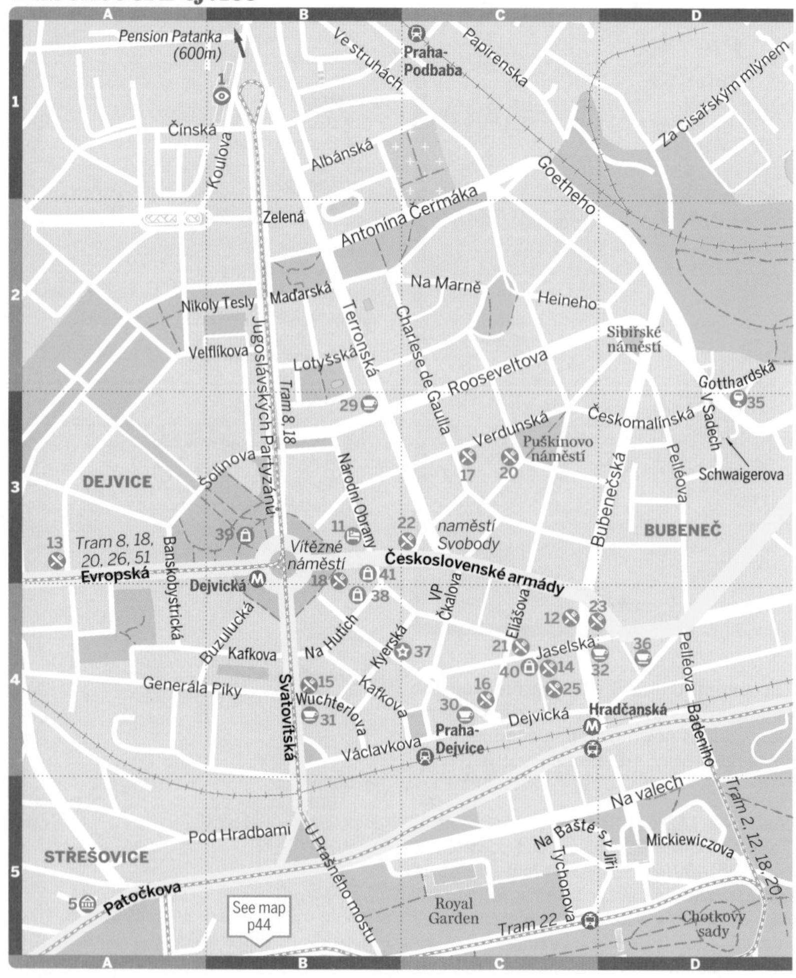

Výstaviště exhibition grounds, or from Letenské náměstí follow Čechova třída north to a ridge over the park and walk down.

Výstaviště CULTURAL CENTRE

(Exhibition Grounds; Map p98; ☎220 103 111; www.incheba.cz; Areál Výstaviště; ⏰9am-11pm; 🚋12, 17) This is a sprawling area of attractions and buildings of various architectural styles that was first laid out for the 1891 Jubilee Exhibition. These days it holds mainly trade fairs (see the website for a calendar), but also has a branch of the National Museum, a singing fountain, the city's biggest aquarium and a slightly scruffy amusement park that's open daily from April to October.

Křižík's Fountain FOUNTAIN

(Křižíkova fontána; Map p98; ☎723 665 694; www.krizikovafontana.cz; U Výstaviště 1,; 230Kč; ⏰performances hourly 7-11pm Mar-Nov; 👪; 🚋12, 17) Each evening from spring to late autumn the musical Křižík's Fountain performs its computer-controlled light-and-water dance. Performances range from classical music such as Dvořák's *New World Symphony* to rousing

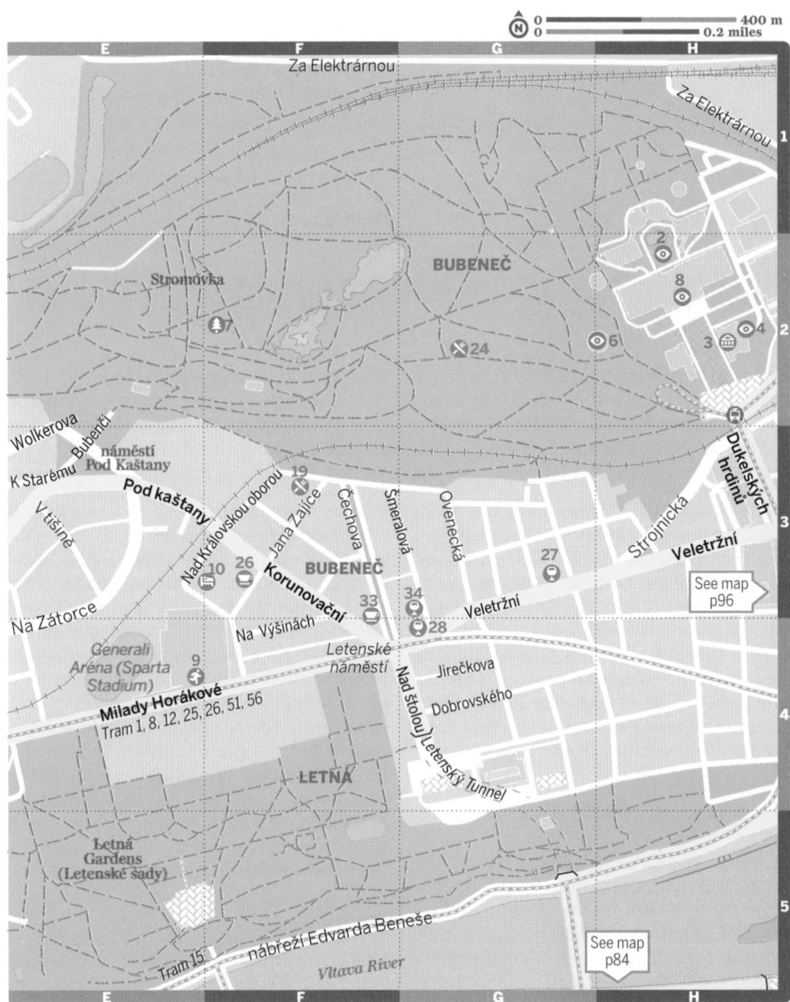

Bubeneč & Dejvice

Sights
1 Hotel International ... B1
2 Křižík's Fountain ... H2
3 Lapidárium ... H2
4 Mořský Svět ... H2
5 Museum of Public Transport ... A5
6 Prague Planetarium ... H2
7 Stromovka ... F2
8 Výstaviště ... H2

Activities, Courses & Tours
9 Generali Aréna ... E4

Sleeping
10 Art Hotel ... F3
Hotel International ... (see 1)
11 Hotel Meda ... B3

Eating
12 Argument ... C4
13 Âu Cơ ... A3
14 Bistro à Table ... C4
15 Budvarká ... B4
16 Café Záhorský ... C4
17 Da Emanuel ... C3
18 Kulat'ák ... B3
19 Lokál Nad Stromovkou ... F3
20 Na Urale ... C3
Nahoře a Dole ... (see 38)
21 Restaurace U Veverky ... C4
22 Sakura ... C3
23 U mě dobrý ... C4
24 Vozovna Stromovka ... G2
25 YamYam ... C4

Drinking & Nightlife
26 Alchymista ... F3
27 Elbow Room ... G3
28 Fraktal ... G4
29 Kabinet ... B3
30 Kafemat ... C4
31 Kavárna Alibi ... B4
32 Kavárna Místo ... D4
33 Kavárna pod Lipami ... F3
34 La Bodega Flamenca ... G3
35 Na Slamníku ... D3
36 Potrvá ... D4

Entertainment
37 Spejbl & Hurvínek Theatre ... C4

Shopping
38 Antikvita ... B4
39 Dejvice Farmers Market ... B3
40 Starožitnosti Robert Pavlů ... C4
41 Wine Food Market ... B3

works performed by Andrea Bocelli, Queen or the Scorpions. Check the website for what's on. The show is best after sunset – from May to July go for later shows.

Lapidárium MUSEUM

(Map p98; ☎702 013 372; www.nm.cz; U Výstaviště 1; adult/concession 50/30Kč; ⏰10am-4pm Wed, noon-6pm Thu-Sun May-Nov; 🚋12, 17) An outlying branch of the National Museum and an often-overlooked gem, the Lapidárium is a repository for some 400 sculptures from the 11th to the 19th centuries. The exhibits include Bohemia's oldest surviving stone sculpture, parts of the Renaissance Krocín Fountain that once stood on Old Town Square, and several original statues from Charles Bridge.

Mořský Svět AQUARIUM

(Sea World; Map p98; ☎220 103 275, special events 736 649 558; www.morskysvet.cz; U Výstaviště 1; adult/concession 280/180Kč; ⏰10am-7pm; 👪; 🚋12, 17) The Czech 'Sea World' has the largest water tank in the country, with a capacity of around 100,000L. Some 4500 living species of fish and sea creatures are on display, with a good (and suitably scary) set of sharks. The cramped interior will be disappointing if you're used to larger marine-themed amusement parks around the world, though kids will certainly enjoy the experience. Special feeding shows and other special events are held through the week. See the website.

Prague Planetarium PLANETARIUM

(Planetárium Praha; Map p98; ☎220 999 001; www.planetarium.cz; Královská obora 233; adult/concession 150/75Kč, English headphones 50Kč; ⏰8.30am-6pm Mon, to 8pm Tue-Thu & Sat, 10.30am-6pm Sun, closed Fri; 🚋12, 17) The planetarium in Stromovka park (p98), just west of Výstaviště, presents various slide and video presentations in addition to daily star shows. Most shows are in Czech only, but one or two of the more popular ones are offered in English and English-language headphones are available on request. There's also an astronomical exhibition in the main hall. Opening hours tend to be sporadic throughout the year, so check the website before heading out.

Dejvice

Museum of Public Transport MUSEUM

(Map p98; ☎296 128 900; www.dpp.cz; Patočkova 4; adult/child 35/20Kč; ⏰9am-5pm Sat & Sun Mar-Nov, closed Dec-Feb; 🚋1, 2, 25) The Public Transport

Authority's museum is funner than it sounds. There are plenty of old-timer streetcars to climb on and the old maps section, showing how the system has changed over the decades, is fascinating. There's a small restaurant here to grab a bite to eat or coffee or beer.

Hotel International ARCHITECTURE
(Map p98; ☎296 537 111; www.internationalprague.cz; Koulová 15; ⏰lobby open 24hr; 🚋8, 18) For architecture buffs, the impressive silhouette of this huge Stalin-era building in Dejvice will be familiar to anyone who has visited Moscow. The Hotel International was built in the 1950s to a design inspired by a tower of Moscow University, right down to the Soviet-style star on top of the spire. The interior is just as impressive.

Smíchov & Vyšehrad

The Vyšehrad fortress is the main sight in this neighbourhood. It's not one building, but rather a complex of ruins, churches and a picturesque cemetery that serves as the final resting place for many of the country's best-known personalities.

★**Vyšehrad Citadel** FORTRESS
See p104.

★**Vyšehrad Cemetery** CEMETERY
(Vyšehradský hřbitov; Map p106; ☎274 774 835; www.praha-vysehrad.cz; K Rotundě 10, Vyšehrad; ⏰8am-7pm May-Sep, shorter hours Oct-Apr; Ⓜ Vyšehrad) FREE Vyšehrad Cemetery is a main attraction for many visitors, being the final resting place for dozens of Czech luminaries, including Antonín Dvořák, Bedřich Smetana and Alfons Mucha. Many tombs and headstones are works of art – Dvořák's is a sculpture by Ladislav Šaloun, the art-nouveau sculptor who created the Jan Hus monument in Old Town Square.

Futura Gallery GALLERY
(Centre for Contemporary Art Futura; Map p102; ☎604 738 390; www.futuraproject.cz; Holečkova 49, Smíchov; admission by donation; ⏰11am-6pm Wed-Sun; 🚋9, 12, 15, 20) The Futura Gallery focuses on all aspects of contemporary art, ranging from painting, photography and sculpture to video, installations and performance art. In the garden, you'll find a rather shocking and amusing permanent installation by David Černý, called **Brownnosers** (Map p102; Holečkova 49, Futura Gallery, Smíchov; 🚋9, 12, 15, 20).

Activities

The Czechs have always been keen on sports and outdoor activities, and Prague's extensive green spaces offer plenty of opportunity for exercise. Although hiking, swimming and ice hockey are the traditional favourites, recent years have seen a steady increase in the numbers of cyclists in the city as bike lanes and dedicated cycle trails have been introduced.

Hiking

The Czech Republic is covered by a network of waymarked hiking trails, colour-coded and clearly marked on a range of excellent 1:50,000 and 1:25,000 hiking maps *(turistické mapy)*. Prague has its share of trails – the Klub Českých Turistů (Czech Hiking Club) 1:50,000 map sheet 36, *Okolí Prahy-západ* (Prague & Around, West), covers the best in and around the city, including Beroun and Karlštejn.

For easy walks of an hour or two, you can head for the big parks and nature reserves – Stromovka in the north, Prokopské udolí in the southwest, and Michelský les and Kunratický les in the southeast – or follow

WORTH A TRIP

WORTH A DETOUR: TROJA CHATEAU

Troja Chateau (Zámek Troja; ☎283 851 614; www.ghmp.cz; U Trojského Zámku 1, Troja; adult/concession 120/60Kč; ⏰10am-6pm Tue-Sun, from 1pm Fri Apr-Oct, closed Nov-Mar; 🚌112, Ⓜ Nádraží Holešovice) is a 17th-century baroque palace that was built for the Šternberk family, and inspired by Roman country villas seen by the architect on a visit to Italy. A visit to the chateau can easily be combined with a trip to **Prague Zoo** (p97), as the two are side by side. It's a pleasant 20-minute walk from Stromovka park, including crossing a dramatic footbridge over the Vltava.

The sumptuously decorated palace now houses collections of the Prague City Gallery and exhibits explaining the sculptures and frescoes that adorn the palace itself. There's free admission to the grounds, where you can wander in the beautiful French gardens.

Smíchov

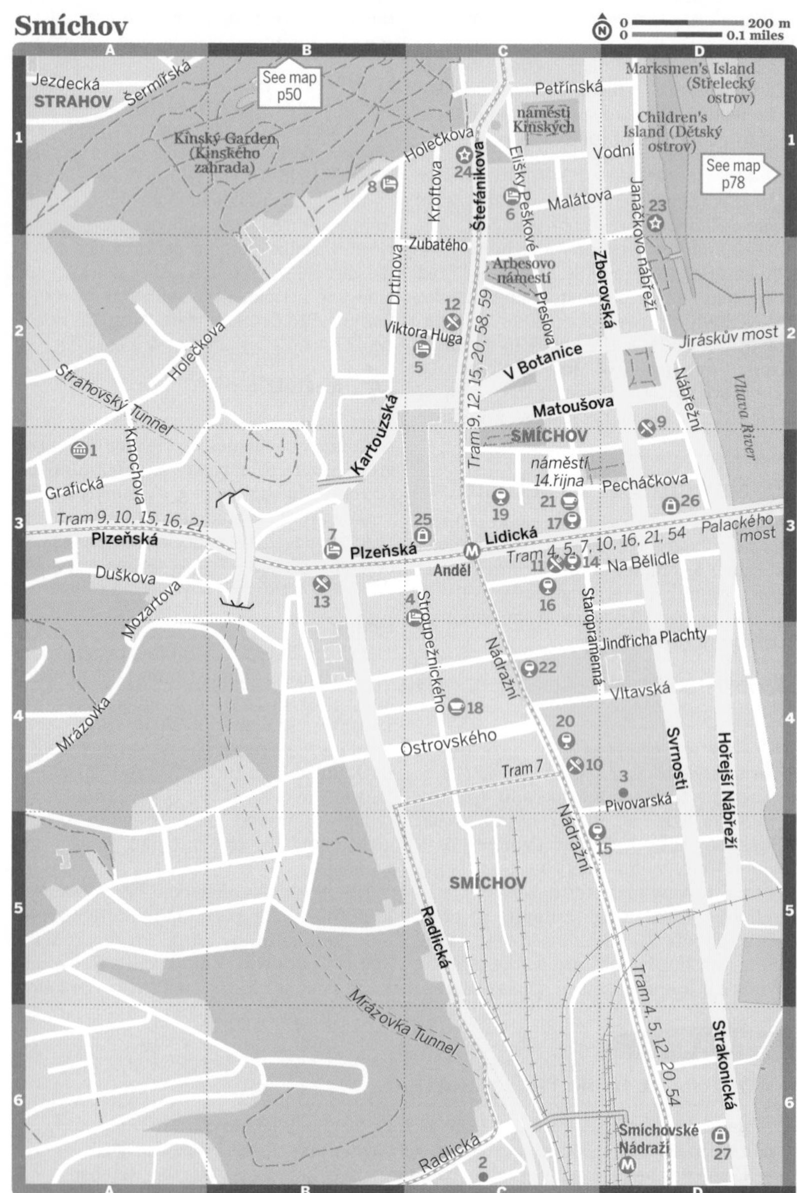

the riverbank trails north from Prague Zoo to the little ferry at Roztoky, and return to the city by train.

A more challenging day hike, which takes in a visit to Karlštejn Castle, begins at the town of Beroun to the southwest of the city. From Beroun train station follow a red-marked trail east for 6km to the Monastery of St John under the Rock (Klášter sv Jan pod Skálou), situated in a spectacular limestone gorge. From here, continue on the red trail through wooded hills for

Smíchov

Sights

Brownnosers (David Černý).........(see 1)
1 Futura Gallery..A3

Activities, Courses & Tours

2 AVE Bicycle Tours C6
3 Staropramen Brewery D4

Sleeping

4 Anděl's By Vienna House.....................C3
5 Hotel Arbes...C2
6 Hotel Julian... C1
7 Ibis Praha Malá Strana........................B3
8 Red & Blue Design Hotel...................... B1

Eating

9 Bejzment...D2
10 Na Verandách.. C4
11 U Bílého lva C3
12 U Míkuláše Dačíckého..........................C2
13 Zlatý klas...B3

Drinking & Nightlife

14 Back Doors C3
15 Dog's Bollocks...C5
16 Hells Bells...C3
17 Hospoda U Buldoka..............................C3
18 Kavárna co hledá jméno C4
19 Lokal Blok C3
20 Phenomen... C4
21 Pitomá Kavárna C3
22 Prolog C4

Entertainment

23 Jazz Dock... D1
24 Švandovo Divadlo Na Smíchově......... C1

Shopping

25 Nový Smíchov C3
26 Tribo D3
27 Wine Food Market................................ D6

another 8km to Karlštejn, where you can catch another train back to the city centre. Allow five hours from Beroun to Karlštejn.

Cycling

Prague has a long way to go before it's a cycling town comparable with big cities in Germany, or even Vienna. Nevertheless, there's a group of hardcore cyclists at work promoting things like commuter cycling, extending bike paths and raising driver awareness. Their efforts are starting to bear fruit. Prague now has a relatively complete, if disjointed, network of bike paths – signposted in yellow – that criss-cross the city centre and fan out in all directions.

Recreational cyclists will probably be content just to putz around on one of the tours offered by the bike-rental companies. More serious cyclists should consider buying a good map, hiring a bike and hitting the outlying trails for a day or two. See www.prahounakole.cz (partly in English) for information.

The most popular bike trail is undoubtedly the riverside route that leads south from the city centre on the east bank of the **Vltava River** (waymarked A2); at Radotin you can cross the river and continue on a combination of signposted trails and minor roads to Karlštejn Castle (total 35km one way). **Biko Adventures** (Map p106; ☎733 750 990; www.bikoadventures.com; Vratislavova 3, Vyšehrad; standard rental per day 450Kč, group tours per person from 1250Kč; ⏰9am-6pm Apr-Oct; 🚋2, 3, 7, 17, 21) offers an excellent guided bike tour on this route, returning by train.

Another good route leads north along the Vltava in the direction of Germany, with a nearly complete trail as far as the town of **Kralupy nad Vltavou** (20km from Prague; it's possible to return by rail). From here you can continue on back roads to Mělník. There are plenty of bridges and ferries to take you back and forth across the river, and some really great trails leading inland along the way.

There's also the **Prague Circle** (Pražské kolo), an 80km loop around the city limits (waymarked 8100 and A50).

Most large bookstores stock *cycloturisticka mapa* (cycling maps). One of the best ones to look out for is Freytag & Berndt's *Praha a Okolí* (Prague & Surroundings; 1:75,000), which costs about 157Kč. Another good choice is *Z prahy na kole* (Around Prague by Bike; 1:65,000), a series of five maps covering the city. Remember to pack water and sunscreen and always watch out for cars. Czech drivers, inexplicably, are rabidly anti-cyclist.

Running

The Prague Marathon (www.runczech.com), established in 1989, is held annually in mid-to late May. It's considered to be one of the world's top 10 city marathons, attracting in excess of 10,000 entrants. There's also a half-marathon, held in late March. If you'd like to compete, you can register online or obtain entry forms from the website.

Tours

Prague offers so much intriguing history and culture that it's easy to feel overwhelmed. A guided tour can ease you into an aspect of the city that reflects your interests. The Prague City Tourism (p170) office in the Old Town Hall provides details of tours.

TOP SIGHT
VYŠEHRAD CITADEL

The complex of buildings and structures that make up the Vyšehrad Citadel has played an important role in Czech history for more than 1000 years. While not many of the ancient buildings have survived to the present day (indeed, most structures date from the 18th century), the citadel is viewed as Prague's spiritual home. Part of the fun is simply to stroll the grounds and admire the views.

The Birthplace of Prague

Legend has it this high hill is the very place where Prague was born. According to myth, a wise chieftain named Krok built a castle here in the 7th century, and his daughter Libuše famously prophesied a great city would rise someday in the valley of the Vltava.

While there's scant physical evidence for Libuše's prophesy, it does make for a nice story. According to the legend, Libuše went on to marry a ploughman named Přemysl, who founded both the city of Prague and the Přemysl dynasty. That last part may be true since there really was a Přemysl dynasty, but records from these days are scarce.

Indeed, the early Přemysl rulers seemed to like Vyšehrad; Boleslav II (r 972–99) may have lived here once. By mid-11th century there was a fortified settlement, and Vratislav II (r 1061–92) moved his court here from Hradčany, beefing up the walls and adding a castle and religious buildings. His successors stayed until 1140, when Vladislav II returned to Hradčany.

While little physical evidence remains of Vyšehrad from the period, a hint of the area's magnificent past is seen at the 11th-century Rotunda of St Martin (Rotunda sv Martina; Map p106; ☎224 911 353; www.praha-vysehrad.cz; V Pevnosti, Vyšehrad; ⏲mass at 6pm

DON'T MISS

- Brick Gate & Casements
- Northern and southern ramparts
- Gothic Cellar
- Church of Sts Peter & Paul
- Rotunda of St Martin

PRACTICALITIES

- Map p106
- ☎261 225 304
- www.praha-vysehrad.cz
- information centre at V pevnosti 159/5b
- admission to grounds free
- ⏲grounds 24hr
- Ⓜ Vyšehrad

Mon, Wed, Thu, Fri, Sat; M Vyšehrad), Prague's oldest surviving building. The door and frescoes date from a renovation made about 1880. In addition, the Gothic Cellar (Gotický sklep; Map p106; ☎ 261 225 304; www.praha-vysehrad.cz; Vyšehradské sady, Vyšehrad; adult/child 60/30Kč; ⌚ 9.30am-6pm Apr-Oct, to 5pm Nov-Mar; M Vyšehrad) houses a permanent exhibition called 'The Historic Faces of Vyšehrad', which focuses on both the myths and facts concerning the origins of Vyšehrad.

Ups and Downs

After Vladislav II moved the court back to Hradčany, Vyšehrad faded into the background for around two centuries. It took the reign of Charles IV, in the 14th century, to recognise the complex's symbolic importance to the Bohemian kingdom. He repaired the walls and joined them to those of his new town, Nové Město. He built a small palace (now gone) and decreed that the coronations of Bohemian kings should begin with a procession from here to Hradčany.

While the Gothic-spired Church of Sts Peter & Paul (Kostel sv Petra a Pavla; Map p106; ☎ 261 225 304; www.praha-vysehrad.cz; K Rotundé 10, Vyšehrad; adult/child 30/10Kč; ⌚ 9am-noon & 1-5pm Wed-Mon; M Vyšehrad) certainly looks like it may have come from Charles IV's day, the church has in fact been built and rebuilt several times over the centuries. The arresting twin spires are visible from around the city and have become the symbol of Vyšehrad. They date from the end of the 19th century and the brief architectural craze that gripped Prague at that time known as neo-Gothic.

Unfortunately, nearly everything truly ancient was wiped out during the Hussite Wars of the 15th century. The fortress remained a ruin – except for a ramshackle township of artisans and traders – until after the Thirty Years' War, which ended in 1648, when Habsburg Emperor Leopold I once again refortified it.

A Baroque Fortress

While most associate Vyšehrad with the very early founding of the city, much of what you see today dates from the 17th and 18th centuries, when it was used by the Austrian Habsburgs to secure their western and northern borders from Prussian and French advances. Both the French and the Prussians did occupy Vyšehrad for brief periods in the mid-18th century and contributed to the citadel's development as a fort.

This military history of Vyšehrad is on display at the Brick Gate & Casements (www.praha-vysehrad.cz; adult/child 60/30Kč; ⌚ 9.30am-6pm Apr-Oct, to 5pm Nov-Mar), situated on the northern side of the fortress. The highlight is the barrel-vaulted Gorlice Hall, which was once used as a place for troops to muster in secret. Now it is home to six of the original baroque statues from Charles Bridge.

ACCESSING THE CITADEL

The main entrance to the Vyšehrad Citadel is through a series of gates on the eastern side. The first is the narrow Tábor Gate (Táborská brana; ☎ 261 225 304; M Vyšehrad), followed by the grander 17th-century Leopold Gate (Leopoldova Brána; M Vyšehrad). Between these two main gates, you'll see the only surviving remnants of the 14th-century Gothic **Peak Gate** (Špička brána; Map p106; M Vyšehrad), which now houses the Špička Information Centre (www.praha-vysehrad.cz; V pevnosti 159/5b; ⌚ 9.30am-5pm M Vyšehrad). From here, there's no prescribed viewing route. Beside the southwestern bastion are the foundations of a **royal palace** that was built by Emperor Charles IV in the 14th century but dismantled in 1655.

Be sure to check out the ramparts on the northern and southern sides of the complex, which have wonderful views out over the city in the distance.

EARLY RESIDENTS

Archaeological digs at Vyšehrad have turned up proof that the site was permanently settled from at least the 9th century, and possibly even earlier.

Vyšehrad

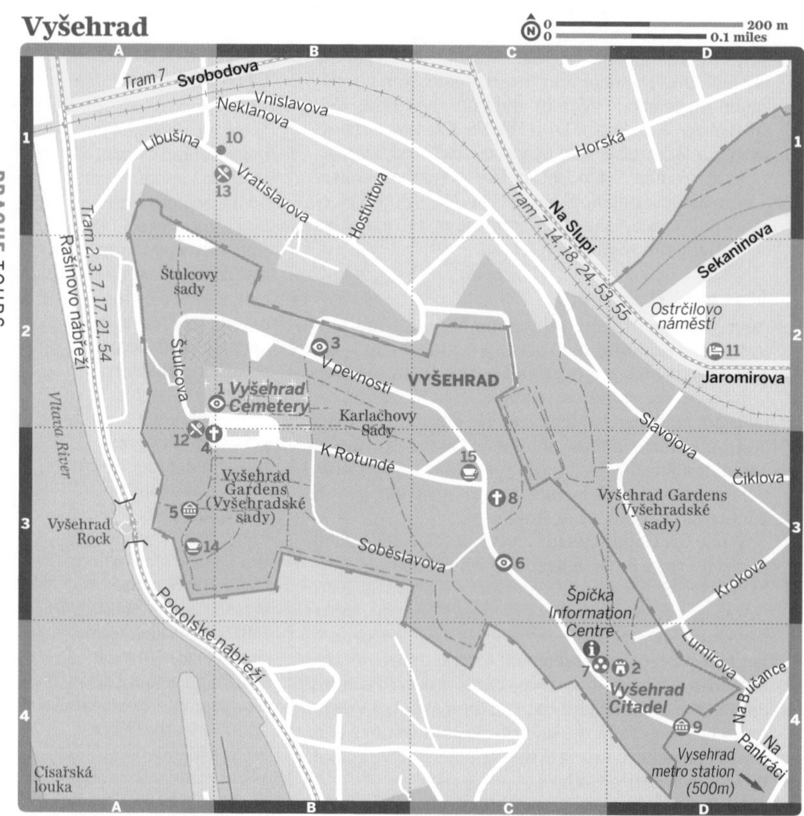

Vyšehrad

Top Sights
1 Vyšehrad Cemetery B2
2 Vyšehrad Citadel D4

Sights
3 Brick Gate & Casements B2
4 Church of Sts Peter & Paul A3
5 Gothic Cellar A3
6 Leopold Gate C3
7 Peak Gate C4
8 Rotunda of St Martin C3
9 Tábor Gate D4

Activities, Courses & Tours
10 Biko Adventures Prague B1

Sleeping
11 Hotel Union D2

Eating
12 Rio's Vyšehrad A3
13 U Kroka B1

Drinking & Nightlife
14 Cafe Citadela A3
15 V Cafe C3

Walking Tours

The corner of Old Town Square outside the Old Town Hall is usually clogged with dozens of people touting for business as walking guides; the quality varies, but some of the better ones are listed here. Most operators don't have an office – you can join a walk by just turning up at the starting point and paying your money.

★ **AlenaGuide** TOURS
(☎724 129 201; www.alenaguide.com; tours from 2300Kč) Alena Vopalkova is a graduate of La Salle University in Philadelphia, USA, who has returned to Prague to lead

BIKE TOURS

Biko Adventures (p103) Excellent guided tours, on either road or mountain bikes, ranging from a half-day urban tour of Prague's communist-era tower blocks to a full-day trip to Karlštejn (returning by train). Also offers proper off-road mountainbiking, trail running and (in winter) cross-country skiing.

Praha Bike (p300) Offers a 2½-hour guided cycling tour through the city or an easy evening pedal through the parks. Tours depart at 11.30am mid-March to October and also at 2.30pm May to September. Trips outside the city can also be arranged, including a full-day tour to Karlštejn Castle (returning by train; 1240Kč).

AVE Bicycle Tours (p300) Operates a full-day guided bicycle tour from Prague to Karlštejn Castle (one-way), including hotel pick-up, bike hire, lunch at Karlštejn and a train ticket back to the city. It also offers bike trips to Konopiště and one-week tours through the Czech countryside.

private, customised tours of her home city. Subjects range from general sightseeing to more specialised tours covering the Jewish Museum, food or shopping, and from three-hour walking tours to day trips exploring off-the-beaten-track spots such as the scenic Český raj (Bohemian Paradise).

Context Tours TOURS

(☎246 019 648; www.contexttravel.com/cities/prague; per person 1500Kč) US-based outfit that employs specialist guides to lead three-hour walking tours (maximum six persons) exploring various aspects of Prague – architecture, art, history, Jewish Prague and communism. Book online.

Pragulic TOURS

(☎725 314 930; www.pragulic.cz; per person from 250Kč; ⌚various times) Get a glimpse of another side of Prague with one of these social enterprise tours, led by guides who haved lived rough on the city streets. Their insights reveal aspects of Prague that you might never have noticed, and shine a light on the experience of homeless people in the Czech capital.

Royal Walk Free Tour WALKING

(www.discover-prague.com; ⌚hourly 10am-3pm) FREE One of Prague's most popular and highly rated walking tours, operated on a tips-only basis, provides an entertaining introduction to the city's history. No booking needed, just turn up at the Astronomical Clock (p68).

World War II in Prague TOURS

(☎605 918 596; www.ww2inprague.com; per person 600Kč; ⌚10am & 2pm) Highly recommended tour for anyone interested in military history, with a chance to visit the underground HQ of the Prague resistance, and compare archive photos of WWII Prague with their present-day locations. Departs from the Powder Gate (p75).

Prague Special Tours WALKING

(Map p62; ☎777 172 177; www.prague-specialtours.com; Malé náměstí 11; per person 600Kč; ⌚10.30am & 2.30pm daily) Offers a range of historical tours – their communism tour visits a genuine 1950s underground nuclear bunker, containing a small museum, beneath Parukářka hill in ŽIžkov. All tours start from the office, in a passage off Malé náměstí near Old Town Square.

Food Tours

★Taste of Prague FOOD & DRINK

(☎775 577 275; www.tasteofprague.com; per person 2700Kč) Locals Jan and Zuzi are passionate about Prague's restaurant scene. They lead four-hour foodie tours of the city, tasting trad and modern Czech dishes and drinks in a variety of venues, with intriguing asides on Czech history and culture along the way. Private one- or two-day tasting tours of Moravian vineyards can also be arranged.

Eating Prague FOOD & DRINK

(☎228 885 011; www.eatingpraguetours.com; adult/child 2350/1400Kč, beer-tasting tour 1820Kč; ⌚12.30pm & 1.20pm Mon-Sat) These guys lead a four-hour walking tour of central Prague that takes in tastings of classic Czech dishes such as *chlebíčky* (open sandwiches), *svíčková* (braised beef and dumplings with cream sauce) and *perníček* (decorated gingerbread) at various eateries.

A 3½-hour beer-tasting tour of Prague's beer gardens (2.30pm Tuesday to Saturday) is also available.

Boat Tours

Prague Boats BOATING

(Evropská Vodní Doprava; Map p62; ☎224 810 032; www.prague-boats.cz; Čechův most; 1hr cruise adult/child 290/180Kč, 2hr cruise 450/290Kč; ⏱9am-10pm; 🚋17) Offers a one-hour cruise to Charles Bridge and back, with views of the castle, departing half-hourly from 10am to 10pm April to October (hourly 11am to 7pm November to March); and a two-hour cruise to Vyšehrad and back, departing at 3pm year-round, and 4.30pm April to October.

Prague Steamboat Co BOATING

(Pražská Paroplavební Společnost, PPS; Map p78; ☎224 931 013; www.praguesteamboats.com; Rašínovo nábřeží 2; ⏱Mar-Oct; Ⓜ Karlovo Náměstí) Runs a photogenic one-hour cruise taking in the National Theatre, Štrelecký island and Vyšehrad, departing at 11am, 2pm, 4pm, 5pm and 6pm April to September (adult/child 250/150Kč). Also offers a 1¼-hour boat trip to Troja (near the zoo; 190/140Kč one-way, 290/180Kč return) departing four times daily from May to August, and three times daily at weekends only in April and September.

Prague Venice BOATING

(Map p62; ☎776 776 779; www.prague-venice.cz; Křižovnické náměstí 3; per person 290Kč; ⏱10.30am-10pm Jul & Aug, to 8pm Apr-Jun & Sep, to 6pm Oct-Mar; 🚋2, 17, 18) Runs entertaining 45-minute cruises in small boats under the hidden arches of Charles Bridge and along the Čertovka millstream in Kampa.

LOCAL KNOWLEDGE

PRAGUE SPRING

First held in 1946, the **Prague Spring** (Pražské jaro; ☎box office 227 059 234, program 257 314 040; www.festival.cz; ⏱May) international music festival is the Czech Republic's best-known annual cultural event. It begins on 12 May, the anniversary of composer Bedřich Smetana's death, with a procession from his grave at Vyšehrad to the **Municipal House** (p72), and a performance there of his patriotic song cycle *Má vlast* (My Homeland). The festival runs until 3 June, and the beautiful concert venues are as big a drawcard as the music.

Tickets can be obtained through the official **Prague Spring Box Office** (Map p62; ☎227 059 234; www.festival.cz; náměstí Jana Palacha, Rudolfinum; ⏱10am-6pm Mon-Fri; Ⓜ Staroměstská) in the Rudolfinum, or from any branch of **Ticketpro** (www.ticketpro.cz; Pasáž Lucerna, Štěpánská 61; ⏱5-8.30pm Mon-Fri; 🚋3, 5, 6, 9, 14, 24).

If you want a guaranteed seat at a Prague Spring concert, book it by mid-March at the latest, though a few seats may still be available as late as the end of May.

Tram Tours

Nostalgic Tram No 91 TOURS

(☎233 343 349; www.dpp.cz/en/nostalgic-tram-line-no-91; Public Transport Museum, Patočkova 4, Střešovice; adult/child 35/20Kč; ⏱departs hourly noon-5.30pm Sat, Sun & holidays Mar–mid-Nov) Vintage tram cars dating from 1908 to 1924 trundle along a special route, starting at the Public Transport Museum and going via stops at Prague Castle, Malostranské náměstí, the National Theatre, Wenceslas Square, náměstí Republiky and Štefánikův, with most finishing at Výstaviště. You can get on and off at any stop, and buy tickets on board (ordinary public transport tickets and passes are not valid).

Jewish-Interest Tours

Wittmann Tours TOURS

(Map p62; ☎222 252 472; www.wittmann-tours.com; Novotného lávka 5; tour per person 880Kč; ⏱Josefov tours 10.30am & 2pm Sun-Fri mid-Mar–Dec; 🚋2, 17, 18) The experts on Jewish Prague offer a three-hour walking tour of Josefov and seven-hour day trips to Terezín (1500Kč per person), daily May to October, four times a week April, November and December. Private tours are also available (from 1300Kč per hour).

Precious Legacy Tours TOURS

(Map p62; ☎222 321 954; www.legacytours.net; Kaprova 13; tour per person 880Kč; ⏱tours 10.30am & 2pm Sun-Fri; Ⓜ Staroměstská) Offers a three-hour walking tour of Prague's Josefov district (the fee includes admission to the Prague Jewish Museum complex, but not the Old-New Synagogue – this is 200Kč extra). There's also a daily six-hour excursion to Terezín (1600Kč per person; departs 10am).

WORTH A TRIP

DIVOKÁ ŠÁRKA

If you're in the mood to get away from it all, plan an outing to one of the city's prettiest and most remote nature parks, **Divoká Šárka** (☎603 723 501; www.koupaliste-sarka.webnode.cz; Evropská, Dejvice; adult/concession 80/60Kč; ⏱swimming pool 10am-6pm Jun-Aug; ; 20, 26). The park is best known for its eerie lunar landscape of barren rocks and hills at its western end, but it actually stretches for kilometres through forests and valleys along the Šárecký potok (Šárka Creek). The easiest way to access the park is by tram; lines 20 and 26 from Vítězné náměstí terminate at the edge of the park. You can return by tram the way you came or walk a 7km trail that circles back towards the Vltava, from where you can catch another tram.

The park is named after the mythical warrior Šárka, who is said to have thrown herself off a cliff here after the death of her enemy, the handsome Ctirad – whom she either seduced and murdered (committing suicide afterwards to avoid capture), or fell in love with and failed to protect (killing herself out of grief and guilt), depending on which version of the legend you prefer.

In addition to hiking, the area is perfect for spreading out a picnic blanket. In summer, there's an unheated swimming pool (with icy cold water), and a number of pubs.

To hike back towards town, find the red-marked trail that runs all the way to the suburb of Podbaba, where the creek empties into the Vltava. Once you've hit the river, look for the tower of the unmissable Hotel Crowne Plaza (with a gold star on top). Head towards the hotel, from where you can pick up tram 5 or 8, which brings you back to the Dejvická metro station, or stay aboard all the way to Náměstí Republiky.

Festivals & Events

Prague has an active festival season, with weekends from April through October often packed with food and street fests, musical events and happenings of all kinds. Below is a short list of the main events. **Prague City Tourism** maintains a comprehensive list on its website at www.prague.eu/en/events.

Prague Marathon SPORTS
(www.runczech.com; ⏱May) The Prague Marathon, established in 1989, is held annually in mid- to late May. It's considered to be one of the world's top 10 city marathons, attracting in excess of 10,000 entrants. There's also a half-marathon, held in late March. If you'd like to compete, you can register online or obtain entry forms from the website.

Prague Fringe Festival ART
(www.praguefringe.com; ⏱late May/early Jun) A wild week of happenings, theatre pieces, concerts and comedy shows, much of it is in English.

Christmas Market CHRISTMAS MARKET
(⏱1-24 Dec) From early December a Christmas market centred around a huge Christmas tree takes over Old Town Square.

Sleeping

Prague Castle & Hradčany

Hradčany is the place to stay if you're looking for peace and quiet. You'll be within a short walk of the castle, but when the crowds ebb away at the end of the day the streets are almost deserted.

★**Domus Henrici** HOTEL €€
(Map p44; ☎220 511 369; www.domus-henrici.cz; Loretánská 11; s/d/ste 3150/3600/4400Kč; @📶; 22) This historic building in a quiet corner of Hradčany is intentionally nondescript out front, hinting that peace and privacy are top priorities here. There are eight spacious and stylish rooms, half with private fax, scanner/copier and internet access (via wi-fi and ethernet port), and all with polished wood floors, large bathrooms, comfy beds and fluffy bathrobes.

Hotel Monastery HOTEL €€
(Map p44; ☎233 090 200; www.hotelmonastery.cz; Strahovské nádvoří 13; d/f from 3650/5490Kč; P⊖@📶; 22) Ancient meets modern at this small hotel, where the only noise likely to disturb you is the occasional tolling of a church bell. The 12 quirkily shaped rooms in this 17th-century building

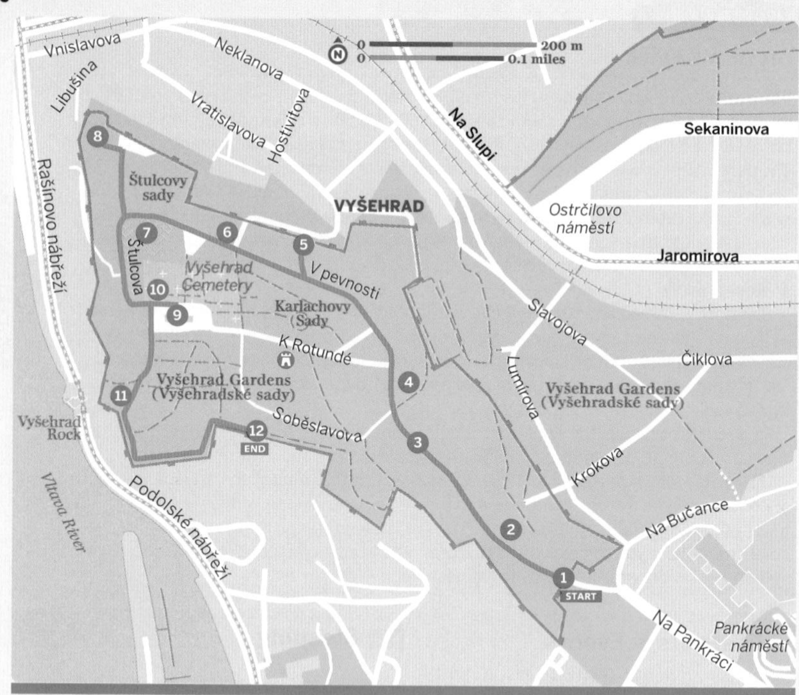

City Walk
Discovering the Roots of Prague

START TÁBOR GATE
END VYŠEHRAD FORTRESS'S SOUTHERN WALL
LENGTH 2KM; TWO HOURS

The first entrance into Vyšehrad fortress, 1 **Tábor Gate** (p105), can be found 200m west of the Vyšehrad metro stop. Just beyond it, you'll find the helpful 2 **Špička Information Centre** (p105). From here, continue along the road and walk through the larger and more impressive 3 **Leopold Gate** (p105).

Once inside the fortress proper, bear right to find the 4 **Rotunda of St Martin** (p104), dating from the 11th century.

Continue along the main path to locate the fortress's 5 **northern ramparts** for stunning views out over Prague below.

Retrace your steps and bear right to see the 6 **Brick Gate & Casemates** (p105). Guided tours here take you inside some of the old mustering chambers in the fortress. These hold a small exhibition on the structure's military history as well as a few original statues that once stood on Charles Bridge.

From there, walk west in the direction of the neo-Gothic 7 **New Provosts' Residence**. Bear right to reach the fortress's northwestern corner, which holds the 8 **Letní scéna**, a small amphitheatre with dramatic views. It's worth coming back in the evening to see a concert or dramatic presentation here.

Trace the fortress's western wall to reach the Rio's Vyšehrad restaurant, then round the bend to see the impressive facade of the 9 **Church of Sts Peter & Paul** (p105). Look inside to see the energetic interior, complete with early-20th-century frescoes. Just to the left of the church is the entrance to 10 **Vyšehrad Cemetery** (p101), the final resting place of a host of Czech luminaries from the 19th and 20th centuries.

Next walk south through an archway to enter a large park where a path leads to the right to the 11 **Gothic Cellar** (p105), which holds a permanent exhibition on Vyšehrad's history.

You'll find more photo ops and dramatic views along the 12 **southern wall** of the fortress. Trace the southern ramparts to the east, which will eventually loop you back to Leopold Gate and then the metro.

have been given a bright, modern makeover with polished wood floors, plain white walls hung with photos of Prague, and a splash of colour from the bedspread and sofa.

★**Romantik Hotel U Raka** HOTEL €€€
(Map p44; ☎220 511 100; www.romantikhotel-uraka.cz; Černínská 10, Hradčany; s/d from 2840/4450Kč; ; 22) Concealed in a manicured rock garden in a quiet corner of Hradčany, this historic hotel is an atmospheric, late-18th-century timber cottage with just six elegant, low-ceilinged doubles, complete with timber beams, wood floors and red-brick fireplaces. With its cosy bedrooms, attentive staff, artistic decor and farmhouse-kitchen–style breakfast room, it's ideal for a romantic getaway. Book at least a few months ahead.

Malá Strana

Lots of Malá Strana's lovely old Renaissance and baroque buildings have been converted into hotels and apartments, making this a good district to stay in if you're looking for a romantic atmosphere. You'll also be within walking distance of Charles Bridge and surrounded by lots of good restaurants and bars.

Little Quarter Hostel HOSTEL €
(Map p50; ☎257 212 029; www.littlequarter.com; Nerudova 21; dm/tr from 420/1800Kč; @; 12, 15, 20, 22) This place is not your average hostel – it's gleamingly clean, reception is staffed 24 hours, the six- or eight-bed dorms have mostly single beds (only a few bunks) with secure storage underneath, and there's working wi-fi on every floor. Add the fact that it's halfway between Charles Bridge and the castle, and you'll see the need to get your booking in early.

Little Town Budget Hotel HOTEL €
(Map p50; ☎242 406 965; www.littletownhotel.cz; Malostranské náměstí 11; dm 550Kč, s/d/tr 1750/2000/2400Kč; @; 12, 15, 20, 22) A brilliant location in Malá Strana reveals excellent-value rooms arrayed around a quiet, central courtyard. Rooms are simply furnished with whitewashed walls and have a relaxed ambience verging on monastic. The more expensive three- and four-person self-contained rooms/apartments with kitchen and bathroom are excellent value for groups.

★**Dům U Velké Boty** PENSION €€
(Map p50; ☎257 532 088; www.dumuvelkeboty.cz; Vlašská 30; s/d from 2160/2850Kč; ; 12, 15, 20, 22) Location, location, location – those three little words that mean so much. The quaint little 'House at the Big Boot' is set on a quiet square, just five minutes' walk from the castle, and the same from Charles Bridge. The warren of ancient rooms is furnished in an understated and elegant way, with a period atmosphere (no TVs), and the owners are unfailingly helpful .

For families, there is a suite with two neighbouring doubles that share a bathroom.

TAKE A STROLL THROUGH STAROPRAMEN BREWERY

Though Plzeň and České Budějovice are better known as beer towns, Prague has a major brewery of its own: Staropramen. Tours of the **Staropramen Brewery** (Map p102; ☎273 132 589; www.staropramen.com; Pivovarská 9, Smíchov; tour 200Kč; 10am-6pm; M Anděl, 4, 5, 12, 20) in Smíchov are offered daily. It's actually more of a museum visit than a brewery tour, as the presentation focuses on the 100-plus years of history of the brewery. The reward for your time, though, is a glass of Staropramen at the end and the chance to drink plenty more at the brewery pub. See the website or check tour times on the door. English tours are normally conducted at 10am, 1pm and 4pm, though the times of tours can differ by the day.

Lokál Inn INN €€
(Map p50; ☎257 014 800; www.lokalinn.cz; Míšeňská 12; d/ste from 3800/4600Kč; ; 12, 15, 20, 22) Polished parquet floors and painted wooden ceilings abound in this 18th-century house designed by Prague's premier baroque architect, Kilian Dientzenhofer. The eight rooms and four suites are elegant and uncluttered, and the rustic, stone-vaulted cellars house a deservedly popular pub and restaurant run by the same folk as Lokál (p125), a busy Czech beer hall in Staré Město.

Best ask for a quiet room if you plan to be in bed before the pub shuts.

Design Hotel Sax HOTEL €€
(Map p50; ☎775 859 694; www.hotelsax.cz; Jánský vršek 3; s/d from 2850/3650Kč; @; 12, 15, 20, 22) Set in a quiet corner of Malá Strana, amid embassies and monastery gardens, the Sax is refreshingly different. The building is 18th-century on the

ROOM RATES & SEASONS

A double room in a midrange hotel in central Prague costs around 4000Kč (€160) in high season; outside the centre, this might fall to about 3000Kč. Top-range hotels cost from 4000Kč up, with the best luxury hotels charging 6000Kč and more. Budget options charge less than 2000Kč for a double room.

Note that some midrange and top-end hotels quote rates in euros. At these hotels you can pay cash in Czech crowns if you like, but the price will depend on the exchange rate on the day you settle the bill.

We provide high-season rates, which generally cover April to June, September and October, and the Christmas/New Year holidays. July and August are midseason, and the rest of the year is low season, when rates can drop by 30% or 40%.

Even high-season rates can be inflated by up to 15% on certain dates, notably at New Year, Easter, during the Prague Spring festival, and at weekends (Thursday to Sunday) in May, June and September.

outside, but the interior has been remodelled with classic furniture and design from the 1950s, '60s and '70s. There's a dramatic glass-roofed atrium where the courtyard used to be; bold and colourful retro decor; stylish, uncluttered bedrooms; and impeccable service.

Hunger Wall Residence APARTMENT €€
(Map p50; 257 404 040; www.hungerwall.eu; Plaská 8; 2-person apt from 3100Kč; ; 9, 12, 15, 20) The Hunger Wall offers bright, stylish, modernised apartments at reasonable short-stay rates. From the smiling welcome at reception to the spotlessly clean rooms, the atmosphere here is resolutely 'new Prague', with facilities that include an excellent cafe (p122), conference room and a tiny gym. Located in the quieter southern part of Malá Strana, only two tram stops from Malostranské náměstí.

★ **Golden Well Hotel** HOTEL €€€
(Map p50; 257 011 213; www.goldenwell.cz; U Zlaté studně 4; d/ste from 4750/14,900Kč; P @; M Malostranská, 12, 15, 20, 22) The Golden Well is one of Malá Strana's hidden secrets, tucked away at the end of a cobbled cul-de-sac – a Renaissance house that once belonged to Emperor Rudolf II, perched on the southern slope of the castle hill. The rooms are quiet and spacious, with polished wood floors, reproduction period furniture, and luxurious bathrooms with underfloor heating and whirlpool baths.

Many rooms have a superb outlook over the city or the Palace Gardens below, as does the hotel's excellent restaurant (p125) and terrace.

Hotel Aria BOUTIQUE HOTEL €€€
(Map p50; 225 334 111; www.ariahotel.net; Tržiště 9; d/ste from 5250/13,400Kč; P @; 12, 15, 20, 22) The Aria offers five-star luxury with a musical theme – each of the four floors is dedicated to a musical genre (jazz, opera, classical and contemporary), and each room celebrates a particular artist or musician and contains a selection of their music that you can enjoy on the in-room hi-fi system.

Service is professional and efficient, and the rooms are furnished with crisp bed linen, plump continental quilts, Molton Brown toiletries and complimentary chocolates.

Staré Město

Staré Město offers a wide range of accommodation, from backpacker hostels to some of the city's most luxurious hotels, with everything in between. Be aware that a lot of pensions and midrange hotels have been squeezed into historic old buildings with no room for a lift – be prepared for a bit of stair climbing.

Ahoy! Hostel HOSTEL €
(Map p62; 773 004 003; www.ahoyhostel.com; Na Perštýně 10; dm/tw 460/1350Kč; @; M Národní Třída, 2, 9, 18, 22) No big signs or branding here, just an inconspicous card by the blue door at No 10. But inside is a very pleasant, welcoming and peaceful hostel (definitely not for the party crowd), with eager-to-please staff, some self-consciously 'arty' decoration, clean and comfortable six- or eight-bed dorms, and a couple of private twin rooms. Ideal location too.

Old Prague Hostel HOSTEL €
(Map p62; ☎224 829 058; www.oldpraguehostel.com; Benediktská 2; dm from 380Kč, s/d 1100/1300Kč; ; Náměstí Republiky) Cheerful and welcoming, with colourful homemade murals brightening the walls, this is one of Prague's most sociable hostels, with a good mix of people from backpackers to families. Facilities are good, with lockers in the dorms, luggage storage and 24-hour reception, though the mattresses on the bunks are a bit on the thin side.

The staff are very helpful and the location could hardly be more central, just a five-minute walk east of Old Town Square.

★U Zeleného Věnce PENSION €€
(Map p62; ☎222 220 178; www.uzv.cz; Řetězová 10; s/d/tr 2400/2700/3300Kč; ; 2, 17, 18) Located on a quiet side street, the 'Green Garland' is a surprisingly rustic retreat right in the heart of the city. The bedrooms vary in size – some cramped and some spacious – but all are spotlessly clean, and simply but appealingly decorated, with exposed medieval roof beams in the attic rooms. The English-speaking owner is unfailingly polite and helpful.

Set in a restored 14th-century building, the pension takes its name from the house-sign above the door, and is only a few minutes' stroll from Old Town Square.

Design Hotel Jewel BOUTIQUE HOTEL €€
(Map p62; ☎224 211 699; www.hoteljewelprague.com; Rytířská 3; s/d from 2300/3100Kč; ; Můstek) Housed in a medieval building that was once home to a royal jeweller (check out the early-20th-century painted ceiling with gemstone motifs in the cafe-bar), this diamond of a hotel is themed around jewels. Comfort and service are as dazzling as the decor, with rooms named after precious stones, gold and silver detailing, glittering crystals and mirror mosaic tiles. There's no elevator.

Perla Hotel BOUTIQUE HOTEL €€
(Map p62; ☎221 667 707; www.perlahotel.cz; Perlová 1; s/d from 3760/4030Kč; ; Můstek) The 'Pearl' is typical of the slinky, appealing designer hotels that have sprung up all over central Prague. Here the designer has picked – surprise, surprise – a pearl motif that extends from the giant pearls that form the reception desk to the silky, lustrous bedspreads and huge screen prints on the bedroom walls.

The rooms are on the small side, but the decor is sleek and modern with muted colours offset by bright-red lacquered chairs and glossy black-tiled bathrooms.

Design Hotel Josef BOUTIQUE HOTEL €€
(Map p62; ☎221 700 111; www.hoteljosef.com; Rybná 20; r from 4000Kč; ; Náměstí Republiky) Designed by London-based Czech architect Eva Jiřičná, the Josef is one of Prague's most stylish contemporary hotels. The minimalist theme evident in the stark, white lobby (with its glass spiral staircase) is continued in the bedrooms, where things are kept clean and simple with plenty of subtle neutral tones. The glass-walled en suites are especially attractive, boasting extra-large rainfall shower heads and glass bowl basins.

★Savic Hotel HOTEL €€€
(Map p62; ☎224 248 555; www.savic.eu; Jilská 7; r from 4800Kč; ; Můstek) From the complimentary glass of wine when you arrive to the comfy king-size beds, the Savic certainly knows how to make you feel pampered. Housed in the former monastery of St Giles, the hotel is bursting with character and full of delightful period details including old stone fireplaces, beautiful painted timber ceilings and fragments of frescoes.

The huge bedrooms are furnished in antique style with parquet floors, dark wooden furniture, wingback armchairs and plush sofas, while the bathrooms are lined with polished marble.

Residence Karolina APARTMENT €€€
(Map p62; ☎224 990 990; www.residence-karolina.com; Karoliny Světlé 4; 2-/4-person apt 4100/6300Kč; ; 2, 9, 18, 22) We're going to have to invent a new category of accommodation – boutique apartments – to cover this array of 20 beautifully furnished flats. Offering one- or two-bedroom options, all apartments have spacious seating areas with comfy sofas and flat-screen TVs, sleek modern kitchens and dining areas.

The location is good too, set back on a quiet street but close to a major tram stop,

RESERVATIONS

Booking your accommodation in advance is strongly recommended (especially if you want to stay in or near the centre), and there are dozens of agencies that will help you find a place to stay. The more reliable agencies should be able to find you a bed even if you turn up in peak periods without a booking.

and just two blocks from a Tesco supermarket for your self-catering supplies.

Nové Město

Although there are one or two grand old luxury hotels here, Nové Město's accommodation is mostly in modern chain hotels and upgraded 1930s establishments. What they might lack in historical atmosphere and romantic appeal they make up for in spaciousness and facilities. Those on Wenceslas Square are right in the thick of things, but there are quiet corners to be found as well, especially in southern Nové Město (such as Charles Square and its surrounds).

★ Sophie's Hostel HOSTEL €

(Map p78; 246 032 621; www.sophieshostel.com; Melounova 2; dm from 400Kč, d/apt from 1800/2400Kč; M IP Pavlova) This hostel makes a pleasant change from the usual characterless backpacker hive. There's a touch of contemporary style here, with oak-veneer floors and stark, minimalist decor, along with neutral colours, chunky timber and quirky metal-framed beds – the place is famous for its 'designer' showers, with autographed glass screens and huge rainfall shower heads.

Sophie's Bar, in the basement, serves an all-you-can-eat breakfast buffet for 150Kč, and the 24-hour reception is staffed by a young, multilingual crew who are always eager to help.

ArtHarmony PENSION, HOSTEL €

(Map p78; 222 542 931; www.artharmony.cz; Ječná 12; dm/d from 440/1800Kč; 4, 6, 10, 16, 22) Quirkily decorated with colourful wall paintings, rustic timber and real silver-birch trees, this pension stands out from the crowd. The atmosphere is easygoing, family-friendly and vaguely hippy-ish, and you can choose to stay in a shared room (from three to six people, doesn't really feel like a dorm), a private room with shared bathroom, or a private room with en suite.

Staff are super-helpful, and there's a lounge and communal kitchen. Note – reception is on the 2nd floor, and there's no elevator.

★ Fusion Hotel BOUTIQUE HOTEL €€

(Map p84; 226 222 800; www.fusionhotels.com; Panská 9; r from 2650Kč; 3, 5, 6, 9, 14, 24) Fusion has style in abundance, from the revolving bar and spaceship-like UV corridor lighting, to the individually decorated bedrooms that resemble miniature modern-art galleries. As well as doubles, triples and family rooms, there are 'theme rooms' decorated in vintage or romantic style, with works by young Czech artists; one even offers a communal bed for up to six people!

★ Hotel 16 HOTEL €€

(Map p78; 224 920 636; www.hotel16.cz; Kateřinská 16; s/d from 2400/3500Kč; 4, 6, 10, 16, 22) Hotel 16 is a friendly, family-run little place with just 14 rooms, tucked away in a very quiet corner of town where you're more likely to hear birdsong than traffic. The rooms vary in size and are simply but smartly furnished; the best, at the back, have views onto the peaceful terraced garden. Staff are superb, and can't do enough to help.

Buffet breakfast is included in the price, and the hotel is equipped with a lift. It's near the Botanic Gardens and about five minutes' walk from Štěpánská tram stop or IP Pavlova metro station.

Moods Hotel BOUTIQUE HOTEL €€

(Map p84; 222 330 100; www.hotelmoods.com; Klimentská 28; r from 3300Kč; 6, 8, 15, 26) Staff here play a huge part in the visitor experience: they're welcoming, friendly and helpful. One of the best examples of Prague's 'design hotels', Moods is sharply styled and tech savvy, with clever colour schemes, adjustable mood lighting and intriguing quotations gracing the walls.

The location is off the beaten track, but still only 10 minutes' walk from Old Town Square, with the option of a scenic stroll along the bank of the Vltava.

Mosaic House HOTEL, HOSTEL €€

(Map p78; 221 595 350; www.mosaichouse.com; Odborů 4; dm/tw from 370/2400Kč; 5) A blend of four-star hotel and boutique hostel, Mosaic House is a cornucopia of designer detail, from the original 1930s mosaic in the entrance hall to the silver spray-painted tree branches used as clothes racks. The backpackers dorms are kept separate from the private rooms, but have the same high-quality decor and design, as does the in-house music bar and lounge.

The top-floor private bedrooms cost about a third more than standard doubles but are worth it for the spacious balconies with city views, and the relative peace and quiet. All have incredibly stylish bathrooms with water-efficient rain showers; other green technology includes the use of intelligent heating systems, solar panels and grey-water recycling.

Hotel Suite Home APARTMENT €€

(Map p78; ☎222 230 833; www.hotelsuitehomeprague.com; Příčná 2; 2-person ste from 3660Kč; P ⊜ ❄ @ ☎; M Karlovo Náměstí) Straddling the divide between apartment and hotel, this place offers the space and convenience of a suite with private bathroom and kitchen along with hotel facilities such as 24-hour reception, cleaning service and breakfast room. It's a good choice for families, with suites for up to six; the rooms are pleasantly old-fashioned, and some on the upper floors have good views towards the castle.

There's a lift, though it's a bit on the small side – important, as the building has five floors. Check the website for special rates.

Hotel Union HOTEL €€

(Map p106; ☎261 214 812; www.hotelunion.cz; Ostrčilovo náměstí 4, Vyšehrad; s/d 1800/3000Kč; P ⊜ ❄ @ ☎; 🚋7, 14, 18, 24) A grand old hotel from 1906, the Union was nationalised by the communists in 1958 and returned to the former owner's family in 1991. Comfortably renovated, with a few period touches left intact, the hotel is at the foot of the hill below Vyšehrad fortress. Bedrooms are plain but pleasant.

Ask for one of the deluxe corner rooms, which are huge and have bay windows with a view of either Vyšehrad or distant Prague Castle.

★Radisson Blu Alcron Hotel HISTORIC HOTEL €€€

(Map p78; ☎222 820 000; www.radissonblu.com/en/hotel-prague; Štěpánská 40; r from 4500Kč; ⊜ ☎; 🚋3, 5, 6, 9, 14, 24) Located just a few minutes' walk from Wenceslas Square, the five-star Radisson is the modern reincarnation of the 1930s Alcron Hotel, and has long been favoured by celebrities and diplomats. Many of the original art-deco marble-and-glass fittings have been preserved, including the beautiful Michelin-starred Alcron restaurant, and the renovations have been far more tastefully executed than in many other refurbished Prague hotels.

★Icon Hotel BOUTIQUE HOTEL €€€

(Map p78; ☎221 634 100; www.iconhotel.eu; V Jámě 6; r from 3800Kč; ❄ @ ☎; 🚋3, 5, 6, 9, 14, 24) Staff clothes by Diesel, computers by Apple, beds by Hästens – pretty much everything in this gorgeous boutique hotel has a designer stamp on it. Appearing on Europe's trendiest hotels lists, the Icon's sleekly minimalist rooms are enlivened with a splash of imperial purple from the silky bedspreads, while the curvy, reproduction art-deco armchairs are supplied by Modernista (p165).

Hi-tech touches include iPod docks, Skype phones and fingerprint-activated safes, while the in-house Asian spa offers relaxing massages and beauty treatments.

Dancing House Hotel BOUTIQUE HOTEL €€€

(Map p78; ☎720 983 172; www.dancinghousehotel.com; Jiráskovo náměstí 6; r from 4400Kč; ☎; 🚋5, 17) It's been a long time coming, but it had to happen – Milunić and Gehry's icon of modern architecture, first opened in 1996, now houses a 21-room luxury hotel. Rooms range from stylish doubles overlooking the river to stunning suites in the curvy, glass-clad half of the building with breathtaking views of the castle.

Vinohrady & Vršovice

Vinohrady is a great place to stay. Not only is it relatively close to the centre, with good metro connections from Náměstí Míru and Jiřího z Poděbrad metro stations, but there are lots of pleasant places to stroll around and stop for a beer or bite to eat. One drawback is the shortage of parking.

★Czech Inn HOSTEL, HOTEL €

(Map p88; ☎reception 267 267 612, reservations 267 267 600; www.czech-inn.com; Francouzská 76, Vršovice; dm 280-450Kč, s/d 1200/1600Kč, apt from 3000Kč; P ⊜ @ ☎; 🚋4, 22) The Czech Inn calls itself a hostel, but a boutique label wouldn't be out of place. Everything seems sculpted by an industrial designer, from the iron beds to the brushed-steel flooring and minimalist square sinks. It offers a variety of accommodation, from standard hostel dorm rooms to good-value doubles (with or without private bathroom) and apartments.

A cosy coffee bar in the lobby and an excellent buffet breakfast in the adjoining bar round out the charms. The nearest metro station is 10 minutes on foot or a short tram ride away.

Holiday Home PENSION €

(Map p88; ☎222 512 710; www.holidayhome.cz; Americká 37, Vinohrady; s/d from 1200/1400Kč; P ⊜ @ ☎; M Náměstí Míru) This popular family-owned pension offers excellent value in one of the city's choicest residential neighbourhoods. The secret here is no frills: simple, plain rooms and small beds at an unbeatable price.

EXPERIENCE PRAGUE LIKE A LOCAL

Central Prague can often feel like it's populated entirely by tourists. So where are all the locals? If it's the weekend, they're probably out picking wild mushrooms, watching a football or ice-hockey match, or browsing the stalls at one of the city's excellent farmers markets.

Root Like a Local

Czechs are inveterate sports fans, with football (soccer) and ice hockey being the most popular. It's easy to combine a trip to Prague with a chance to root for the home team.

Ice Hockey

It's a toss-up whether football or ice hockey inspires more passion in the hearts of Prague sports fans, but hockey probably wins. Games are fast and furious, and the atmosphere can be electrifying – it's well worth making the effort to see a game, and take part in a genuinely Czech experience.

Prague's two big hockey teams are **HC Sparta Praha** (www.hcsparta.cz), which competes in the 14-team national league (known as the Extraliga), and **HC Slavia Praha** (www.hc-slavia.cz), which is in the second-tier WSM Liga. Gifted young players are often lured away by the promise of big money in North America's National Hockey League, and there is a sizeable Czech contingent in the NHL. Both Sparta and Slavia Praha play at **O2 Arena** (www.o2arena.cz; Českomoravská 17, Vysočany; ⌚box office 10am-6pm Mon-Fri, from 10am day of event; Ⓜ Českomoravská); the season runs from September to early April. Buy tickets online at www.ticketportal.cz, or at the stadium box office before matches.

Football

Prague's two big football (soccer) clubs are **SK Slavia Praha** (www.slavia.cz) and their great rivals **AC Sparta Praha** (www.sparta.cz), with fiercely partisan supporters all over the country. Two other Prague-based teams – **FC Bohemians** (www.bohemians1905.cz) and **FK Viktoria Žižkov** (www.fkvz.cz) – attract fervent local support. The season runs from August to May, and matches are mostly played on Wednesday, Saturday and Sunday afternoons. You can buy tickets (100Kč to 400Kč) at stadium box offices on match days.

Generali Aréna (Sparta Stadium; Map p98; ☎296 111 400; www.sparta.cz; Milady Horákové 98, Bubeneč; tickets 100-400Kč; ⌚box office 9am-noon Mon, 1-5pm Tue-Wed, 1-7pm Thu, 9am-noon & 1-5pm Fri; 🚋1, 8, 12, 25, 26) is home ground for Sparta, the winner of the top Czech football league several times in the past decade. It's also the field of choice for many international matches and friendlies. Slavia plays its home matches at Vršovice's **Eden Aréna** (SK Slavia Praha; ☎725 707 295, tickets 272 118 311; www.edenarena.cz; U Slavie 2a, Vršovice; match tickets 160-310Kč; 🚋6, 7, 22, 24). While Slavia often plays second fiddle to Sparta Praha, Slavia actually has the longer lineage of the two, dating back to 1892. It's even an honorary member of England's Football Association.

Celebrate Like a Local

Easter

Come Easter, the country celebrates with a mirthful rite of spring: Czech boys swat their favourite girls on the legs with braided willow switches (you'll see them on sale in street

The manager is super-friendly. The location is ideal, just a short walk to several nearby cafes and the Náměstí Míru metro stop.

Arkada BOUTIQUE HOTEL €€
(Map p88; ☎242 429 111; www.arkadahotel.cz; Balbínová 8, Vinohrady; s/d from 1750/2250Kč; P ⊜ @ 🛜; Ⓜ Muzeum, 🚋11, 13) This 35-room hotel in Vinohrady offers a great combination of style, comfort and location. The rooms are well appointed, with a retro-1930s feel that fits the style of the building. Rooms have flat-screen TVs, free internet access and minibars. Ask to see a couple before choosing, as the decor differs from room to room.

The location is about five minutes by foot to the top of Wenceslas Square and is within easy walking distance of some of the best Vinohrady restaurants and clubs.

markets) or splash them with water, and the girls respond with gifts of hand-painted eggs, after which the whole family parties – the culmination of several days of serious spring-cleaning, cooking and visiting relatives and friends.

May Day

The May Day holiday (Svátek práce) on 1 May – once the communist 'holy' day, marked by huge parades – is now just a chance for a picnic or a day in the country. To celebrate the arrival of spring, many couples lay flowers at the statue of the 19th-century poet Karel Hynek Mácha (author of *Máj*, a poem about unrequited love) on Petřín.

Majáles

Prague students celebrate the first weekend of May as Majáles, a festival dating back to at least the early 19th century, which was banned under communism but revived in 1997. It starts with a midday parade – with bands, students in fancy dress, and a float bearing the Kral Majáles (King of Majáles) and Miss Majáles – from Wenceslas Square to Stromovka park, and there's an open-air party including live bands, student theatre and nonstop sausages and beer. For dates and details, check www.majales.cz.

Relax Like a Local

Forage for Fun

It's estimated that Czechs pick more than 20 million kilograms of wild mushrooms each year. From May to October, foraging for fungi and wild berries is one of the nation's most popular pastimes, when Prague's **Divoká Šárka** (p109) and **Michelský Les** woodlands (southeast of the city centre) are thronged with locals clutching wicker baskets. Czechs learn young how to identify edible fungi, so unless you've mastered the art of mushroom identification you'd better tag along with a local expert; otherwise you can sample the fruits of the forest at a farmers market, or at restaurants advertising *hřiby* or *lesní houby*.

Picnic in the Park

Get a taste for local produce by browsing the weekend farmers markets at **Dejvice** (p168) or **Náplavka** (p166) and putting together the makings of a picnic. Then join the crowds at **Riegrovy sady** (p88) in Vinohrady for an alfresco lunch (there's a beer garden here, too), or head down to Havlíčkovy sady, where you can sample Czech wine at **Viniční Altán** (p151). From Náplavka, climb up to **Vyšehrad** – a favourite spot for weekend strolls – for a picnic with a view.

Head to the Riverfront

From late April to September, as evening approaches, the river embankment at **Náplavka** in Nové Město, south of the National Theatre, swells with crowds of walkers and gawkers, cyclists and strollers who throng here to take in various live-music events, evening drinks on quayside boats, and the breathtaking views towards floodlit Prague Castle.

Hotel Luník HOTEL €€

(Map p88; ☎224 253 974; www.hotel-lunik.cz; Londýnská 50, Vinohrady; s/d from 1800/2800Kč; P ⊜ @ ☜; M Náměstí Míru, IP Pavlova) Clean, attractive and smallish, Hotel Luník is on a quiet residential street a block from Peace Sq, between the Náměstí Míru and IP Pavlova metro stations. The lobby and public areas exude a quiet sophistication, while the rooms are homey and slightly old-fashioned, with attractive green-tiled bathrooms. The friendly receptionist may be willing to negotiate room rates on slow nights.

Ametyst BOUTIQUE HOTEL €€

(Map p88; ☎222 921 921; www.hotelametyst.cz; Jana Masaryka 11, Vinohrady; s/d from €90/130; P ⊜ ❄ @ ☜; M Náměstí Míru) The polished

Ametyst straddles the line between boutique and hotel, with just enough style points in the lobby (nice retro flagstone) and the rooms (hardwood floors, arty lamps and flat-screen TVs) to put it in the boutique camp. Rooms in the more expensive 'deluxe' category were fully renovated in 2015.

There are dozens of places to relax within easy walking distance in one of the nicest parts of leafy Vinohrady. Note, rack rates have risen steeply in the past couple of years, but the hotel does offer frequent discounts on its website.

Louren Hotel BOUTIQUE HOTEL €€
(Map p88; 224 250 025; www.louren.cz; Slezská 55, Vinohrady; s/d/ste 2400/3200/4200Kč; ; M Jiřího z Poděbrad, 10, 16) Popular with business travellers, this small luxury hotel with 27 rooms, including several suites, is set in a grand 19th-century apartment building. Stylish decor and attentive service are accompanied by thoughtful touches such as bathrobes and fresh flowers. The rooms are decorated in restful, neutral tones (lots of cream and light wood).

The building dates from 1889 and has been restored to its former grandeur. Service can't be faulted, and the staff are courteous and very helpful. Rates are sometimes discounted on its website.

Orion APARTMENT €€
(Map p88; 222 521 706; www.okhotels.cz; Americká 9, Vinohrady; 2-/4-person apt 1800/2400Kč; P; M Náměstí Míru) Good-value apartment rentals in an upmarket section of Vinohrady, within easy walking distance of Peace Sq and Havlíčkovy sady. The 26 apartments are equipped with a small kitchen, including a fridge and coffee maker. Several have multiple rooms and can accommodate groups. Ask to see a couple of rooms as they are slightly different; some come with hardwood floors, others carpet.

Hotel Anna HOTEL, PENSION €€
(Map p88; 222 513 111; www.hotelanna.cz; Budečská 17, Vinohrady; s/d from €60/80, ste from €100; P; M Náměstí Míru) This small, friendly hotel has helpful and knowledgeable employees. The late-19th-century building retains many of its original art-nouveau features, and the bedrooms are bright and cheerful, with floral bedspreads and arty black-and-white photos of Prague buildings on the walls. There are two small suites on the top floor, one of which has a great view towards the castle.

The hotel is tucked away on a quiet backstreet but is close to the metro and lots of good restaurants and bars; you can walk to the top end of Wenceslas Square in 10 minutes.

★ Le Palais Hotel HOTEL €€€
(Map p88; 234 634 111; www.lepalaishotel.eu; U Zvonařky 1, Vinohrady; r from €180, ste from €280; P; 6, 11, 13) Le Palais is housed in a gorgeous belle-époque building dating from the end of the 19th century that was once home to Czech artist Luděk Marold (1865–98; his former apartment is now rooms 407 to 412). It has been beautifully restored, complete with original floor mosaics, period fireplaces, marble staircases, wrought-iron balustrades, frescoes, painted ceilings and delicate stucco work.

The luxury bedrooms are decorated in warm shades of yellow and pink, while the various suites – some located in the corner tower, some with a south-facing balcony – make the most of the hotel's superb location, perched on top of a bluff with views of the Vyšehrad fortress. Within easy walking distance of bars and restaurants in Vinohrady and about 15 minutes by foot from the top of Wenceslas Square.

Žižkov & Karlín

If you're looking for somewhere inexpensive but not far from the city centre, then Žižkov and Karlín are your best bet. The slightly run-down air of these districts puts a lot of people off, but they are as safe as anywhere else in the city and only a couple of tram stops from Staré Město. Some of the accommodation here can be mediocre, but things are improving all the time – Žižkov has some of Prague's best hostels, and we'd be surprised if Karlín doesn't sprout some cool designer hotels in the next few years.

★ Brix Hostel HOSTEL €
(Map p92; 222 742 700; www.brixhostel.com; Roháčova 15, Žižkov; dm/d from 300/1200Kč; ; 133, 175, 207) Created by a group of friends who all previously worked in other hostels, this place benefits hugely from their experience – everything is focused on making your stay enjoyable, from the warm welcome to the custom-built bunks and clean, modern bathrooms. The hostel's own bar is open 24/7, and is a great place to make new acquaintances.

Hostel Elf HOSTEL €
(Map p92; ☎222 540 963; www.hostelelf.com; Husitská 11, Žižkov; dm/d from 280/570Kč; 📶; 🚌133, 175, 207) Young, hip and sociable, Hostel Elf welcomes a steady stream of party-hearty backpackers to its well-maintained dorms, and many end up staying longer than they planned. The dorms, sleeping up to 12 people, are immaculately clean and brightly decorated with graffiti art or the odd mural. There's a little beer-garden terrace and cosy lounge, with free tea and coffee and cheap beer.

Hostel Lípa HOSTEL €
(Map p92; ☎602 211 182; www.hostellipa.com; Tachovské náměstí 6, Žižkov; dm/d from 300/750Kč; P@📶; 🚌133, 175, 207) Several good hostels have opened in Žižkov in recent years, but this place is a little gem, run by a young Czech couple (with good English). It feels more like a shared apartment, consisting of only three dorms (maximum six beds), three private rooms and a modern fitted kitchen. It's upstairs from the excellent pub U Slovanské Lípy (p152).

Hotel Theatrino HOTEL €€
(Map p92; ☎227 031 894; www.hoteltheatrino.cz; Bořivojova 53, Žižkov; r from 2700Kč; 🚭📶; 🚋5, 9, 15, 26) The design of some hotels could be described as theatrical, but there can't be too many that were actually designed as a theatre. Dating from 1910, the art-nouveau building that houses this hotel was originally a cultural centre – you can enjoy an excellent buffet breakfast in what was once the theatre auditorium.

The rooms are plain and modern, but the public areas are filled with beautiful period features from wrought-iron railings to stained-glass windows.

Pentahotel Prague HOTEL €€
(Map p92; ☎222 332 800; www.pentahotels.com; Sokolovská 112, Karlín; r from 3400Kč; P❄📶; MKřižíkova) This German hotel chain is aimed at business and independent travellers, with sleek, modern styling, quality beds and bathrooms, a large gym and a 'pentalounge' – a combined reception, bar, cafe and sitting area where guests can meet and mingle. The Karlín location has good tram and metro connections, and there are many good restaurants and bars in the vicinity.

Hotel Alwyn HOTEL €€
(Map p92; ☎222 334 200; www.hotelalwyn.cz; Vítkova 26, Karlín; s/d from 2900/3400Kč; ❄@📶; 🚋3, 8, 24) The Alwyn is the first designer hotel to appear in the up-and-coming district of Karlín. Set on a quiet side street only a few tram stops east of Staré Město, the hotel sports deliciously modern decor in shades of chocolate brown, beige and burnt orange, with lots of polished wood and deco-style sofas in the cocktail bar, and super-comfortable Hästens beds in the rooms.

It's designed for both business and pleasure, with a conference room, gym, sauna and massage centre.

Holešovice

Hotels in this part of town are among the cheapest in Prague and represent excellent value. The best are located in the eastern part of the neighbourhood and easy to reach by tram or metro (red line C: Praha-Holešovice).

Sir Toby's Hostel HOSTEL €
(Map p96; ☎246 032 611; www.sirtobys.com; Dělnická 24; dm 270-400Kč, s/d 1000/1400Kč; P🚭@📶; 🚋1, 6, 12, 25) Set in a refurbished apartment building with a spacious kitchen and common room, Sir Toby's is about 10 minutes north of the city centre by tram. The dorms have between five and 12 bunks, including a six-bed, all-female room, and the bigger dorms are some of the cheapest in Prague. All rooms are light and clean, but don't expect anything fancy.

The mattresses are a little thin, but all sheets and blankets are provided at no extra cost. There's a communal kitchen for self-caterers, a lounge and a relaxing garden where you can sit back and chat.

Plus Prague Hostel HOSTEL €
(Map p96; ☎220 510 046; www.plusprague.com; Přívozní 1; dm 280-400Kč, r 1100Kč; P🚭@📶🏊; MNádraží Holešovice, 🚋6, 12) The cheerful Plus Prague Hostel is one tram stop from Nádraží Holešovice. Cheap rates, clean private rooms with en suite bathrooms, friendly staff and an indoor swimming pool make this a special place. It also offers four- to eight-bed female-only dorm rooms, outfitted with hair dryers and fluffier towels.

Autocamp Trojská CAMPGROUND €
(☎283 850 487; www.autocamp-trojska.cz; Trojská 157, Troja; site per person 100Kč, plus per tent/car 150/90Kč; ⏲year-round; P📶; MNádraží Holešovice then bus 112 to Kazanka) The most comfortable and secure of half a dozen campgrounds in this quiet northern suburb,

Trojská offers a garden bar and restaurant, laundry and on-site shop.

Hotel Extol Inn HOTEL €

(Map p96; 220 802 549; www.extolinn.cz; Přístavní 2; s/d from 800/1500Kč; P ⊖ @ ; 6, 12) The bright, modern Extol Inn provides budget accommodation in an up-and-coming neighbourhood within easy reach of the city centre by tram. The cheapest rooms (on the upper floors) are basic, no-frills affairs with shared bathrooms. More expensive three-star rooms (doubles from 1800Kč) have private bathrooms, TVs, minibars and free use of the hotel spa. Wheelchair-accessible. On-site parking costs 150Kč.

Hotel Leon HOSTEL, HOTEL €

(Map p96; 220 941 351; www.leonhotel.eu; Ortenovo náměstí 26; s/d from 700/900Kč; P ⊖ @ ; M Nádraží Holešovice, 6, 12) The Hotel Leon advertises itself as something between a hostel and a small hotel. In truth, it's actually much nicer than a standard hostel and not much more expensive (especially if you share a three- or four-bed room). The rooms are basic, with no TV or much of anything else, but are quiet and clean, with adjoining bathrooms.

If noise is an issue, ask for a quieter room overlooking the back garden. It's one tram stop (Ortenovo náměstí) from the Nádraží Holešovice train and metro station.

Absolutum Hotel BOUTIQUE HOTEL €€

(Map p96; 222 541 406; www.absolutumhotel.cz; Jablonského 639/4; s/d 1800/2600Kč; P ⊖ ❄ @ ; M Nádraží Holešovice, 6, 12, Praha-Holešovice) A highly recommended, eye-catching boutique hotel, the Absolutum is located across from Nádraží Holešovice metro station. While the industrial neighbourhood wouldn't win a beauty contest, the hotel compensates with a nice list of amenities, including smartly designed rooms with exposed brickwork, well-appointed modern bathrooms (some rooms have a tub), air-conditioning, an excellent restaurant, a wellness centre and free parking.

The friendly receptionist is sometimes willing to cut rates if you happen to arrive on a slow night. The hotel restaurant is close enough to Praha-Holešovice train station that you could jump over for a quick meal if you have to wait for a train.

Parkhotel Praha HOTEL €€

(Map p96; 225 117 861; www.parkhotel-praha.cz; Veletržní 20; s/d/ste from 1800/2200/3000Kč; P ⊖ @ ; 6, 17) The owners play on the current mania for all thing retro by embracing the hotel's futuristic, communist-era architecture and airy '70s-style lobby. The rooms come in two sizes – 18 and 25 sq metres – and two classes, with the higher-end 'Maple' rooms offering better views and higher-end amenities like robes and slippers.

Plaza Alta Hotel HOTEL €€

(Map p96; 220 407 011; www.plazahotelalta.com; Ortenovo náměstí 22; s/d from 1800/2400Kč; P ⊖ ❄ @ ; M Nádraží Holešovice, 6, 12) The snazziest hotel in this part of town draws mostly business clientele and travellers looking for a full-service property within easy reach (one tram stop) of the Praha-Holešovice train station and the Nádraží Holešovice metro station. The rooms have a tasteful contemporary look, with comfy mattresses and bold, striped bedspreads. All rooms have air-conditioning and minibar.

It's great value if you manage to snag a good deal on the hotel's website. The '7 Tacos' restaurant off the lobby (open until 11pm) serves Mexican food and is not a bad option if you're arriving late and don't have the energy to go back out.

Bubeneč & Dejvice

While the pensions and hotels in Bubeneč and Dejvice can't offer amenities like window views of Prague Castle, they tend to be cheaper than properties in the centre. The western parts of Bubeneč and Dejvice have another big advantage: they're within easy reach of the airport. Metro and tram connections to the centre are generally very good.

Pension Patanka PENSION €

(602 151 558; www.patanka.cz; Paťanka 4; s/d 700/1200Kč; 8, 18) This family-run guesthouse is the perfect spot if you're looking to save money and don't care too much about a central location. The pension's position, on the northern fringe of Bubeneč, is ideal for a hike in Divoká Šárka park (p109), a tram ride away from anything else. It's simple, friendly, spotlessly clean and there's a restaurant on-site.

Hotel Meda HOTEL €

(Map p98; 603 373 242; www.hotelmeda.cz; Národní Obrany 33, Dejvice; s/d from 1400/1800Kč; P ⊖ @ ; M Dejvická) This small, family-run hotel in a turn-of-the-century apartment building on a quiet side street has been thoroughly renovated and represents excellent value for money. Rooms have nice thick mattresses, flat-screen TVs, minibars and high-speed wi-fi. The location has always been a plus, just a few minutes' walk to the Dejvická metro stop, as well as convenient to the airport.

Hotel International HOTEL €€

(Map p98; 296 537 111; www.internationalprague.cz; Koulova 15, Dejvice; d from €80; P; 8, 18) This stunning socialist realist palace was built in the 1950s in the style of Moscow University, complete with Soviet star atop the tower. The rooms are mostly standard chain-hotel style, with all the necessities but not many luxuries. The deluxe rooms, on the higher floors, are more spacious and have good views over the city.

The building itself is really something special, covered in polished marble, bas-reliefs and frescoes of the noble worker. The socialist-style 'luxury' extends to the beautiful lobby. Tram 5 or 8 can take you to the city centre in about 15 minutes.

Art Hotel BOUTIQUE HOTEL €€

(Map p98; 233 101 331; www.arthotel.cz; Nad Královskou oborou 53, Bubeneč; s/d from 1700/2500Kč; P; 1, 8, 12, 25, 26) There are lots of word-of-mouth recommendations for this small, well-managed hotel in a normally quiet neighbourhood behind Generali Aréna, where Sparta Praha plays football (soccer). The hotel has sleek, modern styling, with a display of contemporary Czech art in the lobby and art photography in the rooms. The location, behind the stadium, is tricky to find the first time.

Smíchov & Vyšehrad

Smíchov has gone upmarket in recent years and now boasts some of the city's nicest hotels. While it's not truly within easy walking distance of the centre (despite what hotel brochures might say), the metro connection from Anděl is excellent and puts you at Můstek, at the foot of Wenceslas Square, in 10 minutes.

Ibis Praha Malá Strana HOTEL €

(Map p102; 221 701 700; www.ibishotel.com; Plzeňská 14, Smíchov; r from €70; P; M Anděl) Offering a little splash of the neighbourhood's more upscale properties, but at half the price. Never mind that it's nowhere near Malá Strana (but nice try by the marketing department), Smíchov's Ibis hotel is a great addition to the neighbourhood. The rooms are standard-issue, but they have air-conditioning and free wi-fi. Breakfast not included. It's an easy walk to public transport.

Hotel Arbes HOTEL €

(Map p102; reception 251 116 555; www.hotelarbes.cz; Viktora Huga 3, Smíchov; s/d from 1800/2000Kč; P; M Anděl) Clean, quiet and excellent value, the Arbes is a down-to-earth tonic to the high-rise, flashier hotels in Smíchov. The hotel is family-run and friendly, and the rooms are basic, with modern furnishings and clean bathrooms. Ask for a courtyard room if noise is an issue. There's limited street parking, but there's paid parking near the hotel (per night 375Kč).

Anděl's By Vienna House BOUTIQUE HOTEL €€

(Map p102; 296 889 688; www.viennahouse.com; Stroupežnického 21, Smíchov; r from €110; P; M Anděl) This sleek designer hotel, all stark contemporary in white with black and red accents, has floor-to-ceiling windows, in-room music players and modern art in every room. The bathrooms are a wonderland of polished chrome and frosted glass. The website offers packages with significant discounts from the rack rate. The location is a short walk from the Anděl metro station.

Red & Blue Design Hotel HOTEL €€

(Map p102; 220 990 100; www.redandbluehotels.com; Holečkova 13, Smíchov; s/d from €90/110; ; 9, 12, 15, 20) This designer boutique sports 26 rooms done out in tasteful red highlights and 26 in blue. The setting is a smartly renovated 19th-century townhouse. The overall style might be termed contemporary minimalist, though the lobby cafe-bar is a riot of colour. Whichever colour scheme, the rooms are similar, with thick carpets, modern furnishings and baths, and air-conditioning.

Hotel Julian HOTEL €€

(Map p102; 257 311 144; www.hoteljulian.com; Elišky Peškové 11, Smíchov; s/d from €105/130; P; 9, 12, 15, 20) This deservedly popular small hotel has helpful staff and a quiet location south of Malá Strana. The smart, well-kept bedrooms are decorated with relaxing pastels and pine-topped furniture. The public areas include a clubby drawing room with a library. If you're travelling with kids, there are family rooms that can accommodate up to six people. There's also a wheelchair-accessible room.

Eating

In the last decade the number, quality and variety of Prague's restaurants has expanded beyond all recognition. You can now enjoy a wide range of international cuisine, from Afghan to Argentinian, Korean to

Vietnamese, and even expect service with a smile in the majority of eating places. However, don't let this kaleidoscope of cuisines blind you to the pleasures of good old-fashioned Czech grub.

Prague Castle & Hradčany

Most of the restaurants in the castle district are aimed squarely at the tourist crowds, though there are a few which are a cut above the rest in regards to character and cuisine and are worth seeking out. The whole area becomes pretty quiet in the evenings after the castle closes.

Malý Buddha ASIAN €

(Map p44; 220 513 894; www.malybuddha.cz; Úvoz 46; mains 100-300Kč; noon-10.30pm Tue-Sun; ; 22) Candlelight, incense and a Buddhist shrine characterise this intimate, vaulted restaurant that tries to capture the atmosphere of an oriental tearoom. The menu is a mix of Asian influences, with authentic Thai, Chinese and Vietnamese dishes, many of them vegetarian, and a drinks list that includes ginseng wine, Chinese rose liqueur and all kinds of tea. Credit cards are not accepted.

Host INTERNATIONAL €€

(Map p44; 728 695 793; www.hostrestaurant.cz; Loretánská 15; mains 325-425Kč; 11.30am-10pm Mon-Sat, to 9pm Sun; ; 22) Hidden away down a narrow staircase between streets, Host impresses with its sleekly modern dining room, decorated with old monochrome photos, and the stunning view from its outdoor terrace. Friendly staff will guide you through a competent menu that ranges from steaks and burgers to traditional Czech dishes to Asian favourites such as spring rolls and Thai-style prawn stir-fry.

Villa Richter CZECH, FRENCH €€

(Map p44; 702 205 108; www.villarichter.cz; Staré zamecké schody 6; mains 150-300Kč, 3-course dinner 945Kč; 11am-11pm Mar-Oct; M Malostranská) Housed in a restored 18th-century villa in the middle of a replanted medieval vineyard, this place is aimed squarely at the hordes of tourists thronging up and down the Old Castle Steps. But the setting is special – outdoor tables on terraces with one of the finest views in the city – and the menu of classic Czech dishes doesn't disappoint.

If you want something fancier, the Piano Nobile restaurant (open year-round) with in the villa itself offers a French-influenced fine-dining menu.

Lobkowicz Palace Café CAFE €€

(Map p44; 233 312 925; Jiřská 3; mains 200-300Kč; 10am-6pm; ; 22) This cafe, housed in the 16th-century Lobkowicz Palace, is the best eatery in the castle complex by an imperial mile. Try to grab one of the tables on the balconies at the back – the view over the city is superb, as is the goulash. The coffee is good too, and service is fast and friendly.

U Zlaté Hrušky CZECH €€

(Map p44; 220 941 244; www.restauranturlatehrusky.cz; Nový Svět 3; mains 390-490Kč; 11am-1am; 22) 'At the Golden Pear' is a cosy, wood-panelled gourmets' corner, serving Bohemian fish, fowl and game dishes and frequented by locals and visiting dignitaries as well as tourists (the Czech foreign ministry is just up the road, and Margaret Thatcher once dined here). In summer get a table in its leafy *zahradní restaurace* (garden restaurant) across the street.

Malá Strana

You'll be spoilt for choice looking for somewhere to eat in Malá Strana. The tourist crowds are joined by hungry office workers from the district's many embassies and government offices, and this well-heeled clientele ensures that there are lots of quality restaurants offering a wide range of cuisines. Many of the best restaurants take advantage of a riverside location, or are perched on a hillside with a view over the city.

Café Lounge CZECH €

(Map p50; 257 404 020; www.cafe-lounge.cz; Plaská 8; mains 150-390Kč; 7.30am-10pm Mon-Fri, 9am-10pm Sat, 9am-5pm Sun; ; 9, 12, 15, 20, 22) Cosy and welcoming, Café Lounge sports an art-deco atmosphere, superb coffee, exquisite pastries and an extensive wine list. The all-day cafe menu offers freshly made salads and sandwiches, while lunch and dinner extends to dishes such as braised rabbit with dumplings, or vegetable moussaka. Great breakfasts too (served until 11am weekdays, all day on weekends).

Cukrkávalimonáda EUROPEAN €

(Map p50; 257 225 396; www.cukrkavalimonada.com; Lázeňská 7; mains 100-200Kč; 9am-7pm; 12, 15, 20, 22) A cute little cafe-restaurant that combines minimalist modern styling with Renaissance-era painted timber roof-beams,

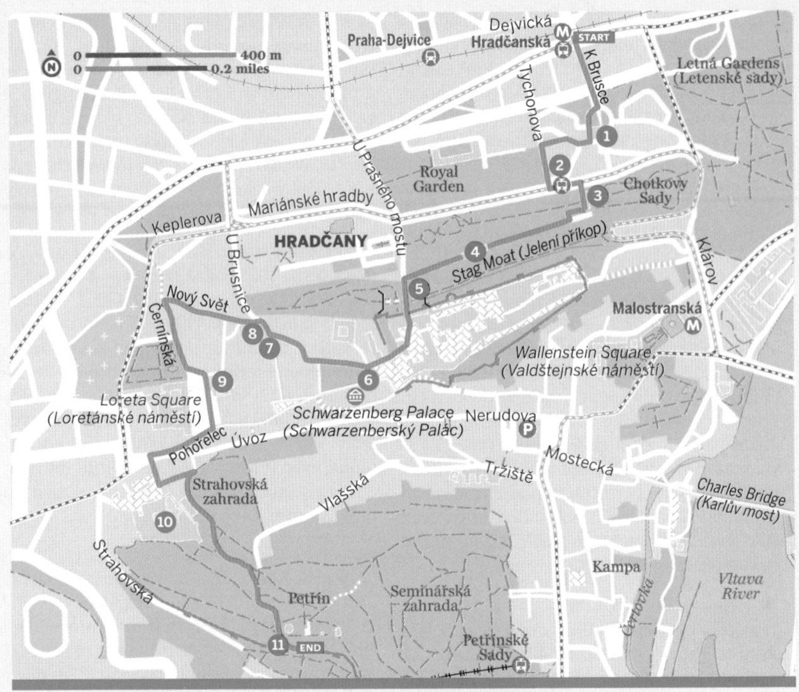

City Walk
Castle Gardens & Hradčany Backstreets

START HRADČANSKÁ METRO STATION
END PETŘÍN
LENGTH 2.5KM; ONE HOUR

From the metro station follow K Brusce towards the stone portal of the 1 **Písek Gate**. This baroque gateway, decorated with carved military emblems, was built in 1721 as part of Prague's new fortifications; the streets on either side still follow the outlines of the bastions.

Turn right on U Písecké Brány, and then left onto Tychonova. Here you will pass two 2 **cubist houses** designed by Josef Gočár. Cross Mariánské hradby and enter the Royal Garden (open April to October only) beside the beautiful Renaissance 3 **Summer Palace** (p37).

Turn right, continue past the stunning 4 **Ball-Game House** (p37), and follow the upper rim of the Stag Moat to the western end of the gardens. Go through the gate and turn left to enter the Second Courtyard of Prague Castle via the 5 **Powder Bridge**.

Leave the courtyard via the second gate on the right, which leads into 6 **Hradčany Square**, once the heart of the aristocratic quarter. At the far end bear right on Kanovnická, past the 7 **Church of St John Nepomuk**, built in 1729 by the king of Prague baroque, Kilian Dientzenhofer.

Turn left into Nový Svět, a picturesque cluster of cottages once inhabited by court artisans. 8 **No 1 Nový Svět** was the home of astronomer Tycho Brahe and, after 1600, his successor Johannes Kepler. Turn left on Černínská to the pretty square in front of the extravagantly baroque 9 **Loreta** (p47); opposite is the imposing facade of the Černín Palace, dating from 1692.

Turn right into Pohořelec – a staircase between Nos 8 and 9 leads into the courtyard of 10 **Strahov Monastery** (p47), where you can visit the library before going through the gate at the eastern end of the courtyard into the gardens above Malá Strana. Turn right on the footpath (signposted 'Rozhledna & Bludiště') and finish with a stroll along to the 11 **Petřín Lookout Tower** (p61).

CKL offers fresh, homemade pastas, frittatas, ciabattas, salads and pancakes (sweet and savoury) by day and a slightly more sophisticated bistro menu in the early evening. There's also a good breakfast menu offering ham and eggs, croissants, and yoghurt, and the hot chocolate is to die for.

Since you ask, the name means 'sugar, coffee, lemonade' – the phrase is the Czech equivalent of 'eeny-meeny-miny-moe'.

★Pastař ITALIAN €€

(Map p50; ☎777 009 108; www.pastar.cz; Malostranské nábřeží 1; mains 230-385Kč; ⏰11am-10pm Mon-Thu, to 10.30pm Fri, noon-10.30pm Sat, noon-10pm Sun; 🚊9, 12, 15, 20, 22) This new Italian restaurant has been getting rave reviews from Prague foodies with its combination of freshly made pasta and intense Mediterranean flavours in dishes such as cannelloni filled with pumpkin purée, pecorino Romano and baked almonds. There's an in-house deli so you can take away its homemade pasta and imported Italian cheeses, salamis and wines.

★Ichnusa Botega Bistro ITALIAN €€

(Map p50; ☎605 375 012; www.ichnusabotegabistro.cz; Plaská 5; mains 200-540Kč; ⏰11am-midnight Mon-Fri, 4pm-midnight Sat; 📶; 🚊9, 12, 15, 20, 22) 'Ichnusa' is the ancient name for Sardinia, which is where owner Antonella Pranteddu sources all of the meats, cheeses and wines he serves in this inviting, family-run bistro. Let the server run through the day's starters and mains (we love the prawns with tomato, garlic and red pepper). The grilled tuna is Prague's best. Reservations essential.

★Café Savoy EUROPEAN €€

(Map p50; ☎257 311 562; http://cafesavoy.ambi.cz; Vítězná 5; mains 200-400Kč; ⏰8am-10.30pm Mon-Fri, 9am-10.30pm Sat & Sun; 📶; 🚊9, 12, 15, 20, 22) The Savoy is a beautifully restored belle-époque cafe, with smart, suited waiting staff and a Viennese-style menu of hearty soups, salads, roast meats and schnitzels. There's also a 'gourmet menu' (mains 400Kč to 700Kč) where the star of the show is Parisian steak tartare mixed at your table, and a superb wine list (ask the staff for recommendations).

The Savoy is also a good bet for breakfast, with plenty of healthy choices including a 'Full English', an American breakfast, and eggs cooked half-a-dozen ways.

Bar Bar CZECH, EUROPEAN €€

(Map p50; ☎257 312 246; www.bar-bar.cz; Všehrdova 17; mains 140-305Kč; ⏰11am-11pm; 🚭; 🚊9, 12, 15, 20, 22) This friendly cellar bar is frequented more by locals than tourists, but the healthy-eating menu is chalked on a blackboard in both Czech and English. It ranges from braised beef cheeks with potato and chive mash, to roast trout with lime risotto, with a couple of good veggie alternatives. The weekday lunch menu offers soup and a main course for 156Kč.

Restaurant Nebozízek INTERNATIONAL €€

(Map p50; ☎257 315 329; www.nebozizek.cz; Petřínské sady 411; mains 150-420Kč; ⏰11am-10pm; 🚊Nebozizek) This 17th-century conservatory restaurant halfway up Petřín has a designer interior with lots of pale Nordic furniture and Singapore orchids, as well as a modern international menu seasoned with a few Czech specialities. The views are fabulous, even if the place feels a little touristy.

It's also accessible by footpath, in case you don't want to take the funicular.

Noi THAI €€

(Map p50; ☎257 311 411; www.noirestaurant.cz; Újezd 19; mains 210-325Kč; ⏰11am-1am; 📶; 🚊12, 15, 20, 22) A restaurant that feels more like a club, Noi is super-stylish with a chilled-out atmosphere and oriental design. The decor is based around lotus blossoms, lanterns and soft lighting, and the menu follows the Asian theme with competent Thai dishes such as chicken in red curry, and pad thai noodles, which – unusually for a Prague restaurant – has a hefty chilli kick.

Café de Paris FRENCH €€

(Map p50; ☎603 160 718; www.cafedeparis.cz; Maltézské náměstí 4; mains 245-470Kč; ⏰11.30am-midnight; 🚊12, 15, 20, 22) A little corner of France tucked away on a quiet square, the Café de Paris is straightforward and unpretentious. So is the menu – onion soup or foie gras terrine to start, followed by entrecôte steak with chips, salad and a choice of sauces (they're very proud of the Café de Paris sauce, made to a 75-year-old recipe).

There are also one or two seasonal specials, including a vegetarian alternative.

★Augustine CZECH, EUROPEAN €€€

(Map p50; ☎266 112 280; www.augustine-restaurant.cz; Letenská 12, Augustine Hotel; mains 350-590Kč, 4-course tasting menu 1350Kč; ⏰7am-11pm; 📶; 🚊12, 15, 20, 22) Hidden away in the historic Augustine Hotel (check out the ceiling fresco in the bar), this sophisticated yet relaxed restaurant is well worth seeking out. The menu ranges from down-to-earth but delicious dishes such as pork cheeks braised in the hotel's own St Thomas beer, to inventive dishes built around fresh Czech produce. The two-course business lunch costs 380Kč.

Terasa U Zlaté Studně EUROPEAN, ASIAN €€€
(Map p50; ☎257 533 322; www.terasauzlatestudne.cz; U Zlaté studně 4, Golden Well Hotel; mains 900-1350Kč; ⊙noon-11pm; Ⓜ Malostranská, 🚊12, 15, 20, 22) Perched atop a Renaissance mansion within a champagne cork's pop of the castle, 'At the Golden Well' combines some of Prague's finest dining with one of the finest settings in the city. Weather will dictate whether you sit in the plush dining room or on the outdoor terrace – both command a stunning panorama across the red-tiled rooftops of Malá Strana.

The kitchen, which has French, Mediterranean and Asian influences, conjures up dishes such as Canadian lobster on cuttlefish risotto, and its signature dish of Argentinian steak with foie gras and truffles.

Hergetova Cihelná MEDITERRANEAN, ASIAN €€€
(Map p50; ☎296 826 103; www.kampagroup.com; Cihelná 2b; mains lunch 200-400Kč, dinner 400-700Kč; ⊙11.30am-4pm & 6pm-1am; 📶 👪; Ⓜ Malostranská) Housed in a converted 18th-century *cihelná* (brickworks), this place enjoys one of Prague's hottest locations, with a riverside terrace offering sweeping views of Charles Bridge. The menu is as sweeping as the view, ranging from fish and steak to Czech game dishes such as saddle of venison and wild boar ragout. There's also a decent kids menu and play area.

U Modré Kachničky CZECH €€€
(Map p50; ☎257 320 308; www.umodrekachnicky.cz; Nebovidská 6; mains 475-600Kč; ⊙noon-4pm & 6.30pm-midnight; 📶; 🚊12, 15, 20, 22) A plush and chintzy 1930s-style hunting lodge hidden away on a quiet side street, 'At the Blue Duckling' is a pleasantly old-fashioned place with quiet, candlelit nooks perfect for a romantic dinner. The menu is heavy on traditional Bohemian duck and game dishes, such as roast duck with *slivovice* (plum brandy), plum sauce and potato pancakes.

Staré Město

The Old Town is littered with tourist traps, especially around Old Town Square, but there are also plenty of excellent restaurants to discover. The maze of streets leading away from Old Town Square contains many hidden gems, and in recent years Dlouhá street has seen a concentration of top-notch eateries, especially at its eastern end around the new development of Gurmet Pasáž Dlouhá (p163).

★ Mistral Café BISTRO €
(Map p62; ☎222 317 737; www.mistralcafe.cz; Valentinská 11; mains 130-250Kč; ⊙10am-11pm; 📶 👪; Ⓜ Staroměstská) Is this the coolest bistro in the Old Town? Pale stone, bleached birchwood and potted shrubs make for a clean, crisp, modern look, and the clientele of local students and office workers clearly appreciate the competitively priced, well-prepared food. Fish and chips in crumpled brown paper with lemon and black-pepper mayo – yum!

Naše Maso STEAK €
(Our Meat; Map p62; ☎222 311 378; http://nasemaso.ambi.cz; Dlouhá 39; mains 80-215Kč; ⊙8.30am-1pm Mon-Sat; 🚊6, 8, 15, 26) 🍃 Little more than a clutch of stand-up tables at the front of a butchers shop, this place is at the forefront of Prague's rush to embrace the foodie philosophy of high-quality, locally sourced meat. The menu offers some of the best steak tartare, hamburger and handmade sausages you'll taste in the city – expect to queue at lunchtime.

Lokál CZECH €
(Map p62; ☎222 316 265; http://lokal-dlouha.ambi.cz; Dlouhá 33; mains 115-235Kč; ⊙11am-1am Mon-Sat, noon-midnight Sun; 📶; 🚊6, 8, 15, 26) Who'd have thought it possible? A classic Czech beer hall (albeit with slick modern styling); excellent *tankové pivo* (tanked Pilsner Urquell); a daily-changing menu of traditional Bohemian dishes; and smiling, efficient, friendly service! Top restaurant chain Ambiente has turned its hand to Czech cuisine, and the result has been so successful that the place is always busy, mostly with locals.

Maitrea VEGETARIAN €
(Map p62; ☎221 711 631; www.restaurace-maitrea.cz; Týnská ulička 6; mains 200-240Kč, weekday lunch 135Kč; ⊙11.30am-11.30pm Mon-Fri, noon-11.30pm Sat & Sun; 🌿 👪; Ⓜ Staroměstská) Maitrea (a Buddhist term meaning 'the future Buddha') is a beautifully designed space full of flowing curves and organic shapes, from the sensuous polished-oak furniture and fittings to the blossom-like lampshades. The menu is inventive and wholly vegetarian, with dishes such as Tex-Mex quesadillas, spicy goulash with wholemeal dumplings, and spaghetti with spinach, crispy shredded tofu and rosemary pesto.

Banh Mi Makers VIETNAMESE €

(Map p62; ☎732 966 621; www.facebook.com/banhmimakers; Hradební 1; mains 80-120Kč; ⏰11am-10pm Mon-Fri, noon-9pm Sat; ; 🚋6, 8, 15, 26) This small and friendly fast-food joint bakes its own *banh mi* (crusty baguette rolls) fresh on the premises twice daily, and serves them with a range of tasty fillings such as grilled duck with soy and sesame. Wash one down with iced jasmine tea.

Home Kitchen INTERNATIONAL €

(Map p62; ☎774 905 802; www.homekitchen.cz; Kozí 5; mains 160-200Kč; ⏰8am-10pm Sun-Wed, to 11pm Thu-Sat; Ⓜ Staroměstská) Chunky timber tables, bare brick and industrial light fittings set the scene around the central open kitchen here, where the conceit is that there is no menu – you choose from the range of dishes available that day, displayed on a side table. The food is simple, hearty and very, very good – burgers with honey barbecue sauce and herb dumplings, roast pork knuckle with pumpkin purée.

Pho Viet VIETNAMESE €

(Map p62; ☎777 724 489; Národní třída 25; mains 70-120Kč; ⏰10am-11pm; Ⓜ Národní Třída) Tucked away in the far corner of a shopping arcade, this unassuming little place serves up fresh *nem tuoi* (prawn rolls) and aromatic *pho* (beef and noodle soup with coriander) with searingly hot chillis. No prizes for decor – think workers' canteen – but the price/tastiness ratio can't be beat.

Country Life VEGETARIAN €

(Map p62; ☎224 213 366; www.countrylife.cz; Melantrichova 15; mains 90-180Kč; ⏰10.30am-7.30pm Mon-Thu, to 3.30pm Fri, noon-6pm Sun; ; Ⓜ Můstek) Prague's first-ever health-food shop opened in 1991, and is now an all-vegan cafeteria and sandwich bar offering inexpensive salads, sandwiches, pizzas, vegetarian goulash, sunflower-seed burgers and soy drinks (food is sold by weight, around 30Kč per 100g). There is plenty of seating in the rear courtyard but it can still get crowded at lunchtime; go early or buy sandwiches to go.

Bakeshop Praha BAKERY €

(Map p62; ☎222 316 823; www.bakeshop.cz; Kozí 1; sandwiches 75-200Kč; ⏰7am-9pm; Ⓜ Staroměstská) This fantastic bakery sells some of the best bread in the city, along with pastries, cakes and takeaway sandwiches, wraps, salads and quiche. Very busy at lunchtime.

Culinaria DELICASTESSEN €

(Map p62; www.culinaria.cz; Skořepká 9; mains 100-200Kč; ⏰8am-7pm; ; Ⓜ Národní Třída) This health-food delicatessen sells handmade bread, pastries, homemade soup and freshly made sandwiches, lasagne, salads and a good range of vegetarian dishes.

★**La Bottega Bistroteka** ITALIAN €€

(Map p62; ☎222 311 372; www.bistroteka.cz; Dlouhá 39; mains 265-465Kč; ⏰9am-10.30pm Mon-Sat, to 9pm Sun; 🚋6, 8, 15, 26) You'll find smart and snappy service at this stylish deli-cum-bistro, where the menu makes the most of all that delicious Italian produce artfully arranged on the counter; the beef cheek cannelloni with parmesan sauce and fava beans, for example, is just exquisite. It's best to book, but you can often get a walk-in table at lunchtime.

Divinis ITALIAN €€

(Map p62; ☎222 325 440; www.divinis.cz; Týnská 21; mains 400-550Kč; ⏰noon-3pm Mon-Fri, 6pm-midnight Mon-Sat; 🚋6, 8, 15, 26) This restaurant has a playful decor in shades of cream enlivened with feature mirrors and splashes of cerise, and a homely clutter of shelves stacked with books, vases and odds and ends. The uncomplicated menu offers a choice of around eight starters and main courses, from king crab salad with cucumber ice cream, to veal osso buco with gremolata and garlic risotto.

Kafka Snob Food ITALIAN €€

(Map p62; ☎725 915 505; www.facebook.com/kafkasnobfood; Široká 12; mains 150-300Kč; ⏰8am-10pm; ; Ⓜ Staroměstská) A favourite hang-out for fashion-conscious employees of the Old Town's many designer boutiques, this smoky bistro models a self-consciously hip look that combines turquoise-painted panelling and tan leather banquettes with brushed steel ducting and painted brick. The menu offers authentically Italian pasta and risotto dishes, plus great cakes and coffee. And no, we don't know what the name means either.

Indian Jewel INDIAN €€

(Map p62; ☎222 310 156; www.indianjewel.cz; Týn 6; mains 300-400Kč; ⏰11am-11pm; ; Ⓜ Staroměstská) A long, vaulted room in a medieval building makes an elegant setting for one of Prague's best Indian restaurants, with marble floors, chunky wooden chairs, copper tableware and restrained oriental decor. Tables spill into the courtyard in summer. The food impresses, too, with light and flaky parathas, richly spiced sauces and plenty of fire in the hotter curries.

Vino di Vino ITALIAN €€

(Map p62; ☎222 311 791; www.vinodivinopraha.cz; Štupartská 18; mains 290-530Kč; ⏲11.30am-10pm Mon-Fri, noon-10.30pm Sat & Sun; 📶; Ⓜ Náměstí Republiky) This Italian wine shop and delicatessen doubles as a restaurant, with a menu that makes the most of all those imported goodies – bresaola with smoked mozzarella, spaghetti with scampi, pistachios and saffron sauce, and rabbit stuffed with olives and Italian sausage. There's a good list of Italian wines too, including excellent Montepulciano d'Abbruzzo (from 610Kč a bottle).

Monarch Gastrobar TAPAS €€

(Map p62; ☎224 239 602; www.monarch.cz; Na Perštýně 15; tapas 70-190Kč, mains 260-380Kč; ⏲5pm-midnight Mon-Sat; Ⓜ Národní Třída) The Monarch is one of the best tapas bars in town (the Argentinian head chef previously ran a Michelin-starred restaurant in Spain). The menu extends beyond mere tapas to take in paella, octopus, calamari and roast suckling lamb, and the wine list is one of the most extensive in town (including a good range of cava and champagne).

Ambiente Pizza Nuova ITALIAN €€

(Map p62; ☎221 803 308; www.pizzanuova.ambi.cz; Revoluční 1; mains 200-500Kč; ⏲11.30am-11.30pm; 📶👪; Ⓜ Náměstí Republiky) This cool 1st-floor space filled with big tables and banquettes with picture windows overlooking náměstí Republiky showcases a good idea from the Ambiente team: for a fixed price (298Kč per person before 6pm, 385Kč after) you get an all-you-can-eat pasta and pizza deal. (Adding an antipasti buffet to the pizza-pasta deal costs 485/578Kč.) Wine by the glass is 88Kč to 198Kč.

Lehká Hlava VEGETARIAN €€

(Map p62; ☎222 220 665; www.lehkahlava.cz; Boršov 2; mains 200-240Kč; ⏲11.30am-11.30pm Mon-Fri, noon-11.30pm Sat & Sun; 🌶👪; 🚋2, 17, 18) Tucked away down a narrow cul-de-sac, Lehká Hlava (the name means 'clear head') exists in a little world of its own. There are two exotically decorated dining rooms, both with a vaguely psychedelic vibe – tables lit from within, studded with glowing glass spheres or with a radiant wood-grain effect. In the kitchen the emphasis is on healthy, freshly prepared vegetarian and vegan dishes.

Kolkovna CZECH €€

(Map p62; ☎224 819 701; www.vkolkovne.cz; V Kolkovně 8; mains 120-390Kč; ⏲11am-midnight; 📶; Ⓜ Staroměstská) Owned and operated by the Pilsner Urquell Brewery, Kolkovna is a stylish, modern take on the traditional Prague pub, with decor by top Czech designers, and posh (but hearty) versions of classic Czech dishes such as goulash, roast duck and Moravian sparrow, as well as the Czech favourite, roast pork knuckle. All washed down with exquisite Urquell beer, of course.

U Prince INTERNATIONAL €€

(Map p62; ☎737 261 842; www.hoteluprince.com; Staroměstské náměstí 29; mains 230-550Kč; ⏲11am-11pm; Ⓜ Můstek) Guests are offered the standard array of Caesar and chef salads, plus burgers, grilled chicken breast and other ubiquitous mains; nevertheless, the focus here was never intended to be on the plate, but rather the awesome view over Old Town Square. Book your terrace seat well in advance.

★ **Field** CZECH €€€

(Map p62; ☎222 316 999; www.fieldrestaurant.cz; U Milosrdných 12; mains 590-620Kč, 6-course tasting menu 2800Kč; ⏲11am-2.30pm & 6-10.30pm Mon-Fri, noon-3pm & 6-10.30pm Sat, noon-3pm & 6-10pm Sun; 🚋17) 🍃 Prague's third Michelin-starred restaurant is its least formal and most fun. The decor is an amusing art-meets-agriculture blend of farmyard implements and minimalist chic, while the chef creates painterly presentations from the finest of local produce along with freshly foraged herbs and edible flowers. You'll have to book at least a couple of weeks in advance to have a chance of a table.

★ **Kalina** FRENCH €€€

(Map p62; ☎222 317 715; www.kalinarestaurant.cz; Dlouhá 12; mains 500-900Kč; ⏲noon-3pm & 6-11.30pm; 📶; 🚋6, 8, 15, 26) Setting a trend for taking the best of fresh Czech produce and giving it the French gourmet treatment, this smart but unfailingly friendly little restaurant offers dishes such as Prague snails with beef marrow and parsley purée, and roast sweetbreads with glazed salsify and black truffles. Weekday lunch specials are good value at 150Kč to 300Kč.

V Zátiší CZECH, INDIAN €€€

(Map p62; ☎222 221 155; www.vzatisi.cz; Liliová 1; 2-/3-course meal 990/1190Kč; ⏲noon-3pm & 5.30-11pm; 📶; 🚋2, 17, 18) 'Still Life' is one of Prague's top restaurants, famed for the quality of its cuisine. The decor is bold and modern, with quirky glassware, boldly patterned wallpapers and cappuccino-coloured crushed-velvet chairs. The menu ranges from high-end Indian cuisine to gourmet versions of traditional

Czech dishes – the South Bohemian duck with white cabbage and herb dumplings is superb.

If the three-course dinner is not enough, you can lash out on the five-course dégustation menu (1490Kč; plus 790Kč extra for wine pairings).

Francouzská Restaurace FRENCH €€€
(Map p62; 222 002 770; www.francouzskarestaurace.cz; Náměstí Republiky 5, Municipal House; mains 695Kč; noon-11pm; M Náměstí Republiky) The French Restaurant in the Municipal House (p72) is a stunning art-nouveau dining room offering gourmet cuisine, from caviar and foie gras to lobster bisque and saddle of veal. It's hugely popular with visitors, so book to avoid disappointment. The à la carte menu is complemented by a two-/three-course set menu for 1050/1350Kč.

George Prime Steak STEAK €€€
(Map p62; 226 202 599; http://georgeprimesteak.com; Platnéřská 19; mains bar 200-400Kč, restaurant 600-1100Kč; noon-2.30pm & 6-10.30pm; ; M Staroměstská) The 100% Black Angus USDA Prime Beef imported from the American Midwest is the name of the game here, whether you order a charcoal-broiled T-bone steak in the elegant surroundings of the main restaurant, or opt for a house burger in the less formal bar. The presence on the menu of the 999Kč 'Oligarch Burger' (with foie gras and gold leaf) gives a clue as to the target market.

Bellevue INTERNATIONAL €€€
(Map p62; 224 221 443; www.bellevuerestaurant.cz; Smetanovo nábr 18; mains 845Kč, 3-course set menu 1490Kč; 11am-11pm; ; 2, 17, 18) Book a table on the terrace and come to enjoy the fabulous views of the river and castle while tucking into gourmet cuisine. Bellevue offers a Eurasian choice of dishes from roasted veal loin in black-truffle crust to New Zealand lamb chops marinated in lemon thyme. Best value is the three-course set menu.

Nové Město

The New Town has an eclectic collection of eating places, with cafes and traditional Czech pubs as well as a range of international restaurants. The main eating areas are Wenceslas Square and Na Příkopě, lined with restaurants offering cuisines from across the world; there are also lots of less obvious and more appealing eateries hidden in the backstreets between Wenceslas Square and the river. Since the opening of Sansho in northern Nové Město in 2011, the area around Petrské náměstí has sprouted several good eating places.

Styl & Interier CAFE €
(Map p78; 222 543 128; www.stylainterier.cz/kavarna; Vodičkova 35; mains 100-200Kč; 9.30am-9pm Mon-Sat, to 8pm Sun; ; 3, 5, 6, 9, 14, 24) A passage opposite the Vodičkova entrance to the Lucerna Palace leads to this secret retreat, a rustic cafe with a high-walled garden where local shoppers gather in wicker armchairs beneath the trees to enjoy coffee and cake, or a lunch of lasagne, quiche and salad, or slow-cooked lamb with red wine gravy. Best to book a table.

Maso a Kobliha GASTROPUB €
(Map p84; 224 815 056; www.masoakobliha.cz; Petrská 23; mains 185-210Kč; 9am-4pm Tue, to 10pm Wed-Fri, 10am-4pm Sat & Sun; ; 3, 8, 14, 24) Established by the British chef at Sansho, across the street, this pub-style eatery (and butcher shop; the name means 'Meat and Doughnuts') serves hearty pub-style food prepared using locally grown, seasonal, organic produce – it's famous for its Scotch eggs, beef shin pies and freshly made doughnuts filled with vanilla cream. All-day brunch at weekends.

U Ferdinanda CZECH €
(Map p78; 775 135 575; www.ferdinanda.cz; cnr ulice Opletalova & Politických Vězňů; mains 150-250Kč; 11am-11pm Mon-Sat; M Muzeum) Welcome to a thoroughly modern spin on a classic Czech pub with beer courtesy of the Ferdinand brewery from nearby Benešov. Quirky gardening implements in corrugated iron decorate the raucous interior, and a younger local clientele crowds in for well-prepared and well-priced traditional Czech food.

Globe Bookstore & Café CAFE €
(Map p78; 224 934 203; www.globebookstore.cz; Pštrossova 6; mains 150-300Kč; 10am-11pm; ; M Karlovo Náměstí) This appealing expat bookshop-cafe serves nachos, burgers, chicken wings and salads until 11pm nightly, and also offers an excellent brunch menu (9.30am to 3pm Saturday and Sunday) that includes an American classic (bacon, egg and hash browns), full English fry-up, blueberry pancakes and freshly squeezed juices. Lighter breakfasts are served from 10am to noon weekdays.

★ **Room** SPANISH €€

(Map p78; ☎221 634 103; www.tapasroom.cz; V Jámě 6, Icon Hotel; tapas 80-250Kc; ⏰bar 7am-1am, tapas 11am-11pm; 📶; 🚋3, 5, 6, 9, 14, 24) Cool, angular and precise in shades of grey, black and avocado green, Room provides the perfect setting for some of Prague's most carefully crafted flavours. With an accomplished kitchen team working from a menu created by actor Tommy Lee Jones's personal chef, it's no surprise that the food – *gambas pil pil,* Argentinian beef skewers, grilled octopus with fava beans – is top-notch.

★ **Sansho** ASIAN, FUSION €€

(Map p84; ☎222 317 425; www.sansho.cz; Petrská 25; lunch mains 190-245Kč, 6-course dinner 900-1200Kč; ⏰11.30am-2pm Tue-Fri, 6-11pm Tue-Sat, last orders 10pm; 📶; 🚋3, 8, 14, 24) 🌿 'Friendly and informal' best describes the atmosphere at this groundbreaking restaurant where British chef Paul Day champions Czech farmers by sourcing all his meat and vegetables locally. There's no menu as such – the waiter will explain what dishes are available, depending on market produce. Typical dishes include curried rabbit, pork belly with watermelon and hoisin, and 12-hour beef rendang. Reservations recommended.

The gastropub Maso a kobliha, just across the road, was established by the same chef.

Black Dog Cantina TEX-MEX €€

(Map p78; ☎735 750 050; www.blackdogs.cz; Gorazdova 1; mains 180-300Kč; ⏰11am-midnight Mon-Fri, noon-midnight Sat, noon-10pm Sun; 📶👪; Ⓜ Karlovo Náměstí) Black Dog's super-tasty and fiery-hot Tex-Mex food blew a few minds (and taste buds) when it first opened in the provincial town of Beroun in 2010. It has now finally made the move to Prague with this big, buzzy informal eatery offering a mouth-watering menu of chipotle-marinated barbecue pork ribs, chilli con carne, chicken wings, burgers and steaks.

Art Restaurant Mánes FRENCH, CZECH €€

(☎730 150 772; www.manesrestaurant.cz; Masarykovo nábřeží 1; mains 285-525Kč; ⏰11am-midnight; 🚋5, 17) Hidden around the back of the striking late-1920s functionalist facade of the Mánes Gallery (p86), this gorgeous restaurant manages to be both welcoming and sophisticated, its angular art-deco lines decorated with original ceiling frescoes by avant-garde Czech artist Emil Filla. The menu has strong French influences, but also lends a gourmet touch to a handful of Czech classics.

Mangal TURKISH €€

(Map p78; ☎222 210 382; www.mangalrestaurant.cz; Václavské náměstí 64; mains 150-400Kč; ⏰11am-11pm Mon-Sat, noon-11pm Sun; 📶👪; Ⓜ Muzeum) An unexpected sanctuary just a few paces from the brash bustle of Wenceslas Square, this family restaurant is 100% authentically Turkish, from the sizzling kebabs and meatballs to the crisp and savoury *pide* (Turkish 'pizza' filled with minced lamb and/or cheese).

Brasserie La Gare FRENCH €€

(Map p84; ☎222 313 712; www.lagare.cz; V Celnici 3; mains 265-525Kč; ⏰8am-midnight; 📶👪; Ⓜ Náměstí Republiky) It might not impress a Parisian, but La Gare is a passable imitation of a bustling French brasserie, offering classics such as fish soup, frog legs, coq au vin and bœuf Bourguignon. Downstairs is Brasserie Sklep, an Alsace-themed cellar serving *tartes flambées,* a traditional, wood-fired Alsatian dish that resembles a thin and crispy pizza. Family-friendly breakfast is served daily from 8am to 11am.

Al Forno ITALIAN €€

(Map p84; ☎222 316 011; www.al-forno.cz; Petrské náměstí 4; mains 175-500Kč; ⏰11am-11pm; 📶; 🚋3, 8, 14, 24) As the name suggests ('al forno' means 'cooked in the oven'), this rustic Italian place with warm yellow walls, old wooden furniture and checked tablecloths sports a wood-fired oven that turns out authentic pizza, focaccia, lasagne, cannelloni and a range of roast meat dishes. There's a wide choice of reasonably priced Italian wines, and desserts include tiramisu and panna cotta.

Café Imperial INTERNATIONAL €€

(Map p84; ☎246 011 440; www.cafeimperial.cz; Na poříčí 15; mains 225-385Kč; ⏰7am-11pm; 📶; Ⓜ Náměstí Republiky, 🚋3, 8, 14, 24) First opened in 1914, and given a complete facelift in 2007, the Imperial is a tour de force of art-nouveau tiling – the walls and ceiling are covered in original ceramic tiles, mosaics, sculptured panels and bas-reliefs, with period light fittings and bronzes scattered about. The menu ranges from American breakfasts to Czech classics to roast quail.

Lemon Leaf ASIAN €€

(Map p78; ☎224 919 056; www.lemon.cz; Myslíkova 14; mains 160-240Kč; ⏰11am-11pm Mon-Fri, noon-11pm Sat & Sun; 📶; 🚋5) It's a bit off the beaten tourist path, but with its high-ceilinged rooms, atmospheric lighting and arty photographs, the Lemon Leaf is certainly making an effort to pull in the visitors. And it's worth a visit for excellent, authentic Thai dishes, including a rich and fragrant green curry with a decent kick of chilli heat.

Klub Cestovatelů MIDDLE EASTERN €€
(Map p78; ☎734 322 729; www.klubcestovatelu.cz; Masarykovo nábřeží 22; mains 200-330Kč; ⊙11am-11pm Mon-Thu, to midnight Fri, noon-midnight Sat, noon-10pm Sun; 📶📝👪; 🚋5, 17) This restaurant and tearoom cultivates a relaxed and welcoming atmosphere, with its wicker chairs, oriental knick-knacks and library of travel guidebooks. The menu is mostly Lebanese – baba ganoush, falafel, hummus and lamb kebabs – with a couple of Indian dishes thrown in. There's also a huge range of speciality teas to choose from.

Siam Orchid THAI €€
(Map p84; ☎222 319 410; www.siamorchid.cz; Na poříčí 21; mains 180-320Kč; ⊙10am-10pm; 📶; 🚋3, 8, 14, 24) The setting – a scatter of plastic tables and chairs on a 1st-floor balcony hidden up a passage beside a department store – looks none too promising, but this tiny restaurant, tucked away beside a Thai massage studio, offers some of the city's most authentic Thai cuisine.

From the crisp, grease-free *po-pia thot* (spring rolls with pork and black mushrooms) to the fiery *kaeng khiao wan kai* (chicken in green curry with basil), pretty much everything on the menu is a delight.

Kogo ITALIAN €€
(Map p84; ☎221 451 259; www.kogo.cz; Slovanský dům, Na příkopě 22; mains 250-680Kč; ⊙11am-11pm; 📶👪; Ⓜ Náměstí Republiky) Chic and businesslike, but also relaxed and family-friendly (highchairs provided), Kogo is a stylish restaurant serving top-notch pizza, pasta, and Italian meat and seafood dishes – the rich, tomatoey *zuppa di pesce* (fish soup) is delicious, as is the *risotto alla pescatora* (made with squid, mussels, shrimp and octopus). On summer evenings, candle-lit tables filled with conversation spill over into the leafy courtyard.

Ginger & Fred FRENCH €€€
(Map p78; ☎221 984 160; www.ginger-fred-restaurant.cz; 7th fl, Rašínovo nábřeží 80, Dancing Building; mains 300-700Kč; ⊙11.30am-11pm; 📶; Ⓜ Karlovo Náměstí) Located on the 7th floor of the spectacular Dancing House (p86), Ginger & Fred's dining room and outdoor terrace offer stunning views across the river to Malá Strana and Prague Castle. The atmosphere is crisply formal and the cuisine is French, with the accent on seafood and meat dishes (only one vegetarian main course on the menu here).

Vinohrady & Vršovice

Outside the centre, Vinohrady has Prague's largest concentration of good restaurants, and the choice is only getting better as the area continues to move upmarket. Most are clustered around náměstí Míru and residential street Mánesova, which parallels Vinohradská from the Muzeum to Jiřího z Poděbrad metro stops.

Vinohradský Parlament CZECH €
(Map p88; ☎224 250 403; www.vinohradskyparlament.cz; Korunní 1, Vinohrady; mains 180-250Kč; ⊙11am-midnight Mon-Wed, to 1am Thu-Sat, 11.30am-11.30pm Sun; 📶; Ⓜ Náměstí Míru) This clean, bright and well-run pub features both a handsome early-modern, art-nouveau interior and a daring, inventive cooking staff who are willing to look beyond the standard pork and duck to other traditional Czech staples such as goose, rabbit and boar. Perfect for both lunch and dinner, but phone ahead to book a table as it's often jammed.

Dish BURGERS €
(Map p88; ☎222 511 032; www.dish.cz; Římská 29, Vinohrady; burgers 170-210Kč; ⊙11am-11pm Mon-Sat, noon-10pm Sun; 📶; Ⓜ Náměstí Míru) The burger wars are heating up, but Dish has emerged as the city's favourite. The 'Dish' burger is a classic bacon and cheese, but other varieties feature mushrooms, lamb, red beets or even highly aromatic cheese from Olomouc. The homemade buns are shiny, brioche-style. The chips (fries) are served with inventive sauces like lime-cilantro mayonnaise. Reservations essential.

The Tavern BURGERS €
(Map p88; www.eng.thetavern.cz; Chopinova 26, Vinohrady; burgers 140-200Kč; ⊙11.30am-10pm Mon-Fri, brunch from 11am Sat & Sun; 📶; Ⓜ Jiřího z Poděbrad, 🚋11, 13) This cosy sit-down burger joint is the dream of a husband-and-wife team of American expats who wanted to create the perfect burger using organic products and free-range, grass-fed beef. Great pulled-pork sandwiches, fries and bourbon-based cocktails too. Reservations are taken (via the website) for dinner on Thursday, Friday and Saturday only.

Javánka & Co INDONESIAN €

(Map p88; ☎223 013 630; www.facebook.com/javankaandco; Máchova 22, Vinohrady; mains 130-180Kč; ⏱11am-10pm Mon-Fri, noon-9pm Sun, closed Sat; 📶🌶; 🚋4, 22) Simple, good-value Indonesian food, such as a fragrant rendang (slow-cooked beef), served in a casual, family-friendly atmosphere. There's lots on offer for vegetarians and the home-baked pies and cakes are impossible to resist for dessert. Queue up at the bar to order during lunch; dinners feature a more orderly table service. Reservations are essential at any time of day.

Cafe Jen BREAKFAST €

(Map p88; ☎reservations 604 329 904; www.cafe-jen.cz; Kodaňská 37; mains 80-120Kč; ⏱7.30am-8pm Mon-Fri, 9am-6pm Sat & Sun; 📶🌶👪; 🚋4, 22) This warm, inviting bakery and cafe is best known for its big, good-value breakfasts and friendly vibe. Arrive early and prepare to queue on Saturday and Sunday mornings (or reserve, though you'll likely still have to wait). Other days, the pace is more tranquil.

Plevel VEGETARIAN €

(Map p88; ☎273 160 041; www.restaurace plevel.cz; Krymská 2, Vršovice; mains 135-185Kc; ⏱10am-midnight Mon-Sat, to 10pm Sun; 📶🌶; 🚋4, 22) This warm, rustic spot with big wooden tables and exposed beams opened in 2013 to cement the Krymská corridor as the centre of Prague hipsterdom. It has arguably the best hummus in the city and many other great choices, like vegan kebabs and grilled peppers. Daily lunch specials.

Cafe Sladkovský INTERNATIONAL €

(Map p88; ☎776 772 478; www.cafesladkovsky.cz; Sevastopolská 17, Vršovice; mains 135-160Kč; ⏱10am-1am Mon-Fri, 5pm-1am Sat, 11am-1am Sun; 📶🌶; 🚋4, 22) Every Prague neighbourhood could use a Cafe Sladkovský. By day, a quiet spot to meditate over a meal of tapas, burgers, or falafel and hummus; by night, the same great food, but more of a party or pub vibe, filled with students and neighbours. The interior is old-school Viennese cafe, with high ceilings, tiled floors and faded print wallpaper.

Las Adelitas MEXICAN €

(Map p88; ☎222 542 031; www.lasadelitas.cz; Americká 8, Vinohrady; mains 150-200Kč; ⏱11am-midnight Mon-Fri, from noon Sat & Sun; 📶🌶; Ⓜ Náměstí Míru) This small, informal restaurant run by a group of friends from Mexico offers the closest thing to authentic Tex-Mex you're likely to find in Prague. Delicious tacos, burritos and enchiladas are crafted with love from handmade tortillas. The ambience is a little sterile, but no one is here for a candlelit dinner – just very good, good-value nosh.

Madame Lyn VIETNAMESE €

(Map p88; ☎606 307 777; www.facebook.com/madamelynrestaurant; Šafaříkova 18, Vinohrady; mains 130-230Kč; ⏱11am-10pm Mon-Fri, from noon Sat & Sun; 📶🌶; Ⓜ IP Pavlova, 🚋6, 11, 13) Very good Vietnamese and Thai restaurant. The daily luncheon specials offer good value, as do the hearty *pho bo* (beef noodle) and *pho ga* (chicken noodle) soups, and the fresh and fried spring rolls. The service is friendly and attentive. The clean and bright modern interior is a step up from the usual Vietnamese restaurant in Prague.

Pho Vietnam Tuan & Lan VIETNAMESE €

(Map p88; www.facebook.com/photuanlan; Slavíkova 1, Vinohrady; mains 80-120Kč; ⏱10am-10pm; 🌶; Ⓜ Jiřího z Poděbrad) This stand-up Vietnamese joint gets jammed at lunchtime for arguably the best *pho* in the immediate vicinity, and at reasonable prices. Snippets from the menu include spicy beef with green beans, and beef with *pho bo* rice noodles. There are plenty of items for vegetarians. Takeaway available.

Ha Noi VIETNAMESE €

(Map p88; ☎222 521 430; www.restaurace hanoi.webnode.cz; Slezská 57, Vinohrady; mains 80-150Kč; ⏱10am-10pm Mon-Fri, 2-11pm Sat; Ⓜ Jiřího z Poděbrad, 🚋10, 16) Ha Noi was one of the first Vietnamese restaurants to open in Prague and is still one of the best. Decent spring rolls, both fresh and fried, and two types of seasoned *pho* are on offer. The unremarkable set-up – just a few wooden tables and oriental kitsch – make it better suited to a hearty lunch than a special night out.

Pizzeria Grosseto ITALIAN €

(Map p88; ☎224 252 778; www.grosseto.cz; Francouzská 2, Vinohrady; mains 130-230Kč; ⏱11.30am-11pm; 📶🌶; Ⓜ Náměstí Míru) This bustling Vinohrady pizzeria serves very good pizzas, with inventive toppings such as asparagus and ricotta cheese, as well as homemade pastas and original desserts. The garden terrace at the back is a secluded hideaway and something of a local secret.

Mozaika Burger & Co BURGERS €

(Map p88; ☎725 422 862; www.mozaikaburger.cz; Nitranská 13, Vinohrady; burgers 185-225Kč;

⌚5pm-midnight Tue-Fri, noon-11pm Sat & Sun; 📶; Ⓜ Jiřího z Poděbrad) Artisanal burgers ground on the premises from Uruguayan beef. The house 'Mozaika' comes topped with cheese, mushrooms and homemade mayo, while the 'Hell' burger eschews the local preference for mild food, going for spicy mangoes and habanero peppers. The setting is upscale for a burger joint. Advance book for evening meals.

Café FX VEGETARIAN €

(Map p88; ☎603 193 711; www.radostfx.cz; Bělehradská 120, Vinohrady; mains 120-250Kč; 📶 ✍; Ⓜ IP Pavlova) For more than two decades Café FX has been a vegetarian beacon in the gritty but slowly gentrifying neighbourhood surrounding the IP Pavlova metro station. The food – mostly salads, Mexican, stir-fries and veggie burgers – is reliably good, though the menu has changed little since opening day.

Loving Hut VEGETARIAN €

(Map p88; ☎222 515 006; www.lovinghut.cz; Londýnská 35, Vinohrady; mains under 100Kč; ⌚11am-9pm Mon-Sat; 📶 ✍; Ⓜ Náměstí Míru, IP Pavlova) Part of a citywide chain of no-alcohol vegan/vegetarian restaurants. The menu includes items such as curry soup, vegetarian sushi and other Asian-inspired vegetarian dishes. There's a great-value self-service buffet on weekdays from 11am to 4pm.

★**Osteria Da Clara** ITALIAN €€

(Map p88; ☎271 726 548; www.daclara.com; Mexická 7, Vršovice; mains 200-350Kč; ⌚11am-3pm & 6-11pm Mon-Fri, noon-3.30pm & 6-11pm Sat, noon-4pm Sun; 📶 ✍; 🚊4, 22) This minuscule Tuscan-style trattoria offers some of the most authentic and best-value Italian cooking in the city, though it will take a good map to find the place. The menu varies, but expect a handful of creative pasta dishes and main courses built around duck, beef, pork and seafood. Reserve in advance – there are only a few tables.

Bad Jeff's BARBECUE €€

(Map p88; ☎774 402 235; www.badjeffs.cz; Americká 32, Vinohrady; mains 175-365Kč; ⌚6-11pm Mon, noon-3pm & 6-11pm Tue-Fri, noon-11pm Sat; 📶 ✍; Ⓜ Náměstí Míru) Owner and head chef Jeff Cohen vowed to bring American-style barbecue to Prague and has largely succeeded. Diners enjoy relative rarities like shrimp and grits (cornmeal), Southern (US)-style chicken and the house pride and joy: slow-cooked barbecued beef brisket. The minimalist interior feels more upscale than you'd expect from a BBQ joint, making it a nice choice for a special dinner.

Restaurace U Bulínů CZECH €€

(Map p88; ☎224 254 676; www.ubulinu.cz; Budečská 2, cnr Francouzká, Vinohrady; mains 190-300Kč; ⌚11am-11pm; 📶 👪; Ⓜ Náměstí Míru, 🚊4, 22) Delicious traditional Czech cooking served in a clean, warm setting. This is the place to try duck liver pâté, rabbit, venison, *strapačky* (small flour-potato dumplings often served with sheep's cheese) and other local specialities, cooked by a kitchen that knows what it's doing. There's a small terrace at the back. Book in advance.

Originál 1869 CZECH €€

(Restaurace Kravín; Map p88; ☎222 540 524; www.restauracekravin.cz; náměstí Míru 18, Vinohrady; mains 140-395Kč; ⌚11am-midnight Mon-Thu, to 1.30am Fri, noon-1.30am Sat, noon-11pm Sun; 📶; Ⓜ Náměstí Míru) The Gambrinus brewery purchased and renovated this long-time traditional pub on a corner of náměstí Míru, giving it a fresh coat of paint, a swanky modern interior and a new lease on life. Daily lunch specials of Czech favourites such as grilled chicken livers or pork schnitzels are excellent value. It's slightly fancier (and pricier) at night, but still fun.

Kofein SPANISH €€

(Map p88; ☎273 132 145; www.ikofein.cz; Nitranská 9, Vinohrady; 3 tapas plates about 270Kč; ⌚11am-midnight Mon-Fri, from 5pm Sat & Sun; 📶 ✍; Ⓜ Jiřího z Poděbrad, 🚊11, 13) One of the hottest restaurants in town is this Spanish-style tapas place not far from the Jiřího z Poděbrad metro station. Descend into a lively space to see a red-faced chef minding the busy grill. Local faves include marinated trout with horseradish and pork belly confit with celeriac. Service is prompt and friendly. Book ahead.

Zelená Zahrada CZECH €€

(Map p88; ☎222 518 159; www.zelena-zahrada.eu; Šmilovského 12, Vinohrady; mains 150-390Kč; ⌚11am-11.30pm Sun-Thu, to 1am Fri & Sat; 📶; Ⓜ Náměstí Míru, 🚊4, 22) This secluded, upscale restaurant draws a star-studded crowd, including on at least one occasion – judging by the photos on the wall – crooner Karel Gott. Book in advance to snag one of the coveted garden seats. There are great luncheon specials, including a very good beef tartare served with capers for 165Kč.

U Bílé Krávy STEAK €€

(Map p88; ☎224 239 570; www.bilakrava.cz; Rubešova 10, Vinohrady; mains 180-450Kč; ⌚11.30am-11pm Mon-Fri, 5-11pm Sat; Ⓜ Muzeum, IP Pavlova) This French-run, Lyonnais-styled bistro has some of the best steaks at the best prices in town. The name 'White Cow' refers to the Charollais breed of white cows from Burgundy, the source of the restaurant's signature steaks. Added charms include an authentic bistro feel and an excellent wine selection.

Pastička CZECH €€

(Map p88; ☎222 253 228; www.pasticka.cz; Blanická 25, Vinohrady; mains 150-330Kč; ⌚11am-1am Mon-Fri, noon-midnight Sat; 📶; Ⓜ Jiřího z Poděbrad, 🚊11, 13) A warm, inviting ground-floor pub with a little garden out the back, Pastička is great for a beer or a meal. The interior design is part 1920s Prague and part Irish pub. Most come for the beer, but the mix of international and traditional Czech dishes is very good.

Aromi ITALIAN €€€

(Map p88; ☎222 713 222; www.aromi.cz; Náměstí Míru 6, Vinohrady; mains 400-600Kč; ⌚noon-3pm & 5-11pm Mon-Sat, noon-10pm Sun; 📶; Ⓜ Náměstí Míru) High ceilings, polished parquet floors and stylish, contemporary decor make this one of the city's prime venues to see and be seen. Aromi has a well-earned reputation for authentic, excellent Italian cuisine, at a price. The mood is brisk and businesslike at lunchtime, romantic in the evening. Advance booking essential.

Ristorante Sapori ITALIAN €€€

(Map p88; ☎222 523 533; www.saporirestaurace.cz; Americká 20, Vinohrady; mains 225-550Kč; ⌚11am-11pm; Ⓜ Náměstí Míru) This elegant Italian restaurant is the best in the immediate vicinity for a proper tablecloth dinner with all the trimmings. Local favourites include the calamari with arugula garlic and cherry tomatoes. Offers daily lunch specials with mains priced around 150Kč. Handsome light decor with hardwood floors; excellent wine list.

Žižkov & Karlín

Žižkov is more famous for its pubs than its restaurants, but there are new places springing up every year to add to the stalwarts that have been around for ages. As well as the restaurants, it's worth checking out Pivovarský Klub (p152), a drinking venue that serves good traditional pub grub.

In the last few years Karlín's restaurant scene has really taken off, with some of the city's best new restaurants and cafes. And don't miss the neighbourhood's weekly farmers market for a more laid-back alternative to Nové Město's Náplavka.

★ Můj Šálek Kávy CAFE €

(Map p92; ☎725 556 944; www.mujsalekkavy.cz; Křižíkova 105, Karlín; mains 80-160Kč; ⌚9am-10pm Mon-Sat, 10am-6pm Sun; 📶👪; Ⓜ Křižíkova) A symbol of Karlín's up-and-coming, neighbourhood-to-watch status, 'My Cup of Coffee' uses Direct Trade beans prepared by expert baristas, and serves what is probably the city's best caffeine hit. Add on a friendly, laid-back atmosphere and superb breakfast and lunch dishes, and you can see why it's often full – reservations are recommended at weekends.

Lokál Hamburk CZECH €

(Map p92; ☎222 310 361; http://lokal-hamburk.ambi.cz; Sokolovská 55, Karlín; mains 150-220Kč; ⌚11am-midnight Mon-Thu, to 1am Fri, noon-1am Sat, noon-11pm Sun; 📶👪; 🚊3, 8, 24) The success of the original Lokál (p125) in Stáre Město has seen the winning formula transferred to Karlín – basically a traditional, family-friendly neighbourhood pub with excellent tanked Pilsner Urquell and a crowd-pleasing menu of classic pub grub including hamburger, steak tartare, schnitzel and goulash.

Café Pavlač CAFE €

(Map p92; ☎222 721 731; www.cafepavlac.cz; Víta Nejedlého 23, Žižkov; mains 120-200Kč; ⌚10am-11pm Mon-Fri, 11am-11pm Sat & Sun; 📶👪; 🚊5, 9, 15, 26) This smart and stylish cafe-bar is emblematic of the new Žižkov, forsaking spit-and-sawdust earthiness for designer metalwork, edgy art and architectural magazines. It serves excellent coffee and hot chocolate, and the food menu runs from breakfast (ham and eggs, croissants or muesli with yoghurt), to lunch specials, to dinner dishes of pasta, salads and steaks.

Restaurace Akropolis INTERNATIONAL €

(Map p92; ☎296 330 990; www.palacakropolis.com; Kubelíkova 27, Žižkov; mains 110-270Kč; ⌚11am-10pm; 📶🌶👪; 🚊5, 9, 15, 26) The cafe in the famous Palác Akropolis club is a Žižkov institution, with its eccentric combination of marble panels, quirky metalwork light fittings and weird fish tank installations designed by local artist František Skála. The menu has a good selection of vegetarian dishes, from salads to gnocchi, plus great fajitas, searingly hot buffalo wings and steak tartare. It can be smoky inside.

★Nejen Bistro BISTRO €€
(Map p92; ☎222 960 515; www.nejenbistro.cz; Křižíkova 24, Karlín; mains 200-380Kč; ⏲10am-11pm; 🚊3, 8, 24) Nejen (Not Only) is emblematic of the new breed of restaurant that is transforming Karlín into one of Prague's hottest neighbourhoods, its quirky interior nominated for a slew of design awards. But just as much attention is lavished on the food, which makes the most of the kitchen's fancy Josper grill, turning out superb steaks, beef ribs and Nejen's signature Black Angus burger.

Eska CZECH €€
(Map p92; ☎731 140 884; www.eska.ambi.cz; Pernerova 49, Karlín; mains 140-350Kč; ⏲11.30am-3pm & 5.30-11.30pm Mon-Fri, 9am-11.30pm Sat & Sun; 📶✍; Ⓜ Křižíkova) Part of a beautifully converted warehouse that now houses gleaming modern offices, Eska is a combined artisanal bakery and industrial-chic restaurant that does some very original and interesting things with the most basic of Czech ingredients – potatoes cooked in ash with smoked fish, dried egg yolk and kefir (yoghurty grains) is an Eska classic. Excellent brunch served at weekends.

Krystal Bistro BISTRO €€
(Map p92; ☎222 318 152; www.krystal-bistro.cz; Sokolovská 99, Karlín; mains 240-465Kč; ⏲11.30am-3pm & 5-11pm Mon-Fri, noon-11pm Sat & Sun; Ⓜ Křižíkova) The first of the new wave of restaurants to open in Karlín back in 2010, Krystal remains popular for its unpretentious way with fine food, adding a twist of French sophistication to quality local produce. This is one of the best places in town to order the classic Czech dessert *švestkový kynutý knedlík* (plum dumplings).

Indian by Nature INDIAN €€
(Map p92; ☎222 968 622; www.ibn-restaurant.cz; Pernerova 1, Karlín; mains 220-320Kč; ⏲11am-11pm Mon-Thu, to 11.30pm Fri, noon-11.30pm Sat, noon-10pm Sun; 📶✍; 🚊3, 8) Prague's selection of Indian and Pakistani restaurants just keeps getting better, and this place – hidden away in a corner of Karlín – is one of the best. Classic curry dishes are fragrant with fresh herbs and zinging with ginger, chilli and spices, while the authentic tandoor turns out tender chicken tikka and fluffy naan breads. All-you-can-eat buffet 11am to 3pm weekdays.

Kuře V Hodinkách CZECH, INTERNATIONAL €€
(Map p92; ☎222 734 212; www.kurevhodinkach.eu; Seifertova 26, Žižkov; mains 160-330Kč; ⏲11am-1am; 📶; 🚊5, 9, 15, 26) This music-themed pub is decked out in rock memorabilia, and with a choice of buzzing street-level bar or more intimate brick-vaulted basement, it's more upmarket than most Žižkov pubs and has a classy kitchen to match. The menu includes chicken Caesar salad, barbecued steak with Dijon mustard sauce, and a rich, dark and tasty goulash with bacon dumplings.

The pub is named after a 1972 album by Czech jazz-rock band Flamengo, which was banned by the communist authorities (it means 'Chicken in the Watch' – hey, it was the '70s, psychedelic drugs and all that...).

Hanil JAPANESE, KOREAN €€
(Map p92; ☎222 715 867; www.hanil.cz; Slavíkova 24, Žižkov; sushi per piece 70-120Kč, mains 320-560Kč; ⏲11am-2.30pm & 5.30-11pm Mon-Sat; Ⓜ Jiřího z Poděbrad) White walls, lattice screens, paper lanterns and polished granite tables create a relaxed and informal setting where a mixed crowd of businesspeople, locals and expats enjoys authentic Japanese and Korean cuisine. Tuck into a bowl of *bibimbap* (rice topped with meat and pickled vegetables spiced with hot pepper paste), or order a sashimi platter – the sushi here is among the best in town.

Holešovice

Holešovice is known around town as something of a culinary wasteland (and that's not far from the truth). There are some notable exceptions, but for the most part you're likely to eat here only if you happen to be staying somewhere nearby. The busy area around the tram hub at Strossmayerovo náměstí offers the best selection.

Phill's Corner INTERNATIONAL €
(Map p96; ☎731 836 988; www.facebook.com/phillscornercafe; Komunardů 32; mains 100-180Kč; ⏲7.30am-10pm Mon-Fri, 9am-6pm Sat & Sun; 📶✍; 🚊1, 6, 12, 14, 25) This tight, airy corner restaurant draws design inspiration from Holešovice's industrial past and its culinary cues from kitchens around the world, including Asia and the Middle East. The menu is well marked for food allergies, and there are

ample gluten-free and other choices available. The daily lunch menu of soup and main course for around 150Kč is a great deal.

Tràng An Restaurace VIETNAMESE €
(Map p96; ☎220 560 041; www.facebook.com/asijskebistropodosmickou; Bubenské nábřeží 306, Bldg 5, Holešovická tržnice/Pražská tržnice; mains 100-130Kč; ⏲9am-7pm Mon-Sat; 🚊1, 12, 14, 25) This low-key Vietnamese restaurant is the single best reason to trundle out to the sprawling Holešovická tržnice (p168). Line up with everyone else at the counter and choose from a large picture menu on the wall. There's plenty of indoor seating and outside picnic tables in nice weather. Try to visit before or after typical meal times to avoid a wait.

Mr Hot Dog HOT DOGS €
(Map p96; ☎732 732 404; www.mrhotdog.cz; Kamenická 24; hot dogs 80-100Kc; ⏲11.30am-10pm; 🚊1, 8, 12, 25, 26) The city's leader in the global push for gourmet hot dogs. It has excellent regular and chilli dogs as well as sliders (mini hamburgers) and cheese fries. Eat in or take away. The location is handy for dropping in before or after a sojourn at the nearby Letná Beer Garden (p153).

Bistro 8 INTERNATIONAL €
(Map p96; ☎777 871 878; www.facebook.com/bistro8; Veverkova 8; ⏲8am-9.30pm Mon-Fri, 10am-4pm Sat & Sun; 📶; 🚊1, 6, 8, 12, 17, 25, 26) This tiny bistro, bakery and cafe solidifies this tiny street's claim to being the coolest spot in Holešovice. The menu consists mainly of fresh-made soups and sandwiches, plus a tempting array of cakes and excellent coffees. There are a few tables inside and some sidewalk spots to sit in nice weather.

Bohemia Bagel AMERICAN €
(Map p96; ☎220 806 541; www.bohemiabagel.cz; Dukelských hrdinů 48; mains 120-210Kč; ⏲10am-11pm; 📶; 🚊6, 17) This hamburger, bagel and breakfast outfit remains the best all-round place to grab a light meal in this barren stretch (at least from a culinary standpoint) of Holešovice. It has a popular brunch on weekends and inexpensive daily lunch specials, such as baked cod or grilled peppers (around 140Kč), on weekdays.

Letenský Zámeček CZECH €€
(Brasserie Ullmann; Map p96; ☎233 378 208; www.letenskyzamecek.cz; Letenské sady 341; mains 175-395Kč; ⏲11am-11pm; 📶; 🚊1, 8, 12, 25, 26) An upscale brasserie occupying the ground floor of a 19th-century chateau next to the Letná Beer Garden (p153). It's open year-round but comes into its own from May to September, with the terrace open and the spires of the Old Town stretching out in the distance. The kitchen is strong on Czech specialities such as rabbit confit and beef in cream sauce with dumplings.

Sasazu ASIAN €€
(Map p96; ☎284 097 455; www.sasazu.com; Bubenské nábřeží 306, Hall 25, Pražská tržnice; mains 220-460Kč; ⏲noon-midnight Sun-Wed, to 1am Thu-Sat; 📶; Ⓜ Vltavská, 🚊1, 12, 14, 25) This upmarket Asian restaurant (connected to the club of the same name) has by many accounts the best high-end Asian-fusion cooking in Prague. While prices for individual entrées are not outrageous for what's on offer, portions are on the small side. Book in advance, especially on weekends.

Peperoncino ITALIAN €€
(Map p96; ☎233 312 438; www.restaurant-peperoncino.cz; Letohradská 34; mains 180-390Kč; ⏲11am-11pm; 📶🖉; 🚊1, 8, 12, 25, 26) The insider's choice for good, reasonably priced Italian cooking in the western end of Holešovice. The grilled octopus and beans starter is a neighbourhood favourite, but the beef or tuna carpaccio is also reliably good. The pastas and main courses are all excellent, and the wine list has lots of affordable Czech and Italian choices. Beautiful, bucolic garden in summer. Reservations recommended.

Molo 22 INTERNATIONAL €€
(Map p96; ☎220 514 612; www.molo22.cz; U Průhonu 22; mains 160-360Kč; ⏲11am-11pm; 📶; 🚊6, 12) This Staropramen brewery–run restaurant has a clean, modern interior and an upscale international menu of Caesar salads, chicken wraps, pastas and steaks. It draws a lively lunch crowd on work days, and makes for a decent dinner before a night spent clubbing at nearby nightspots.

Pivovar Marina CZECH, ITALIAN €€€
(Map p96; ☎220 571 183; www.pivovarmarina.cz; Jankovcova 12; mains 260-650Kč; ⏲11am-midnight; 📶; 🚊6, 12) An unlikely but welcome combination: an excellent Czech microbrewery and the best Italian cooking in eastern Holešovice. For beers, the wheat beer and 10° *Přístavní* lager are certainly worth trying. The food includes high-end pastas and mains such as lamb chops served with pea purée and roast potatoes. During the warmer months, the outdoor tables afford relaxing views over the river.

ALEXABELOV/GETTY IMAGES ©

J. LEKAVICIUS/SHUTTERSTOCK ©

1. Charles Bridge (p54)
The famous baroque statues on medieval Charles Bridge stare down with stony indifference on buskers, jazz bands and postcard sellers.

2. Wenceslas Square (p77)
A silent witness to a great deal of Czech history, the fall of communism was announced in Wenceslas Square in 1989.

3. John Lennon Wall (p59)
Following his murder in 1980, John Lennon became a pacifist hero for many young Czechs and his image was painted on this wall. The original painting is long gone, but the wall now features other Lennon images, peace messages and inconsequential tourist graffiti.

4. Vintage Trams (p108)
Trams dating from the early 20th century trundle along a special route in the city.

3

TOM PERKINS/GETTY IMAGES ©

1. Puppets
Puppetry is an old Czech tradition and many towns and cities have marionette shows on offer.

2. Prague Castle (p36)
The changing of the guard at Prague Castle takes place every hour on the hour.

3. Church of St Nicholas (p70)
The Church of St Nicholas in Staré Město's Old Town Square was built in the 1730s by Kilian Dientzenhofer.

4. Prague (p32)
Prague offers a range of dance and performance art entertainment.

3

ROSSHELEN/SHUTTERSTOCK ©

Bubeneč & Dejvice

For a relatively prosperous, residential part of town, there are few – if any – true destination restaurants in these parts. That said, there are plenty of good neighbourhood spots to grab a bite, including some of the best pub food in the city.

★**Restaurace U Veverky** CZECH €
(Map p98; ☎603 781 997; www.uveverky.com; Eliášova 14, Dejvice; mains 139-240Kč; ⊙11am-11pm; Ⓜ Hradčanská) This highly rated traditional pub has some of the best-tasting and best-value lunches in the city and is worth a detour. The set-up is classic, with a drinking room out the front and two big dining rooms in the back. The restaurant is filled with the welcoming smell of grilled onions and beer. Reserve in advance.

Âu Cơ VIETNAMESE €
(Map p98; ☎721 056 639; www.facebook.com/aucovietnamrestaurant; Studentská 1, Dejvice; mains 130-200Kč; ⊙10am-9.30pm Mon-Sat; 📶📝; Ⓜ Dejvická) Dejvice's best Vietnamese restaurant is situated on a quiet corner, close to both the Technical University and metro station. The beef and chicken *pho* are standouts, prepared by a long-time star chef in the Vietnamese community. The casual interior is geared more towards lunch than a candlelit dinner; try to book in advance if you're arriving around noon.

Lokál Nad Stromovkou CZECH €
(Nad Královskou Oborou; Map p98; ☎220 912 319; www.ambi.cz; Nad Královskou oborou 31, Bubeneč; mains 115-210Kč; ⊙11.30am-midnight Mon-Thu & Sat, to 1am Fri, to 11pm Sun; 📶; 🚊1, 8, 12, 25, 26) This lovingly restored, traditional Czech pub is part of the Lokál chain, which has a commitment to high-quality ingredients and, naturally, perfectly tended Pilsner Urquell beer. The menu features simple Czech cooking, such as grilled trout or chicken schnitzels, done well. Pair a visit here with a stroll through nearby Stromovka park. Book in advance.

Na Urale CZECH €
(Map p98; ☎224 326 820; www.dejrest.cz/na-urale; Uralská 9, Dejvice; mains 120-230Kč; ⊙11am-midnight; 📶; Ⓜ Dejvická, 🚊8, 18) Na Urale has greatly cleaned up its act in recent years, adding beautiful crimson walls and stone-tile floors, to spruce up what had been an ordinary pub. The kitchen has also had an upgrade, but the prices for well-done Czech dishes (such as goulash and roast pork) are barely higher than at a typical workers' pub.

U Mě Dobrý CZECH €
(Map p98; ☎739 162 490; Bubenečská 16, Bubeneč; mains 90-150Kč; ⊙11am-midnight Mon-Sat, to 10pm Sun; Ⓜ Hradčanská) This popular neighbourhood pub and beer garden has a welcoming atmosphere and very good 11° Svijany on tap for a bargain 35Kč. The menu includes many simple, home-cooked Czech specialities, such as *pečené hovězí* (roast beef and gravy) and the house goulash served on a potato pancake. The garden makes for a welcome respite in summer.

YamYam ASIAN €
(Map p98; ☎774 844 446; www.yamyam.cz; Mařákova 8, Dejvice; mains 125-195Kč; ⊙11am-11pm; 📶📝; Ⓜ Hradčanská) This warm, inviting Thai-influenced Asian spot serves well-prepared curry, rice and noodle dishes, featuring shrimp, duck, chicken and beef as well as a nice range of vegetarian options. The mixed appetiser plate, with tiger prawns, chicken satay and fresh spring rolls, is big enough for a meal in itself. Daily lunch specials offer an appetiser and main for around 140Kč.

Argument INTERNATIONAL €€
(Map p98; ☎607 075 487; www.argument-restaurant.cz; Bubenečská 19, Bubeneč; mains 225-500Kč; ⊙11.30am-11.30pm Mon-Sat; 📶; Ⓜ Hradčanská) Upscale dining in Prague 6 that perennially gets mentioned alongside the city's best restaurants, with a strong suit being steaks and fresh seafood. There's no defining culinary theme here, more a hodgepodge of international favourites plus a terrific burger. The interior is classy but still casual. Reserve in advance.

Café Záhorský INTERNATIONAL €€
(Map p98; ☎724 969 911; www.cafezahorsky.cz; Eliášova 1, Dejvice; mains 165-225Kč; ⊙8am-11pm Mon-Fri, 9am-11pm Sat, 10am-8pm Sun; 📶; Ⓜ Hradčanská) This airy, modern-minimalist space is more than just a place to grab a quick cup. There's a big French-inspired bakery on the premises, and the menu is especially strong on breakfasts, salads and sandwiches. The highly praised, monochrome black-and-white interior is enlivened by colourful red and cream chairs strewn about, lending an Instagram-inspired filter effect.

Bistro à Table FRENCH €€

(Map p98; ☎211 152 619; www.facebook.com/atablebistro; Mařákova 10, Dejvice; mains 150-300Kč; ⏰7.30am-11pm Mon-Fri, 10am-11pm Sat; 📶; Ⓜ Hradčanská) As the name implies, this is traditional French bistro food – think soups, salads and steak frites – served in a bright, upbeat setting of big wooden tables and white walls. Ideal for lunch or a bite in the evening if you happen to be staying nearby, though not necessarily worth a trip across town. Excellent table wines available. Book in advance.

Vozovna Stromovka INTERNATIONAL €€

(Map p98; ☎725 123 705; www.vozovna-stromovka.cz; Královská obora 2, Bubeneč; mains 160-280Kč; ⏰10am-7pm; 📶👪; 🚋12, 17) This garden restaurant in the middle of Stromovka park is often standing-room-only with mums and dads, while kids play in the adjacent playground. The menu borrows heavily from around Europe, with spicy ground beef from the Balkans next to grilled salmon and a very good paella with chorizo sausage. The location is about 200m west of Prague Planetarium.

Nahoře a Dole INTERNATIONAL €€

(Kavárna Nahoře a Restaurace Dole; Map p98; ☎727 891 986; www.nahoreadole.cz; Na Hutích 9, Dejvice; mains 140-280Kč; ⏰restaurant 11.30am-11pm Mon-Sat, cafe 9am-midnight Mon-Thu, 9am-1am Fri, 2pm-midnight Sat, 5pm-midnight Sun; 📶; Ⓜ Dejvická, 🚋8, 18, 20, 26) Walk down a flight of stairs to find this handsome, contemporary restaurant serving a welcome mix of Czech and international dishes, such as leg of rabbit pâté served with pistachios. The minimalist space, with concrete walls, wood floors, and colourful, playful chairs and tables, sets a trendy tone. Retire to the ground-level cafe for an after-meal espresso.

Kulat'ák CZECH €€

(Map p98; ☎773 973 037; www.kulatak.cz; Vítězné náměstí 12, Dejvice; mains 170-270Kč; ⏰11am-midnight; 📶; Ⓜ Dejvická, 🚋8, 18, 20, 26) The local branch of a Pilsner Urquell–run chain does not disappoint, offering decent Czech cooking in an authentic but spiffed-up pub atmosphere. This is a good place to try specialities such as *svíčková na smetaně* (braised beef with cranberries and dumplings) or *Moravský vrabec* (Moravian 'sparrow' – a cut of roast pork with a side of bread dumplings).

Budvarká CZECH €€

(Map p98; ☎222 960 820; www.budvarkadejvice.cz; Wuchterlova 22, Dejvice; mains 160-320Kč; ⏰11am-midnight; 📶; Ⓜ Dejvická, 🚋8, 18, 20, 26) Handsome Czech pub owned and operated by the Budvar brewery. You'll find the complete 'Budweiser' family of beers here, including the hard-to-find yeast and dark varieties. There's also excellent Czech pub food, heavy on pork and chicken, served in an accurate rendition of a 19th-century taproom.

Sakura JAPANESE €€

(Map p98; ☎774 785 077; www.sakuradejvice.cz; náměstí Svobody 1, Dejvice; mains 200-360Kč; ⏰11am-10pm; 📶👪; Ⓜ Dejvická, 🚋8, 18, 20, 26) This is one of the best sushi places in Prague. It occupies a smart 1930s functionalist building, and the open interior is a blend of contemporary Japanese and Czech modern. The 'volcano' roll features spicy tuna; the 'crunch' roll comes lightly fried, with gently cooked salmon tucked inside. There's a small children's play area.

Da Emanuel ITALIAN €€€

(Map p98; ☎224 312 934; www.daemanuel.cz; Charlese de Gaulla 4, Dejvice; mains 390-530Kč; ⏰11am-11pm Mon-Fri, 9am-11pm Sat & Sun; 📶; Ⓜ Dejvická, 🚋8, 18) This small, elegant Italian restaurant, on a quiet residential street, is one of Dejvice's true destination restaurants. The main dining room, perched romantically below an arched brick ceiling, holds around a dozen tables, each with a vase of fresh flowers. The menu features homemade pastas as well as grilled meats and fish. Book in advance.

Smíchov & Vyšehrad

Of the two districts, Smíchov and Vyšehrad, the former offers more variety. The area around Anděl metro station has exploded with restaurants in recent years. Many are chains, but there are several good, traditional pubs to choose from too. Offerings are more limited in Vyšehrad.

Bejzment BURGERS €

(Map p102; ☎731 406 163; www.bejzment.cz; Lesnická 8, Smíchov; burgers 150-200Kč; ⏰11am-11pm; 📶; Ⓜ Anděl) This popular American-themed burger joint gets crowded at meal times, so be sure to reserve in advance. The burgers, grilled in a smoky kitchen at the back, are some of the best in Prague, but they also serve excellent BBQ chicken wings, hot dogs and Caesar salads.

The US number plates on the wall add a touch of authenticity.

U Bílého lva CZECH €
(Map p102; ☎257 316 731; www.ubileholva.eu; Na Bělidle 30, Smíchov; mains 135-240Kč; ⊗11am-11.30pm; ; M Anděl) There's been a pub here since 1883, and everything at the 'White Lion' certainly feels authentic, down to the hardwood bench seating and shiny taps at the bar. The menu is a greatest hits list of traditional dishes, including local 'Smíchovský' goulash, served with fresh onions on top and big bread dumplings on the side.

U Kroka CZECH €€
(Map p106; ☎775 905 022; www.ukroka.cz; Vratislavova 12, Vyšehrad; mains 170-295Kč; ⊗11am-11pm; ; 2, 3, 7, 17, 21) Cap a visit to historic Vyšehrad Citadel with a hearty meal at this traditional pub that delivers not just excellent beer but very good food as well. Classic dishes like goulash, boiled beef, rabbit and duck confit are served in a festive setting. Daily lunch specials (around 140Kč) are available from 11am to 3pm. Reservations (advisable) are only possible after 3pm.

Rio's Vyšehrad MEDITERRANEAN €€
(Map p106; ☎224 922 156; www.riorestaurant.cz; Štulcova 2, Vyšehrad; mains 250-600Kč; ⊗10am-midnight; ; M Vyšehrad) Located opposite the Church of Sts Peter & Paul, this is an attractive modern restaurant set in an ancient building. There's an elegant indoor dining room, but the main drawcard is the garden, a lovely spot for an outdoor meal in summer. The international gourmet menu includes dishes such as grilled octopus salad, veal saltimbocca and chargrilled Argentinian beef.

Na Verandách CZECH €€
(Map p102; ☎257 191 200; www.phnaverandach.cz; Nádražní 84, Smíchov; mains 150-280Kč; ⊗11am-midnight Mon-Wed, to 1am Thu-Sat, to 11pm Sun; ; M Anděl, 4, 5, 12, 20) This pub and restaurant, managed by the Potrefená husa chain, is inside the Staropramen Brewery, and while lots of people come here to eat, it's perfectly fine to come in just for a super-fresh beer (there are seven varieties on tap). The menu is high-end fast food: ribs, burgers and chicken breasts, as well as standard Czech dishes.

Zlatý Klas CZECH €€
(Map p102; ☎251 562 539; www.zlatyklas.cz; Plzeňská 9, Smíchov; mains 140-280Kč; ⊗11am-11pm Sun-Thu, 11.30am-1am Fri & Sat; M Anděl) This very popular pub and restaurant offers well-done Czech grub such as roast pork, goulash and fried chicken breast in a kitsch but comfortable space. Zlatý klas also offers fresh unpasteurised beer *(tankové pivo)* from Plzeň, a local badge of honour. The service is fast and friendly, but you'll have to book in advance in the evening.

U Míkuláše Dačíckého CZECH €€
(Map p102; ☎257 322 334; www.umikulasedacickeho.com; Victora Huga 2, Smíchov; mains 150-300Kč; ⊗11am-midnight; M Anděl) This is an honest-to-goodness, old-fashioned *vinárna* (wine bar) – complete with traditional atmosphere and excellent local cooking. The food here is classic Czech, with well-prepared roast pork and duck main courses, as well as grilled sausages and goulash. The owners have gone for the 'Ye Olde Middle Ages' look, with dark woods and red tablecloths. Reserve in advance.

Drinking & Nightlife

Bars in Prague go in and out of fashion with alarming speed, and trend spotters are forever flocking to the latest 'in' place only to desert it as soon as it becomes mainstream. The best areas to go looking for good drinking dens include Vinohrady, Žižkov, Karlín, Holešovice, the area south of Národní třída in Nové Město and the lanes around Old Town Square in Staré Město.

Prague Castle & Hradčany

This is a fairly quiet district, with drinking venues limited to laid-back cafes, a couple of traditional pubs and the excellent Klášterní pivovar Strahov.

Klášterní Pivovar Strahov BREWERY
(Strahov Monastery Brewery; Map p44; ☎233 353 155; www.klasterni-pivovar.cz; Strahovské nádvoří 301; ⊗10am-10pm; 22) Dominated by two polished copper brewing kettles, this convivial little pub in Strahov Monastery serves up two varieties of its St Norbert beer – *tmavý* (dark), a rich, tarry brew with a creamy head, and *polotmavý* (amber), a full-bodied, hoppy lager; both cost 65Kč per 0.4L. There's also a strong (6.3% abv) IPA-style beer.

The modern microbrewery opened in 2000 on the site of a monastic brewery that was in operation from 1628 to 1907.

Pivnice U Černého Vola PUB

(Map p44; ☎220 513 481; Loretánské náměstí 1; ⏰10am-10pm; 🚋22) Many religious people make a pilgrimage to the Loreta, but just across the road, the 'Black Ox' is a shrine that pulls in pilgrims of a different kind. This surprisingly inexpensive beer hall is visited by real-ale aficionados for its authentic atmosphere and lip-smackingly delicious draught beer, Velkopopovický Kozel (31Kč for 0.5L), brewed in a small town southeast of Prague.

Kafe U Zelených Kamen BAR

(Map p44; ☎776 282 226; www.uzelenychkamen.cz; Úvoz 6; ⏰11am-8pm; 📶; 🚋12, 20, 22) A superb little cafe-bar barely five minutes' walk from the castle, with a cosy, antique atmosphere, serving freshly roasted coffee, homemade Guinness cake, and tasty panini and tortilla wraps. Foaming Žatecky Pivovar beer is 35Kč a glass, and Tom Waits grumbles on the sound system.

Malá Strana

Malá Strana is the place to go for sidewalk table people-watching, with lots of cafes and bars spilling out onto the streets – especially on Malostranské náměstí and on Nerudova, which leads up to the castle. Places here range from cute teahouses and cafes to traditional cellar-pubs and funky bars.

Vinograf WINE BAR

(Map p50; ☎604 705 730; www.vinograf.cz; Míšeňská 8; ⏰4pm-midnight Mon-Sat, 2-10pm Sun; 📶; 🚋12, 15, 20, 22) A smaller and more intimate branch of the pioneering Nové Město wine bar (p147), this place specialises in the best of Bohemian and Moravian wines, and offers a selection of cheese and charcuterie on the side.

Malostranská Beseda BAR, CLUB

(Map p50; ☎257 409 123; www.malostranska-beseda.cz; Malostranské náměstí 21; shows 120-250Kč; ⏰bar 4pm-1am, box office 5-9pm Mon-Sat, to 8pm Sun; 🚋12, 15, 20, 22) Malá Strana's four-storey pleasure palace includes a fabled music club on the 2nd floor, with a lively roster of cabaret acts, jazz and old Czech rockers. There's also an art gallery on the top floor, a bar and restaurant on the ground floor, and a big beer hall in the basement serving Pilsner Urquell and Velkopopovický Kozel at 39Kč per 0.5L.

Blue Light COCKTAIL BAR

(Map p50; ☎257 533 126; www.bluelightbar.cz; Josefská 1; ⏰6pm-3am Mon-Fri, 7pm-3am Sat & Sun; 🚋12, 15, 20, 22) The Blue Light is a dark and atmospheric hang-out, as popular with locals as with tourists, where you can sip a caipirinha or cranberry colada as you cast an eye over the vintage jazz posters, records, old photographs and decades worth of scratched graffiti that adorn the walls. The background jazz is recorded rather than live, and never overpowers your conversation. Often heaving on weekend nights.

Hostinec U Kocoura PUB

(Map p50; ☎257 530 107; Nerudova 2; ⏰noon-10.30pm; 🚋12, 15, 20, 22) 'The Tomcat' is a long-established traditional pub, still enjoying its reputation as a former favourite of the late president Václav Havel, and still managing to pull in a mostly Czech crowd despite being in the heart of touristville (maybe it's the ever-present pall of cigarette smoke). It has relatively inexpensive beer for this part of town – 35Kč for 0.5L of draught Pilsner Urquell.

Mlýnská Kavárna BAR

(Map p50; ☎257 313 222; Všehrdova 14; ⏰noon-midnight; 📶; 🚋9, 12, 15, 20, 22) This cafe-bar in Kampa park has existed in various guises since the communist era, and you might still hear it called Tato Kejkej, its previous incarnation, or just Mlýn (the mill). A wooden footbridge leads from Kampa to the smoky, dimly lit interior which is peopled with local artists (David Černý is a regular), writers and politicians.

U Malého Glena BAR

(Map p50; ☎257 531 717; www.malyglen.cz; Karmelitská 23; ⏰10am-2am Sun-Thu, to 3am Fri & Sat, music from 8.30pm; 📶; 🚋12, 15, 20, 22) 'Little Glen's' is a long-standing American-owned bar where hard-swinging local jazz or blues bands play every night in the cramped and steamy stone-vaulted cellar. There are Sunday-night jam sessions where amateurs are welcome (as long as you're good!) – it's a small venue, so get here early if you want to see as well as hear the band.

Klub Újezd BAR

(Map p50; ☎251 510 873; www.klubujezd.cz; Újezd 18; ⏰2pm-4am; 🚋9, 12, 15, 20, 22) Klub Újezd is one of Prague's many 'alternative' bars, spread over three floors (DJs in the cellar, and a cafe upstairs) and filled with

DRINKING & NIGHTLIFE BY NEIGHBOURHOOD

Prague Castle & Hradčany The area has a couple of interesting cafes and pubs, but becomes very quiet in the evenings.

Malá Strana A lively drinking scene with smart, modern bars and plenty of live music.

Staré Město Classic outdoor tables around Old Town Square, and snug atmospheric bars and jazz joints in the backstreets.

Nové Město A hotbed of sports bars, Irish pubs and girlie bars much frequented by visiting stag parties.

Vinohrady & Vršovice Trendy neighbourhoods where you can seek out the latest cocktail bars and cool cafes.

Žižkov & Karlín Žižkov is best for down-to-earth pubs packed with locals; Karlín for sophisticated wine bars.

Holešovice Working-class neighbourhood that's big on pubs and some surprisingly classy cafes.

Bubeneč & Dejvice Aside from a few pockets of life, residents here tend to turn in early.

Smíchov & Vyšehrad Smíchov has the rowdiest pubs per square metre in Prague; in Vyšehrad, you can hear a pin drop at night.

a fascinating collection of original art and weird wrought-iron sculptures. Clamber onto a two-tonne bar stool in the agreeably grungy street-level bar, and sip on a beer beneath a scaly, fire-breathing sea monster.

Staré Město

The Old Town is tourist central, with crowded pubs and prices to match. But all you have to do is explore the narrow backstreets that radiate from Old Town Square to find hidden cocktail bars, cool jazz joints and smoky student cafes.

Bokovka WINE BAR

(Map p62; ☎731 492 046; www.bokovka.com; Dlouhá 37; ⏲3pm-1am Mon-Sat; 🚋6, 8, 15, 26) Founded by a syndicate of oenophiles, including film directors Jan Hřebejk and David Ondříček, Bokovka has moved from its original New Town location to this hidden courtyard – look for the red wine droplet sign; the door is opposite it on the right. The crumbling, atmospheric cellar bar is a great place to sample the best of Czech wines.

The bar is named after the movie *Sideways* (*bokovka* in Czech), which was set in California vineyards.

Hemingway Bar COCKTAIL BAR

(Map p62; ☎773 974 764; www.hemingwaybar.eu; Karolíny Světlé 26; ⏲5pm-1am Mon-Thu, to 2am Fri, 7pm-2am Sat, 7pm-1am Sun; 📶; 🚋2, 17, 18) The Hemingway is a snug and sophisticated hideaway with dark leather benches, a library-like back room, flickering candlelight, and polite and professional bartenders. There's a huge range of quality spirits (especially rum), first-class cocktails, champagne and cigars.

U Zlatého Tygra PUB

(Map p62; ☎222 221 111; www.uzlatehotygra.cz; Husova 17; ⏲3-11pm; Ⓜ Staroměstská) Novelist Bohumil Hrabal's favourite hostelry, the 'Golden Tiger' is one of the few Old Town drinking holes that has hung on to its soul – and its reasonable prices (45Kč per 0.45L of Pilsner Urquell), considering its location close to Old Town Square. A thick fug of cigarette smoke keeps many tourists away.

This was the place that Václav Havel took Bill Clinton in 1994 to show him a real Czech pub.

Black Angel's Bar COCKTAIL BAR

(Map p62; ☎737 261 842; www.blackangelsbar.cz; Staroměstské náměstí 29; ⏲5pm-3am; 📶; Ⓜ Staroměstská) Hidden away in the vaulted cellars of Hotel U Prince in one of Prague's most crowded corners (opposite the Astronomical Clock on Old Town Square), the Black Angel pulls off the trick of seeming like a secret discovery. A cosy cluster of mirrored bars, leather Chesterfields and crystal lamps recreates the atmosphere of a 1930s cocktail bar.

Red Pif WINE BAR

(Map p62; 222 232 086; www.redpif.cz; Betlémská 9; 4.30-11.30pm Tue-Sat; 2, 17, 18) This welcoming wine bar is a great place to try out wines from the Czech Republic and around the world – there's no wine list, just tell the staff what you're interested in and they'll help you choose the right bottle. It's a shop too, so if you want to take a bottle or two away with you, no problem.

T-Anker BEER GARDEN

(Map p62; 722 445 474; www.t-anker.cz; 5th fl, Kotva Bldg, náměstí Republiky 8; 11am-11pm; M Náměstí Republiky) Down a beer or two while soaking up one of the best views over the Old Town at this roof-terrace bar and restaurant, with up to nine Czech and guest beers on tap. Access is from the 5th floor of Kotva department store, or direct by elevator from Kralodvorská street, above the entrance to the underground car park. Best to book a table.

Tricafe CAFE

(Map p62; 222 210 326; www.facebook.com/tricafepraha; Anenská 3; 8.30am-8pm Mon-Sat, 10am-6pm Sun; 2, 17, 18) A cosy corner of convivial chatter, furnished like your eccentric granny's living room with a mishmash of vintage furniture and quirky art, and serving some of the best espresso in the Old Town.

U Tří Růží BREWERY

(Map p62; 601 588 281; www.u3r.cz; Husova 10; 11am-11pm Sun-Thu, to midnight Fri & Sat; 2, 17, 18) In the 19th century there were more than 20 breweries in Prague's Old Town, but by 1989 there was only one left (U Medvidku). The Three Roses brewpub, on the site of one of those early breweries, helps revive the tradition, offering six beers on tap, including a tasty *světlý ležák* (pale lager; 56Kč per 0.4L), good food and convivial surroundings.

Tretter's New York Bar BAR

(Map p62; 224 811 165; www.tretters.cz; V Kolkovně 3; 7pm-2am; M Staroměstská) This sultry 1930s Manhattan-style cocktail bar harks back to gentler times when people went out for nightcaps – and when the drinks were stiff and properly made. Regularly cited as one of the city's top bars, Tretter's brings in the beautiful people and has prices to match. Book your table in advance.

U Rudolfina PUB

(Map p62; 222 328 758; Křižovnická 10; 11am-10pm; M Staroměstská) A rare Old Town *pivnice* that doesn't actively woo tourists, but gets them regardless. Belly up to the downstairs bar, often filled with Czechs, and have a pint of the very good Pilsner Urquell beer on tap (42Kč per 0.5L).

Prague Beer Museum PUB

(Map p62; 732 330 912; www.praguebeermuseum.com; Dlouhá 46; noon-3am; ; 6, 8, 15, 26) Although the name seems aimed at the tourist market, this lively and always-heaving pub pulls in some locals too, especially at lunchtime. There are no fewer than 30 Czech-produced craft beers on tap (plus a beer menu with tasting notes to guide you). Try a sample board – a wooden platter with five 0.15L glasses containing five beers of your choice.

James Joyce PUB

(Map p62; 224 818 851; www.jamesjoyceprague.cz; U obecního dvora 4; 11am-12.30am Sun-Thu, to 2am Fri & Sat; ; 6, 8, 15, 26) You probably don't go to Prague to visit an Irish bar, but if you're here in winter this friendly pub offers something rarely seen in Prague

BEER TYPES

There are two main varieties of beer: *světlé* (light) and *tmavy* or *černé* (dark). The *světlé* is a pale amber or golden lager-style beer with a crisp, refreshing, hoppy flavour. Dark beers are sweeter and more full-bodied, with a rich, malty or fruity flavour.

Czechs like their beer served at cellar temperature (around 6°C to 10°C) with a tall, creamy head (known as *pěna*, meaning 'foam'). Americans and Australians may find it a bit warm, but this improves the flavour. Most draught beer is sold in *půl-litr* (0.5L) glasses; if you prefer a small beer, ask for a *malé pivo* (0.3L). Some bars confuse the issue by using 0.4L glasses, while others offer a German-style 1L mug known as a *tuplák*.

Prague pubs traditionally offered just three beers on tap, all from one large brewery such as Pilsner Urquell; some pioneering bar owners added a *čtvrtá pípa* ('fourth pipe') to allow them to offer a rotating range of guest beers from various independent regional breweries. Many now have five, six or even more pipes.

PUB ETIQUETTE

There's an etiquette to be observed if you want to sample the atmosphere in a traditional *hospoda* (pub) without drawing disapproving stares from the regulars. First off, don't barge in and start rearranging chairs – if you want to share a table or take a spare seat, first ask *'je tu volno?'* (is this free?). It's normal practice in crowded Czech pubs to share tables with strangers.

Take a beer mat from the rack and place it in front of you, and wait for the bar staff to come to you; waving for service is guaranteed to get you ignored. When the waiter approaches, just raise your thumb for one beer, thumb and index finger for two etc – it's automatically assumed that you're here for the beer. Even just a nod will do. The waiter will keep track of your order by marking a slip of paper that stays on your table; whatever you do, don't write on it or lose it (you'll have to pay a fine if you do).

As soon as the level of beer in your glass falls to within a couple of centimetres of the bottom, the eagle-eyed waiter will be on their way with another. But never, as people often do in Britain, pour the dregs of the old glass into the new – this is considered to be deeply uncivilised behaviour.

If you don't want any more beer brought to your table, place a beer mat on top of your glass. When you want to pay up and go, get the waiter's attention and say *'zaplatím'* (I'll pay). They will total up the marks on your slip of paper, and you pay there, at the table.

bars: an open fire. Toast your toes while sipping a Guinness (99Kč a pint), or downing the all-day Irish breakfast fry, including Clonakilty black pudding.

Grand Cafe Orient CAFE

(Map p62; ☎224 224 240; www.grandcafeorient.cz; Ovocný trh 19; ⏰9am-10pm Mon-Fri, 10am-10pm Sat & Sun; Ⓜ Náměstí Republiky) Prague's only cubist cafe, the Orient was designed by Josef Gočár in 1912 and flaunts its cubist styling down to the smallest detail, including the lampshades and coat hooks. It was restored and reopened in 2005, having been closed since 1920. Decent coffee and inexpensive cocktails, but occasionally surly service.

Café Kampus CAFE

(Map p62; ☎775 755 143; www.cafekampus.cz; Náprstkova 10; ⏰10am-1am Mon-Fri, noon-1am Sat, noon-11pm Sun; 📶; 🚋2, 17, 18) This cool cafe doubles as an art gallery and occasional music venue, and is hugely popular with students from nearby Charles University. There are Czech newspapers and books to leaf through, chilled tunes on the sound system, and a menu of gourmet teas and coffees to choose from.

Kozička BAR

(Map p62; ☎224 818 308; www.kozicka.cz; Kozí 1; ⏰4pm-4am Mon-Thu, 5pm-5.30am Fri, 6pm-5.30am Sat, 7pm-3am Sun; 📶; Ⓜ Staroměstská) The 'Little Goat' is a buzzing, red-brick basement bar decorated with cute steel goat sculptures, serving Krušovice on tap at 55Kč for 0.5L (though watch out – the bartenders will occasionally sling you a 1L *tuplák* if they think you're a tourist). It fills up later in the evening with a mostly Czech crowd, and makes a civilised setting for a late-night session.

Čili Bar COCKTAIL BAR

(Map p62; ☎724 379 117; www.cilibar.cz; Kožná 8; ⏰6pm-2am; 📶; Ⓜ Můstek) This tiny cocktail bar could not be further removed in atmosphere from your typical Old Town drinking place. Cramped and smoky – there are Cuban cigars for sale – with battered leather armchairs competing for space with a handful of tables, it's friendly, relaxed and lively. Try the speciality of the house – rum mixed with finely chopped red chillis (minimum three shots).

Literární Kavárna Řetězová CAFE

(Map p62; ☎222 220 681; www.facebook.com/literarnikavarnaretezova; Řetězová 10; ⏰noon-11pm Mon-Fri, 5-11pm Sat & Sun; 🚋2, 17, 18) This is the kind of place where you can imagine yourself tapping out the Great Prague Novel on your laptop with a half-finished coffee on the table beside you. It's a plain, vaulted room with battered wooden furniture, a scatter of rugs on the floor, old black-and-white photos on the wall and a relaxed – if smoky – atmosphere.

U Medvídků BEER HALL

(At the Little Bear; Map p62; 224 211 916; www.umedvidku.cz; Na Perštýně 7; beer hall 11.30am-11pm, museum noon-10pm; ; Národní Třída, 2, 9, 18, 22) The most micro of Prague's microbreweries, with a capacity of only 250L, U Medvídků started producing its own beer in 2005, though its trad-style beer hall has been around for many years. What it lacks in size, it makes up for in strength – the dark lager, marketed as X-Beer, is the strongest in the country, with an alcohol content of 11.8%.

Available in bottles (133Kč for 0.33L), it's a malty, bitter-sweet brew with a powerful punch; handle with caution! There's also Budvar on tap (42Kč for 0.5L).

Duende BAR

(Map p62; 775 186 077; www.barduende.cz; Karolíny Světlé 30; 1pm-midnight Mon-Fri, 3pm-midnight Sat, 4pm-midnight Sun; 2, 17, 18) Barely five minutes' walk from Charles Bridge but half a world away in atmosphere, this cute little bar is the opposite of touristy – a bohemian drinking den that pulls in an arty, mixed-age crowd of locals. Here you can enjoy a drink while casting an eye over the fascinating photos and quirky art that cover the walls, or listen to live guitar or violin.

Kavárna Slavia CAFE

(Map p62; 224 220 957; www.cafeslavia.cz; Národní třída 1; 8am-midnight Mon-Fri, 9am-midnight Sat & Sun; ; 2, 9, 18, 22) The Slavia is the most famous of Prague's old cafes, a cherrywood-and-onyx shrine to art-deco elegance, with polished limestone-topped tables and big windows overlooking the river. It has been a celebrated literary meeting place since the early 20th century – Rainer Maria Rilke and Franz Kafka hung out here, and it was frequented by Václav Havel and other dissidents in the 1970s and '80s.

Friends CLUB

(Map p62; 226 211 920; www.friendsclub.cz; Bartolomějská 11; 7pm-6am; ; Národní Třída, 2, 9, 18, 22) Friends is a welcoming gay bar and club serving excellent coffee, cocktails and wine. It's a good spot to sit back with a drink and check out the crowd, or join in the party spirit on assorted theme nights, which range from Czech pop music and movies to beach parties and comedy nights (see the website for listings).

Kavárna Obecní Dům CAFE

(Map p62; 222 002 763; www.kavarnaod.cz; náměstí Republiky 5, Municipal House; 7.30am-11pm; ; Náměstí Republiky) The spectacular cafe in Prague's opulent Municipal House (p72) offers the opportunity to sip your cappuccino amid an orgy of art-nouveau splendour.

Nové Město

Nové Město, particularly the area around Wenceslas Square, is still a bit of a magnet for stag parties and groups of young lads on the piss – best avoided if you're looking for a quiet drink. But there are plenty of off-the-beaten-track drinking places too. Check out the streets south of Národní třída near the river, where you'll find lots of studenty cafes, quirky wine bars and trendy new drinking spots; the area around Petrské náměstí in northern Nové Město is also worth a look.

★Vinograf WINE BAR

(Map p84; 214 214 681; www.vinograf.cz; Senovážné náměstí 23; 11.30am-midnight Mon-Sat, 5pm-midnight Sun; ; 3, 5, 6, 9, 14, 24) With knowledgeable staff, a relaxed atmosphere and an off-the-beaten-track feel, this appealingly modern wine bar is a great place to discover Moravian wines. There's good finger food to accompany your wine, mostly cheese and charcuterie, with food and wine menus (in Czech and English) on big blackboards behind the bar. Very busy at weekends, when it's worth booking a table.

There's another branch in Malá Strana (p143).

Pivovarský Dům BREWERY

(Map p78; 296 216 666; www.pivovarskydum.com; cnr Ječná & Lipová; 11am-11.30pm; 4, 6, 10, 16, 22) While the tourists flock to U Fleků (p148), locals gather here to sample the Štěpán classic Czech lager (44Kč per 0.5L) that is produced on the premises, as well as wheat beer and a range of flavoured beers (including coffee, banana and cherry; 44Kč per 0.3L). The pub itself is a pleasant place to linger, decked out with polished copper vats and brewing implements.

EMA Espresso Bar CAFE

(Map p84; 730 156 933; www.emaespressobar.cz; Na Florenci 3; 8am-8pm Mon-Fri, 10am-6pm Sat & Sun; ; 3, 6, 14, 15, 24, 26) Prague's answer to hipster espresso bars, EMA serves fine artisanal coffee in a cool, white, high-ceilinged, art-gallery-like space, with a big communal table in the middle where a dozen start-ups have surely been hatched. Freshly roasted beans and cofffee-making equipment are on sale too.

Red Room BAR

(Map p78; 602 429 989; www.redroom.cz; Myslíkova 28; 5pm-3am Sun-Thu, to 5am Fri & Sat; ; 5) The American-expat owners of this tiny bar, just off of Karlovo náměstí, are musicians, so most nights you can count on some impromptu guitar playing or an open-mic night. Other times it's quieter and a good spot to start or end your night over a beer and friendly conversation. Draws mainly students and backpackers.

Hoffa COCKTAIL BAR

(Map p84; 601 359 659; www.hoffa.cz; Senovážné náměstí 22; 11am-2am Mon-Fri, 6pm-2am Sat, 6pm-midnight Sun; ; 3, 5, 6, 9, 14, 24) One of Prague's first entirely smoke-free bars, Hoffa matches clean air with clean design: a long (12m long!) bar fronts a room with sleek, functional decor and a wall of windows looking out onto Senovážné náměstí's fountain of dancing sprites. Friendly staff, accomplished cocktails and good food – you'll be struggling to find a table at lunchtime.

Friends Coffee House CAFE

(Map p78; 272 049 665; www.milujikavu.cz; Palackého 7; 9am-9pm Mon-Fri, noon-8pm Sat & Sun; ; 3, 5, 6, 9, 14, 24) It's easy to walk past this place, but it's worth seeking out – head through the back to find a couple of relaxing rooms, one fitted out as a library, with well-spaced tables and comfy chairs. They take their coffee seriously here, using only freshly roasted and ground coffee beans (counter service only). Excellent, freshly prepared sandwiches are also available.

U Fleků BREWERY

(Map p78; 224 934 019; www.ufleku.cz; Křemencová 11; 10am-11pm; 5) A festive warren of drinking and dining rooms, U Fleků is a Prague institution, although it's usually clogged with tour groups high on oompah music and the tavern's home-brewed, 13-degree black beer (59Kč for 0.4L), known as Flek. Purists grumble but go along anyway because the beer is good, though tourist prices have nudged out many locals.

Beware the waiter asking if you want to try a Becherovka (Czech liqueur) – it's not a great accompaniment to beer, and it'll add 79Kč to the bill.

Kávovarna CAFE

(Map p78; 296 236 233; www.facebook.com/kavovarna; Pasáž Lucerna, Štěpánská 61; 9am-11pm Mon-Fri, 2-11pm Sat, 2-10.30pm Sun; 3, 5, 6, 9, 14, 24) This retro-styled place has bentwood chairs and curved wooden benches in the dimly lit front room (there's another room beyond the bar), with exhibitions of arty B&W photography on the walls. The coffee is good and reasonably priced, and the service is friendly, if somewhat relaxed.

Kavárna Velryba CAFE

(Map p78; 224 931 444; www.kavarnavelryba.cz; Opatovická 24; 11am-11pm Mon-Fri, noon-11pm Sat & Sun; ; 2, 9, 18, 22) The 'Whale' is an arty cafe-bar – usually quiet enough to have a real conversation – with vegetarian-friendly snacks, a smoky back room and a basement art gallery. A clientele of Czech students, local office workers and foreign backpackers attracted by the low prices keep the place jumping.

Jáma BAR

(Map p78; 222 967 081; www.jamapub.cz; V Jámě 7; 11am-1am Tue-Sun, to midnight Mon; ; 3, 5, 6, 9, 14, 24) Jáma ('the Hollow') is a popular American-expat bar plastered with old rock-gig posters ranging from Led Zep and REM to Kiss and Shania Twain. There's a little beer garden out the back shaded by lime and walnut trees, smiling staff serving up a rotating selection of regional beers and microbrews, and a menu that includes good burgers, steaks, ribs and chicken wings.

Cafe Louvre CAFE

(Map p78; 224 930 949; www.cafelouvre.cz; 1st fl, Národní třída 22; 8am-11.30pm Mon-Fri, 9am-11.30pm Sat & Sun; 2, 9, 18, 22) The French-style Cafe Louvre is arguably the most amenable of Prague's grand cafes, as popular today as it was in the early 1900s when it was frequented by the likes of Franz Kafka and Albert Einstein. The atmosphere is wonderfully olde-worlde, and it serves good food as well as coffee. Check out the billiard hall, and the ground-floor art gallery.

Kavárna Lucerna CAFE

(Map p78; 224 215 495; www.restaurace-monarchie.cz/en/cafe-lucerna; Pasáž Lucerna, Štěpánská 61; 10am-midnight; ; 3, 5, 6, 9, 14, 24) The least touristy of Prague's grand cafes, the Lucerna is part of an art-nouveau shopping arcade designed by the grandfather of ex-president Václav Havel. Filled with faux marble, ornamental metalwork and glittering crystal lanterns (*lucerna* is Czech for lantern), this 1920s gem has arched windows overlooking David Černý's famous sculpture Kun (p81), hanging beneath the glass-domed atrium.

Cellarius WINE BAR

(Map p78; 224 210 979; wwwcellarius.cz; Pasáž Lucerna, Štěpánská 61; 9.30am-9pm Mon-Fri, 11am-9pm Sat, 3-9pm Sun; 3, 5, 6, 9, 14, 24) Take a break from Czech beer with a visit to this cute vinotheque and sample some good Czech wine (such as a Frankovka red or Veltlínské zelené white) at a table in the heart of Prague's most famous art-nouveau shopping arcade.

Vinohrady & Vršovice

Vinohrady is a great area for bar- and cafe-hopping. Check out the streets surrounding náměstí Míru (Peace Sq), particularly along Americká and Jiřího z Poděbrad, as well as those around Riegrovy sady, which has one of Prague's best beer gardens. Vinohrady is also the centre of Prague's gay life. The vibe is scruffier – and trendier – in adjoining Vršovice. Repair here for after-hours drinking.

Over the years Vinohrady has evolved into the unofficial centre of gay Prague, and you'll find many of the city's better gay-friendly cafes and clubs in this area.

★ **Beer Geek** PUB

(Map p88; https://beergeek.cz; Vinohradská 62, Vinohrady; 3pm-2am; ; Jiřího z Poděbrad) One of the most successful of a new generation of multi-tap pubs in Prague to offer the best beers from local Czech producers as well as brewers from around the world. They have 32 taps in all, and regularly rotate in obscure and hard-to-find labels. The 'geek' part of the name extends to the cool, lab-like presentation of the pub.

Oliveira WINE BAR

(Map p88; reservations 608 812 230; www.oliveira.cz; Čermákova 4, Vinohrady; 4-11pm Tue-Fri, from 1pm Sat & Sun; ; Náměstí Míru) Cosy, corner wine bar specialising in excellent Portuguese wines, spirits and coffees, with a small tapas menu (bruschetta, spicy chorizo sausages) in case you get the munchies. The staff is more than happy to recommend a glass or bottle of wine to try and will even hold the place open late if the place is still buzzing at closing time.

Vinohradský Pivovar PUB

(Map p88; 222 760 080; www.vinohradskypivovar.cz; Korunní 106, Vinohrady; 11am-midnight; ; 10, 16) This popular and highly recommended neighbourhood pub and restaurant offers its own home-brewed lagers as well as a well-regarded IPA. There's seating on two levels and a large events room at the back for concerts and happenings. The restaurant features classic Czech pub dishes (like *Wienerschnitzel* and pork medallions) at reasonable prices (180Kč to 230Kč). Book in advance for an evening meal.

Ráno Kavu Večer Víno CAFE

(Map p88; 774 673 732; www.ranokavuvecervino.cz; Kodaňská 4, Vršovice; 7.30am-noon & 5-10pm Mon-Fri, 5-10pm Sat; ; 4, 22) The name translates as 'Morning Coffee, Evening Wine' and the reality is just as good as the concept. Slide into this tiny space in the morning to get a home-roasted cup, prepared according to your preferred method. In the evening, choose a glass from a number of carefully selected bottles. The downside: there are only a few places to sit.

Cafe Zenit BAR

(Map p88; 267 314 903; www.zenitcafe.cz; Krymská 24, Vršovice; 4pm-3am; ; 4, 22) Coffee, cocktails, speciality beers...Whatever you're in the mood for, this chill, Berlin-style Vršovice hang-out has the answer. Part-owned by Czech author Petra Hůlová, Zenit brings a cultural component in the form of regular happenings, readings and DJ nights. The mismatched chairs, trippy chandeliers and exposed brick walls fit this part of town's relaxed DIY vibe to a tee.

DRINKING HABITS

Even in these times of encroaching coffee culture, *pivo* (beer) remains the lifeblood of Prague. Many people drink at least one glass of beer every day – local nicknames for beer include *tekutý chleb* (liquid bread) and *živá voda* (life-giving water) – and it's still possible to see people stopping off for a small glass of beer on their way to work in the morning. And come the evening, beer reigns supreme. There's nothing Praguers enjoy more than getting together in a local bar and swapping stories over a *pivo* or two. Or three...

VINOHRADY PUB CRAWL

The district of Vinohrady may be named for vineyards, but these days beer is clearly king. In the recent past, several major pubs have opened along the perimeter of central náměstí Míru (Peace Sq). If you'll pardon the pun, we're starting to wonder when they're going to rename náměstí Míru as 'náměstí Beeru'...

The proximity of the pubs makes for a perfect, low-energy pub crawl, and since there's a handy metro station nearby, it's a feasible destination no matter where you're staying. If you're still standing by the end of the night, there are dozens of additional watering holes within easy walking distance at which to carry on.

It's a toss-up where to start, as all three pubs serve decent food too. **Vinohradský Parlament** (p130), on the square's eastern end, is clean, brightly lit and serves excellent and inventive Czech food, mixing staples such as pork and duck with more unusual entrées like venison and rabbit. It's a Staropramen pub, but usually has a couple of experimental brews on hand, and the Staropramen unfiltered and 11-degree lagers are both very drinkable.

From here, wend your way to the Vinohrady branch of the **Prague Beer Museum** (p151) on the square's southern side. Though the bar food is above average, this place really excels at serious drinking. There's no fewer than 33 beers on tap here, including excellent Czech regional labels such as Primátor, Svijany, Klášter and Rychtář.

Finish up the evening with a Gambrinus across the street at **Originál 1869** (p132), which keeps the doors open until 2am on Friday and Saturday. The 10-degree Gambrinus lager remains the most popular beer in the country – not so much because it's great, but because it goes down like water. At this stage in the evening, that might be all you're looking for.

Coffee Source CAFE
(Coffee House; Map p88; ☎226 531 277; www.coffeesource.eu; Francouzská 100, Vršovice; ⌚8am-5pm Mon-Fri; 📶; 🚋4, 22) They call themselves 'Coffee Source' and the sign on the outside says 'Coffee House', but whatever the name, this is Vršovice's best coffee, bar none. High-quality beans are used plus various roasting and filtering techniques to deliver the perfect cup every time. Light breakfasts, such as croissants, are served and there's a pretty garden out back for warm weather days.

Riegrovy Sady Beer Garden BEER GARDEN
(Map p88; Riegrovy sady, Vinohrady; ⌚noon-1am Apr-Oct; Ⓜ Jiřího z Poděbrad, 🚋11, 13) There's a good-natured rivalry between this beer garden and the one across the river at Letná as to which one is the best. We're not sure, but this one is pretty good. Order beers at the bar and carry them to your table. To find it, go to Polská, turn up Chopínova, and enter the park across from Na Švíhance.

Bad Flash Bar PUB
(Map p88; ☎273 134 609; www.badflash.cz; Krymská 2, Vršovice; ⌚5pm-1am Mon-Sat, to midnight Sun; 📶; 🚋4, 22) This popular brew-pub offers seven varieties of its homemade beer, including some very bold IPAs and a killer 17° beer called 'Prague Inspiration' (around 8% alcohol). Not surprisingly, the vibe here gets frothy on a Friday or Saturday night. Beers and ciders from around the world are also served, as well as takeaway bottles if you want to continue the party elsewhere.

Bio Zahrada CAFE
(Map p88; ☎reservations 734 266 315; www.bio-zahrada.cz; Belgická 33, Vinohrady; ⌚8.30am-9pm Mon-Thu, to 10pm Fri, 10am-8pm Sat; 📶; Ⓜ Náměstí Míru) This organic coffee shop serves high-end coffees and pastries in a welcoming, rustic setting with a big garden out back. Light food items are also served, including daily, good-value lunch specials like veggie curries and risottos, for around 130Kč. There's a small shop at the front that specialises in organic food items, including pastries, grains, dairy products and tofu.

Le Caveau CAFE
(Map p88; ☎775 294 864; www.broz-d.cz; náměstí Jiřího z Poděbrad 9, Vinohrady; ⌚8am-10.30pm Mon-Fri, 9am-10.30pm Sat, 2-8.30pm Sun; 📶; Ⓜ Jiřího z Poděbrad) This charming French cafe, perched on a corner of náměstí Jiřího z Poděbrad, is a perfect spot to relax with coffee or one of the excellent French wines. It also serves French pastries, sandwiches and cheeses, and has a small bakery counter for

takeaway. The 1920s-inspired interior, with stylish hanging lamps and wood flooring, is ideal for an intimate meet-up.

Cafe V Lese CAFE

(Map p88; ☎reservations 731 413 964; www.cafevlese.cz; Krymská 12, Vršovice; ⏰4pm-2am; 📶; 🚋4, 22) The epicentre of the Vršovice hipster revival is this popular student cafe, bar and alternative music club (downstairs). It's always packed and fun; arrive early in the evening to get a table. Check the website for musical happenings or events, such as blues nights, trance DJs and other funky stuff. Concerts start at 8pm, and admission is usually 100Kč.

Kavárna Šlágr CAFE

(Map p88; ☎607 277 688; www.kavarnaslagr.cz; Francouzská 72, Vršovice; ⏰9am-8pm; 📶; 🚋4, 22) Walking into this evocative, old-fashioned bakery-cafe is like stepping back into the last century and the time of the First Republic, when Czechoslovakia was a young, prosperous democracy. There's a big pastry counter at the front (our favourite has to be the calorie-bomb Czech cream puff called *větrník*) and several cosy, secluded tables at the back.

Prague Beer Museum PUB

(Map p88; ☎reservations 775 994 698; www.praguebeermuseum.com; Americká 43, Vinohrady; ⏰noon-3am; 📶; Ⓜ Náměstí Míru) The Vinohrady branch of a popular pub chain that started in the Old Town. The idea is to highlight smaller, regional beers from around the country, rather than pledge allegiance to a big national brewer. They normally keep 33 labels on tap, including lights, darks, IPAs and just about everything else. Decent bar food too.

Bar & Books Mánesova COCKTAIL BAR

(Map p88; ☎222 724 581; www.barandbooks.cz; Mánesova 64, Vinohrady; ⏰5pm-3am Sun-Wed, to 4am Thu-Sat; 📶; 🚋11, 13) This upmarket New York–style cocktail and cigar bar occupies a former rugby pub and couldn't be more different in terms of atmosphere. Check the website for special themed nights, such as burlesque and whisky tastings. There's occasional live music. Try to book a table in advance.

Blatouch CAFE

(Map p88; ☎222 328 643; www.facebook.com/kavarnablatouch; Americká 17, Vinohrady; ⏰11am-1am Mon-Fri, 1pm-1am Sat & Sun; 📶; Ⓜ Náměstí Míru) This popular cafe is an excellent choice in which to relax, surf the net on free wi-fi, and enjoy a good coffee or glass of wine. The vibe is student-friendly and relaxed. There are also some light food items available, such as salads and sandwiches.

Viniční Altán WINE BAR

(Gröbovka; Map p88; ☎222 516 887; www.vinicni-altan.cz; Havlíčkovy sady 1369, Vršovice; ⏰11am-11pm Apr-Oct, 11am-9pm Mon-Wed, Sat & Sun Nov-Mar; Ⓜ Náměstí Míru) Prague's nicest open-air wine garden claims to be its oldest too – apparently established by Emperor Charles IV himself. Enjoy a glass of locally made white or red on a refurbished wooden gazebo overlooking the vineyards and the Nusle valley. There's no easy way to get here; try cutting through Vinohrady, following Americká and then continuing through Havlíčkovy sady.

Kavárna Zanzibar CAFE

(Map p88; ☎222 520 315; www.kavarnazanzibar.cz; Americká 15, Vinohrady; ⏰8am-11pm Mon-Fri, 10am-11pm Sat & Sun; 📶; Ⓜ Náměstí Míru) Zanzibar started out years ago as a place to buy newspapers and tobacco products. Over the years it's evolved into a homey space that serves as a cafe, bar or informal restaurant, depending on your mood. The terrace out the front is pleasant in nice weather.

Café Kaaba CAFE

(Map p88; ☎reservations 222 254 021; www.kaaba.cz; Mánesova 20, Vinohrady; ⏰8am-midnight Mon-Fri, from 9am Sat, from 10am Sun; 📶; 🚋11, 13) Café Kaaba is a stylish little cafe-bar with retro furniture and pastel-coloured decor that comes straight out of the 1959 Ideal Homes Exhibition. It serves up excellent coffee made with freshly ground imported beans. Wi-fi is only free for customers from opening until 6pm.

Saints BAR

(Map p88; ☎222 250 326; www.facebook.com/thesaintsbar; Polská 32, Vinohrady; ⏰7pm-4am; Ⓜ Jiřího z Poděbrad) Sealing the deal on Prague's booming 'gay quarter' in Vinohrady, this British-run bar is laid-back, friendly and serves good drinks. With a multinational staff speaking many languages, for newcomers it's the perfect entrée to the local scene.

Žlutá Pumpa PUB

(Map p88; ☎608 184 360; www.zluta-pumpa.info; Belgická 11, Vinohrady; ⏰11.30am-12.30am; 📶; Ⓜ Náměstí Míru, IP Pavlova) There aren't many student watering holes left in trendy Vinohrady, but the 'Yellow Pump' has been a neighbourhood fixture for over a decade. There's a tiny bar area and several adjacent small rooms, and normally every seat in the house is filled. There's a complete range of beers, wines and cocktails, plus average but edible Mexican food.

Hospůdka Obyčejný Svět PUB

(Map p88; 224 257 161; Korunní 96, entry on Chorvatská, Vinohrady; 11.30am-1am Mon-Fri, 1pm-1am Sat, 1pm-midnight Sun; ; M Náměstí Jiřího z Poděbrad, 10, 16) This traditional pub has something of a darkly lit, British gentlemen's club feel about it. There's an excellent range of beers on hand, including harder-to-find varieties from Ježek and Lobkowicz, plus decent traditional Czech food and a friendly, welcoming atmosphere.

Mama Coffee CAFE

(Map p88; 773 263 333; www.mamacoffee.cz; Londýnská 49, Vinohrady; 8.30am-8pm Mon-Fri, 10am-6pm Sat & Sun; ; M Náměstí Míru) One of several Mama Coffee branches around town that specialise in home-roasted, fair-trade coffees imported from around the world. Mama Coffees are famously laid-back as well as being stroller- and kid-friendly.

Dobrá Trafika CAFE

(Map p88; 724 146 218; www.dobratrafika.cz; Korunní 42, Vinohrady; 7.30am-11pm Mon-Fri, 8am-11pm Sat, 9am-11pm Sun; ; M Náměstí Míru, 10, 16) From the outside you'd never know there was a cute little coffee shop tucked behind this tobacconist on busy Korunní. The shop is a great place to buy teas, sweets and gifts. At the back there's a small room for drinking coffee and a larger garden for just hanging out. Popular with students.

Sokolovna PUB

(Map p88; 222 524 525; www.restaurantsokolovna.cz; Slezská 22, Vinohrady; 11am-midnight; ; M Náměstí Míru) It might be a little unfair to consign Sokolovna to the 'pub' category; after all, it's also a pretty good restaurant, serving excellent traditional Czech food, including a good-value luncheon special. But it's a great beer joint too, with unpasteurised Pilsner Urquell (*tankové pivo)* on tap, served in a dignified 1930s interior.

Al Cafetero CAFE

(Map p88; 777 061 161; www.alcafetero.cz; Blanická 24, Vinohrady; 9am-10pm Mon-Thu, to 6pm Fri; ; M Náměstí Míru, Muzeum, 11, 13) This quirky little cafe and wine bar, just between Vinohradská and náměstí Míru, has several things going for it, including arguably the best coffee drinks in Prague. There's an excellent wine selection and it's comfortable for lingering over the newspaper.

Café Celebrity CAFE

(Map p88; 222 511 343; www.celebritycafe.cz; Vinohradská 40, Vinohrady; 8am-1am Mon-Fri, 5pm-2am Sat; ; M Náměstí Míru, 11, 13) This cafe is part of the cluster of gay-friendly places that make up the old Radio Palác building. The Celebrity offers early-morning breakfasts on weekdays and a more relaxed brunch on weekends. At other times, it's great for coffee and people-watching.

Galerie Kavárna Róza K CAFE

(Map p88; 222 544 696; Belgická 17, Vinohrady; 11am-1am Mon-Fri, 5pm-midnight Sat & Sun; ; M Náměstí Míru, IP Pavlova) This cosy, out-of-the-way cafe is popular with students, who come for the relaxed mood, decent cakes and an interior fitted out like your auntie's drawing room.

Žižkov & Karlín

Žižkov is famous for having more pubs per head of population than any other city district in Europe, and – depending on your tastes – offers the most authentic or the most terrifying pub-crawling experience in Prague. Be prepared for smoke, sticky floors, wall-to-wall noise and some heroically drunk companions.

Up-and-coming Karlín has a great choice of trad pubs, trendy wine bars and artisanal coffee shops.

★U Slovanské Lípy PUB

(Map p92; 734 743 094; www.uslovanskelipy.cz; Tachovské náměstí 6, Žižkov; 11am-midnight; ; 133, 175, 207) A classic Žižkov pub, plain and unassuming in and out, 'At the Linden Trees' (the linden is a Czech and Slovak national emblem) is something of a place of pilgrimage for beer lovers. The reason is its range of artisan brews (from 28Kč for 0.5L), such as those from the Kocour brewery, including their superb Sumeček 11° (Catfish pale ale).

★Pivovarský Klub PUB

(Map p92; 222 315 777; www.pivovarskyklub.com; Křižíkova 17, Karlín; 11.30am-11.30pm; M Florenc) This bar is to beer what the

Bodleian Library is to books – wall-to-wall shelves lined with more than 200 varieties of bottled beer from all over the world, and six guest beers on tap. Perch on a bar stool or head downstairs to the snug cellar and order some of the pub's excellent grub (such as authentic *guláš* with bacon dumplings) to soak up the beer.

Veltlin WINE BAR

(Map p92; 725 535 395; www.veltlin.cz; Křižíkova 115, Karlín; 5-11pm Mon-Sat; M Křižíkova) This fun and friendly bar focuses its attention on wines from the countries of the former Habsburg empire – mainly Austria, Hungary, the Czech Republic and Slovakia, plus a bit of northern Italy and the Balkans. The clued-up staff can provide you with an easy introduction to this less-frequented corner of the oenophile atlas.

U Kurelů PUB

(Map p92; www.ukurelu.cz; Chvalova 1, Žižkov; 5-11pm Tue-Sun; ; 5, 9, 15, 26) This reinvention of a classic Žižkov pub, originally opened in 1907, is the brainchild of the good folk at the Tavern (p130), and the well-priced Pilsner Urquell (46Kč for 0.5L) and range of Czech microbrews is underpinned by the Tavern's famous smokehouse burgers, nachos and quesadillas.

Bukowski's COCKTAIL BAR

(Map p92; 773 445 280; www.facebook.com/bukowskisbar; Bořivojova 86, Žižkov; 7pm-3am; 5, 9, 15, 26) Like many of the drinking dens that are popular among expats, Bukowski's is more a cocktail dive than a cocktail bar. Named after hard-drinking American writer Charles Bukowski, it cultivates a dark and slightly debauched atmosphere – the decor is self-consciously 'interesting' (when you can see it through the smoke-befogged candlelight) – but it peddles quality cocktails and cigars, and has friendly bartenders and cool tunes.

Hospoda Parukářka PUB

(Map p92; http://parukarka.cz; Olšanské náměstí, Žižkov; 2pm-1am Apr-Oct, to midnight Nov-Mar; ; 5, 9, 15, 26) This friendly community pub is little more than a ramshackle wooden hut in a park overlooking Žižkov, where locals, accompanied by kids and/or dogs, gather for a chat at the outdoor tables. There's Žatec and Kozel beers on tap (only 28Kč per 0.5L), a hot-dog stand in summer, occasional live music, and lots of sweet-smelling smoke wafting about in the evenings.

Fatal Music Club BAR

(Map p92; 222 716 122; www.fatalclub.cz; Rokycanova 29, Žižkov; 2pm-2am Mon-Thu, to 5am Fri & Sat, 5pm-2am Sun; 5, 9, 15, 26) Some of the more hardcore Žižkov clubs can be a bit intimidating for nonlocals, but this much-loved venue is scruffy, laid-back, eclectic and great fun. There's a lively cafe-bar at street level, plus a cavern-like club venue downstairs that hosts local DJs and live music from heavy metal to acoustic singer-songwriters.

U Vystřeleného Oka PUB

(Map p92; 222 540 465; www.uvoka.cz; U Božích Bojovníků 3, Žižkov; 4.30pm-1am Mon-Sat; 133, 175, 207) You've got to love a pub that has vinyl pads on the wall above the gents' urinals to rest your forehead on. 'The Shot-Out Eye' – the name pays homage to the one-eyed Hussite hero atop the hill – is a bohemian hostelry with a raucous Friday night atmosphere where the cheap Pilsner Urquell (38Kč per 0.5L) pulls in a typically heterogeneous Žižkov crowd.

U Sadu PUB

(Map p92; 222 727 072; www.usadu.cz; Škroupovo náměstí 5, Žižkov; 8am-4am Tue-Sat, to 2am Sun & Mon; M Jiřího z Poděbrad) Escape the overpriced tyranny of central Prague at this neighbourhood pub in grungy Žižkov, where 0.5L beers cost from only 29Kč. With its ragtag collection of memorabilia, including communist-era posters of forgotten politicians, nothing's really changed here in the last few decades.

Holešovice

Holešovice may be a working-class district at heart, but it has some of the city's best cafes and a couple of excellent clubs. Most of the better cafes are in the western side of the district, while the clubs are on the eastern side.

★ Letná Beer Garden BEER GARDEN

(Map p96; 233 378 208; www.letenskyzamecek.cz; Letenské sady 341; 11am-11pm May-Sep; 1, 8, 12, 25, 26) No accounting of watering holes in the neighbourhood would be complete without a nod towards the city's best beer garden, with an amazing panorama, situated at the eastern end of the Letná Gardens (p94). Buy a takeaway beer from a small kiosk and grab a picnic table, or sit on a small terrace where you can order beer by the glass and decent pizza.

★ Cross Club CLUB

(Map p96; ☎736 535 010; www.crossclub.cz; Plynární 23; admission free-200Kč; ⊙cafe noon-2am, club 6pm-4am; 📶; Ⓜ Nádraží Holešovice) An industrial club in every sense of the word: the setting in an industrial zone; the thumping music (both DJs and live acts); and the interior, an absolute must-see jumble of gadgets, shafts, cranks and pipes, many of which move and pulsate with light to the music. The program includes occasional live music, theatre performances and art happenings.

Cobra BAR

(Map p96; ☎778 470 515; www.barcobra.cz; Milady Horákové 8; 📶; 🚋1, 6, 8, 12, 17, 25, 26) This all-purpose cafe, lunch spot and light-night bar has something for everyone: very good coffee and tea, hard-to-find microbrews and IPAs, and well-made cocktails, including a hard-to-pass-up 'Bloody Beet', made from vodka, tabasco and beet juice. There's also an open kitchen at the back that serves up a daily soup and main-course lunch. The menu is filled with vegan options.

Phill's Twenty7 CAFE

(Map p96; ☎605 444 528; www.twenty7.cz; Přístavní 27; ⊙8.30am-10pm Mon-Fri, 10am-10pm Sat & Sun; 📶; 🚋1, 6, 12, 14, 25) Stylish cafe in the industrialised eastern end of Holešovice, featuring excellent coffees – among them fragrant Vietnamese Trung Nguyen filtered coffees – homemade lemonades and chai. Also serves breakfasts (85Kč to 120Kč) and an ambitious range of light bites, including a 'Japanese' hot dog with wasabi. The service is excellent and the clientele tilts towards trendy professionals.

Sasazu CLUB

(Map p96; ☎778 054 054; www.sasazu.com; Bubenské nábřeží 306, Hall 25, Pražská tržnice; admission 200-1000Kč; ⊙9pm-5am; 📶; Ⓜ Vltavská, 🚋1, 12, 14, 25) One of the most popular dance clubs in the city, Sasazu attracts the fashionable elite and hangers-on in equal measure. If you're into big dance floors and long lines (hint: go early), this is your place. Check the website for occasional big-name acts (such as Bastille or Morcheeba). Book a table in advance by phone (10am to 6pm Monday to Friday, 4pm to 10pm Saturday).

Café Jedna CAFE

(Map p96; ☎778 440 877; www.cafejedna.cz; Dukelských Hrdinů 47; ⊙9.30am-10pm; 📶👪; Ⓜ Vltavská, 🚋1, 6, 8, 12, 17, 25, 26 to Strossmayerovo náměstí) The Veletržní Palác's home cafe is just as starkly minimalist and pleasantly trendy as you'd expect. Long rows of unadorned tables fan out in an oversized, airy space. There's excellent coffee and some light sandwiches if you're hungry. There's a pretty play area in the corner and plenty of space for the kids to run around in.

Kavárna Liberál CAFE

(Map p96; ☎732 222 880; www.facebook.com/kavarnaliberal; Heřmanova 6; ⊙9am-midnight Mon-Sat, 2pm-midnight Sun; 📶; Ⓜ Vltavská, 🚋1, 6, 8, 12, 17, 25, 26) This Viennese-style coffee house captures something of Prague in the 1920s. By day, it's a quiet spot for coffee and connecting with the wi-fi; evenings bring out a more pub-like feel. There are occasional live bands in the basement. The menu includes coffee, beer and wine, and light foods like salads and omelettes. Often it will have excellent sweets such as cheesecake and apple strudel.

Park Cafe & Bar CAFE

(Map p96; ☎603 193 003; www.parkcafebar.cz; Kamenická 56; ⊙5pm-1am Mon-Sat, to 11pm Sun; 📶; 🚋1, 8, 12, 25, 26) This laid-back, alternative cafe is just what the doctor ordered. Two simply adorned rooms with big wooden tables and wood-plank flooring provide the perfect setting for a relaxing coffee or glass of wine. There's not much in the way of food, but the toasted panini-style cheese, ham and arugula sandwiches hit the spot.

Hells Bells PUB

(Map p96; ☎733 734 918; www.hellsbells.cz; Letohradská 50; ⊙11am-12.30am Mon-Thu, 11am-2am Fri & Sat, noon-10pm Sun; 📶; 🚋1, 8, 12, 25, 26) This raucous beer pub with a mostly student-age clientele makes a good place to move on to after the Letná Beer Garden closes. There's decent Czech food as well, including good-value daily lunch specials.

Ouky Douky CAFE

(Map p96; ☎266 711 531; www.oukydouky.cz; Janovského 14; ⊙8am-midnight; 📶; 🚋1, 6, 8, 12, 17, 25, 26) This was the original home of the legendary Globe Bookstore & Café (p167) in the 1990s, and a kind of eclectic, San Francisco funkiness lingers. Today it houses a used bookstore, with a worn-out selection of Czech-language books, and an inviting cafe filled with students and a wandering expat or two (possibly still looking for the Globe).

Erhartova Cukrárna CAFE

(Map p96; ☎233 312 148; www.erhartovacukrarna.cz; Milady Horákové 56; ⏰10am-7pm; 📶; 🚋1, 8, 12, 25, 26) This stylish 1930s-era cafe and sweet shop in a refurbished functionalist building is adjacent to the local branch of the public library. It draws a mix of students, older folk and mothers with strollers, attracted mainly by the cookies, doughnuts and cinnamon rolls, as well as ice cream in hot weather.

Klášterní Pivnice PUB

(Map p96; ☎723 026 104; Ovenecká 15; ⏰9.30am-9.30pm; 🚋1, 8, 12, 25, 26) Not for the mild mannered, this old man's pub serves excellent, hard-to-find Klášter beer. The main drinking room gets pretty smoky and crowded with crusty regulars, and indeed, a whole day can go by without a single female visitor, but you can't argue with the beer. A perfectly preserved Prague pub undisturbed by modern life.

Kumbal CAFE

(Map p96; ☎604 959 323; www.kumbal.cz; Heřmanova 12; ⏰8am-9.30pm Mon-Fri, 9am-9.30pm Sat & Sun; 📶👪; 🚋1, 6, 8, 12, 17, 25, 26) This stylish coffee bar in a 1930s functionalist building manages to be both hip and comfortable at the same time. There's good coffee and tea, though not much on the menu aside from a few simple sandwiches and a daily soup (usually vegetarian). Breakfast is served every day until 11.30am.

Bubeneč & Dejvice

The adjoining neighbourhoods of Bubeneč and Dejvice are mainly residential and lack traditional sights. Nevertheless, Bubeneč, with its embassies and stately turn-of-the-20th-century mansions, is considered one of the city's top addresses, and Stromovka park – which lies within Bubeneč's boundaries – is arguably Prague's nicest park. The relative proximity to the airport makes this a good choice for hotels. The two neighbourhoods also have their share of upscale restaurants.

★Kavárna Pod Lipami CAFE

(Map p98; ☎777 568 658; www.facebook.com/kavarnapodlipami; Čechova 1, Bubeneč; ⏰11am-10pm; 📶; 🚋1, 8, 12, 25, 26) This local branch of the citywide Mama Coffee chain offers fair-trade coffees, as well as teas, other drinks and light meals (such as hummus, soups and salads) in a comfortably dressed-down setting of tiled floors, white walls and light bulbs simply hanging on wires from the ceiling. It's popular with students and there's a terrace out front in summer.

Elbow Room COCKTAIL BAR

(Map p98; www.facebook.com/elbowroomletna; Veletržní 40, Bubeneč; ⏰7pm-3am Mon-Sat, to midnight Sun; 📶; 🚋1, 8, 12, 25, 26) This small cocktail bar, tucked away on an assuming block, busy Veletržní, feels like a secret speakeasy. There are few signs on the door, but push through to find yourself in a cramped but cosy front room (there's a quieter second room at the back). Very good and good-value cocktails, including Prague's best 'Dark & Stormy' (rum and ginger beer).

Alchymista CAFE

(Map p98; ☎732 938 046; www.alchymista.cz; Jana Zajíce 7, Bubeneč; ⏰10.30am-9.30pm; 📶; 🚋1, 8, 12, 25, 26) This old-fashioned coffee house with an adjacent art gallery is an oasis in the culturally barren neighbourhood behind Sparta Stadium. Freshly ground coffee, a serious selection of teas (no Lipton tea bags here), and freshly made cakes and strudels draw a mostly local crowd. Beautiful garden out back in summer.

Kavárna Místo CAFE

(Map p98; ☎727 914 535; www.mistoprovas.cz; Bubenečská 12, Dejvice; ⏰9am-10pm Mon-Sat, 10am-6pm Sun; 📶; Ⓜ Hradčanská) This modern, minimalist coffee bar and restaurant uses premium beans from local roaster DoubleShot. There's an elaborate coffee menu, with several different preparation methods available. Servers are knowledgeable and encourage experimentation (no simple 'Americanos' here). In addition, there's a light food menu and full bakery of cakes and sweets, including some gluten-free options. Try to book because this place is popular.

Kafemat CAFE

(Map p98; ☎721 536 200; www.facebook.com/kafematdejvice; Dejvická 3; ⏰8am-6pm Mon-Fri, 9.30am-6pm Sat; 📶; Ⓜ Hradčanská) This little hole-in-the-wall reputedly serves some of the city's best coffee. Order at the bar and take one of the few seats scattered around or grab your cup to go. In addition to coffee, it serves chai, lemonade and morning pastries.

Potrvá CAFE

(Map p98; ☎reservations 222 963 707; www.potrva.cz; Srbská 2, Bubeneč; ⏰3pm-midnight; 📶; Ⓜ Hradčanská) This relaxing cafe just a short walk across the railway tracks from the Hradčanská metro station is a good place for quiet reflection during the day. The menu consists mostly of coffee and drinks, but small bites such as soups and sandwiches (60Kč to 90Kč) are also served. Occasional live music and open-mic nights in the evening.

Kabinet CAFE
(Map p98; ☎233 326 668; www.facebook.com/kavarnakabinet; Terronská 25, Dejvice; ⏰noon-10pm Mon-Fri, 3-10pm Sat & Sun; 📶; Ⓜ Dejvická, 🚋8, 18) A retro, 1920s-style coffee house, Kabinet is situated in a cool cubist building in a pleasantly residential part of Dejvice. Old cameras, posters and photographs lend a throwback feel. To add to the nostalgic setting, the name of the cafe, for Czechs, recalls early school days – a 'kabinet' being a teacher's office.

Na Slamníku PUB
(Map p98; ☎233 322 594; www.koncertynaslamniku.wz.cz; Wolkerova 12, Bubeneč; ⏰noon-midnight; 🚌131 to Sibiřské náměstí) A great traditional Czech pub and beer garden dating from the 19th century, Na Slamníku is tucked away in a small valley in Bubeneč, just behind the sprawling Russian embassy. There are a couple of drinking rooms inside, and a peaceful shady garden in front in summer. Check the website for occasional live music from around 8pm.

Fraktal BAR
(Map p98; ☎777 794 094; www.fraktalbar.cz; Šmeralová 1, Bubeneč; ⏰11am-midnight; 📶; 🚋1, 8, 12, 25, 26) This subterranean space under a corner house near Letenské náměstí is easily the friendliest bar this side of the Vltava. This is especially true for English speakers, as Fraktal serves as a kind of unofficial expat watering hole. There's also good bar fare such as burgers (mains 120Kč to 300Kč). The only drawback is the early closing time (last orders at 11.30pm).

Kavárna Alibi CAFE
(Map p98; www.alibi.cz; Svatovítská 6, Dejvice; ⏰9am-midnight Mon-Fri, 2pm-midnight Sat & Sun; 📶; Ⓜ Dejvická, 🚋Vítězné Náměstí) Lively, smoky coffee house that is usually packed with students. It's a perfect spot to curl up with a coffee or a beer, write some postcards, read your book or have a heart-to-heart with your travelling companion.

La Bodega Flamenca BAR
(Map p98; ☎233 374 075; www.labodega.cz; Šmeralová 5, Bubeneč; ⏰4pm-1am Sun-Thu, to 3am Fri & Sat; 🚋1, 8, 12, 25, 26) La Bodega resides in an atmospheric, red-brick cellar. With the Latin music turned down low, the crowd seems a bit more reflective (at least compared with the rest of the bars in the neighbourhood). Most people come for a beer or sangria, but there's also a nice selection of tapas on hand. Live music and dance some nights.

🍷 Smíchov & Vyšehrad

Smíchov continues to surprise, with every year bringing at least one or two new bar or cafe openings. Most of the action is clustered near Anděl metro station, anchored by Nový Smíchov shopping centre. Vyšehrad is a different story. There's no real nightlife to speak of here, though there are a couple of cafes in which to relax as you take in the sights.

Kavárna Co Hledá Jméno CAFE
(Cafe That's Looking for a Name; Map p102; ☎775 466 330; www.facebook.com/kavarnacohledajmeno; Stroupežnického 10; ⏰8am-10pm Mon-Fri; 📶; Ⓜ Anděl) One of the most eye-catching of a slew of industrial-style, hipsterish cafes to open around town in the past couple of years. Light bulbs hanging from cords, mix-and-match chairs, plank flooring and an enormous tree-trunk bar are just some of the elements that lend a casual, 'found object' vibe. In addition to coffee drinks, there's a modest kitchen with good-value lunch deals.

Lokal Blok PUB
(Map p102; ☎251 511 490; http://lokalblok.cz; náměstí 14, října 10, Smíchov; ⏰noon-1am Mon-Fri, 4pm-1am Sat & Sun; 📶; Ⓜ Anděl) The perfect Prague combination: a raucous pub and a state-of-the-art climbing wall (though presumably you're supposed to climb before you drink and not vice versa). Most nights there's a lively crowd, fuelled by Pilsner Urquell on tap and some good Mexican eats, such as nachos and quesadillas. Highly recommended.

Prolog COCKTAIL BAR
(Map p102; ☎775 005 007; www.prologbar.cz; Nádražní 57a, Smíchov; ⏰2pm-2am Mon-Sat, to midnight Sun; 📶; Ⓜ Anděl) Arguably Smíchov's most upscale watering hole, this classy cocktail bar, with a subdued interior of dark woods and black leather, draws an after-work crowd from the nearby office complexes. There's an inventive cocktail menu

plus high-end snacks, such as blinis and oysters, to enjoy with your drink.

Hospoda U Buldoka PUB

(At the Bulldog; Map p102; ☎257 329 154; www.ubuldoka.cz; Preslova 1, Smíchov; ⊙bar 11am-midnight Mon-Thu, 11am-1am Fri, noon-midnight Sat, noon-11pm Sun, club 8pm-4am Wed-Sat; 📶; Ⓜ Anděl) The Bulldog pub has it all: a quiet setting with good beer and decent Czech pub food during the day, while evenings bring out a rowdier vibe (women drink free on Wednesday nights). By night the Bulldog morphs into a college-style dance club, with DJs and theme nights; depending on the crowd it can go well into the wee hours.

Cafe Citadela CAFE

(Map p106; Vyšehrad Citadel, Vyšehrad; ⊙9.30am-6pm Apr-Sep, 10am-5pm Wed-Sun Oct-Mar; Ⓜ Vyšehrad) This relaxed beer garden and cafe is the perfect place to cool off under the trees. You'll find it just on the edge of the sculpture garden, south of the cathedral. Most come for coffee or beer, but there's also a small menu of salads, omelettes and sweets.

V Cafe CAFE

(Map p106; ☎725 740 717; K Rotundě 3, Vyšehrad; ⊙11am-9.30pm; 📶; Ⓜ Vyšehrad) This pretty summer terrace may be the nicest place within the Vyšehrad citadel area to relax over a coffee, beer or light meal of grilled sausages.

Dog's Bollocks BAR

(Map p102; ☎775 736 030; www.dogsbollocks.cz; Nádražní 82, Smíchov; ⊙5pm-3am Tue-Thu, to 5am Fri & Sat; 🚊4, 5, 12, 20) This classy bar, restaurant and nightspot is not far from the Staropramen Brewery and is a great choice if you're staying in the area and don't want to go far for your fun. In spite of the English-friendly name, it draws mostly Czech students and young professionals letting loose.

Pitomá Kavárna CAFE

(Map p102; ☎774 608 971; www.pitomakavarna.sweb.cz; Preslova 3, Smíchov; ⊙8am-11pm Mon-Fri, 10am-11pm Sat & Sun; 📶; Ⓜ Anděl) This likeable and popular neighbourhood cafe has friendly service and a quiet back room that's perfect for writing postcards home or having a friendly chat over coffee and a piece of cake. In summer it serves delicious homemade iced teas and ice-cream shakes.

Phenomen CLUB

(Map p102; ☎774 366 636; www.phenomen.cz; Nádražní 84, Smíchov; ⊙7pm-3am Tue-Thu, to 4am Fri & Sat; 📶; Ⓜ Anděl, 🚊4, 5, 12, 20) This upscale dance club draws a well-heeled crowd in their 20s and 30s who come for the cocktails, champagne, DJ theme nights and occasional live music. Pretty decent bar food such as burgers, wings and salads too (the kitchen closes at 2am).

Hells Bells BAR

(Map p102; ☎722 302 559; www.hellsbells.cz; Na Bělidle 27, Smíchov; ⊙5pm-3am Mon-Sat, to midnight Sun; Ⓜ Anděl) In spite of the glitzy office towers, Smíchov is still a down-and-dirty kind of place, and this Goth-friendly, heavy-metal bar is where the locals let it all hang out. Loud, crowded and fun – the late closing time makes it a perfect ticket for that last drink of the night.

Back Doors BAR

(Map p102; ☎257 315 824; www.backdoors.cz; Na Bělidle 30, Smíchov; ⊙11am-3pm & 6pm-1am Mon-Fri, 6pm-3am Sat; Ⓜ Anděl) This upmarket cellar/bar/restaurant/club is inspired by similar spaces in New York and Amsterdam (though the subterranean Gothic-cellar look could only be Prague). It offers decent Czech DJs and a relaxed vibe most nights, though it can get stuffy on a crowded weekend night. If you're hungry, there's a full menu of well-done international dishes.

☆ Entertainment

Across the spectrum, from ballet to blues, jazz to rock and theatre to film, there's a bewildering range of entertainment on offer in this eclectic city. Prague is now as much a European centre for jazz, rock and hip-hop as it is for classical music. The biggest draw, however, is still the Prague Spring festival of classical music and opera.

☆ Staré Město

Smetana Hall CLASSICAL MUSIC

(Smetanova síň; Map p62; ☎222 002 101; www.obecnidum.cz; náměstí Republiky 5, Municipal House; tickets 400-900Kč; ⊙box office 10am-6pm; Ⓜ Náměstí Republiky) The Smetana Hall, centrepiece of the stunning Municipal House (p72), is the city's largest concert hall, with seating for 1200 beneath an art-nouveau glass dome. The stage is framed by sculptures representing the Vyšehrad legend (to the right) and Slavonic dances (to the left). This is the home venue of the Prague Symphony Orchestra

ENTERTAINMENT BY NEIGHBOURHOOD

Prague Castle & Hradčany Very little happens in this neighbourhood after dark – best head elsewhere!

Malá Strana Good selection of small, intimate live-music venues.

Staré Město Home to many classical-music venues and old-school jazz clubs.

Nové Město Prague State Opera and the National Theatre rub shoulders with sports bars and stag parties.

Vinohrady & Vršovice The heart of Prague's gay scene also has lots of trendy clubs and bars.

Žižkov & Karlín Žižkov is the place for classic, sticky-floored, down-and-dirty rock joints.

Holešovice Home to up-and-coming nightclubs and experimental venues.

Bubeneč & Dejvice Few entertainment options here, but catching a Sparta Praha football match is usually pretty entertaining.

Smíchov & Vyšehrad Some good experimental venues in Smíchov; open-air classical concerts in Vyšehrad.

(Symfonický orchestr hlavního města Prahy; www.fok.cz), and also stages performances of folk dance and music.

Dvořák Hall CONCERT VENUE
(Dvořákova síň; Map p62; ☎227 059 227; www.ceskafilharmonie.cz; náměstí Jana Palacha 1, Rudolfinum; tickets 120-900Kč; ⊙box office 10am-12.30pm & 1.30-6pm Mon-Fri; Ⓜ Staroměstská) The Dvořák Hall in the neo-Renaissance Rudolfinum (p72) is home to the world-renowned Czech Philharmonic Orchestra (Česká filharmonie). Sit back and be impressed by some of the best classical musicians in Prague.

Estates Theatre OPERA, BALLET
(Stavovské divadlo; Map p62; ☎224 902 322; www.narodni-divadlo.cz; Ovocný trh 1; tickets 100-990Kč; ⊙box office 10am-6pm; Ⓜ Můstek) The Estates is the oldest theatre in Prague, famed as the place where Mozart conducted the premiere of *Don Giovanni* on 29 October 1787. This, and other Mozart operas, are regularly performed here, along with a range of classic opera, ballet and drama productions.

Theatre on the Balustrade THEATRE
(Divadlo Na Zábradlí; Map p62; ☎222 868 868; www.nazabradli.cz; Anenské náměstí 5; tickets 300-380Kč; ⊙box office 2-8pm Mon-Fri, 2hr before show starts Sat & Sun; 🚊2, 17, 18) The theatre where Václav Havel honed his skills as a playwright four decades ago is now the city's main venue for serious Czech-language drama, including works by a range of foreign playwrights translated into Czech. There are occasional performances in English, though most are in Czech with English subtitles. Closed for renovations until summer 2017.

National Marionette Theatre PERFORMING ARTS
(Národní divadlo marionet; Map p62; ☎224 819 323; www.mozart.cz; Žatecká 1; adult/child 590/490Kč; ⊙box office 10am-8pm; Ⓜ Staroměstská) Loudly touted as the longest-running marionette show in the city – performed almost continuously since 1991 (a fact, some say, that is reflected in the enthusiasm of the performances) – *Don Giovanni* is a life-sized puppet version of the Mozart opera, and has spawned several imitations around town. Younger kids' attention might begin to wander fairly early on during this two-hour show.

Ta Fantastika PERFORMING ARTS
(Map p62; ☎222 221 366; www.tafantastika.cz; Karlova 8; tickets 720Kč; ⊙box office 10am-9.30pm; Ⓜ Staroměstská) Established in New York in 1981 by Czech émigré Petr Kratochvil, Ta Fantastika moved to Prague in 1989. The company has produced black-light theatre based on classic literature and legends such as *Excalibur, The Picture of Dorian Gray* and *Joan of Arc,* but the program is now dominated almost entirely by *Aspects of Alice,* based on *Alice in Wonderland.*

Roxy LIVE MUSIC
(Map p62; ☎224 826 296; www.roxy.cz; Dlouhá 33; tickets 150-700Kč; ⊙7pm-5am; 🚊6, 8, 15, 26) Set in the ramshackle shell of an art-deco cinema, the legendary Roxy has nurtured

the more independent and innovative end of Prague's club spectrum since 1987 – this is the place to see the Czech Republic's top DJs. On the 1st floor is NoD, an 'experimental space' that stages drama, dance, performance art, cinema and live music. Best nightspot in Staré Město.

Jazz Republic LIVE MUSIC
(Map p62; ☎221 183 552; www.jazzrepublic.cz; Jilská 1a; admission free; ⏰8pm-late, music 9.15pm-midnight; Ⓜ Národní Třída) Despite the name, this relaxed club stages all kinds of live music, including rock, blues, reggae and fusion as well as jazz. Bands are mostly local, and the music is not overpowering – you can easily hold a conversation – which means it won't please the purists (sssshh!).

Vagon LIVE MUSIC
(Map p62; ☎733 737 301; www.vagon.cz; Národní třída 25, Palác Metro; gigs 100-200Kč, cover after midnight free; ⏰7pm-5am Mon-Thu, to 6am Fri & Sat, to 1am Sun; 📶; Ⓜ Národní Třída, 🚋2, 9, 18, 22) Vagon is more like a student-union bar than a club as such, but it always has a friendly, chilled-out atmosphere. There's live music pretty much every night, from local blues artists, to Pink Floyd and Led Zep tribute bands, to classic Czech rock bands. From midnight into the small hours the dancing continues as a DJ-hosted 'rockothèque'.

Blues Sklep JAZZ
(Map p62; ☎221 466 138; www.bluessklep.cz; Liliová 10; cover 100-150Kč; ⏰bar 7pm-2.30am, music 9pm-midnight; 🚋2, 17, 18) One of the city's newer jazz clubs, the Blues Sklep (*sklep* means 'cellar') is a typical Old Town basement with dark, Gothic-vaulted rooms that provide an atmospheric setting for regular nightly jazz sessions. Bands play anything from trad New Orleans jazz to bebop, blues, funk and soul.

AghaRTA Jazz Centrum JAZZ
(Map p62; ☎222 211 275; www.agharta.cz; Železná 16; cover 250Kč; ⏰7pm-1am, music 9pm-midnight; Ⓜ Můstek) AghaRTA has been staging top-notch modern jazz, blues, funk and fusion since 1991, but moved into this central Old Town venue only in 2004. A typical jazz cellar with red-brick vaults, the centre also has a music shop (open 7pm to midnight) which sells CDs, T-shirts and coffee mugs. As well as hosting local musicians, AghaRTA occasionally stages gigs by leading international artists.

☆ Nové Město

National Theatre OPERA, BALLET
(Národní divadlo; Map p78; ☎224 901 448; www.narodni-divadlo.cz; Národní třída 2; tickets 100-1290Kč; ⏰box offices 10am-6pm; 🚋2, 9, 18, 22) The much-loved National Theatre provides a stage for traditional opera, drama and ballet by the likes of Smetana, Shakespeare and Tchaikovsky, sharing the program alongside more modern works by composers and playwrights such as Philip Glass and John Osborne. The box offices are in the Nový síň building next door, in the Kolowrat Palace (opposite the Estates Theatre) and at the State Opera.

Prague State Opera OPERA, BALLET
(Státní opera Praha; Map p78; ☎224 901 448; www.narodni-divadlo.cz; Wilsonova 4; ⏰box office 10am-6pm; Ⓜ Muzeum) The impressive neo-rococo home of the Prague State Opera provides a glorious setting for performances of opera and ballet. The building is closed for renovation work until 2018.

Wonderful Dvořák CLASSICAL MUSIC
(Kouzelný Dvořák; Map p78; www.facebook.com/musictheatre; Ke Karlovu 20, Vila Amerika; tickets 595Kč; ⏰concerts 8pm Tue & Fri May-Oct; Ⓜ IP Pavlova) The pretty little Vila Amerika was built in 1717 as an aristocrat's immodest summer retreat. These days it's home to the Dvořák Museum (p87) and from May to October it stages performances of Dvořák's works by a chamber orchestra, complete with period costume. Tickets are available at www.pragueexperience.com and www.pragueticketoffice.com.

Archa Theatre THEATRE
(Divadlo Archa; Map p84; ☎221 716 333; www.archatheatre.cz; Na poříčí 26; tickets 230-900Kč; ⏰box office 10am-6pm Mon-Fri, plus 2hr before performances; 📶; 🚋3, 8, 14, 24) The Archa (Ark) has been described as Prague's alternative National Theatre, a multifunctional venue for the avant garde and the experimental. As well as contemporary drama (occasionally in English) – Václav Havel's *Leaving* has been performed here – dance and performance art, the theatre stages TV shows and live music, from Indian classical to industrial noise.

Minor Theatre THEATRE
(Divadlo Minor; Map p78; ☎222 231 351; www.minor.cz; Vodičkova 6; adult/child 150/100Kč; ⏰box office 10am-1.30pm & 2.30-8pm Mon-Fri,

ART-HOUSE CINEMA

Prague has more than 30 cinemas, some showing first-run Western films (usually in English), some showing Czech films, and several excellent art-house cinemas, where Czech films are often screened with English subtitles. Czech-language films with English subtitles are listed as having *anglický titulky*.

Movies are normally screened twice in the evening, at around 7pm and 9pm, though multiplexes show films all day. Most cinemas screen matinees on weekends. For cinema listings check www.prague.tv. The best art-house cinemas include:

Kino Světozor (Map p78; 224 946 824; www.kinosvetozor.cz; Vodičkova 41; tickets 60-120Kč; ; Můstek) Emphasis on classic cinema, documentary and art-house films screened in their original language – everything from *Battleship Potemkin* and *Casablanca* to *Annie Hall* and *The Motorcycle Diaries* – plus critically acclaimed box office hits.

Bio Oko (Oko Cinema; Map p96; box office 233 382 606, ticket reservations 608 330 088; www.biooko.net; Františka Křížka 15; tickets from 100Kč; ; 1, 6, 8, 12, 17, 25, 26) Repertory cinema shows a varied program of underground films, selections from film festivals, documentaries, big-budget movies, and classics from around the world. Most films are shown in the original language (not necessarily English), with Czech subtitles.

Kino Aero (Map p92; 271 771 349; www.kinoaero.cz; Biskupcova 31, Žižkov; tickets 60-120Kč; ; 1, 9, 10, 11, 16) The Aero is Prague's best-loved art-house cinema, with themed programs, retrospectives and unusual films, often in English or with English subtitles.

11am-6pm Sat & Sun; Karlovo Náměstí) Divadlo Minor is a wheelchair-accessible children's theatre that offers a fun mix of puppets, clown shows and pantomime. There are performances (in Czech) at 3pm Saturday and Sunday, and at 6pm Thursday and Friday, and you can usually get a ticket at the door.

Laterna Magika PERFORMING ARTS

(Map p78; 224 901 417; www.narodni-divadlo.cz; Nová Scéna, Národní třída 4; tickets 260-690Kč; box office 9am-6pm Mon-Fri, 10am-6pm Sat & Sun; 2, 9, 18, 22) Laterna Magika has been wowing audiences since its first cutting-edge multimedia show caused a stir at the 1958 Brussels World Fair. Its imaginative blend of dance, music and projected images continues to pull in the crowds. Nová Scena, the futuristic building next to the National Theatre, has been home to Laterna Magika since it moved here from its birthplace in the Adria Palace in the mid-1970s.

Image Theatre PERFORMING ARTS

(Divadlo Image; Map p78; 222 314 448; www.imagetheatre.cz; Národní 25; tickets 480Kč; box office 10am-8pm; Staroměstská) Founded in 1989, this company uses creative black-light theatre along with pantomime, modern dance and video – not to mention liberal doses of slapstick – to tell its stories. The staging can be very effective, but the atmosphere is often dictated by audience reaction.

Lucerna Music Bar LIVE MUSIC

(Map p78; 224 217 108; www.musicbar.cz; Palác Lucerna, Vodičkova 36; cover 100-500Kč; hours vary; Můstek) Nostalgia reigns supreme at this atmospheric old theatre, now looking a little dog-eared. It hosts a hugely popular 1980s and '90s video party from 9pm every Friday and Saturday night, with crowds of young locals bopping along to Duran Duran and Gary Numan.

There's an impressively eclectic program of live bands on midweek nights, with everything from Slovakian ska and Belgian pop-rock to Dutch electro-funk and US heavy metal.

Rock Café LIVE MUSIC

(Map p78; 224 933 947; www.rockcafe.cz; Národní třída 20; cover free-500Kč; 10am-3am Mon-Fri, 5pm-3am Sat, 5pm-1am Sun; Národní Třída) Not to be confused with the Hard Rock Café, this multifunction club is the offspring of the influential Nový Horizont art movement of the 1990s. It sports a stage for DJs, comedians and live rock bands, funkily decorated 'rock cafe', cinema, theatre, art gallery and CD shop.

Live bands are mostly local, ranging from nu-metal to folk rock to Doors and Sex Pistols tribute bands. Music from 7.30pm.

Reduta Jazz Club JAZZ
(Map p78; ☎224 933 487; www.redutajazzclub.cz; Národní třída 20; cover 330-490Kč; ⊙9pm-3am; 📶; Ⓜ Národní Třída) The Reduta is Prague's oldest jazz club, founded in 1958 during the communist era – it was here in 1994 that former US president Bill Clinton famously jammed on a new saxophone presented to him by Václav Havel. It has an intimate setting, with smartly dressed patrons squeezing into tiered seats and lounges to soak up the big-band, swing and Dixieland atmosphere.

☆ Vinohrady & Vršovice

Techtle Mechtle CLUB
(Map p88; ☎222 250 143; www.techtle-mechtle.cz; Vinohradská 47, Vinohrady; ⊙6pm-5am Tue-Sat; 📶; Ⓜ Náměstí Míru, 🚋11, 13) A popular cellar dance bar on Vinohrady's main drag. The name translates to 'hanky panky' in Czech, and that's what most of the swank people who come here are after. In addition to a well-tended cocktail bar, you'll find a decent restaurant and dance floor, and occasional special events. Arrive early to get a good table.

Radost FX CLUB
(Map p88; ☎224 254 776, 603 193 711; www.radostfx.cz; Bělehradská 120, Vinohrady; cover 100-250Kč; ⊙10pm-6am; 📶; Ⓜ IP Pavlova) Though not quite as trendy as it once was, slick and shiny Radost is still capable of pulling in the crowds, with themed dance parties each night of the week. The regular Thursday night hip-hop and R&B party remains the most popular. The place has a chilled-out, bohemian atmosphere, with an excellent lounge and vegetarian restaurant (p132).

Termix CLUB
(Map p88; ☎222 710 462; www.club-termix.cz; Třebízského 4a, Vinohrady; ⊙9pm-6am Wed-Sun; Ⓜ Jiřího z Poděbrad, 🚋11, 13) Termix is one of Prague's most popular gay dance clubs, with an industrial hi-tech vibe (lots of shiny steel, glass and plush sofas) and a young crowd that includes as many tourists as locals. The smallish dance floor fills up fast and you may have to queue to get in.

Le Clan CLUB
(Map p88; www.leclan.cz; Balbínova 23, Vinohrady; cover 100Kč, free before 3am Sat & Sun; ⊙10pm-3am Wed & Thu, 11.30pm-noon Sat & Sun; Ⓜ Muzeum) A French-accented after-party club, with DJs on two floors, lots of bars, cosy armchairs and myriad rooms stuffed with people who want to party until dawn. It's usually got a good, decadent vibe, and tends to get more (not less) crowded as the night wears on.

Infinity CLUB
(Map p88; ☎731 109 639; www.infinitybar.cz; Chrudimská 2a, Vinohrady; ⊙8pm-3am Tue-Thu, to 4.30am Fri & Sat; Ⓜ Flora) Smart-casual clubbing gear is the order of the day in this mid-sized cellar with exposed-brick walls and sophisticated lighting. Alternating between upbeat happy house and nostalgic '60s to '90s nights, it's much more enjoyable than its reputation as the second-biggest pick-up joint in Prague might suggest.

☆ Holešovice

La Fabrika THEATRE, PERFORMING ARTS
(Map p96; ☎box office 774 417 644; www.lafabrika.cz; Komunardů 30; admission 200-400Kč; ⊙box office 2-7.30pm Mon-Fri; 🚋1, 6, 12, 14, 25) The name refers to a 'factory', but this is actually a former paint warehouse that's been converted into an experimental performance space. Depending on the night, come here to catch live music (jazz or cabaret), theatre, dance or film. Consult the website

GOING TO THE THEATRE

Most Czech drama is, not surprisingly, performed in Czech. However, there are some English-language productions, as well as many predominantly visual shows where language is not a barrier. There's also the **Prague Fringe Festival** (p109), which takes place in early June and offers plenty of English-language theatre.

Prague is famous for its black-light theatre – occasionally called just 'black theatre' – a hybrid of mime, drama, dance and special effects in which actors wearing fluorescent costumes do their thing in front of a black backdrop lit only by ultraviolet light. It's a growth industry in Prague, with at least half a dozen venues; **Ta Fantastika** (p158) and **Image Theatre** (p160) are two of the longest-running. An even older Czech tradition is puppetry, and the city has several marionette shows on offer.

CLASSICAL MUSIC

There are half a dozen concerts of one kind or another in Prague almost every day during the summer, making a fine soundtrack to accompany the city's visual delights. Many of these are chamber concerts performed by aspiring musicians in the city's churches – gorgeous but chilly (take an extra layer, even on a summer day), and not always with the finest of acoustics. However, a good number of concerts, especially those promoted by people handing out flyers in the street, are second-rate, despite the premium prices that foreigners pay. If you want to be sure of quality, go for a performance by one of the city's professional orchestras.

Box offices are open from 30 minutes to one hour before the start of a performance. For classical music, opera and ballet listings, check out www.czechopera.cz and www.pragueevents calendar.com.

for the latest program. Try to reserve in advance as shows typically sell out.

Alfred Ve Dvoře THEATRE
(Map p96; ☎233 382 433; www.alfredvedvore.cz; Františka Křížka 36; tickets 100-150Kč; ⊙box office 5.30-11pm Mon-Fri; 🚋1, 6, 8, 12, 17, 25, 26) An artistic treasure in an unlikely spot in Holešovice, the Alfred regularly stages demanding works of drama, dance, cabaret and movement theatre, including occasional performances in English. Check the website to see what's on and buy tickets.

☆ Žižkov & Karlín

★**Palác Akropolis** LIVE MUSIC
(Map p92; ☎296 330 913; www.palacakropolis.cz; Kubelíkova 27, Žižkov; tickets free-250Kč; ⊙club 6.30pm-5am; 📶; 🚋5, 9, 15, 26) The Akropolis is a Prague institution, a smoky, labyrinthine, sticky-floored shrine to alternative music and drama. Its various performance spaces host a smorgasbord of musical and cultural events, from DJs to string quartets to Macedonian Roma bands to local rock gods to visiting talent – Marianne Faithfull, the Flaming Lips and the Strokes have all played here.

☆ Bubeneč & Dejvice

Spejbl & Hurvínek Theatre THEATRE
(Divadlo Spejbla a Hurvínka; Map p98; ☎box office 224 316 784; www.spejbl-hurvinek.cz; Dejvická 38, Dejvice; tickets 110-220Kč; ⊙box office 1-6pm Mon, 9am-2pm & 3-6pm Tue-Fri, 9.30-11.30am & noon-5pm Sat & Sun; 👪; Ⓜ Dejvická) Created in 1930 by puppeteer Josef Skupa, Spejbl and Hurvínek are the Czech marionette equivalents of Punch and Judy, though they are father and son rather than husband and wife. The shows are in Czech, but most can be followed regardless of which language you speak.

☆ Smíchov & Vyšehrad

Švandovo Divadlo Na Smíchově THEATRE
(Švandovo Theatre in Smíchov; Map p102; ☎box office 257 318 666; www.svandovodivadlo.cz; Štefánikova 57, Smíchov; tickets 150-300Kč; ⊙box office 2-8pm Mon-Fri, plus 2hr before performances Sat & Sun; 🚋9, 12, 15, 20) This experimental theatre space, where Czech and international dramatic works are performed, is admired for its commitment to staging 'English-friendly' performances. It also hosts occasional live music and dance, as well as regular 'Stage Talks', unscripted discussions with noted personalities.

Jazz Dock JAZZ
(Map p102; ☎774 058 838; www.jazzdock.cz; Janáčkovo nábřeží 2, Smíchov; tickets 150-300Kč; ⊙4pm-3am; 📶; Ⓜ Anděl, 🚋9, 12, 15, 20) Most of Prague's jazz clubs are smoky cellar affairs, but this riverside club is a definite step up, with clean, modern decor and a decidedly romantic view out over the Vltava. It draws some of the best local talent and occasional international acts. Go early or book to get a good table. Shows normally begin at 7pm and 10pm.

MeetFactory LIVE PERFORMANCE
(☎251 551 796; www.meetfactory.cz; Ke Sklárně 15, Smíchov; ⊙1-8pm, varies according to event; 🚋4, 5, 12, 20) FREE David Černý's MeetFactory is a remarkable project that unites artists from around the world to live and create in an abandoned factory south of Smíchovské nádraží. The space is used for exhibitions, happenings, film screenings, theatrical performances and concerts. The location is out of the way, so be sure to check the website for the program before heading out.

Shopping

In the past decade or so, Prague's shopping scene has changed beyond recognition. An influx of global brand names and glitzy new malls has left the city's main shopping streets looking very much like those of any other European capital, while a new generation of young Czechs have created their own fashion and design boutiques in the backstreets of Stáre Město.

Prague Castle & Hradčany

Houpací Kůň TOYS

(Map p44; ☎603 515 745; Loretánské náměstí 3; ⏰9.30am-6.30pm; 🚋22) The 'Rocking Horse' toy shop houses a collection of wooden folk dolls, 1950s wind-up tractors, toy cars and – surprise – even a couple of rocking horses. There are quality toys and art supplies you won't find anywhere else in Prague, but for a typically Czech souvenir try the famous and ubiquitous Little Mole cartoon character, available here in several guises.

Malá Strana

Although Mostecká and Nerudova streets are lined with souvenir shops, Malá Strana is not really a shopping district. That said, there are some gems to be discovered among the tourist tat, and a few design shops and fashion boutiques are beginning to make an appearance in the neighbourhood, especially on Tržiště and U Lužického semináře.

★ **Shakespeare & Sons** BOOKS

(Map p50; ☎257 531 894; www.shakes.cz; U Lužického semináře 10; ⏰11am-9pm; 🚋12, 15, 20, 22) Though its shelves groan with a formidable range of literature in English, French and German, this is more than just a bookshop (with Prague's best range of titles on East European history) – it's a congenial literary hang-out with knowledgeable staff, occasional author events, and a cool downstairs space for sitting and reading.

Chemistry DESIGN

(Map p50; ☎604 293 385; www.facebook.com/thechemistrydesignstore; U Lužického semináře 11; ⏰9am-7pm; 🚋12, 15, 20, 22) Spreading through several ground-floor rooms of a Malá Strana townhouse, this 'pop-up shop' run by the Chemistry Gallery (p96) showcases the best of Czech art and design, both contemporary and retro, from sculpture and graphic art to ceramics and jewellery.

Artěl GLASS, INTERIOR DESIGN

(Map p50; ☎251 554 008; www.artelglass.com; U Lužickeho semináře 7; ⏰10am-7pm; 🚋12, 15, 20, 22) Traditional Bohemian glass-making meets modern design in this stylish shop founded by US designer Karen Feldman. In addition to hand-blown designer crystal, you can find a range of vintage and modern items of Czech design, from jewellery and ceramics to toys and stationery.

Marionety Truhlář ARTS & CRAFTS

(Map p50; ☎602 689 918; www.marionety.com; U Lužického semináře 5; ⏰10am-9pm; 🚋12, 15, 20, 22) This palace of puppetry stocks traditional marionettes from more than 40 workshops around the Czech Republic, as well as offering DIY puppet kits, courses on puppet-making, and the chance to order a custom-made marionette in your own (or anyone else's) likeness.

Staré Město

The elegant avenue of Pařížská is lined with international designer houses including Dior, Boss, Armani and Louis Vuitton, while the backstreets to its east are home to lots of little boutiques operated by Czech fashion designers. In contrast, the winding lanes between Old Town Square and Charles Bridge are thronged with tacky souvenir shops flaunting puppets, Russian dolls and 'Czech This Out' T-shirts.

Gurmet Pasáž Dlouhá FOOD & DRINKS

(Gourmet Arcade; Map p62; www.gurmetpasazdlouha.eu; Dlouhá 39; ⏰9am-10pm) Prague's foodie scene attains its apotheosis in this upmarket arcade dedicated to fine food. As well as eateries such as Nase Maso and Banh Mi Makers, you'll find shops selling fine wines, artisanal cheeses, handmade chocolate and imported seafood.

Dušní 3 FASHION & ACCESSORIES

(Map p62; ☎234 095 870; www.dusni3.cz; Dušní 3; ⏰10am-7pm Mon-Sat; Ⓜ Staroměstská) Established as an alternative to the superbrand stores on nearby Pařížská, this welcoming boutique offers a range of ready-to-wear fashion and accessories from a range of international designers, including clothes by Tara Jarmon, Ilaria Nistri and Vivienne

‑stwood, bags by Lulu Guinness, shoes by ‑llow Yellow, sunglasses by Victoria Beckham and perfumes by Andrea Maack.

Leeda FASHION & ACCESSORIES

(Map p62; 775 601 185; www.leeda.cz; Bartolomějská 1; 11am-7pm Mon-Sat; 2, 9, 18, 22) This original Czech label, created by two young Prague designers, Lucie Kutálková and Lucie Trnkov, has established a well-earned reputation for turning out colourful, hip and stylish clothes, from T-shirts to designer dresses – and all at very reasonable prices.

TEG1 FASHION & ACCESSORIES

(Map p62; 222 327 358; www.timoure.cz; V Kolkovně 6; 10am-7pm Mon-Fri, 11am-5pm Sat; M Staroměstská) TEG (Timoure et Group) is the design team created by Alexandra Pavalová and Ivana Šafránková, two of Prague's most respected fashion designers. This boutique showcases their quarterly collections, which feature a sharp, imaginative look that adds zest and sophistication to everyday, wearable clothes. There's a second branch near Národní třída.

Denim Heads FASHION & ACCESSORIES

(Map p62; 224 283 974; www.denimheads.cz; Konviktská 30; 11am-7pm Mon-Sat; 2, 9, 18, 22) Probably the city's best outlet for denim goods, this stylish boutique stocks more than two dozen brands from around the world, including Denim Demon and Indigofera from Sweden, and quality Japanese jeans from Momotaro and Japan Blue.

Material GLASS

(Map p62; 608 664 766; www.i-material.com; Týn 1; 10am-8pm; M Náměstí Republiky) Material puts a modern twist on the Czech crystal industry, with its oversized contemporary vases, bowls and Dale Chihuly–like ornaments, candle holders, chandeliers and glasses. The firm boasts its 'drunken sailor' glass is spill-proof. Yet, despite well-spaced displays, it's a store where you immediately fear breaking something – and when you check the prices you realise you should!

Pohádka TOYS

(Map p62; 224 239 469; www.czechtoys.cz; Celetná 32; 9am-9pm; M Náměstí Republiky) This store is sometimes beset by souvenir-hunting tour groups and it stocks plenty of *matryoshky* (Russian stacking dolls) – objects that actually have nothing to do with Prague. Surprisingly, then, it's also a pretty good place to shop for genuine Czech toys, from marionettes and costumed dolls to finger puppets, rocking horses and toy cars.

TEG2 FASHION & ACCESSORIES

(Map p62; 224 240 737; www.timoure.cz; Martinská 4; 10am-7pm Mon-Fri, 11am-5pm Sat; M Národní Třída) TEG (Timoure et Group) is the design team created by Alexandra Pavalová and Ivana Šafránková, two of Prague's most respected fashion designers. The main branch, TEG1, is near Old Town Square.

Talacko MUSIC

(Map p62; 224 813 039; www.talacko.cz; Rybná 29; 10am-6pm Mon-Fri, to 4pm Sat; M Náměstí Republiky) Pick up the score for Mozart's *Don Giovanni* or Dvořák's *New World Symphony* at this eclectic sheet-music shop. Or you might enjoy some popular music favourites – how about '101 Beatles Songs for Buskers'?

Le Patio Lifestyle HOMEWARES

(Map p62; 222 310 310; www.lepatiolifestyle.com; Dušní 8; 10am-7pm Mon-Sat, 11am-7pm Sun; M Staroměstská) There are lots of high-quality household accessories here, from wrought-iron chairs and lamps forged by Bohemian blacksmiths to scented wooden chests made by Indian carpenters. Plus you'll find funky earthenware plant pots, chunky crystal wine glasses in contemporary designs, and many more tempting items that you just *know* will fit into your already crammed suitcase…

Bohème FASHION & ACCESSORIES

(Map p62; 224 813 840; www.boheme.cz; Dušní 8; 11am-7pm Mon-Fri, to 5pm Sat; M Staroměstská) This boutique showcases the designs of Hana Stocklassa and her associates, with collections of knitwear, leather and suede clothes for women. Sweaters, turtlenecks, suede skirts, linen blouses, knit dresses and stretch denim suits seem to be the stock in trade, and there's a range of jewellery to choose from as well.

Maximum Underground MUSIC

(Map p62; 724 307 198; www.maximum.cz; Jílská 22; 11am-7pm Mon-Sat; M Můstek) On the 1st floor in an arcade just off Jílská, this place is stocked with CDs and LPs of indie, punk, hip-hop, techno and other genres. It also has a selection of new and secondhand street and club wear for those seeking that Central European grunge look.

Art Deco Galerie ANTIQUES
(Map p62; ☎224 223 076; www.artdecogalerie-mili.com; Michalská 21; ⊙2-7pm Mon-Fri, to 6pm Sat; Ⓜ Můstek) Specialising in early-20th-century items, this shop has a wide range of 1920s and '30s stuff, including clothes, handbags, jewellery, glassware and ceramics, along with knick-knacks such as the kind of cigarette case you might imagine Dorothy Parker pulling out of her purse.

Modernista HOMEWARES
(Map p62; ☎222 002 102; www.modernista.cz; náměstí Republiky 5, Municipal House; ⊙10am-6pm; Ⓜ Náměstí Republiky) Modernista specialises in reproduction 20th-century furniture, ceramics, glassware and jewellery in classic styles ranging from art-deco and cubist to functionalist and Bauhaus. This branch, located in the Municipal House information centre, is strong on jewellery and ceramics; the main showroom, in Vinohradský Pavilon (p167), has sensuously curved chairs that are a feature of the Icon Hotel, and an unusual chaise lounge by Adolf Loos.

Klara Nademlýnská FASHION & ACCESSORIES
(Map p62; ☎224 818 769; www.klaranademlynska.cz; Dlouhá 3; ⊙10am-7pm Mon-Fri, to 6pm Sat; Ⓜ Staroměstská) Klara Nademlýnská is one of the Czech Republic's top fashion designers, having trained in Prague and worked for almost a decade in Paris. Her clothes are characterised by clean lines, simple styling and quality materials, making for a very wearable range that covers the spectrum from swimwear to evening wear via jeans, halter tops, colourful blouses and sharply styled suits.

Bric A Brac ANTIQUES
(Map p62; ☎222 326 484; Týnská 7; ⊙11am-6pm; Ⓜ Náměstí Republiky) This is a wonderfully cluttered cave of old household items, glassware, toys, apothecary jars, 1940s leather jackets, cigar boxes, typewriters and stringed instruments and much, much more. Despite the junky look of the place, the knick-knacks are surprisingly expensive, but the affable Serbian owner can give you a guided tour around every piece in his extensive collection.

Kubista HOMEWARES
(Map p62; ☎224 236 378; www.kubista.cz; Ovocný trh 19; ⊙10am-6.30pm Tue-Sun; Ⓜ Náměstí Republiky) Appropriately located in Prague's finest cubist building, this shop specialises in limited-edition reproductions of distinctive cubist furniture and ceramics, and designs by masters of the form such as Josef Gočár and Pavel Janák. It also has a few original pieces for serious collectors with serious cash to spend.

Manufaktura ARTS & CRAFTS
(Map p62; ☎601 310 611; www.manufaktura.cz; Melantrichova 17; ⊙10am-8pm; Ⓜ Můstek) There are several Manufaktura outlets across town, but this small branch near Old Town Square seems to keep its inventory especially enticing. You'll find great Czech wooden toys, beautiful-looking (if extremely chewy) honey gingerbread made from elaborate medieval moulds, and seasonal gifts such as hand-painted Easter eggs.

Botanicus COSMETICS
(Map p62; ☎234 767 446; www.botanicus.cz; Týn 3; ⊙10am-6.30pm Nov-Mar, to 8pm Apr-Oct; Ⓜ Náměstí Republiky) Prepare for olfactory overload in this always-busy outlet for natural health and beauty products. The scented soaps, herbal bath oils and shampoos, fruit cordials and handmade paper products are made using herbs and plants grown on an organic farm at Ostrá, east of Prague.

Frey Wille JEWELLERY
(Map p62; ☎272 142 228; www.frey-wille.com; Havířská 3; ⊙10am-7pm Mon-Sat, noon-6pm Sun; Ⓜ Můstek) An Austrian jewellery maker famed for enamel work, Frey Wille produces a distinctive range of highly decorative pieces. Its traditional paisley and Egyptian designs are complemented by a range of art-nouveau designs based on the works of Alfons Mucha.

St Vol GLASS
(Map p62; ☎224 814 099; www.stvol.eu; Valentinská 11; ⊙10am-6pm Mon-Fri, 11am-5pm Sat & Sun; Ⓜ Staroměstská) This gallery-shop is a showroom for the striking and colourful glassware of Czech designers, including Jiří Pačínek and Bořek Šípek. Their work may not be to everyone's taste, but their eccentric creations are certainly eye-catching.

Granát Turnov JEWELLERY
(Map p62; ☎222 315 612; www.granat.eu; Dlouhá 28-30; ⊙10am-6pm Mon-Fri, to 1pm Sat; Ⓜ Náměstí Republiky) Part of the country's biggest jewellery chain, Granát Turnov specialises in Bohemian garnet, and has a huge range of gold and silver rings, brooches, cufflinks and necklaces featuring these small,

SHOPPING BY NEIGHBOURHOOD

Prague Castle & Hradčany There's not much in the way of shopping here.

Malá Strana Mostly tourist-oriented shopping, with a few designer boutiques and bookshops tucked away in back alleys.

Staré Město The best area in the city for Czech designer fashion.

Nové Město This is the main shopping area, with all the big European high-street names from Marks & Spencer to Mothercare.

Vinohrady & Vršovice Upmarket neighbourhoods with chic arty-crafty shops, designer furniture and antiques.

Žižkov & Karlín As yet, there's not much of interest here for the dedicated shopper.

Holešovice Home to the city's biggest open-air market, but more interesting for people-watching than actually buying.

Bubeneč & Dejvice Some interesting specialist shops, plus the city's oldest farmers market.

Smíchov & Vyšehrad Home to Nový Smíchov, one of Prague's biggest and busiest shopping malls.

dark blood-red stones. There's also pearl and diamond jewellery, and less expensive pieces set with the dark green semiprecious stone known in Czech as *vltavín* (moldavite).

Havelská Market MARKET

(Map p62; Havelská; ⏲7.30am-6pm Mon-Fri, 8.30am-6pm Sat & Sun; Ⓜ Můstek) Souvenirs have insinuated themselves among the fruit and veg of this formerly produce-only market. While the shops on either side of the street are selling entirely resistible tat, the market stalls are worth a quick browse for fresh honey or sweets, as well as colourfully painted eggs sold in the run-up to Easter.

Nové Město

Nové Město is the focus of central Prague's mainstream shopping scene, with big-name department stores and high-street shops clustered along Wenceslas Square and Na Příkopě. Here you'll find international brands, from Marks & Spencer to Mothercare, Levi to Lacoste, and big Czech stores such as Bat'a (shoes), Bontonland (music) and Moser (glassware).

★ Náplavka Farmers Market MARKET

(Map p78; www.farmarsketrziste.cz; Rašínovo nábřeží; ⏲8am-2pm Sat; 2, 3, 7, 17, 21) Stretching along the embankment from Trojická to Výton, this weekly market makes the most of its riverside setting with live music and outdoor tables scattered among stalls selling freshly baked bread, organic locally grown vegetables, homemade cakes and pastries, wild mushrooms (in season), herbs, flowers, wild honey, hot food, Czech cider, coffee and a range of arts and crafts.

Palladium Praha Shopping Centre SHOPPING CENTRE

(Map p84; www.palladiumpraha.cz; náměstí Republiky; ⏲9am-10pm Mon-Sat, to 9pm Sun; Ⓜ Náměstí Republiky) Central Prague's biggest shopping mall, with five floors of internationally branded stores, a dozen restaurants and a couple of coffee shops.

Baťa SHOES

(Map p78; ☎221 088 478; www.bata.cz; Václavské náměstí 6; ⏲9am-9pm Mon-Sat, 10am-9pm Sun; Ⓜ Můstek) Established by Tomáš Baťa in 1894, the Baťa footwear empire is still in family hands and is one of the Czech Republic's most successful companies. The flagship store on Wenceslas Square, built in the 1920s, is considered a masterpiece of modern architecture, and houses six floors of shoes (including international brands as well as Baťa's own), handbags, luggage and leather goods.

Bontonland MUSIC

(Map p84; ☎601 309 183; www.bontonland.cz; Václavské náměstí 1, Koruna Palác; ⏲9am-8pm Mon-Fri, 10am-8pm Sat, 10am-7pm Sun; ; Ⓜ Můstek) Supposedly the biggest music megastore in the Czech Republic, with pretty much everything including Western chart music, classical, jazz, dance and heavy metal, as well as an extensive collection of Czech pop. It also sells Blu-ray discs and DVDs, iPods and accessories, and has a large PlayStation arena and internet cafe.

Moser GLASS

(Map p84; ☎224 211 293; www.moser-glass.com; Na příkopě 12; ⊙10am-8pm Mon-Fri, to 7pm Sat & Sun; Ⓜ Můstek) One of the most exclusive and respected of Bohemian glassmakers, Moser was founded in Karlovy Vary in 1857 and is famous for its rich and flamboyant designs. The shop on Na Příkopě is worth a browse as much for the decor as for the goods – it's in a magnificently decorated, originally Gothic building called the House of the Black Rose (dům U černé růže).

Globe Bookstore & Café BOOKS

(Map p78; ☎224 934 203; www.globebookstore.cz; Pštrossova 6; ⊙10am-midnight Mon-Fri, 9.30am-1am Sat & Sun; 📶; Ⓜ Karlovo Náměstí) A popular hang-out for book-loving expats, the Globe is a cosy English-language bookshop with an excellent cafe-bar (p128) in which to peruse your purchases. There's a good range of new fiction and nonfiction, a big selection of secondhand books, and newspapers and magazines in English, French, Spanish, Italian, German and Russian. Plus art exhibitions and film screenings.

Belda Jewellery JEWELLERY

(Map p78; ☎224 933 052; www.belda.cz; Mikulandská 10; ⊙11am-6pm Mon-Fri; Ⓜ Národní Třída) Belda & Co is a long-established Czech firm dating from 1922. Nationalised in 1948, it was revived by the founder's son and grandson, and continues to create gold and silver jewellery of a very high standard. Its range includes its own angular, contemporary designs, as well as reproductions based on art-nouveau designs by Alfons Mucha.

Bazar MUSIC

(Map p78; ☎602 313 730; www.cdkrakovska.cz; Krakovská 4; ⊙11am-7pm Mon-Fri; Ⓜ Muzeum) There's a vast selection of secondhand CDs, LPs and videos to browse here, representing a wide range of genres. Czech and Western pop jostle with jazz, blues, heavy metal, country and world music, though with most LPs costing around 300Kč to 450Kč, this place is not exactly what you'd call a bargain basement.

Palác Knih Neo Luxor BOOKS

(Map p78; ☎296 110 368; www.neoluxor.cz; Václavské náměstí 41; ⊙8am-8pm Mon-Fri, 9am-7pm Sat, 10am-7pm Sun; 🚋3, 5, 6, 9, 14, 24) Palác Knih Neo Luxor is Prague's biggest bookshop – head for the basement to find a wide selection of fiction and nonfiction in English, German, French and Russian, including Czech authors in translation. You'll also find internet access, a cafe and a good selection of international newspapers and magazines.

Jan Pazdera PHOTOGRAPHY

(Map p78; ☎737 762 506; www.fotopazdera.cz; Vodičkova 28; ⊙10am-6pm Mon-Fri, to 1pm Sat; 🚋3, 5, 6, 9, 14, 24) The friendly and knowledgeable staff members at this long-standing shop are happy to show you around their impressive stock of secondhand cameras, darkroom gear, lenses, binoculars and telescopes. Models range from the basic but unbreakable Russian-made Zenit to expensive Leicas.

Vinohrady & Vršovice

Vinohrady is largely residential and most shops here are of the everyday variety. Still, one of the main boulevards, Vinohradska, has some handsome home-furnishing shops, with the largest cluster at Vinohradský Pavilon. The farmers market above the Jiřího z Poděbrad metro station is a fun diversion and a handy place to pick up farm-fresh picnic food.

Obchod s Uměním ART, ANTIQUES

(Map p88; ☎224 252 779; Korunní 34, Vinohrady; ⊙11am-5pm Mon-Fri; Ⓜ Náměstí Míru, 🚋10, 16) The 'Shop with Art' specialises in original paintings, prints and sculpture from 1900 to 1940, when Czech artists were at the forefront in movements such as constructivism, surrealism and cubism. Naturally, these artworks fetch astronomical prices these days, but it's still fun to drop by and browse.

Vinohradský Pavilon HOMEWARES

(Vinohradská tržnice; Map p88; www.pavilon.cz; Vinohradská 50, Vinohrady; ⊙10am-7.30pm Mon-Fri, to 6pm Sat; Ⓜ Jiřího z Poděbrad, 🚋11, 13) Vinohrady's grand old market hall dates from 1902, but in recent times it has struggled to find a purpose. The interior has now been given a lavish makeover, however, to display high-end home and furniture design. Stroll the upper floors to see the best modern lighting, tables and furnishings from Italian, German and local designers.

Jiřího z Poděbrad Farmers Market MARKET

(Farmářské tržiště; Map p88; www.farmarsketrziste.cz; náměstí Jiřího z Poděbrad, Vinohrady;

8am-6pm Wed-Fri, to 2pm Sat; ; M Jiřího z Poděbrad) Food vendors and farmers descend on to the grassy square above the Jiřího z Poděbrad metro station four times a week to sell their fresh fruits and vegetables, as well as baked goods, coffees, meats and cheeses. It's fun for the whole family.

Karel Vávra MUSIC

(Map p88; 222 518 114; www.housle-vavra.cz; Lublaňská 65, Vinohrady; 9am-5pm Mon-Fri; M IP Pavlova) Handmade fiddles decorate the interior of this old-fashioned violin workshop where Karel and his assistants beaver away making and repairing these instruments in time-honoured fashion. Even if you are not in search of a custom-made violin, it's worth a look just for the time-warp atmosphere.

Dům Porcelánu GLASS

(Map p88; 221 505 320; www.dumporcelanu.cz; Jugoslávská 16, Vinohrady; 9am-7pm Mon-Fri, to 5pm Sat, 2-5pm Sun; M IP Pavlova, Náměstí Míru) The 'House of Porcelain' is a kind of factory outlet for the best Czech porcelain makers, including Haas & Czjzek and Thun, both of which are based in western Bohemia. The flatware, china, blue onion pattern porcelain and other items are priced to draw in local buyers – not tourists.

Žižkov & Karlín

As yet, Žižkov and Karlín are not really geared up towards shopping, though a few galleries and design shops are beginning to make an appearance, notably along Bořivojova street in Žižkov and around Karlín's Karlínské náměstí.

Karlín Farmers Market FOOD & DRINKS

(Karlínské farmářské trhy; Map p92; Karlínské náměstí, Karlín; 8am-2pm Sat; M Křižíkova, 3, 8, 24) With a lovely setting amid the plane trees beside the striking Church of Sts Cyril & Methodius, Karlín's farmers market is a great place to browse stalls selling artisanal produce, or just to enjoy an alfresco breakfast of coffee and croissants while listening to the local buskers.

Holešovice

Both Veletržní Palác (p94) and the DOX Centre for Contemporary Art (p96) have excellent gift shops, the latter specialising in hard-to-find art and architecture books. Hall 22 of the Holešovická tržnice has farm-fresh fruit and veg through the week, but otherwise not much of value to buy.

BENDOX BOOKS

(Map p96; 295 568 114; www.dox.cz; Poupětova 1; 10am-6pm Mon, 11am-7pm Wed, Thu & Fri, 10am-6pm Sat & Sun, closed Tue; ; 6, 12) One of the city's best art and architecture bookshops is located on the upper floor of the DOX Centre for Contemporary Art. There's a wide selection of books in both English and Czech. In addition to art books, it sells journals, sketchbooks and high-quality notebooks.

Pivní Galerie FOOD & DRINKS

(Map p96; 220 870 613; www.pivnigalerie.cz; U Průhonu 9; 11.30am-7pm Mon-Fri; 6, 12) If you think Czech beer begins and ends with Pilsner Urquell, a visit to the tasting room at Pivní Galerie (the Beer Gallery) will lift the scales from your eyes. Here you can sample and purchase a huge range of Bohemian and Moravian beers – nearly 150 varieties from 30 different breweries – with expert advice from the owners.

Holešovická Tržnice MARKET

(Pražská tržnice, Prague Market; Map p96; 220 800 592; www.holesovickatrznice.cz; Bubenské nábřeží 306; 7am-6pm Mon-Fri, to 2pm Sat; 1, 12, 14, 25) Almost a suburb in itself, Holešovice's sprawling, slightly depressing city market includes a large open-air area selling fresh fruit, vegetables and flowers (Hall 22), and dozens of stalls selling everything from cheap clothes to garden gnomes. Note that it's officially called Pražská tržnice, but better known locally as Holešovická tržnice (Holešovice Market).

Bubeneč & Dejvice

Most of the shops in this neighbourhood are of the workaday variety, geared towards residents. There are a couple of interesting antique shops, however, and the Saturday-morning farmers market, above the Dejvická metro station, is a fun diversion.

Dejvice Farmers Market MARKET

(Farmářský trh; Map p98; Vítězné náměstí, Dejvice; 8am-2pm Sat Mar-Nov; M Dejvická) Every Saturday morning from March to November, farmers from the surrounding countryside descend on the grassy square adjacent to the Dejvická metro station to sell their fruits and vegetables, as well as fresh bread and other baked goods, meats and cheeses. Come early to avoid the crowds.

The market has evolved into more than just a chance to buy fresh produce. A sunny morning usually brings hundreds of people onto the square and the atmosphere becomes something akin to a carnival. It's a great outing for the whole family.

Starožitnosti Robert Pavlů ANTIQUES
(Map p98; ☎224 318 952; Jaselská 19, Dejvice; ⏲10am-5pm Mon-Thu; Ⓜ Hradčanská) Reputable dealer of antiques, including watches, furniture, glass and other decorative items, displayed in several rooms that stretch nearly a block. The holdings are especially rich in early modern, functionalist and art-deco styles from the early decades of the 20th century.

Antikvita ANTIQUES
(Map p98; ☎233 336 601; www.antikvita.cz; Na Hutích 9, Dejvice; ⏲9.30am-5pm Mon-Fri; Ⓜ Dejvická) This antique shop is a collector's delight, crammed with cases and cabinets overflowing with vintage toys, model trains, dolls, coins, medals, jewellery, clocks, watches, militaria, postcards, porcelain figures, glassware and much more. If you have something to sell, Antikvita holds buying sessions on Wednesday and Thursday.

Wine Food Market FOOD
(Map p98; ☎252 540 660; www.winemarket.cz; Národní Obrany 29, Dejvice; ⏲9am-8pm; 📶; Ⓜ Dejvická) The Dejvice branch of a small citywide chain of high-end Italian food and wine shops is a great place to stock up on meats, cheeses and wines for a day out or to take back to your hotel. There are also a few tables for a quick coffee or bite in-house.

Smíchov & Vyšehrad

Smíchov is a lively commercial quarter with a large shopping centre and plenty of street-level shops around the Anděl metro station that sell mainly everyday items.

★ **Wine Food Market** FOOD
(Map p102; ☎733 338 650; www.winemarket.cz; Strakonická 1, Smíchov; ⏲7am-11pm Mon-Sat, 8am-11pm Sun; 📶; Ⓜ Smíchovské Nádraží) This rather unpromising, industrial corner in a forgotten Smíchov neighbourhood holds arguably the city's best Italian market, with all manner of breads, cheeses, meats and Italian goodies such as marinated mushrooms and peppers. It's the perfect spot to assemble a picnic lunch. There's a dining room in the back where you can treat yourself to the spoils. A real treasure.

Tribo ARTS & CRAFTS
(Map p102; ☎736 689 472; www.tattooshop.cz; Lidická 8, Smíchov; ⏲10am-8pm Mon-Fri, to 5pm Sat; Ⓜ Anděl, 🚊4, 5, 7, 10, 16, 21) Though Tribo advertises itself as a tattoo shop, it feels more like an artists' collective, selling an eclectic range of handmade goods, ranging from urban streetwear to funky diaries and journals, composed of artisanal paper and found objects such as old postcards and tram tickets. They also do tattoos and piercings.

Nový Smíchov SHOPPING CENTRE
(Map p102; ☎251 101 061; www.novysmichov.eu; Plzeňská 8, Smíchov; ⏲9am-9pm, restaurants to 10pm; 📶; Ⓜ Anděl) Nový Smíchov is a vast shopping centre that occupies an area the size of several city blocks. It's an airy, well-designed space with plenty of fashion boutiques and niche-market stores. Besides all the big brand names, there's a large computer store, food court, virtual-games hall, 12-screen multiplex cinema and well-stocked Tesco hypermarket.

ℹ Information

EMERGENCY

EU-Wide Emergency Hotline (☎112) English- and German-speaking operators are available.

Prague Municipal Police (☎156)

State Police (☎158)

ÚAMK (Central Automobile & Motorcycle Club; ☎1230; www.uamk.cz) For emergency breakdowns, the ÚAMK provides nationwide assistance 24 hours a day.

INTERNET ACCESS

Nearly all hotels and many restaurants and cafes offer free wi-fi. You may have to ask for the password. There are several internet cafes sprinkled around the centre, including the following:

Globe Bookstore & Café (☎224 934 203; www.globebookstore.cz; Pštrossova 6, Nové Město; per min 1Kč; ⏲10am-midnight Mon-Thu, 9.30am-1am Fri-Sun; 📶; Ⓜ Karlovo Náměstí) No minimum usage and free wi-fi.

Relax Café-Bar (☎224 211 521; www.relaxcafebar.cz; Dlážděná 4; per 10min 10Kč; ⏲8am-10pm Mon-Fri, 2-10pm Sat; 📶; Ⓜ Náměstí Republiky) A conveniently located internet cafe. Wi-fi is free.

MEDICAL SERVICES

The quality of medical care in Prague is high, and rest assured, if you do suffer a medical emergency you will receive proper care. Prague has several large hospitals, with trained staff used to dealing with foreign visitors.

Canadian Medical Care (call centre 235 360 133, emergency 24hr 724 300 301; www.cmcpraha.cz; Veleslavínská 1, Veleslavín; initial consultation 1500-2500Kč; 8am-6pm Mon & Fri, to 8pm Tue-Thu, 9am-2pm Sat; M Nádraží Veleslavín) A pricey but professional private clinic with English-speaking doctors.

Lékárna U Sv Ludmily (222 513 396; www.lekarnabelgicka.cz; Belgická 37, Vinohrady; 7am-7pm Mon-Fri, 8am-noon Sat; M Náměstí Míru) Has a 24-hour pharmacy window.

Na Homolce Hospital (257 271 111; www.homolka.cz; 5th fl, Foreign Pavilion, Roentgenova 2, Motol; 167, 168 to Nemocnice Na Homolce) Widely considered to be the best hospital in Prague, equipped and staffed to Western standards, with staff who speak English, French, German and Spanish.

Polyclinic at Národní (Poliklinika na Národní; 222 075 119, 24hr emergencies 155; www.poliklinika.narodni.cz; Národní třída 9; 8.30am-5pm Mon-Fri; M Národní Třída, 2, 9, 18, 22) A central clinic with staff who speak English, German, French and Russian. Expect to pay around 900Kč to 2000Kč for an initial consultation.

MONEY

You'll find ATMs all around Prague. There are ATMs on the concourse of Prague's main train station as well as at both arrivals terminals at Prague airport.

ETIQUETTE ON PUBLIC TRANSPORT

On metro escalators, stand on the right-hand side and only use the left side if you want to walk up or down. Failure to observe this nicety can cause consternation among other users, especially during rush hour.

The large seatless area at the tail end of older trams or in the middle section of newer trams is generally reserved for baby strollers – be sure to make room here if someone boards with a pram.

Except in the oldest trams, you have to press a green button (marked *dveře*) to make the doors open; if you're at the front of the queue, press it quickly if you don't want to incur the wrath of those behind!

Most ATMs accept any credit or debit card, provided you have a four-digit PIN code.

POST

The Czech Postal Service (*Česká Pošta;* www.cpost.cz) is efficient, though post offices can be tricky to negotiate since signage is only in Czech. For mailing letters and postcards, be sure to get into the proper line, identified as '*listovní zásilky*' (correspondence).

Prague's **main post office** (Map p84; 221 131 445; www.cpost.cz; Jindřišská 14, Nové Město; 2am-midnight; M Můstek) is centrally located not far from Wenceslas Square in Nové Město. It uses an automated queuing system: take a ticket from one of the machines in the entrance corridors – press button No 1 for stamps, letters and parcels; then watch the display boards in the main hall – when your ticket number appears (flashing), go to the desk number shown.

- A standard postcard or letter up to 20g costs about 20Kč to other European countries and 30Kč for destinations outside Europe.
- Buy stamps at post offices but be sure to have the letter weighed to ensure proper postage.

TOURIST INFORMATION

Prague City Tourism branches are scattered around town, including at both airport arrivals terminals at Václav Havel Airport Prague. Offices are good sources of maps and general information; they also sell Prague Card discount cards and can book guides and tours.

The **Czech Tourism Information Centre** (Map p62; 224 861 476; www.czechtourism.cz; Staroměstské náměstí 5; 9am-6pm Mon-Fri, 10am-5pm Sat & Sun), on Old Town Square, provides tourist information on cities and regions around the Czech Republic, outside of Prague.

Prague City Tourism (Prague Welcome; Map p62; 221 714 714; www.prague.eu; Staroměstské náměstí 5, Old Town Hall; 9am-7pm; M Staroměstská) The busiest of the Prague City Tourism branches occupies the ground floor of the Old Town Hall (enter to the left of the Astronomical Clock).

Prague City Tourism (Prague Welcome; Map p62; 221 714 444; www.prague.eu; Rytířská 12, Staré Město; 9am-7pm; M Můstek) Conveniently situated near the Můstek metro station. In addition to the usual services, such as handing out maps and advice, this office is a good place to buy tickets for various events around town.

Prague City Tourism – Wenceslas Square (Map p78; 221 714 714; www.prague.eu; Václavské náměstí 42; 10am-6pm; M Můstek, Muzeum) Handy tourist information kiosk on the busiest square in the city. Hands out free maps and advice, and is the place to buy Prague Card discount cards and arrange guides and tours.

Prague City Tourism (Prague Welcome; ☎221 714 714; www.prague.eu; Terminals 1 & 2, Václav Havel Airport Prague, Ruzyně; ⏰8am-8pm; 🚌100, 119) Prague's official tourist information office has branches at both arrivals terminals at Václav Havel Airport Prague. These branches are great places to pick up a city map and get the latest info on special events happening during your visit. The Prague Card discount card can be bought here.

Getting There & Away

For information on international travel to and from Prague, as well as travel around the Czech Republic, see the general Transport section of the Survival Guide, p289.

Getting Around

TO/FROM THE AIRPORT

For information on getting to and from Václav Havel Airport Prague, see 'Getting There & Away' under the Transport section of the Survival Guide, p297.

BICYCLE

Several parts of Prague have marked bike lanes (look for yellow bike-path signs). Still, with its cobblestones, tram tracks and multitudes of pedestrians, Prague has a long way to go to catch up with far-bike-friendlier cities such as Vienna or Amsterdam.

- Nearly everyone wears a helmet, and this is always a good idea.
- The black market for stolen bikes is thriving, so don't leave bikes unattended for longer than a few minutes and always use a sturdy lock.
- Cycling is prohibited in pedestrian zones such as on Charles Bridge. Technically you could be fined up to 1000Kč, but more often than not, the police will simply tell you to dismount.
- Bikes are transported free of charge on the metro, but cyclists are required to obey certain rules. Bikes can only ride near the last door of the rear carriage, and only two bikes are allowed per train. Bikes are not permitted if the carriage is full, or if there's already a pram in the carriage.

BUS & TRAM

To supplement the metro, the Prague Public Transport Authority (DPP; p296) operates a comprehensive system of trams (streetcars) and buses that reach virtually every nook and cranny in the city. The DPP website has a handy 'Journey Planner' tab in English to enable you to plan your route.

> **KEY TRAM ROUTES**
>
> **No 22** The classic tram line that climbs to Prague Castle from Malá Strana, though you can board it in Vinohrady, at Národní třídá, or Národní Divadlo (National Theatre) too.
>
> **No 9** One of Prague's busiest cross-city tram routes, linking Žižkov, the main train station, Wenceslas Square, the National Theatre and Smíchov. Transfer to line No 22 at Národní třídá, Národní Divadlo or Újezd.

- Trams are convenient for crossing the river and moving between neighbourhoods.
- Buses are less useful for visitors and normally connect far-flung residential neighbourhoods to nearby metro stations or the centre.
- The system uses the same tickets as the metro and metro rides can be combined with rides on both trams and buses, provided the ticket is still valid.
- Always validate an unstamped ticket on entering the tram or bus.
- Trams and buses run from around 5am to midnight daily. After the system shuts down, a smaller fleet of night trams (51 to 59) and night buses rumbles across the city about every 40 minutes (only full-price 32Kč tickets are valid on these services).

CAR & MOTORCYCLE

If you've brought your own car, don't even think about trying to use it for getting around Prague. Car travel in the centre is often restricted, and the warren of one-way streets takes years of driving to get to know well. The only exception might be to destinations outside the centre or to cross town, but even then you'll have to contend with soul-crushing traffic jams. Instead, find a secure place to leave your vehicle for the duration of your stay and use public transport.

Car Hire

Small local firms tend to offer better prices than major international companies, but are less likely to have fluent, English-speaking staff. It's often easier to book by email than by phone. Typical rates for a Škoda Fabia are around 800Kč a day, including unlimited kilometres, collision-damage waiver and value-added tax (VAT). Bring your credit card as a deposit. A motorway tax coupon is included with most rental cars.

Most of the major international car-hire companies operate in Prague and have desks at Václav Havel Airport Prague (p297).

USING AUTOMATED TICKET MACHINES

The automated ticket machines at metro and some tram stops can be tricky to use. To get started, first press the button for the ticket you need – probably the 32Kč PLNOCENNÁ (full fare) at the top left – once for one ticket, twice for two etc. You will see the price clocking up in the display. Put your coins in the slot – as soon as the correct fare (or more) has been inserted, your tickets will be printed, and change given if necessary. If you make a mistake, press the STORNO (cancel) button and start again.

METRO

Prague's excellent metro is operated by the Prague Public Transport Authority (p296), which has information desks in both terminals of Prague's Václav Havel airport and in several metro stations, including the Můstek, Anděl, Hradčanská and Nádraží Veleslavín stations. The metro operates daily from 5am to midnight.

The metro has three lines:

Line A (shown on transport maps in green) Links the airport bus to Malá Strana, Old Town Square, Wenceslas Square and Vinohrady.

Line B (Yellow) Cross-river route from Smíchov in the southwest to central Náměstí Republiky and Florenc bus station.

Line C (Red) Links main train station to Florenc bus station, Wenceslas Square and Vyšehrad.

Convenient stops for visitors include Staroměstská (closest to Old Town Square), Malostranská (Malá Strana), Můstek (Wenceslas Square), Muzeum (National Museum) and Hlavní nádraží (main train station).

Tickets & Passes

A valid ticket or day pass is required for travel on all metros, trams and buses. Tickets and passes are sold from machines at metro stations and some tram stops (coins only), as well as at newspaper kiosks and DPP information offices at the Můstek, Anděl, Hradčanská and Nádraží Veleslavín stations.

➡ You must validate (punch) your ticket before descending on the metro escalators or on entering a tram or bus (day passes must be stamped the first time you use them). For the metro, you'll see stamping machines at the top of the escalators. In trams and buses there will be a stamping machine in the vehicle by the door.

➡ A full-price ticket costs 32Kč per adult. A discounted ticket of 16Kč is available to children aged six to 15 years and seniors aged 65 to 70 (kids under six ride free). Full-price tickets are valid for 90 minutes of unlimited travel, including transfers.

➡ For shorter journeys, buy short-term tickets that are valid for 30 minutes of unlimited travel. These cost 24/12Kč per adult/child and senior. You'll also need a 16Kč ticket if you're carrying a dog or for each large suitcase or backpack (more than 25cm x 45cm x 70cm); a 24-hour or three-day pass includes one such item of luggage.

➡ Bikes (metro only) and prams travel free.

➡ Day passes are available for one or three days and make sense if you're planning on staying more than a few hours. One-day passes cost 110/55Kč per adult/child and senior; three-day passes cost 310Kč (no discounts available for children or seniors).

➡ While ticket inspections are infrequent, getting caught without a validated ticket can be expensive. The fine if paid on the spot is 800Kč, or 1500Kč if paid later at a police station.

TAXI

Taxis in Prague are an easy and relatively affordable way to get around town, though taxi scams are an ever-present risk. The official rate for licensed cabs is 40Kč flag fall plus 28Kč per kilometre and 6Kč per minute while waiting. On this basis, any trip within the city centre – say, from Wenceslas Square to Malá Strana – should cost no more than 200Kč. A trip to the suburbs, depending on the distance, should cost 200Kč to 300Kč, and to the airport between 400Kč and 600Kč.

When flagging a cab, look for a cab with its yellow roof lamp lit and raise your hand. Establish your destination and a likely fare before getting in, and make sure the meter is switched on. Only hail official, registered cabs – these are yellow, have a permanently installed roof lamp with the word 'TAXI' on it, and have the driver's name and licence number printed on both front doors.

Alternatively, call or ask someone to call a radio taxi, as they're better regulated and more responsible. Companies with honest drivers, 24-hour service and English-speaking operators include AAA Radio Taxi (p298), ProfiTaxi (p302) and City Taxi (p302).

WALKING

Walking is the best way to see the centre of the city. Indeed, much of the centre is closed to vehicular traffic, meaning walking is sometimes the only option for getting around. Cars and vehicles are prohibited from crossing Charles Bridge. Cobblestones and the long hill on the approach to Prague Castle play havoc with heels, though. The best bet is to opt for comfortable walkers or sneakers.

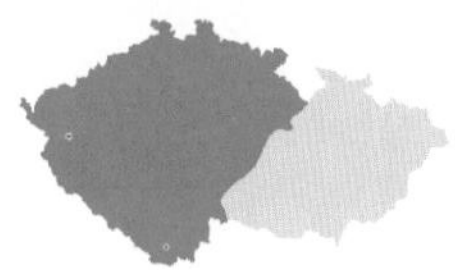

Bohemia

Includes ➡

Karlštejn Castle 174
Konopiště Chateau 176
Kutná Hora 179
Terezín 182
České Budějovice 185
Český Krumlov 192
Třeboň 198
Tábor 201
Plzeň 205
Karlovy Vary 211
Mariánské Lázně 219

Best Places to Eat

- ➡ Medité (p223)
- ➡ Naše farma (p188)
- ➡ Šupina & Šupinka (p201)
- ➡ Nonna Gina (p196)
- ➡ Goldie (p205)
- ➡ Embassy Restaurant (p217)

Best Places to Sleep

- ➡ Pension Villa Rosa (p215)
- ➡ Krumlov House (p195)
- ➡ U Tří hrušek (p187)
- ➡ Villa Patriot (p222)
- ➡ Penzion Havlíček (p180)

Why Go?

Beyond the serried apartment blocks of Prague's outer suburbs, the city gives way to the surprisingly green hinterland of Bohemia, a land of rolling hills, rich farmland and thick forests dotted with castles, chateaux and picturesque towns. Rural and rustic, yet mostly within two to three hours' drive of the capital, the Czech Republic's western province has for centuries provided an escape for generations of city-dwellers.

It's a region of surprising variety. Český Krumlov, with its riverside setting and Renaissance castle, is in a class by itself, but lesser-known towns such as Třeboň in the south and Loket in the west exude an unexpected charm. Big cities like České Budějovice and Plzeň offer great museums and restaurants, while the famed 19th-century spa towns of western Bohemia retain an old-world lustre.

When to Go

Terezín

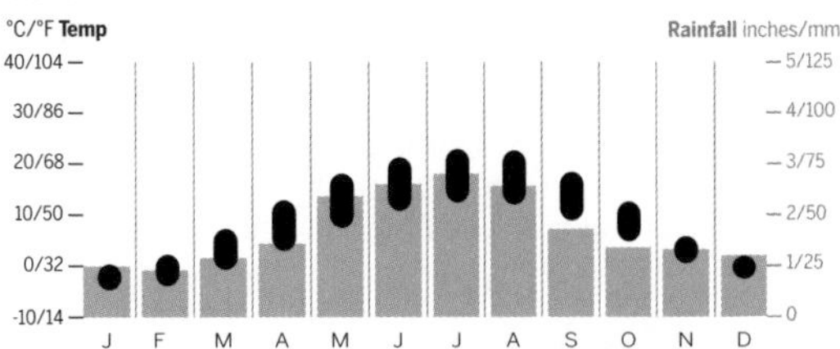

Apr Spring brings blossoms to the trees, and castles and museums reopen.

Jun–Aug Plenty of warm, sunny days to enjoy city strolls and countryside walks.

Sep & Oct Regional cultural hubs like Plzeň or České Budějovice reawaken after a summer slumber.

LIPSKIY/SHUTTERSTOCK ©

TOP SIGHT
KARLŠTEJN CASTLE

Rising above the village of Karlštejn, 30km southwest of Prague, Karlštejn Castle is rightly one of the top attractions in the Czech Republic. This fairy-tale medieval fortress is in such good shape that it wouldn't look out of place on Disney World's Main Street. Unfortunately, the crowds that throng its courtyards come in theme-park proportions too.

History

Perched high on a crag overlooking the Berounka River, Karlštejn was born of a grand pedigree, starting life in 1348 as a hideaway for the crown jewels and treasury of the Holy Roman Emperor Charles IV. Run by an appointed burgrave, the castle was surrounded by a network of landowning knight-vassals, who came to the castle's aid whenever enemies moved against it.

Karlštejn again sheltered the Bohemian and the Holy Roman Empire crown jewels during the Hussite Wars of the early 15th century, but fell into disrepair as its defences became outmoded. Considerable restoration work in the late 19th century has returned the castle to its former glory – most notably by Josef Mocker, the king of Prague's neo-Gothic architecture.

Guided Tours

Admission to the castle is by guided tour only; there are three tours available in English. Tour 1 (adult/child 270/180Kč, 50 minutes) passes through the Knight's Hall, still daubed with the coats-of-arms and names of the

DON'T MISS

- Chapel of the Holy Cross
- Knight's Hall
- Charles IV's Bedchamber
- Audience Hall
- Jewel House
- The Great Tower views

PRACTICALITIES

- Hrad Karlštejn
- tour bookings 311 681 617
- www.hradkarlstejn.cz
- adult/child Tour 1 270/180Kč, Tour 2 330/230Kč, Tour 3 150/100Kč
- 9am-6.30pm Jul & Aug, 9.30am-5.30pm Tue-Sun May, Jun & Sep, to 5pm Apr, to 4.30pm Oct, to 4pm Mar, shorter hrs Sat & Sun only Dec-Feb

knight-vassals, Charles IV's Bedchamber, the Audience Hall and the Jewel House, which includes treasures from the Chapel of the Holy Cross and a replica of the St Wenceslas Crown.

Tour 2 (adult/child 330/230Kč, 70 minutes, May to October only) must be booked in advance and takes in the Marian Tower, with the Church of the Virgin Mary and the Chapel of St Catherine, then moves on to the Great Tower for the castle's star attraction, the exquisite Chapel of the Holy Cross. Designed by Charles IV for the safekeeping of the crown jewels of the Holy Roman Empire, and of sacred relics of the Crucifixion, the chapel's walls and vaulted ceiling are adorned with thousands of polished semiprecious stones set in gilt stucco in the form of crosses, and with religious and heraldic paintings. For Tour 2, book as far ahead as possible.

Tour 3 (adult/child 150/100Kč, 40 minutes, daily June to August, weekends only May and October) visits the upper levels of the Great Tower, the highest point of the castle, which provides stunning views over the surrounding countryside.

Tours run to a complicated timetable; however, when you purchase your tickets online, you can select the time of your tour.

Getting There & Away

Trains from Prague's main train station to Beroun (via Praha-Smíchov) stop at Karlštejn (103Kč return, 45 minutes, half-hourly). Note that trains are shown as departing from platform 1J, which means the southern (jih in Czech) end of platform 1. From the train station or the main car park, it's a 20- or 30-minute uphill walk to the castle.

WHEN TO GO

In summer Karlštejn is mobbed with visitors. If at all possible, visit midweek or out of season, and avoid the queues at the castle ticket office by purchasing your tickets in advance via the link on the castle's website. Thankfully, the peaceful surrounding countryside offers views of Karlštejn's stunning exterior that rival anything you'll see on the inside.

Get away from the hordes milling up and down the main route to the castle at the appealing Restaurace Pod Dračí Skálou (☎311 681 177; www.poddraciskalou.eu; Karlštejn 130; mains 100-250Kč; ⏲11am-11pm Mon-Sat, to 8pm Sun; P 📶 👪), which has outdoor tables and a barbecue grill.

A RIDE IN THE COUNTRY

Karlštejn is a straightforward 35km bike ride from Prague, mostly on dedicated cycle tracks, and with no hills. Biko Adventures (p300) offers a leisurely, guided day trip by bike, stopping to swim in the river or pick cherries on the way, and returning to Prague by train. For noncyclists, a full-day trip involving travel by minibus and a little bit of easy hiking, but no biking, can also be arranged.

TOP SIGHT
KONOPIŠTĚ CHATEAU

Konopiště Chateau is not only a monument to the obsessions of early-20th-century Habsburg aristocrats, but also an insight into one of the most famous names in European history – the Archduke Franz Ferdinand d'Este, heir to the Austro-Hungarian throne, whose assassination in 1914 sparked WWI.

You'll need a full day to make the most of a visit here: do one of the guided tours of the chateau (Tour 3 is the best), and leave time to explore the beautiful landscaped grounds that surround it.

The Chateau

Konopiště is a testament to the archduke's twin obsessions – hunting and St George. Having renovated the massive Gothic and Renaissance building in the 1890s and installed all the latest technology – including electricity, central heating, flush toilets, showers and a lift – Franz Ferdinand decorated his home with his hunting trophies.

His game books record that he shot about 300,000 creatures. About 100,000 animal trophies adorn the walls. The crowded Trophy Corridor (Tour 1 and 3), with a forest of mounted animal heads, and the antler-clad Chamois Room (Tour 3), with its 'chandelier' fashioned from a stuffed condor, are truly bizarre sights.

The archduke's collection of art and artefacts relating to St George amounts to 3750 items, many of which are in the St George Museum (muzeum sv Jiří; Konopiště 1; admission incl with chateau ticket; ⏲10am-5pm Tue-Sun Jun-Aug, to 4pm Apr, May & Sep, to 3pm Oct, closed Oct-May).

DON'T MISS

- ➡ Chamois Room
- ➡ Trophy Corridor
- ➡ St George Museum

PRACTICALITIES

- ➡ Zámek Konopiště
- ➡ ☎ 317 721 366
- ➡ www.zamek-konopiste.cz
- ➡ adult/child Tour 1 or 2 220/150Kč, Tour 3 320/220Kč
- ➡ ⏲10am-5pm Tue-Sun Jun-Aug, to 4pm Apr, May & Sep, to 3pm Oct, to 3pm Sat & Sun only Nov, closed Dec-Mar
- ➡ P

Guided Tours

There are three guided tours in English. Tour 3 (adult/child 320/220Kč) is the most interesting, visiting the private apartments used by the archduke and his family, which have remained unchanged since the state took possession of the chateau in 1921. Tour 2 (adult/child 220/150Kč) takes in the Great Armoury, one of the most impressive collections of weapons in Europe, while Tour 3 (adult/child 220/150Kč) visits the grand apartments of the south wing. Tours depart hourly, on the hour.

Getting There & Away

Konopiště is 2km west of Benešov. Local bus 2 (12Kč, six minutes, hourly) runs from a stop on Dukelská, 400m north of the train station (turn left out of the station, take first right on Tyršova and then first left), to the castle car park. If you'd rather walk, turn left out of the train station, go left across the bridge over the railway, and follow the yellow markers west along Konopištská street.

There are buses from Prague's Roztyly metro station to Benešov (112Kč return, 40 minutes, twice hourly) – their final destination is usually Pelhřímov or Jihlava. There are also buses from Prague's Florenc bus station (104Kč return, 40 minutes, eight daily).

Trains run from Prague's Hlavní nádraží to Benešov u Prahy (146Kč return, one hour, hourly). Konopiště is 2km west of Benešov. Walk to the chateau or take local bus 2.

From April to October, a tourist 'train' called the Ekovlaček (www.ekovlacekbenesov.cz) shuttles between Benešov train station and the chateau (per person 20Kč, 15 minutes, three to five times daily). Board at the Sokolovna stop, just north of the station.

EATING

There's a cafe in the chateau courtyard. Or for a proper meal, head down the hill to **Stará Myslivna** (☎317 700 280; www.staramyslivna.com; Konopiště 2; mains 170-350Kč; ⏰11am-9pm; 📶), a Czech restaurant set in a 19th-century gamekeeper's lodge.

Escape the crowds at the chateau by taking a 30-minute walk around the ornamental lake to the west of the castle.

Bohemia Highlights

1 **Český Krumlov** (p192) Discovering Krumlov's fairy-tale castle and medieval townscape.

2 **Pilsner Urquell Brewery** (p207) Imbibing the wisdom of the brewer's art at the fountainhead of the world's finest beer.

3 **Tábor** (p201) Taking in the history of this pretty Renaissance town and former Hussite stronghold.

4 **Loket** (p218) Wandering the cobbled lanes up to the castle that dominates this impossibly picturesque village.

5 **Sedlec Ossuary** (p179) Sending a shiver up your spine among the artfully arranged human bones in Bohemia's creepiest crypt.

6 **Kutná Hora** (p179) Venturing underground to explore the silver mines beneath this historic town.

7 **Karlštejn** (p174) Hiking the wooded hills around Bohemia's most famous and photogenic castle.

KUTNÁ HORA

POP 74,500

Enriched by the silver ore that veined the surrounding hills, the medieval city of Kutná Hora became the seat of Wenceslas II's royal mint in 1308, producing silver *groschen* that were then the hard currency of Central Europe. Boom-time Kutná Hora rivalled Prague in importance, but by the 16th century the mines began to run dry, and its demise was hastened by the Thirty Years' War and a devastating fire in 1770. The town became a Unesco World Heritage Site in 1996, luring visitors with a smorgasbord of historic sights. It looks its flower-bedecked best in May and June but is worth a full day's visit at any time of year.

Sights

★Sedlec Ossuary CHURCH

(Kostnice; ☎information centre 326 551 049; www.ossuary.eu; Zámecká 127; adult/concession 90/60Kč; ⏲8am-6pm Mon-Sat, 9am-6pm Sun Apr-Sep, 9am-5pm Mar & Oct, 9am-4pm Nov-Feb) When the Schwarzenbergs purchased Sedlec monastery (2.5km northeast of the town centre) in 1870 they allowed local woodcarver František Rint to get creative with the bones piled in the crypt (the remains of around 40,000 people), resulting in this remarkable 'bone church'. Garlands of skulls and femurs are strung from the vaulted ceiling like Addams Family Christmas decorations, while in the centre dangles a vast chandelier containing at least one of each bone in the human body.

Four giant pyramids of stacked bones squat in the corner chapels, and crosses, chalices and monstrances of bone adorn the altar. There's even a Schwarzenberg coat-of-arms made from bones, and Rint signed his name in bones at the foot of the stairs.

★Cathedral of St Barbara CHURCH

(Chrám sv Barbora; ☎775 363 938; www.khfarnost.cz; Barborská; adult/concession 85/40Kč; ⏲9am-6pm Apr-Oct, 10am-5pm Mon-Fri, 10am-6pm Sat & Sun Nov-Dec, 10am-4pm Jan-Mar) Kutná Hora's greatest monument is the Gothic Cathedral of St Barbara. Rivalling Prague's St Vitus in size and magnificence, its soaring nave culminates in elegant, six-petalled ribbed vaulting, and the ambulatory chapels preserve original 15th-century frescoes, some of them showing miners at work. Take a walk around the outside of the church; the terrace at the eastern end enjoys the finest view in town.

Construction was begun in 1380, interrupted during the Hussite Wars and abandoned in 1558 when the silver began to run out. The cathedral was finally completed in neo-Gothic style at the end of the 19th century.

Gallery of Central Bohemia GALLERY

(Galerie Středočeského kraje; Map p180; ☎327 311 135; www.gask.cz; Barborská 53; adult/child 80/40Kč; ⏲10am-6pm Tue-Sun) The town's 17th-century former Jesuit College has been restored and now houses this regional gallery devoted to 20th- and 21st-century art. There's also a gallery shop that showcases the work of young Czech artists and designers.

Barborská STREET

(Map p180) Barborská street runs along the front of the 17th-century former Jesuit College, with glorious views over the valley below, and is decorated with a row of 13 baroque statues of saints, an arrangement inspired by the statues on Prague's Charles Bridge. All are related to the Jesuits and/or the town; the second statue – the woman holding a chalice, with a stone tower at her side – is St Barbara, the patron saint of miners and therefore of Kutná Hora.

Czech Silver Museum MUSEUM

(České muzeum stříbra; Map p180; ☎327 512 159; www.cms-kh.cz; Barborská 28; adult/concession Tour 1 70/40Kč, Tour 2 120/80Kč, combined 140/90Kč; ⏲10am-6pm Jul & Aug, 9am-6pm May, Jun & Sep, 9am-5pm Apr & Oct, 10am-4pm Nov, closed Mon year-round) Originally part of the town's fortifications, the Hrádek (Little Castle) was rebuilt in the 15th century as the residence of Jan Smíšek, administrator of the royal mines, who grew rich from silver mined illegally right under the building. It now houses the Czech Silver Museum. Visiting is by guided tour, which includes the chance to visit an ancient silver mine.

Tour 1 (one hour) leads through the main part of the museum where the exhibits celebrate the mines that made Kutná Hora wealthy, including a huge wooden device once used to lift loads weighing as much as 1000kg from the 200m-deep shafts. Tour 2 (1½ hours) allows you to don a miner's helmet and explore 500m of medieval mine shafts beneath the town. Kids must be aged at least seven for this tour.

Kutná Hora

Sights

1 Barborská ... A3
2 Czech Silver Museum ... A3
3 Gallery of Central Bohemia ... A3
4 Italian Court ... C2

Sleeping

5 Hotel Zlatá Stoupa ... D2
6 Penzion Havlíček ... C2

Eating

7 Piazza Navona ... C1
8 Pivnice Dačický ... A2
9 U Sňeka Pohodáře ... C1

Italian Court HISTORIC BUILDING

(Vlašský dvůr; Map p180; ☎327 512 873; www.guideskutnahora.com/italian-court; Havlíčkovo náměstí 552; adult/concession full tour 105/65Kč, mint only 70/50Kč; ⊙9am-6pm Apr-Sep, 10am-5pm Mar & Oct, 10am-4pm Nov-Feb) Just east of St James Church (kostel sv Jakuba; 1330) lies the Italian Court, the former Royal Mint – it gets its name from the master craftsmen from Florence brought in by Wenceslas II to kick-start the business, and who began stamping silver coins here in 1300. The original treasury rooms hold an exhibit on coins and minting.

The full guided tour (in English) visits all the historical rooms open to the public, notably the Royal Mint itself, the Royal Chapel, and the 15th-century Audience Hall, with two impressive 19th-century murals depicting the 1471 election of Vladislav Jagiello as king of Bohemia, and the Decree of Kutná Hora being proclaimed by Wenceslas IV and Jan Hus in 1409.

Sleeping

Kutná Hora is an easy day trip from Prague, but there are plenty of sleeping options if you want to stay the night, especially in the pensions and small hotels range; what's missing are hostels and luxury hotels.

★**Penzion Havlíček** PENSION €

(Map p180; ☎723 561 530; www.cafehavlicekpenzion.cz; Havlíčkovo náměstí 572; s/d/tr incl breakfast 1000/1400/1800Kč) This historic house, just across the street from the Italian Court, sports a stylish cafe and five freshly converted bedrooms – the attic room (No 4), with its massive exposed timber beams and view across to St James Church, has the most character. Excellent breakfasts are served in the cafe.

Hotel U Zvonu HOTEL €
(☎777 680 992; www.uzvonu.cz; Zvonařská 286; s/d 930/1290Kč; P 📶) Service with a smile is the secret of this small, family-run hotel just a short walk north of the main square, along with bright, spotlessly clean, Ikea-furnished bedrooms and a good-value restaurant.

Penzión Barbora PENSION €
(☎327 316 327; www.penzionbarbora.cz; Kremnická 909; s/d/tr from 1400/1800/2500Kč; P 🚭 📶) A friendly family pension with a lovely (and quiet) location near St Barbara's Cathedral; it's worth paying a little extra for one of the two deluxe rooms with balconies overlooking the cathedral. Check in at the restaurant. Secure parking available.

Hotel U Kata HOTEL €
(☎327 515 096; www.ukata.cz; Štefánikova 92; s/d/tr 990/1390/1990Kč; P @ 📶) You won't lose your head over the rates at this good-value family hotel called the 'Executioner'. Rooms are clean and brightly decorated, and the mostly English-speaking staff are friendly and helpful. Facilities include a sauna, steam room and 'beer spa', plus bike rental (250Kč per day). There's a welcoming Czech beer hall and restaurant too.

Hotel Zlatá Stoupa HOTEL €€
(Map p180; ☎327 511 540; www.zlatastoupa.cz; Tylova 426; s/d from 1350/2150Kč; P 📶) Formerly the top hotel in town, the elegantly furnished but determinedly old-fashioned 'Golden Mount' is resting on its laurels somewhat these days, though friendly staff, secure parking, and a location halfway between the town centre and KH Město train station mean that it is still a reasonable choice.

Eating & Drinking

Kutná Hora is a bit of a gastronomic black hole – there are no outstanding places to eat, just a handful of decent Czech pubs and Italian restaurants.

Piazza Navona ITALIAN €
(Map p180; ☎327 512 588; www.piazzanavona.cz; Palackého náměstí 90; mains 100-260Kč; ⏰9am-10pm Sun-Thu, to midnight Fri & Sat; 📶) Feed up on authentic thin, crispy pizza at this homey Italian cafe-bar, plastered with Ferrari flags and Inter Milan pennants. Tables spill onto the main square in summer.

U Sňeka Pohodáře ITALIAN €
(Map p180; ☎327 515 987; www.usneka.cz; Vladislavova 11; mains 110-270Kč; ⏰11am-10pm Sun-Thu, to 11pm Fri & Sat; 📶) This cosy local favourite is very popular for takeaway or dine-in pizza and pasta, washed down with draught Bernard beer. And no, we don't know why it's called 'The Contented Snail'.

Pivnice Dačický PUB FOOD €€
(Map p180; ☎327 512 248; www.dacicky.com; Rakova 8; mains 160-330Kč; ⏰11am-11pm Sun-Thu, to midnight Fri & Sat; 📶 👪) Get some froth on your moustache at this old-fashioned, wood-panelled Bohemian beer hall, where you can dine on dumplings and choose from five draught beers including Pilsner Urquell, Primátor yeast beer and local Kutná Hora lager. Popular with coach parties so book ahead.

Information

Kutná Hora Tourist Office (Informační centrum; Map p180; ☎327 512 378; http://destinace.kutnahora.cz; Palackého náměstí 377; ⏰9am-6pm Apr-Sep, 9am-5pm Mon-Fri, 10am-4pm Sat & Sun Oct-Mar) Books accommodation, rents bicycles (per day 220Kč; April to October only) and offers internet access (per minute 1Kč, minimum 15Kč).

Sedlec Tourist Office (Informační centrum Sedlec; ☎326 551 049; www.ossuary.eu; Zámecká 279; ⏰9am-6pm Apr-Sep, to 5pm Mar & Oct, to 4pm Nov-Feb) Branch office near Sedlec Ossuary.

Getting There & Away

BUS

There are hourly buses on weekdays (three or four on Saturday) from Háje bus station on the southern edge of Prague to Kutná Hora (136Kč return, 1¾ hours); the train is a better bet.

TRAIN

There are direct trains from Prague's main train station to Kutná Hora hlavní nádraží every two hours (209Kč return, 55 minutes). It's a 10-minute walk from here to Sedlec Ossuary, and a further 2.5km (30 minutes) to the Old Town.

Alternatively, five minutes after the arrival of the Prague train (and before the departure of return trains) a bright yellow-and-green rail car shuttles from platform 1 to Kutná Hora Město station (six minutes). To use this option, make sure you buy a return train ticket to Kutná Hora Město, rather than Kutná Hora hlavní nádraží.

BOHEMIA IN ...

One Week

Focus your efforts: choose between the historic castle towns of the south or the spa resorts of the west. **Český Krumlov** (p194) deserves two nights, with your remaining time split between **Třeboň** (p198) and České Budějovice. If you opt for the west, spend a night in Plzeň and divide the rest of the week between Karlovy Vary and Mariánské Lázně.

Two Weeks

Two weeks is enough time to fully explore the province. Spend one week in the south, enjoying Český Krumlov and České Budějovice. For the second week, head west: book a long stay at a spa and treat yourself like royalty.

TEREZÍN

POP 2900

After the beauty of many Czech towns, the imposing double fortress of Terezín comes as a moving reminder of the more tragic aspects of Central Europe's past. The massive bastion of stone and earth was built in 1780 by Emperor Joseph II to keep the Prussians at bay, and could accommodate up to 11,000 soldiers. The fortress was never used in wartime, instead serving as a prison in the mid-19th century. Gavrilo Princip, the Serb nationalist who assassinated Archduke Franz Ferdinand in 1914 to ignite WWI, died in the prison in 1918.

But the place is best known to history for its role as a notorious WWII concentration camp. Around 150,000 men, women and children, mostly Jews, passed through on their way to the extermination camps of Auschwitz-Birkenau – 35,000 of them died here of hunger, disease or suicide; only 4000 survived.

History

A massive bulwark of stone and earth, the fortress of Terezín (Theresienstadt in German) was built in 1780 by Emperor Joseph II with a single purpose: to keep the enemy out. Ironically, it is more notorious for keeping people in – it served as a political prison in the later days of the Habsburg empire. Gavrilo Princip, the assassin who killed Archduke Franz Ferdinand in 1914, was incarcerated here during WWI, and when the Germans took control during WWII, the fortress became a grim holding pen for Jews bound for extermination camps. In contrast to the colourful, baroque face of many Czech towns, Terezín is a stark but profoundly evocative monument to a darker aspect of Europe's past.

The bleakest phase of Terezín's history began in 1940 when the Gestapo established a prison in the Lesser Fortress. Evicting the inhabitants from the Main Fortress the following year, the Nazis transformed the town into a transit camp through which some 150,000 people eventually passed en route to the death camps. For most, conditions were appalling. Between April and September 1942 the ghetto's population increased from 12,968 to 58,491, leaving each prisoner with only 1.65 sq metres of space and causing disease and starvation on a terrifying scale. In the same period, there was a 15-fold increase in the number of deaths within the prison walls.

Terezín later became the centrepiece of one of the Nazis' more extraordinary public relations coups. Official visitors to the fortress, including representatives of the Red Cross, saw a town that was billed as a kind of Jewish 'refuge', with a Jewish administration, banks, shops, cafes, schools and a thriving cultural life – it even had a jazz band – in a charade that twice completely fooled international observers. In reality Terezín was home to a relentlessly increasing population of prisoners, regular trains departing for the gas chambers of Auschwitz, and the death by starvation, disease or suicide of some 35,000 people.

Sights

While it's possible to visit Terezín on a guided day trip from Prague, in our experience these tours tend to be a bit rushed. Our advice is to allow a full day, bring a picnic lunch, and begin by visiting the Terezín Museum (p184), the Ghetto Museum (p184), where you can pick up information leaflets and maps, and the Magdeburg Barracks (p184). It's worth walking past the old railway siding to see the crematorium before crossing the river to take a self-guided tour of the Lesser Fortress

Lesser Fortress HISTORIC SITE

(Malá Pevnost; ☎416 782 576; www.pamatnik-terezin.cz; Pražská; adult/child 175/145Kč, combined with

Ghetto Museum 215/165Kč; ⏲8am-6pm Apr-Oct, to 4.30pm Nov-Mar) Terezín's Lesser Fortress, which served as a prison and concentration camp, lies 700m east of the town centre. The best way to see it is to take a **self-guided tour** through the prison barracks, isolation cells, workshops and morgues, past execution grounds and former mass graves. The Nazis' mocking slogan, *Arbeit Macht Frei* (Work Makes You Free), hangs above the gate to the inner yard. It would be hard to invent a more menacing location.

In front of the fortress is a **National Cemetery**, established in 1945 for the victims exhumed from the Nazis' mass graves.

WORTH A TRIP

WINE WITH A VIEW AT MĚLNÍK CHATEAU

Tiny Mělník sprawls over a rocky promontory surrounded by the flat Central Bohemian plains, with its picturesque old town appealingly sited atop a steep hill overlooking the confluence of the Vltava and Labe (Elbe) Rivers. The vines in the small vineyard below the old town are supposedly descendants of the first vines introduced to Bohemia, by Charles IV in the 14th century. They're now used to make the Mělník Chateau's own wines.

Mělník makes an easy day trip by bus from Prague. Plan on taking the chateau tour in the morning, followed by lunch and then a stroll around the other sites – they're all close together. Don't miss the terrace on the far side of the chateau, with superb views across the river.

Mělník Chateau (Zámek Mělník; ☎315 622 121; Svatováclavská 19; adult/concession 110/80Kč; ⏲10am-6pm Mar-Sep, 9.30am-5pm Oct-Feb) was acquired by the noble Lobkowicz family in 1739, and they opened it to the public in 1990. You can wander through the former living quarters, which are crowded with a rich collection of baroque furniture and 17th- and 18th-century paintings, on a self-guided tour with English text. A separate tour descends to the 14th-century wine cellars where you can taste the chateau's wines; a shop in the courtyard sells the chateau's own label and hosts wine-tasting sessions (120Kč to 280Kč).

Additional rooms have changing exhibits of modern works and a fabulous collection of 17th-century maps and engravings detailing Europe's great cities.

Next to Mělník Chateau is the 15th-century **Church of Sts Peter & Paul** (kostel sv Petra a Pavla; ☎315 622 337; Na Vyhlídce; tower adult/child 50/25Kč; ⏲tower 10am-12.30pm & 1.15-5pm Tue-Sat, 11am-12.30pm & 1.15-5pm Sun Mar-Oct), a Gothic church, with baroque furnishings and remnants of its Romanesque predecessor incorporated into the rear of the building. Climb to the top of the church tower (Vyhlídková věž) for superlative views.

The church crypt is now an **ossuary** (Kostnice; Na Vyhlídce; adult/child 30/20Kč; ⏲9.30am-4pm Tue-Fri, 10am-4pm Sat & Sun Mar-Oct, closed 12.30-1.15pm), packed with the bones of around 10,000 people, dug up to make room for 16th-century plague victims. The bones are arranged in the shapes of anchors, hearts and crosses (symbols of faith, love and hope). This crypt is much more visceral and claustrophobic than the Sedlec Ossuary in Kutná Hora; the floor is of beaten earth, and you literally rub shoulders with the bones.

Part of the fun of a trip here is to sample the local wines, both white and red. The better wines are called **Ludmilla**, after the saint and grandmother of St Wenceslas. One of the best places to taste and buy them is in the chateau itself.

Don't miss a coffee or tea at **Galerie/Café Ve Věži** (☎721 414 909; www.facebook.com/cafevevezi; ulice 5 května; ⏲2-11pm), an atmospheric cafe and art gallery inside the medieval Prague Gate tower. Guests are served by an ingenious dumbwaiter: write your order on the notepad, ding the bell, and the tray goes down, returning moments later with your order. Choose from a range of freshly ground coffees, exotic teas, local wines, beer and *medovina* (mead).

Buses run to Mělník from the bus stop outside Prague's Ládví metro station (46Kč, 40 minutes, every 15 to 30 minutes weekdays, hourly weekends); buy your ticket from the driver (one-way only, no return tickets). The bus station is 800m east of the town centre.

Terezín Museum MUSEUM

(Retranchement 5; ☎775 711 881; www.terezin.cz; entrance on Dlouhá; adult/child 80/50Kč; ⏲9am-5pm) This new museum, housed in a restored bastion at the northwest corner of the Main Fortress, is dedicated to the history of Terezín, from its construction in the late 18th century up to the present day, and is a good place to begin your visit to the town. There's a visitor centre here, and you can book a guided tour of the fortifications and its underground tunnels.

Main Fortress HISTORIC SITE

(Hlavní pevnost) FREE From the ground, the sheer scale of the maze of walls and moats that surrounds the town of Terezín is impossible to fathom. Take a peek at the aerial photograph in the town's Ghetto Museum, or wander past the walls en route to the Lesser Fortress, however, and a very different picture emerges – that of a massive 18th-century artillery fortification.

At the heart of the Main Fortress is the neat grid of streets that makes up the town of Terezín, with a central square that looks no different from a hundred other old town centres. There's little to look at except the chunky, 19th-century **Church of the Resurrection**, the arcaded former **Commandant's office**, the neoclassical administrative buildings on the square, and the surrounding grid of houses with their awful secrets. South of the square are the anonymous **remains of a railway siding**, built by prisoners, via which loads of further prisoners arrived – and departed.

Ghetto Museum MUSEUM

(Muzeum Ghetta; ☎416 782 225; www.pamatnik-terezin.cz; Komenského 151; adult/child 175/145Kč, combined with Lesser Fortress 215/165Kč; ⏲9am-6pm Apr-Oct, to 5.30pm Nov-Mar) The Ghetto Museum explores the rise of Nazism and life in the Terezín ghetto. The building once accommodated the camp's 10- to 15-year-old boys; haunting images painted by them still decorate the walls. The former **Magdeburg Barracks** (Magdeburská kasárna), which served as the seat of the Jewish 'town council', houses an annex to the main museum. Here you can visit a reconstructed dormitory and see exhibits on the rich cultural life that somehow flourished against this backdrop of fear.

There is also a small exhibit in the grim Crematorium in the Jewish Cemetery just off Bohušovická brána, about 750m south of the main square.

The Ghetto Museum has multilingual pamphlets and tour guides (some of them ghetto survivors) to offer assistance.

Crematorium HISTORIC SITE

(Krematorium; admission incl in Ghetto Museum ticket; ⏲10am-6pm Sun-Fri Apr-Oct, to 4pm Sun-Fri Nov-Mar) There is a small memorial in the grim crematorium, where around 30,000 people were cremated between 1942 and 1945. It's in the Jewish Cemetery just off Bohušovická brána, about 750m south of the main square.

Sleeping

With its harrowing history and unpleasant associations, few people choose to spend a night in Terezín apart from those on dedicated coach tours. If you do need to stay overnight, it's nicer to stay in one of the small hotels or pensions in nearby Litoměřice.

Eating

It's hard to recommend a pleasant place to eat in Terezín, as the atmosphere is so tragic. Rather than squeeze into one of the town's crowded tourist restaurants, take a bus or taxi to attractive Litoměřice, 3km to the north. The town square there has several good eateries.

Restaurace Atypik CZECH €

(☎416 782 780; www.atypik.cz; Máchova 91; mains 75-140Kč; ⏲9.30am-9pm Mon-Fri, 11am-1pm Sat, 11am-6pm Sun) Atypik by name but rather typical by nature, this always busy place offers all the predictable local favourites, with an emphasis on stodge and unapologetic meatiness.

Information

Terezín Visitor Centre (☎775 711 881; www.terezin.cz; entrance on Dlouhá; ⏲9am-5pm; 📶) Part of Terezín Museum; housed in a restored bastion of the old fortress.

Getting There & Away

Direct buses from Prague to Litoměřice (168Kč return, one hour, hourly) stop at Terezín. They depart from the bus station outside Praha-Holešovice train station. There are buses between Litoměřice bus station and Terezín (15Kč, eight minutes, at least hourly).

From Prague, 60km from Terezín, head north on the D8 and leave at junction 45 at Lovosice.

Go north on route 247, then east on 15 to reach Terezín. The drives takes about an hour.

ČESKÉ BUDĚJOVICE

POP 190,850

České Budějovice (pronounced chesky *bood*-yo-vit-zah or simply 'Budweis') is the provincial capital of southern Bohemia and a natural base for exploring the region. Transport connections to nearby Český Krumlov are good, meaning you could easily take in both places on an overnight excursion from Prague. While České Budějovice lacks top sights, it does have one of Europe's largest main squares and a charming labyrinth of narrow lanes and winding alleyways, some of which hug a sleepy but atmospheric canal. It's also the home of 'Budvar' beer (aka Czech 'Budweiser'), and a brewery tour usually tops the 'must-do' list.

Sights

Náměstí Přemysla Otakara II SQUARE

(Map p186; náměstí Přemysla Otakara II) The attractive arcaded buildings grouped around Samson's Fountain (Samsonova kašna; 1727) constitute the biggest town square in the country, 133m on each side. Among the architectural treats is the 1555 Renaissance town hall (Radnice), which received a baroque facelift in 1731. The figures on the balustrade – Justice, Wisdom, Courage and Prudence – are matched by an exotic quartet of bronze gargoyles.

Black Tower TOWER

(Černá věž; Map p186; 386 352 508; U Černé věže 70/2; adult/concession 30/20Kč; 10am-6pm daily Jul-Aug, Tue-Sun Apr-Jun, Sep & Oct) The dominating, 72m Gothic-Renaissance Black Tower was built in 1553. Climb its 225 steps (yes, we counted them) for fine views. The tower's two **bells** – the Marta (1723) and Budvar (1995; a gift from the brewery) – are rung daily at noon.

Beside the tower is the **Cathedral of St Nicholas** (Katedrála sv Mikuláše), built as a church in the 13th century, rebuilt in 1649, then made a cathedral in 1784.

Budweiser Budvar Brewery BREWERY

(Budějovický Budvar; 387 705 347; www.visitbudvar.cz; cnr Pražská & K Světlé; adult/child 120/60Kč; 9am-5pm daily Mar-Dec, Tue-Sat Jan & Feb; 2 to Budvar) One of the highlights of a trip to České Budějovice is a chance to see where original Budweiser beer was born. Brewery tours depart daily at 2pm (plus 11am July and August, less frequently from November to March). The tour highlights modern production methods, with the reward being a glass of Budvar in the brewery's chilly cellars. The brewery is 2km north of the main square.

South Bohemian Motorcycle Museum MUSEUM

(Jihočeské Motocyklové muzeum; Map p186; 723 247 104; www.motomuseum.cz; Piaristické náměstí; adult/concession 60/30Kč; 10am-6pm Tue-Sun Mar-Oct) There are dozens of historic bikes on display in this museum, housed in the unlikely setting of a 16th-century Gothic granary, later used as a salt warehouse. In addition to motorbikes, there are old-time bicycles and model aeroplanes.

Museum of South Bohemia MUSEUM

(Jihočeské muzeum; Map p186; www.muzeumcb.cz; Dukelská 1; adult/child 60/35Kč; 9am-5.30pm Tue-Sun) Founded in 1877, the recently revamped Museum of South Bohemia holds an enormous collection of historic books,

AROUND THE OLD TOWN

Part of the fun of a trip to České Budějovice is the chance to poke around amid the tiny alleyways that radiate from gigantic náměstí Přemysla Otakara II. The Old Town is surrounded by a picturesque canal, **Mlýnská stoka**, and the **Malše River**, as well as extensive gardens where the town walls once stood. Only a few bits of Gothic fortifications remain, including **Rabenštejn Tower** (Rabenštejnská věž; Map p186; 387 022 511; cnr Hradební & Panská; adult/concession 20/10Kč; 10am-4pm Mon-Fri, 9am-noon Sat Jun-Sep), and 15th-century **Iron Maiden Tower** (Železná Pana; Map p186; 603 711 977; Zátkovo nábřeží; adult/concession 30/15Kč; 1-6pm May-Oct), a crumbling former prison. Along Hroznová, on Piaristické náměstí, is the **Church of St Mary's Oblation** (Kostel Obětování Panny Marie; Map p186; www.bcb.cz; Piaristická náměstí; sightseeing tours 10Kč; 10am-5pm May-Oct) and a former Dominican monastery, with a splendid pulpit.

České Budějovice

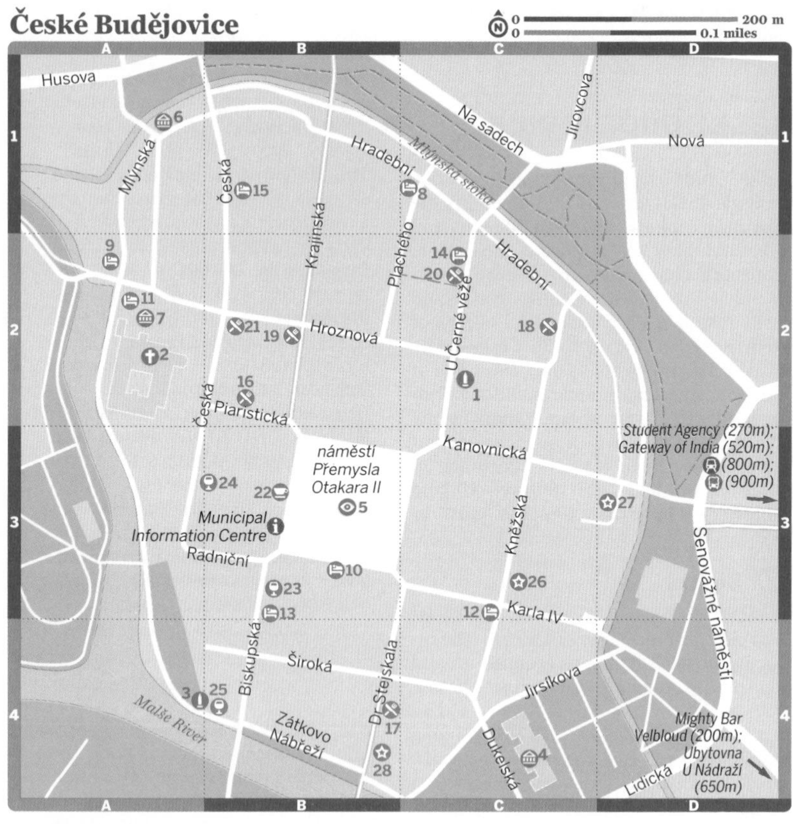

České Budějovice

Sights

1 Black Tower C2
2 Church of St Mary's Oblation A2
3 Iron Maiden Tower A4
4 Museum of South Bohemia C4
5 Náměstí Přemysla Otakara II B3
6 Rabenštejn Tower A1
7 South Bohemian Motorcycle Museum A2

Sleeping

8 Hotel Bohemia C1
9 Hotel Budweis A2
10 Hotel Dvořak B3
11 Hotel Klika A2
12 Hotel Malý Pivovar C3
13 Penzión Centrum B3
14 Residence u černé věž C2
15 U Tří hrušek B1

Eating

16 Gateway of India B2
17 Hospůdka U Divadla B4
18 Life is Dream C2
19 Masné Krámy B2
20 Naše farma C2
21 U Tři Sedláku B2

Drinking & Nightlife

22 Cafe Plaza B3
23 Modrý Dveře Jazz & Blues B3
24 Singer Pub B3
25 Staré Časy B4

Entertainment

26 Chamber Philharmonic Orchestra of South Bohemia C3
27 Conservatory D3
28 South Bohemian Theatre B4

coins, militaria, folk art and displays on natural history and archaeology, with a focus on the local region.

Sleeping

České Budějovice has a good selection of places to stay in and around the old town, ranging from cute family pensions to luxurious apartments and business hotels, all within easy walking distance of the town square.

Hotel Bohemia HOTEL €
(Map p186; ☎380 427 999; http://bohemia.restaurant; Hradební 20; s/d/tr 820/1220/1620Kč; P ⊖ ☎) Carved wooden doors open to the beautifully restored interior of these two 16th-century burghers' houses set on a quiet street. Rooms are basic but have been given a bit of character, and there's a good restaurant on the ground floor. The location near the canal is atmospheric, but the centre is just a short stroll away.

Penzión Centrum PENSION €
(Map p186; ☎387 311 801; www.penzioncentrum.cz; Biskupská 130/3; s/d/tr 1100/1400/1700Kč; ⊖ @ ☎) Spacious rooms with satellite TV, queen-sized beds with crisp, white linen, and thoroughly professional staff all make this a top spot near the main square. Call ahead or try to arrive before 8pm since the reception desk closes early.

Ubytovna U Nádraží HOSTEL €
(☎734 200 826; www.ubytovnacb.cz.cz; Dvořákova 161/14; s/d from 400/720Kč; P ⊖ @ ☎) This unattractive but clean tower block, just behind the bus station and about 200m from the train station, is popular with long-stay students but also offers good-value accommodation with shared bathrooms (usually sharing with just one other room) for independent travellers.

★U Tří hrušek PENSION €€
(Three Pears; Map p186; ☎386 322 141; www.utrihrusek.cz; Česká 23; s/d/tr from 1200/1700/2300Kč; P ⊖ ☎) This cleverly adapted historic building on a peaceful street offers smart, stylish and good-value accommodation, ranging from pension-style bedrooms (breakfast included) to more luxurious apartments. It even manages to squeeze in an elevator and a tiny parking garage for up to four cars (book in advance).

★Residence u černé věže APARTMENT €€
(Map p186; ☎725 178 584; www.residenceucerneveze.cz; U Černé věže 13; 2-person apt from 1700Kč; P ⊖ ❄ ☎) Four centrally located townhouses have been given a thoroughly 21st-century makeover to create 18 furnished, self-contained apartments. The decor is crisply modern with high ceilings, spotless bathrooms and fully equipped kitchens.

Hotel Budweis HOTEL €€
(Map p186; ☎389 822 111; www.hotelbudweis.cz; Mlýnská 6; s/d 2490/2990Kč; P ⊖ ❄ @ ☎) Opening its doors in 2010, the Hotel Budweis was converted from an old grain mill and has a picturesque canal-side setting. The owners have opted for a smart contemporary look. All the rooms have air-con and are wheelchair accessible. There are two good restaurants in-house, and the central location puts other eating and drinking options just a short walk away.

Hotel Klika HOTEL €€
(Map p186; ☎387 318 171; www.hotelklika.cz; Hroznová 25; s/d/apt 1200/1690/2500Kč; P ⊖ ☎) This is an excellent, good-value option, with an attractive riverside location; anywhere that integrates 14th-century walls into its design is OK by us. The modern rooms are light and airy, and there's a double apartment complete with private sauna.

Hotel Malý Pivovar HOTEL €€
(Map p186; ☎386 360 471; www.malypivovar.cz; Karla IV 8-10; s/d 1450/1850Kč; P ⊖ @) With a cabinet of sports trophies and sculpted leather sofas, the lobby here resembles a gentlemen's club, and the atmosphere throughout is rather old-fashioned. However, the traditionally furnished rooms are comfortable enough, the location is good, and it's just a few paces to the cosy Budvarka beer hall downstairs.

Hotel Dvořák HOTEL €€
(Map p186; ☎386 322 349; www.hoteldvorakcb.cz; náměstí Přemysla Otakara II 36; s/d 1490/1990Kč; P @ ☎) Don't be fooled by the elegant facade: the Dvořák's rooms are modern and clean, but a bit lacking in character. Still, the friendly staff and good-value last-minute specials (up to 40% off) make this a worthwhile standby, and the location on the main square is excellent.

Eating

Long famed for its hearty traditional pub grub – Masné Kramy (p188) is the epitome of South Bohemian beer halls – České Budějovice is developing the fine dining side of its restaurant scene, with new places such as Naše farma championing fresh local produce prepared with a bit of style.

Gateway of India INDIAN €

(Indická Restaurace; ☎386 359 355; www.indickarestaurace.cz; Chelčického 121/10; mains 130-230Kč; ⏰11am-11pm Mon-Sat; 📶) Oddly for a city of its size, České Budějovice has two Indian restaurants. We prefer this smaller, more intimate place close to the train and bus stations; the other **branch** (Indická Restaurace; Map p186; ☎387 203 844; www.indickarestaurace.cz; Piaristická 22; mains 130-230Kč; ⏰11am-11pm Mon-Sat; 📶) is near the main square. Climb the stairs to the cosy dining room, infused with the smell of curries cooking. The lamb madras is our favourite, but all the dishes are good and authentic.

U Tři Sedláku CZECH €

(Map p186; ☎387 222 303; www.utrisedlaku.cz; Hroznová 488; mains 100-170Kč) Although the interior is lacking in historic atmosphere, the menu hasn't changed much at 'The Three Farmers' since its opening in 1897 and the traditional Czech food is among the best in town. Choose meaty dishes such as lamb, venison or rabbit to go with the Pilsner Urquell that's constantly being shuffled to busy tables.

★ Naše farma CZECH €€

(Map p186; ☎605 228 803; www.nasefarma.cz; U Černé věže 15; mains 120-280Kč; ⏰11am-9pm Mon-Thu, to 10pm Fri-Sat) The name of this restaurant (Our Farm) is a statement of its priorities – serving fresh local produce (mainly pork and beef) raised on organic farms in the surrounding region. Dishes are simple but delicious, focusing on the main event – grilled pork chop with hollandaise sauce, pea purée and cauliflower florets, or meatloaf of confit beef with creamed potatoes and horseradish.

Hospůdka U Divadla CZECH €€

(Map p186; ☎607 078 486; www.hospudkaudivadla.cz; Dr Stejskala 13; mains 145-285Kč; ⏰11am-10pm Mon-Sat; ❄📶) Hospůdka means 'little pub' in Czech, but this refined restaurant is much more than that. The highlight here is fish, sourced locally and served fresh, but there are also a few traditional meat dishes. The daily lunch specials, served 11am to 3pm on weekdays with mains priced around 145Kč, are particularly good value. Try the microbrew Glokner beer.

Life is Dream INTERNATIONAL €€

(Map p186; ☎733 609 225; www.lifeisdream.cz; Kněžská 31; mains 190-360Kč; ⏰11am-11pm Mon-Fri, 11.30am-11pm Sat, 11.30am-10pm Sun; 📶🌶) This eclectic restaurant traditionally scores high on user-generated websites, but more for the cosy atmosphere and friendly staff than the quality of the food. The menu ranges around the globe, from Turkish pilaf to paella to kangaroo steaks, and several dishes incorporate tofu and seitan, making this a good choice for vegetarians.

Masné Krámy CZECH €€

(Map p186; ☎387 201 301; www.masne-kramy.cz; Krajinská 13; mains 150-280Kč; ⏰10.30am-11pm Mon-Thu, to midnight Fri & Sat, to 9pm Sun) No visit to České Budějovice would be complete without stopping at this local institution (open since 1954), a renovated 16th-century meat market serving excellent Czech food and cold Budvar beer. You'll find all the Czech staples, including the house 'brewer's goulash', and superb unfiltered yeast beer. It's often crammed with coach parties; advance booking is essential.

Drinking & Nightlife

Staré Časy PUB

(Map p186; ☎728 873 434; Zátkovo nábřeží 13; ⏰1-11pm Mon-Fri, 3-11pm Sat & Sun; 📶) It's hard to pinpoint why exactly, but we love this smoky old-style pub by the canal. Maybe it's the wood-panelled walls, dotted with old photos and maps, the hidden tables that invite long chats, or the friendly service. Even the Platan 11° lager (29Kč) is pretty good. In summer, try to grab a wobbly table by the water.

Cafe Plaza CAFE

(Map p186; ☎728 272 958; www.cafeplaza.cz; náměstí Přemysla Otakara II 4; ⏰8am-10pm Mon-Fri, 9am-10pm Sat & Sun; 📶) The kind of breezy, busy cafe that every big town needs, right on the main square next to the Municipal Information Centre. Run in for a quick coffee, soft drink, beer or wine, or cake and ice cream. The wi-fi signal is fast and reliable and the service is friendly.

WORTH A TRIP

A WHIFF OF WINDSOR AT HLUBOKÁ NAD VLTAVOU

The delightful confection known as **Hluboká Chateau** (387 843 911; www.zamek-hluboka.eu; Zámek; adult/child Tour 1 250/160Kč, Tour 2 230/160Kč, Tour 3 230/160Kč, Tour 4 170/80Kč, castle tower 40/25Kč; 9am-5pm Tue-Sun May & Jun, daily Jul & Aug, shorter hr Sep-Apr, closed 20 Dec-1 Jan) is one of the most popular day trips from České Budějovice. Buses make the journey to the main square in **Hluboká nad Vltavou** every 30 to 60 minutes (21Kč, 25 minutes).

A raven pecking the eyes from a Turk's head (the grisly crest of the Schwarzenberg family) is a recurrent motif of the chateau's decor, but this image is at odds with the building's overt romanticism. Built by the Přemysl rulers in the latter half of the 13th century, Hluboká was taken from the Protestant Malovec family in 1662 as punishment for supporting an anti-Habsburg rebellion, and then sold to the Bavarian Schwarzenbergs. Two centuries later, they gave the chateau its English Tudor makeover, modelling its exterior on Britain's Windsor Castle.

Crowned with crenellations and surrounded by landscaped gardens, Hluboká is too prissy for some, but it remains the second-most visited chateau in Bohemia after Karlštejn, and with good reason.

The main one-hour English-language **Tour 1** (called 'Representation Rooms' on the website) focuses on the Schwarzenberg family's ornate reception rooms, including the grandiose dining room and library, and the private apartments of Duchess Eleonora. **Tour 2** is a shorter winter itinerary, while **Tours 3** and **4** explore more suites of apartments and the castle's massive kitchen, respectively. There is separate admission to the **castle tower**. Tours in Czech are 100Kč cheaper.

An annual **music festival** (www.sinfonie.cz) is held in the chateau grounds in late summer. Performances range from Czech folk to jazz and chamber music.

The exquisite **South Bohemian Aleš Gallery** (Alšova jihočeská galérie; 387 967 041; www.ajg.cz; Zámek 144; adult/concession 70/35Kč; 9am-6pm Apr-Oct, to 4pm Nov-Mar) is housed in a former *jízdárna* (riding school) next to the chateau. On display is a fabulous permanent collection of Czech religious art from the 14th to 16th centuries, plus 17th-century Dutch masters and changing exhibits of modern art.

While most visitors treat Hluboká as a day outing, it is possible to stay the night. The **Hotel Bakalář** (730 585 463; www.hotel-bakalar.cz; Masarykova 69; s/d 400/750Kč; P), at the far end of the main street, has functional rooms and a decent pub-restaurant on-site, and rents out bikes (per day 200Kč). Alternatively, the **Tourist Information Centre** (387 966 164; www.hluboka.cz; cnr Masarykova & Zborovská; 9am-6pm Apr-Oct, to 5pm Tue-Sun Nov-Mar;), which has internet access and a useful map, can recommend private rooms (also watch for *'Zimmer frei'* or *'privát'* signs along the main street, Masarykova).

There are a few restaurants scattered about that cater to day trippers. An easy in-out option is **Pizzerie Ionia** (387 966 109; www.pizzerieionia.cz; Masarykova 35; pizza 120-170Kč; 11am-10pm Mon-Sat, noon-5pm Sun), just near the information centre.

Modrý Dveře Jazz & Blues BAR

(Map p186; 386 359 958; www.modrydvere.cz; Biskupská 1; 10am-midnight Mon-Sat, noon-midnight Sun;) By day Modrý Dveře is a welcoming bar-cafe with vintage pics of Sinatra. At dusk the lights dim for live music – blues and jazz on Thursday (from 8pm; admission 50Kč to 80Kč), and DJs on most Friday nights. Pop in for a drink even if there's nothing on the cards; it's one of the few lively bars near the centre.

Singer Pub PUB

(Map p186; 386 360 186; www.singerpub.cz; Česká 7; 3pm-1am Mon-Fri, 7pm-1am Sat & Sun;) With Czech and Irish beers and good cocktails, don't be surprised if you get the urge to rustle up something on the Singer sewing machines scattered around here. If not, challenge the regulars to a game of foosball to a soundtrack of noisy rock.

1

DALIU/SHUTTERSTOCK ©

2

4

1. Hluboká Chateau (p189)
Delightful Hluboká Chateau, in neo-Gothic style, was created by the noble Schwarzenberg family, who consciously modelled their home after Windsor Castle in the UK.

2. Karlštejn (p174)
Karlštejn village is most well-known for Karlštejn Castle, a fairy-tale medieval fortress that rises above the village.

3. Pilsner Urquell Brewery (p207)
In operation since 1842, Pilsner Urquell Brewery in Plzeň is arguably home to the world's best beer.

4. Český Krumlov (p192)
Located in Bohemia's deep south, Český Krumlov is a picturesque Unesco World Heritage Site with a stunning castle above the Vltava River, an old town square and Renaissance and baroque architecture.

3

Entertainment

Mighty Bar Velbloud LIVE MUSIC
(www.velbloud.info; U Tří lvů 4; 7pm-2am Tue-Sat) A loud and fun club with an eclectic schedule of live music, covering anything from neo-punk to Roma DJs to German rockabilly. Check the website to see what's on offer during your visit.

Chamber Philharmonic Orchestra of South Bohemia CLASSICAL MUSIC
(Jihočeská komorní filharmonie; Map p186; box office 386 321 084; www.jcfilharmonie.cz; Kněžská 6; tickets around 180Kč; box office 1-5pm Mon-Fri) A highlight of a visit to České Budějovice is attending a concert at this former church that's been converted into a concert hall. The repertoire ranges from baroque all the way to modern, and there are also regular performances of folk and pop music. Buy tickets at the box office or the Municipal Information Centre (p192).

South Bohemian Theatre THEATRE
(Jihočeské divadlo; Map p186; 386 356 925; www.jihoceskedivadlo.cz; Dr Stejskala 19; tickets 190-260Kč; box office 10am-7pm Mon-Fri) The main building of the South Bohemian Theatre mostly stages dramatic works and small operas. The plays are normally performed in Czech.

Conservatory CLASSICAL MUSIC
(Konzervatoř; Map p186; 386 352 089; www.konzervatorcb.cz; Kanovnická 22; admission free) This music academy hosts regular classical performances.

Information

Municipal Information Centre (Městské Informarční Centrum; Map p186; 386 801 413; www.cb-info.cz; náměstí Přemysla Otakara II 2; 8.30am-6pm Mon-Fri, to 5pm Sat, 10am-4pm Sun May-Sep, shorter hours Oct-Apr) Books tickets, tours and accommodation, and has free internet.

Oberbank (www.oberbank.cz; náměstí Přemysla Otakara II 4) Handy bank ATM located just on the main square next to the Municipal Information Centre.

Getting There & Away

BUS

Student Agency (386 111 000; www.studentagency.cz; Lannova 27; 9am-6pm Mon-Fri) buses leave from Prague's Na Knížecí bus station (165Kč, 2½ hours, hourly) at the Anděl metro station (Line B). There are decent bus services from České Budějovice to Český Krumlov (32Kč, 40 to 50 minutes), Tábor (70Kč, 1½ hours) and Třeboň (36Kč, 40 minutes). České Budějovice's **bus station** (266 014 111; Nádražní 1759) is about 500m east of the centre, near the train station.

TRAIN

České Budějovice is a major rail hub with frequent train services from Prague (234Kč, 2½ hours, hourly). Regular (slow) trains trundle to Český Krumlov (51Kč, 45 minutes). České Budějovice's **train station** (Vlakové nádraží; 840 112 113; www.cd.cz; Nádražní) is about 500m east of the centre; by foot, follow pedestrianised Lannova street for 10 to 15 minutes.

ČESKÝ KRUMLOV

POP 61,100

Český Krumlov, in Bohemia's deep south, is one of the most picturesque towns in Europe. It's a little like Prague in miniature – a Unesco World Heritage Site with a stunning castle above the Vltava River, an old town square, Renaissance and baroque architecture, and hordes of tourists milling through the streets – but all on a smaller scale; you can walk from one side of town to the other in 20 minutes. There are plenty of lively bars and riverside picnic spots – in summer it's a popular hang-out for backpackers. It can be a magical place in winter, though, when the crowds are gone and the castle is blanketed in snow.

Český Krumlov is best approached as an overnight destination; it's too far for a comfortable day trip from Prague. Consider staying at least two nights, and spend one of the days hiking or biking in the surrounding woods and fields.

Sights

There's no neatly prescribed plan for exploring Český Krumlov, so the best strategy is simply to follow your nose. The basic layout will soon become clear: a giant Renaissance castle on top and a web of backstreets and alleyways, bridges and riverbanks below. The centre of the Old Town (also known as the Inner Town, or Vnitřní Město) is defined by náměstí Svornosti, with its 16th-century Town Hall and Marian Plague Column, dating from 1716. Several buildings on the square feature valuable stucco and painted decorations: note the hotel at No 13 and the house at No 14.

Český Krumlov

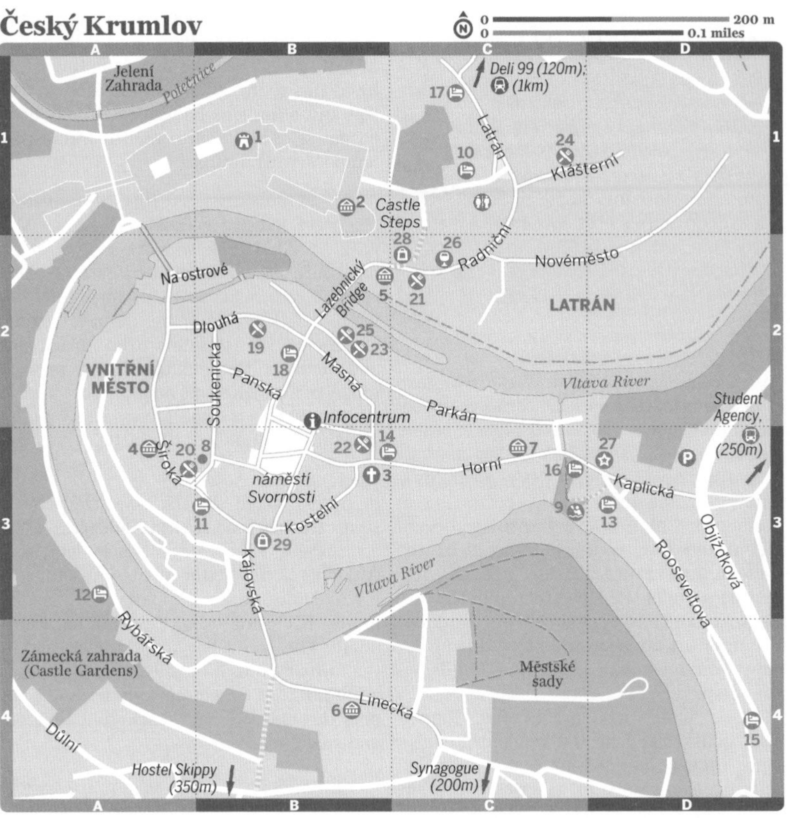

Český Krumlov

Top Sights
1 Český Krumlov State Castle B1

Sights
2 Castle Museum & Tower B1
3 Church of St Vitus B3
4 Egon Schiele Art Centrum A3
5 Marionette Museum B2
6 Museum Fotoateliér Seidel B4
7 Regional Museum C3

Activities, Courses & Tours
8 Expedicion B3
9 Maleček C3

Sleeping
10 Castle Apartments C1
11 Hospoda Na Louži B3
12 Hostel Postel A3
13 Hotel garni Myší Díra D3
14 Hotel Konvice B3
15 Krumlov House D4
16 Pension Barbakán C3
17 Pension Danny C1
18 U Malého Vítka B2

Eating
19 Cikánská Jizba B2
Hospoda Na Louži .... (see 11)
20 Jakub A3
21 Kolektiv C2
22 Krčma v Šatlavské B3
23 Laibon B2
24 Nonna Gina C1
25 U Dwau Maryí B2

Drinking & Nightlife
Egon Schiele Café .... (see 4)
26 Zapa Cocktail Bar C2

Entertainment
Divadelní Klub Ántré .... (see 27)
27 Městské Divadlo D3

Shopping
28 Antique na Zámeckých schodech C2
29 Koh-I-Noor B3

ℹ ČESKÝ KRUMLOV CARD

Pick up the **Český Krumlov Card** (www.ckrumlov.cz/card; adult/child 300/150Kč) to get reduced entry into several popular attractions, including the Castle Museum and Tower, Regional Museum, Museum Fotoateliér Seidel and Egon Schiele Art Centrum. Buy it at the **Infocentrum** (p198) or the various attractions. It's valid for one year after the first use.

★Český Krumlov State Castle CASTLE
(Map p193; ☎380 704 711; www.zamek-ceskykrumlov.eu; Zámek 59; adult/concession Tour 1 250/160Kč, Tour 2 240/140Kč, Theatre Tour 300/200Kč; ⏲9am-6pm Tue-Sun Jun-Aug, to 5pm Apr, May, Sep & Oct) Český Krumlov's striking Renaissance castle, occupying a promontory high above the town, began life in the 13th century. It acquired its present appearance in the 16th to 18th centuries under the stewardship of the noble Rožmberk and Schwarzenberg families. The interiors are accessible by guided tour only, though you can stroll the grounds on your own.

Three main **tours** are offered: Tour 1 (one hour) takes in the opulent Renaissance rooms; Tour 2 (one hour) visits the Schwarzenberg portrait galleries and their 19th-century apartments. The Theatre Tour (40 minutes, 10am to 4pm Tuesday to Sunday May to October) explores the chateau's remarkable rococo theatre.

Castle Museum & Tower MUSEUM, TOWER
(Map p193; ☎380 704 711; www.zamek-ceskykrumlov.eu; Zámek 59; combined entry adult/child 130/60Kč, museum only 100/50Kč, tower only 50/30Kč; ⏲9am-5pm Jun-Aug, to 4pm Apr, May, Sep & Oct, to 3pm Tue-Sun Nov-Mar) Located within the castle complex, this small museum and adjoining tower is an ideal option if you don't have the time or energy for a full castle tour. Through a series of rooms, the museum traces the castle's history from its origins to the present day. Climb the tower for the perfect photo ops of the town below.

Egon Schiele Art Centrum MUSEUM
(Map p193; ☎380 704 011; www.schieleartcentrum.cz; Široká 71; adult/child under 6yr 160Kč/free; ⏲10am-6pm Tue-Sun) This excellent private gallery houses a small retrospective of the controversial Viennese painter Egon Schiele (1890–1918), who lived in Krumlov in 1911, and raised the ire of the townsfolk by hiring young girls as nude models. For this and other sins he was eventually driven out. The centre also houses interesting temporary exhibitions.

Regional Museum MUSEUM
(Regionální muzeum v Českém Krumlové; Map p193; ☎380 711 674; www.museum-krumlov.eu; Horní 152; adult/concession 50/25Kč; ⏲9am-noon & 12.30-5pm Tue-Sun) This small museum features folk art from the Šumava region, archaeology, history, fine arts, furnishings and weapons. The highlight is a room-sized model of Český Krumlov c 1800. Just next to the museum is a small grassy area with an amazing view out over the castle.

Marionette Museum MUSEUM
(Map p193; ☎380 711 175; www.marionettemuseum.cz; Latrán 6; adult/child 80/40Kč; ⏲10am-6pm Jun-Aug, to 5pm May & Sep, to 4pm Apr & Oct) This is the better of two museums in town dedicated to puppetry and marionettes. It's a branch of the National Marionette Theatre in Prague and is housed in the former Church of St Jošt. On display is a full range of Czech marionettes and puppets through the ages, including theatres and stage sets.

Graphite Mine MINE
(Grafitový důl; ☎380 711 199; www.grafitovydul.cz; Chvalšinská ul 243; tour in English 200/150Kč; ⏲9am-6pm Jul & Aug, to 4pm Jun & Sep, to 3pm May) Don a hard hat and ride a clanking electric wagon through 2km of underground workings in the Czech Republic's last graphite mine, only recently abandoned. Tours are available in English and German or, for a lower admission fee (150Kč) in Czech with a text handout in your own language. The mine is signposted 1.5km northwest of the town centre.

Museum Fotoateliér Seidel MUSEUM
(Map p193; ☎736 503 871; www.seidel.cz; Linecká 272; adult/child 100/40Kč; ⏲9am-noon & 1-6pm May-Sep, to 5pm Apr & Oct-Dec, to 5pm Tue-Sun Jan-Mar) This photography museum presents a moving retrospective of the work of local photographers Josef Seidel and his son František. Especially poignant are the images recording early-20th-century life in nearby villages. In the high season you should be able to join an English-language tour; if not, let the pictures tell the story.

Church of St Vitus CHURCH
(kostel sv Víta; Map p193; ☎380 711 336; www.farnostck.bcb.cz; Horní 156; ⊙9am-6pm) FREE This pretty church, with its signature neo-Gothic tower, is worth a peek inside. The church occasionally hosts classical music concerts; ask at the nearby tourist office (p198) on the main square.

Synagogue SYNAGOGUE
(☎605 335 353; www.synagoga-krumlov.cz; Za Soudem 282; adult/concession 60/30Kč; ⊙10am-6pm Apr-Dec) Český Krumlov's renovated synagogue was built in neo-Romanesque style in 1909. The building survived the Nazi occupation in WWII and was used as a nondenominational place of worship by American soldiers shortly after the war. It's now used to house photo exhibitions and has a cute cafe around the corner. Buy entry tickets at the cafe.

Activities

Český Krumlov is more than a pretty face. The Vltava River, here close to its source, is ideal for kayaking, and the surrounding woods and hills make a pretty backdrop for hiking and cycling outings.

Expedicion ADVENTURE
(Map p193; ☎720 107 171; www.expedicion.cz; Soukenická 33; ⊙9am-7pm) Expedicion rents bikes (per day 290Kč), arranges horse riding (per hour 250Kč), and operates action-packed day trips (per person 450Kč) involving a rafting trip down the Vltava River to Zlatá Koruna and returning by bike.

Maleček CANOEING
(Map p193; ☎380 712 508; www.malecek.cz; Rooseveltova 28; per person from 250Kč; ⊙9am-5pm) In summer, messing about on the river is a great way to keep cool. Rent a canoe and splash around locally, or take a full-day trip down the river from the town of Rožmberk to Český Krumlov (per person 500Kč, six to eight hours).

Slupenec Stables HORSE RIDING
(☎723 832 459; www.jk-slupenec.cz; Slupenec 1; horse riding per hr 500Kč; ⊙Apr-Oct) Slupenec Stables, 2.5km south of town, hires horses for lessons and guided treks through the local forests and meadows. Book through the Infocentrum (p198).

Sebastian Tours TOURS
(☎607 100 234; www.sebastianck-tours.com; 5 Května ul, Plešivec) Sebastian Tours can get you discovering South Bohemia on guided minibus tours including day trips that take in České Budějovice and Hluboká nad Vltavou (per person 600Kč). Shuttle bus service to destinations further afield, such as Linz, Vienna and Salzburg in Austria, is also possible.

Sleeping

There are thousands of beds in Český Krumlov, but accommodation is still tight in summer. Winter rates drop by up to 30%. Accommodation can be noisy in the Old Town, and parking expensive. Consider alternative accommodation a short walk out of town. For budget accommodation, expect to pay from 450Kč per person for a private room, often with breakfast included. The Infocentrum (p198) can recommend furnished apartments in the midrange bracket.

★**Krumlov House** HOSTEL €
(Map p193; ☎380 711 935; www.krumlovhostel.com; Rooseveltova 68; dm/d/tr 335/785/935Kč; ⊕@📶) 🍃 Perched above the river, Krumlov House is friendly and comfortable, and has plenty of books, DVDs and local information to feed your inner wanderer. Accommodation is in a six-bed en suite dorm as well as private double and triple rooms or private, self-catered apartments. The owners are English-speaking and traveller-friendly.

Hostel Skippy HOSTEL €
(☎380 728 380; www.hostelskippy.webs.com; Plešivecká 123; dm 350-390Kč, d 900Kč; P⊕📶) This riverside hostel is about 15 minutes' walk south of the historic centre. The owners are a musician and artist and the hostel has a relaxed, indie vibe. Unlike some places with racks of bunks, Skippy is more like hanging out at a friend's place. It's small, so you'll need to book ahead.

Hospoda Na Louži HOTEL €
(Map p193; ☎380 711 280; www.nalouzi.cz; Kájovská 66; d/tr 1450/1850Kč; ⊕📶) Eleven cosy rooms situated above a great pub in the absolute centre of town. The interiors couldn't be more pleasant, with big wooden, period-piece beds, wood floors and modernised bathrooms. Noise from the pub is a nonissue. Accommodation is tight in summer; winter rates may drop by up to 40%.

Pension Danny PENSION €
(Map p193; ☎380 712 710; www.pensiondanny.cz; Latrán 72; d/tr 1190/1790Kč; ⊕📶) Exposed

timber roof beams plus restored brickwork equals rustic charm in this atmospheric 17th-century building; try to get an attic room for maximum character. As with many other places in town, the pension tends to fill up in summer, but it is much emptier and cheaper in winter.

Hostel Postel HOSTEL €
(Map p193; ☎776 720 722; www.hostelpostel.cz; Rybářská 35; dm from 300Kč, tw 700Kč; ⏰closed Jan-Mar; ⊖@📶) Situated near a couple of good local pubs, Hostel Postel has a sunny courtyard with shady umbrellas to help you wake up slowly after a big night. All accommodation is in super-clean, two- to six-bed rooms.

★**Hotel garni Myší Díra** HOTEL €€
(Map p193; ☎380 712 853; http://cz.ubytovani.ceskykrumlov-info.cz; Rooseveltova 28; s/d/tr 2150/2450/2950Kč; P📶) This place has a superb location overlooking the river, and bright, spacious rooms with lots of pale wood and quirky handmade furniture; room No 12, with a huge corner bath and naughty decorations on the bed, is our favourite. Limited parking in front of the hotel costs 190Kč.

Hotel Konvice HOTEL €€
(Map p193; ☎380 711 611; www.boehmerwaldhotels.de; Horní 144; s/d 1800/2000Kč; P⊖📶) An attractive old-fashioned hotel with romantic rooms and period furnishings. Many rooms, such as No 12, have impressive wood-beamed ceilings, and all have homey architectural quirks that lend atmosphere. The service is reserved but friendly. The cook at breakfast is more than happy to whip up an egg on request (to go with the usual cold cuts and cheeses).

Castle Apartments APARTMENT €€
(Map p193; ☎380 725 110; www.zameckaapartma.cz; Zámek 57; 2-person apt 1690-2990Kč; ⏰reception 9am-6pm; ⊖📶) Several apartments situated in three historic buildings near the castle district have been transformed into comfortable short-term rental units that offer wood floors and modern kitchenettes and bathrooms (no additional charge for the romantic views). The central reception is located just inside the castle entrance off Latrán.

Pension Barbakán PENSION €€
(Map p193; ☎380 717 017; www.barbakan.cz; Kaplická 26; r 1700-2100Kč; ⊖@📶) Originally the town's gunpowder arsenal, Barbakán now creates fireworks of its own with super-comfy rooms featuring bright and cosy wooden decor, perched high above the Vltava. Sit out on the sunny hotel terrace and watch the tubing and rafting action on the river below.

U Malého Vítka HOTEL €€
(Map p193; ☎380 711 925; www.vitekhotel.cz; Radnični 27; s/d 1050/1600Kč; P⊖📶) We like this small hotel in the heart of the Old Town. The simple room furnishings are of high-quality, hand-crafted wood, and each room is named after a traditional Czech fairy-tale character. The downstairs restaurant and cafe are very good too.

Eating

Although there are dozens of places to eat in town, the large number of visitors means that booking ahead for dinner is recommended from April to October and on weekends year-round.

★**Nonna Gina** ITALIAN €
(Map p193; ☎380 717 187; www.pizzerianonnagina.wz.cz; Klášteriní 52; mains 100-200Kč; ⏰11am-11pm) Authentic Italian flavours from the Massaro family feature at this long-established pizzeria, where the quality of food and service knocks the socks off more expensive restaurants. Superb antipasti, great pizza and Italian wines at surprisingly low prices make for a memorable meal. Grab an outdoor table and pretend you're in Naples, or retreat to the snug and intimate upstairs dining room.

Kolektiv CAFE €
(Map p193; ☎776 626 644; www.bistrokolektiv.cz; Latrán 13; mains 80-100Kč; ⏰8am-9pm; 📶) This stylish modern cafe is a good place to grab a breakfast of ham and eggs or coffee and croissants, enjoy a light lunch of homemade soup or quiche, or chat over a glass of prosecco or homemade lemonade. After 5pm there's more of a wine-bar vibe.

Hospoda Na Louži CZECH €
(Map p193; ☎380 711 280; www.nalouzi.cz; Kájovská 66; mains 120-240Kč) Nothing's changed in this wood-panelled *pivo* (beer) parlour for almost a century. Locals and tourists pack Na Louži for huge plates of Czech staples such as chicken schnitzels or roast pork and dumplings, as well as dark (and light) beer from the local Eggenberg brewery. Get

the fruit dumplings for dessert if you see them on the menu.

U Dwau Maryí CZECH €
(Map p193; ☎380 717 228; www.2marie.cz; Parkán 104; mains 150-200Kč; 📶) The 'Two Marys' medieval tavern recreates old Bohemian recipes and presents an opportunity to try dishes made with buckwheat and millet (all tastier than they sound). Wash the food down with a goblet of mead or choose a 21st-century Eggenberg. In summer it's a tad touristy, but the stunning riverside castle views easily compensate.

Laibon VEGETARIAN €
(Map p193; ☎775 676 654; www.laibon.cz; Parkán 105; mains 130-200Kč; ⏰11am-11pm; 📶🖊) One of the town's rare meat-free zones, this snug veggie oasis offers great hummus, couscous, curry and pasta dishes, and local specialities such as *bryndzové halušky* (tiny potato dumplings with sheep's-milk cheese). Book in advance in summer and request an outside table with a view of the castle.

Cikánská Jizba CZECH €
(Map p193; ☎380 717 585; www.cikanskajizba.cz; Dlouhá 31; mains 130-280Kč; ⏰1pm-midnight May-Sep, 5pm-midnight Mon-Sat Oct-Apr) At the 'Gypsy Room' there's often live Roma music at the weekends to go with the menu of meaty Czech favourites. Reserve a table in advance during summer, especially over weekends.

Deli 99 SANDWICHES €
(☎721 750 786; www.hostel99.cz/deli-99; Latrán 106; mains 50-90Kč; ⏰7am-7pm Mon-Fri, 8am-7pm Sat, 8am-5pm Sun; 📶🖊) Bagels, sandwiches, good strong espresso, organic juices and wi-fi all tick the box marked 'Slightly Homesick Traveller' at this hostel deli. It's just inside the city gate, at the northern end of town.

★ Krčma v Šatlavské CZECH €€
(Map p193; ☎380 713 344; www.satlava.cz; Horní 157; mains 150-325Kč; ⏰11am-midnight) This medieval barbecue cellar is hugely popular with visitors and your table mates are much more likely to be from Austria or China than from the town itself, but the grilled meats served up with gusto in a funky labyrinth illuminated by candles are excellent and perfectly in character with Český Krumlov. Advance booking is essential.

Jakub CZECH €€
(Map p193; ☎380 725 912; www.jakubrestaurant.cz; Kájovská 54; mains 200-350Kč; ⏰11am-10pm, closed late Nov-Mar; 👪) Classical decor provides a formal setting for classic South Bohemian dishes such as *kulajda* (dill soup with mushrooms and a poached egg), rabbit with mustard sauce, and local freshwater fish including carp and pike-perch. Try to get a table in the right-hand dining room (as you enter) – it's decorated with murals inspired by the original medieval paintings on the restaurant's facade.

DON'T MISS

INTERNATIONAL MUSIC FESTIVAL

Český Krumlov's most important cultural event is the month-long **International Music Festival** (Mezinárodní hudební festival; ☎380 711 797; www.festivalkrumlov.cz; ⏰concerts mid-Jul–Aug), a celebration of classical music, with a nod to other genres such as folk, pop and jazz. Concerts are scattered around town, though most take place inside the castle or on the surrounding grounds. Consult the website for program details. Buy tickets through **TicketStream** (www.ticketstream.cz).

Drinking & Nightlife

Český Krumlov tends to be a bit on the quiet side after dark, with nightlife confined to a couple of bars, many serving local beer from the town's Eggenberg Brewery. For a livelier scene you're better off in České Budějovice.

Zapa Cocktail Bar COCKTAIL BAR
(Map p193; ☎380 712 559; www.zapabar.cz; Latrán 15; ⏰6pm-1am; 📶) Most of Český Krumlov empties out after dinner, but Zapa keeps going until after midnight. Expect a relaxed vibe and the town's best cocktails.

Egon Schiele Café CAFE
(Map p193; ☎380 704 011; www.egonschielecafe.cz; Široká 71; ⏰10am-6pm Tue-Sun; 📶) A lovely cafe housed in the art gallery, with ancient oak floorboards, mismatched furniture and a grand piano with sawn-off legs serving as a coffee table. Good Lavazza coffee, homemade ginger ale and freshly baked apple pie are on the menu.

Entertainment

Divadelní Klub Ántré LIVE MUSIC
(Map p193; ☎605 882 342; www.divadlo.ckrumlov.cz; Horní 2; 📶) The best up-and-coming

Czech bands often include the Ántré on their national schedules. The website is not very helpful, so ask at the theatre box office or the tourist office in the town square to see if anything's on during your visit.

Městské Divadlo THEATRE
(Map p193; ☎380 727 370; www.divadlo.ckrumlov.cz; Horní 2) The town theatre holds regular performances. Check the website for the current program.

Shopping

Koh-I-Noor ARTS & CRAFTS
(Map p193; ☎731 627 867; www.koh-i-noor.cz; Kostelní 169; ⌚9am-5pm Mon-Fri, 10am-3pm Sat) Founded in Vienna in 1790, world-famous Koh-I-Noor has been making pencils in České Budějovice since 1848, based on South Bohemia's abundant graphite deposits. This colourful shop, redolent with the scent of pencil shavings, stocks the company's full range of coloured pencils, pastels, paints and other art supplies.

Antique na Zámeckých schodech ANTIQUES
(Map p193; ☎380 711 228; www.starozitnosti-ceskykrumlov.cz; Zámecké schody 8; ⌚10am-6pm) This cramped corner at the foot of the castle steps is crammed with a mixture of militaria, old musical instruments, collectables and genuine antiques. If the object of your desire is too big for your bag, they ship worldwide.

Information

Infocentrum (Map p193; ☎380 704 622; www.ckrumlov.info; náměstí Svornosti 2; ⌚9am-7pm Jun-Aug, to 6pm Apr, May, Sep & Oct, to 5pm Nov-Mar, closed lunch Sat & Sun) One of the country's best tourist offices. Good source for transport and accommodation info, maps, internet access (per five minutes 5Kč) and audio guides (per hour 100Kč). A guide for disabled visitors is also available.

Getting There & Away

BUS

Student Agency (☎841 101 101; www.studentagency.cz; Nemocniční 586) coaches (200Kč, three hours, hourly) leave from Prague's Na Knížecí bus station at Anděl metro station (Line B). Book in advance for weekends or in July and August. Český Krumlov **bus station** (Autobusové nádraží; Nemocniční 586) is about a 10-minute walk east of the historic centre.

CAR & MOTORCYCLE

The drive from Prague is a strenuous three hours along mostly two-lane highway. Take the D1 motorway in the direction of Brno, and turn south on Hwy E55.

TRAIN

The train from Prague (275Kč, 3½ hours, four to six daily) requires a change in České Budějovice. There's regular train service between České Budějovice and Český Krumlov (51Kč, 45 minutes). It is quicker and cheaper to take the bus. Český Krumlov **train station** (Vlakové nádraží; ☎840 112 113; www.cd.cz; Třída Míru 1) is located 2km north of the historic centre. A taxi from the station will run around 100Kč and is a better option if you're arriving after dark or in bad weather.

TŘEBOŇ

POP 8400

Třeboň is known throughout the Czech Republic for its many traditional fish ponds, which produce much of the carp consumed around the country on Christmas Eve. The ponds have been used to raise carp since the 15th century, but these days they're also prized for aesthetic reasons: they make a picturesque backdrop while hiking or biking through the Třeboňsko Protected Landscape region, which has been designated a Unesco Biosphere Reserve.

Třeboň itself is a nicely preserved period piece of Bohemian Renaissance architecture, mixed in with a handful of sights and some decent hotels. It can be visited as an easy day trip from České Budějovice.

Sights

Třeboň's main attractions are its lovely lakeside setting on the shore of Rybník Svět, its Renaissance chateau, and the Renaissance and baroque houses on the square and within the town walls (which date from 1527). Don't miss the Town Hall on the square, St Giles Church (kostel sv Jiljí) and the Augustine monastery.

Třeboň Chateau CASTLE
(Zámek; Map p199; ☎384 721 193; www.zamek-trebon.eu; Zámek 115; guided tour in English adult/child 180/100Kč; ⌚9am-5.15pm Tue-Sun Jun-Aug, to 4pm Apr-May & Sep-Oct) Třeboň's main attraction is its Renaissance chateau, which includes a museum displaying furniture and weapons. Today's chateau dates from 1611, the replacement for a Gothic

Třeboň

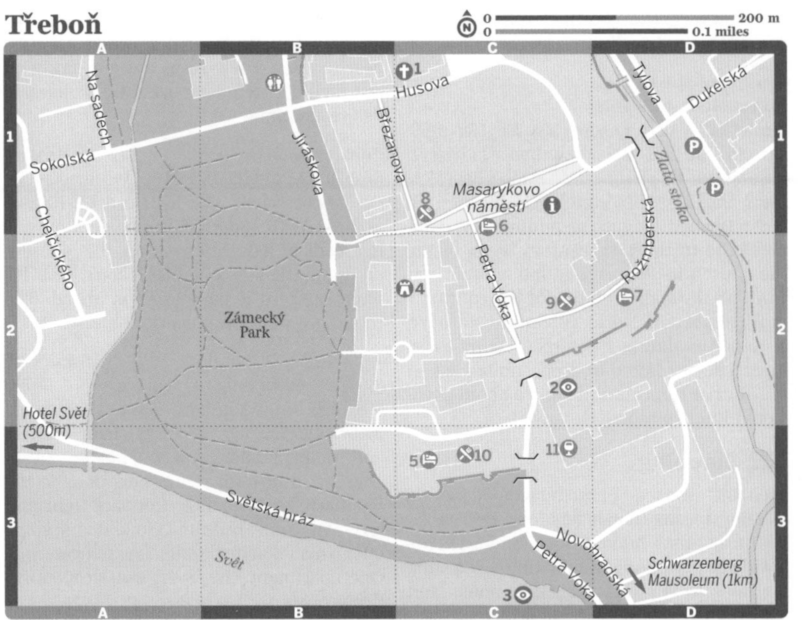

Třeboň

Sights
1 Church of the Virgin Mary & St Giles....C1
2 Regent Brewery....C2
3 Rybník Svět....C3
4 Třeboň Chateau....C2

Sleeping
5 Apartmány Šupina....C3
6 Hotel Zlatá Hvězda....C1
7 Penzion Modrá Růže....D2

Eating
8 Restaurace Vratislavský dům....C1
9 Rožmberská Bašta....C2
10 Šupina & Šupinka....C3

Drinking & Nightlife
11 Zbrojnice....C3

castle destroyed by fire. Originally built by the Rožmberk family, it then became one of the main residences of the Schwarzenbergs.

Entry is by one of three guided tours (prices are for Czech-language tours): tour A (100Kč) takes you through the castle's Renaissance interiors; tour B (100Kč) focuses on the Schwarzenberg family's 19th-century private apartments; and tour C (70Kč; July and August only) the stables, kennels, cellars and casemates.

Schwarzenberg Mausoleum MAUSOLEUM
(Švarcenberská Hrobka; ☎384 721 193; www.zamek-trebon.eu; Park U Hrobky; adult/child 60/40Kč, guided tour in English 100/70Kč; ⌚9am-5pm Tue-Sun Jun-Aug, to 4pm Apr-May & Sep-Oct) Many Schwarzenbergs are buried in this grand neo-Gothic mausoleum, dating from 1877, located in Park U Hrobky on the other side of the pond from Třeboň. The crypt is about a 15-minute walk from the centre along well-marked paths. Guided tours in English are possible but must be arranged in advance.

Regent Brewery BREWERY
(Pivovar Bohemia Regent; Map p199; ☎384 721 319; www.pivovar-regent.cz; Trocnovské náměstí 124; tour per person 120-200Kč; ⌚10am-9pm Mon-Sat, 11am-5pm Sun Jun-Aug, shorter hours Sep-May) Třeboň's municipal brewery was founded in 1379, and still turns out excellent beers sold under the 'Bohemia Regent' label. Brewery tours need to be prebooked by telephone or email. Prices depend on the time of day and number of people; check the website for tour times (in Czech)

or ask at reception (on the left as you enter the gate).

Church of the Virgin Mary & St Giles CHURCH

(Kostel Panny Marie Královny a sv Jiljí; Map p199; ☎tours 732 251 103; www.trebon.farnost.cz; Husova; tour per person 30Kč; ⊙tours 3pm Mon, Tue & Thu-Sat) This stately Gothic church and attached Augustine monastery complex date to the 14th century. Peek inside the church to see original late-Gothic artwork on the walls and one of the country's most important works of Gothic statuary, a Madonna dating from 1400. Daily tours in Czech are offered at 3pm, though ask at the Tourist Information Centre about occasional English tours.

Sleeping

Třeboň's wooded parkland and lakeside location means that it has long been a favourite summer holiday destination. There's a wide choice of accommodation, from snug pensions to sprawling lakeside hotels and spa complexes, but it's a good idea to book ahead in summer and at weekends.

Hotel Svět HOTEL €

(☎384 721 394; www.hotelsvet.com; U Světa 750; s/d 910/1550Kč; P 📶) This large resort hotel on the shore of the Svět pond sports a cool, 1980s retro vibe. The rooms are spacious and many have balconies, while a sandy beach is just a few steps away, along with spa facilities, tennis courts and a lakeside fish restaurant.

Penzion Modrá Růže PENSION €

(Map p199; ☎603 768 819; www.modra-ruze.cz; Rožmberská 39; s 450-740Kč, d 720-1000Kč; ⊖@📶) With super-helpful owners providing loads of local information, this pension on a quiet lane is one of Třeboň's best. It's often busy, so it pays to book ahead. The rooms are simple but comfortable.

Apartmány Šupina APARTMENT €€

(Šupina Apartments; Map p199; ☎720 993 825; www.supina.cz; Valy 155; s/d/tr 1600/2400/3600Kč; P⊖📶) Four stylish and well-appointed apartments are available for short-term rental next door to the Šupina restaurant. The units are light and airy, with comfy beds and wood floors; some offer small kitchen units for self-catering. One apartment, the 'Svět', can sleep up to five people.

Hotel Zlatá Hvězda HOTEL €€

(Map p199; ☎384 757 111; www.zlatahvezda.cz; Masarykovo náměstí 107; s/d 1400/2400Kč; P⊖@📶) Třeboň's smartest offering has flash rooms, a small bowling alley and a spa centre, all in a 430-year-old building right on the main square. The helpful reception desk serves as a second tourist information office and can suggest good hikes and cycling tours. Bikes are available for hire (per day 300Kč).

TOURING A CARP POND

The area around Třeboň is dotted with literally hundreds of fish ponds, many dating back several centuries when fish-farming techniques were first being developed. Eating fish is near and dear to the hearts of land-locked Czechs. Indeed, the most important meal of the year, at Christmas Eve, is centred around carp, and much of the nation's carp is raised right here. One of the main fishponds, **Rybník Svět** (Svět Pond; Map p199), is an easy 10-minute walk south of Třeboň's central square. There's a well-marked trail that borders the pond for several kilometres. Part of the edge of the pond is lined with working fish foundries, where you can see how the fish are stored and harvested for that all-important Christmas meal (the carp are fried and served with potato salad, while sundry inedible bits are boiled-up to make carp soup).

Eating & Drinking

Třeboň is *the* place to try Czech freshwater fish dishes, notably carp from the local fish ponds – *Třeboňský kapr* (Třeboň carp) has been awarded the EU's PGI (Protected Geographical Indication) status. Carp is a traditional family Christmas dish, but it is eaten year-round in the form of *kapří hranolky* (carp chips), strips of fish dipped in batter and deep-fried until golden and crispy.

Restaurace Vratislavský dům INTERNATIONAL €

(Map p199; ☎384 392 595; www.vratislavskydum.cz; Masarykovo náměstí 97; mains 85-140Kč; ⊙10am-10pm Tue-Sat, to 8pm Sun & Mon; 📶🖋) Giant, thin-crust pizzas are the name of the game here. Enjoy your slice on the outdoor terrace in main-square splendour, or head indoors to enjoy the vaulted ceilings and antique decor of this 16th-century Renaissance building.

★ Šupina & Šupinka SEAFOOD €€
(Map p199; ☎384 721 149; www.supina.cz; Valy 155; mains 200-500Kč; ⏲10.30am-11pm;) Many people come to Třeboň just to eat here, possibly the best fish restaurant in southern Bohemia (even the menu is bound in fish skin). Šupina is the fancier option, while Šupinka is cheaper and family-oriented. Both feature freshwater fish such as pike, trout, eel and Třeboň carp. The *kapří hranolky* (pieces of carp battered and fries) are a national treasure.

Rožmberská Bašta CZECH €€
(Map p199; ☎731 175 902; www.rozmberska-basta.cz; Rožmberská 59; mains 140-250Kč; ⏲11am-10pm) You'll find good fish dishes at this homespun little restaurant, on a quiet side street near the main square. The speciality is grilled or fried *candat* (pike-perch). There's a small open-air terrace out the back in summer.

Zbrojnice PUB
(Map p199; ☎722 347 606; www.pivovar-regent.cz; Trocnovské náměstí 124, Bohemia Regent Brewery; ⏲3-10pm) The Bohemia Regent Brewery is home to a few watering holes, including this smoky beer cellar (on the right, just inside the main gate). A half-litre of beer here is cheaper – and better – than in Prague; our favourite is the Regent 11° light lager (25Kč for 0.5L).

Information

ČSOB (Ceskoslovenska obchodni banka; www.csob.cz; Masarykovo náměstí 104) Centrally located bank ATM situated just next to the Tourist Information Centre.

Tourist Information Centre (Turistické informační centrum; Map p199; ☎384 721 169; www.itrebon.cz; Masarykovo náměstí 103; ⏲9am-6pm May-Sep, 9am-noon & 12.45-4pm Mon-Fri Oct-Apr) Centrally located tourist information centre hands out maps and flyers and can advise on accommodation and transportation options.

Getting There & Away

BUS

There is one direct bus a day from Florenc bus station in Prague to Třeboň (138Kč, two hours 50 minutes). Hourly buses run from České Budějovice (31Kč, 30 minutes). The bus station is a 10-minute walk from the centre.

WALKING THE TŘEBOŇSKO PROTECTED LANDSCAPE

Much of the area around Třeboň, with its wooded areas and fish ponds, has been designated as a protected landscape. A good walk through the region begins at Třeboň's Masarykovo náměstí. Follow the blue-marked trail northeast to **Na Kopečku** (1.5km, 30 minutes). From Na Kopečku, keep on the blue-marked trail to **Hodějov Pond** (7.5km, 2½ hours). A yellow trail then runs west to **Smítka** (2km, 45 minutes) where it joins a red trail heading north to **Klec** and a primitive campground (6km, two hours).

From there, for a further 13km (four hours), the red trail runs north, past more fish ponds, forests and small villages to **Veselí nad Lužnicí**, a major railway junction where you can catch a train back to Třeboň. Camping is allowed only in official campgrounds throughout the protected landscape region.

TRAIN

There are six or seven services daily from Prague's main train station to Třeboň (211Kč, 2¾ hours); all require a change of train at Veselí nad Lužnicí.

TÁBOR

POP 102,370

Tábor earned its place in Czech history in the 15th century as home to the most radical wing of the Hussite movement. These days, there aren't many radicals left, but Tábor makes for a convenient lunch-and-a-stroll stopover on the trip south towards České Budějovice and Český Krumlov. The most interesting sights here are Hussite-related: there's a museum of Hussite history on the town's pretty main square, and some centuries-old underground passages have been opened to the public.

With a steep hillside dropping off into dense woodland on three sides of the old town, Tábor's natural defences are as formidable today as they would have been when the Hussites first set up shop here some 600 years ago. But while the town's picture-postcard appeal is blatantly apparent, Tábor is no fossil. With a youthful *joie*

Tábor

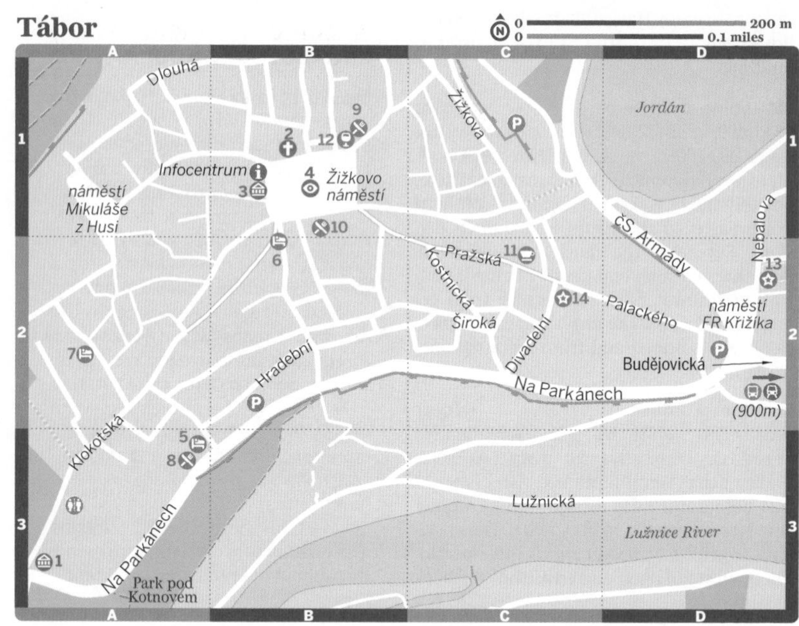

Tábor

Sights

1 Bechyně Gate & Kotnov Tower A3
2 Church of Our Lord's Transfiguration on Mt Tábor B1
3 Hussite Museum B1
Underground Passages .... (see 3)
4 Žižkovo Náměstí B1

Sleeping

5 Hotel Dvořák A3
6 Hotel Nautilus B2
7 Staroměstský Penzion A2

Eating

Goldie .... (see 6)
8 La Cave A3
9 Tandoor B1
10 U Zlatého lva B1

Drinking & Nightlife

11 Moccacafe C2
12 MP7 .... B1

Entertainment

13 Kino Svět D2
14 Oskar Nedbal Theatre C2

de vivre permeating its streets, it remains as vibrant as it is venerable.

Sights

Tábor's Old Town is a beautifully preserved medieval townscape. Be sure to leave time for some aimless wandering through the labyrinth of cobbled lanes. The confusing street plan was originally devised to thwart invaders; these days it serves mainly to charm visitors.

Žižkovo Náměstí SQUARE

(Map p202; Žižkovo náměstí) Tabor's handsome main square is lined with late-Gothic, Renaissance and baroque houses. In the middle is a fountain (1567) and a commanding statue of the Hussite leader Jan Žižka, after whom the square is named. The two stone tables in front of the Hussite Museum (p203) on the square's western end may have been used by the Hussites for religious services.

Underground Passages TUNNEL

(Podzemní Chodby; Map p202; ☎381 254 286; www.husitskemuzeum.cz; Žižkovo náměstí 1; adult/concession 50/30Kč, combined with Hussite Museum 100/60Kč; ⌚9am-5pm daily Apr-Sep, Wed-Sat Oct-Mar) At the Hussite Museum (p203) in the former Town Hall, you'll find the entrance to a fascinating 650m stretch of underground passageways, which you can visit by guided tour only. The passages, constructed in the 15th century as refuges during fires and times of war, were also used to store food and to mature beer.

Hussite Museum MUSEUM
(Husitské muzeum; Map p202; ☎381 254 286; www.husitskemuzeum.cz; Žižkovo náměstí 1; adult/concession 60/40Kč, combined with Undergroud Passages 100/60Kč; ⏲9am-5pm daily Apr-Sep, Wed-Sat Oct-Mar) Situated in Tábor's former late-Gothic Town Hall (Stará radnice), this museum traces the origins and history of the Hussite movement in the Czech Republic. Here you'll also find the entrance to the underground passages (p202) below the Old Town.

Bechyně Gate & Kotnov Tower MUSEUM
(Bechyňská brána & věž Kotnov; Map p202; ☎381 252 788; www.husitskemuzeum.cz; Klokotská; adult/concession 30/20Kč; ⏲9am-5pm May-Sep) The Bechyně Gate, just next to the ruins of Kotnov Castle, is the last of the town's original Gothic portals to remain standing, and it still retains the look it had some 500 years ago. It houses a small museum with a permanent exhibition entitled 'Life and Work in Medieval Society', focused mainly on how peasants lived. Climb to the top of the adjacent 15th-century **Kotnov Tower** for a broad view over the city and the Lužnice River.

Church of Our Lord's Transfiguration on Mt Tábor CHURCH
(Děkanský kostel Proměnění Páně na hoře Tábor; Map p202; ☎381 251 226; Žižkovo náměstí; tower adult/concession 50/20Kč; ⏲10am-5pm daily May-Aug, check with tourist office Sep-Apr) There has been a church here, on the square's northern side, for several centuries. This building dates from the mid-15th century and replaced a wooden structure. The basic style is Gothic, though reconstructions over the years have added Renaissance and baroque elements. The **tower** soars some 75m (200 steps) and offers sweeping views over Tábor.

Sleeping

If you do decide to overnight in Tábor (most people stop for a lunchtime visit on the way south to Český Krumlov), the Infocentrum (p205) can help with finding beds in seasonal hostels and privately rented rooms.

★**Staroměstský Penzion** PENSION €
(Map p202; ☎737 864 819; www.staromestsky-penzion.com; Křížová 8; s/d/ste from 600/1100/2200Kč; ⊖) Nothing fancy here, just a well-run, spotlessly clean pension on a quiet street a few metres away from the main square. There are just four rooms, including a suite that sleeps up to four, so you'll have to book well in advance in summer. Drop the owners an email ahead of arrival so they meet you at the door.

Hotel Dvořák HOTEL €€
(Map p202; ☎381 207 211; www.dvoraktabor.cz; Hradební 3037; s/d 1850/2350Kč; P⊖@🛜) The Dvořák occupies a renovated former brewery, just near to the Kotnov Tower and a short walk from the town centre. It has a spa and wellness centre (with special beer massages) as well as clean, fashionable rooms and one of the city's better

THE BLIND GENERAL JAN ŽIŽKA

Hussite Count Jan Žižka, the legendary blind general, was born in Trocnov, just outside České Budějovice, in 1376. He spent his youth at King Wenceslas IV's court and fought as a mercenary in Poland, but returned to the Czech kingdom at the beginning of the Reformation and became the leader of the radical wing of the Hussite movement, the Taborites. His military genius was responsible for all of the Hussite victories, from the 1420 Battle of Žižkov onwards. After losing both eyes in two separate battles, Žižka eventually died of the plague in 1424.

Žižka's army was highly organised and was the first to use a system of wagons with mounted artillery – the earliest tanks in history. These vehicles allowed him to choose where to draw up position, taking the initiative away from the crusaders and making them fight where he wanted. The technique proved almost invincible.

The Hussites successfully held off their enemies for a decade following Žižka's death, but were defeated by a combined army of the rival Hussite faction of the Utraquists and the Holy Roman Empire in 1434. Surprisingly, Žižka's invention was not incorporated into other armies until Sweden's King Gustavus II Adolphus adopted it two centuries later.

A BACKGROUNDER ON THE HUSSITES

Tábor is often regarded as the spiritual home of the radical Hussite movement. The movement's history can be traced back to the 15th century and the decision by Catholic authorities to murder Czech religious reformer Jan Hus, who was famously burned at the stake in Constance, Germany, in 1415. The consequences of this act were far greater than the Catholic authorities could have foreseen. Hus's death caused a religious revolt among the Czechs, who had viewed his decision to preach in Czech language as a step towards religious and national self-determination.

Hus himself had not intended such a drastic revolution, focusing on a translation of the Latin rite, and the giving of bread and wine to all the congregation instead of to the clergy alone. But for many, the time was ripe for church reform.

Hus was born around 1372 in Husinec, in southern Bohemia. From a poor background, he managed to become a lecturer at Charles University in Prague and in 1402 was ordained a preacher. He dreamt of a return to the original doctrines of the church – tolerance, humility, simplicity – but such a message had political overtones for a church that treated forgiveness as an opportunity to make money.

Tried on a trumped-up charge of heresy at Constance, Hus's murder was doubly unjust in that he had been granted safe conduct by the Holy Roman Emperor Sigismund.

In Bohemia many nobles offered to guarantee protection to those who practised religion according to Hus's teachings, and Hussite committees became widespread. The movement split over its relationship with the secular authorities, with the moderate Utraquists siding in 1434 with the Catholic Sigismund.

The more radical Taborites, seeing themselves as God's warriors, fought the Catholics in every way. As the military base for the Hussites, Tábor – named after the biblical Mt Tabor – was successfully defended by a mainly peasant army under the brilliant Jan Žižka and Prokop Holý.

The movement also attracted supporters from other Protestant sects in Europe. Many converged on Tábor and the groups joined against the crusading armies of the Holy Roman Empire.

Hussite ideals were never fully extinguished in Bohemia. Although the Utraquists became the dominant force after defeating (with the help of Sigismund's Catholic forces) the Taborites at the Battle of Lipany in 1434, the resulting peace guaranteed religious freedom for the movement. It took almost 200 years before Protestantism was fully suppressed in the Czech lands by the Catholic Habsburg rulers following the Battle of White Mountain, near Prague, in 1620.

restaurants, La Cave (p205). Good value for money.

Hotel Nautilus BOUTIQUE HOTEL €€
(Map p202; 380 900 900; www.hotelnautilus.cz; Žižkovo náměstí 20; s/d from 2450/3300Kč;) From the effortlessly cool bar to the elegant rooms decorated with original art, Tábor's first and only real boutique hotel is pure class, and surprisingly affordable for such international ambience right on the main square. Maybe it's time for a mini-splurge?

Eating

There are several pleasant eateries dotted around the main square, plus a couple of top-end hotel restaurants.

U Zlatého lva CZECH, PIZZA €
(The Golden Lion; Map p202; 381 252 397; www.facebook.com/zlatylevtabor.cz; Žižkovo náměstí 16; mains 100-280Kč; 11am-10pm;) From the outside, it's an ordinary looking pub serving Budweiser beer from České Budějovice, but locals know it for its excellent, Italian-inspired thin-crust pizza, using fresh ingredients and authentic mozzarella cheese.

Tandoor INDIAN €€
(Indická Restaurace; Map p202; 381 213 250; www.tabor.indicka.cz; Žižkovo náměstí 8; mains 130-230Kč; 11am-10pm Mon-Sat;) Tábor's highly regarded Indian restaurant offers a spicy alternative to the schnitzels and pizzas on offer at most other places in town, and also has a large and delicious

section devoted to vegetarian food. Enjoy quality curries and tandoor dishes in a casual, smoke-free environment.

La Cave CZECH €€

(Map p202; ☎381 207 211; www.dvoraktabor.cz; Hradební 3037, Hotel Dvořák; mains 215-360Kč; 11.30am-3pm & 6-10pm;) One of the better dining choices around town is the restaurant in the courtyard of the Hotel Dvořák (p203), which takes its food very seriously indeed. The menu is filled with treasures such as smoked duck with sour cherries, pork cheeks braised in apple juice with chestnut purée, and confit of rabbit with mustard potato dumplings; a seven-course tasting menu costs 650Kč.

★ **Goldie** CZECH €€€

(Map p202; ☎380 900 900; www.hotelnautilus.cz; Žižkovo náměstí 20, Hotel Nautilus; mains 255-565Kč; 8am-10pm;) The in-house restaurant of the nicest hotel in town also happens to be head and shoulders above everything else around. Head chef Martin Svatek has built a menu around traditional Czech mains such as duck, rabbit and even horse cheeks, but gives them a lighter touch. It's frequently named on national 'Top 10' lists. Dress up and book in advance in summer.

Drinking & Nightlife

Tábor is a sleepy little town come evening, with just a handful of bars where you might catch some live music on weekends.

★ **Moccacafe** CAFE

(Map p202; ☎725 054 239; www.moccacafe.cz; Pražská 232; 9am-7pm Mon-Sat, 10am-7pm Sun;) You won't find a better flat white anywhere in town, or for miles around for that matter (Moccacafe uses specially roasted beans). It also serves excellent breakfasts, cakes and a wide variety of high-end ice cream. An ideal spot to plant yourself after a day spent hiking around the Old Town.

MP7 BAR

(Map p202; ☎606 856 994; www.facebook.com/cafemp7; Žižkovo náměstí 7; 1-11.30pm Tue-Thu, to 2am Fri & Sat, 2-10.30pm Sun;) Dance music, jazz, reggae and house all occasionally feature at this art gallery/garden cafe/cocktail bar. It's a good spot to ask about live gigs around town too.

Entertainment

Kino Svět CINEMA

(Map p202; ☎381 252 200; www.kinosvettabor.cz; náměstí FR Křižíka 129; cafe 1-10.30pm Mon-Thu, 1pm-1am Fri, 3pm-midnight Sat, 3-10pm Sun) See Hollywood favourites and chat about them afterwards at the cinema's funky, laid-back cafe.

Oskar Nedbal Theatre THEATRE, LIVE MUSIC

(Divadlo Oskara Nedbala; Map p202; ☎box office 381 254 070; www.divadlotabor.cz; Divadelní 218; box office 3-6pm Mon-Fri, plus 1hr before performances) Everything from jazz and classical music to Czech theatre.

Information

Infocentrum (Map p202; ☎381 486 230; www.taborcz.eu; Žižkovo náměstí 2; 8.30am-7pm Mon-Fri, 10am-4pm Sat & Sun May-Sep, 8am-4pm Mon-Fri Oct-Apr) The official city tourism office is located on the main square. It provides all the usual services, including maps and sightseeing suggestions, and advice on transport and accommodation.

Oberbank (www.oberbank.cz; Pražská třída 211; 8.30am-5pm Mon-Thu, to 2.30pm Fri) Conveniently located ATM a short walk from the main square.

Getting There & Away

BUS

There are frequent buses to Tábor from Prague's Florenc bus station (101Kč, 1½ hours) and Roztyly metro station (84Kč, 1½ hours), the former in a more comfortable intercity coach. Tábor's bus station is 1km east of the historic centre.

TRAIN

There are hourly trains from Prague's main station to Tábor (147Kč, 1½ hours), but they are generally more expensive and less convenient than the bus. Tábor's train station is 1km east of the historic centre, near the bus station.

PLZEŇ

POP 188,190

Plzeň (Pilsen in German) is famed among beer-heads worldwide as the mother lode of all lagers, the fountain of eternal froth – Pilsner lager was invented here in 1842. It's the home of Pilsner Urquell (Plzeňský prazdroj), the world's first and finest lager beer – 'Urquell' (in German; *prazdroj* in Czech)

Plzeň

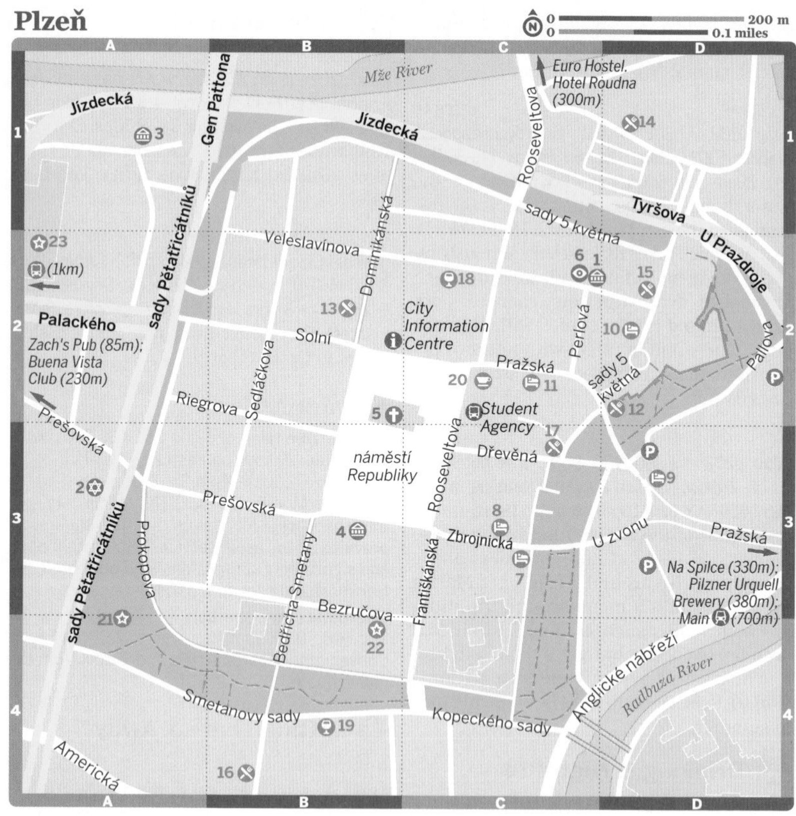

Plzeň

Sights
1 Brewery Museum C2
2 Great Synagogue A3
3 Patton Memorial Pilsen A1
4 Puppet Museum B3
5 St Bartholomew Church B2
6 Underground Plzeň C2

Sleeping
7 Hotel Continental C3
8 Hotel Rous C3
9 Hotel U Zvonu D3
10 Pension City D2
11 U Salzmannů C2

Eating
12 Aberdeen Angus Steakhouse D2
13 Buffalo Burger Bar B2
14 Groll Pivovar D1
15 Na Parkánu D2
16 Slunečnice B4
17 U Mansfelda C3

Drinking & Nightlife
18 Galerie Azyl C2
19 Měšťanská Beseda B4
20 Olala Cafe C2

Entertainment
21 JK Tyl Theatre A4
22 Music Bar Anděl B4
23 New Theatre A2

means 'original source' – and beer drinkers from around the world flock to worship at the Pilsner Urquell brewery.

The second-biggest city in Bohemia after Prague, and the EU's choice of 'Cultural Capital' in 2015, Plzeň's other attractions include a pretty town square and historic underground tunnels, while the Techmania Science Centre joins the zoo and puppet museum to make this a kid-friendly destination. The city is close enough to Prague to see the sights in a long day trip, but you'll enjoy the outing much more if you plan to spend the night.

Sights

★Pilsner Urquell Brewery BREWERY

(Prazdroj; ☎377 062 888; www.prazdrojvisit.cz; U Prazdroje 7; guided tour adult/child 200/120Kč; ⏲8.30am-6pm Apr-Sep, to 5pm Oct-Mar, English tours 1pm, 2.45pm & 4.30pm) Plzeň's most popular attraction is the tour of the Pilsner Urquell Brewery, in operation since 1842 and arguably home to the world's best beer. Entry is by guided tour only, with three tours in English available daily. Tour highlights include a trip to the old cellars (dress warmly) and a glass of unpasteurised nectar at the end.

Reservations are possible only for groups of 10 or more. Email the brewery to arrange.

Underground Plzeň TUNNEL

(Plzeňské historické podzemí; Map p206; ☎377 235 574; www.plzenskepodzemi.cz; Veleslavínova 6; tour in English adult/child 120/90Kč; ⏲10am-6pm Apr-Sep, to 5pm Oct-Dec & Feb-Mar, closed Jan, English tour 2.20pm daily Apr-Oct) This extraordinary tour explores the passageways below the old city. The earliest were probably dug in the 14th century, perhaps for beer production or defence; the latest date from the 19th century. Of an estimated 11km that have been excavated, some 500m of the tunnels are open to the public. Bring extra clothing – it's a chilly 10°C underground.

Plzeň's wealthier set used to have wells in their cellars. Overuse led to severe water shortages. When wells dried up they were often filled with rubbish and buried; these have yielded an amazing trove of artefacts. English-language audio guides are available in case you miss the English tour.

Brewery Museum MUSEUM

(Map p206; ☎377 224 955; www.prazdrojvisit.cz; Veleslavínova 6; guided tour adult/child 120/90Kč, English text 90/60Kč; ⏲10am-6pm Apr-Sep, to 5pm Oct-Mar) The Brewery Museum offers an insight into how beer was made (and drunk) in the days before Pilsner Urquell was founded. Highlights include a mock-up of a 19th-century pub, a huge wooden beer tankard from Siberia and a collection of beer mats. All have English captions and there's a good printed English text available for those not taking the tour.

St Bartholomew Church CHURCH

(kostel sv Bartoloměje; Map p206; ☎377 226 098; www.katedralaplzen.org; náměstí Republiky; adult/child church 35/15Kč, tower 50/25Kč; ⏲10am-4pm Wed-Sat Apr-Sep, Wed-Fri Oct-Dec) Gigantic, Gothic St Bartholomew Church looms over the surrounding facades from the centre of náměstí Republiky. Look inside at the delicate marble 'Pilsen Madonna' (c 1390) on the main altar, or climb the 301 steps to the top of the tower (weather permitting) for serious views. Ask at the City Information Centre (p210) about guided tours.

Puppet Museum MUSEUM

(Muzeum Loutek; Map p206; ☎378 370 801; www.muzeumloutek.cz; náměstí Republiky 23; adult/concession 60/30Kč; ⏲10am-6pm Tue-Sun) Plzeň's museum of marionettes and puppetry is well done and certainly worth a look, especially if you're travelling with younger children. The exhibits are understandably heavy on Czech puppet tradition, but there's ample signage in English and even some impromptu puppet performances to keep young ones interested.

Great Synagogue SYNAGOGUE

(Velká Synagoga; Map p206; ☎377 223 346; www.zoplzen.cz; sady Pětatřicátníků 11; adult/child 70/40Kč; ⏲10am-6pm Sun-Fri Apr-Oct) The Great Synagogue, west of the Old Town, is the third-largest in the world – only those in Jerusalem and Budapest are bigger. It was built in the Moorish style in 1892 by the 2000 Jews who lived in Plzeň at the time. The building is now used for concerts and art exhibitions.

Patton Memorial Pilsen MUSEUM

(Map p206; ☎378 037 954; www.patton-memorial.cz; Pobřezni 10; adult/concession 60/40Kč; ⏲9am-1pm & 2-5pm Tue-Sun) The Patton Memorial details the liberation of Plzeň in May 1945 by the American army, under General George S Patton. Especially poignant are the handwritten memories of former American soldiers who have returned to Plzeň over the years, and the museum's response to the communist-era revisionist fabrications that claimed Soviet troops, not Americans, were responsible for the city's liberation.

Outside the Centre

★Techmania Science Centre MUSEUM

(☎737 247 585; www.techmania.cz; cnr Borská & Břeňkova, Areál Škoda; adult/child incl 3D planetarium 180/110Kč; ⊙8.30am-5pm Mon-Fri, 10am-7pm Sat, 10am-6pm Sun; P 👪; 🚌15, 17) Kids will have a ball at this high-tech, interactive science centre where they can play with infrared cameras, magnets and many other instructive and fun exhibits. There's a 3D planetarium (included in the full-price admission) and a few full-sized historic trams and trains manufactured at the Škoda engineering works. Take the trolleybus; it's a 2km hike southwest from the city centre.

Fans of Czech visual artist David Černý will want to see his epic **Entropa** installation, mounted on a giant wall in the main exhibition room. It's a subtle (or not so subtle) critique of the EU and originally hung in Brussels during the Czech presidency of the EU in 2009. Presciently, in view of Britain's vote to leave the EU, the artist represented the UK with an empty space.

Zoo Plzeň ZOO

(☎378 038 325; www.zooplzen.cz; Pod Vinicemi 9; adult/concession 90/60Kč, combined ticket with DinoPark 220/150Kč; ⊙8am-7pm Apr-Oct, 9am-5pm Nov-Mar; 👪; 🚌1, 4) Plzeň's zoo is one of the best in the country, with a sizeable collection of exotic animals, including rhinos, hippos and giraffes. You can buy a combined ticket for both the zoo and DinoPark next door.

DinoPark AMUSEMENT PARK

(☎378 774 636; www.dinopark.cz; Nad ZOO 1; adult/child 100/70Kč, combined ticket with Zoo Plzeň 220/150Kč; ⊙8am-6pm Apr-Oct; 👪; 🚌1, 4) This dinosaur park has life-sized replicas of some 30 dinosaurs, as well as films and playgrounds. You can buy a combined-entry ticket for both the DinoPark and the adjacent Zoo Plzeň (p208).

DEPO2015 ARTS CENTRE

(☎702 019 508; www.depo2015.cz; Presslova 14; ⊙11am-7pm Mon-Fri, 10am-6pm Sat & Sun) FREE Housed in a former tram depot, this 'makerspace' is a creative hub that provides working space for tech start-ups, artists and craftspeople, and houses various exhibitions of art, design and ideas for alternative lifestyles. There's also a good cafe, and a street food festival that takes place two or three times a year. It's just over 1km south of the town centre.

Sleeping

The city has a decent range of pensions, budget and midrange hotels, many aimed at business and student visitors. The City Information Centre (p210) can find and book accommodation for a small fee.

Hotel Continental HISTORIC HOTEL €

(Map p206; ☎377 235 292; www.hotelcontinental.cz; Zbrojnická 8; s/d from 1190/1890Kč; P 📶) This historic hotel has survived being hit by an Allied bomb in WWII and playing host to Gerard Depardieu and John Malkovich. Other former guests include Marlene Dietrich, General Patton and Ingrid Bergman. Finally the Continental's art-deco glory has been resurrected and newly renovated suites are tinged with Asian design features, making it again one of the best places in town. Unrenovated older rooms are also good value.

Hotel Roudna HOTEL €

(☎377 259 926; www.hotelroudna.cz; Na Roudné 13; s/d 1150/1400Kč; P @ 📶) Perhaps the city's best-value lodging, across the river to the north of the old town, the Roudna's exterior isn't much to look at, but inside the rooms are well proportioned with high-end amenities such as flat-screen TV, minibar and desk. Breakfasts are fresh and ample, and reception is friendly. Note there's no lift.

Euro Hostel HOSTEL €

(☎377 259 926; www.eurohostel.cz; Na Roudné 13; per person 450Kč; 📶) Housed in a grand old corner building, this place is pretty basic and lacking in atmosphere, but the location is good (just 400m from Plzeň's old town) and the rooms are clean. Walk north on Rooseveltova across the river and veer right on Luční. You'll need to check in at the Hotel Roudna nearby.

Hotel U Zvonu HOTEL €€

(Map p206; ☎378 011 855; www.hotel-uzvonu.cz; Pražská 27; s/d 1850/2250Kč; P ⊖ ❄ @ 📶) This place is similar to a high-end chain in that it's super clean and modern. It's also conveniently located, close to all the main sights. The rooms are spacious and well endowed; some are equipped with small kitchenettes, and one room is barrier-free for travellers with disabilities. There's ample parking out front.

U Salzmannů PENSION €€

(Map p206; ☎377 235 476; www.usalzmannu.com; Pražská 8; s/d 990/1690Kč, 4-person ste 2490Kč;

) This pleasant pension, right in the heart of town, sits above a very good historic pub. The standard rooms are comfortable but basic; the more luxurious 'suites' have antique beds and small sitting rooms, as well as kitchenettes. The pub location is convenient if you overdo it; to reach your bed, just climb the stairs.

Hotel Rous BOUTIQUE HOTEL €€
(Map p206; 602 320 294; www.hotelrous.cz; Zbrojnicka 113/7; s/d from 1750/2150Kč;) This 600-year-old building combines the historic character of the original stone walls alongside modern furnishings. Bathrooms are art-deco cool in black and white. Breakfast is taken in a garden cafe concealed amid remnants of Plzeň's defensive walls. Downstairs, the Caffe Emily serves very good coffee.

Pension City PENSION €€
(Map p206; 377 326 069; www.pensioncityplzen.cz; Sady 5 kvetna 52; s/d 1400/1820Kč;) On a quiet street near the river, Pension City has comfortable rooms and friendly, English-speaking staff armed with lots of local information.

Eating

Plzeň is a good place to try traditional Czech pub grub, washed down with excellent local Pilsner Urquell beer.

Na Parkánu CZECH €
(Map p206; 377 324 485; www.naparkanu.com; Veleslavínova 4; mains 100-330Kč; 11am-11pm Mon-Thu, to 1am Fri & Sat, to 10pm Sun;) Don't overlook this pleasant pub-restaurant, attached to the Brewery Museum. It may look a bit touristy, but the traditional Czech food is top-rate, and the beer, naturally, could hardly be better. Try to snag a spot in the summer garden. Don't leave without trying the *nefiltrované pivo* (unfiltered beer). Reservations are an absolute must.

Slunečnice VEGETARIAN €
(Map p206; 377 236 093; www.slunecniceplzen.cz; Jungmannova 4; mains 110-230Kč; 11am-11pm Mon-Sat, to 8pm Sun;) This casual restaurant specialises in organic and healthy foods, including many vegetarian entrées such as quesadillas with spinach, veggie pastas and burgers made from tempeh.

★ **Buffalo Burger Bar** AMERICAN €€
(Map p206; 733 124 514; buffaloburgerbar@gmail.com; Dominikánská 3; mains 165-385Kč; 11am-11pm;) Tuck in to some of the best burgers in the Czech Republic at this American-style diner, with cool timber decor the colour of a well-done steak. Everything is freshly made, from the hand-cooked tortilla chips, zingy salsa and guacamole, to the perfect French fries, coleslaw and the juicy burgers themselves.

★ **Aberdeen Angus Steakhouse** STEAK €€
(Map p206; 725 555 631; www.angussteakhouse.cz; Pražská 23; mains 215-715Kč; 11am-11pm Sun-Thu, to midnight Fri & Sat;) For our money, this may be the best steakhouse in all of the Czech Republic. The meats hail from a nearby farm, where the livestock is raised organically. There are several cuts and sizes on offer; lunch options include a tantalising cheeseburger. The downstairs dining room is cosy; there's also a creekside terrace. Book in advance.

Na Spilce CZECH €€
(377 062 755; www.naspilce.com; U Prazdroje 7; mains 150-300Kč; 11am-10pm Sun-Thu, to 11pm Fri & Sat;) The Pilsner Urquell Brewery (p207) tour often ends with a meal (and several more beers, naturally) at this pub, situated within the confines of the brewery itself. The traditional Czech-style cooking, such as venison stew flavoured with red wine, is reasonably priced and well above average, and the beer is fresh from tanks next door.

Groll Pivovar CZECH €€
(Map p206; 602 596 161; www.pivovargroll.cz; Truhlářska 10; mains 130-400Kč; 11am-10pm Sun-Thu, to 11pm Fri-Sat;) If you've come to Plzeň on a beer pilgrimage, then another essential port of call is a beer garden lunch at this spiffy microbrewery. Meals include well-priced steaks and salads but the highlight is the drinks menu: homemade light and dark beers, including a very good 11° nonfiltered, nonpasteurised light lager.

U Mansfelda CZECH €€
(Map p206; 377 333 844; www.umansfelda.cz; Dřevěná 9; mains 150-350Kč; 11am-11pm Mon-Thu, to midnight Fri & Sat, noon-10pm Sun;) Sure, it's a pub – remember you're in Plzeň now – but it's also more refined and has more interesting food than many other places. Try Czech cuisine such as wild boar *guláš* (spicy meat and potato soup). Downstairs from the beer-fuelled terrace is a more relaxed *vinárna* (wine bar).

GETTING AROUND

Plzeň has a good city network of tram and trolleybus services with fares starting at 16Kč for a single journey. See www.pmdp.eu for routes and timetables.

Drinking & Nightlife

Plzeň is a big student town, and there are plenty of good places to kick back with your beverage of choice. The streets between the main square and the gardens to the south at Smetanovy sady are crammed with lively bars and cafes that fill up in the early evening.

★Měšťanská Beseda PUB
(Map p206; ☎378 035 415; http://web.mestanska-beseda.cz; Kopeckého sady 13; ⏰9am-10pm Mon-Fri, 11am-10pm Sat & Sun; 📶) Cool heritage cafe, sunny beer garden, expansive exhibition space and occasional art-house cinema – the elegant art-nouveau Mêšťanská Beseda is hands-down Plzeň's most versatile venue. The beautifully restored 19th-century pub is perfect for a leisurely beer or cafe. Check out who's performing at the attached theatre.

Olala Cafe CAFE
(Map p206; ☎378 609 699; www.olalacafe.cz; Pražská 2; ⏰8am-10pm Mon-Fri, 9am-10pm Sat, 9am-9pm Sun; 📶) This clean, modern cafe right on the central square is a lifesaver if you need a strong cup and/or good wi-fi. A nice selection of cakes, sweets and ice-cream dishes is also on offer.

Galerie Azyl BAR
(Map p206; ☎377 235 507; www.galerieazyl.cz; Veleslavínova 17; ⏰8am-11pm Mon-Thu, to 1am Fri, 6pm-1am Sat; 📶) Locals kick-off the morning with an excellent espresso here. Later in the day, Galerie Azyl morphs into Plzeň's classiest cocktail bar. Quirky artwork surrounds conversation-friendly booths.

Entertainment

★New Theatre THEATRE
(Nová Scéna; Map p206; ☎box office 378 038 059; www.djkt.eu; Palackého náměstí 30; tickets 230-450Kč) Plzeň's stint as European 'Cultural Capital' in 2015 saw the opening of this jaw-dropping new theatre building, which stages drama, opera, ballet and musicals. There's also a smaller stage (Malá Scéna, or Black Box) that presents more intimate performances of music and drama.

Buena Vista Club LIVE MUSIC
(☎377 921 291; www.buenavistaclub.cz; Kollárova 20; concert tickets 100-200Kč; ⏰11am-3am Mon-Sat; 📶) This funky multipurpose space, in a studenty area filled with pubs, hosts everything from emerging Czech live acts to an eclectic range of DJs. English-language movies are occasionally screened.

JK Tyl Theatre THEATRE
(Velké divadlo; Map p206; ☎box office 378 038 190; www.djkt.eu; Prokopova 14; performances 130-400Kč; ⏰9am-6pm Mon-Fri) Plzeň's main theatre, dating from 1902, stages regular performances of Czech drama, ballet, opera and classical music. Check the website for what's on during your visit. Buy tickets online, at the theatre box office or at the City Information Centre.

Zach's Pub LIVE MUSIC
(☎377 223 176; www.zachspub.cz; Kollárova 6; ⏰1pm-1am Mon-Thu, to 2am Fri, 5pm-2am Sat, 5pm-midnight Sun; 📶) Head to Zach's for live music and a suitably studenty atmosphere. There's a big garden for open-air drinking in summer. It's about a 15-minute walk west of the city centre.

Music Bar Anděl LIVE MUSIC
(Map p206; ☎377 323 226; www.andelcafe.cz; Bezručova 7; shows 50-200Kč; ⏰6pm-2am Mon-Thu, to 4am Fri & Sat, 11am-midnight Sun; 📶) By day a cool, hip cafe, the Anděl is transformed after dark into a rocking live-music venue featuring the best of touring Czech bands and occasional international acts.

Information

City Information Centre (Informační centrum města Plzně; Map p206; ☎378 035 330; www.pilsen.eu/tourist; náměstí Republiky 41; ⏰9am-7pm Apr-Sep, to 6pm Oct-Mar; 📶) Plzeň's well-stocked tourist information office is a first port of call for visitors. Staff here can advise on sleeping and eating options, and there are free city maps and a stock of brochures on what to see and do.

Getting There & Away

BUS

From Prague, **Student Agency** (Map p206; ☎841 101 101; www.studentagency.cz; náměstí Republiky 9; ⏰9am-6pm Mon-Fri) runs half-hourly buses during the day to Plzeň (100Kč, one hour). Most buses leave Prague from Zličín station, the last stop on metro line B (yellow). Plzeň **bus station** (Centrální autobusové nádraží, CAN; ☎377 237 237; www.csadplzen.cz; Husova 60), marked on maps and street signs as CAN, is 1km west of the centre.

TRAIN

Several trains leave daily from Prague's main train station (Hlavní nádraží; 160Kč, 1½ hours) to Plzeň's **train station** (Plzeň hlavní nádraží; www.cd.cz; Nádražní 102), which is 1km east of the historic centre. There are also frequent trains from Plzeň to select cities in Moravia with Student Agency's Regiojet service.

KARLOVY VARY

POP 116,340

Karlovy Vary (Carlsbad), or simply 'Vary' to Czechs, has stepped up its game in recent years, thanks largely to a property boom spurred by wealthy Russian investors. Indeed, the first thing you'll notice is the high number of Russian visitors, all following in the footsteps of Tsar Peter the Great, who stayed here for treatments in the early 18th century. Day trippers come to admire the grand 19th-century spa architecture and to stroll the impressive colonnades, sipping on the supposedly health-restoring sulphurous waters from spouted ceramic drinking cups.

Despite its exalted spa reputation, Karlovy Vary is not entirely welcoming to walk-ins looking for high-end treatments such as exotic massages and peelings; these services are available but make sure to book in advance.

Sights

★Mill Colonnade SPRING

(Mlýnská kolonáda; Map p212; www.karlovyvary.cz/en/colonnades-and-springs; ⌚24hr) FREE The most impressive piece of architecture in Karlovy Vary is the neo-Renaissance Mill Colonnade (built 1871–81), with five different springs, rooftop statues depicting the months of the year, and a little bandstand. The Petra Restaurant, opposite, is the spot (but not the original building) where Peter the Great allegedly stayed in 1711.

★Hot Spring Colonnade SPRING

(Vřídelní kolonáda; Map p212; www.karlovyvary.cz/en/colonnades-and-springs; ⌚9am-5pm Mon-Fri, 10am-5pm Sat & Sun) FREE The Hot Spring Colonnade is in an incongruous concrete-and-glass functionalist structure built in 1975 and once dedicated to Soviet cosmonaut Yuri Gagarin. It houses the most impressive of the town's geysers, Pramen Vřídlo, which spurts some 12m into the air; people lounge about inhaling the vapours or sampling the waters from a line of taps in the main hall.

HIKING THE HILLS

Once you've wearied of walking around town and taking the waters, a scenic network of trails lies in the hills to the west of the main spa area waiting for exploration. One of the most popular trails ascends 1.5km from just beside the **Grandhotel Pupp** to the hilltop **Diana Lookout Tower** (Map p212; ☎353 222 872; http://dianakv.cz/en; ⌚9am-7pm May-Sep, to 6pm Apr & Oct, to 5pm Feb, Mar, Nov & Dec, closed Jan) FREE. The woods on the way to the lookout are peppered with follies and monuments, a testament to the trail's popularity for several centuries.

If you'd like to skip the hike up, the **Diana Funicular Railway** (Map p212; ☎353 222 638; www.dpkv.cz; Mariánská; one-way/return adult 45/80Kč, child 25/40Kč; ⌚9am-7pm Jun-Sep, to 6pm Apr, May & Oct, to 5pm Feb, Mar, Nov & Dec) can whisk you to the top from its base station just at the entrance to the trail, near the Grandhotel Pupp. The trip takes about five minutes. Just next to the lookout tower, the rustic **Diana Restaurant** (p216), a former hunting lodge, is a great spot for lunch or a cup of coffee.

Stag's Leap (Jelení skok), the promontory from where legend has it that Charles IV, or rather his dogs, first discovered the town's healing waters, is 500m northeast of an intermediate stop on the Diana Funicular Railway. This is a wonderful photo-op spot and even sports an over-the-top **monument** to Russia's Peter the Great, who apparently greatly enjoyed his visits to the spa in the early 18th century. If you're feeling energetic, it's a 15km hike on a blue-marked trail via the Diana Lookout Tower and along the Ohře River to the romantic castle and village of **Loket**.

Karlovy Vary

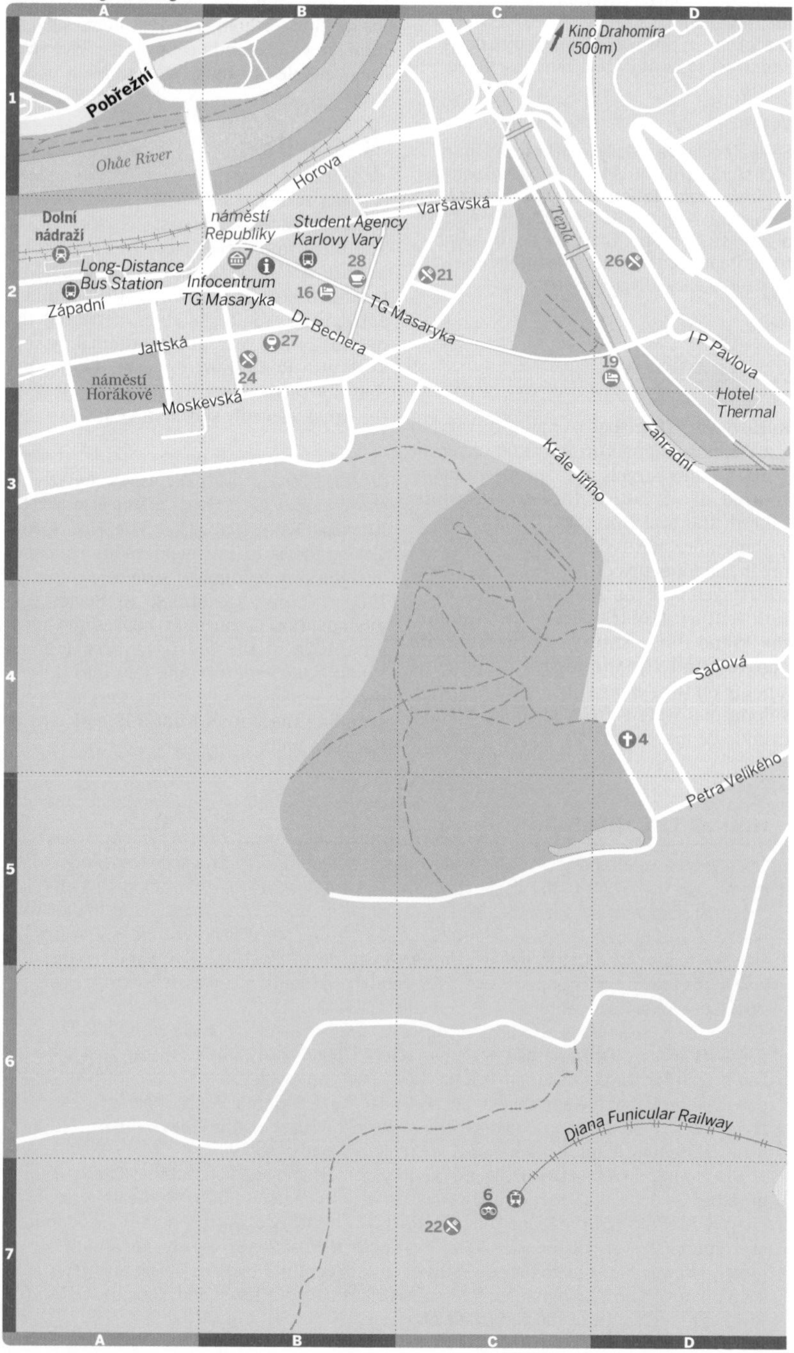

A B C D

1 2 3 4 5 6 7

Kino Drahomíra (500m)

Pobřežní

Ohře River

Horova

Varšavská

Teplá

Dolní nádraží

náměstí Republiky

Student Agency Karlovy Vary

7

28

21

26

Long-Distance Bus Station

Infocentrum TG Masaryka

16

Západní

TG Masaryka

Dr Bechera

Jaltská

27

I P Pavlova

19

24

náměstí Horákové

Moskevská

Hotel Thermal

Zahradní

Krále Jiřího

Sadová

4

Petra Velikého

Diana Funicular Railway

6

22

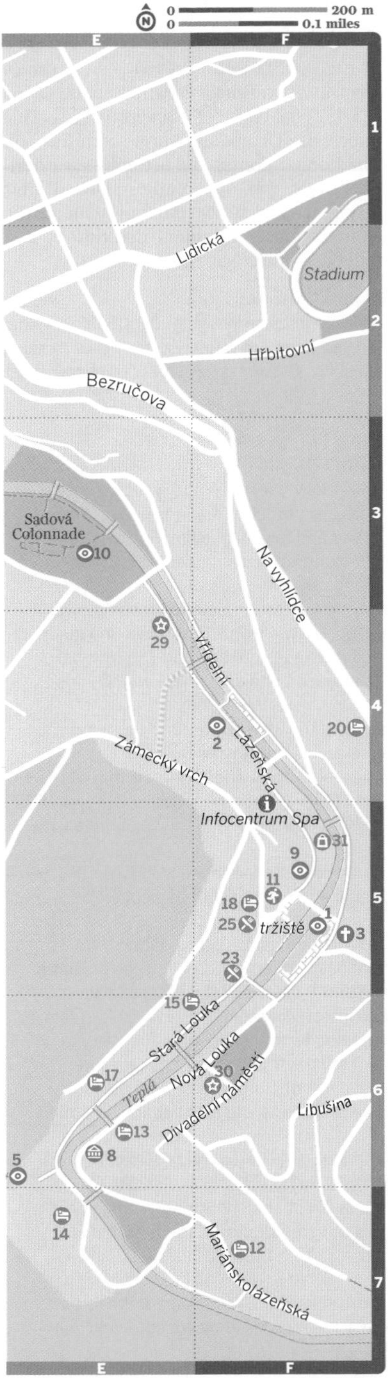

Karlovy Vary

Top Sights
1 Hot Spring Colonnade F5
2 Mill Colonnade F4

Sights
3 Church of Mary Magdalene F5
4 Church of Sts Peter & Paul D4
5 Diana Funicular Railway E6
6 Diana Lookout Tower C7
7 Jan Becher Museum B2
8 Karlovy Vary Museum E6
9 Market Colonnade F5
10 Park Colonnade E3

Activities, Courses & Tours
11 Castle Spa F5

Sleeping
12 Carlsbad Plaza F7
13 Embassy Hotel E6
14 Grandhotel Pupp E7
15 Hotel Boston E6
16 Hotel Kavalerie B2
17 Hotel Maltézský Kříž E6
18 Hotel Romance Puškin F5
19 Hotel Romania D2
20 Pension Villa Rosa F4

Eating
21 Charleston C2
22 Diana Restaurant C7
Embassy Restaurant (see 13)
23 Hospoda U Švejka F5
24 Kus Kus B2
25 Promenáda F5
26 Tandoor D2

Drinking & Nightlife
27 Barracuda B2
28 Republica Coffee B2

Entertainment
29 Karlovy Vary Symphony Orchestra E4
30 Town Theatre F6

Shopping
31 Moser Glasswork Shop F5

Park Colonnade SPRING

(Sadová kolonáda; Map p212; www.karlovyvary.cz/en/colonnades-and-springs; 24hr) FREE Also known as the Garden Colonnade, this elegant wrought-iron structure dates from 1880 and is the first of the main colonnades that you reach as you enter the spa zone from the north. It was designed by the Viennese architectural firm of Fellner & Helmer, the same company that designed the Market Colonnade (p214).

Church of Mary Magdalene CHURCH

(Kostel sv Máří Magdaléná; Map p212; ☎353 223 668; www.farnost-kv.cz; náměstí Svobody 2; crypt tour in English adult/child 120/100Kč; ⏰church 9am-6pm, crypt 9am-5pm Jun-Aug, 10am-4pm May & Sep) FREE Karlovy Vary's most important Catholic church and one of its grandest baroque buildings, this imposing, twin-steepled structure in the heart of the spa dates from the 1730s and is the work of baroque master Kilian Dientzenhofer, the architect of St Nicholas Church in Prague's Malá Strana.

The **crypt** contains an underground altar and an ossuary containing the bones from the 18th-century graveyard that once surrounded the church. Buy tickets in the nearby Hot Spring Colonnade (p211).

Church of Sts Peter & Paul CHURCH

(Chrám svatých Petra a Pavla; Map p212; ☎353 223 451; Krále Jiřího; ⏰9am-6pm) FREE This impressive Orthodox Church, with five polished onion domes and art-nouveau exterior murals, was apparently modelled after a similar church near Moscow. One of the church's most prominent decorations is a relief depicting Tsar Peter the Great.

Moser Glass Museum MUSEUM

(Sklářské muzeum Moser; ☎353 416 132; www.moser-glass.com; Kpt Jaroše 19; adult/child museum 80/50Kč, glassworks 120/70Kč, combined ticket

STROLLING THE COLONNADES

As you'll soon discover, there's not much to do in Karlovy Vary except to walk, gawk and sip the sulphurous spring waters from a traditional porcelain drinking cup (called a *lázeňský pohárek*). So why not give it a go yourself and take a little strolling tour of the spa area? Buy your own cup from any one of a hundred souvenir shops and kiosks around town (100Kč to 130Kč).

There are 15 mineral springs housed in or near the four main *kolonády* (colonnades) along the Teplá River. Each spring has its own purported medicinal properties and gushes forth at various temperatures, ranging from lukewarm to scalding hot. The **Infocentrum** (p219) has a chart of the springs and temperatures, and can advise on the various health benefits of the waters.

You can fill your cup for free at public springs along the way, but watch how much you sip, as too much 'health' has been known to cause occasional gastric distress.

The main spa begins at the northern end of the resort area, whose entry is marked by the functionalist, communist-era Hotel Thermal (1976) sanatorium across the river. Walk south past the hotel and through a small park to find the first of the colonnades, the **Park Colonnade** (p213).

Further on is the biggest and most impressive, the neo-Renaissance **Mill Colonnade** (p211), with five different springs, a small bandstand and rooftop statues depicting the months of the year.

Straight up Lázeňská onto Tržiště is a gorgeous art-nouveau building dating from 1900 called **Dům Zawojski**, now reopened as a classy boutique hotel. You can do some very upmarket window-shopping along Lázeňská and Tržiště, including at the **Moser Glasswork Shop** (Map p212; ☎353 235 303; www.moser-glass.com; Tržiště 7; ⏰10am-7pm Mon-Fri, to 6pm Sat & Sun). The Moser company opened its first shop in Karlovy Vary in 1857, and by 1893 had established a glassworks in the town. Less than a decade later Moser became the official supplier to the imperial court of Franz Josef I, who obviously put in a good word to his English friend King Edward VII, as Moser also became the official supplier of glass to British royalty in 1907.

Across the road is the impressive **Market Colonnade** (Tržní kolonáda; Map p212; www.karlovyvary.cz/en/colonnades-and-springs; Lázeňská; ⏰24hr) FREE with its delicately fretted woodwork: one of its two springs, the *pramen Karla IV* (Charles IV Spring), is the spa's oldest. Just beyond the Market Colonnade stands the granddaddy of them all, the **Hot Spring Colonnade** (p211), now housed in a hulking 1970s brutalist building that was once dedicated to cosmonaut Yuri Gagarin.

The street Stará Louka continues south for more splendour. At the end of the stroll stands the magnificent **Grandhotel Pupp** (p216), the resort's choicest hotel and still the favoured choice of well-heeled visitors.

180/100Kč; 9am-5pm, glassworks to 2.30pm; 1) The Moser Glass Museum on the western edge of town has more than 2000 items on display. Tours of the adjacent glassworks and combined tickets are also available. There is a shop here, too, but the prices are not anything special, and there's another shop in town. To get here catch bus 1 from the Tržnice bus station.

Jan Becher Museum MUSEUM
(Map p212; 359 578 142; www.becherovka.cz; TG Masaryka 57; adult/child 120/30Kč; 9am-5pm) This museum deals with all things Becherovka, the town's famed herbal liqueur. Entry is by guided tour only, which must be booked in advance at the museum cash desk. Most tours are in Czech or Russian, but there's at least one tour a day in English.

Karlovy Vary Museum MUSEUM
(Krajské muzeum Karlovy Vary; Map p212; 353 226 253; www.kvmuz.cz; Nová Louka 23; adult/concession 60/30Kč; 9am-noon & 1-5pm Wed-Sun) The Karlovy Vary Museum, set to reopen in spring 2017 after a major renovation, has extensive exhibits on the town's development as a spa resort, Czech glasswork and the region's natural history.

Activities

Castle Spa SPA
(Zámecké Lázně; Map p212; 353 225 502; www.zamecke-lazne.com; Zámecký vrch 1; 30min massage from 700Kč; 7.30am-7.30pm) Most Karlovy Vary accommodation offers some kind of spa treatment for a fee, but if you're just a casual visitor or day tripper, consider this modernised spa centre complete with a subterranean thermal pool. Visit the website for a full menu of treatments and massages.

Sleeping

Accommodation prices in Karlovy Vary have risen in recent years to be similar to those in Prague, especially in July during the film festival. Indeed, if you're planning a July arrival, make sure to book well in advance. Infocentrum (p219) can help with hostel, pension and hotel bookings.

Hotel Kavalerie HOTEL €
(Map p212; 353 229 613; www.kavalerie.cz; TG Masaryka 43; s/d from 1000/1300Kč;) Quiet, homey and central, the Kavalerie is probably the best-value hotel in town, provided you don't mind a bit of walking. It's a five-minute walk from the lower train and bus stations, and 20 minutes from the spa area. It's on a pedestrianised street, so if you're driving you'll have to carry your bags around 300m from the nearest parking.

OPLATKY: A WAFER WITH YOUR SULPHUR DRINK

To quote Monty Python, 'Do you get wafers with it?' The answer is a resounding 'yes' according to Karlovy Vary locals, who prescribe the following method of taking your spring water: have a sip from your *lázeňský pohárek* (spa cup), then dull the sulphurous taste with big, round, sweet wafers called *oplatky*. *Oplatky* are sold for around 10Kč each at speciality shops all over the spa area.

★**Pension Villa Rosa** PENSION €€
(Map p212; 353 239 121; www.villarosa.cz; Na Vyhlídce 22; s/d from 1300/1800Kč; P) Perched high above the river, the family-run Villa Rosa combines traditionally furnished rooms and hearty breakfasts with a spectacular location – go for the more expensive doubles (2200Kč) and suites (2500Kč), which have balconies with stunning views over the town (reached via a footpath below the building).

★**Hotel Romance Puškin** HOTEL €€
(Map p212; 353 222 646; www.hotelromance.cz; Tržiště 37; s/d 2700/3600Kč;) In a great location just across from the Hot Spring Colonnade, the Puškin has renovated rooms with fully updated baths and very comfortable beds. These are just some of the charms at one of the nicest midrange hotels in the spa area. The breakfast is a treat; the usual sausage and eggs is supplemented by inventive salads and smoked fish.

Embassy Hotel HOTEL €€
(Map p212; 353 221 161; www.embassy.cz; Nová Louka 21; s/d from 2590/3590Kč; @) Karlovy Vary's not short of top-end hotels, but most lack the personal touch of the family-owned Embassy, with its riverside location and perfectly pitched heritage rooms, some with canopy beds. The hotel's pub and restaurant have seen visits from plenty of film-fest luminaries.

DON'T MISS

KARLOVY VARY FILM FESTIVAL

The **Karlovy Vary International Film Festival** (www.kviff.com; Jul) in early July always features the year's top films as well as attracting plenty of (B-list) stars. It's rather behind the pace of the likes of Cannes, Venice and Berlin but is well worth the trip.

Hotel Maltézský Kříž HOTEL €€
(Map p212; 353 169 011; www.maltezskykriz.cz; Stará Louka 50; s/d 1650/2800Kč;) This small hotel on the promenade offers very good value, given its upmarket location in the heart of the spa area and the nicely appointed rooms with oriental rugs and wood floors. The bathrooms are decked out in warm, earthy tones. Request an upper room overlooking the river for the best views.

Hotel Boston HOTEL €€
(Map p212; 353 362 711; www.boston.cz; Luční vrch 9; s/d from 2100/2400Kč;) Tucked away down a quiet lane, this family-owned hotel offers very good value, with spacious rooms decorated in bright colours and updated bathrooms. Upper-floor rooms have a view out the back towards the forest.

Hotel Romania HOTEL €€
(Map p212; 353 222 822; www.romania.cz; Zahradni 49; s/d 1200/1800Kč;) This is one of Karlovy Vary's better deals if you want to be close to the modern town rather than the spa area. The view out the front door towards the ugly monolith of the Hotel Thermal could be better, but the rooms themselves are spacious and tidy. The English-speaking staff is very helpful.

Grandhotel Pupp HOTEL €€€
(Map p212; 353 109 631; www.pupp.cz; Mírové náměstí 2; s/d from 4500/4700Kč;) The sumptuous 18th-century Pupp covers nearly the whole of the spa's southern end and oozes old-world glamour. It was featured in the James Bond film *Casino Royale* and inspired Wes Anderson's *Grand Budapest Hotel*. These days it's a budget-blower, but worth the splurge if you can snag one of the rooms in period style (you have to ask).

Even if you're not staying here, take a peek inside; the restaurants are very good, and the historic atmosphere is perfect.

Carlsbad Plaza HOTEL €€€
(Map p212; 353 225 501; www.carlsbadplaza.cz; Mariánskolázeňská 23; s/d 5000/6080Kč;) Seriously stylish, this sprawling neo-baroque hotel has raised the bar with olde-worlde elegance complemented by soothingly modern treatment facilities, spacious suites and facilities that include a pool, gym, casino and a health-conscious restaurant.

Eating

With a few notable exceptions listed here, Karlovy Vary's dining scene is bland. Prices tend to be higher in the spa area than in other parts of town.

Tandoor INDIAN €
(Map p212; 608 701 341; www.tandoor-kv.cz; IP Pavlova 25; mains 90-190Kč; noon-9pm Mon-Sat;) Occupying a well-hidden location in the courtyard of a block of flats, Tandoor turns out a winning combo of authentic Indian flavours, Gambrinus beer and smooth, creamy lassis. Vegetarian options abound, or if you're after a serious chilli hit, order the chicken phall.

Kus Kus VEGETARIAN €
(Map p212; 777 066 477; www.kus-kus.cz; Bělehradská 8; mains 60-90Kč; 9am-2pm Mon-Fri;) This cosy cafe-bakery serves salads, pasta and homemade desserts with an organic and vegetarian vibe. It also offers daily vegetarian lunch mains (89Kč) such as soya noodles or stuffed baked potatoes. Note the limited menu and opening hours.

★ **Charleston** CZECH €€
(Map p212; 353 230 797; www.charleston-kv.cz; Bulharská 1; mains 170-430Kč; 10am-midnight Mon-Sat, from noon Sun;) Karlovy Vary, alas, is not a food paradise, but this 1920s-themed restaurant in the modern town is the best of the lot. In addition to stalwarts such as roast pork, the menu lists more inventive mains such as venison ragout and a true *Wienerschnitzel* (made with veal, not pork). Book ahead as the seating area is small.

Diana Restaurant CZECH €€
(Map p212; 777 774 040; www.dianakv.cz; Vrch přátelství 1; mains 160-450Kč; 11am-7pm May-Sep, to 6pm Apr & Oct, to 5pm Nov-Mar; ; Diana Funicular Railway top station) This rustic hunting lodge is a wonderful choice for lunch if you're hiking up on the hill. The menu is strong on Czech classics like pork and chicken, with venison and wild boar

tossed in perhaps as a nod to the restaurant's hunting heritage. There are two big rooms, with the interior portion boasting a roaring, wood-burning fire.

Hospoda U Švejka CZECH €€
(Map p212; ☎353 232 276; www.svejk-kv.cz; Stará Louka 10; mains 170-360Kč; ⊙11am-11pm) Located right in the heart of the spa centre, this is a great choice for lunch or dinner. Though the presentation borders on kitsch, the food is actually very good and the atmosphere not unlike a classic Czech pub. The only ouch factor comes when you receive the bill: a 0.5L glass of beer here costs a whopping 75Kč.

★**Embassy Restaurant** CZECH €€€
(Map p212; ☎353 221 161; www.embassy.cz; Nová Louka 21; mains 350-580Kč; ⊙11am-11pm; 📶) The in-house restaurant of the Embassy Hotel (p215) is a destination in its own right, often patronised by big-name stars attending the film festival. The dining room is richly atmospheric and the food, mostly Czech standards such as roast pork or duck, is top-notch.

Promenáda INTERNATIONAL €€€
(Map p212; ☎353 225 648; www.hotel-promenada.cz; Tržiště 31; mains 300-500Kč; ⊙noon-11pm) The house restaurant of the Hotel Promenáda has appeared in some 'best of' lists for the Czech Republic and is a perennial favourite on online forums. The elegant dining area is conducive to a memorable evening, and the food is very good (though perhaps not always worthy of the steep prices).

Drinking & Nightlife

Karlovy Vary is home to Becherovka, an alcoholic herbal liqueur invented in 1807 and

WORTH A TRIP

THE 'THIRD SPA' OF FRANTIŠKOVY LÁZNĚ

When people talk of western Bohemia's spas, it's usually only the two big ones that are mentioned: Karlovy Vary and Mariánské Lázně. There is, however, a third spa town, Františkovy Lázně (frantish-kovee *lahz*-nyeh), which is worth a day trip from Mariánské Lázně if you're in the area and have the time.

Indeed, with its sunny veneer of yellow paint, well-tended parklands with statues and springs, and spa patients and tourists walking around ever so slowly, Františkovy Lázně may better fulfil your expectations of what a real spa town should look like.

Beethoven and Goethe were Františkovy Lázně's most famous guests, but they were more likely drawn by the lively cafe society than the spa, which was best known for the treatment of female infertility. Czech author Milan Kundera was obviously intrigued by the idea of so many young women concentrated in such a small town that he set his tragic-comic 1970s novel *The Farewell Waltz* here. These days that kind of action (or indeed any action at all) is entirely missing. The walks and pavement cafes are soporific, but in a pleasing, relaxing sort of way.

Like its two big-brother spas, Františkovy Lázně is rather short on must-sees. The biggest attraction is simply to stroll the main drag, Národní, admiring the impossibly cute spa architecture and stopping for coffee or cake every couple of hours or so. The key sights are the **Church of the Ascension of the Cross** (kostel Povýšení sv Kříže) on Ruská, and the town's central spring, the **Františkův pramen**, at the southern end of Národní. To get a better understanding of the spa's history, drop by the **City Museum** (Městské muzeum; ☎354 542 344; www.muzeum-frantiskovylazne.cz; Dlouhá 4, Františkovy Lázně; adult/child 35/25Kč; ⊙10am-5pm Tue-Sun). You can also hire a boat at the small pond, the **Rybník Amerika**, about 1km from the city centre.

For a good meal, try **Restaurant Goethe** (☎354 500 180; www.franzensbad-casino.com; Národní 1, Františkovy Lázně; mains 140-385Kč; ⊙11.30am-2.30pm & 6–11pm, cafe 9am–7pm; 📶) for well-prepared international dishes served by waiters decked out in period-piece garb. Hotels line the main drag, though most of these are fancy four-star affairs booked by the week for those seeking spa treatments.

You can get to Františkovy Lázně by bus or train from Plzeň (two hours via Cheb) or Mariánské Lázně (around an hour). Alternatively, the largish city of Cheb is just 30 minutes away by bus: from here you can catch regular trains back to Prague.

WORTH A TRIP

THE 'ELBOW' OF LOKET NAD OHŘE

Surrounded by a wickedly serpentine loop in the Ohře River, the picturesque village of **Loket** may as well be on an island. According to the local tourist office, it was Goethe's favourite town, and after a lazily subdued stroll around the gorgeous main square and castle, it may be yours as well.

Loket's German name is Elbogen (meaning 'elbow', after the extreme bend in the river) – a name synonymous with the manufacturing of porcelain since 1815. Shops in town have a fine selection of the local craftsmanship. The neighbouring towns of Horní Slavkov (Schlackenwald) and Chodov (Chodan) also make porcelain.

Most people visit Loket as a day trip from Karlovy Vary, but it's also a sleepy place to ease off the travel accelerator for a few days, especially when the day trippers have departed. Loket also makes a good base for visiting Karlovy Vary: the bus to/from Karlovy Vary (30Kč) stops across the bridge from the Old Town. Walk across the bridge to reach the castle, accommodation and **Infocentrum** (Loket Information Centre; ☎352 684 123; www.loket.cz; TG Masaryka 12; ⏲10.30am-12.30pm & 1-5.30pm), which hands out maps and can advise on transport and sightseeing options.

The main site in town is the beautiful castle, **Hrad Loket** (Loket Castle; ☎352 684 648; www.hradloket.cz; Hrad; adult/concession with English guide 150/125Kč, with English text 100/80Kč; ⏲9am-6.30pm Jun-Aug, to 5pm Apr, May, Sep & Oct, to 4pm Nov-Mar). It was built on the site of an earlier Romanesque fort, of which the only surviving bits are the tall, square tower and fragments of a rotunda and palace.

The castle was regarded as very defensively secure in earlier times, and was known as 'the key to Bohemia'. Its present late-Gothic look dates from the late 14th century. From 1788 to 1947 it was used as the town prison. Highlights of the tour include two rooms filled with the town's lustrous porcelain and views from the castle tower (96 steps). There's also a gleefully gruesome torture chamber, complete with stereophonic sound effects.

Ask at the Infocentrum about hiking (p219) possibilities in the surrounding forests, including a semi-ambitious day hike to Karlovy Vary (around four hours) along a 17km blue-marked trail. Karlovy Vary is also the destination for rafting trips.

There are several decent pensions in town. The nicest hotel is the **Hotel Císař Ferdinand** (☎352 327 130; www.hotel-loket.cz; TG Masaryka 136; s/d 1300/1850Kč; P ⊖ ≋ ≋), right across from the Infocentrum. This former post office has recently renovated rooms and the best little microbrewery in town.

originally marketed as an 'aid to digestion'. However, the town's health-conscious reputation means there's not much in the way of night-time frolics beyond taking a stroll along the promenades, or maybe catching an early-evening concert in one of the town's bandstands.

★Republica Coffee CAFE
(Map p212; ☎720 347 166; www.facebook.com/republicacoffee; TG Masaryka 28; ⏲7am-6pm Mon-Fri, 8am-6pm Sat & Sun; ≋) This cool upstairs space with modern art on bare brick walls, '80s tunes on the sound system and comfortable armchairs serves the best coffee in town, from espressos to flat whites all expertly made using freshly ground beans (they roast their own). Food is limited to a small selection of pastries.

Barracuda COCKTAIL BAR
(Map p212; ☎608 100 640; www.barracuda-bar.cz; Jaltská 7; ⏲7pm-1am Mon-Thu, to 3am Fri & Sat) This Caribbean-themed cocktail bar away from the spa area has been going strong for many years. It's about the only place in town you can be assured of late-night drinking, dancing to cheesy DJs, and all that goes with it.

☆ Entertainment

Karlovy Vary Symphony Orchestra CLASSICAL MUSIC
(Karlovarský symfonický orchestr; Map p212; ☎353 228 707; www.kso.cz; Mlýnské nábřeží 5, Windsor Spa Hotel) The town's highly regarded orchestra stages a regular program of concerts; check the website for what's on during your visit. Concerts are held in the

Windsor Hotel's concert hall in the main spa area. You can buy tickets at the hotel's box office or the tourist offices in town.

Kino Drahomíra CINEMA
(Kino Panasonic; ☎353 222 963; http://kinodrahomira.cz; Vitězná 50; ⌚box office from 11am Mon-Fri, from 3pm Sat & Sun; 📶) This compact art-house cinema has a good cafe with free wi-fi access. It's 500m northeast of the modern town centre.

Town Theatre THEATRE
(Karlovarské městské divadlo; Map p212; ☎353 225 537; www.karlovarske-divadlo.cz; Divadelní náměstí 21; ⌚box office 10-11.30am & noon-5.30pm) Drama, comedy and musicals all feature here. Tickets are available from the theatre box office or at the town's tourist offices.

Information

Česká Spořitelna (☎956 748 000; www.csas.cz; TG Masaryka 14; ⌚8.30am-4pm Mon-Fri)

Infocentrum Spa (Infocentrum Lázeňská; Map p212; ☎355 321 176; www.karlovyvary.cz; Lázeňská 14; ⌚8am-6pm; 📶) The main tourist information office within the main spa area. Can provide maps and advice on accommodation, events, transport info and spa treatments.

Infocentrum TG Masaryka (Infocentrum TGM; Map p212; ☎355 321 171; www.karlovyvary.cz; TG Masaryka 53; ⌚8am-6pm Mon-Fri, 9am-1pm & 1.30-5pm Sat & Sun) This branch of the main tourist information office is within easy walk of the bus and train stations. Can provide maps and advice on accommodation, events, transport info and spa treatments.

Getting There & Away

BUS

Buses from Prague (160Kč, 2¼ hours, hourly) arrive at Karlovy Vary's **bus station** (Map p212). The most popular coach operator is **Student Agency** (Map p212; ☎353 176 333; www.studentagency.cz; TG Masaryka 34; ⌚9am-6pm Mon-Fri), which maintains a branch in Karlovy Vary. Check www.vlak-bus.cz for timetables.

TRAIN

Trains from Prague (323Kč, 3¼ hours, every two hours) take a circuitous route that is much slower and more expensive than the bus. Unless you have nothing else to do, it's not recommended.

MARIÁNSKÉ LÁZNĚ

POP 13,225

Mariánské Lázně (mari-*ahn*-skay *lahz*-nyeh; known internationally as Marienbad) is smaller, less urban and arguably prettier than Karlovy Vary, making it feel more like a classic spa destination (but also meaning there's even less to do in the evening). In its heyday, Mariánské Lázně attracted celebrities such as Goethe, Thomas Edison, Britain's King Edward VII and even American author Mark Twain. These days, many visitors are day trippers from Germany hauled in by coach to stroll the gardens and colonnades before repairing to a cafe for the inevitable *Apfelstrudel* and then the ride back home. Besides the colonnades, the town is ringed by deep forests that make for great walks.

Sights

Hlavní třída, as the name implies (*hlavní* means 'main'), is the spa town's central avenue, lined on one side by big hotels, cafes and resorts, and on the other by a long, sloping park. The main attraction here, besides the cafes and the tourist office, is a the small Chopin Museum (p221) dedicated to Polish-French composer Frédéric Chopin, who visited the spa in 1836.

Singing Fountain FOUNTAIN
(Zpívající fontána; Map p220; www.marianskelazne.cz; Hlavní kolonáda; ⌚7am-10pm May-Oct) FREE The Singing Fountain sashays to coloured lights and recorded music – anything from Dvořák to Celine Dion – every two hours on the odd hour, with the last two performances normally at 9pm and 10pm. An information board details the musical schedule.

Colonnade HISTORIC BUILDING
(Hlavní kolonáda; Map p220; Masarykova; ⌚6am-6pm) FREE The cast-iron Colonnade, built in neo-baroque style in 1889, is the spa's visual centrepiece. Classical and brass-band concerts are performed here two or three times a day in the high season. Also here, in its own pavilion, is the **Cross Spring** (Křížový pramen), the spa's first spring. Choose from a galaxy of souvenir porcelain mugs or bring along a plastic bottle.

Church of the Assumption of the Virgin Mary CHURCH
(Kostel Nanebevzetí Panny Marie; Map p220; ☎354 622 434; www.farnostml.cz; Goethovo náměstí 31; ⌚9am-noon Tue-Fri, 2.30-4.30pm

Mariánské Lázně

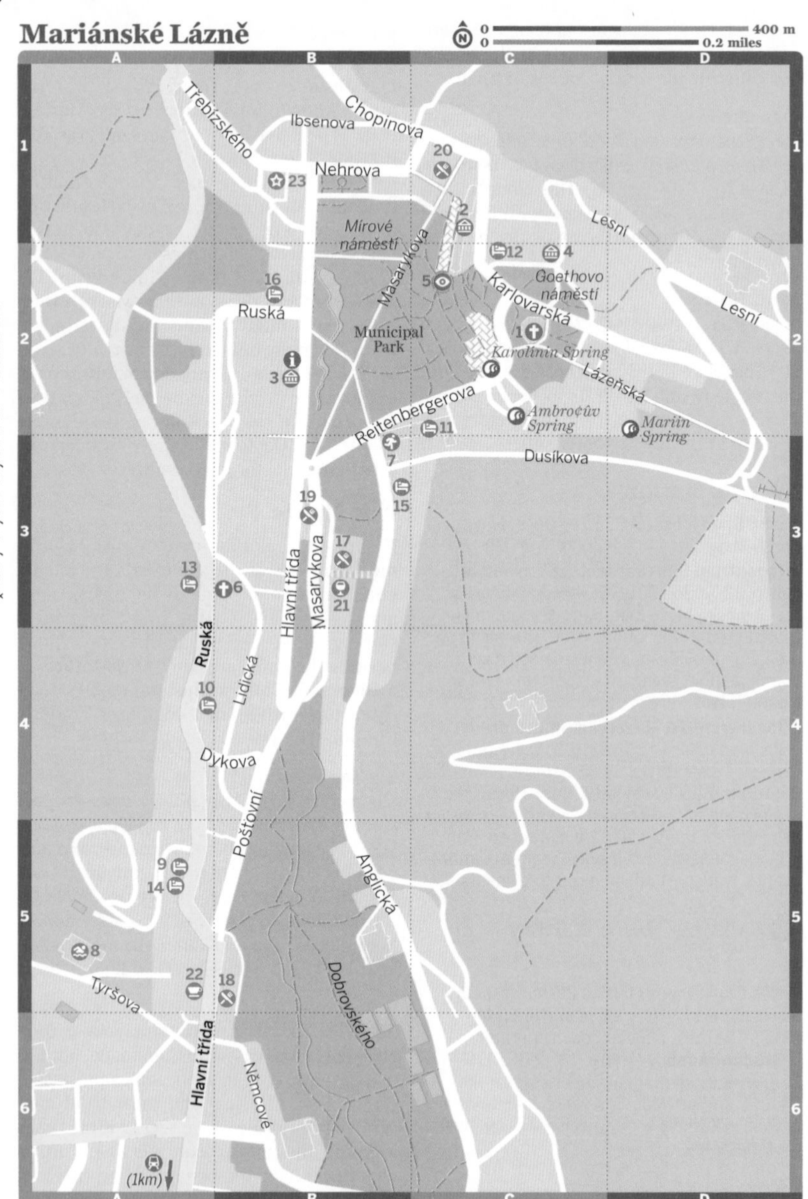

Sat & Sun) FREE This imposing twin-towered white-and-yellow structure is the most important Roman Catholic Church in Mariánské Lázně. It dates from the mid-19th century and is an example of neo-Byzantine style.

Municipal Museum MUSEUM

(Městské muzeum; Map p220; ☎354 622 740; www.muzeum-ml.cz; Goethovo náměstí 11; adult/concession 60/30Kč; ⏰9.30am-5.30pm Tue-Sun) The tiny Municipal Museum occupies the house where Goethe stayed during his last

Mariánské Lázně

Sights
1 Church of the Assumption of the Virgin Mary ... C2
2 Colonnade ... C1
3 Fryderyk Chopin Memorial Museum ... B2
4 Municipal Museum ... C2
5 Singing Fountain ... C2
6 St Vladimír Church ... B3

Activities, Courses & Tours
7 Danubius Health Spa Resort Nové Lázně ... B3
8 Public Swimming Pool ... A5

Sleeping
9 Hostel Milano ... A5
10 Hotel Grand MedSpa Marienbad ... A4
11 Hotel Nové Lázně ... C2
12 Hotel Paris ... C2
13 Hotel Richard ... A3
14 Pension Edinburgh ... A5
15 Villa Patriot ... B3
16 Villa-Art ... B2

Eating
17 Česká Hospůdka ... B3
18 Medité ... B5
19 Rybí Restaurace U Pidlý ... B3
20 U Zlaté Koule ... C1

Drinking & Nightlife
21 Irish Pub ... B3
22 New York Barcaffe ... A5

Entertainment
23 Městské Divadlo ... B1

visit to Mariánské Lázně. The exhibits cover the visits of Goethe and Britain's King Edward VII, local geology and natural history, and are labelled mostly in Czech. Perhaps the most interesting thing is a 20-minute video in English on the history of the spa (filmed in 1987 and comically dated in parts).

Fryderyk Chopin Memorial Museum MUSEUM
(Map p220; ☎354 622 617; www.chopinfestival.cz; Hlavní třída 47; admission 30Kč; ⏰2-5pm Tue, Thu & Sun Apr-Sep) This small museum, next door to the tourist office, displays personal effects and information on the life of Polish-French composer Frédéric Chopin, who visited the spa in 1836. Chopin's music is played in the background.

St Vladimír Church CHURCH
(kostel sv Vladimíra; Map p220; www.kostelml.cz; Ruská 347-49; admission 20Kč; ⏰9.30am-noon & 1-5pm May-Oct, 9.30-11.30am & 2-4pm Nov-Apr) The 1901 red-and-yellow brick St Vladimír Church is a plush, Byzantine-style Orthodox church with an amazing porcelain iconostasis.

Activities

Most people come here to stroll the grounds and take a drinking cure by sipping mineral water from the various springs using a spouted, porcelain sipping cup (called a *lázeňský pohárek*). The town website (www.marianskelazne.cz) has information in English on the properties of the various springs. Dozens of hotels and resorts offer various spa treatments for guests and occasionally walk-ins, though often these are more of the medical (and not the pampering) variety.

Outside the spa area, there are hundreds of kilometres of marked hiking trails that spread out in all directions.

Royal Golf Club of Mariánské Lázně GOLF
(☎354 624 300; www.golfml.cz; Mariánské Lázně 582; greens fees 1600-1800Kč; ⏰7am-9pm May-Sep) Mariánské Lázně is known around the country for its challenging and beautiful 5.6 m, par-72 golf course, which lies 2.5km east of town. The course has a long history, going back more than 100 years. You can hire clubs from the pro club; book in advance.

Danubius Health Spa Resort Nové Lázně SPA
(Map p220; ☎354 644 111; www.danubiushotels.cz; Reitenbergerova 53; 1hr full-body massage 990Kč; ⏰7am-7pm depending on treatment) The Danubius chain manages many of the hotels and resorts in town. Consult the website for a full menu of spa treatments, aimed at both longer-term (two weeks) or short-term (overnight) visitors. The chain's main resort is the Hotel Nové Lázně (p223), which has pools and saunas.

Public Swimming Pool SWIMMING
(Plavecký bazén; Map p220; ☎354 623 579; www.marianskelazne.cz; Tyršova 6; per 2hr adult/concession 120/60Kč; ⏰9am-8pm Wed & Fri-Sun, 1-4pm & 6-8pm Mon & Thu, 1-8pm Tue) The indoor public pool is southwest of the city centre.

WORTH A TRIP

A TRIP TO 'BEER WELLNESS LAND'

In the village of Chodová Planá, 20 minutes by bus south of Mariánské Lázně, the beer spa at the **Chodovar Brewery** (374 617 100; www.chodovar.cz; Pivovarská 107, Chodová Planá; treatments from 660Kč; 9am-5pm) is the perfect spot to simultaneously explore both of western Bohemia's claims to fame: world-class spas and beer.

Beer spa treatments at Chodovar's self-proclaimed 'Beer Wellness Land' include a couple of glasses of the village's liquid gold. There are other tantalising menu options, including massages, hot stones and even a 'beer bath for two'. Couples can book in for special Valentine's Day packages.

The beer spa experience goes something like this: after disrobing, you sink yourself into a hoppy bath of warm beer. Confetti-sized fragments of hops and yeast stud the water, and the overriding aroma features the grassy, zesty tones of world-renowned hops from nearby Žatec.

The bath is heated to a comfy 34°C (93°F), and you're even allowed to sup on a glass of the Chodovar Brewery's fine golden lager for the duration. After a relaxing soak of around 30 minutes, an attendant brings you your robe and leads you into some granite tunnels (used for 'lagering' beer as far back as the 12th century) for yet more rest and relaxation.

According to the brewery's marketing spiel, the procedures will have 'curative effects on the complexion and hair, relieve muscle tension, warm-up joints and support the immune system of the organism'. In the attached gift shop there's beer soap, shampoo and cosmetics.

After all that hoppy goodness, visitors can even the score with tasty meat-heavy dishes and more brews in the subterranean restaurant and beer hall. Another above-ground restaurant features official beer sommeliers who can instruct in different types of beer.

Sleeping

While one-night stays are possible, most of the big hotels and resorts in town are geared for longer-term (one- to two-week) bookings, including full wellness packages. In practice that means reception desks are not always prepared to handle walk-in requests for a one- or two-night stay. You'll get better service (and often better prices) if you reserve a room in advance.

★Villa-Art PENSION €

(Map p220; 739 082 358; Ruská 315; s/d from 1200/1500Kč; P) Owner Miroslav Paral has transformed this 19th-century villa into a cosy but modest pension in the spa's upper end. Rooms are situated on two levels, with some upper-level rooms sporting balconies and shared kitchens. The baths have had a makeover and are gleaming. Rooms have wood floors and solid-wood beds and desks. Guests take their breakfast at the downstairs cafe.

Pension Edinburgh PENSION €

(Map p220; 354 620 804; www.pensionedinburgh.com; Ruská 56; s/d 860/1280Kč, apt 1460Kč; P@) This friendly, centrally located pension offers five idiosyncratically decorated rooms and one apartment, each equipped with bathrobes, armchairs and a well-stocked minibar, tucked away above the Scottish Pub, a cosy spot for an evening drink. The owners offer transport around town and further afield.

Hostel Milano HOSTEL €

(Map p220; 774 417 065; http://ubytovani.newyorkml.cz/milano/en; Ruská 309; s/tw from 350/600Kč; P) The cheapest accommodation in town, this hostel features Ikea-furnished rooms and modern art. There's a well-equipped shared kitchen if you're watching your budget. It's run by the same people who own the popular New York Barcaffe (p224).

★Villa Patriot HOTEL €€

(Map p220; 354 673 143; villa-patriot.cz; Dusíkova 62; s/d from 1900/2400Kč) A modern building finished in neoclassical style, this hotel provides great-value accommodation in spacious, elegant rooms with gleaming modern bathrooms. Breakfast is served in the ground-floor restaurant, which has an outdoor terrace and a reputation for fine dining. There's no lift.

Hotel Paris HOTEL €€

(Map p220; ☎354 628 897; www.hotelparis.cz; Goethovo náměstí 3; s/d 1450/2400Kč; P ⊖ ☎ ≋) An attractive 19th-century hotel, located just down from the Colonnade in the heart of the spa district. The rooms are on the spare side, but are spotlessly clean and most have balconies. The hotel offers a full range of spa treatments; see the website for details. Prices for treatments here are lower than for more glamorous resort hotels.

Hotel Richard HOTEL €€

(Map p220; ☎354 696 111; www.hotelrichard.com; Ruská 487/28; s/d incl breakfast 1850/2890Kč; P ⊖ ❄ ☎ ≋) This modern hotel is situated just to the west of the main spa area and has a nice view onto the nearby St Vladimír Church. The rooms are done up in a bland, contemporary style, but they are nevertheless clean and well cared for. The main selling point is the comprehensive and good-value menu of spa and treatment options.

Hotel Grand MedSpa Marienbad HOTEL €€€

(Map p220; ☎354 929 397; www.falkensteiner.com; Ruská 123; s/d from 3400/5800Kč; P ⊖ ❄ @ ☎ ≋) This massive complex towers over the spa resort in more ways than one. The hotel is situated in a sensitively renovated 19th-century spa palace and offers every conceivable amenity. It will help arrange spa treatments too; check the website for special deals and weekend packages.

Hotel Nové Lázně HOTEL €€€

(Map p220; ☎354 644 300; www.danubiushotels.cz; Reitenbergerova 53; s/d from 3600/6100Kč; P ⊖ ❄ ☎ ≋) They say 'five star', but we reckon one of Mariánské Lázně's best hotels is a very good 'four star'. Either way you're guaranteed an elegant stay in this 19th-century confection that sits atop the 'new baths'. Exemplary spa services are virtually on tap as you're ushered into the gilded lobby. See the website for spa packages (p221).

Eating & Drinking

Although it's far from being a gourmet hotspot, Mariánské Lázně has a couple of above-average restaurants to keep its well-heeled clients happy. Apart from those, eating out here is mostly cafe lunches and midrange hotel restaurant fare.

★ **Medité** SPANISH €€

(Map p220; ☎354 422 018; www.medite.cz; Hlavní třída 7/229; tapas 100-200Kč, mains 300-450Kč; ⊙11am-11pm; ☎ 🖉) Czech owner David Böhm has transformed this unassuming spot into the best tapas restaurant in the Czech Republic. Choose from a small menu of hot and cold tapas dishes, as well as authentic paella and pastas, and pair them with carefully selected Spanish wines. The decor is colourful and minimalist – a welcome change from the spa's overwrought baroque.

Česká Hospůdka CZECH €€

(Map p220; ☎720 121 500; www.ceskahospudkaml.cz; Klíčová 179; mains 130-330Kč; ⊙11am-10pm; ☎) A cosy Czech pub with a wood-burning fire and excellent, inventive local cooking is just the ticket for an enjoyable evening meal. Opt for something standard like a very good beef goulash or step out

HIKING AROUND MARIÁNSKÉ LÁZNĚ

Mariánské Lázně is surrounded by dense forest, with dozens of trails winding through the woods and past pavilions and springs. The **Town Information Centre** (p224) hands out a free hiking map that traces out four of the most popular, shorter hikes.

The longest and most satisfying of these is the 6km-long **Edward Trail** (Edwardova cesta), which is marked in blue and begins from behind the **Hotel Nové Lázně**. It climbs quickly and then circles around the southern end of the spa all the way out to the **Royal Golf Club of Mariánské Lázně**.

Another worthwhile path, the 5km-long **Metternich Trail** (Metternichova cesta), marked in green, covers the lesser-explored western side of the spa area and takes in several springs. Find it at the southern end of the spa area, just near the **Public Swimming Pool**. It wends northward and drops you off at the far northern end of the spa, near the top of Hlavní třída.

But these hikes are just the tip of the iceberg. Beyond the immediate spa region, trails link Mariánské Lázně to further-flung locales like **Františkovy Lázně** and a wooded monastery at **Teplá**.

a bit with roast leg of venison or marinated pork ribs served in a garlic-honey sauce. The beers on tap include an excellent nonpasteurised Gambrinus.

Rybí Restaurace U Pidlý SEAFOOD €€
(City Cafe; Map p220; ☎777 301 634; www.upidly.cz; Masarykova 626; mains 150-380Kč; ⊙10am-10pm) This is arguably the best traditional fish restaurant in town, with a menu of freshwater fish ranging from carp and trout to eel and pike-perch. Try the mouth-watering grilled trout lightly coated in herbs and breadcrumbs. It also does fish burgers, cod and chips, and a handful of beef and pork dishes.

U Zlaté Koule CZECH €€€
(Map p220; ☎354 624 455; www.uzlatekoule.com; Nehrova 26; mains 250-630Kč; ⊙noon-11pm) A stunning cocktail of five-star class and cosy informality, the swish 'Golden Globe' features creaking wooden beams, crisp table linen, sparkling glassware and antiques. The game-rich menu effortlessly whips up the 'wow' factor. Order a day in advance for roast goose with apple stuffing and bread-and-bacon dumplings.

New York Barcaffe CAFE
(Map p220; ☎776 007 921; www.newyorkml.cz; Hlavní třída 233; mains 90-170Kč; ⊙9.30am-11pm Sun-Thu, to 1am Fri & Sat; 📶) One of those tough-to-pigeonhole places, this is a popular cafe most of the day, but transforms into a lively bar at night. We like it because they also do light international food items such as salads and pastas – the kind of good (and quick) food that isn't easy to find in Mariánské Lázně.

Irish Pub PUB
(Map p220; ☎777 303 838; www.irish-pub.cz; Poštovni 96; ⊙5pm-1am; 📶) Old typewriters and vintage green bicycles create a suitably Irish ambience for the best craic in Mariánské Lázně. Lots of Irish whiskeys are on hand, as well as light food and pizza. Follow the signs that say 'Irish Pub' up the steps and to the right.

Entertainment

Městské Divadlo THEATRE
(Municipal Theatre; Map p220; ☎354 622 036; www.kisml.cz/en/town-theatre; Třebízského 106) Check the website for musical and theatrical performances. Get information and buy tickets from the Tourist Information Centre.

Information

Československá Obchodní Banka (☎354 601 611; www.csob.cz; Hlavní třída 81/10; ⊙9am-5pm Mon-Fri) Bank ATM and currency exchange.

Town Information Centre (Map p220; ☎354 622 474; www.marianskelazne.cz; Hlavní třída 47; ⊙9am-7pm Mar-Oct, to 6pm Nov-Feb) Sells theatre tickets, bus tickets and maps, books accommodation, and has internet access and a left-luggage service.

Getting There & Away

BUS

Services from Prague's Zličín bus station (200Kč, four hours, up to five per day) require changes at Plzeň and Tachov.

TRAIN

Several fast trains per day run from Prague (261Kč, three hours) with a change at Plzeň. Regular (slow) trains link Mariánské Lázně and Karlovy Vary (66Kč, 1¾ hours). Trolleybuses 5 and 7 (12Kč) run from the station to the spa area, or you can walk (30 minutes).

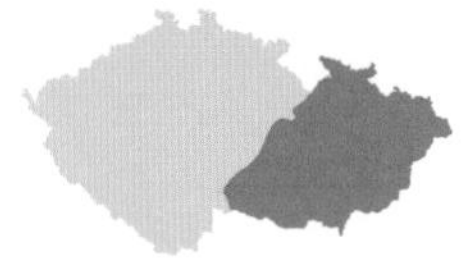

Moravia

Includes ➡

Brno 227
Telč 235
Třebíč 237
Mikulov 238
Valtice-Lednice 244
Znojmo 246
Olomouc 248
Kroměříž 254

Best Places to Eat

- Pavillon (p232)
- Veselá 13 (p247)
- Restaurant Coqpit (p238)
- Sojka & Spol (p241)
- Svatováclavský Pivovar (p252)

Best Places to Sleep

- Hostel Mitte (p230)
- Hotel Templ (p240)
- Hotel Mario (p245)
- Hotel Lahofer (p247)
- Penzión Na Hradě (p252)

Why Go?

The Czech Republic's easternmost province, Moravia, is yin to Bohemia's yang. If Bohemians love beer, Moravians love wine. If Bohemia is about towns and cities, Moravia is all rolling hills and pretty landscapes. The capital, Brno, has the museums, but the northern city of Olomouc has captivating architecture. The lesser-visited south is dominated by vineyards and, naturally, wine-drinking day-tipplers. This was the former stomping ground of some of the wealthiest families of the Austro-Hungarian empire, and you can still see the glint of this old money at former noble piles in Mikulov, Valtice and Lednice.

When to Go

Brno

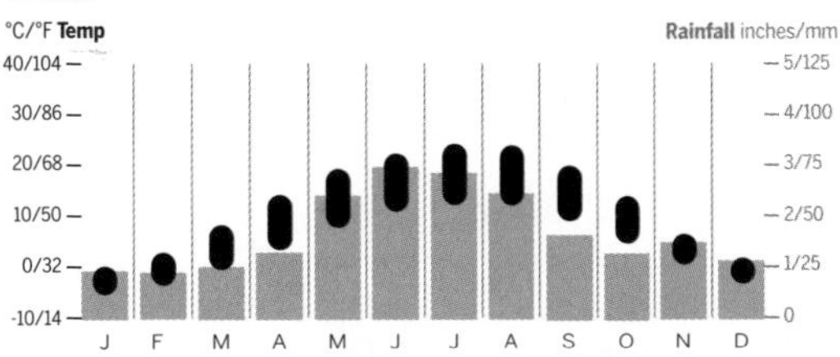

Apr Trees bud and flowers bloom in pretty towns like Olomouc.

Jul Warm, sunny days are perfect for urban strolls or hiking or biking the countryside.

Sep Toast the grape harvest with new wine in Valtice or at the Znojmo wine festival.

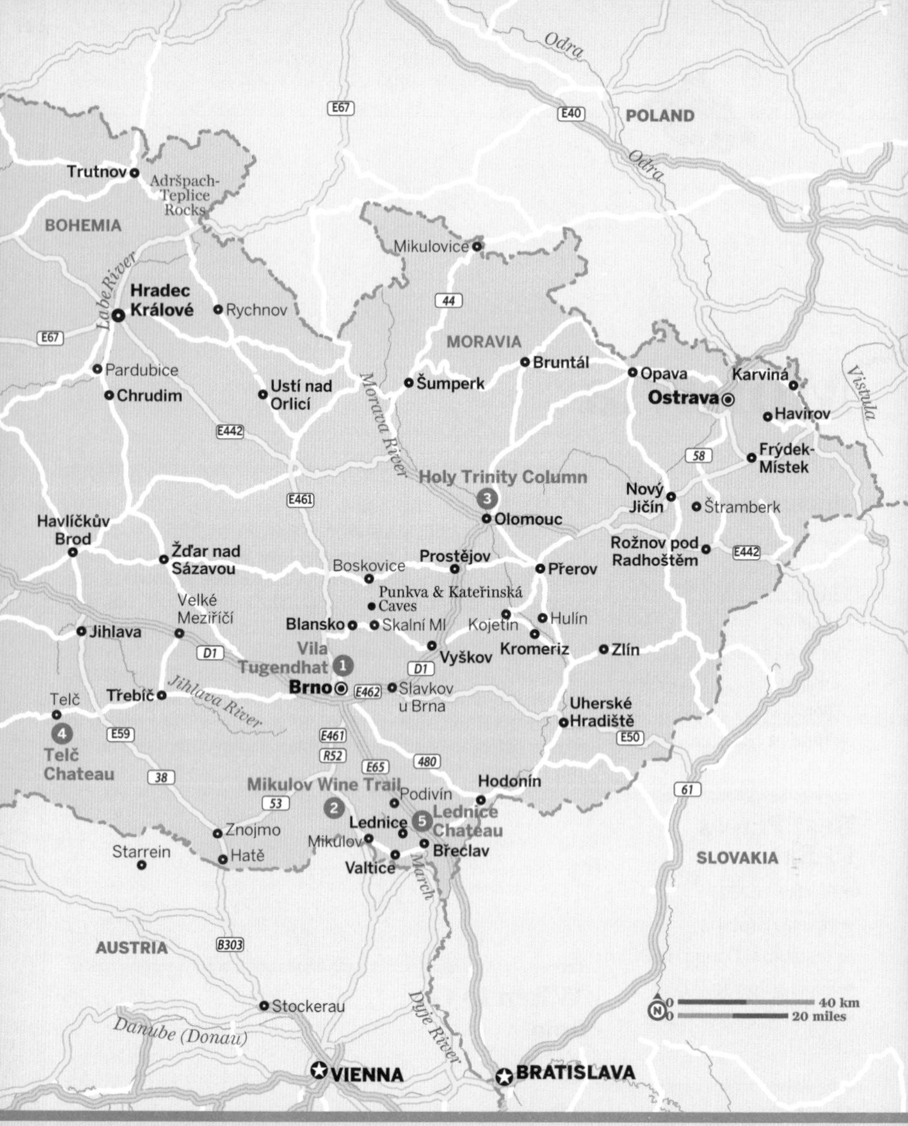

Moravia Highlights

❶ **Vila Tugendhat** (p230) Appraising the value, aesthetically speaking, of a functionalist masterwork.

❷ **Mikulov Wine Trail** (p240) Hiking, biking or simply sipping your way through the hills and dales of southern Moravian wine country.

❸ **Holy Trinity Column** (p248) Admiring the intricacies of Central Europe's most riveting piece of baroque statuary.

❹ **Telč Chateau** (p235) Taking in the palatial splendour amid the country's most perfectly preserved Renaissance townscape.

❺ **Lednice Chateau** (p244) Gawking at the magnificent folly of the Liechtenstein family's ancestral spread, complete with a mock minaret.

BRNO

POP 370,440

Among Czechs, Moravia's capital has a dull rep: a likeable enough place where not much actually happens. That 'nothing to do here' feel was cemented in the early 2000s by the hit local film *Boredom in Brno (Nuda v Brně)*, and, sadly, not many people have gone back to reappraise their opinions. The reality, however, is very different. Tens of thousands of students who attend university here ensure a lively cafe and club scene that easily rivals Prague's. The museums are great too. And if you add in some excellent microbreweries and at least two of the country's best restaurants, there's plenty to reward more than a transit stop.

Brno was one of the leading centres of experimental architecture in the early 20th century, and the Unesco-protected Vila Tugendhat is considered a masterwork of functionalist design.

Sights

Špilberk Castle CASTLE

(Hrad Špilberk; ☎542 123 611; www.spilberk.cz; Špilberk 210/1; combined entry adult/concession 280/170Kč, casements only 90/50Kč, tower only 50/30Kč; ⏲9am-5pm May & Jun, 10am-6pm Jul-Sep, 9am-5pm Tue-Sun Oct-Apr) Brno's spooky hilltop castle is considered the city's most important landmark. Its history stretches back to the 13th century, when it was home to Moravian margraves and later a fortress. Under the Habsburgs in the 18th and 19th centuries, it served as a prison. Today it's home to the **Brno City Museum**, with several temporary and permanent exhibitions.

The menu of visiting options is confusing at first glance. You can choose to visit the exhibitions individually or buy a combined entry ticket to all the sights. The most popular sights are the **casements**, dating from the 18th century, and the **lookout tower**. Interesting permanent exhibitions include 'From Castle to Fortress', about the castle's history, and 'Prison of Nations', on the role Špilberk played as an impenetrable prison.

Cathedral of Sts Peter & Paul CHURCH, TOWER

(katedrála sv Petra a Pavla; Map p228; ☎543 235 031; www.katedrala-petrov.cz; Petrov Hill; tower adult/concession 40/30Kč; ⏲8am-6.30pm Mon-Sat, noon-6.30pm Sun; 🚋1, 12) This 14th-century cathedral atop Petrov Hill was originally built on the site of a pagan temple to Venus, and has been reconstructed many times since. The highly decorated 11m-high main altar with figures of Sts Peter and Paul was carved by Viennese sculptor Josef Leimer in 1891. You can climb the tower for dramatic views.

The Renaissance Bishop's Palace (closed to the public) adjoins the cathedral. To the left is the pleasant Denisovy sady, a verdant park sweeping around Petrov Hill.

Cabbage Market & Around

The **Cabbage Market** (Zelný trh) is the heart of the Old Town. Today it functions as a fruit-and-vegetable market, but at its centre

BRNO'S QUIRKY OLD TOWN HALL

No visit to Brno would be complete without a peek inside the city's medieval **Old Town Hall** (Stará radnice; Map p228; ☎542 427 150; www.ticbrno.cz; Radnická 8; tower adult/concession 60/30Kč; ⏲10am-6pm; 🚋4, 8, 9), parts of which date back to the 13th century. The oddities start right at the entrance on Radnická. Take a look at the Gothic portal made by Anton Pilgram in 1510 and notice the crooked middle turret. According to legend, this was intentional: Pilgram was not paid the agreed amount by the council so, in revenge, he left the turret more than slightly bent.

Take a stroll inside to see the corpse of the legendary **Brno 'dragon'** that supposedly once terrorised the city's waterways. The animal, in fact (well at least we've been told), is an Amazon River crocodile, donated by Archprince Matyáš in 1608. Near the dragon, you'll see a **wooden wagon wheel** hanging on the wall. It was apparently crafted by an enterprising cartwright from Lednice. In 1636 he bet a mate that he could fell a tree, build a wheel and roll it 50km to Brno – all before dusk. He was successful, and the hastily made and quickly rolled wheel has been on display ever since. Unfortunately, someone started the dodgy rumour that the cartwright had received assistance from the devil and he died penniless when his customers went elsewhere.

Brno

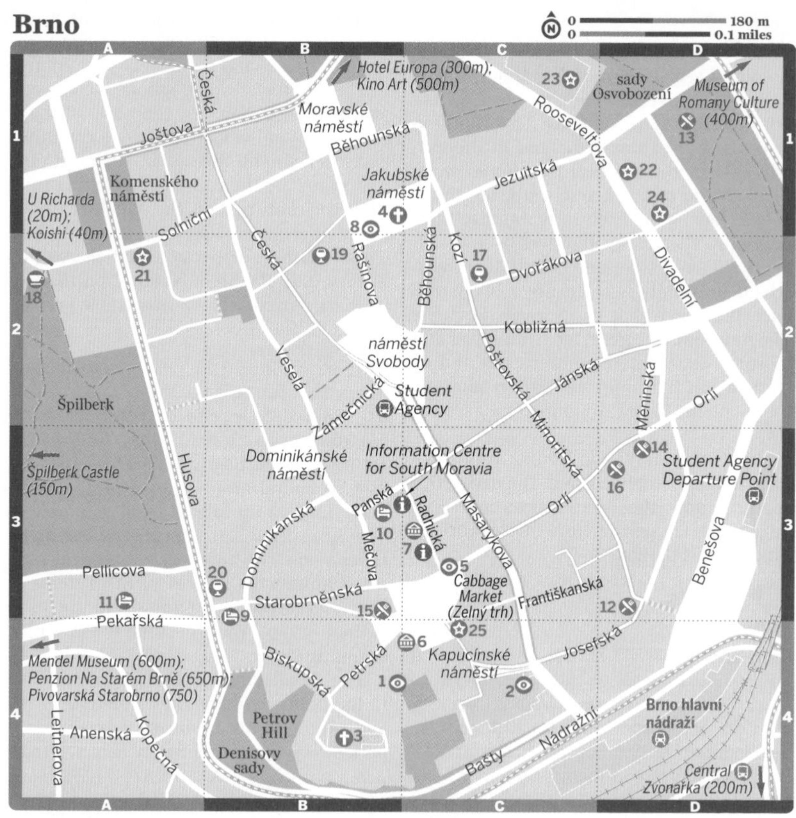

Brno

Sights
1 Bishop's Court B4
2 Capuchin Monastery C4
3 Cathedral of Sts Peter & Paul B4
4 Church of St James B1
5 Labyrinth under the Cabbage Market C3
6 Moravian Museum C4
7 Old Town Hall C3
8 Ossuary at St James B1

Sleeping
9 Barceló Brno Palace B3
10 Hostel Mitte B3
11 Hotel Pod Špilberkem A3

Eating
12 Annapurna D3
13 Pavillon D1
14 Rebio D3
15 Špaliček B3
16 Spolek D3

Drinking & Nightlife
17 Bar, Který Neexistuje C2
18 Cafe Podnebi A2
19 Pivnice Pegas B2
20 Super Panda Circus B3

Entertainment
21 Brno Philharmonic Orchestra A2
22 Desert D1
23 Janáček Theatre C1
24 National Theatre Box Office D1
25 Reduta Theatre C4

is the curious baroque **Parnassus Fountain** (1695). The images here depict Hercules restraining the three-headed Cerberus, watchdog of the underworld. The three female figures represent the ancient empires of Babylon (crown), Persia (cornucopia) and Greece (quiver of arrows). The triumphant woman on top symbolises Europe.

Labyrinth under the Cabbage Market TUNNELS
(Brněnské podzemí; Map p228; ☎542 427 150; www.ticbrno.cz; Zelný trh 21; adult/concession 160/80Kč; 9am-6pm Tue-Sun; 4, 8, 9) In recent years, the city has opened several sections of extensive underground tunnels to the general public. This tour takes around 40 minutes to explore several cellars situated 6m to 8m below the Cabbage Market, which has served as a food market for centuries. The cellars were built for two purposes: to store goods and to hide in during wars.

Capuchin Monastery CEMETERY
(Kapucínský klášter; Map p228; ☎511 145 796; www.kapucini.cz; Kapucínské náměstí; adult/concession 70/35Kč; 9am-noon & 1-6pm Mon-Sat, 11am-5pm Sun Apr-Oct, 10am-4pm Mon-Sat, 11am-4.30pm Sun Nov-Mar; 4, 8, 9) One of the city's leading attractions is this ghoulish cellar crypt that holds the mummified remains of several city noblemen from the 18th century. Apparently, the dry, well-ventilated crypt has the natural ability to turn dead bodies into mummies. Up to 150 cadavers were deposited here prior to 1784, the desiccated corpses including monks, abbots and local notables.

Moravian Museum MUSEUM
(Moravské zemské muzeum; Map p228; ☎533 435 220; www.mzm.cz; Zelný trh 8; adult/concession 150/75Kč; 9am-3pm Tue, 9am-5pm Wed-Fri, 1-6pm Sat & Sun; 4, 8, 9) This natural history and ethnographic museum holds some six million pieces and is the country's second-largest. Exhibits straddle the intellectual gulf between extinct life and the medieval village. In a courtyard next to the museum is the **Bishop's Court** (Biskupský dvůr; Map p228; ☎533 435 220; www.mzm.cz; Muzejní 1; adult/concession 50/30Kč; 9am-5pm Tue-Fri, 1-6pm Sat & Sun; 8, 9), housing the largest freshwater aquarium in the country with plenty of info on Moravian wildlife.

Náměstí Svobody & Around

Spacious **náměstí Svobody** is the city's bustling central hub. It dates from the early 13th century, when it was called Dolní trh (lower market). The **plague column** here dates from 1680, and the **House of the Lords of Lipá** (Dům Pánů z Lipé) at No 17 is a Renaissance palace (1589–96) with a 19th-century sgraffito facade and arcaded courtyard. On the eastern side of the square at No 10 is the **House of the Four Mamlases** (Dům U čtyř mamlasů). The facade here is supported by a quartet of well-muscled but clearly moronic 'Atlas' figures, each struggling to hold up the building and their loincloths at the same time.

AHEAD OF THEIR TIME

The bells of the **Cathedral of Sts Peter & Paul** (p227) disconcertingly ring noon an hour early, at 11am. Legend has it that the practice dates to when Swedish soldiers laid siege to the city during the Thirty Years' War in 1645. Their commander, General Torstenson, who had been frustrated by Brno's defences for more than a week, decided to launch a final attack, with one caveat: if his troops could not prevail by noon, he would throw in his hand.

By 11am the Swedes were making headway, but the cathedral's tower-keeper had the inspired idea to ring noon early. The bells struck 12, the Swedes withdrew, and the city was saved.

Church of St James CHURCH
(kostel sv Jakuba; Map p228; ☎542 212 039; www.svatyjakubbrno.wz.cz; Jakubská 11; 8am-6pm; 4, 8, 9) FREE This austere 15th-century church contains a baroque pulpit with reliefs of Christ dating from 1525. But the biggest draw is a small stone figure known as the 'Nehaňba' (The Shameless): above the 1st-floor window on the southern side of the clock tower at the church's western end is the figure of a man baring his buttocks towards the cathedral. Local legend claims this was a disgruntled mason's parting shot to his rivals working on Petrov Hill.

Ossuary at St James CATACOMB
(Kostnice u sv Jakuba; Map p228; ☎542 427 150; www.ticbrno.cz; Jakubské náměstí; adult/concession 140/70Kč; 9.30am-6pm Tue-Sun; 4, 8, 9) This ghoulish 20-minute tour through the former burial grounds and crypts below the Church of St James displays the collected bones and remains of some 50,000 people who perished from wars, famines and plagues over the centuries. The remains were

BRNO WITH KIDS

Brno will be a tough sell for kids. After the charms of the Brno 'dragon' and the wagon wheel in the Old Town Hall have worn off, you'll have to come up with some more inspired ideas. One possibility is the **Brno Observatory & Planetarium** (☎541 321 287; www.hvezdarna.cz; Kraví hora 2; adult/concession 125/100Kč; ⏲7.30am-3pm Mon & Tue, 7.30am-7.30pm Wed-Fri, 9am-7.30pm Sat, 9am-4pm Sun; 🚋4). While most of the shows are in Czech, it may be possible to arrange an English presentation if you contact the staff in advance. The **City Zoological Garden** (Zoologická zahrada; ☎546 432 311; www.zoobrno.cz; Bystrc-Mniší hora; adult/concession 100/70Kč; ⏲9am-4pm Nov-Feb, to 5pm Mar & Oct, to 6pm Apr-Sep; 🚋1, 3, 11), on the outskirts of town, occupies a lovely setting and has a wide variety of animals. Brno's **Technical Museum** (Technické muzeum vs Brně; ☎541 421 411; www.technicalmuseum.cz; Purkyňova 105; adult/concession 130/70Kč⏲9am-5pm Tue-Fri, 10am-6pm Sat & Sun; 🚋12) is worth a half day of anyone's time. Don't miss the panopticon on the 1st floor; this huge wooden stereoscope allows up to 20 viewers to look at 3D images from antique glass slides that are changed on a regular basis.

discovered in 2001 during the renovation of the square and opened to the public in 2013.

Outside the Centre

★Vila Tugendhat ARCHITECTURE

(Villa Tugendhat; ☎515 511 015, tour bookings 731 616 899; www.tugendhat.eu; Černopolni 45; adult/concession basic tour 300/180Kč, extended tour 350/210Kč; ⏲10am-6pm Tue-Sun Mar-Dec, 9am-7pm Wed-Sun Jan & Feb; 🚋3, 5, 9) Brno had a reputation in the 1920s as a centre for modern architecture in the Bauhaus style. Arguably the finest example is this family villa, designed by modern master Mies van der Rohe for Greta and Fritz Tugendhat in 1930. The house was the inspiration for British author Simon Mawer in his 2009 bestseller *The Glass Room*. Entry is by guided tour booked in advance by phone or email. Two tours are available: basic (one hour) and extended (1½ hours).

Because of the high demand for tickets, it's recommended to book at least two months in advance. If you can't book a tour, the front of the house is still worth a look for how sharply it contrasts with many of the other contemporaneous buildings in the neighbourhood. To find the villa, take the tram from Moravské náměstí up Milady Horákové to the Dětská nemocnice stop, then walk 300m north.

Museum of Romani Culture MUSEUM

(Muzeum romské kultury; ☎545 571 798; www.rommuz.cz; Bratislavská 67; adult/concession 80/40Kč; ⏲10am-6pm Tue-Fri & Sun, closed Mon & Sat; 🚋2, 4, 11) This excellent museum provides an overdue positive showcase of Romany culture. Highlights include a couple of music-packed videos, period photographs from across Europe and regular special exhibitions.

Mendel Museum MUSEUM

(☎549 496 669; www.mendel-museum.com; Mendlovo náměstí 1a; adult/concession 60/40Kč; ⏲10am-6pm Tue-Sun Apr-Oct, to 5pm Nov-Mar; 🚋1, 2, 6, 8, 9, 10, 12) Gregor Mendel (1822–84), the Augustinian monk whose studies of pea plants and bees at Brno's Abbey of St Thomas established modern genetics, is commemorated here in a series of photographs and displays (with plenty of information in English). In the garden are the foundations of Mendel's original greenhouse.

Sleeping

Brno is a popular venue for international trade fairs, and hotels routinely jack up rates by 40% to 100% during large events (in February, April, August, September and October especially). Check www.bvv.cz for event dates and try to plan your visit for an off week. Always book ahead if possible.

★Hostel Mitte HOSTEL €

(Map p228; ☎734 622 340; www.hostelmitte.com; Panská 22; dm 400-500Kč, s/d 1000/1300Kč, all incl breakfast; ⊖@; 🚋4, 8, 9) Set in the heart of the Old Town, this clean and stylish hostel smells and looks brand new. The rooms are named after famous Moravians (eg Milan Kundera) or famous events (Austerlitz) and decorated accordingly. There are six-bed dorms and private singles and doubles. Cute cafe on the ground floor.

Penzion Na Starém Brně PENSION €
(543 247 872; www.pension-brno.com; Mendlovo náměstí 1a; s/d incl breakfast 1010/1360Kč; ; 1, 2, 3, 5, 6, 10) The atmospheric Augustinian monastery where Gregor Mendel first experimented with pea plants also holds a simple but good-value pension. The five compact rooms are bare bones but clean and comfortable. The Mendlovo náměstí location is convenient to several tram lines.

Hotel Europa HOTEL €€
(515 143 100; www.hotel-europa-brno.cz; třída kpt Jaroše 27; s/d 1400/1800Kč; ; 3, 5, 9) Set in a quiet neighbourhood a 10-minute walk from the city centre, this self-proclaimed 'art' hotel (presumably for the futuristic lobby furniture) offers clean and tastefully furnished modern rooms in a historic 19th-century building. Rooms come in 'standard' and more expensive 'superior', with the chief difference being size. There is free parking out the front and in the courtyard.

Hotel Pod Špilberkem HOTEL €€
(Map p228; 543 235 003; www.hotelpodspilberkem.cz; Pekařská 10; s/d/tr incl breakfast 1400/1600/2200Kč; @; 1, 3, 4, 5, 6, 9) This small, family-run and family-friendly pension is located on a busy street just below Špilberk Castle. The rooms are clean, simply appointed with bed and desk, and relatively quiet (ask for one facing the courtyard). Breakfast is the average spread of cold cuts and cheeses. The secure car park is a good option for self-drive travellers.

Barceló Brno Palace LUXURY HOTEL €€€
(Map p228; national hotline 800 222 515, reception 532 156 777; www.barcelo.com; Šilingrovo nám 2; r from 3600Kč; @; 1, 12) Five-star heritage luxury comes to Brno at the Barceló Brno Palace. The lobby blends glorious 19th-century architecture with thoroughly modern touches, and the spacious rooms are both contemporary and romantic. The location on the edge of Brno's Old Town is excellent.

Eating

As the second-biggest city in the Czech Republic, Brno also has some of the country's best restaurants – at prices to match. For travellers on a budget, there are plenty of cafes and pubs where you can grab cheaper – but still very good – grub.

Spolek CZECH €
(Map p228; 774 814 230; www.spolek.net; Orli 22; mains 80-180Kč; 9am-10pm Mon-Fri, 10am-10pm Sat & Sun; ; 4, 8, 9) You'll get friendly, unpretentious service at this coolly 'bohemian' (yes, we're in Moravia) haven with interesting salads and soups, and a concise but diverse wine list. Photojournalism on the walls is complemented by a funky mezzanine bookshop. It has excellent coffee too.

Annapurna INDIAN €
(Map p228; 774 995 122; www.indicka-restaurace-annapurna.cz; Josefská 14; mains 140-220Kč; 10.30am-10.30pm Mon-Fri, noon-10.30pm Sat & Sun; ; 1, 2, 4, 8, 9, 10, 12) The weekday lunch specials (110Kč for soup, main, rice and salad) are absolutely mobbed at this cramped space not far from the train station. People come for the very good Indian food and prompt service. It's less crowded at other times but still worth a trip for curries and lots of varied vegetarian dishes.

Špalíček CZECH €
(Map p228; 542 211 526; www.facebook.com/restaurace.spalicek; Zelný trh 12; mains 80-160Kč; 11am-11pm; ; 4, 8, 9) Brno's oldest (and maybe its 'meatiest') restaurant sits on the edge of the Cabbage Market. Ignore the irony and dig into huge Moravian meals, partnered with a local beer or something from the decent list of Moravian wines. The old-school tavern atmosphere is authentic and the daily lunch specials are a steal.

MORAVIA IN ...

One Week

Spend two days in **Brno** (p227) to experience the culture, modern architecture and nightlife. From there, head north to **Olomouc** (p248) for two days, with a day trip to **Štramberk** (p254), or head south to **Mikulov** (p238), to enjoy the wine and nature.

Two Weeks

In two weeks, you can see everything. Spend four days in **Brno** and at least a couple in **Olomouc**, before heading south to **Znojmo** and **Mikulov**. Rent a bike, hope for sun and spend the days on the Mikulov wine trail and nights at a wine cellar.

WORTH A TRIP

CAVING IN MORAVIA

The area to the immediate north of Brno has some of the Czech Republic's best caving in a region known as the **Moravian Karst** (Moravský kras). Carved with canyons and some 400 caves, the landscape is very pretty, with lots of woods and hills.

The karst formations here resulted from the seepage of faintly acidic rainwater through limestone, which over millions of years slowly dissolves it, creating hollows and fissures. In the caves themselves, the slow dripping of this water has produced extraordinary stalagmites and stalactites.

The organisational centre for any caving expedition is the town of **Blansko**, which has a good **tourist information office** (Blanenská Informační Kancelář; ☎516 410 470; www.blansko.cz; Rožmitálova 6, Blansko; ⏲9am-6pm Mon-Fri, to noon Sat) that sells maps and advance tickets to two of the main caves: the Punkva and Kateřinská Caves. The office can also field transport questions and help with accommodation. On weekends, particularly in July and August, cave-tour tickets sell out in advance, so try to book ahead with the tourist information office.

The most popular tour is through the **Punkva Cave** (Punkevní jeskyně; ☎516 413 575; www.caves.cz; Skalní Mlýn; adult/child 180/100Kč; ⏲8.40am-2pm Tue-Sun Jan-Mar, 10am-4pm Mon, 8.20am-4pm Tue-Sun Apr-Sep, 8.40am-2pm Tue-Sun Oct-Dec). It involves a 1km walk through limestone caverns to the bottom of the Macocha Abyss, a 140m-deep sinkhole. Small, electric-powered boats then cruise along the underground river back to the entrance.

Another popular tour is to the **Kateřinská Cave** (Kateřinská jeskyně; ☎516 413 161; www.caves.cz; Skalní Mlýn; adult/child 90/70Kč; ⏲8.20am-4pm daily May-Aug, 9am-4pm Tue-Sun Apr & Sep, 9am-2pm Tue-Sun Oct, 10am-2pm Tue-Fri Mar & Nov, closed Dec-Feb). It's usually a little less crowded than the Punkva option. The 30-minute tour here explores two massive chambers, including the very large Main Dome.

Though it's easiest to explore the cave region with your own wheels, it's possible with some advance planning to see the caves on a day trip from Brno using public transport. Trains make the run to Blansko (40Kč, 30 minutes) hourly most days. After that, it's about an 8km hike to the caves, though from May to September special tour buses are available. Before setting out, be sure to arrange transport at the **Information Centre for South Moravia** (Informační centrum – Jižní Morava; Map p228; ☎542 427 170; www.jizni-morava.cz; Radnická 2; ⏲9am-5pm Mon-Fri) in Brno.

Rebio VEGETARIAN €
(Map p228; ☎542 211 110; www.rebio.cz; Orli 26; mains 80-110Kč; ⏲8am-7pm Mon-Fri, 10am-3pm Sat; 📶🌿; 🚋4, 8, 9) Healthy risottos and veggie pies stand out at this self-service spot that changes its tasty menu every day. Time your arrival outside traditional mealtimes, or you'll end up standing in line and looking for a table.

★ **Pavillon** INTERNATIONAL €€
(Map p228; ☎541 213 497; www.restaurant-pavillon.cz; Jezuitská 6; mains 250-385Kč; ⏲11am-11pm Mon-Sat, noon-10pm Sun; 📶🌿; 🚋1, 2, 4, 8) High-end dining in an elegant, airy space that recalls the city's heritage in functionalist architecture. The menu changes with the season, but usually features one vegetarian entrée as well as mains with locally sourced ingredients, such as wild boar or lamb raised in the Vysočina highlands. Daily lunch specials (200Kč) including soup, main and dessert are a steal.

Bistro Franz CZECH €€
(☎720 113 502; www.bistrofranz.cz; Veveří 14; mains 155-220Kč; ⏲8am-11pm Mon-Fri, 10am-11pm Sat, 10am-9pm Sun; 📶🌿; 🚋1, 3, 9, 11, 12) Colourfully retro Bistro Franz is one of a new generation of restaurants that focuses on locally sourced, organic ingredients. The philosophy extends to the relatively simple menu of soups, baked chicken drumsticks, curried lentils and other student-friendly food. The wine is carefully chosen and the coffee is sustainably grown. Excellent choice for morning coffee and breakfast.

Koishi ASIAN €€€
(☎777 564 744; www.koishi.cz; Údolní 11; mains 400-700Kč; ⏲11am-10pm Tue-Sat, sushi served

only noon-2pm & 5-10pm; ; 4) Sushi master Noritada Saito and head chef Petr Fučík have combined forces to bring one of the country's top restaurants to Brno. Sushi is the highlight, but the menu includes traditional Czech dishes with an Asian twist, such as pike-perch served with barley risotto and apple-vinegar foam. The wine selection is excellent. Book ahead.

Drinking & Nightlife

Whether your beverage of choice is coffee, beer or cocktails, Brno has you covered. Thousands of students mean dozens of watering holes, and the cafes are every bit as cool as Prague's and the cocktail bars are even better. Central Dvořákova is a popular street for clubs and bars.

★Cafe Podnebi CAFE
(Map p228; 542 211 372; www.podnebi.cz; Údolní 5; 8am-midnight Mon-Fri, from 9am Sat & Sun; ; 4) This homey, student-oriented cafe is famous citywide for its excellent hot chocolate, but it also serves very good espresso drinks. There are plenty of baked goods and sweets to snack on. In summer the garden terrace is a hidden oasis, and there's a small play area for kids.

Super Panda Circus COCKTAIL BAR
(Map p228; 734 878 603; www.superpandacircus.cz; Šilingrovo náměstí 3, enter from Husova; 6pm-2am Mon-Sat; ; 1, 12) From the moment the doorman ushers you through an unmarked door into this bar, you feel you've entered a secret world like out of the movie *Eyes Wide Shut*. The dark interior, lit only in crazy colours emanating from the bar, and inventive drinks add to the allure. Hope for an empty table since it's not possible to book.

Bar, Který Neexistuje COCKTAIL BAR
(Map p228; 734 878 602; www.barkterynee xistuje.cz; Dvořákova 1; 5pm-2am; ; 4, 8, 9) 'The bar that doesn't exist' boasts a long, beautiful bar backed by every bottle of booze imaginable. It anchors a row of popular, student-oriented bars along trendy Dvořákova. For a bar that 'doesn't exist', it gets quite crowded, so it's best to book ahead.

U Richarda PUB
(775 027 918; www.uricharda.cz; Údolní 7; 3.30pm-2.30am Mon-Sat; ; 4) This microbrewery is highly popular with students, who come for the great house-brewed, unpasteurised yeast beers, including a rare cherry-flavoured lager, and decent bar food like burgers and ribs (mains 110Kč to 149Kč). Book ahead.

Pivovarská Starobrno PUB
(543 420 130; www.pivovarskabrno.cz; Mendlovo náměstí 20; 10am-11pm; 1, 2, 6, 8, 9, 10, 12) Brno's longest-established brewery is at its best in the beer garden on a warm summer's evening – especially if there is a band playing live music. To pair with the beers, there's a big menu of Czech traditional favourites like leg of duck, goulash and pork knee (200Kč to 300Kč). Catch nearly any tram to Mendlovo náměstí.

Pivnice Pegas PUB
(Map p228; 542 210 104; www.hotelpegas.cz; Jakubská 4; 11am-midnight; 8, 9) *Pivo* melts that old Moravian reserve as the locals become pleasantly noisy. Don't miss the 12° wheat beer with a slice of lemon. Try to book a table in advance, or grab a spot at one of Brno's longest bars. The food's pretty good too – mainly Czech pub staples like grilled meats, braised beef and goulash (140Kč to 220Kč).

Entertainment

Brno has a great live-music scene, and on any given evening, you can catch some of the best local and international rock and indie acts at clubs around town. For something a bit more high-brow there's opera and dance at the **Národní divadlo Brno** (Brno National Theatre) and the **Brno Philharmonic Orchestra**.

Fléda LIVE MUSIC
(533 433 432; www.fleda.cz; Štefánikova 24; tickets 200-400Kč; 7pm-2am; 1, 2, 4, 6, 8) Brno's best up-and-coming bands, occasional touring performers and DJs all rock the stage at Brno's top music club. Buy tickets at the venue. Shows start around 9pm. Take the tram to the Hrnčirská stop.

Janáček Theatre OPERA, BALLET
(Janáčkovo divadlo; Map p228; tickets 542 158 120; www.ndbrno.cz; Rooseveltova 1-7, sady Osvobození; 1, 11) This modern performance hall dating from the early 1960s is home to the National Theatre's highly acclaimed opera and ballet companies. Performances are held several times weekly in season; check the website for a current schedule. Buy tickets at the **National Theatre box office** (Národní Divadlo v Brně Prodej

Vstupnek; Map p228; 542 158 120; www.ndbrno.cz; Dvořákova 11, cnr Rooseveltova; 8.30am-6pm; 1, 2, 4, 8) or at the theatre 45 minutes before a performance.

Reduta Theatre CLASSICAL MUSIC, OPERA
(Reduta divadlo; Map p228; 542 158 286; www.ndbrno.cz; Zelný trh 4; tickets 120-170Kč; box office 10am-2pm Mon-Fri, plus 1hr before performances; 4, 8, 9) One of the main venues of the Národní divadlo Brno (Brno National Theatre), with an emphasis on opera and classical music. Buy tickets online or at the venue box office.

Desert LIVE MUSIC
(Map p228; 776 865 383; www.dodesertu.cz; Rooseveltova 11; 4pm-3am Mon-Sat, 6pm-1am Sun; 1, 2, 4, 8) Part cool bar-cafe and part intimate performance venue, Desert features some of Brno's most eclectic live late-night line-ups. Gypsy bands, neofolk – anything goes.

Kino Art CINEMA
(541 213 542; http://kinoart.cz; Cihlářská 19; tickets 100-120Kč; 1, 6) Screens art-house films and has a handy cafe for before or after the movie. Check the website for the program.

Brno Philharmonic Orchestra CLASSICAL MUSIC
(Besední dům; Map p228; tickets 539 092 811; www.filharmonie-brno.cz; Komenského náměstí 8; tickets 290-390Kč; box office 9am-2pm Mon & Wed, 1-6pm Tue, Thu & Fri, plus 1hr before performances; 12, 13) The Brno Philharmonic is the city's leading orchestra for classical music. It conducts some 40 concerts each year, plus tours around the Czech Republic and Europe. It's particularly strong on Moravian-born, early-20th-century composer Leoš Janáček. Most performances are held at Besední dům concert house. Buy tickets at the box office, located around the corner from the main entrance on Besední.

Stará Pekárna LIVE MUSIC
(773 834 538; www.starapekarna.cz; Štefánikova 8; tickets 80-150Kč; 5pm-late Mon-Sat; 1, 2, 4, 6, 8, 9, 12) Old and new music including blues, world beats, DJs and rock. Gigs usually kick off at 8pm. Catch the tram to Pionýrská.

Information

Tourist Information Centre (TIC Brno; Map p228; 542 427 150; www.gotobrno.cz; Radnická 8, Old Town Hall; 8.30am-6pm Mon-Fri, 9am-6pm Sat & Sun) Brno's main tourist office is located within the Old Town Hall complex. The office has loads of great information on the city in English, including events calendars and walking maps, and staff can help find accommodation. Lots of material on the city's rich architectural heritage is also available, as well as self-guided tours. There's a free computer for checking emails.

Getting There & Away

AIR

The small **Brno-Tuřany airport** (p298) is located in Tuřany, about 8km southeast of the centre. It's serviced by a handful of budget carriers and has regular service to the UK and Germany; there is no service to Prague. Brno city bus No 76 connects the airport and the **main train station**.

BUS

Brno's central bus station, **Zvonařka** (ÚAN Zvonařka; 543 217 733; www.vlak-bus.cz; Zvonařka; information 5am-8pm Mon-Fri, 5.45am-4.15pm Sat & Sun), is the arrival and departure point for most regional coach services in and out of the city. The main exceptions are **Student Agency** (Map p228; Brno office 539 000 860, national hotline 800 100 300; www.studentagency.cz; náměstí Svobody 17; 9am-6pm Mon-Fri) buses, which use a small **departure point** (Map p228; 841 101 101; www.studentagency.cz; Benešova; 4.30am-9.30pm Mon-Fri, 5.30am-9pm Sat & Sun) in front of the main train station.

The Zvonařka station is situated behind the main train station. Access from the centre is through a tunnel that begins below the train station and runs through a shopping centre.

There's regular coach service throughout the day to Prague (210Kč, 2½ hours), Bratislava (180Kč, two hours), Olomouc (100Kč, one hour) and Vienna (200Kč, two hours). Student Agency buses serve Prague, as well as other domestic and international destinations.

TRAIN

Brno's hulking **train station** (Brno hlavní nádraží; 221 111 122; www.cd.cz; Nádražní 1) is a major domestic and international train hub, with regular service to Prague, as well as Vienna, Bratislava and Budapest. There are domestic and international ticket offices, train information, a left-luggage office and lockers, as well as several places to stock up on train provisions.

Express trains to Brno depart Prague's Hlavní nádraží (main train station; 219Kč, three hours) every couple of hours during the day. Brno is a handy junction for onward train travel to Vienna (220Kč, two hours) and Bratislava (210Kč, 1½ hours).

TELČ

POP 6000

The Unesco heritage town of Telč, perched on the border between Bohemia and Moravia, possesses one of the country's prettiest and best-preserved historic squares. The main attraction is the beauty of the square itself, lined by Renaissance and baroque burgers' houses, with their brightly coloured yellow, pink and green facades. Spend part of your visit simply ambling about, taking in the classic Renaissance chateau on the square's northwestern end and the parklands and ponds that surround the square on all sides.

Sights

Begin your exploration at Telč's gorgeous town square, **náměstí Zachariáše z Hradce**, with its long row of townhouses sporting street-level arcades and high gables and all painted in a riot of pastel colours. Most houses here were built in Renaissance style in the 16th century after a fire levelled the town in 1530.

Famous houses on the square include No 15, which shows the characteristic Renaissance sgraffito. The house at No 48 was given a baroque facade in the 18th century. No 61 has a lively Renaissance facade rich in sgraffito. The **Marian column** in the middle of the square dates from 1717, and is a relatively late baroque addition.

Telč Chateau CASTLE

(Zámek; Map p236; ☎567 243 943; www.zamek-telc.cz; náměstí Zachariáše z Hradce 1; adult/concession Route A 120/80Kč, Route B 90/70Kč; ⏰10am-3pm Tue-Sun Apr & Oct, to 4pm May, Jun & Sep, to 4.30pm Jul & Aug) Telč's sumptuous Renaissance chateau guards the northern end of the Telč peninsula. The chateau was rebuilt from the original Gothic structure in the 16th century and remains in fine fettle, with immaculately tended lawns and beautifully kept interiors. In the ornate Chapel of St George (kaple sv Jiří) are the remains of the chateau's builder, nobleman Zachariáš z Hradce.

Entry to the chateau is by guided tour only. Two tours are available. Route A (about 50 minutes) passes through the Renaissance halls and includes the chateau's most impressive interior, the Golden Hall. Route B (around 40 minutes) explores the castle's residence rooms on the 1st floor, last occupied by the Podstatský family of Liechtenstein in the late 19th and early 20th centuries.

DON'T MISS

FOLK MUSIC FESTIVAL

The town explodes into life during the **Prázdniny v Telči Folk Music Festival** (www.prazdninyvtelci.cz; ⏰Jul & Aug), a two-week celebration of the best of Czech folk, held at the end of July and beginning of August. Accommodation can be hard to find, though, so book ahead.

Church of the Holy Spirit CHURCH

(kostel sv Ducha; Map p236; ☎567 112 407; www.telc.eu; Palackého; tower adult/concession 15/10Kč; ⏰7am-6pm) FREE The church and adjoining tower date from the late-Romanesque period of the early 13th century. The church has been rebuilt several times over the centuries, but the 49m tower is original and the town's oldest surviving building. Climb around 100 steps to the top for pretty views out over the historic core and surrounding area.

Church of St James CHURCH

(kostel sv Jakuba; Map p236; ☎604 985 398; www.telc.eu; náměstí Jana Kypty 72; adult/concession 30/25Kč; ⏰10am-noon & 1-6pm Tue-Sun Jun-Aug, 1-5pm Sat & Sun May & Sep) The Church of St James's impressive 60m-high Gothic tower dominates the central square. This 15th-century church replaced an older building dating from the 14th century that burned to the ground. It's been remodelled several times over the years and its modern appearance owes much to the neo-Gothic craze of the 19th century.

Sleeping

Penzin Kamenné Slunce PENSION €

(Map p236; ☎732 193 510; www.kamenne-slunce.cz; Palackého 27; r from 800Kč; P ⊖ ☎) Lots of brick, exposed beams and warm wood floors make this a very welcoming spot just off the main square. Hip bathrooms with colourful tiles add weight to claims that this is arguably Telč's coolest place to stay. Breakfast costs 100Kč.

Penzión Petra PENSION €

(☎567 213 059; www.penzionpetra.cz; Srázná 572; s 300-500Kč, d 600-1000Kč; P ⊖ ☎ ≋) This modern house just across the bridge from the town square has brightly coloured

Telč

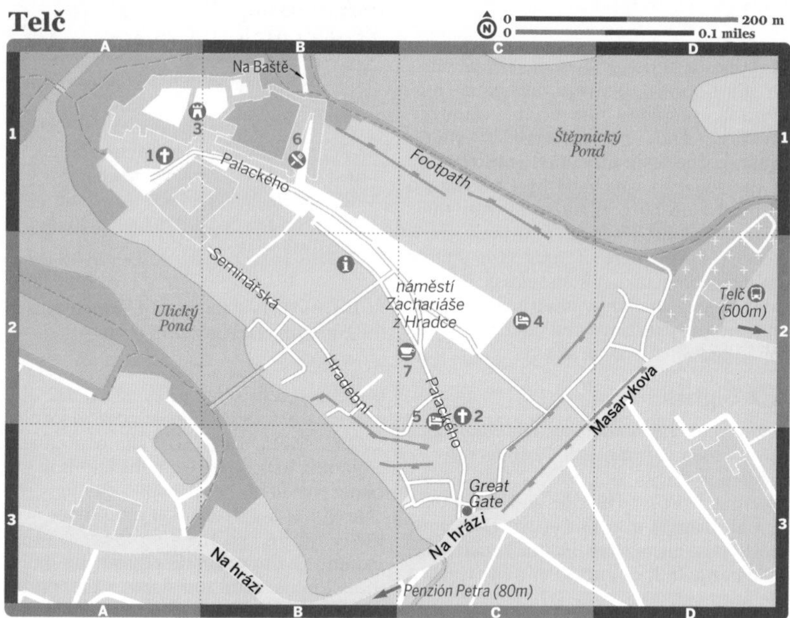

Telč

Sights

1 Church of St James A1
2 Church of the Holy Spirit C2
3 Telč Chateau A1

Sleeping

4 Hotel Celerin C2
5 Penzin Kamenné Slunce C2

Eating

6 Restaurant Švejk Na Zámecké B1

Drinking & Nightlife

7 Kavarná Antoniana C2

rooms, spotless bathrooms and a wading pool in the garden. The separate 'Garden House' (300Kč to 500Kč per person) sleeps up to five and has its own kitchen.

Hotel Celerin HOTEL €€

(Map p236; ☎567 243 477; www.hotelcelerin.cz; náměstí Zachariáše z Hradce 43; s/d 980/1700Kč;) Variety is king in the Celerin's 12 comfortable rooms, with decor ranging from cosy wood to white-wedding chintz (take a look first). Rooms 4, 5, 9 and 10 have views out onto the square. The hotel sometimes closes in winter.

Eating & Drinking

Restaurant Švejk Na Zámecké CZECH €€

(Map p236; ☎567 213 151; www.svejk-telc.cz; náměstí Zachariáše z Hradce 1; mains 120-200Kč; 10am-10pm;) Classic Czech cooking in a pub-like setting next to the castle. The names of menu items, unsurprisingly, are taken from the classic WWI anti-war book, *The Good Soldier Švejk*. 'Cadet Biegler' chicken, for example, turns out to be a schnitzel that's stuffed with ham and cheese. The outdoor terrace is popular in nice weather.

Kavarná Antoniana CAFE

(Map p236; ☎603 519 903; www.facebook.com/kafac.telc; náměstí Zachariáše z Hradce 23; coffee 30-40Kč, cake 40Kč; 8am-2am) The best coffee on the square, plus beer and other alcoholic drinks, and inspirational B&W photos of Telč plastered on the wall. There are only limited food options, but the late opening hours mean it's one of the few places in the centre where you can get a drink in the evening.

Information

Tourist Information Office (Informační Středisko; Map p236; ☎567 112 407; www.telc.eu; náměstí Zachariáše z Hradce 10, Town Hall; ⏱8am-6pm Mon-Fri, 10am-6pm Sat & Sun Jun-Aug, 8am-5pm Mon-Fri, 10am-5pm Sat & Sun Apr, May, Sep & Oct, 8am-4pm Mon-Fri Nov-Apr) Located inside the town hall. Staff here can book accommodation and there's a computer for checking email (first 15 minutes free).

Getting There & Away

BUS

There are a handful of daily buses that make the run from Prague's Florenc bus station (175Kč, 2½ hours), though many connections require a change in Jihlava. The situation is marginally better for travel from Brno (125Kč, two hours), which is served by around four daily Student Agency buses.

Telč's **bus station** (Telč AN; www.student-agency.cz; Masarykova) is located just south of the train station, about 800m east of the central square.

TRAIN

The **train station** (☎725 754 757; www.cd.cz; Masarykova 156) is located next to the bus station, about 800m east of the central square. Though the station is handy for picking up a rental bike, passenger train services to Telč have been greatly scaled back and are not recommended.

TŘEBÍČ

POP 36,880

In the past, the medium-sized Moravian city of Třebíč rarely made it onto travellers' itineraries. This changed in 2003 when Unesco placed the city's nearly perfectly preserved former Jewish Quarter on its list of protected World Heritage Sites. While the quarter is small, it's unique in the Czech Republic and worth searching out if you're coming this way. In addition, take in the impressive St Procopius' Basilica, another Unesco site. Třebíč is best approached as a day trip from Brno or Telč, though there are a couple of decent overnight options if you want to stay.

Sights

Most visitors come to see the remains of the town's once-thriving Jewish community, which dates back to the 14th century. The former **Jewish Quarter**, the best-preserved ghetto in the Czech Republic and a Unesco World Heritage Site, is situated along the northern bank of the Jihlava River, about a five-minute walk from the centre. Most of Třebíč's Jews perished in WWII, but the buildings here, including two synagogues, survived and are being slowly refurbished.

Rear (New) Synagogue SYNAGOGUE
(Zadní (Nová) synagóga; ☎568 610 023; www.mkstrebic.cz; Subakova 1/44; adult/concession 100/70Kč; ⏱9am-5pm Jan-Jun & Sep-Nov, to 6pm Jul & Aug, to 4pm Dec) Dating from 1669, this Renaissance synagogue is the highlight of the Jewish Quarters with its beautifully restored frescoes and a wonderful historical model of the ghetto as it appeared in the mid-19th century. Entry is by 30-minute guided tour, with tours scheduled at least once an hour.

Jewish Cemetery CEMETERY
(Židovský hřbitov; ☎737 180 813; www.mkstrebic.cz/pamatky/zidovsky-hrbitov; Hrádek; ⏱9am-6pm Mar-Oct, to 4pm Nov-Feb) FREE The 17th-century burial ground on Hrádek, about 600m north of the Jewish Quarter, is the largest in the country, with more than 11,000 graves. The oldest dates back to 1641.

St Procopius' Basilica CHURCH
(Bazilika sv Prokopa; Map p92; ☎568 610 022; www.mkstrebic.cz/pamatky/bazilika-sv-prokopa; Zámek 1; adult/concession 80/50Kč; ⏱9am-5pm Mon-Fri, 12.30-6pm Sat & Sun Jun-Sep, 9am-5pm Mon-Thu, 9am-3pm Fri, 12.30-5pm Sat & Sun Oct-May) There was a chapel on this site way back in the early 12th century, when the church was connected to a Benedictine monastery. Although the church has been remodelled many times since then, parts still show signs of the Gothic renovation the structure received in 1260. Today it's a Unesco World Heritage Site.

Sleeping

Most visitors head to Třebíč as a day trip from Brno or Telč, though it's a big enough city to support several hotels and pensions.

Penzión u Synagogy PENSION €
(☎775 707 506; www.mkstrebic.cz/ubytovani/penzion-u-synagogy; Subakova 43; s/d incl breakfast 500/800Kč; ⊖ 📶) Seven simple rooms in an atmospheric location near the Rear (New) Synagogue. Note that the reception desk is

only staffed until 5pm and the pension does not take credit cards.

Grand Hotel HOTEL €€
(☎568 848 540; www.grand-hotel.cz; Karlovo náměstí 5; s/d/tr incl breakfast 1380/1780/2500Kč; P ⊖ @ ☜ ≋) The city's nicest hotel is a modern, four-star offering on the main square, an easy five-minute walk from the Jewish Quarter. There's a good restaurant in-house, plus extras such as a music club, pool, fitness centre and even a bowling alley! The rooms are plain, but clean and very comfortable. Excellent value.

Eating & Drinking

★ **Restaurant Coqpit** CZECH €€
(☎607 160 027; www.restaurant-coqpit.cz; Havlíčkovo nábřeží 146/39; mains 180-280Kč; ⊙11am-11pm Mon-Sat, to 4pm Sun; ☜) One of the best restaurants in this part of Moravia stands on the edge of the Jewish Quarter. The bare-bones interior belies a highly skilled kitchen. Popular and well-executed mains include the braised pork tenderloin flavoured in plum sauce with gingerbread, and baked garlic soup served as a starter. The homemade cheesecake is perfection.

Kavárna Vrátka CAFE
(☎776 840 468; www.vratka.cz; L Pokorného 29/42; coffee 30-60Kč; ⊙10am-5pm Tue-Sun; ☜) This family-friendly coffee house has excellent coffee concoctions and homemade cakes, and is just steps away from the Rear (New) Synagogue.

Information

Tourist Information Centre – Jewish Quarter (TIC Zadní synagoga; ☎568 610 023; www.mkstrebic.cz; Subakova 1/44; adult/concession short tour 150/100Kč, long tour 180/120Kč; ⊙9am-5pm Jan-Jun & Sep-Nov, to 6pm Jul & Aug, to 4pm Dec) The smaller branch of the main tourist office is located at the Rear (New) Synagogue and has lots of information about the Jewish Quarter. Two walking tours of the former ghetto are on offer: a shorter, 1½-hour walk around the area, and a longer two- to three-hour tour that includes a visit to the Jewish Cemetery. Book tours at least two days in advance by phone or email.

Tourist Information Centre – Národní Dům (TIC, Turistická Informační Centra; ☎568 847 070; www.mkstrebic.cz; Karlovo náměstí 47, Národní dům; ⊙9am-6pm Jul & Aug, 9am-5pm Mon-Sat, to 1pm Sun May, Jun & Sep, 9am-5pm Mon-Fri, to 1pm Sat Oct-Apr) Hands out maps and advises on transport, restaurants and accommodation. A computer is available for rent for 15 minutes of gratis web-surfing.

Getting There & Away

BUS

Buses run regularly to/from Brno (75Kč, 1¼ hours) and several times daily direct to Prague (165Kč, three hours). The main **bus station** (Autobusové nádraží Třebíč; Sucheniova, cnr Komenského náměstí) is located about 500m west of the centre.

TRAIN

From Brno, trains leave every hour or so for Třebíč (92Kč, 1¼ hours). Train travel is not recommended from Prague, with most connections requiring at least two changes. The **train station** (Železniční stanice; ☎221 111 122; www.cd.cz; Nádražní) is located about 1km south of the centre.

MIKULOV

POP 7370

The 20th-century Czech poet Jan Skácel (1922–89) bequeathed Mikulov a tourist slogan for the ages when he penned that the town was a 'piece of Italy moved to Moravia by God's hand'. Mikulov is arguably the most attractive of the southern Moravian wine towns, surrounded by white, chalky hills and adorned with an amazing hilltop Renaissance chateau, visible for kilometres around. Mikulov was also once a thriving cultural centre for Moravia's Jewish community, and the former Jewish Quarter is slowly being rebuilt. Once you've tired of history, explore the surrounding countryside (on foot or bike) or relax with a glass of local wine.

Sights

Mikulov is filled with beautiful buildings, many still sporting impressive Renaissance and baroque facades. The long main square, called simply Náměstí (square), has many houses of interest, including the Town Hall at No 1. The town was a leading centre of Jewish culture for several centuries until WWII. There's a small former synagogue here as well as the highly evocative Jewish Cemetery, a 10-minute walk north of the tourist information office.

Mikulov

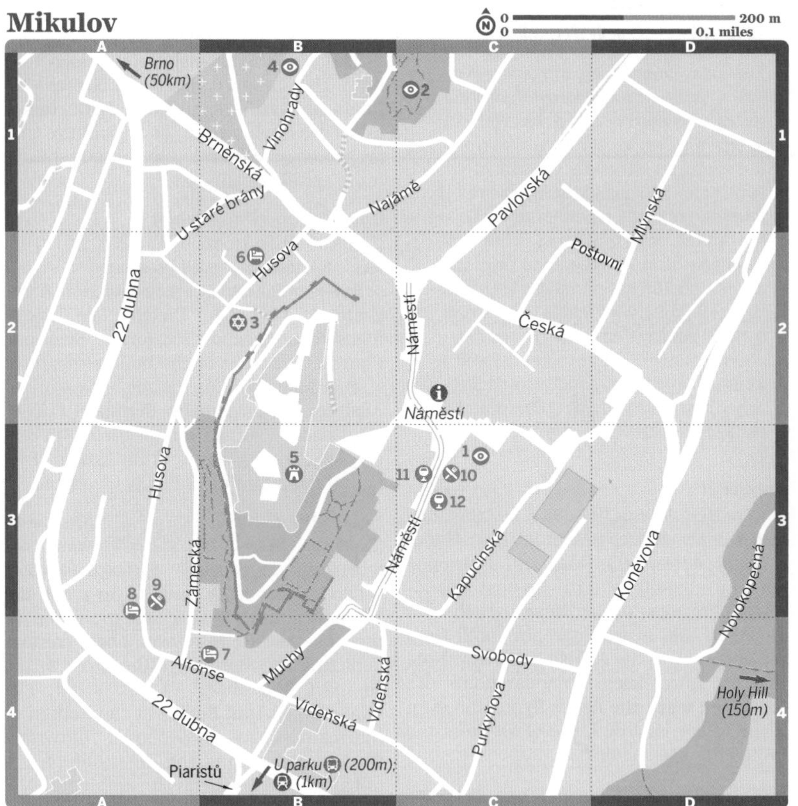

Mikulov

Sights
1 Dietrichstein Burial Vault C3
2 Goat Hill C1
3 High Synagogue B2
4 Jewish Cemetery B1
5 Mikulov Chateau B3

Sleeping
6 Boutique Hotel Tanzberg B2
7 Fajká Penzion B4
8 Hotel Templ A3

Eating
9 Hospůdka Pod Zámkem A3
Restaurace Templ .... (see 8)
10 Sojka & Spol C3

Drinking & Nightlife
11 Dobrý Ročník C3
12 Vinařské Centrum C3

Jewish Cemetery CEMETERY
(Židovský hřbitov; Map p239; tours 731 484 500; info@zidovskyhrbitovmikulov.cz; Hřbitovní náměstí; adult/concession 30/20Kč; 10am-4pm Tue-Fri Apr & Oct, to 5pm May, to 6pm Jun-Sep) The size of Mikulov's forlorn Jewish cemetery, numbering 4000 tombstones, is a testament to the importance of the community to the town over the centuries. The oldest surviving headstone dates to 1605. Enter through the former **Ceremonial Hall**, which holds a small exhibition on Jewish history and burial traditions. Guided tours can be arranged by phone or email.

DON'T MISS

THE MIKULOV WINE TRAIL

The 82km-long hiking and biking **Mikulov Wine Trail** (Mikulovská vinařská stezka; www.stezky.cz) is a pleasant way to visit smaller, local vineyards across the rolling countryside. The tourist information office in Mikulov can recommend rides along either part of or the entire circuit that takes in the nearby chateaux at **Valtice** and **Lednice**. It's signposted in yellow. **Rentbike** (☎519 510 692; www.rentbike.cz; Husova 8; rental per day from 340Kč) hires out good-quality mountain bikes, as well as electronic bikes, scooters and Segways. It can also advise on trails and deliver bikes to your hotel.

Goat Hill HILL, LOOKOUT

(Kozí hrádek; Map p239; ☎608 002 976; Kozí hrádek; tower adult/concession 20/10Kč; ⏲tower 9am-6pm May-Sep) Goat Hill is topped with an abandoned 15th-century lookout tower offering stunning views over the Old Town. To find it, walk steeply uphill from the entrance to the Jewish Cemetery. Note that the tower keeps irregular hours: it's only open when the flag is flying. But even if the tower is closed, the views from the hilltop are spectacular.

High Synagogue SYNAGOGUE

(Horní synagoga; Map p239; ☎727 914 223; www.rmm.cz; Husova 11; adult/concession 50/25Kč; ⏲9am-6pm daily Jul & Aug, 9am-5pm Tue-Sun May, Jun & Sep, 9am-4pm Fri-Sun Apr, Oct & Nov, closed Dec-Mar) The main synagogue dates from around 1550 and is said to be the only synagogue in Moravia of the 'Polish' style. It was rebuilt after a fire in 1719 and renovated several times since then, most recently in the years to 2014. Today it houses a small exhibition on the Jews of Mikulov.

Mikulov Chateau CASTLE

(Zámek; Map p239; ☎777 061 230; www.rmm.cz; Zámek 1; adult/concession 150/75Kč; ⏲9am-6pm daily Jul & Aug, 9am-5pm Tue-Sun May, Jun & Sep, 9am-4pm Fri-Sun Apr, Oct & Nov, closed Dec-Mar) This chateau was the seat of the Dietrichstein family from 1575 to 1945, and played an important role in the 19th century, hosting on separate occasions French Emperor Napoleon, Russia's Tsar Alexander and Prussia's King Frederick. Much of the castle was destroyed by German forces in February 1945: the lavish interiors are the result of a painstaking reconstruction.

The castle is accessible by guided tour only. The standard tour takes around 1½ hours and visits significant castle rooms as well as exhibitions on viticulture and archaeology. Several specialised shorter tours are also available.

Dietrichstein Burial Vault MAUSOLEUM

(Dietrichštejnská hrobka; Map p239; ☎720 151 793; Náměstí 5; adult/concession 80/50Kč; ⏲9am-6pm Jun-Sep, 10am-5pm Apr, May & Oct, closed Nov-Mar) The Dietrichstein family mausoleum occupies the former St Anne's Church. The front of the building features a remarkable baroque facade – the work of Austrian master Johann Bernhard Fischer von Erlach – dating from the early 18th century. The tombs, dating from 1617 to 1852, hold the remains of 45 family members.

Holy Hill HILL, CHURCH

(Svatý kopeček; ☎737 382 622; www.farnostimikulovska.cz; Svobody; ⏲church 9am-5pm Sat, to 1pm Sun Jun-Aug) FREE To reach the 363m peak of Holy Hill, take the 1km path through a nature reserve and past grottoes depicting the Stations of the Cross to the compact **Church of St Sebastian**. The blue-marked trail begins at the bottom of the main square on Svobody. The whitewashed church and the limestone on the hill give it a Mediterranean ambience.

Sleeping

Mikulov has some beautiful small hotels and pensions, and is a good choice for an overnight stay. Most of the better properties are clustered along Husova in the former Jewish Quarter. Many properties offer sightseeing tours and wine tastings and have bikes to rent; ask when booking.

Fajká Penzion PENSION €

(Map p239; ☎732 833 147; www.fajka-mikulov.cz; Alfonse Muchy 18; s/d 700/1100Kč; P ⊜) These brightly decorated rooms sit above a cosy wine bar. Out the back is a garden restaurant if you really, really like the local wine. The pension rents bikes for 350Kč per day.

★ **Hotel Templ** HOTEL €€

(Map p239; ☎519 323 095; www.templ.cz; Husova 50; s/d from 1390/1650Kč; P ⊜ ⓦ) This beautifully reconstructed, family-run hotel comprises a main building and an annexe, two doors down. The updated rooms are done out in cheerful tiles and stained glass, and the baths are just as stylish. Some rooms (such as No 11 in the annexe) open onto a secluded patio with tables for relaxing in the evening. There's a very good restaurant on-site.

Boutique Hotel Tanzberg BOUTIQUE HOTEL €€

(Map p239; 519 510 692; www.hotel-tanzberg.cz; Husova 8; d 1800Kč;) The simply furnished rooms don't exactly scream 'boutique' but the Tanzberg is worth a look for the excellent location, close to Mikulov's Jewish sights. The decent restaurant here plays on the theme, offering Jewish-style (but not kosher) dishes, as well as the in-house pub – U Golema – named after the clay creature of Jewish lore.

Eating & Drinking

For a town its size, Mikulov is blessed with a couple of truly excellent restaurants, including unassuming Sojka & Spol, specialising in locally sourced, organic foods. Several cafes around town feature tastings of locally produced wine.

★Sojka & Spol INTERNATIONAL €

(Map p239; 518 327 862; www.sojkaaspol.cz; Náměstí 10; mains 120-160Kč; 9am-8pm Mon-Wed, to 9pm Thu-Sun;) This light, airy bistro situated above a food shop on central Náměstí is a must, both for the quality of the ingredients (fresh, locally grown and organic) and the inventiveness of the menu. Expect anything from tomato soup to lamb burgers, Thai green curry or French-style coq au vin. There are normally several vegetarian options as well.

Hospůdka Pod Zámkem CZECH €

(Map p239; 607 879 965; www.hospudkapodzamkem.cz; Husova 49; daily special 80Kč; 11am-10pm Tue-Sun, from 3pm Mon;) This funky combination of old-school pub and coffee bar serves simple but very good Czech meals, usually limited to a few daily specials such as soup plus roast pork or chicken drumsticks. It's also the unlikely home of Mikulov's best coffee and serves very good 11° Gambrinus beer to boot.

Restaurace Templ CZECH €€

(Map p239; 519 323 095; www.templ.cz; Husova 50; mains 180-300Kč; 11am-10pm;) A leading contender for the best restaurant in town features an appetising mix of duck, beef and fish dishes, plus a fine wine list specialising in local varietals. Choose from either the formal restaurant or the relaxed wine garden. There's also a small terrace out the back for dining alfresco on warm evenings.

DISCOVERING MORAVIAN WINE

Compared to the wine regions of France, California, Australia or New Zealand, the Moravian wine tourism experience is much more low-key and homespun. Rather than flash boutique hotels or Michelin-star restaurants, the wine scene here is more likely to involve energetic harvest festivals and leisurely cycle touring between family-owned vineyards.

South from Brno towards the borders with Austria and Slovakia, the Moravian wine region accounts for more than 90% of the total area under vine in the Czech Republic. Traditionally, robust red wines were part of the Moravian rural diet, but in recent years, late-ripening white wines have taken centre stage. With grape ripening occurring at a slower pace, the emphasis is on full-bodied, aromatic and often spicy wines.

The Mikulov subregion is characterised by the proximity of the Pavlovské hills, creating a local terrain rich in limestone and sand. Wines to look for during your visit include the mineral-rich white varietals of Rulandské šedé, Ryzlink vlašský (better known by its German name of Welschriesling) and Veltlínské zelené (Grüner Veltliner). Müller-Thurgau and chardonnay grapes also do well.

Further west, the Znojmo subregion is situated in the rain shadow of the Bohemian and Moravian highlands, and the soils are more likely to be studded with gravel and stones. Aromatic white wines including sauvignon, Pálava and Ryzling rýnský (Riesling) are of notable quality, and red wines, especially Frankovka (Blaufränkisch), are also worth trying.

3

ANTON GVOZDIKOV/SHUTTERSTOCK ©

1. Moravia (p225)
The Czech Republic's easternmost province, Moravia is all rolling hills and pretty landscapes.

2. Holy Trinity Column (p248), Olomouc
The Unesco-protected Holy Trinity Column is the pride and joy of the town of Olomouc. Built between 1716 and 1754, the 35m-high baroque sculpture dominates the main square, Horní náměstí.

3. Telč Chateau (p235)
Telč's beautiful Renaissance chateau guards the northern end of the Telč peninsula. It was rebuilt from the original Gothic structure in the 16th century and remains in fine condition.

54115341/SHUTTERSTOCK ©

Dobrý Ročník WINE BAR
(Map p239; www.dobryrocnik.eu; Náměstí 27; ⌚10am-9pm Mon-Sat, to 5pm Sun; 📶) A pleasant little wine and coffee bar, serving local wines by the glass or the bottle.

Vinařské Centrum WINE BAR
(Map p239; ☎777 922 600; www.vinarskecentrum.com; Náměstí 11; ⌚9.15am-noon & 1.15-6.15pm Mon-Sat, 10am-12.15pm Sun) This drinking room has an excellent range of local wines available in small tasting glasses (20Kč to 60Kč), or whole bottles when you've made up your mind.

Information

Tourist Information Office (Map p239; ☎519 510 855; www.mikulov.cz; Náměstí 1; ⌚9am-6pm Jun-Sep, to 5pm Apr, May & Oct, to 4pm Nov, 8am-4pm Mon-Fri Dec-Mar) This helpful tourist office has public toilets (5Kč) and a computer for short-term web-surfing. Maps and brochures are also available, including the comprehensive 'Tourist Guide' (free), which lists all the main sights and is printed annually. Staff can also help organise wine tours and tastings as well as advise on accommodation.

Getting There & Away

BUS

The bus is generally the best way to access Mikulov from Brno (75Kč, 1½ hours), with coaches leaving hourly. Regional bus service is also good, with frequent buses to both Valtice and Lednice (20Kč, 30 minutes). Buses depart from a tiny **station** (Nádražní) near the train station or at another stop, closer to the centre, called **U parku** (Piaristů).

TRAIN

Mikulov is poorly served by train and lacks direct lines to major cities, though there are a few handy connections. Several daily trains run to both Valtice (20Kč, 15 minutes) and Znojmo (70Kč, 50 minutes). Trains running in the Valtice direction normally terminate at busy Břeclav junction, which has onward connections to Prague, Brno and Vienna.

The tiny **train station** (Mikulov na Moravě; ☎221 111 122; www.vlak-bus.cz; Nádražní) is a 20- to 30-minute walk southwest of the centre. See the timetable online.

VALTICE-LEDNICE

POP 6000

The Unesco-protected historic landscape of Valtice-Lednice is a popular weekend destination for Czechs, who tour the historic architecture, including two world-class royal palaces, as well as hike and bike and sample the region's wines. The two towns are about 10km apart, connected by regular buses and a scenic footpath. Neither Valtice nor Lednice offer much in terms of nightlife, so they're best visited as a day trip from either Mikulov or Brno. If you've got more time, either town makes a perfect base for exploring the rolling hills of the southern Moravian wine country: hundreds of kilometres of walking and cycling trails crisscross a mostly unspoiled landscape.

Sights & Activities

This region was the major stomping ground of the noble Lichtenstein family, one of the wealthiest aristocratic clans of the former Austro-Hungarian empire. Both family piles, the Lednice and Valtice chateaux, are worth a peek inside to see how the upper 'one percent' of their day spent their leisure time. For moving between the sights or seeing the surrounding wine country, rent bikes by the day or longer at **Cykloráj** (☎605 983 978; www.cykloraj.com; Petra Bezruče 1125, Valtice; rental per day 200-300Kč; ⌚9am-5pm Mon-Fri) in Valtice.

★**Lednice Chateau** CASTLE
(Zámek; ☎519 340 128; www.zamek-lednice.com; Zámek, Lednice; adult/child Tour 1 230/175Kč, Tour 2 200/155Kč; ⌚9am-5pm Tue-Sun May-Sep, 9am-4pm Sat & Sun Apr & Oct, 10am-4pm Sat & Sun Feb, Mar & Nov to mid-Dec, closed Jan) Lednice's massive neo-Gothic chateau, owned by the Liechtenstein family from 1582 to 1945, is one of the country's most popular weekend destinations. The crowds come for the splendid interiors and extensive gardens, complete with an exotic-plant greenhouse, lakes with pleasure boats, and a mock Turkish minaret – architectural excess for the 19th-century nobility.

Entry is by guided tour only, with two main tours (50 minutes each) available. Tour 1, the 'Representative Tour', visits the chateau's major rooms, including the famous wooden spiral staircase. Tour 2, the 'Princely Apartments', concentrates on the Liechtenstein's living quarters; the highlight is the lovely 19th-century Chinese salon. Check the website for additional smaller tours.

Valtice Chateau CASTLE
(Zámek; ☎778 743 754; www.zamek-valtice.cz; Zámek 1, Valtice; standard tour adult/concession 160/90Kč; ⌚9am-5pm Tue-Sun Apr-Sep, to 3pm

Oct, 10am-2pm Sat & Sun Nov, closed Dec-Mar) Valtice's 12th-century castle, the seat of the wealthy Liechtenstein family, is one of the country's finest baroque structures, the work of JB Fischer von Erlach and Italian architect Domenico Martinelli. Entry is by guided tour only, with several different tours on offer (in Czech, with English text available). The grounds and gardens are free to explore during opening times.

The standard 55-minute tour visits around 20 lavish castle rooms. Highlights include belongings left behind when the Liechtensteins fled the advancing Soviets in 1945. Notice the walls themselves, plastered with kilos of gold. A shorter 45-minute tour (adult/concession 90/60Kč) highlights the castle's baroque theatre.

Assumption of the Virgin Mary CHURCH
(kostel Nanebevzetí Panny Marie; náměstí Svobody, Valtice; 8am-5pm) FREE Valtice's most significant church is this early baroque work, dating from the middle of the 17th century. Take a look inside to admire the rare baroque organ from the 18th century. Behind the main altar are two significant paintings: the larger is a copy of a Rubens, but the smaller one above it, depicting the Holy Trinity, is a Rubens original.

Sleeping

Pension Klaret PENSION €
(733 348 305; www.pensionklaret.cz; Střelecká 106, Valtice; s/d incl breakfast 1000/1500Kč; P) This pristine modern pension set amid grassy lawns has 12 rooms and two larger apartments. The cosy, brick-lined wine cellar is slightly less modern; it dates back to 1890.

★ **Hotel Mario** HOTEL €€
(731 607 210; www.hotelmario.cz; ul 21 dubna 55, Lednice; r incl breakfast 1600-2000Kč; P@) The fully renovated Hotel Mario stands head and shoulders above any of the smaller hotels or pensions in the Valtice-Lednice area. The immaculate rooms are furnished in muted contemporary style, with thick cotton sheets on the beds and tastefully updated bathrooms. There's a small wine cellar in the basement and a few garden tables out the back.

Hotel Hubertus HOTEL €€
(530 503 465; www.hotelhubertus.cz; Zámek 1, Valtice; s/d incl breakfast 1300/1600K; P@) Valtice's most unusual lodging option is to sleep in the chateau itself. While the facilities are not quite as bedazzling as the website might indicate, and there is a slight whiff of neglect about the place, the setting is amazing and the price affordable. The rooms are simply furnished, in stark contrast to the opulence of the rest of the chateau.

DON'T MISS

SAMPLING VALTICE'S WINES

The **National Wine Centre** (519 352 744; www.vinarskecentrum.cz; Zámek 1, Valtice; tastings 100-400Kč; 9.30am-5pm Tue-Thu, 10.30am-6pm Fri, 10.30am-5pm Sat & Sun Jun-Sep) wine salon, in the cellar of Valtice Chateau, is the place to buy local varietals. It is dedicated to promoting Czech wines, with a full menu of wine tastings and experts on hand to guide you through your selections. Tastings by the glass are available, as well as extended tastings, lasting up to 1½ hours, where guests are invited to sample to their heart's (and head's) content.

Eating & Drinking

There is no shortage of places in either town to stop for lunch or dinner. The grounds of the Lednice Chateau are surrounded by outdoor terrace restaurants in warm weather.

Albero CZECH €
(519 352 615; www.alberovaltice.cz; náměstí Svobody 12, Valtice; mains 130-180Kč; 10.30am-10pm Mon-Sat, to 6pm Sun;) This lively Czech restaurant and pub, with a raucous terrace in summer, is the place to enjoy grilled meats and local favourites, washed down with wine or beer.

Grand Moravia CZECH €€
(519 340 130; www.grandmoravia.cz; ul 21 dubna 657, Lednice; mains 140-300Kč; 11am-10pm;) This restaurant, part of a hotel complex, is arguably Lednice's best (out of an admittedly meagre bunch). You'll find nicely done local specialities, including a couple of fish entrées such as trout and pike-perch. Many of the menu items are given a special twist, such as the baked lamb with a hint of rosemary, served with leaf spinach. Book on weekends.

Vinotéka V Zámecké Bráně WINE BAR
(606 712 128; www.wineofczechrepublic.cz; Zámek 1, Valtice; 4-6pm Fri, 10am-6pm Sat &

Sun, 10am-3pm Mon) Situated just to the right of the front of the Valtice Chateau, this little wine shop and bar is a friendly place to sip the local varietals.

Information

Lednice Tourist Information Centre (Lednice Informační Centrum; 519 340 986; www.lednice.cz; Zámecké náměstí 68, Lednice; 8am-6pm Mon-Fri, 9am-6pm Sat & Sun Jul & Aug, 8-11am & noon-5pm Mon-Fri, 10am-noon & 12.30-5pm Sat & Sun Apr-Jun & Sep, 8-11am & noon-3pm Mon-Fri Nov-Mar) Decent tourist information office with plenty of brochures, maps and tips. Buses for Valtice and other regional towns arrive at and depart from the parking lot here.

Valtice Tourist Information Centre (Turistické Informační Centrum; 519 352 978; www.valtice.eu; náměstí Svobody 4, Valtice; 9am-5pm daily Apr-Sep, 7am-3.30pm Mon-Fri Oct-Mar) Well-stocked tourist information office offering lots of ideas for what to do in town and where to go for wine. There's a computer terminal for web-surfing (20Kč per 20 minutes).

Getting There & Getting Away

BUS

The bus is the ultimately the best way to reach both Valtice and Lednice, as well as to move between the two towns (20Kč, 15 minutes, hourly). In Lednice, buses leave from the parking lot in front of the tourist information centre. In Valtice, buses arrive at and depart from a small **stop** (www.vlak-bus.cz; cnr Za Radnicí & Sobotní, Valtice) one block northwest of the Valtice Chateau.

Connections to/from Brno are complicated and sometimes require both bus and train. To get to Lednice from Brno, take the train to Podivín (70Kč, 30 minutes) and then a bus (15Kč, 10 minutes) from there.

Hourly buses make the 30km journey from Mikulov to Lednice (around 40Kč, 40 minutes). Regular service between Valtice and Mikulov takes about 15 minutes (20Kč).

TRAIN

Valtice has regular train service to/from Mikulov (20Kč, 15 minutes) and Znojmo (80Kč, 70 minutes), but otherwise Valtice and Lednice are poorly served by train. The Mikulov trains use the ever so tiny **Město Valtice train station** (Stanice Valtice město; 221 111 122; www.vlak-bus.cz; Petra Bezruče, Valtice), about 2km north of the centre along the main road to Lednice.

ZNOJMO

POP 33,760

The border town of Znojmo is one of southern Moravia's most beloved day trips, particularly for travellers from neighbouring Austria. People come for the wine and to stroll the town's village-like alleys, linking intimate plazas with bustling main squares. Znojmo lies midway between Prague and Vienna and could easily be covered in a few hours as a stopover en route. Alternatively, there are some very nice small hotels and pensions here, and Znojmo is a convenient base for exploring the entire southern Moravian wine region.

Sights

Znojmo Castle CASTLE
(Znojemský hrad; 515 222 311; www.muzeumznojmo.cz; Hrad; adult/concession 40/30Kč; 9am-5pm Tue-Sun May-Sep, Sat & Sun only Apr) Znojmo has traditionally occupied a strategic position on the border between Austria and Moravia, and there's been a fortress here since the 11th century. The castle has served as a residence for Moravian nobles, a garrison, and even housed a brewery in the 18th century. In 1335, King John of Luxembourg held a wedding ceremony for his daughter, Anne, here.

Entry is by guided tour only. Tours leave at the top of the hour, with the day's last tour at 4pm. Tours are normally in Czech, but English and German text is provided on request.

Znojmo Underground TUNNEL
(Znojemské podzemí; 515 221 342; Slepičí trh 2; classic tour adult 70-100Kč, concession 50-60Kč, adrenaline tours 120-200Kč; 9am-5pm daily May-Sep, 10am-5pm Mon-Sat, 1-4pm Sun Oct-Apr) Znojmo's labyrinth of underground corridors below the old town is one of the most extensive in Central Europe, snaking around for some 27km. Two types of guided tours are offered: the 'classic' tour is designed for families and features fairy-tale characters; the 'adrenaline' tour is more hardcore and involves actually climbing walls and crawling through tunnels.

Three types of adrenaline tours (blue, red and black) are available and ranked by difficulty (black is the hardest). Hard hats and proper outer gear are provided. Children under 15 are not permitted on the red and black tours.

Rotunda of Our Lady & St Catherine CHURCH
(Rotunda Panny Marie a sv Kateřiny; ☎515 222 311; www.muzeumznojmo.cz; Hrad; 90Kč; ⏲9.15am-5pm Tue-Sun May-Sep) This 11th-century church is one of the republic's oldest Romanesque structures and contains a beautiful series of 12th-century frescoes depicting the life of Christ. Because of the sensitive nature of the frescoes, visitors are limited to groups of 10 or fewer, and are allowed in for 15 minutes at a time twice per hour (at quarter to and quarter past the hour).

Church of St Nicholas CHURCH
(kostel sv Mikuláše; www.farnostznojmo.cz; náměstí Mikulášské; ⏲8am-6pm) FREE This beautiful 13th-century church was originally Romanesque and was rebuilt in Gothic style. Towards the front on the right-hand side is the 'Bread Madonna' chapel. According to legend, during the Thirty Years' War a box beneath the image was always found to be full of food. Beside the church is the small St Wenceslas Chapel (kaple sv Václava).

Sleeping

Znojmo has several good-value pensions located in the historic centre and in the very picturesque area near Znojmo Castle.

Cyklopenzion Café Kulíšek PENSION €
(☎608 811 313; www.pensionkulisek.cz; Velká Michalská 7; s/d/tr 700/1300/1950Kč;) This family-run pension built over a cafe has lots of charm. The public areas and corridors have an antique-shop feel, and the rooms retain many old-world touches such as period lamps and elegant crown mouldings. The location, at the edge of the historic area, is not particularly beautiful, but the sights are a few minutes' walk away. Breakfast costs 100Kč.

★**Hotel Lahofer** HOTEL €€
(☎515 220 323; www.lahofer.cz; Veselá 13; s/d/ste 1400/2100/2800Kč;) This small hotel, connected to a winery of the same name, is one of the nicest lodging options in this part of the country. The setting is a renovated 14th-century house, a three-minute walk from the main square. The selling points include fresh, contemporary styling and attention to detail that extends to the excellent restaurant. Bikes are available for hire (220Kč per day).

Rezidence Zvon PENSION €€
(☎775 611 128; www.rezidence-zvon.cz; Klácelova 61/11; s/d incl breakfast from 1200/1500Kč;) Concealed in a restored 18th-century residence near the castle are six comfortable rooms featuring wood floors, flat-screen TVs and modern furniture. The central location couldn't be better or more picturesque. The minor downside is that there are lots of steps. There's no reception desk, so be sure to agree on an arrival time so someone can meet you with the keys.

Eating & Drinking

Central Znojmo has plenty of pubs for beer drinking. Most restaurants also offer local wines for sampling.

Na Věčnosti VEGETARIAN €
(☎776 856 650; www.navecnosti.cz; Velká Mikulášská 11; mains 80-160Kč, lunch 90Kč; ⏲11am-10pm Sun-Thu, to midnight Fri & Sat;) An excellent vegetarian restaurant with a couple of fish dishes on the menu. Mains such as Thai noodles and dhal (spiced lentils) are well above average for these parts, and the intimate dining room, with wood-plank walls, red brick and lots of plants, is very cosy. There's also a club with occasional touring bands.

Veselá 13 CZECH €€
(☎515 220 323; www.lahofer.cz; Veselá 13, Hotel Lahofer; mains 185-400Kč; ⏲11am-10pm Mon-Sat, to 8pm Sun;) The in-house restaurant of the Hotel Lahofer is a real treat. The chef is talented at turning out great regional cooking with an international twist, such as grilled trout served with fresh rosemary. Menu items are paired with wines from the Lahofer winery. Book a table in advance.

La Casa Navarra MEDITERRANEAN €€
(☎515 266 815; www.lacasanavarra.cz; Kovářská 10; mains 100-230Kč; ⏲11am-10pm Sun-Thu, to 11pm Fri & Sat;) La Casa Navarra is well

ZNOJMO WINE FESTIVAL

The **Znojmo Wine Festival** (Znojemské vinobraní; ☎515 222 552; www.znojemskevinobrani.cz; ⏲mid-Sep) is the region's biggest annual fest dedicated to wine. In addition to wine tastings, there are musical performances, parades and general merriment scattered all around town.

known locally for homemade gnocchi (usually served with cheese), but the pastas, grilled meats and steaks are also very good. The small dining room is warm and inviting, with lots of red brick centred on a fireplace. There aren't many tables, so it's a good idea to book ahead or visit outside standard mealtimes.

Deci Deci WINE BAR

(☎511 146 714; www.decideci.cz; Pražská 25; ⏲10am-midnight Mon-Fri, 6pm-midnight Sat) Stylish wine and coffee bar, with a nice selection of wines from the Znojmo wine-growing region. To pair with the wines, there's plenty of cheeses, homemade pâtés and spreads, as well as more substantial soups and sandwiches. Look out for special wine-tasting events.

Information

Tourist Information Centre (☎515 222 552; www.znojmocity.cz; Obroková 10; ⏲8am-6pm Mon-Fri, 9am-5pm Sat, 10am-5pm Sun May, Jun, Sep & Oct, longer hours Jul & Aug, shorter hours Nov-Apr) Well-stocked, centrally located tourist office with maps and lots of information on activities. Can suggest hiking and biking outings (as well as where to rent bikes), wine tastings and cultural events, and has a computer terminal on hand for web-surfing.

Getting There & Away

BUS

Znojmo lies near the major north–south E59 highway and has hourly bus service most days from Brno (80Kč, one hour), plus a couple of direct buses each day from Prague (200Kč, three hours). The **bus station** (Autobusové nádraží; www.vlak-bus.cz; Dr Milady Horákové) is located next to the train station, about 1km southeast of the centre.

TRAIN

The bus is better for reaching Znojmo from Brno or Prague, but there is regular train service to Mikulov (70Kč, 50 minutes) and Valtice (80Kč, 70 minutes). There are also several trains daily to Vienna (400Kč, 1½ hours). The **train station** (Železniční stanice Znojmo; ☎840 112 113; www.cd.cz; 28 října) is located about 1km southeast of the historic centre.

OLOMOUC

POP 100,154

Olomouc is a sleeper. Practically unknown outside the Czech Republic and underappreciated even at home, the city is surprisingly majestic. The main square is among the country's nicest, surrounded by historic buildings and blessed with a Unesco-protected trinity column. The evocative central streets are dotted with beautiful churches, testament to the city's long history as a bastion of the Catholic church. Explore the foundations of ancient Olomouc Castle at the must-see Archdiocesan Museum, then head for one of the city's many pubs or microbreweries, fuelled by thousands of students who attend university here. Don't forget to try the cheese, *Olomoucký sýr* or *tvarůžky*, reputedly the smelliest in the Czech Republic.

Sights

Most of the sights are located within the historic centre, comprised of two great central squares that fan out below the Town Hall, and on old cobbled alleys that lead off in all directions. Public transport cannot access all of these older, tiny streets, but everything is fairly close together and within easy walking distance.

Horní Náměstí & Around

Olomouc's main square, Horní ('upper') náměstí, is home to the Town Hall as well as the city's most important sight: a gargantuan trinity column. The square also contains two of the city's six baroque fountains: the **Hercules Fountain** (Herkulova kašna) dates from 1688 and features the muscular Greek hero standing astride a pit of writhing serpents, while the **Caesar Fountain** (Caeserova kašna), east of the town hall, was built in 1724 and is Olomouc's biggest. The tradition of building fountains was continued in 2002 when an **Orion Fountain** featuring turtles and a graceful dolphin was erected on the square.

Holy Trinity Column MONUMENT

(Sloup Nejsvětější Trojice; Map p250; Horní náměstí; ⏲closed to the public) The town's pride and joy is this 35m-high baroque sculpture that dominates Horní náměstí and is a popular meeting spot for local residents. The trinity column was built between 1716 and 1754 and is allegedly the biggest single baroque sculpture in Central Europe. In 2000 the column was added to Unesco's World Heritage Site list.

The individual statues depict a bewildering array of Catholic religious motifs, including the Holy Trinity, the 12 Apostles, the assumption of Mary, and some of the

WORTH A TRIP

THE FUNCTIONALIST ARCHITECTURE OF ZLÍN

In the early 20th century, Moravia was a hotbed of groundbreaking modern architecture. Brno is recognised as the centre of this action, but the smaller industrial town of Zlín (pronounced 'zleen') was also home to some radical and fascinating experimentation in functionalist town planning, following the vision of philanthropist shoe millionaire Tomáš Baťa ('bah-tya').

Adhering to Baťa's plan, the factories, offices, shopping centres and houses all used lookalike red bricks and a functionalist template to provide 'a total environment' to house, feed and entertain the workers at Baťa's massive shoe factory. Wide avenues and planned gardens produce a singular ambience, giving Zlín an expansive and unnervingly modern appearance, in contrast with the sometimes-saccharine historical centres of other towns.

The **tourist information office** (Městské Informační a Turistické Středsiko; ☎577 630 222; www.ic-zlin.cz; náměstí Míru 12, Zlín; ⏰7.30am-6pm Mon-Thu, to 5pm Fri year-round, plus 9am-3pm Sat May-Sep) in Zlín has lots of information on the town's architectural heritage, including maps and walking tours (in English) of the most important buildings.

For a taste of the importance of Bat'a and his ideas to the town, stop by **Building 14|15** (14|15 Baťův Institut; ☎573 032 111; www.14-15.cz; Vavrečkova 7040, Bldg 14/15, Bat'a Institute; adult/concession 130/60Kč; ⏰10am-6pm Tue-Sun) of the Baťa Complex to see a permanent exhibition titled 'The Baťa Principle: Today Fantasy, Tomorrow Reality'. There are tonnes of interesting and interactive displays on the history of Zlín and the Bat'a shoe company, filled with old photos, machinery and maps (and, of course, lots of shoes over the ages).

The best way to reach Zlín is by bus: there are regular links with Brno (110Kč, two hours) and Olomouc (90Kč, one hour).

best-known saints. There's a small chapel at the base of the column that's sometimes open during the day for you to poke your nose in.

St Moritz Cathedral CHURCH
(Chrám sv Mořice; Map p250; www.moric-olomouc.cz; Opletalova 10; ⏰tower 9am-5pm Mon-Sat, noon-5pm Sun; 🚊2, 3, 4, 6) FREE This vast Gothic cathedral is Olomouc's original parish church, built between 1412 and 1540. The western tower is a remnant of its 13th-century predecessor. The cathedral's amazing sense of peace is shattered every September with an International Organ Festival; the cathedral's organ is Moravia's mightiest. The tower (more than 200 steps) provides the best view in town.

Town Hall TOWER
(Radnice; Map p250; www.tourism.olomouc.eu; Horní náměstí; tower 30Kč; ⏰guided tours 11am & 3pm) FREE Olomouc's Town Hall dates from the 14th century and is home to one of the quirkier sights in town: an astronomical clock from the 1950s, with a face in socialist realist style. The original was damaged in WWII. At noon the figures put on a little performance. The tower is open twice daily for guided tours.

Dolní Náměstí & Around

Dolní náměstí, or 'lower' square, runs south of Horní náměstí, and is lined by shops and restaurants. It sports its own **Marian Plague Column** (Mariánský morový sloup; Map p250; Dolní náměstí) and baroque fountains dedicated to Neptune and Jupiter.

St Michael's Church CHURCH
(kostel sv Michala; Map p250; www.svatymichal.cz; Žerotínovo náměstí 1; ⏰8am-6pm) FREE This beautiful church on Žerotínovo náměstí is topped by an ageing green dome and a robust baroque interior with a rare painting of a pregnant Virgin Mary. Wrapped around the entire block is an active Dominican seminary (Dominikánský klášter).

Chapel of St Jan Sarkander CHURCH
(kaple sv Jana Sarkandra; Map p250; Žerotínovo náměstí; ⏰10am-noon & 1-5pm) FREE This tiny, rounded chapel is named after a local priest who died under torture in 1620 for refusing to divulge confessions. It's built on the site

Olomouc

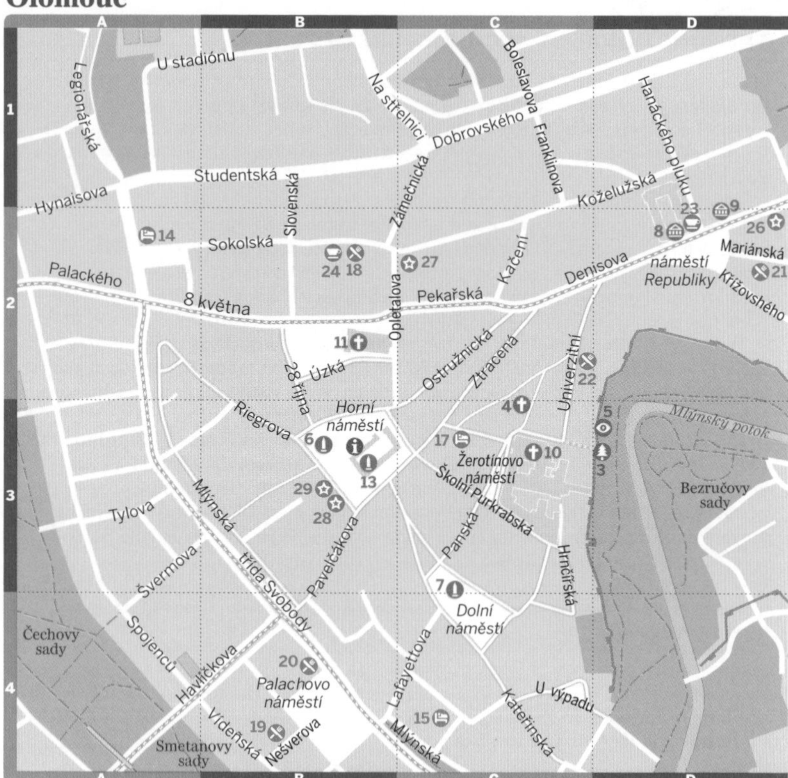

of the jail where he died, part of which is preserved in the cellar. Downstairs is an exhibition about his pious life.

Náměstí Republiky & Around

Museum of Modern Art MUSEUM

(Muzeum moderního umění; Map p250; 585 514 111; www.olmuart.cz; Denisova 47; adult/child 70/35Kč, Sun & 1st Wed of month free, combined admission with Archdiocesan Museum 100/50Kč; 10am-6pm Tue-Sun; 2, 3, 4, 6) On two floors, the museum showcases art from the 20th century under the heading 'A Century of Relativity'. The top floor focuses on movements from the first half of the century, including expressionism, cubism and surrealism. A second part, one floor below, features postwar movements such as abstraction and Czech trends from the 1970s and '80s.

Regional History Museum MUSEUM

(Vlastivědné muzeum; Map p250; 585 515 111; www.vmo.cz; náměstí Republiky 5; adult/child 60/30Kč; 9am-6pm Tue-Sun Apr-Sep, 10am-5pm Wed-Sun Oct-Mar; 2, 3, 4, 6) Housed in a former convent, this is part ethnographic museum and part natural history museum. One section focuses on the history of Olomouc from the 6th century to modern times, while the second section focuses on the geology of the region, as well as photos of scenic landscapes and information on endangered species. There are films and interactive displays, though not everything is signposted in English.

Václavské Náměstí & Around

Václavské náměstí, northeast of the centre, was where Olomouc began. A thousand years ago, it was the site of Olomouc Castle, and you can see the castle foundations

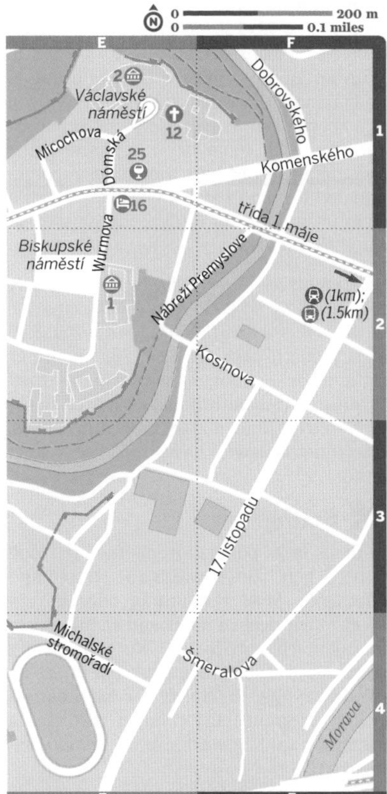

Olomouc

Sights

1	Archbishop's Palace	E2
2	Archdiocesan Museum	E1
3	Bezručovy Sady	D3
4	Chapel of St Jan Sarkander	C3
5	Civil Defence Shelter	D3
6	Holy Trinity Column	B3
7	Marian Plague Column	C3
8	Museum of Modern Art	D2
9	Regional History Museum	D2
10	St Michael's Church	C3
11	St Moritz Cathedral	B2
12	St Wenceslas Cathedral	E1
13	Town Hall	B3

Sleeping

14	Cosy Corner Hostel	A2
15	Pension Křivá	C4
16	Pension Royal	E1
17	Penzión Na Hradě	C3

Eating

18	Aroma	B2
19	Moritz	B4
20	Plan B	B4
21	Svatováclavský Pivovar	D2
22	Vila Primavesi	C2

Drinking & Nightlife

23	Cafe 87	D2
24	Té & Café Kratochvíle	B2
25	The Black Stuff	E1

Entertainment

26	Hospoda u Musea	D2
27	Jazz Tibet Club	C2
28	Moravian Philharmonic Olomouc	B3
29	Moravské Divadlo	B3

in the lower levels of the Archdiocesan Museum. The area still holds Olomouc's most venerable buildings and darkest secrets; Czech King Wenceslas III (Václav III) was murdered here in 1306 under circumstances that are still not clear to this day.

Archdiocesan Museum MUSEUM
(Arcidiecézni muzeum; Map p250; ☎585 514 111; www.olmuart.cz; Václavské náměstí 3; adult/concession 70/35Kč, Sun free, combined admission with Museum of Modern Art 100/50Kč; ⏰10am-6pm Tue-Sun; 🚋2, 3, 4, 6) The impressive holdings of the Archdiocesan Museum trace the history of Olomouc back 1000 years. The thoughtful layout, with helpful English signage, takes you through the original Romanesque foundations of Olomouc Castle, and highlights the cultural and artistic development of the city during the Gothic and baroque periods. Don't miss the magnificent Troyer Coach, definitely the stretch limo of the 18th century.

St Wenceslas Cathedral CHURCH
(dóm sv Václava; Map p250; Václavské náměstí; ⏰8am-6pm; 🚋2, 3, 4, 6) FREE This magnificent cathedral, the seat of the Olomouc Archbishop, was originally a Romanesque basilica that was first consecrated way back in 1131. It was rebuilt several times, before finally (in the 1880s) having the neo-Gothic makeover you see today.

Archbishop's Palace MUSEUM
(Arcibiskupský palác; Map p250; ☎587 405 421; www.arcibiskupskypalac.cz; Wurmova 9; adult/concession 60/30Kč; ⏰10am-5pm Tue-Sun May-Sep, 10am-5pm Sat & Sun Apr & Oct; 🚋2, 3, 4, 6) This expansive former residence of the

archbishop was built in 1685. Entry to see the lavish interiors is by guided tour only (a free audio guide is provided in English). It was here that Franz Josef I was crowned Emperor of Austria in 1848 at the tender age of 18.

Outside the Centre

The centre is ringed by **Bezručovy sady** (Map p250; Bezručovy sady; 24hr) FREE, a pretty city park with walking trails, playgrounds and secluded spots to admire the town and enjoy the meandering Mlýnský potok (Mill Stream).

Civil Defence Shelter HISTORIC SITE
(Kryt Civilní Obrany; Map p250; www.tourism.olomouc.eu; Bezručovy sady; 30Kč; tours 10am, 1pm & 4pm Thu & Sat mid-Jun–mid-Sep) Olomouc is all about centuries-old history, but this more-recent relic of the Cold War is also worth exploring on a guided tour. The shelter was built between 1953 and 1956 and was designed to keep a lucky few protected from the ravages of a chemical or nuclear strike. Tours are arranged by Olomouc Information Centre (p254), which is also where they start.

Sleeping

Cosy Corner Hostel HOSTEL €
(Map p250; 777 570 730; www.cosycornerhostel.com; 4th fl, Sokolská 1; dm/s/d 300/700/900Kč; ; 2,3,4,6) The Australian-Czech couple who mind this friendly and exceptionally well-run hostel are a wealth of local information. There are dorms in eight-bed rooms, as well as private singles and doubles. Bicycles can be hired for 100Kč per day. In summer there's sometimes a two-night minimum stay, but Olomouc is worth it, and there's plenty of day-trip information on offer.

★ **Penzión Na Hradě** PENSION €€
(Map p250; 585 203 231; www.penzionnahrade.cz; Michalská 4; s/d 1490/1990Kč;) In terms of price/quality ratio, this may be Olomouc's best deal, and worth the minor splurge if you can swing it. The location, tucked away in the shadow of St Michael's Church, is ideally central and the sleek, cool rooms have a professional design touch. There's also a small garden terrace for relaxing out the back. Book ahead in summer.

Pension Royal PENSION €€
(Map p250; 734 200 602; www.pension-royal.cz; Wurmova 1; r 1600/2000Kč; P; 2, 3, 4, 6) With antique furniture, crisp white duvets and Oriental rugs on wood floors, the Royal is a spacious and splurge-worthy romantic getaway. Each room has a separate name and unique furnishings, though all go for an updated old-world feel. To get here catch a tram from the train station, jumping off at the U Domú stop.

Pension Křivá PENSION €€
(Map p250; 585 209 204; www.pension-kriva.cz; Křivá 8; s/d 1550/2000Kč; ; 1, 3, 7) This modern pension gets a lot of things right: spacious rooms with cherry-wood furniture, flash bathrooms with even flasher toiletries, and a cosy cafe downstairs. The quiet laneway location doesn't hurt either.

Eating

With its large population of students, food options here tend towards the simple and affordable. Most restaurants offer a very good lunch deal of soup and main course for not much more than 100Kč. Nearly every restaurant will offer some version of the local cheese (*Olomoucký sýr* or *tvarůžky*), a stringy, fragrant dairy product that makes for either a filling starter or an accompaniment to beer.

Aroma INDIAN €
(Map p250; 775 053 097; www.aromaindianrestaurant.cz; Sokolská 38; mains 100-180Kč; 11am-10pm Mon-Fri, noon-10pm Sat & Sun; ; 2, 3, 4, 6) This popular Indian spot offers an all-you-can-eat lunch buffet (110Kč), making it the go-to spot for Olomouc's large student crowd. Choose from a couple of mains as well as basmati rice, curried potatoes, soup and a salad. Try to arrive just before noon to get a seat. It's quieter – though still recommendable – by evening, when it reverts to being a casual, family-friendly Indian restaurant.

★ **Svatováclavský Pivovar** CZECH €€
(Map p250; 585 207 517; www.svatovaclavsky-pivovar.cz; Mariánská 4; mains 180-290Kč; 9am-midnight Mon-Fri, 11am-midnight Sat, 11am-10pm Sun; ; 2, 3, 4, 6) This warm and inviting pub makes its own beer and serves plate-loads of Czech specialities such as duck confit and beer-infused goulash. Stop by for lunch midweek for an

excellent-value soup and main course for around 150Kč. Speciality beers include unpasteurised wheat and cherry-flavoured varieties. Useful for washing down some *tvarůžky*.

Plan B CZECH €€
(Map p250; 773 046 454; www.bar-planb.cz; Palachovo náměstí 1; mains 150-250Kč; 11am-midnight Mon-Fri, 4pm-midnight Sat; ; 1, 3, 4, 6, 7) This homey, low-key bistro puts the emphasis on organic, locally sourced ingredients and traditional recipes. The daily lunch specials served during the week (11am to 2pm) feature a choice of four to five entrées (at least one vegetarian) plus soup for 120Kč. The evening menu changes week to week, so check the door or the website to see what's cooking during your visit.

Moritz CZECH €€
(Map p250; 585 205 560; www.hostinec-moritz.cz; Nešverova 2; mains 120-260Kč; 11am-11pm Sun-Thu, to midnight Fri & Sat; ; 1, 3, 4, 6, 7) This microbrewery and restaurant is a local favourite. We reckon it's a combination of the terrific beers, good-value food and nonsmoking policy. In summer the beer garden's the only place to be. Advance booking is a must. The location is about a 10-minute walk south of the town centre, across the busy street, třída Svobody.

Vila Primavesi INTERNATIONAL €€
(Map p250; 585 204 852; www.primavesi.cz; Univerzitní 7; mains 160-280Kč; 11am-11pm Mon-Sat, to 4pm Sun; 2, 3, 4, 6) In an art-nouveau villa that played host to Austrian artist Gustav Klimt in the early 20th century, the Vila Primavesi enjoys one of Olomouc's most exclusive settings. On summer evenings enjoy meals such as tuna steak and risotto on the terrace overlooking the city gardens. Lunch specials are better value than evening meals.

Drinking & Nightlife

Lots of students usually equates to lots of good cafes and drinking spots, and Olomouc has more than its share. And although this is mainly wine country, the number of microbreweries and restaurants that revolve around good beer is impressive.

★ **Cafe 87** CAFE
(Map p250; 585 202 593; www.cafe87.cz; Denisova 47; coffee 40Kč; 7.30am-9pm Mon-Fri, 8am-9pm Sat & Sun; ; 2, 3, 4, 6) Locals come in droves to this funky cafe beside the Olomouc Museum of Modern Art for coffee and its famous chocolate pie (50Kč). Some people still apparently prefer the dark chocolate to the white chocolate. When will they learn? It's a top spot for breakfast and toasted sandwiches too. Seating is over two floors and there's a rooftop terrace.

Té & Café Kratochvíle CAFE
(Map p250; 603 564 120; www.kratochvilecajovna.cz; Sokolská 36; 11am-11pm Mon-Fri, 3-11pm Sat & Sun; ; 2, 3, 4, 6) A global array of tea and coffee, an interesting selection of beers and wines, and a laid-back Zen ambience make this a good spot to recharge.

The Black Stuff PUB
(Map p250; 774 697 909; www.blackstuff.cz; 1 máje 19; 4pm-2am Mon-Fri, 5pm-3am Sat, 5-11pm Sun; ; 2, 3, 4, 6) Cosy, old-fashioned Irish bar with several beers on tap and a large and growing collection of single malts and other choice tipples. Attracts a mixed crowd of students, locals and visitors.

Entertainment

Jazz Tibet Club LIVE MUSIC
(Map p250; 585 230 399; www.jazzclub.olomouc.com; Sokolská 48; tickets 100-300Kč;) Blues, jazz and world music, including occasional international acts, feature at this popular spot, which also incorporates a good restaurant and wine bar. See the website for the program during your visit. Buy tickets at the venue on the day of the show or in advance at the Olomouc Information Centre.

Moravské Divadlo OPERA, BALLET
(Map p250; box office 585 500 500; www.moravskedivadlo.cz; Horní náměstí 22; tickets 150-250Kč; box office 9am-6pm Mon-Fri) From opera to ballet, all affordably priced. Consult the website or ask at the Olomouc Information Centre to see what's on during your visit. Buy tickets online or at the theatre box office.

Moravian Philharmonic Olomouc CLASSICAL MUSIC
(Moravská Filharmonie Olomouc; Map p250; 585 206 520, tickets 585 513 392; www.mfo.cz; Horní náměstí 23; tickets 80-220Kč) The local orchestra presents regular concerts and hosts Olomouc's International Organ Festival. Buy tickets one week in advance at the Olomouc Information Centre or at the venue one hour before the performance starts.

WORTH A TRIP

THE VILLAGE OF ŠTRAMBERK

The village of Štramberk, nestled on the slopes of White Mountain (Bílá hora), is a pristine slice of northern Moravia that's reachable from Olomouc by bus or car, via the town of Nový Jičín.

The main attractions here are the undisturbed rural setting and a ruined clifftop castle you can hike to for views across the surrounding valleys. Oh, and there's a terrific microbrewery here too, so you'll have somewhere to recover after you've finished your walk.

The path up Bílá hora starts north of Štramberk's main square and passes through a stone gate inscribed 'Cuius Regio – Eius Religio – 1111' ('Whose Place – His Place – 1111'). On the slopes are the remains of the Gothic castle walls; climb the 166 steps up the tower.

The **Štramberk Municipal Brewery** (Městský Pivovar; 602 759 256; www.relaxvpodhuri.cz/cs/gastronomie/mestsky-pivovar-stramberk; náměstí 5; mains 100-200Kč; noon-10pm Sun-Thu, to midnight Fri & Sat;) is the real centre of activity, offering its own light and dark beers as well as bar snacks and full meals. Be sure to try *Štramberské uši* (Štramberk ears), conical ginger biscuits with honey and spices, usually served with cream. According to legend, the ears originally belonged to unfortunate Tatar prisoners of war.

The **Štramberk Municipal Information Centre** (Městské informační centrum; 558 840 617; www.stramberk.cz; náměstí 9; 8am-noon & 12.30-5pm May-Sep, to 4pm Tue-Sat Oct-Apr) is situated near the square. Staff can help to find and book accommodation.

Buses for Štramberk leave hourly most days from Nový Jičín (a stopover on most Olomouc–Ostrava buses). The ride takes about 20 minutes and costs about 25Kč.

Hospoda u Musea LIVE MUSIC
(Ponorka; Map p250; www.ponorka.com; třída 1. máje 8; 10am-2am Mon-Fri; 2, 3, 4, 6) Usually known by its nickname 'Ponorka' (literally 'submarine'), this is possibly the loudest, smokiest and most crowded rock club-pub in the Czech Republic (and that's saying something). The scene is mostly ageing rockers and punks still living in the good ol' days, but on occasional evenings there are legendary concerts.

Information

Olomouc Information Centre (Olomoucká Informační Služba; Map p250; 585 513 385; www.tourism.olomouc.eu; Horní náměstí; 9am-7pm) Though Olomouc's information centre is short on language skills, it's very helpful when it comes to securing maps, brochures and tickets for events around town. It also offers regular daily sightseeing tours of the Town Hall (30Kč), and from mid-June to mid-September daily guided one-hour sightseeing tours of the city centre (70Kč).

Getting There & Away

BUS

Olomouc is connected by around 15 buses daily to/from Brno (90Kč, 1¼ hours). Regional bus service is excellent. The best way of getting to Prague, however, is by train. The **bus station** (Autobusové nádraží Olomouc; 585 313 848; www.vlak-bus.cz; Sladkovského 142/37; 1, 2, 3, 4, 5, 6, 7) is located just behind the train station, about 2km east of the centre.

TRAIN

Olomouc is on a main international rail line, with regular services from both Prague (220Kč, two to three hours) and Brno (100Kč, 1½ hours). From Prague, you can take normal trains or faster, high-end private trains run by **Student Agency's RegioJet** (RegioJet; 841 101 101; www.studentagency.cz; Riegrova 28; 9am-6pm Mon-Fri; 2, 3, 4, 6) or **LEO Express** (220 311 700; www.le.cz; Jeremenkova 23, Main Train Station; 5.45am-9.45pm; 1, 2, 3, 4, 5, 6, 7). Buy tickets online or at ticket counters in either train station. Olomouc's **train station** (Olomouc hlavní nádraží; 221 111 122; www.cd.cz; Jeremenkova; 1, 2, 3, 4, 5, 6, 7) is around 2km east of the centre and accessible via several tram lines.

KROMĚŘÍŽ

POP 29,035

Sleepy Kroměříž is worth a detour if you happen to be in this part of the country. The main draw is the sumptuous baroque Archbishop's Chateau, with its commanding tower, rococo interiors and even a certifiable masterpiece: Titian's *The Flaying of Marsyas*. The palace is a Unesco World Heritage Site and a great place to while away a few hours. Outside the palace, there are some attractive Renaissance and baroque churches and other buildings scattered about, and two lovely gardens: the formal Flower Garden and a sprawling park below the chateau itself. Kroměříž is also home to an excellent microbrewery, an essential retreat once you've taken in the sights.

Sights

Most visitors come to see the Archbishop's Chateau. After you've done that, meander over to the town's impressive main square, Velké náměstí. The 16th-century Renaissance town hall stands on the corner with Kovářská. At No 30 is the town's oldest pharmacy, U Zlatého lva, established in 1675. The cobblestone square also has a decorative fountain and plague column.

Archbishop's Chateau CASTLE
(Arcibiskupský zámek; ☎573 502 011; www.zamek-kromeriz.cz; Zámek; main tour in English adult/concession 300/200Kč, picture gallery 90/60Kč; ⏲9am-4.30pm Tue-Sun Jul-Aug, to 3.30pm Tue-Sun May, Jun & Sep, to 2.30pm Sat & Sun only Apr & Oct) The Unesco-protected Archbishop's Chateau dates from the late 17th century and is Kroměříž's big-ticket sight. Its 84m-high baroque tower, visible for kilometres around, is the main attraction, along with impressive interiors, boasting baroque and rococo murals, an impressive art gallery with works by the Venetian master Titian (including *The Flaying of Marsyas*) and other luminaries, as well as the castle grounds.

Entry is by guided tour only, and several different tours are available (see the website). Most visitors will be satisfied with the 50-minute main tour of the historic rooms and tower, referred to as the *'reprezentační sály'* tour. The beautiful gardens below the castle are open year-round and free to visit.

Kroměříž Museum MUSEUM
(muzeum Kroměřížska; ☎573 338 388; www.muzeum-km.cz; Velké náměstí 38; adult/concession 60/30Kč; ⏲9am-noon & 1-5pm Tue-Sun) The biggest draw here is a permanent collection of the works of Czech painter and graphic artist Max Švabinský, who was born in Kroměříž in 1873. Several rooms of Švabinský's paintings and sketches are located on the 1st floor, while the top floor is dedicated to wildlife. The cellar holds an interesting exhibition of archaeological finds (information only in Czech).

Flower Garden GARDENS
(Květná zahrada; ☎cash desk 723 962 891; www.zamek-kromeriz.cz; ulice Gen Svobody; adult/concession 70/45Kč; ⏲9am-6.30pm May-Sep, to 5.30pm Apr, to 4.30pm Oct & Mar, to 3.30pm Nov & Feb) This 17th-century baroque garden is managed by the Archbishop's Chateau, but is located on the opposite side of town, about a 15-minute walk west of the chateau. The appeal here is an immaculately kept formal garden. The main sights are a frequently photographed rotunda and colonnade. Enter from Gen Svobody street.

Sleeping

Kroměříž has a handful of pleasant, reasonably priced hotels and pensions. Book in advance over summer weekends; otherwise, landing a room is not difficult.

Hotel Excellent HOTEL €
(☎737 122 849; www.excellent.tunker.com; Riegrovo náměstí 163/7; s/d 900/1300Kč;) This hotel offers brightly furnished rooms and a big buffet breakfast, with a central location on a quiet square about a five-minute walk from the Archbishop's Chateau. While it lacks the polish of a couple of other places in town, it's nevertheless good value and a decent choice for a short stay.

Hotel Černý Orel HOTEL €€
(☎573 332 769; www.cerny-orel.eu; Velké náměstí 24; s 1000-1300Kč, d 1200-1600Kč;) One of the nicest hotels in town just happens to occupy prime real estate above the town's highly recommended restaurant-microbrewery (p256). The rooms have a clean, modern look and are equipped with fancy baths and high-end amenities such as flat-screen TVs and DVD players. Book in advance on weekends in summer.

Hotel La Fresca BOUTIQUE HOTEL €€
(☎573 335 404; www.lafresca.cz; Velké náměstí 109/55; s 1100-1300Kč, d 1400-1800Kč;) La Fresca occupies a beautifully restored 16th-century burgher's house, retaining some of the original interior elements such as wood floors, high ceilings and exposed brick in some rooms. The apartments feature furnishings that recall 19th-century Biedermeier and art-nouveau styles. The in-house restaurant is very good. Book well in advance in summer.

Hotel Octárna HOTEL €€
(☎573 505 655; www.octarna.cz; Tovačovského 318; s 1150-1400Kč, d 1500-2050Kč; P ⊖ @ ☕) This small hotel is tucked away inside a quiet, shaded courtyard that once belonged to a Franciscan monastery. From the original Max Švabinský paintings on the garden wall to the clean and modern rooms, everything feels classy and well taken care of. The location is a short stroll from the main square.

Eating & Drinking

Radniční Sklípek CZECH €
(☎608 117 226; www.radnicnikm.cz; Kovářská 20/2; mains 80-140Kč; ⊙10am-10pm Mon-Fri, to midnight Sat, to 6pm Sun) This cute and cosy subterranean space just off Velké náměstí offers good-value Czech dishes such as chicken schnitzel served with potato salad. The homemade soups are brought to the table in big tureens for the whole family. An excellent choice for lunch.

Green Bar VEGETARIAN €
(☎724 176 926; www.greenbar.717.cz; Ztracená 68; mains 50-80Kč; ⊙11.30am-4pm Mon-Thu, to 2.30pm Fri; ✎ 👪) Salads and veggie main dishes and vegan entrées, a nonsmoking environment and a kids' play area add up to a family-friendly joint.

★**Černý Orel** CZECH €€
(☎573 332 769; www.pivovar-kromeriz.cz; Velké náměstí 24; mains 160-300Kč; ⊙11am-midnight; ☕) Some of the best food in this part of Moravia is served at this microbrewery on the main square. Choose from appetisers such as duck crackling and liver to a full range of duck, pork and venison mains. Pair your meal with one of the house brews, such as the 17° dark with hints of caramel and coffee. Reservations essential.

Information

Tourist Information Centre (Informační Centrum Kroměříž; ☎573 321 408; www.kromeriz.eu; Velké náměstí 115; ⊙9am-5pm Mon-Fri year-round, plus 9am-5pm Sat & Sun May-Sep, 9am-2pm Sat Oct-Apr) This extremely helpful tourist information office can provide free maps, advise on eating and sleeping options, and help sort out onward transport, including selling tickets on Student Agency buses to Zlín and Brno. There's a computer for free web-surfing (maximum 15 minutes).

Getting There & Away

BUS

Buses are generally more frequent and direct than trains. There are regular buses, including Student Agency coaches, to/from Brno (85Kč, 1¼ hours) and Olomouc (60Kč, 1½ hours). The **bus station** (Stoličkova, cnr Nádražní) is a 10-minute walk northeast of the centre, next to the train station. Buy tickets at the tourist information centre.

TRAIN

Train service to Kroměříž is infrequent and almost always requires a change; it makes more sense to take a direct bus. From Brno (80Kč, 1½ hours) change in Kojetín and from Olomouc (75Kč, one hour) change in Kojetín, or Hulín. See www.vlak-bus.cz for timetables. The **train station** (Vlakové nádraží; ☎221 111 122; www.cd.cz; Nádražní 3) is a 10-minute walk northeast of the centre.

Understand the Czech Republic

PRAGUE & THE CZECH REPUBLIC TODAY. 258

Amid a rapidly changing world political landscape, Czechs are struggling to find their own direction.

HISTORY 260

From the centre of the Holy Roman Empire to a Habsburg backwater, Prague and the Czech Republic are back on top.

CZECH LIFE. 269

Czechs find themselves coping with ethnic diversity while trying to remain true to their first love: ice hockey.

ARTS IN THE CZECH REPUBLIC 273

Prague counts as one of Europe's great musical capitals and the country has a rich tradition in sculpture and photography.

ARCHITECTURE 278

From Gothic to art nouveau, a trip to Prague is like taking a crash course in European architecture.

THE CZECH REPUBLIC ON PAGE & SCREEN. . . . 282

The territory of today's Czech Republic was home to Franz Kafka, Milan Kundera and Miloš Forman.

A NATION OF BEER LOVERS 286

Czech beer is widely considered the world's best, and Czechs lead the league in per capita beer consumption.

Prague & the Czech Republic Today

These days the Czech Republic finds itself caught up in the wider international debate over the benefits of EU membership and cross-border immigration. Three decades after the Velvet Revolution, visitors aren't likely to notice anything other than a thriving economy and bustling tourism sector, though the country's overall direction feels less certain than it has since the fall of communism.

Best on Film

Amadeus (1985) Mozart's love affair with Bohemia gets brilliant treatment.

Kolya (1996) Velvet Revolution–era Prague never looked lovelier.

Loves of a Blonde (1965) Miloš Forman's 'New Wave' classic.

Burning Bush (2013) HBO miniseries on Jan Palach, the Czech student who immolated himself in 1969.

Anthropoid (2016) Big-budget WWII spectacle on the assassination of Nazi leader Reinhard Heydrich.

Best in Print

The Unbearable Lightness of Being (Milan Kundera; 1984) Life before the 1968 Warsaw Pact invasion.

I Served the King of England (Bohumil Hrabal; 1990) Prague's Hotel Paříž is the backdrop to this classic.

The Castle (Franz Kafka; 1926) Wonder which castle Kafka was thinking about?

The Good Soldier Švejk (Jaroslav Hašek; 1923) Hašek's absurdist novel is set throughout the Czech Republic.

My Merry Mornings (Ivan Klíma; 1986) The sweeter side of life under communism.

The Czech Republic & World Politics

Leaders and citizens of the Czech Republic have found themselves grappling with the consequences of the major international events of today, including the historic vote in the UK to leave the EU and the election of Donald Trump as US president.

While it's hard to pigeon-hole Czech President Miloš Zeman – an old-school socialist with political ties that go back to communist times – he's adapting to the new era of world politics. Zeman has embraced the Brexit vote and gone one step further, calling on the Czech Republic to hold a referendum on the country's membership in both the EU and NATO.

To outside observers, Zeman appears to be conforming to a pattern emerging from leaders all around Central Europe. Voters in Poland, Slovakia and Hungary have all brought to power in recent years politicians who remain suspicious of the EU and who place significant emphasis on the perceived negative effects – legitimate or overblown – of rapid social change, multiculturalism and immigration. Here, as with just about everywhere else, Czechs appear to be firmly – and evenly – divided on the issues.

From Economic Crisis to Boom

After wallowing for years in the wake of the global recession, the Czech National Bank took a dramatic decision in 2013 to devalue the currency, the crown, by 5% with respect to the euro. The move took markets by surprise at the time and was roundly criticised as potentially reigniting inflation.

With hindsight, though, it can safely be said that the naysayers have been proved wrong. Boosted by big inflows of foreign investment (including massive, EU-funded capital projects) and a strong demand for Czech exports, the economy has boomed for the past several years. After declining by around 0.5% in 2013, the economy has steadily expanded each year since. At the same time, inflation has flat-lined; prices have risen by just 0.1% during each of the past few years.

Signs of prosperity are everywhere. A near 25-year boom in tourism has helped Prague to become the overall seventh-richest region in the EU. The full benefits of the expansion have not been felt uniformly, though, as parts of northern and western Bohemia, as well as northern Moravia, continue to grapple with the effects of deindustrialisation.

Life after Havel

The death of Václav Havel, the country's first post-communist president and undisputed moral authority of the 1989 Velvet Revolution, in 2011, aged 75, provoked an uncharacteristically intense outpouring of grief from the normally stoic Czech people. Tens of thousands of people placed candles at the statue of St Wenceslas, and thousands more lined up days later to file past his coffin and pay their final respects.

Havel's passing left a moral vacuum at the heart of the country that in many ways has yet to be filled. While he arguably wasn't always an effective president, his conscience was steadfast and his philosophical clarity in murky times is certainly missed. It's a local parlour game to wonder what Havel might have made of the resurgence of nationalist politics around Europe, particularly in Central Europe. To many, especially younger Czechs, the moral component to public life appears to be missing.

In terms of domestic politics, the country continues to ride a knife-edge. Neither major centrist party – the right-leaning Civic Democratic Party (ODS) or the left-leaning Social Democrats (ČSSD) – has been able to cobble together a truly lasting consensus, so the country seems to lurch from side to side and scandal to scandal with each election cycle.

At the time of research, the country was being led by a fragile left-right coalition, linking the Social Democrats with an upstart liberal, pro-business movement called 'ANO' (Yes), headed by a Slovak billionaire with a Czech passport, Andrej Babiš. The country's first-ever direct popular vote for the presidency in 2013 (until then the president was chosen by parliament), swept long-time Social Democratic politician Miloš Zeman into office. Zeman's term in office runs to 2018.

POPULATION: **10.6 MILLION**

AREA: **78,867 SQ KM**

GDP GROWTH (2016): **2.3%**

INFLATION RATE (2016): **1.9%**

AVERAGE MONTHY SALARY (2017): **29,320KČ**

if the Czech Republic were 100 people

86 would be Czech
4 would be Ukranian
2 would be Slovakian
2 would be Russian
1 would be Vietnamese
5 would be other

religion

(% of population)

Agnostic, atheist or irreligious

Roman Catholic

1

Protestant

Other

population per sq km

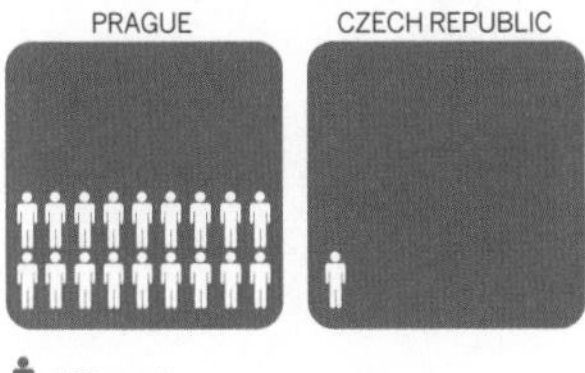

History

While visitors still tend to see the Czech Republic as part of 'Eastern Europe', for more than a thousand years Bohemia and Moravia have stood at the heart of European affairs – in both good times and bad. Over the centuries, Prague has served at various times as Europe's leading city, while the territory of the Czech Republic has found itself, reluctantly, in the middle of the continent's most destructive wars.

The Early Years with the Celts

There's been human habitation on the territory of the modern-day Czech Republic for some 600,000 years, with permanent communities since around 4000 BC, but it's the Celts, who came to the area around 500 BC, that arouse the most interest. The name 'Bohemia' for the western province of the Czech Republic derives from one of the most successful of these Celtic tribes, the Boii. Traces of Boii culture have been found as far away as southern Germany, leading some archaeologists to posit a relationship between Celts here and those in France, and possibly even further afield to tribes in the British Isles.

Archaeologists working near the town of Roztoky, northwest of Prague, have unearthed what may be the largest and oldest of the early Slavic settlements, dating from the early 6th century.

In Come the Slavs

It's unclear what prompted the great migration of peoples across Europe in the 6th and 7th centuries, but during this time large populations of Slavs began arriving in Central Europe from the east, driving out the Celts and pushing German tribes further to the west. The newcomers established several settlements along the Vltava, including one near the present site of Prague Castle and another upriver at Vyšehrad.

It was a highly unstable time, with the new arrivals under threat from incoming peoples such as the Avars. A Frankish trader named Samo briefly succeeded in uniting the Slavs to repel the Avars, but the Slavs quickly resumed their squabbling.

The Myth of Libuše

Fittingly for a country and culture that embrace so much mystery, the origins of the Bohemian (and later Czech) capital are shrouded in a fairy

TIMELINE

500 BC

Celtic tribes thrive in the territory of the modern-day Czech Republic, building settlements whose remains will later be discovered in and around Prague.

AD 500

Slavic tribes enter Central Europe during the Great Migration, forming settlements throughout modern Bohemia and Moravia, and especially along the Vltava River.

Early 600s

Princess Libuše, the fabled founder of the Přemysl dynasty, looks out over the Vltava valley in Prague and predicts that a great city will emerge there someday.

tale. Princess Libuše, the daughter of early ruler Krok, is said to have stood on a hill near Prague's Vyšehrad Citadel one day in the 7th or 8th century and predicted a glorious city would one day rise around her. According to the legend, Libuše needed to find a strong suitor who could yield sturdy heirs to the Bohemian throne. Passing over a field of eligible bachelors, including some sickly looking royals, she selected a simple ploughman: Přemysl. She chose well. The Přemysl dynasty would go on to rule for some 400 years.

In the 9th century, the Přemysl prince Bořivoj selected an outcropping in Prague's Hradčany district to build Prague Castle, the dynasty's seat. Amazingly, the castle – the official seat of the Czech presidency – remains the centre of power to this day.

Christianity became the state religion under the rule of the pious Wenceslas (Václav in Czech), the Duke of Bohemia (r 925–29) and now the chief patron saint of the Czech people (immortalised on horseback at the top of Prague's Wenceslas Square). Wenceslas was the 'Good King Wenceslas' of the well-known Christmas carol, written in 1853 by English clergyman John Mason Neale. Wenceslas's conversion to Christianity is said to have angered his mother and his brother, Boleslav, who ended up killing the young duke in a fit of jealousy.

Despite the dysfunctional family relations, the Přemysls proved to be highly effective rulers. During the 13th century, the Přemysl lands stretched from modern-day Silesia (near the Czech–Polish border) to the Mediterranean Sea. The last Přemysl ruler, King Wenceslas III (Václav III), was murdered in Olomouc in 1306 under circumstances that are still not clear to this day.

Top Castles & Chateaux

- *Český Krumlov State Castle*
- *Karlštejn Castle*
- *Prague Castle*
- *Hluboká Chateau*
- *Mikulov Chateau*

During the 17th and 18th centuries, both Bohemia and Moravia received major baroque facelifts, including the statues on Prague's Charles Bridge and the construction of St Nicholas Church in Malá Strana. This was mainly the work of the Austrians and the Jesuits, eager to mark their triumph.

The Great Moravian Empire

Prague and Bohemia get so much attention from visitors and scholars that it's maybe a surprise to find out that the earliest Slav state in the region actually arose in Moravia, to the east. The Moravian empire formed in the early 9th century and reached its apex under ruler Svatopluk I (r 870–94). It eventually encompassed all of modern-day Moravia, as well parts of the Czech Republic, Slovakia, Poland and Hungary.

It was here in Moravia, where the fabled Bulgarian monks, brothers Cyril (826–69) and Methodius (815–85), carried out their most important work. The brothers were called in to help convert the Slavs to Christianity. They wound up spreading their liturgical language, Old Church Slavonic, and inventing an alphabet, the Glagolitic, that later became the basis for today's Cyrillic script. The brothers are celebrated every year on 5 July – Sts Cyril and Methodius Day.

Alas, the Moravian empire did not last long on the world stage. By the early 10th century, Magyar incursions had eroded much of the empire's

870s

Prince Bořivoj begins construction of Prague Castle in Hradčany to serve as the seat of his Přemysl dynasty – as it will for kings, emperors and presidents for centuries to come.

870–894

The Moravian empire, formed in the early 9th century, reaches its apex under ruler Svatopluk I (r 870–894).

1278

Přemysl King Otakar II is thrashed by the Habsburgs at the Battle of Marchfeld (Moravské Pole in Czech) at the height of the Přemysl dynasty's influence.

1306

The last Přemysl king, Wenceslas III, is murdered, leaving no male heir. The dynasty passes to John of Luxembourg, who will give Bohemia its greatest ruler, his son Charles IV.

external territories. The eastern regions, in today's Slovakia, eventually fell under Hungarian domination. The western area – today's Moravian province – was eventually ceded to the Bohemian kingdom.

Charles IV & the Holy Roman Empire

It's hard to imagine that the Kingdom of Bohemia (including Moravia) will ever exceed the position of power it held in the 14th century, when Prague for a time became the seat of what was known then as the Holy Roman Empire, under Emperor Charles IV (Karel IV; r 1346–78).

The path to glory began predictably enough with the murder of Přemysl ruler Wenceslas III, in 1306, leaving no male successor to the throne. Eventually, John of Luxembourg (Jan Lucemburský to the Czechs) assumed the Bohemian throne through his marriage to Wenceslas III's daughter, Elyška, in 1310.

Following Emperor Sigismund's death, George of Poděbrady (Jiří z Poděbrad) ruled as Bohemia's one and only Hussite king (1452–71), with the backing of moderate Hussites, the Utraquists. By that time, however, the Hussite cause was lost and once-prosperous Bohemia lay in ruin.

Under the enlightened rule of John's son, Charles IV, Prague grew to become one of the continent's largest and most prosperous cities. Charles greatly expanded the limits of the city and commissioned both the bridge that now bears his name and St Vitus Cathedral, among other projects. He also established Charles University as the first university in Central Europe.

The Hussite Wars & Religious Strife

In contrast to the prosperous 14th century, the 15th century brought little but hardship and war to the territory of the Czech Republic. Much of the good of the preceding years was undone in a combination of religion-inspired violence and intolerance. The period witnessed the rise of an impassioned Church-reform movement led by Jan Hus. Hus's intentions to rid Rome's papal authorities of corruption were admirable, but his movement ended up dividing the country. In 1419, supporters of Hussite preacher Jan Želivský stormed Prague's New Town Hall and tossed several Catholic councillors out the windows – thus introducing the word 'defenestration' (throwing someone from a window in order to do him or her bodily harm) into the political lexicon.

The Hussites (as followers of Jan Hus were known) assumed control of Prague after the death of Holy Roman Emperor Wenceslas IV in 1419. The move sparked the first anti-Hussite crusade, launched in 1420 by Emperor Sigismund, with the support of many pro-Catholic rulers around Europe. Hussite commander Jan Žižka successfully defended the city in the Battle of Vítkov Hill, but the religious strife spilled into the countryside. The Hussites were split into factions – those wanting to make peace with the emperor and those wanting to fight to the end. The more radical Hussites, the Taborites, were ultimately defeated in battle at Lipany, east of Prague, in 1434.

1346

John of Luxembourg dies and Charles IV becomes Bohemian king. Later, he adds 'Holy Roman Emperor' to his list of titles. Prague booms as the seat of the empire.

6 July 1415

Religious reformer Jan Hus is burned at the stake at Konstanz, Germany, for refusing to recant his criticisms of the Catholic Church. His death inflames decades of religious strife.

30 July 1419

Angry Hussite supporters rush into the New Town Hall and toss several Catholic councillors out the window, introducing the word 'defenestration' to the world.

15th Century

The Hussite Wars – pitting radical reformers against Catholics and Hussite factions against each other – rage throughout Bohemia.

RELIGIOUS REFORMER JAN HUS

Jan Hus was the Czech lands' foremost (and one of Europe's earliest) Protestant Christian reformers, preceding Martin Luther and the Lutheran reformation by more than a century. Hus was born into a poor family in southern Bohemia in 1372. He studied at the Karolinum (Charles University) and eventually became dean of the philosophy faculty.

Like many of his colleagues at the time, Hus was inspired by the English philosopher and radical reformist theologian John Wycliffe. The corrupt practices of the Roman Catholic clergy proved to be an easy target for Wycliffe's criticisms and fuelled a growing Czech resentment of the wealth and corruption of the clergy.

In 1391 Prague reformers founded the Bethlehem Chapel, where sermons were given in Czech rather than Latin. Hus preached there for about 10 years, while continuing his duties at the university.

Hus's criticisms of the Catholic Church, particularly the practice of selling indulgences, endeared him to his followers but eventually put him in the Pope's black book. In fact, the Pope had him excommunicated in 1410, but Hus continued to preach. In 1415, he was invited to the Council of Constance in modern-day Germany to recant his views with the understanding that he would be granted safe passage. He refused to concede and was burned at the stake on 6 July 1415.

The Habsburgs Take Over

The weakening of the Bohemian kingdom due to the religious wars left both Bohemia and Moravia open to foreign intervention. Austria's Habsburg empire, ruled from Vienna, was able to take advantage and eventually came to dominate both regions. At first, in the mid-16th century, the Habsburgs were invited in by a weary Bohemian nobility weakened by constant warfare. Decades later, in 1620, the Austrians were able to cement their control over the region with a decisive military victory over Czech forces at Bílá Hora, near Prague. The Austrians would continue to rule over Bohemia and Moravia for another 300 years, until the emergence of independent Czechoslovakia at the end of WWI.

Though the Austrians are generally knocked in Czech history books, it must be admitted their leadership established some much needed stability. Indeed, the latter part of the 16th century under Habsburg Emperor Rudolf II (r 1576–1612) is considered a second 'golden age' in Czech history, comparable to Charles IV's rule in the 14th century. Eccentric Rudolf preferred Prague to his family's ancestral home in Vienna and moved the seat of the Habsburg empire to the Bohemian capital for the duration of his reign.

1583

Habsburg Emperor Rudolf II moves the dynasty's seat from Vienna to Prague. This second 'golden age' lasts three decades until Rudolf dies, when Protestant-Catholic tensions boil over.

23 May 1618

A Protestant mob throws two Catholic councillors and their secretary from a window at Prague Castle. This pushes the Habsburgs to start the Thirty Years' War.

1620

Czech soldiers, united under Protestant leader Frederick V, lose a crucial battle to Austrian Habsburg troops at Bílá Hora. It begins 300 years of Austrian rule.

October 1787

Wolfgang Amadeus Mozart, already more popular in Prague than Vienna, conducts the premiere of his opera *Don Giovanni* at the Estates Theatre near Old Town Square.

Rudolf is typically viewed by historians as something of a kook. He had a soft spot for esoteric pursuits such as soothsaying and alchemy, and populated his court with wags and conjurers from around Europe. The English mathematician and occultist John Dee and his less-esteemed countryman, Edward Kelly, were just two of the noted mystics Rudolf kept at the castle in an eternal quest to turn base metals into gold. It's also true, though, that Rudolf's tutelage led to real advances in science, particularly astronomy.

For all his successes, though, Rudolf failed to heal the age-old rift between Protestants and Catholics, and the end of his reign in 1612 saw those tensions again rise to the forefront. The breaking point came in 1618 with the 'Second Defenestration of Prague', when a group of Protestant noblemen stormed into a chamber at Prague Castle and tossed two Catholic councillors and their secretary out the window. The men survived – legend has it they fell onto a dung heap – but the damage was done. The act

JEWS IN THE CZECH LANDS

Both Bohemia and Moravia, for centuries, were relative safe havens for Jews. Prague, in particular, evolved into an important centre of Jewish life and scholarship, but towns like Mikulov and Třebíč in Moravia also developed into influential Jewish settlements.

In Prague, Jews first moved into a walled ghetto north of Old Town Square in about the 13th century, in response to directives from Rome that Jews and Christians should live separately. The Jews generally thrived under Emperor Rudolf II at the end of the 16th century. Rudolf encouraged a flowering of Jewish intellectual life and Mordechai Maisel, the mayor of the ghetto at the time, became Rudolf's finance minister and the city's wealthiest citizen. Another major figure at the time was Judah Loew ben Bezalel (Rabbi Loew), a prominent theologian, chief rabbi and student of the mystical teachings of the Cabbala. He's nowadays known as the creator of the legendary Golem (a kind of proto-robot made from the mud of the Vltava).

When they helped to repel the Swedes on Charles Bridge in 1648, the Jews won the favour of Habsburg Emperor Ferdinand III to the extent he had the ghetto enlarged. But a century later they were driven out of the city, only to be welcomed back later when the residents missed their business.

In the 1780s, Habsburg Emperor Joseph II (r 1780–90) outlawed many forms of discrimination, and in the 19th century the Jews won the right to live wherever they wanted. Many chose to leave the ghetto for nicer areas of the city. At the end of the 19th century, municipal authorities decided to clear the ghetto, which had become a slum.

The ghetto, renamed Josefov in Joseph II's honour, remained the spiritual heart of Prague's Jewish community. That came to a brutal end with the Nazi occupation during WWII. Today Prague is home to roughly 5000 Jews, a fraction of the community's former size.

3 July 1883

German-speaking Jewish writer Franz Kafka is born near Old Town Square. He'll lead a double life: mild-mannered insurance clerk by day, harried father of the modern novel by night.

October 1918

A newly independent Czechoslovakia (for the first time linking Bohemia, Moravia and Slovakia) is proclaimed at Prague's Municipal House (Obecní dům) in the final days of WWI.

1938

European powers meet in Munich, agreeing to Hitler's demand to annex the Sudetenland region. British PM Chamberlain declares 'peace in our time'.

March 1939

German soldiers cross the Czechoslovak frontier and occupy Bohemia and Moravia. Czechoslovak soldiers, ordered in advance not to resist, allow the Germans to enter without firing a shot.

sparked the Thirty Years' War, starting in 1618, that ultimately consumed the whole of Europe and left Bohemia and Moravia again in ruins.

Revival of the Czech Nation

Remarkably, though German was the official language, Czech language and culture managed to endure through the years of Austrian occupation. As the Habsburgs eased their grip in the 19th century, Prague – and to a lesser extent the Moravian capital, Brno – became centres of the Czech National Revival. The revival found its initial expression not in politics – outright political activity was forbidden – but in Czech-language literature and drama. Important figures included linguists Josef Jungmann and Josef Dobrovský, and František Palacký, author of *Dějiny národu českého* (The History of the Czech Nation).

While many of the countries in post-Napoleonic Europe were swept up by similar nationalist sentiments, social and economic factors gave the Czech revival particular strength. Educational reforms by Habsburg Empress Maria Theresa (r 1740–80) had given even the poorest Czechs access to schooling, and a vocal middle class was emerging through the Industrial Revolution.

The Moravian city of Olomouc served briefly (1848–49) as the centre of the Habsburg monarchy during the 1848 revolutions that threatened to topple the Habsburg empire. Emperor Franz Josef I was crowned in Olomouc in 1848 at the tender age of 18.

WWI & Czech Independence

For Czechs, the tragedy of WWI had one silver lining: the defeat of the Central powers, principally Germany and Austria-Hungary, left the Habsburg empire too weak to fight for its former holdings, paving the way for the creation of independent Czechoslovakia in 1918. Czech patriots Tomáš Masaryk and Edvard Beneš had spent part of the war years in the US, where they lobbied ceaselessly with Czech and Slovak émigré communities to win American backing for a joint state, Czechoslovakia, that would link ethnic Czechs (Bohemians and Moravians) with their linguistic cousins, Slovaks, further to the east.

This plea appealed especially to the idealistic American president, Woodrow Wilson, and his belief in the self-determination of peoples. The most workable solution appeared to be a single federal state of two equal republics, and this was spelled out in agreements signed in Cleveland, Ohio, in 1915 and Pittsburgh, Pennsylvania, in 1918 (both cities having large populations of Czechs and Slovaks).

As WWI drew to a close, the newly created Czechoslovakia declared its independence, with Allied support, on 28 October 1918. Prague became the capital and the popular Masaryk, a writer and political philosopher, the new republic's first president.

Austrian archduke and heir to the throne, Franz Ferdinand d'Este – whose 1914 assassination in Sarajevo sparked WWI – had a Czech wife and a main residence in Central Bohemia, Konopiště Chateau. He was not a fan of the imperial capital, Vienna, and preferred to spend as little time there as possible.

27 May 1942

Czechoslovak patriots assassinate German Reichsprotektor Reinhard Heydrich in Prague. They hide in a church but are trapped by Nazi soldiers. Some take their own lives; others are killed.

5 May 1945

Czechs begin an armed uprising against the Germans, liberating the capital city after three days. The Germans are granted free exit in exchange for agreeing not to destroy the city.

9 May 1945

The Soviet Army formally liberates the city, though most German soldiers are already gone. Later the communists recognise this as the official day of liberation.

1948

Communists stage a bloodless coup. Party leader Gottwald proclaims the news in Prague's Old Town Square. The coup leads to four decades of oppressive communist rule.

READING UP ON CZECH HISTORY

The Czech Republic is not lacking in well-written historical accounts in English. Some of the best include:

The Coast of Bohemia (Derek Sayer) The title plays on Shakespeare's comic line from *The Winter's Tale* about the 'coast of Bohemia'. A serious, readable account of the Czechs' struggle over the centuries to define themselves as a people and defend their land.

Under a Cruel Star, A Life in Prague 1941–1968 (Heda Margolius Kovály) The author, Jewish and born in Prague, had the double misfortune of being sent to Auschwitz during WWII, only to survive the war and marry an up-and-coming communist who was executed in the show trials of the 1950s.

Prague in Danger (Peter Demetz) Demetz's work is partly a classical history and partly a lively and moving chronicle of his own family – Demetz's mother was Jewish and died at Terezín.

Prague Winter: A Personal Story of Remembrance and War, 1937–1948 (Madeleine Albright) The former US Secretary of State grew up in Prague and describes her recollections of Czechoslovakia during the Nazi occupation and WWII.

A Taste of Freedom, then Nazi Domination

Czechoslovakia, in the two decades between independence and the 1938 Munich agreement (that paved the way for the Nazi German invasion), was a remarkably successful state. Even now, both Czechs and Slovaks consider the 'First Republic' another golden age of immense cultural and economic achievement.

Czechoslovakia's proximity to Nazi Germany, and its sizeable German minority in the border area known as the Sudetenland, made the country a tempting target for German Nazi leader Adolf Hitler. Hitler correctly judged that neither Britain nor France had an appetite for war, and at a conference in Munich in 1938, Hitler demanded that Germany be allowed to annex the Sudetenland. British Prime Minister Neville Chamberlain acquiesced, famously calling Germany's designs on Czechoslovakia a 'quarrel in a faraway country between people of whom we know nothing'. To this day, the words 'Munich' and 'appeasement' are intertwined in the minds of many Czechs.

On 15 March 1939 Germany occupied all of Bohemia and Moravia, declaring the region a 'protectorate', while Slovakia was permitted 'independence' as long as it remained a Nazi puppet state. During the war, Prague was spared significant physical damage, though the Germans destroyed the Czech resistance. Around two-thirds of Bohemia and Moravia's Jewish population of 120,000 perished in the war.

August 1968

Soviet-led Warsaw Pact forces invade Czechoslovakia to end 'Prague Spring' reforms. Hardliner Gustáv Husák replaces communist leader Alexander Dubček.

January 1969

Student Jan Palach immolates himself at Prague's Wenceslas Square to protest the Warsaw Pact invasion. Thousands visit the square to mark his memory.

1977

Czechoslovakia reaches a political and cultural nadir during 'normalisation'. Dissidents sign Charter 77, demanding that the regime meet its international human rights obligations.

1989

Police violently halt student protests at Prague's Národní třída, sparking mass demonstrations. The communists relinquish power – the 'Velvet Revolution'.

On 5 May 1945, with the war drawing to a close, the citizens of Prague staged an uprising against the Germans. The Red Army was advancing from the east and US troops had made it as far as Plzeň to the west, but were holding back from liberating the city in deference to their Soviet allies. Many people died in the uprising before the Germans pulled out on 8 May, having been granted free passage out in return for an agreement not to destroy more buildings.

In 1945 Czechoslovakia was reconstituted as an independent state. One of its first acts was the expulsion of the remaining Sudeten Germans from the borderlands. By 1947, some 2½ million ethnic Germans had been stripped of their Czechoslovak citizenship and forcibly expelled to Germany and Austria.

Czechoslovakia could have been liberated by the US (instead of the Soviet Union) in WWII. US soldiers, under the command of General George S Patton, had occupied the western Czech city of Plzeň as early as 6 May 1945 and were poised to take the capital. Despite Patton's pleas, US commanders called off the American advance to allow the Russians the 'honour' of liberating Prague.

From Hitler's Arms into Stalin's

Czechoslovak euphoria at the end of the war did not last long. The communists seized power just three years later, in 1948. While these days the takeover is usually viewed as a naked power grab by Stalin's henchmen, the reality is more complicated. For many Czechs, WWII had tarnished the image of the Western democracies, and Stalin's Soviet Union commanded deep respect.

By the 1950s, however, this initial enthusiasm faded as communist economic policies bankrupted the country and a wave of repression sent thousands to labour camps. In a series of Stalin-style purges staged by the KSČ (Communist Party of Czechoslovakia) in the early 1950s, many people, including top members of the party itself, were executed.

In the 1960s, Czechoslovakia enjoyed something of a renaissance, and under the leadership of reform communist Alexander Dubček, became a beacon for idealists wanting to chart a 'third way' between communism and capitalism. The reform movement was dubbed 'Socialism with a Human Face' and mixed elements of democracy with continued state control over the economy. This easing of hardline communism became known around the world as the 'Prague Spring'.

In the end, though, it was the movement's success that eventually undid it. Soviet leaders were alarmed by the prospect of a partially democratic society within the Eastern bloc and any potential spillover it might have in Poland and Hungary. The Prague Spring was eventually crushed by a Soviet-led invasion of Eastern bloc states on the night of 20 and 21 August 1968. While the entire country was invaded, much of the actual fighting took place in Prague, near the top of central Wenceslas Square.

In 1969 Dubček was replaced by hardliner Gustáv Husák and exiled to the Slovak forestry department. Thousands of people were expelled from the party and lost their jobs. Many left the country, while others were

1993

The Czech and Slovak republics agree peacefully to split into independent countries, formally bringing an end to Czechoslovakia. The split becomes known as the 'Velvet Divorce'.

1998

The Czech national ice hockey team defeats Russia 1-0 to win gold at the Nagano Winter Olympics, the nation's first and only Olympic gold medal in the sport.

August 2002

Several Prague districts and the metro tunnels are inundated in the Vltava River's biggest modern-era flood. Damages cost several billion euros and spark redevelopment in hard-hit areas.

1 May 2004

The Czech Republic achieves its biggest foreign policy objective since the Velvet Revolution and joins the EU, along with several other former communist countries.

relegated to being manual labourers and street cleaners. The two decades of stagnation until 1989 are known today as the period of 'normalisation'.

Velvet Revolution & Divorce

Prague was the major objective in the 1968 Warsaw Pact invasion. Soviet special forces, with the help of the Czech secret police, secured Prague airport for Soviet transport planes. At the end of the first day of fighting, 58 people had died.

The year 1989 was a momentous one throughout Eastern Europe as communist governments fell like dominoes in Hungary, Poland, East Germany, Bulgaria and Romania. But the revolution that toppled communism in Czechoslovakia was perhaps the greatest of them all. It remains the gold standard around the world for peaceful anti-government protest.

Ironically, the Velvet Revolution actually had its start in a paroxysm of violence on the night of 17 November, when Czech riot police began attacking a group of peaceful student demonstrators in Prague. The protesters had organised an officially sanctioned demonstration in memory of students executed by the Nazis in 1939, but the marchers had always intended to make this demonstration a protest against the communist regime. What they didn't count on was the fierce resistance of the police, who confronted the crowd of about 50,000 on the city's Národní třída and beat and arrested hundreds of protesters.

Czechs were electrified by this wanton police violence, and the following days saw nonstop demonstrations by students, artists, and finally most of the population, peaking at a rally on Prague's Letná Hill that drew some 750,000 people. Leading dissidents, with playwright and activist Václav Havel at the forefront, formed an anticommunist coalition, which negotiated the government's resignation on 3 December. A 'government of national understanding' was formed with the communists as a minority group. Havel was elected president by the Federal Assembly on 29 December.

After 23 years of complaints that the name 'Czech Republic' was too formal, the government in 2016 finally passed a ruling to give the name 'Czechia' official status. It's been slow to catch on.

Almost immediately after the revolution, problems arose between Czechs and Slovaks. The Slovaks had long harboured grievances against the dominant Czechs, and many Slovaks dreamed of having their own state. On 1 January 1993, amid much hand-wringing on both sides, especially from Havel, the Czechs and Slovaks peacefully divided into independent states.

5 April 2009
US President Barack Obama addresses thousands of well-wishers at a speech near Prague Castle during which he promotes a policy of eventual nuclear disarmament.

2011
Former president and leader of the Velvet Revolution, Václav Havel, dies after a long battle with cancer. The nation goes into prolonged mourning.

January 2013
Miloš Zeman is elected president, replacing Václav Klaus who served 10 years in office, in the country's first-ever direct popular vote for president.

July 2016
Zeman shocks the EU by proposing a referendum be held to determine the Czechs' continued membership in both NATO and the EU.

Czech Life

From the outside, at least, the Czech Republic seems like a straightforward place. But look a little closer and this small, Central European country of just 10 million people reveals its societal complexities. While the Czech Republic is undeniably a country of beautiful churches and cathedrals, these days, the majority of the population are actually atheist or agnostic. And though overwhelmingly populated by Czechs, the country is also home to several immigrant communities, most notably from Vietnam and Ukraine.

A Nation of Czechs & Vietnamese

Compared with Western European countries such as Germany, France and the Netherlands, the Czech Republic remains relatively homogenous. According to the 2011 census, nearly 95% of people living here identify themselves as either Czech or Moravian. (The figures mask the number of Roma in the country, estimated by the Budapest-based European Roma Rights Centre at somewhere between 200,000 and 300,000.) Of the rest, only about 2% are Slovaks, with smaller numbers of Poles, Germans and Hungarians. But it wasn't always this way. Until the start of WWII, the territory of Czechoslovakia was home to around three million ethnic Germans (about 30% of the total population at the time). Many of those people were either killed in the war or forcibly expelled in the months after the war ended.

What the census numbers don't reflect, however, is the increasingly diverse mix of people coming into the Czech Republic to work, either permanently or temporarily. These include relatively large populations of Ukrainians and Russians, and, perhaps most curiously, Vietnamese. Partly because of close ties forged between the former communist government and the government of Vietnam, the Czech Republic has emerged as the destination of choice for Vietnamese people moving to Europe.

Hard numbers are difficult to come by, but it's thought that Vietnamese guest workers may total as many as 90,000. Indeed, the Vietnamese surname Nguyen is one of the more common family names in the country, according to a survey conducted by Czech website www.kdejsme.cz. Most Vietnamese people live in Prague or the western Bohemian city of Cheb. Many make a living by running neighbourhood grocery shops, known in Czech as a *večerka*.

After hundreds of thousands of Syrian refugees crossed into the EU in 2015 and 2016, the Czech Government voted against EU relocation proposals to relieve pressure on countries such as Italy and Greece. By 2016, only 1156 Middle Eastern refugees had applied for asylum in the Czech Republic.

A Modern-Day Lack of Faith

Despite having an active and often violent religious history that stretches back several centuries, Czechs take a much more hands-off approach to the question of organised religion. Surveys indicate that well more than half of all Czechs are either atheists or agnostics. Just 16% or so of the population professes a strong belief in God, according to a 2010 Eurobarometer poll on the subject – that's the lowest percentage in the EU.

The largest church in the country is the Roman Catholic, which claims membership of around a third of the population (including, if the Eurobarometer numbers are to be trusted, a fair number of nonbelievers). This compares to neighbouring Poland, where 90% of the population say they are Catholic, and Slovakia, where the figure is around 70%. Protestant and other denominations make up another 5% or so.

A national scepticism towards organised faith can be traced as far back as Jan Hus in the 15th century. It was Hus, after all, who railed against the excesses of the Catholic Church in his day. In addition, Catholicism has always been bound to some degree with the Austrian conquest and overzealous efforts by Jesuit monks in the 16th and 17th centuries to convert the local population. In more recent times, the former communist government went out of its way to discourage organised religion, going so far as to lock up priests and close down churches.

There are anecdotal signs of a modest rebirth in faith. More and more couples are choosing to be married in a church, and parents are increasingly opting to baptise their children. Also, interest appears to be growing in more esoteric and spiritual beliefs.

Guest Workers by Country

Ukraine (130,000 estimated)

Slovakia (100,000)

Vietnam (90,000)

Russia (40,000)

World Beaters at Ice Hockey

Czechs excel at many international sports, including tennis and speed skating, but they are true masters when it comes to ice hockey. Since the debut of the annual World Hockey Championships in 1920, the Czech and Czechoslovak national teams have won gold no less than 12 times and taken home a total of 45 medals. Ice hockey plays such a role in the country's psyche that if you ask a Czech what the most significant year was in modern history, you might not hear 1989 or 1968, but rather 1998. That was the year the Czechs beat the Russians 1-0 for gold at the Nagano Winter Olympics, and the country erupted with joy.

These successes are no doubt rooted in the competitive nature of the junior leagues all the way up to the country's national hockey league, the Extraliga, where perennial powers HC Sparta Praha (www.hcsparta.cz) and HC Slavia Praha (www.hc-slavia.cz) battle for the top spot.

Czech players are a staple on the rosters of many teams in the North American National Hockey League. Past greats – and still household names – include Jaromír Jágr (b 1972), who won the Stanley Cup with Pittsburgh in 1991 and '92, and who still plays for the NHL's Florida Panthers. Dominik Hašek (b 1965), the 'Dominator', was once regarded as the world's best goaltender after winning a Stanley Cup with the Detroit Red Wings in 2001.

Tennis Too

In addition to ice hockey, Czechs have excelled at international tennis. This is a source of national pride and the reason why nearly every park or field of green in the country has a tennis court nearby. Indeed, two of the sport's all-time greatest players, Ivan Lendl (b 1960) and Martina Navrátilová (b 1956), honed their craft here before moving to the big stage. Lendl dominated the men's circuit for much of the 1980s, winning a total of 11 Grand Slam tennis titles and participating in some 19 finals matches (a record only broken in recent years by Roger Federer).

Navrátilová's feats, if anything, are even more impressive. In the late 1970s and throughout the 1980s, she won some 18 Grand Slam singles titles, including a whopping nine victories at Wimbledon, the last coming in 1990. At one point she won six Grand Slam singles titles in a row.

Czechs continue to do well in the international game. Two top Czech women are currently ranked in the top 10 of world players: Karolína Plíšková (b 1992) was the runner-up at the 2016 US Open and Petra Kvitová (b 1990) won Wimbledon in 2011 and 2014. Another recent star is Tomáš Berdych (b 1985).

Restitution for Churches

For the past 25 years, Czech courts have been busy adjudicating disputes between former property holders, who had their property seized by the communists in the late 1940s and 1950s, and the current owners – often the state.

While the law is complicated, in general if you lost property in the confiscations, you had a decent chance of getting it back. That is, unless you were a church. For years, both Catholic and Protestant groups had been lobbying the government to gain back their nationalised lands, churches and buildings. That effort finally bore fruit in 2015 with the implementation of a landmark government ruling that called for returning to the churches their land and buildings.

While the details are still being worked out, the law so far has provoked some unintended consequences: instead of helping the churches, in some cases it's actually hurt them. While many churches received a windfall in buildings and property, as part of the act they also lost state support for paying their employees. That's left many parishes with a big financial hole to fill.

The communists discouraged priesthood and church attendance. Priests were hounded by the StB (Státní bezpečnost, the Czech secret service) and people who attended services were persecuted. Priests were ordained in secret and performed religious rites behind closed doors.

Where Tolerance Ends: Czechs & Roma

Generally speaking, Czechs are a remarkably tolerant people, with relatively open attitudes when it comes to race, religion and sexual preference. That tolerance tends to fly out the window, however, when discussing the subject of the country's Roma minority.

The Roma, descendants of a tribe that migrated to Europe from India in the 10th century, have never been made to feel particularly welcome. Despite making up just 3% of the population (assuming an estimated 200,000 to 300,000 Roma), they are a perpetual object of prejudice, harassment and occasional incidents of violence.

CZECHS' BEST FRIEND

It's sometimes said 'Russians love their children and Czechs love their dogs'. That's not to say Czechs don't love their kids (of course they do), but dogs occupy a special place in the hearts of many people here. Around 40% of Czech families own a dog (one of the highest ownership rates in Europe), and the most popular breeds remain those adorable apartment-sized ones, such as dachshunds, terriers and schnauzers. Among larger breeds, the most sought-after are German shepherds, Labradors and golden retrievers.

Czechs routinely bring their dogs along when they go out for dinner, and all but the fanciest restaurants normally allow dogs (on a leash) to accompany their owners. Waiters might even bring a bowl of water to the table and, indeed, many restaurants keep doggie water bowls on hand just for those occasions.

While it's normally OK to allow a dog to run free in a park (and leash laws are routinely ignored), there are special occasions when dogs are legally required to be leashed. The most common, of course, is on public transport. Large dogs should also normally be muzzled on trams and metros. In Prague, you're also expected to buy your dog a fare – 16Kč a ride. Fines for not obeying the rules are steep.

About the only time dogs run foul of Czech society is when it comes to soiling footpaths. In recent years, efforts to keep roads and pavements free of dog doo-doo have gained pace, and in many places around the country you'll see stands with paper bags for owners to clean up after their animals.

Oddly, when it comes to naming their dogs, Czechs seem to have a soft spot for English names. As you wander about and see the dogs romping around, don't be surprised to hear 'Joey' or 'Blackie' or 'Jeffie'. That's simply a local resident calling his or her canine in. Most likely, it's time to go home.

Part of the problem stems from communist-era housing policies that tended to group Roma populations together in run-down ghettos in city centres. Some Czechs living near Roma settlements feel that these areas tend to be unsightly, loud and dangerous.

There are no easy answers. Under increased pressure in recent years from international groups, Czech authorities have introduced more enlightened policies to try to educate and mainstream the Roma population. To date, these have had only mixed results.

The Budapest-based European Roma Rights Centre is a watchdog organisation that has kept a close eye on Czech authorities grappling with a rise in anti-Roma violence. The group maintains an informative website at www.errc.org.

The Czech Republic has earned a reputation for its acceptance of homosexuality. The country's first gay-pride march, in Prague in 2011, drew thousands onto the capital's streets. The event, held in August, is now a staple of the summer calendar.

EU Scepticism

For a country that so passionately protested during the 1989 Velvet Revolution to rejoin the West and put itself back in the heart of Europe, it may come as a surprise for visitors to learn how unpopular the EU remains among many Czechs.

A recent survey by the Friedrich Ebert Foundation found some 44% of Czechs believe that the country's membership in the union is disadvantageous. That figure is some 10 percentage points higher than the EU average. While support for the EU continues to drop nearly everywhere in Europe, Czechs rank towards the bottom in supporting the union.

The influence of former President Václav Klaus may be in part responsible for this sentiment. In office for 10 years until stepping down in 2013, Klaus fashioned himself as a disciple of the late British Prime Minister Margaret Thatcher, including the 'Iron Lady's' legendary derision for all things EU. Klaus was, among other things, heavily influential in the country's decision to postpone adoption of the euro until an unspecified point in the future.

The Czech Republic, along with nine other countries mainly from Central and Eastern Europe, joined the EU on 1 May 2004. It was the EU's biggest-ever expansion.

Klaus's successor in office, Miloš Zeman, is similarly wary of the EU. Since taking office in 2013, the populist president has been openly critical of the EU, blaming it for the flow of Syrian refugees into Europe in 2015 and 2016, among other things. In mid-2016, he famously called for a national referendum on both EU and NATO membership, saying that Czechs must be permitted to exercise their opinions on both.

Regardless, the positive effect EU membership has had on the country is undeniable. Since the Czechs joined the bloc in 2004, billions of euros have poured across the border to help improve waste management, air and water quality and food-testing, as well as many other aspects of life. As you travel around the Czech Republic, amid all the construction, you will see that much of it has been funded by the EU.

Arts in the Czech Republic

Czechs have always been active contributors to the arts, and no trip to the country would be complete without a stroll through the museums and galleries to admire the work of local painters, photographers and sculptors. In the evening, you'll be spoiled for choice with offerings of classical music, jazz and rock. Two Czechs, Antonín Dvořák and Bedřich Smetana, are household names in classical music. Czechs are less well known outside the country for visual arts, but are still impressive in this field.

Music

Czechs have eclectic tastes, ranging from the ever-popular Mozart, who conducted the premier of *Don Giovanni* in Prague in 1787, to Elton John, who sold out Prague's 18,000-seat O2 Arena in a matter of hours in 2016.

The rock and pop scene has evolved greatly since 1989, when it was dominated by dissident-era rock bands and highly influential (but well past their prime) international acts like the Velvet Underground and the Rolling Stones. Those bands were soon drowned out by a flood of international acts and newer trends like electronic music, trance, techno, hip-hop, rap, world and indie. One of the surprise bands to emerge in recent years has been Čechomor, which combines harmonies and Czech folk traditions in songs that are simple and yet hauntingly beautiful.

An unavoidable part of the modern Czech music scene is a strong nostalgia for the 1980s and '90s (and not necessarily the hits). Popular radio stations play a syrupy mix of Bryan Adams, Queen, Kylie Minogue and Roxette, among others.

Classical

Classical music has a long, rich tradition in the Czech Republic, and Czechs have basked for centuries in the reputation that they know good music when they hear it. It was audiences in Prague, after all, who first 'discovered' the genius of Mozart long before the listening public in Mozart's home country of Austria warmed to the composer.

Early classical music was heavily influenced by Austrian composers, but began to develop distinctly Czech strains in the mid-19th century with the Czech National Revival. As part of this national awakening, Czech composers consciously drew on Czech folk music and historical legends for their compositions. The best-known composer to emerge from this period was Bedřich Smetana (1824–84). While Smetana wrote several operas and symphonies, his signature work remains his *Moldau* (Vltava) symphony.

Antonín Dvořák (1841–1904) is the composer that most non-Czechs will have heard of. He too was heavily influenced by the Czech National Revival, which inspired his two *Slavonic Dances* (1878 and 1881), the operas *Rusalka* and *Čert a Kača* (The Devil and Kate), and his religious masterpiece, *Stabat Mater*. Dvořák spent four years in the US, where he composed his famous *Symphony No 9, From the New World*.

Mozart actively embraced Czech audiences. Following the premiere of his opera *Don Giovanni* in Prague's Estates Theatre in 1787, he famously said of his adoring Prague public, 'My Praguers understand me'.

Czech mastery of classical music continued into the 20th century, with the compositions of Moravian-born Leoš Janáček (1854–1928). Janáček's music is an acquired taste, though once you have developed an ear for his haunting violin strains, it tends to stay with you. Janáček's better-known compositions include the operas *Cunning Little Vixen* and *Káťa Kabanová,* as well as the *Glagolská mše* (Glagolitic Mass).

In recent times, mezzo-soprano Magdalena Kožená (b 1973) is a leading light in the younger generation of opera singers. She has carved out a career as a major concert and recital artist – performing at the Salzburg, Glyndebourne and Edinburgh festivals, among others – and has recorded best-selling albums of Mozart arias, French baroque music and Bach's St Matthew Passion.

Smetana's *Moldau* (Vltava) is arguably the most-beloved piece of classical music among Czechs and is traditionally played to start the annual Prague Spring music festival.

Jazz

Jazz imported from the US first burst onto the local scene in the 1930s, and has remained a fixture of the Prague music scene ever since (though it was frowned upon by the communist authorities as decadent Western art in the late 1940s and '50s).

Czech jazz came into its own in the 1960s, and one of the top bands of this period was SH Quartet, which played for three years at Reduta Jazz Club, the city's first professional jazz club. The club is still going strong (though it's no longer quite the centre of the jazz scene). Another leading band from this period was Junior Trio, with Jan Hamr (b 1948) and brothers Miroslav and Allan Vitouš, all of whom left for the US after 1968. Hamr became prominent in American music circles in the 1970s and '80s, scoring films and television shows, as Jan Hammer. Hammer's theme music for the popular 1980s TV series, *Miami Vice,* reached number one on the Billboard hits chart in 1985.

Today, the scene feels no less relevant, particularly so in the capital. On any given night in Prague, you can catch a number of decent shows at one of several active jazz clubs.

Guns N' Roses frontman Axl Rose legendarily opened his May 1992 concert at Prague's Strahov stadium with the words, 'OK, you ex-commie bastards, it's time to rock and roll!'

Rock & Pop

Rock has played an outsized role in Czech history, perhaps to an extent unique among European nations. It was rock (or more specifically the rock of the US band the Velvet Underground and clandestine Czech counterparts such as the Plastic People of the Universe) that nurtured and sustained the anticommunist movement in the 1970s and '80s. Late former president Václav Havel was a huge fan, and numbered among his closest friends the members of the Rolling Stones, the late Velvet Underground frontman Lou Reed, and even late absurdist rocker Frank Zappa.

Rock music blossomed during the political thaw of the mid-1960s and home-grown rock acts began to emerge, showing the heavy influence of bands such as the Beatles, the Beach Boys and the Rolling Stones. The local 1967 hit single 'Želva' ('Turtle') by the band Olympic bears the unmistakable traces of mid-decade Beatles. One of the biggest stars of the time was pop singer Marta Kubišová (b 1942). Kubišová was officially banned by the communists after the 1968 Warsaw Pact invasion, though she was rehabilitated after 1989 and still occasionally performs. Her voice and songs, to this day, capture something of that fated optimism of the 1960s, pre-invasion period.

Late former president Václav Havel was a big fan of underground rock in the 1980s, particularly the US-based band the Velvet Underground. Among Havel's closest friends was the band's late frontman Lou Reed.

The Warsaw Pact invasion silenced the rock revolution. Many bands were prohibited from openly performing or recording. In their place, the authorities encouraged more anodyne singers such as Helena Vondráčková (b 1947) and Karel Gott (b 1939). Many popular songs from those days, such as Gott's classic 'Je jaká je' ('She is What She is'), are simply Czech covers of the most innocuous Western music of the day.

Rock became heavily politicised in the 1980s in the run-up to the Velvet Revolution. Hardcore experimental bands such as the Plastic People of the Universe were forced underground and developed big cult followings. Another banned performer, Karel Kryl (1944–94), became an unofficial bard of the people, singing from his West German

ICONIC CZECH SONGS

Czechs tend to be patriotic when it comes to their own music. Pop songs from the 1960s and '70s are beloved because they're sappy and inflected with nostalgia for simpler times. Tunes from the 1990s and 2000s tend to sound more authentic, with a harder edge. Together they form the perfect soundtrack when streaming from your music player as you stroll around town. Here is a highly subjective list of favourites:

Trezor (Safe; 1964) by Karel Gott. The Czech crooner extraordinaire is still going strong today.

Želva (Turtle; 1967) By Olympic. The Czech 'Beatles' in their day had the moves, the tunes and the hair.

Stín Katedrál (1968) By Václav Neckář and Helena Vondráčková. One of the most beautiful pop songs to emerge from the 1960s.

Modlitba pro Martu (Prayer for Marta; 1969) By Marta Kubišová. A sad song that for many Czechs still instantly recalls the 1968 Warsaw Pact invasion and clampdown that followed.

Bratříčku, Zavírej Vrátka (O' Brother, Shut the Door; 1969) By Karel Kryl. 'Shut the door' echoes the hopelessness many felt after the Warsaw Pact invasion.

Sluneční hrob (Sunny Tomb; 1969) By Blue Effect. This progressive rock, jazz fusion hit is arguably the best song to come out of a very good decade for music.

Láska je láska (Love is Love; 1995) By Lucie Bílá. The ballad of mid-'90s Prague from a tough woman with a voice you won't soon forget.

Proměny (2006) By Čechomor. Beautiful music from a band that almost single-handedly made folk music hip again.

Falling Slowly (2007) By Markéta Irglova and Glen Hansard. Addictive Czech/Irish tear-jerker that won an Oscar for the film *Once*.

Pocity (Feelings; 2013) By Tomáš Kluš. Likeable teen pop of the type designed to make young hearts swoon.

exile. His album *Bratříčku, Zavírej Vrátka* (O' Brother, Shut the Door) came to symbolise the hopelessness of the Soviet-led invasion and the decades that followed.

The Velvet Revolution opened the door to a flood of influences from around the world. Early '90s Czech bands such as rockers Lucie and Žlutý pes soon gave way to a variety of sounds, from the Nina Hagen–like screeching of Lucie Bílá to the avant-garde chirping of Iva Bittová, in addition to a flood of mainstream Czech acts. The best of these included Psí Vojáci, Buty, Laura a její tygři, Už jsme doma and Support Lesbiens.

A look at the list of top music acts today shows the charts still dominated by old-schoolers such as Gott and Bílá, but a couple of fresher faces have emerged, including teen idol, pop-rocker Tomáš Kluš, pop balladeer Kryštof, indie folk singer Lenka Dusilová, and hip retro-folk acts like Čechomor and Zrní.

Communist-era crooners Helena Vondráčková and Karel Gott are still going strong today, and if you're lucky, you might be able to catch an occasional performance in Prague.

Visual Arts

Ask about Czech visual arts and many visitors will probably draw a blank. Some may be able to conjure up art-nouveau images by Alfons Mucha, but that's about it. However, the Czech Republic has much more to offer than Mucha's sultry maidens. The country has both a long tradition of avant-garde photography and a rich heritage of public sculpture, ranging from the baroque period to the present day.

Painting

The Czech Republic can look back on at least seven centuries of painting, starting with the luminously realistic 14th-century works of Magister Theodoricus (Master Theodorus). His paintings, which hang in the Chapel of the Holy Cross at Karlštejn Castle and in the Chapel of St Wenceslas in Prague's St Vitus Cathedral, influenced art throughout Central Europe. Another gem of Czech Gothic art is a late-14th-century altar panel by an artist known only as the Master of the Třeboň Altar; what remains of it is at the Convent of St Agnes in Prague's Old Town.

For decades, Mucha's *Slav Epic* was on display in the remote town of Moravský Krumlov, 200km southeast of Prague. For a few years until 2016, the panels were exhibited at Prague's Veletržní Palác. The art works are now on a long-term tour of Asia. Where they'll go after that is anyone's guess.

The Czech National Revival in the 19th century witnessed the return of a Czech style of realism, in particular by Mikuláš Aleš and father and son Antonín and Josef Mánes. The National Revival sought to emphasise the natural beauty of the Czech countryside, and landscape painting from this time is soul-stirringly beautiful. You can see some of it at the National Gallery's Veletržní Palác in Prague.

In the early 20th century, Prague and Brno became centres of avant-garde art. One of the most important groups of early trendsetters was the Prague-based 'Osma' (The Eight). The capital was also a focus for cubist painters, including Josef Čapek (1887–1945) and the aptly named Bohumil Kubišta (1884–1918). The functionalist movement flourished between WWI and WWII in a group called Devětsíl, led by the adaptable Karel Teige (1900–51). Surrealists followed, including Zdeněk Rykr (1900–40) and Josef Šima (1891–1971). Many of the best works from this period hang in the National Gallery's Modern and Contemporary Art Exhibition at Veletržní Palác.

WEIRD ART OF DAVID ČERNÝ

David Černý's sculpture is often controversial, occasionally outrageous and always amusing. Although temporary Černý installations occasionally pop up here and there, the following are permanently on view in Prague:

Quo Vadis (p60; 1991) In the garden of the German embassy in Malá Strana. A Trabant (an East German car) on four human legs serves as a monument to the thousands of East Germans who fled the communist regime in 1989 prior to the fall of the Berlin Wall, and who camped out in the embassy garden seeking political asylum.

Viselec (p77; 1997) Above Husova street, Staré Město. A bearded, bespectacled chap with a passing resemblance to Sigmund Freud, casually dangling by one hand from a pole way above the street.

Kun (p81; 1999) In the Lucerna Palace shopping arcade, Nové Město. Amusing alternative version of the famous St Wenceslas Statue in Wenceslas Square, only this time the horse is upside down.

Miminka (p91; 2000) On the TV Tower, Žižkov. Creepy, giant, slot-faced babies crawling all over a TV transmitter tower – something to do with our attachment to media. We think.

Brownnosers (p101; 2003) In the Futura Gallery, Smíchov. Stick your head up a statue's backside and watch a video of the former Czech president and the director of the National Gallery feeding each other baby food.

Proudy (p58; 2004) In the courtyard of Hergetova Cihelná, Malá Strana. Two guys pissing in a puddle (whose irregular outline, you'll notice, is actually the map outline of the Czech Republic) and spelling out famous quotations from Czech literature with their pee. (Yes, the sculpture moves! It's computer controlled.)

K (p83; 2013) In the courtyard above the Národní třída metro station in Nové Město. This rotating bust of Franz Kafka, carved from 39 tonnes of mirrored stainless steel, plays on notions of Kafka's tortured personality and self-doubt.

Visual arts were driven underground during the Nazi occupation, and in the early years of the communist period painters were forced to work in the official socialist realist style, usually depicting workers and peasants building the workers' state. Underground painters included Jiří Kolář (1914–2002), an outstanding graphic artist and poet whose name when pronounced sounds something like 'collage' – one of his favourite art forms.

Photography

Czech photographers have always been at the forefront of the medium. The earliest photographers, in the late 19th and early 20th centuries, worked in the pictorialist style, which viewed photography as an extension of painting.

It was after independence in 1918 and during the 1920s and '30s that early modern styles captured the Czech imagination. Local photographers seized on trends such as cubism, functionalism, dadaism and surrealism, turning out jarring abstracts that still look fresh today. Two of the best photographers from that time include František Drtikol (1883–1961) and Jaroslav Rössler (1902–90).

During communism, photography was enlisted in the service of promoting the workers' state. Picture books from that time are comically filled with images of tractors, factories and housing projects. Serious photographers turned inward and intentionally chose subjects – such as landscapes and still lifes – that were, at least superficially, devoid of political content. Arguably, the best Czech photographer from this time was Josef Sudek (1896–1976). During a career that spanned five decades, Sudek turned his lens on the city of Prague to absolutely stunning effect.

Current Czech bad-boy photographer Jan Saudek (b 1935) continues to delight his fans (or dismay his critics) with his dreamlike, hand-tinted prints that evoke images of utopia or dystopia – usually involving a nude or semi-nude woman or child.

Street art has long been a legitimate form of dissent in the Czech Republic. In the 1980s, the Lennon Peace Wall in Prague's Malá Strana was a vital anticommunist protest space (long before it became a tourist attraction). The capital's Chemistry Gallery, in Holešovice, exhibits some of the best street art today.

Sculpture

Public sculpture has always played a prominent role in the Czech Republic, from the baroque saints that line the parapets of Charles Bridge in the capital (and churches around the country) to the monumental statue of Stalin that once faced Prague's Old Town from atop Letná Hill. More often than not, that role has been a political one.

In the baroque era, religious sculptures sprouted in public places; they included 'Marian columns' erected in gratitude to the Virgin Mary for protection against the plague or victory over anti-Catholic enemies. One such Marian column stood in Prague's Old Town Square from 1650 until 1918. Perhaps the most impressive of these is the Holy Trinity Column, still standing in Olomouc.

The placing of the statue of St John of Nepomuk on Prague's Charles Bridge in 1683 was a conscious act of propaganda designed to create a new – and Catholic – Czech national hero who would displace the Protestant reformer Jan Hus. And it was successful. John of Nepomuk was canonised in 1729 and the Nepomuk legend, invented by the Jesuits, has passed into the collective memory.

Much of Habsburg Emperor Rudolf II's legendary art collection from the 15th and 16th centuries wound up in the Habsburg family collections in Vienna or as war plunder in Sweden.

The period of the Czech National Revival saw the nation's sculpture take a different tack – to raise public awareness of Czech traditions and culture. One of the most prolific sculptors of this period was Josef Václav Myslbek, whose famous statue of St Wenceslas, the Czech patron saint, dominates the upper end of the capital's Wenceslas Square.

The art-nouveau sculptor Ladislav Šaloun was responsible for one of Prague's most iconic sculptures, the monument to Jan Hus that was unveiled in the Old Town Square in 1915 (to commemorate the 500th anniversary of Hus being burned at the stake).

Architecture

Prague is undeniably a city of beautiful old buildings, some as old as 1000 years, but each century over the past millennium has brought with it its own architectural fads and fashions, and learning the differences between them will help you decode the city's layered and fascinating history.

Historic Prague

Prague's historic architecture, stretching back more than 1000 years, is a major drawcard. The backstreets of Staré Město and Malá Strana are living textbooks of the steady march of European architecture over the years. Thankfully, the city's historic core escaped significant damage in WWII, so it records a millennium of continuous urban development, with baroque facades encasing Gothic houses perched on top of Romanesque cellars – all following a street plan that emerged in the 11th century.

Prague's Best Historical Architecture

Basilica of St George (p39)

St Vitus Cathedral (p43)

Charles Bridge (p54)

Church of St Nicholas (p247)

Municipal House (p72)

Romanesque

Romanesque architecture, characterised by rounded facades, arched doorways and massive walls, was all the rage in Europe from the 10th to the 12th centuries, and was the reigning style during the rise of the early Bohemian kings. The oldest buildings in Prague date from this period, but, regrettably, not many original structures survived intact.

Prague's finest Romanesque building is the Basilica of St George at Prague Castle, but the style is perhaps best preserved in the handful of rotundas (circular churches) that are, amazingly, still standing. The finest examples include the Rotunda of St Longinus, from the early 12th century, in Nové Město and the late-11th-century Rotunda of St Martin in Vyšehrad.

Gothic

Charles Bridge is a good example of two opposing architectural styles – Gothic and baroque – coexisting and teasing out the best from each other. The structure is Gothic, while the statues, which give the bridge its life, are baroque.

Romanesque evolved into Gothic architecture in the 13th and 14th centuries. This is Prague's signature style and is characterised by tall, pointed arches, ribbed vaults, external flying buttresses, and tall, narrow windows with intricate tracery supporting massive stained glass. Gothic architecture flourished in the 14th century during the rule of Charles IV, especially in the hands of architect Peter Parler (Petr Parléř), who was best known for the eastern part of St Vitus Cathedral at Prague Castle. Parler was also responsible for the Gothic design of Charles Bridge and the Old Town Bridge Tower.

Another master builder was Benedikt Rejt, whose finest legacy is the petal-shaped vaulting of Vladislav Hall (1493–1500) in the Old Royal Palace at Prague Castle. The Old Town Hall, with its Astronomical Clock, dates from this period as well.

Curiously, the golden spires that crown the many Gothic steeples around town, including the Church of Sts Peter & Paul at the Vyšehrad Citadel, were not part of the original design. Many of these were were added only in the 19th century, when the craze of neo-Gothic swept the city.

Renaissance

When the Habsburgs assumed the Bohemian throne in the early 16th century, they invited Italian architects to Prague to help create a royal city worthy of their status. The Italians brought a new enthusiasm for classical forms, an obsession with symmetry and a taste for exuberant decoration. The mix of local and Italian styles gave rise to a distinctive 'Bohemian Renaissance', featuring the technique of sgraffito – from the Italian word 'to scrape' – literally creating design patterns by scraping through an outer layer of pale plaster to reveal a darker surface underneath.

The Summer Palace (1538–60), or Belvedere, found in the gardens north of Prague Castle, was built for Queen Anna, the consort of Prague's first Habsburg ruler Ferdinand I. It is almost pure Italian Renaissance. The Schwarzenberg Palace (1546–67) in Hradčany and the House at the Minute (1546–1610) in Staré Město, just to the left of the Astronomical Clock, are good examples of sgraffito.

Nearly all of the statues on Charles Bridge are copies. The originals are too valuable to be exposed to the elements. You can see some of the originals at the Lapidarium and the Brick Gate at the Vyšehrad Citadel.

Baroque

In the aftermath of the Thirty Years' War (1618–48), the Habsburg empire embarked on a campaign to rebuild and re-Catholicise the Czech lands. The ornate baroque style, with its marble columns, florid sculpture, frescoed ceilings and rich ornamentation, was used by the church as an instrument of persuasion.

The most impressive example of baroque style is St Nicholas Church (1704–55) in Malá Strana, the work of Bavarian father and son Kristof and Kilian Ignatz Dientzenhofer. Its massive green dome dominates Malá Strana in a fitting symbol of the Catholic Church's dominance over 18th-century Prague. The final flourish of late baroque was rococo, featuring even more-elaborate decoration. The Kinský Palace (1755–65), overlooking Old Town Square, has a gleaming rococo facade.

Neoclassical & Other 'Neos'

After the exuberance of the 17th and 18th centuries, the architecture of the 19th century was comparatively dull. There was a feeling among architects that baroque and rococo had taken pure decoration as far as it could go and there was a need to simplify styles. They looked to classical Greece and Rome for inspiration. Neoclassical and other 'historicist' styles (in other words, styles that consciously imitate earlier forms such as Gothic and Renaissance; usually given the prefix 'neo') are closely associated with the 19th-century Czech National Revival.

The Estates Theatre (1783) is a good example of neoclassical theatre design. The National Theatre (1888) and National Museum (1891) were built in neo-Renaissance style. The buildings are noteworthy not so much for the architecture, but for what they represented: the chance for Czechs to show they were the equals of their Viennese overlords. The flamboyant Spanish Synagogue (1868) in Josefov is another good example of neoclassicism, though here the style imitated is Moorish, recalling Jewish roots in Spain.

Nerudova is the most atmospheric street in Malá Strana. Many houses here are still known by their names instead of their street addresses, including House at the Three Fiddles, House of the Golden Horseshoe and House of the Two Suns.

Art Nouveau

As the 19th century drew to a close, Czech architects began to tire of linear neoclassical facades and the pompous style of imperial Vienna. They were looking for something new and found inspiration in Paris with art nouveau and its flowing lines and emphasis on natural beauty.

The city's finest expression of art nouveau is the magnificent Municipal House (1906–12). Every aspect of the building's decoration was designed by leading Czech artists of the time, most famously Alfons Mucha, who decorated the Lord Mayor's Hall. Art nouveau was also frequently applied to upmarket hotels, including the Hotel Central (1899–1901) on Hybernská in Nové Město, and the Grand Hotel Evropa (1906) on Wenceslas Square.

Veletržní Palác, a fabled functionalist building from the late 1920s, received only faint praise at the time from modern master Le Corbusier. On seeing the building, he commented it was interesting 'but not yet architecture'.

Cubist

In just one decade (from 1910 to 1920), barely half a dozen architects bequeathed to Prague a unique legacy of buildings that were influenced by the cubist art movement. The cubist style spurned the regular lines of traditional architecture and the sinuous forms of art nouveau in favour of triangular and pyramidal forms, emphasising diagonals rather than horizontals and verticals, and achieving a jagged, almost crystalline effect.

Some have likened the style to a Picasso painting in 3D, and in many ways that was the idea. Many of Prague's finest cubist houses can be seen in the neighbourhood below the Vyšehrad Citadel. Another appealing example is the House of the Black Madonna (1912) at Celetná 34 in

HIGHLIGHTS OUTSIDE OF PRAGUE

Many of the architectural movements that swept through Prague were felt in the countryside as well. From the Gothic splendours of Karlštejn to the breathtaking Renaissance castle at Český Krumlov and the wacky bone church in Kutná Hora, the country's architectural treasures are not limited to the capital.

Karlštejn Castle

Emperor Charles IV had **Karlštejn Castle** (p174) built in the mid-14th century to house the crown jewels. Now it's the most popular destination for day trippers outside of Prague; book your tour in advance and get an early start.

Renaissance Český Krumlov

The soaring Renaissance tower of **Český Krumlov State Castle** (p194), remodelled in the 16th century, dominates the charming riverside town below and is visible for kilometres around. Český Krumlov itself is a nearly perfectly preserved example of Renaissance town planning.

Nineteenth-Century Folly

The 19th century was all about imitation in architecture. The delightful **Hluboká Chateau** (p189), in neo-Gothic style, was created by the noble Schwarzenberg family, who consciously modelled their home after Windsor Castle in the UK.

Spa Architecture

The spa craze that swept Europe in the 19th and early 20th centuries gave the Czech Republic some of the continent's most stunningly beautiful spas, including Karlovy Vary's **Mill Colonnade** (p211) and the main **Colonnade** (p219) in Mariánské Lázně.

The 'Bone Church'

The eerie **ossuary** (p179) at the Sedlec monastery near Kutná Hora, dating from the 19th century, defies easy architectural description, or any other type of description for that matter.

Modern Masterpiece

The Moravian capital Brno had a continental reputation in the 1920s as a centre for modern architecture in the functionalist (similar to Bauhaus) style. The **Vila Tugendhat** (p230), designed by modern master Mies van der Rohe for Greta and Fritz Tugendhat in 1930, is a standout example of austere design, coupled with the use of fine materials and ample light.

Staré Město, which today fittingly houses the Museum of Czech Cubism. Prague also boasts a cubist lamp post (1915).

Modern Prague

While it's true modern architecture (styles from the 1920s to the present) doesn't have the pedigree of the older styles, there are nevertheless several interesting buildings here. Czech modernism got off to a promising start in the 1920s and '30s with functionalism, which was heavily influenced by the German Bauhaus movement. Many of the functionalists' best ideas were co-opted – badly – by the communists from the 1950s to the '80s. The post-'89 period has been relatively disappointing and no single style has dominated.

Prague's Best Modern Architecture

Hotel International (p101)

Veletržní Palác (p94)

TV Tower (p91)

Dancing House (p115)

DOX Centre for Contemporary Art (p96)

Functionalist

The early-modern mantra that 'form follows function' found a receptive audience among a generation of new architects who came of age in the 1920s and '30s. Functionalism – similar to Germany's Bauhaus school – appealed to architects for its conscious rejection of superfluous ornamentation. Instead, functionalist architects tended to prefer natural lighting, clean lines and high-quality materials. Notable functionalist works in Prague include the Baťa shoe store (1929) on Wenceslas Square, Veletržní Palác (1928) in Holešovice, and Adolf Loos's Villa Müller (1930) in the suburb of Střešovice.

Communist

The communists, in power from 1948 to 1989, are usually derided for building ugly, nondescript buildings from cookie-cutter designs and using the cheapest materials available, but some critics are starting to soften their views. It's not that the buildings are good, but at least they're bad in an interesting way.

In the 1950s, architects were forced to design in the bombastic Stalinist, socialist-realist style, as seen in the Hotel International (1954) in Dejvice. In the 1970s, the 'brutalist' style was all the rage, where a building's innards – pipes and ducts and wires – were exposed on the exterior. The TV Tower (1987) in Žižkov dates from the end of the communist period. Its sheer scale dwarfs everything around.

Many people deride brutalist architecture as ugly and, well, 'brutal' to look at, but in the 1970s that style was king. The brutalist Kotva department store on central Náměstí Republiky was highly awarded at the time for its groundbreaking design.

Post-1989

Arguably the most interesting structure of the post–Velvet Revolution period is the so-called Dancing House (1992–96) in Nové Město, designed by Croatian architect Vlado Milunić and American Frank Gehry. The building's resemblance to a pair of dancers spurred the nickname 'Fred and Ginger', after the legendary dancing duo of Astaire and Rogers.

Some of the best new architecture is going up in former industrial districts, such as Smíchov, Karlín and Holešovice, including the refurbishment of a former factory to create a space for the DOX Centre for Contemporary Art (2008).

The Czech Republic on Page & Screen

For a relatively small country, the Czech Republic has made some outsized contributions to world literature and film. One of the most influential authors of the 20th century, Franz Kafka, was born and raised in Prague, while grad-school heavyweight Milan Kundera hails from Brno. In film, the same keen, comic eye for the day-to-day animates directors and film-makers. That sensibility triumphed in the 1960s as the Czech New Wave took the world by storm with its bittersweet take on mundane life in a dysfunctional dictatorship.

Above Milan Kundera in 1984

Czechs in Print

The communist period produced two Czech writers of world standing, both of whom hail originally from Brno: Milan Kundera (b 1929) and Bohumil Hrabal (1914–97). For many visitors, Kundera remains the undisputed champ. His wryly told stories weave elements of humour and sex along with liberal doses of music theory, poetry and philosophy that appeal to both our low- and high-brow literary selves. His best-known book, *The Unbearable Lightness of Being* (also made into a successful film in 1988), is set in Prague in the uncertain days before the 1968 Warsaw Pact invasion. Look out, too, for Kundera's *The Joke* and *The Book of Laughter and Forgetting*.

Ask any Czech who their favourite author is and chances are they will say Hrabal. His writing captures what Czechs like best about themselves – a keen wit, a sense of the absurd and a fondness for beer. Hrabal is also a great storyteller, and popular novels such as *I Served the King of England* (1971) and *The Little Town Where Time Stood Still* (1974) are both entertaining and insightful. Hrabal died in 1997 in classic Czech fashion: falling from a window. In 2014, US-based Archipelago Books published a new translation in English of Hrabal's *Harlequin's Millions*.

Czech contributions to literature are not limited to fiction. Czech poet Jaroslav Seifert (1901–86) won the Nobel Prize for Literature in 1984, though Seifert is not universally considered by Czechs to be their best poet. That distinction often belongs to poet-scientist Miroslav Holub (1923–98).

Other major talents who came of age during the period from the Warsaw Pact invasion in 1968 to the 1989 Velvet Revolution include Ivan Klíma (b 1931) and Josef Škvorecký (1924–2012). Klíma, who survived the WWII Terezín concentration camp as a child and who still lives in Prague, is probably best known for his collections of bittersweet short stories of life in the 1970s and '80s, such as *My First Loves* and *My Merry Mornings*. Klíma's long-awaited memoir *My Crazy Century* was published by Grove Press in 2013.

There's no shortage of new Czech literary talent. Names such as Jáchym Topol (b 1962), Petra Hůlová (b 1979), Michal Viewegh (b 1962), Michal Ajvaz (b 1949), Emil Hakl (b 1958) and Miloš Urban (b 1967) are taking their places among the country's leading authors, pushing out old-guard figures such as Kundera and Klíma, who are now seen as chroniclers of a very different age.

Until relatively recently, few books from these younger novelists had been translated into English. That's changing slowly, however, as the writers start to find an audience in English. In 2013, Portobello Books published Topol's acclaimed *The Devil's Workshop*. This followed successful debuts in English for Hůlová's *All this Belongs to Me*, and Urban's thriller *The Seven Churches*, among others, a couple of years earlier.

Franz Kafka & Jaroslav Hašek

No discussion of 'Czech' literature would be complete without a discussion of Franz Kafka (1883–1924), easily the best-known writer to have

BEST POST-'89 CZECH LITERATURE

More and more books by younger Czech writers are finding English-language publishers. Here's a short list of favourites:

The Seven Churches (Miloš Urban, 2011) A brilliant modern-day Gothic murder story set among the seven major churches of Prague's Nové Město by one of the rising stars of Czech literature.

All this Belongs to Me (Petra Hůlová, 2009) Hůlová's debut novel chronicles the lives of three generations of women living in Mongolia. It was a local sensation on its first Czech printing in 2002.

Bringing Up Girls in Bohemia (Michal Viewegh, 1996) Humorously captures the early years of newly capitalist Prague.

The Devil's Workshop (Jáchym Topol, 2013) Translated by Alex Zucker, this darkly tragi-comic novel weaves in elements of modern-day Terezín, overrun by tourism, with Holocaust memories from nearby Belarus.

ever lived in the country and the author of modern classics *The Trial* and *The Castle,* among many others. Though Kafka was German-speaking and Jewish, he's as thoroughly connected to the Czech capital as any Czech writer could be. Kafka's birthplace is just a stone's throw from Prague's Old Town Square and the author rarely strayed more than a couple of hundred metres in any direction during the course of his short life.

Kafka's Czech contemporary, and polar opposite, was the pub scribe Jaroslav Hašek (1883–1923), author of *The Good Soldier Švejk,* a book that is both loved and reviled in equal doses. For those who get the jokes, it is a comic masterpiece of a bumbling, likeable Czech named Švejk and his (intentional or not) efforts to avoid military service for Austria-Hungary during WWI. Some Czechs, however, tend to bridle at the assertion that an idiot like Švejk could somehow embody any national characteristic.

The 2002 bestseller *Prague* by American writer Arthur Phillips is not actually set in the Czech capital, but in Budapest in the 1990s. Phillips apparently chose the title to reflect the envy his expat characters felt for their countrymen hanging out and partying at the time in the Czech capital.

Czechs on Film

Though films have been made on the territory of the Czech Republic since the dawn of motion pictures in the early 20th century, it wasn't until the 1960s and the Czech New Wave that Czechoslovak film finally caught the attention of international audiences.

Despite being under communism, the 1960s was a decade of relative artistic freedom, and talented young directors such as Miloš Forman and Jiří Menzel crafted bittersweet films that charmed moviegoers with their grit and wit, while at the same time poking critical fun at their communist overlords. During that decade, Czechoslovak films twice won the Oscar for Best Foreign Language Film: *Little Shop on Main Street* in 1965 and *Closely Watched Trains* in 1967. Forman eventually left the country and went on to win Best Picture Oscars for *One Flew Over the Cuckoo's Nest* and *Amadeus*.

After the Velvet Revolution, Czech directors struggled to make meaningful films, given the lack of funding, strong international competition and nonstop critical comparison to the high standards set during the New Wave. That said, younger directors have had some success in crafting smaller, ensemble-driven films that focus on the hardships and moral ambiguities of life in a society rapidly transitioning from communism to capitalism.

Films such as David Ondříček's *Loners* (2000), Jan Hřebejk's *Up and Down* (2004), Sasha Gedeon's *Return of the Idiot* (1999), Bohdan Sláma's *Something Like Happiness* (2005) and Petr Zelenka's *Wrong Side Up*

BEST NEW WAVE FILMS

Many of the best Czech films from the 1960s are available on DVD or through streaming services such as Netflix. A few all-time classics include:

Closely Watched Trains (1966) Jiří Menzel's adaptation of Bohumil Hrabal's comic WWII classic set in a small railway town won an Oscar for best foreign film in 1967 and put the Czech New Wave on the international radar. Watch for the scene where young Miloš gently broaches the subject of premature ejaculation with an older woman while she lovingly strokes the neck of a goose.

Loves of a Blonde (1965) Miloš Forman's bittersweet love story between a naïve girl from a small factory town and her more sophisticated Prague beau. Arguably Forman's finest film, effortlessly capturing both the innocence and the hopelessness of those grey days of the mid-1960s.

Black Peter (1963) This early Forman effort wowed the New York critics on its debut with its cinematic allusions to the French New Wave and its slow but mesmerising teenage-boy-comes-of-age story line.

Books featuring an image of Franz Kafka

(2005) are all different, yet each explores the familiar dark terrain of money, marital problems and shifting moral sands.

A Taste For Historical Films

In more recent years, historical films have made a big comeback, particularly films that explore WWII and the Nazi and communist periods. The best include director Adam Dvořák's *Lidice* (2011), Hřebejk's *Kawasaki Rose* (2009), Tomáš Lunák's *Alois Nebel* (2010), Helena Třeštíková's *Lída Baarová – Doomed Beauty* (2016) and Sean Ellis's *Anthropoid* (2016). The latter was a joint international effort that tells the story of the assassination of Nazi leader Reinhard Heydrich in 1942 and the subsequent hiding and capture of the paratroopers who killed him.

In 2013, HBO released a critically acclaimed three-part miniseries, *Burning Bush,* on Jan Palach, the Czech student who immolated himself in 1969 to protest the Warsaw Pact invasion of the country the previous year. The work of prominent Polish director Agnieszka Holland, the series is widely available on DVD.

Running slightly against this grain – at least in the sense of pursuing a more international audience – has been director Jan Svěrák, who continues to make big-budget films on more general themes. In 1996 he took home the country's first Oscar since the 1960s – for the film *Kolja*.

Czech film-maker Jan Švankmajer is celebrated for his bizarre, surrealist animation work and stop-motion feature films, including his 1988 version of *Alice in Wonderland* (Něco z Alenky) and his 1994 classic, *Faust* (Lekce Faust).

Hollywood Discovers the Czech Republic

In addition to Czech films, the Czech Republic has managed to position itself as a lower-cost production centre for Hollywood films. Part of the pitch has been the excellent production facilities at the Barrandov studios, south of central Prague in Smíchov. The effort has paid off and dozens of big-budget films and television shows, including the first instalment of Tom Cruise's epic *Mission Impossible* (1996), have been filmed here.

A Nation of Beer Lovers

No matter how many times you tell yourself, 'today is an alcohol-free day', Czech beer *(pivo)* will be your undoing. Light, clear, refreshing and cheaper than water, Czech beer is recognised as one of the world's best – the Czechs claim it's so pure it's impossible to get a hangover from drinking it. (Scientific tests conducted by Lonely Planet writers have found this to be not entirely true.) Brewing traditions go back nearly 1000 years, and the beer has only gotten better since then.

Types of Czech Beers

Nearly all Czech beers are bottom-fermented lagers, naturally brewed using Moravian malt and hand-picked hops from Žatec in northwestern Bohemia. The brewing and fermentation process normally uses only natural ingredients – water, hops, yeast and barley – though some brewers these days use a chemically modified hops extract that, regrettably, probably wouldn't pass German purity laws.

According to a 2003 British study, drinking beer does not give you a beer gut.

While both light – *světlé* – and dark – *tmavé* or *černé* – beers are readily available, the overwhelming favourite among Czech drinkers remains the classic golden lager, or pilsner, developed in the city of Plzeň in the mid-19th century. These light lagers are marked by a tart flavour and crisp finish. It's worth pointing out that the word 'light' here refers to colour and is not to be confused with the light, low-calorie beers sold in the US and other countries.

Dark beers are slowly gaining in popularity but run a distant second to light beers at most pubs, and among old-school beer drinkers dark beers still retain a faint wisp of not being entirely a man's drink. It's perfectly acceptable, even common, in pubs to order half and half, a Czech 'black and tan', known locally as *řezané pivo* (literally 'cut' beer). This is an agreeable compromise that reduces the tartness of the pilsner without adding the heaviness of a dark beer.

Czech beer drinkers are conservative, and more exotic brews such as wheat beer *(pšeničné pivo)* and yeast beer *(kvasnicové pivo)* have only recently begun to gain traction. You'll rarely find these at traditional pubs, but they're often a staple at the growing number of brewpubs and at more modern, multi-tap places that specialise in a wider variety of beers.

Best Smaller Breweries

- *Primátor (www.primator.cz)*
- *Klášter (www.pivovarklaster.cz)*
- *Svijany (www.pivovarsvijany.cz)*
- *Bernard (www.bernard.cz)*
- *Únětický (www.unetickypivovar.cz)*

Drinking by Degrees

By tradition, Czech beers are usually labelled either *dvanáctka* (12°) or *desítka* (10°) – or sometimes even a *jedenáctka* (11°) – a designation that can lead to understandable confusion among visitors. This measure does not refer directly to the percentage of alcohol; instead, it's an indicator of specific gravity known as the 'Balling' rating (invented by Czech scientist Karl Josef Balling in the 19th century).

In technical speak, 1° Balling represents 1% by weight of malt-derived sugar in the brewing liquid before fermentation. In practice, a typical

12° brew, such as Pilsner Urquell, tends to be richer in flavour (as well as being slightly stronger in alcohol) than a 10° label, such as Gambrinus, which will be slightly sweeter and less bitter.

Czech beers are also rated according to the alcohol-by-volume (ABV) content, and the law recognises a handful of categories: *'výčepní pivo'* (less than 4.5% ABV), *'ležák'* (4.5% to 5.5% ABV) and 'special' (more than 5.5% ABV).

The Land of the Giants

Although there are more than 100 breweries around the country, the local market is dominated by a handful of giants. The largest and most important remains the Pilsner Urquell brewery in Plzeň, which in December 2016 was sold to Japan's Asahi Group after having been part of SABMiller's beer portfolio for several years. Pilsner Urquell produces not only its signature 12° brew, but also the 10° Gambrinus (often shortened to 'Gambáč' and inexplicably the country's most popular beer) and Velkopopovický Kozel. Pilsner Urquell pubs around the country, including the brewery's own chain of casual restaurants, often called Pilsner Urquell Original, will normally carry the first two beers, and usually the dark version of Kozel.

Czechs drink more beer per capita than anywhere else in the world (around 140L per head per year), and the local *hospoda* or *pivnice* (pub or small beer hall) remains the social hub of the neighbourhood.

The country's number-two brewer is Prague-based Staropramen, owned by American giant Molson Coors. The company's brands include the flagship Staropramen lager and Granát, a semi-dark, as well as international names such as Stella Artois and Hoegaarden, which are produced under licence. Staropramen pubs, including the ubiquitous brewery-owned chain Potrefena Husa, usually carry the brewer's light lagers (including an increasingly popular unfiltered variety), as well as Stella, Hoegaarden and occasionally Leffe. While it was once viewed as nothing short of blasphemy to order a Stella in a Czech pub, we've – gasp – even seen Czechs do it.

Beers made by Budvar (Budweiser) of České Budějovice, the country's third-biggest brewer, are a little harder to find in Prague but are common throughout southern Bohemia and much of the rest of the country. The brewery's 12° premium lager is worth seeking out, as its highly regarded premium dark. The Budvar Brewery is partly state-owned and, despite a long-running battle with the far-larger US-based Budweiser, owned by the Anheuser-Busch InBev group, and persistent rumours of an imminent privatisation, it remains the only major brewery in the country that's still 100% Czech-owned.

Brewery Tours

Pilsner Urquell Brewery (www.prazdrojvisit.cz)

Budweiser Budvar Brewery (www.visitbudvar.cz)

Velké Popovice Brewery (www.kozel.cz)

Staropramen Brewery (www.staropramen.com)

Microbrewers & Multi-Tap Pubs

The takeover of the Czech Republic's breweries by multinational companies has been accompanied by a welcome resurgence of interest in

BEER & BOOKS

Perhaps nowhere else in the world is there a stronger link between beer and literature as in the Czech Republic, and in contrast to many cultures where novels are often concocted in coffee houses or literary salons, as often as not Czech books are written in (and are about) pubs. The great Czech writer Jaroslav Hašek (1883–1923), author of *The Good Soldier Švejk*, wrote many of his best works in a pub. *Švejk* more or less starts out with the main character swilling beers in the neighbourhood saloon.

Bohumil Hrabal (1914–97), arguably the country's favourite writer, was actually raised in a brewery in Nymburk, and recounts many of his funny brewery memories in his book *Cutting It Short*. He spent many an evening whiling away the hours at Prague's famous **U Zlatého Tygra** (p144), before falling from a hospital window to his death in 1997.

THE KING OF BEERS VS THE BEER OF KINGS

In this big wide world, who could have imagined that two major brewers located thousands of kilometres apart on different continents would each want to sell beer by the name 'Budweiser'? As remarkable as it seems, that's the case, and for more than 100 years now, US-based Anheuser-Busch, owned by the Anheuser-Busch InBev group, and the Czech Budvar Budweiser brewery have been locked in a trademark dispute to determine where each brewer can sell their beer and what they can call it.

The dispute arose innocently enough in the 1870s, after the co-founder of the American brewery, Adolphus Busch, returned home from a tour of Bohemia. Busch wanted to create a light lager based on his experience abroad and dubbed his new concoction 'Budweiser' to lend an air of authenticity. Ironically, the American claim may actually predate the Czech one. Though beer has been brewed in the town of České Budějovice for some 800 years, the Czech 'Budweiser' name was apparently only registered in the 1890s.

By the early 20th century, the two brewers, eyeing eventual overseas markets, were already locked in battle. In 1907, they agreed that the American company could use the Budweiser name in North America, while the Czechs could keep it in Europe. That fragile compromise held up remarkably well for decades, though there have been signs for years now that it's fraying around the edges.

Anheuser-Busch InBev sells what many consider its inferior Budweiser brand in parts of Europe under the 'Bud' label. In some markets, including in the UK, the courts have ruled that neither company can claim ownership over the name, allowing both companies to use Budweiser. The American Budweiser is not sold in the Czech Republic. In the US, Czech Budweiser is sold under the somewhat awkward name of 'Czechvar'.

Meantime, rumours abound in the Czech Republic about the eventual privatisation of the state-controlled Czech brewer and its possible sale someday to the far-larger Anheuser-Busch InBev group. Such a move wouldn't shock many people, though true beer lovers would likely shed a few tears into their beer mugs.

traditional beer-making and a growing appreciation for smaller and regional breweries.

The microbrew trend is most pronounced in Prague, which boasts more than a dozen brewpubs where DIY brewers proffer their own concoctions, usually accompanied by decent-to-very-good traditional Czech cooking. Because of the discerning beer-drinking public, standards are remarkably high. Additionally, these pubs are often free to experiment with more exotic variations, such as wheat- and yeast-based beers or fruit-infusions, that bigger breweries seem loathe to take on.

Argentinian expat Max Bahnson has established himself as a local beer expert, and his blog, *Pivní Filosof* (the Beer Philosopher; www.pivni-filosof.com), is a great place to catch up on local trends and beer lore.

Alongside this brew-your-own trend, there's been a similar increase in the number of taverns that offer beers produced by the country's smaller, but highly regarded, regional breweries. This represents a change in how pubs normally operate. Traditionally, the big national brewers have forced exclusivity deals on pubs whereby the pubs agree to sell only that brewer's beer in exchange for publicity material, discounts, and mountains of swag such as beer mats and ashtrays. Increasingly, however, more and more pubs are setting aside a 'fourth tap' (*čtvrtá pípa* in Czech) for dispensing independently sourced smaller brews of invariably excellent quality.

The big brewers are not taking the trends lying down. To compete with the microbrews, the larger breweries have come up with no end of innovations, including offering unfiltered *(nefiltrované)* beer (cloudier and arguably more authentic than its filtered cousin) and hauling beer directly to pubs in supersized tanks (called, unsurprisingly, *tankové pivo*). Tank beer is said to be fresher than beer transported in traditional kegs. Who are we to argue with that?

Survival Guide

DIRECTORY A–Z . . . 290
Accommodation 290
Customs Regulations 292
Discount Cards 292
Electricity 292
Embassies & Consulates 292
GLBTI Travellers 292
Health 293
Insurance 293
Internet Access 293
Legal Matters 293
Money 293
Opening Hours 294
Post 294
Public Holidays 295
Telephone 295
Time 295
Toilets 295
Tourist Information 295
Travellers with Disabilities 296
Visas 296
Volunteering 296

TRANSPORT 297
GETTING THERE & AWAY 297
Air 297
Bus 298
Car & Motorcycle 298
Train 299
GETTING AROUND 300
Air 300
Bicycle 300
Boat 300
Bus 301
Car & Motorcycle 301
Hitching 302
Local Transport 302
Train 302
Walking 303

LANGUAGE 304
Glossary 309

Directory A–Z

Accommodation

Accommodation in the Czech Republic runs the gamut from summer campsites to family pensions to hotels at all price levels. Places that pull in international tourists – Prague, Karlovy Vary and Český Krumlov – are the most expensive and beds can be hard to find during peak periods, but there's rarely any problem finding a place to stay in smaller towns.

Booking Services

Alfa Tourist Service (Map p84; ☎224 230 037; www.alfatourist.cz; Opletalova 38, Nové Město; ⏰9am-5pm Mon-Fri; 🚊5, 9, 15, 26) Can provide accommodation in hostels, pensions, hotels and private rooms.

Happy House Rentals (Map p88; ☎224 947 623; www.happyhouserentals.com; Uruguayská 12, Vinohrady; ⏰9am-6pm Mon-Fri; Ⓜ Náměstí Míru) Specialises in short- and long-term rental apartments.

Hostel.cz (☎415 658 580; www.hostel.cz) Website database of hostels and budget hotels, with a secure online booking system.

Lonely Planet (www.lonelyplanet.com/hotels) For more accommodation reviews and recommendations by Lonely Planet authors; you can also book online here.

Mary's Travel & Tourist Service (☎222 253 511; www.marys.cz; Anny Letenské 17, Vinohrady; ⏰9am-7pm Mon-Fri, 10am-5pm Sat & Sun; Ⓜ Jiřího z Poděbrad, 🚊11, 13) Friendly, efficient agency offering private rooms, hostels, pensions, apartments and hotels in Prague and surrounding areas.

Prague Apartments (☎604 168 756; www.prague-apartment.com) Online service with comfortable, Ikea-furnished flats.

Stop City (Map p88; ☎222 521 233; www.stopcity.com; Belgická 36, Vinohrady; ⏰10am-8pm; Ⓜ Náměstí Míru) Specialises in apartments, private rooms and pensions in the city centre, Vinohrady and Žižkov areas.

BOOK YOUR STAY ONLINE

For more accommodation reviews by Lonely Planet authors, check out www.lonelyplanet.com/czech-republic/hotels You'll find independent reviews, as well as recommendations on the best places to stay. Best of all, you can book online.

Camping

Camping grounds vary greatly; generally there are spaces for caravans and most have basic bungalows, huts or cabins for rent. Often tents are pitched randomly in a big open field in the centre and the cabins are arranged around the edge, near the tree line. Facilities may be basic and run-down, or you might find bars, discos, minigolf and boat rentals in a lakeside location. Most have some food service. Most camping grounds are open from May to October only. **CampCZ** (http://camp.cz) is a good online directory of Czech campsites.

Hostels

A hostel can be anything from a bunk bed in a room of 12 to a double room with shower, the common factor being that you pay by the bed (if you want a double to yourself, you have to pay for two beds). Outside Prague and Český Krumlov there aren't a lot of backpacker-style hostels with nifty internet cafes, games rooms and kitchens. Mostly, what you'll find are basic tourist or worker hostels *(ubytovna)* where sleeping may be dorm style, or you may get a tiny room with shared facilities. In July and August, student dormitories are open to all travellers and provide the cheapest lodging.

PRACTICALITIES

Current Events

Two internet sites, aimed at expats, are good sources of local news in English: **Expats.cz** (www.expats.cz) and **Prague.tv** (www.prague.tv). Foreign newspapers can be found at larger newsagents and bookshops.

Radio

State-run **Radio Prague** (www.radio.cz) offers regular streaming broadcasts in English over its website. The homepage is a good source of local news in English.

Smoking

Smoking is banned in all indoor public places, including schools, offices, hospitals, railway stations and public transport. As of 2017, the ban was extended to restaurants, bars and hotels.

Television

Most hotels offer satellite television with some English-language channels, including CNN International, Eurosport and BBC World. Czech Television (www.ceskatelevize.cz) operates two state-controlled broadcast channels; additionally, there are several private channels. Broadcasts are in Czech.

Tipping

In restaurants, tip 10% to reward good service. Taxi drivers won't expect a tip, but it's fine to round the fare up to the nearest 10Kč increment to reward special service.

Weights & Measures

The Czech Republic uses the metric system.

Hotels

Prague, Český Krumlov and Karlovy Vary have some truly stylish top-end sleeps that are comparable to anywhere in Western Europe (including pricewise). In provincial towns, standards are fairly average, and prices are lower.

The main difference between midrange hotels and pensions the facilities. A hotel will almost always have a restaurant and a bar, and may have business services, a fitness centre and pool. A 'hotel garni' means a hotel with no restaurant (breakfast is usually available, but not lunch or dinner).

Pensions & Private Rooms

Pensions are family-run guesthouses that have breakfast rooms and occasionally small restaurants. Some larger hotels have co-opted the word to sound homey, but, in general, pensions have more character and are smaller than hotels. Depending on the quality of the appointments and the proximity to a town centre, you may pay just as much at one of these as at a hotel.

Keep your eye out for signs on homes advertising *'Zimmer frei'* (German for 'room available') or *'privát'* (private room). Renting rooms in private homes is common near the more popular tourist destinations. You may have to share the bathroom with the family but, more and more, these places are being run like tiny pensions. The local tourist office will usually have a list of private accommodation and you can find some on town and tourist websites.

Rental Accommodation

In Prague, the cost of a short-term stay in a self-catering apartment is comparable with a midrange hotel room and can offer more privacy. Typical rates for a two-person apartment with a combined living room/bedroom, bathroom, TV and kitchenette range from around 2000Kč per night in the outer suburbs, to

SLEEPING PRICE RANGES

The following price ranges refer to the cost of a standard double room per night in high season.

€ less than 1600Kč

€€ 1600Kč to 3700Kč

€€€ more than 3700Kč

around 3500Kč or 4500Kč for an apartment near Old Town Square.

Customs Regulations

Customs formalities have been simplified. On arrival at Prague's Václav Havel airport, if you have nothing to declare, simply walk through the green (customs-free) line. Bags are rarely checked. Formal customs regulations are as follows:

➡ On travel between the Czech Republic and other EU countries, you can import/export 800 cigarettes, 400 cigarillos, 200 cigars, 1kg of smoking tobacco, 10L of spirits, 20L of fortified wine, 90L of wine and 110L of beer, provided the goods are for personal use only (each country sets its own guide levels; these figures are minimums).

➡ Travellers arriving from outside the EU can import or export duty-free a maximum of 200 cigarettes or 100 cigarillos or 50 cigars or 250g of tobacco; 2L of still table wine; 1L of spirits or 2L of fortified wine, sparkling wine or liqueurs; 60mL of perfume; 250mL of eau de toilette; and €175 worth of all other goods (including gifts and souvenirs).

Discount Cards

➡ If you intend to visit several museums during your stay, consider purchasing a **Prague Card** (www.praguecard.com), which offers free or discounted entry to around 50 sights. Included are Prague Castle, the Old Town Hall, the National Gallery museums, the Jewish Museum, the Petřín Lookout Tower and Vyšehrad.

➡ Prague Card passholders are entitled to free public transportation on metros, trams and buses, including the **Airport Express** (AE; ☎296 191 817; www.dpp.cz; ticket 60Kč, luggage free; ⊙5.30am-10.30pm) transfer bus from the airport to the main train station.

➡ The pass is available for two to four days, starting at around 1100/825Kč per adult/child for two days.

➡ Cards can be purchased at **Prague City Tourism** (Prague Welcome; Map p62; ☎221 714 714; www.prague.eu; Staroměstské náměstí 5, Old Town Hall; ⊙9am-7pm; Ⓜ Staroměstská) offices, public transport information centres as well as select hotels and travel agencies around town. They can also be purchased online through the card website.

Electricity

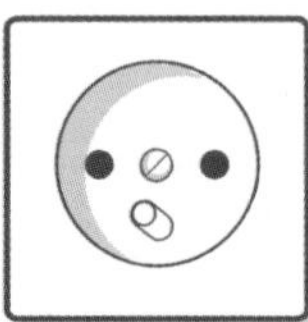

Type E
230V/50Hz

Embassies & Consulates

Australian Consulate (☎221 729 260; www.dfat.gov.au/missions/countries/cz.html; 6th fl, Klimentská 10, Nové Město; 🚋6, 8, 15, 26)

Canadian Embassy (☎272 101 800; www.canadainternational.gc.ca; Ve struhách 2, Bubeneč; 🚌131 to Nemocnice Bubeneč)

French Embassy (☎251 171 711; www.france.cz; Velkopřevorské náměstí 2, Malá Strana; ⊙9am-12.30pm Mon-Fri; 🚋12, 15, 20, 22)

German Embassy (☎257 113 111; www.prag.diplo.de; Vlašská 19, Malá Strana; ⊙8am-5pm Mon-Thu, to 3pm Fri; 🚋12, 15, 20, 22)

Irish Embassy (☎257 011 280; www.dfa.ie; Tržiště 13, Malá Strana; ⊙9am-12.30pm Mon-Fri, 2.30-4.30pm Mon & Wed; 🚋12, 15, 20, 22)

New Zealand Honorary Consulate (☎234 784 777; www.nzembassy.com; Malé náměstí 1, Staré Město; Ⓜ Můstek)

Russian Embassy (☎233 374 093; www.czech.mid.ru; Korunovační 34, Bubeneč; ⊙9am-noon Mon-Fri; 🚌131 to Sibiřské náměstí)

UK Embassy (☎257 402 111; www.gov.uk/government/world/czech-republic; Thunovská 14, Malá Strana; ⊙9am-5pm Mon-Fri; 🚋12, 15, 20, 22)

US Embassy (☎257 022 000; https://cz.usembassy.gov/; Tržiště 15, Malá Strana; ⊙8.15-11.30am Mon-Fri; 🚋12, 15, 20, 22)

GLBTI Travellers

The Czech Republic is a relatively tolerant destination for gay and lesbian travellers. Homosexuality is legal, and since 2006, same-sex couples have been able to form registered partnerships.

Prague has a lively gay scene and is home to Europe's biggest gay pride march (www.praguepride.cz), normally held in August. Attitudes are less accepting outside the capital, but even here homosexual couples are not likely to suffer overt discrimination.

Useful websites include the **Travel Gay Europe** (www.travelgayeurope.com) and **Prague Saints** (www.praguesaints.cz).

Health

Healthwise, the Czech Republic poses no unusual threat or danger, and the worst you'll probably get is a stomach upset or dehydration from too much beer the night before.

Before You Go

HEALTH INSURANCE

The European Health Insurance Card (EHIC) entitles EU citizens to the same emergency health-care benefits as local citizens receive from their national health care; therefore, most emergency care in the Czech Republic will be free for EU citizens, but transporting you to your home country, if you fall ill, will not be covered.

Citizens from other countries should find out if their personal insurance policy covers them abroad. Doctors expect cash if you do not have a national or European health-insurance card; make sure your insurance plan will reimburse your expenses.

Regardless of whether or not you carry an EHIC card, it's always wise to bring cash, a credit card and a valid passport to any hospital or emergency clinic.

VACCINATIONS

There are no specific vaccinations required for entry to the Czech Republic.

The World Health Organization (WHO) recommends that travellers should be covered for diphtheria, tetanus, pertussis, measles, mumps, rubella and polio, as well as hepatitis B, regardless of their destination. Since most vaccines don't produce immunity until at least two weeks after they've been given, visit a physician at least six weeks before departure.

In the Czech Republic

AVAILABILITY & COST OF HEALTH CARE

The level of health care in the Czech Republic is high, and all cities and large towns will have a hospital offering emergency medical treatment. Costs are reasonable and generally lower than in Western Europe, and much lower than in the US.

TAP WATER

Tap water in Prague and other large cities is safe to drink. Opt for bottled water in rural areas.

Insurance

Travel insurance policies covering travel changes, theft, loss and medical problems can be quite helpful. But each has its own caveat, so check the small print. For example, some policies specifically exclude 'dangerous activities' (eg motorcycling, rock climbing, canoeing and even hiking), or require you to return to your home country every 31 days.

Worldwide travel insurance is available at www.lonelyplanet.com/travel-insurance. You can buy, extend and claim online anytime – even if you're already on the road.

Internet Access

The Czech Republic is well wired. Wi-fi (pronounced *vee-fee* in Czech) is ubiquitous. Most hotels, including pensions and youth hostels, offer it free of charge to guests, though occasionally more expensive properties charge (or only offer free wi-fi in the lobby). Many bars, cafes and restaurants offer free wi-fi (usually marked on the door with the international wi-fi sign).

➡ Often the most convenient and reliable places to get wi-fi access in a pinch are big-name fast-food restaurants, which offer free wi-fi around the country.

➡ Many hotels are dropping the practice of making a computer terminal available for guests, though some still do, including most hostels. Larger hotels will sometimes have a business centre for guests to use (for a fee).

➡ For those without a laptop, Prague still has a few internet cafes scattered about the city. Outside the capital, internet cafes are rare, though tourist information offices may have a computer you can use.

Legal Matters

Foreigners in the Czech Republic, as elsewhere, are subject to the laws of the host country. While your embassy or consulate is the best stop in any emergency, bear in mind that there are some things it can't do for you, such as getting local laws or regulations waived, investigating a crime, providing legal advice or representation, getting you out of jail and lending you money.

➡ A consul can usually issue emergency passports, contact relatives and friends, advise on how to transfer funds, provide lists of reliable local doctors, lawyers and interpreters, and visit you if you've been arrested or jailed.

➡ In the Czech Republic, the legal blood-alcohol level for drivers is zero.

➡ Cannabis occupies a legal grey area; it's been decriminalised but is not technically legal. Police will rarely hassle someone for smoking a joint, but always exercise discretion and do not smoke indoors. Buying and selling drugs of any kind, including cannabis, is illegal.

Money

The Czech crown (*Koruna česká*, or Kč) is divided into 100 hellers or *haléřů*. Bank notes come in denominations of 100Kč, 200Kč, 500Kč, 1000Kč, 2000Kč and 5000Kč; coins are of

1Kč, 2Kč, 5Kč, 10Kč, 20Kč and 50Kč. Hellers do not circulate, but prices are sometimes denominated in fractions of crowns. In these instances, the total will be rounded to the nearest whole crown.

Keep small change handy for use at public toilets and tram-ticket machines, and try to keep some small-denomination notes for shops, cafes and bars – getting change for the 2000Kč notes that ATMs often spit out can be a problem.

ATMs

You'll find ATMs all around Prague and in city and town centres around the country. There are ATMs on the concourse of Prague's main train station as well as at both arrivals terminals at Prague airport. Most ATMs accept any credit or debit card, provided you have a four-digit PIN code.

Black Market

Changing money on the black market is illegal and dangerous. Rates are no better than at the banks or ATMs and the chance of getting ripped off is infinitely greater. Firmly decline any offers you may hear to 'change money?'. If you do change money on the street, make sure you receive valid Czech notes in exchange; the black market is flooded with outdated Polish zlotys and other worthless bills.

Changing Money

The main banks – including Komerční banka, Česká spořitelna and UniCredit Bank – are the best places to exchange cash. They normally charge around a 2% commission with a 50Kč minimum fee (but always check, as commissions vary). They will also provide a cash advance on Visa or MasterCard without commission.

Avoid private exchange booths *(směnárna)* in the main tourist areas. They lure you in with attractive-looking exchange rates that turn out to be 'sell' *(prodej)* rates; if you want to change foreign currency into Czech crowns, the 'buy' *(nákup)* rate applies. Moreover, the best rates are usually only for very large transactions, above €500. Check the rates carefully, and ask exactly how much you will get before parting with any money. Similarly, hotel reception desks sometimes exchange money for guests, but seldom offer an attractive rate.

The easiest and cheapest way to carry money is in the form of a credit or debit card from your bank, which you can use to withdraw cash either from an ATM or over the counter in a bank.

Credit & Debit Cards

Visa and MasterCard are widely accepted for goods and services. The only places you may experience a problem are at small establishments or for small transactions (under 250Kč). American Express cards are typically accepted at larger hotels and restaurants, though they are not as widely recognised as other cards.

Taxes & Refunds

Value-added tax (VAT, or DPH in Czech) is applied at 10% to 15% on food (including restaurant meals), books and periodicals, and 21% on the sale of most goods and services. This tax is included in the marked price. Non-EU residents can qualify for a tax refund on large purchases (over 2000Kč), subject to certain conditions.

Look for retailers displaying a 'Tax Free Shopping' sign and then inform the clerk you intend to get a refund. You'll need to save the sales receipt and ensure the goods are not used. Normally you collect the tax at the airport on departure or by mail once you return home. For details, see the Global Blue (www.globalblue.com) website.

Opening Hours

Most places adhere roughly to the hours listed below. Shopping centres and malls have longer hours and are open daily from at least 10am to 8pm.

Banks 9am–4pm Monday–Friday; some banks offer limited hours on Saturday 9am – 1pm.

Bars and clubs 11am–1am Tuesday–Saturday; normally shorter hours Sunday and Monday.

Museums 9am–6pm Tuesday–Sunday; some attractions are closed or have shorter hours October to April.

Post offices 8am–6pm Monday–Friday, 9am–1pm Saturday (varies)

Restaurants 11am–11pm daily; many kitchens close by 10pm.

Shops 9am–6pm Monday–Friday, 9am – 1pm Saturday (varies). Shops that cater mainly to tourists usually have longer hours and are normally open weekends.

Post

The **Czech Postal Service** (Česká Pošta; www.cpost.cz) is efficient, though post offices can be tricky to negotiate since signage is only in Czech. For mailing letters and postcards, be sure to get into the proper line, identified as *'listovní zásilky'* (correspondence). Anything you can't afford to lose should go by registered mail *(doporučený dopis)* or by Express Mail Service (EMS).

➡ A standard postcard or letter up to 20g costs about 20Kč to other European countries and 30Kč for destinations outside Europe. Buy stamps at post offices, but be sure to have the letter weighed to ensure proper postage.

➡ All post offices are open from 8am to 6pm Monday to Friday; post offices in large cities may also have Saturday morning hours.

Public Holidays

Banks, offices, department stores and some shops are closed on public holidays. Restaurants, museums and tourist attractions tend to stay open, though many may close on the first working day after a holiday.

New Year's Day 1 January

Easter Monday March/April

Labour Day 1 May

Liberation Day 8 May

Sts Cyril & Methodius Day 5 July

Jan Hus Day 6 July

Czech Statehood Day 28 September

Republic Day 28 October

Struggle for Freedom & Democracy Day 17 November

Christmas Eve (Generous Day) 24 December

Christmas Day 25 December

St Stephen's Day 26 December

Telephone

Most Czech telephone numbers, both landline and mobile (cell), have nine digits. There are no city or area codes, so to call any Czech number, simply dial the unique nine-digit number.

➡ To call abroad from the Czech Republic, dial the international access code (00), then the country code, then the area code (minus any initial zero) and the number.

➡ To dial the Czech Republic from abroad, dial your country's international access code, then 420 (the Czech Republic country code) and then the unique nine-digit local number.

Mobile Phones

The Czech Republic uses the GSM 900/1800 system, the same system in use around Europe, as well as in Australia and New Zealand. It's not compatible with most mobile phones in North America or Japan (though many mobiles have multiband GSM 1900/900 phones that will work in the Czech Republic). If you have a GSM phone, check with your service provider about using it in the Czech Republic, and beware of calls being routed internationally (expensive for a 'local' call).

➡ If your mobile phone is unlocked, a cheaper and often better option is to buy a prepaid SIM card, available from any mobile-phone shop. Prepaid SIMs allow you to make local calls at cheaper local rates.

➡ The three main mobile operators are **O2** (www.o2.cz), **T-Mobile** (www.t-mobile.cz) and **Vodafone** (www.vodafone.cz). All have service centres scattered around Prague and offer prepaid SIM cards and temporary calling plans at similar prices.

➡ The situation is more complicated if you plan on using a smartphone like an iPhone or Android device that may not be easily unlocked to accommodate a local SIM card. With these phones, it's best to contact your home provider to consider short-term international calling and data plans appropriate to what you might need.

➡ Smartphones can still be used as handy wi-fi devices, even without a special plan. Be sure to switch your phone to 'airplane' mode on arrival, which blocks calls and text messages, but still allows wi-fi. Also turn off your phone's 'data roaming' setting on arrival to avoid unwanted roaming fees.

Phonecards

Local prepaid cards for payphones in the Czech Republic include Smartcall (www.smartcall.cz) and Karta X Plus – you can buy them from hotels, newspaper kiosks and tourist information offices for 300Kč to 1000Kč. To use one, follow the instructions on the card – dial the access number, then the PIN code beneath the scratch-away panel, then the number you want to call (including any international code).

Rates from Prague to the UK, USA and Australia with Smartcall are around 6.6Kč to 10Kč a minute; the more expensive the card, the better the rate.

Time

The Czech Republic lies within the same time zone, GMT/UTC plus one, as most of continental Europe. Czech local time is one hour ahead of London and six hours ahead of New York.

➡ The Czech Republic observes Daylight Saving Time (DST), putting the clock forward one hour at 2am on the last Sunday in March, and back again at 3am on the last Sunday in October.

➡ The 24-hour clock is used for official purposes, including all transport schedules. In everyday conversation, people commonly use the 12-hour clock.

Toilets

In Prague and other large cities, public toilets are free in museums, galleries and concert halls, as well as in train, bus and metro stations. In rural areas and smaller towns, public toilets are rare and you're best advised to seek out a restaurant or pub. Public toilets are normally staffed by attendants who charge 5Kč to 10Kč. Men's are marked *muži* or *páni*, and women's *ženy* or *dámy*.

Tourist Information

Czech Tourism (www.czechtourism.com) maintains a

wonderful website, with a trove of useful information. There's a large English-language section on festivals and events, accommodation and tips on what to see and do all around the country. **Prague City Tourism** (www.prague.eu) and **GoToBrno** (www.gotobrno.cz) are also useful.

Nearly all cities (including Prague and Brno) have decent tourist offices. If you turn up in a city that doesn't have a tourist office, you're pretty much on your own. Local bookshops or newsagents can sometimes sell a local map.

Brno Tourist Information Centre (TIC Brno; Map p228; ☎542 427 150; www.gotobrno.cz; Radnická 8, Old Town Hall; ⏰8.30am-6pm Mon-Fri, 9am-6pm Sat & Sun)

Prague City Tourism (Prague Welcome; Map p62; ☎221 714 714; www.prague.eu; Staroměstské náměstí 5, Old Town Hall; ⏰9am-7pm; Ⓜ Staroměstská)

Travellers with Disabilities

The Czech Republic is behind the curve when it comes to catering to the needs of travellers with disabilities. Cobblestones and high curbs present challenging mobility issues, and many older buildings, including hotels and museums, are not wheelchair accessible. The situation is better with newer buildings, and many big-name fast-food restaurants are wheelchair-friendly.

In terms of public transport, Prague and other large cities are slowly making progress on accessibility. Some buses and trams are low riders and, in theory, should accommodate a wheelchair. These services are marked on timetables with a wheelchair symbol. In Prague, a handful of metro stations, including newer stations, are equipped with lifts. Consult the **Prague Public Transport Authority** (DPP; ☎296 191 817; www.dpp.cz; ⏰7am-9pm) website for details.

➡ **Accessible Travel** (http://lptravel.to/AccessibleTravel) Download Lonely Planet's free Accessible Travel guide.

➡ **Czech Blind United** (Sjednocená Organizace Nevidomých a Slabozrakých v ČR; Map p78; ☎221 462 462; www.sons.cz; Krakovská 21, Nové Město; ⏰9am-noon & 2-4.30pm Mon; Ⓜ Muzeum) Represents the vision-impaired; provides information but no services.

➡ **Prague Wheelchair Users Organisation** (Pražská organizace vozíčkářů; Map p62; ☎224 826 078; www.pov.cz; Benediktská 6; ⏰9am-4pm Mon-Thu, to 3pm Fri; Ⓜ Náměstí Republiky) works to promote barrier-free architecture and improve the lives of disabled persons. Consult the website for online resources.

Visas

➡ Citizens of EU countries can freely enter the Czech Republic and are entitled to apply for visas to stay indefinitely.

➡ Citizens of the US, Canada, Australia, New Zealand, Israel, Japan and many other countries can stay in the Czech Republic for up to 90 days without a visa. Other nationalities should check current visa requirements with the Czech embassy in their home country. There's more information on the **Czech Ministry of Foreign Affairs** (www.mzv.cz) website.

➡ The Czech Republic is a member of the EU's common border and customs area, the Schengen Zone, which imposes its own 90-day visa-free travel limit on visitors from outside the EU. In practice, this means your time in the Czech Republic counts against your stay within the entire Schengen Zone – plan your travel accordingly.

Volunteering

Volunteering options in the Czech Republic usually centre around teaching English, assisting with refugees or displaced persons, or helping people in need. Volunteering organisations sometimes have a religious or Christian undertone, and volunteers are sometimes expected to pay for the experience.

Prague Volunteer (www.praguevolunteer.com) is a nonprofit company that arranges trips and stays for native English speakers with the aim of teaching English and raising language literacy.

Transport

GETTING THERE & AWAY

The Czech Republic sits at the heart of Europe and is well served by air, road and rail.

If you're arriving by air from outside the EU's common border and customs area, the Schengen Zone, you must first go through passport control on arrival at a Czech airport. This includes arrivals from Ireland and the UK. If you're flying in from a European hub within the Schengen Zone, such as Amsterdam or Frankfurt, you will not pass through passport control on arrival in the Czech Republic.

If you're travelling overland by train, bus or car, the Czech Republic is surrounded on all sides by EU Schengen Zone member countries and there are no passport or customs checks on the borders. Always bring your passport, though, on any trip that entails crossing a border, as spot checks on trains, buses and highways are always possible. You'll be detained and sent back if you are found travelling without a valid passport and proper identity documents.

Flights, cars and tours can be booked online at lonelyplanet.com/bookings.

Air

Prague's Václav Havel airport is one of Central Europe's busiest airports, and daily flights connect the Czech capital with major cities throughout Europe, the UK, the Middle East and Asia. It's also possible to fly into the Moravian city of Brno from a handful of cities in the UK and Germany.

Václav Havel Airport Prague

Václav Havel Airport Prague (Prague Ruzyně International Airport; ☎220 111 888; www.prg.aero; K letišti 6, Ruzyně; 📶; 🚌100, 119), 17km west of the city centre, is the main international gateway to the Czech Republic and the hub for the national carrier Czech Airlines, which operates direct flights to Prague from many European cities. There are also direct flights from North America (from April to October) as well as to select cities in the Middle East and Asia.

The airport has two terminals: Terminal 1 for flights to/from non–Schengen Zone countries (including the UK, Ireland and countries outside Europe); Terminal 2 for flights to/from Schengen Zone countries (most EU nations plus Switzerland, Iceland and Norway).

The arrivals halls in both terminals have exchange counters, ATMs, accommodation agencies, public-transport information desks (in Terminal 2 and in the connecting corridor to Terminal 1), tourist information offices,

CLIMATE CHANGE & TRAVEL

Every form of transport that relies on carbon-based fuel generates CO_2, the main cause of human-induced climate change. Modern travel is dependent on aeroplanes, which might use less fuel per kilometre per person than most cars but travel much greater distances. The altitude at which aircraft emit gases (including CO_2) and particles also contributes to their climate change impact. Many websites offer 'carbon calculators' that allow people to estimate the carbon emissions generated by their journey and, for those who wish to do so, to offset the impact of the greenhouse gases emitted with contributions to portfolios of climate-friendly initiatives throughout the world. Lonely Planet offsets the carbon footprint of all staff and author travel.

BORDER CROSSINGS

The Czech Republic shares a border with Germany, Austria, Poland and Slovakia. All are members of the EU's Schengen Zone, and if entering by land (bus, car or train), there are no border stops or passport controls.

taxi services and 24-hour left-luggage counters (Terminal 2 only; per piece per day 120Kč). Car-hire agencies are in the 'Parking C' multistorey car park opposite Terminal 1.

GETTING TO & FROM PRAGUE AIRPORT

To get into Prague from the airport, buy a full-price public transport ticket (32Kč) from the **Prague Public Transport Authority** (DPP; 296 191 817; www.dpp.cz; 7am-9pm) desk (there's one located in each arrivals hall) and take bus 119 (17 minutes, every 10 minutes from 4am to midnight) to Nádraží Veleslavín on metro line A, then continue by metro into the city centre (another 15 minutes; no new ticket needed). Note you'll also need a half-fare (16Kč) ticket for your bag or suitcase (per piece) if it's larger than 25cm x 45cm x 70cm.

If you're heading to the southwestern part of the city, take bus 100, which goes to the Zličín metro station (line B). There's also the **Airport Express bus** (AE; 296 191 817; www.dpp.cz; ticket 60Kč, luggage free; 5.30am-10.30pm), which runs half-hourly to Praha hlavní nádraží (Prague's main train station), where you can connect to metro line C. The trip takes 35 minutes. Buy tickets from the driver.

Alternatively, take a **Cedaz** (Map p84; 220 116 758; www.cedaz.cz; per person 150Kč; Náměstí Republiky) minibus from outside either arrival terminals to the Czech Airlines office near náměstí Republiky (150Kč, 20 minutes, half-hourly from 7.30am to 7pm); buy a ticket at the Cedaz info centre in Terminal 2 or from the driver.

AAA Radio Taxi (14014, 222 333 222; www.aaataxi.cz) Operates a 24-hour taxi service, charging around 500Kč to 650Kč to get to the centre of Prague. You'll find taxi stands outside both arrivals terminals. Drivers usually speak some English and accept credit cards.

Brno-Tuřany Airport

Brno-Tuřany Airport (BRQ; 545 521 310; www.brno-airport.cz; Letiště Brno-Tuřany; 76) handles a small number of mainly budget flights to and from cities in the UK and Germany. It is located in Tuřany, about 8km southeast of the centre. Brno city bus 76 connects the airport and the main train station.

Airlines

The Czech Republic's national carrier is Prague-based **Czech Airlines** (www.czechairlines.com). It operates an extensive network of flights to cities in Europe, as well as a handful of destinations in the Middle East and Asia.

Many national carriers, particularly from Europe and the Middle East, operate regular flights to and from Prague. Additionally, several budget carriers service the Czech market, mainly to and from destinations in Italy, Spain, Germany and the UK. These include **EasyJet** (www.easyjet.com), **EuroWings** (www.eurowings.com), **Ryanair** (www.ryanair.com) and **WizzAir** (www.wizzair.com).

Check the airline websites for the latest information on flights and routes.

Departure Tax

Departure tax is included in the price of a ticket.

Bus

Several bus companies offer long-distance coach service connecting cities in the Czech Republic to cities around Europe. For travel to and from Prague, nearly all international buses (and most domestic services) use the city's renovated and user-friendly **Florenc bus station** (ÚAN Praha Florenc; Map p92; 900 144 444; www.florenc.cz; Křižíkova 2110/2b, Karlín; 5am-midnight; Florenc).

Important international bus operators with ticket offices at the Florenc bus station include **Student Agency** (Map p186; bus information 841 101 101, info 800 100 300; www.studentagency.cz; Křižíkova 2110/2b, ÚAN Praha Florenc; 5am-11.30pm) and **Eurolines** (Map p92; 731 222 111; www.elines.cz; Křižíkova 2110/2b, ÚAN Praha Florenc; 6.30am-7pm Sat-Thu, to 9pm Fri; Florenc).

The Florenc bus station website has a good timetable of buses, both foreign and domestic, arriving in and departing from the capital.

Car & Motorcycle

The Czech Republic has generally good roads, with some limited stretches of four-lane highway. The country is bordered on all sides by EU member states and there are no border or passport controls.

- All drivers, if stopped by the police, must be prepared to show the vehicle's registration, proof of insurance (a 'green' card) and a valid driving licence.
- Visiting foreigners, including EU nationals, are required to show a valid passport (or EU identity card).
- Petrol stations are plentiful.
- In lieu of paying highway tolls, all motorists are

required to display a special prepaid sticker *(dálniční známka)* on car windscreens. Buy these at large petrol stations near the border or immediately after crossing the border. A sticker valid for 10 days costs 310Kč, for 30 days 440Kč, and for a year 1500Kč.

Train

The Czech national railway, **České dráhy** (ČD; www.cd.cz), forms part of the European rail grid, and there are decent connections to neighbouring countries.

The Czech Republic's primary rail gateway is Prague's main station, Praha hlavní nádraží, located in the city centre and connected to the rest of the city via metro and tram.

Frequent international trains connect Prague with German cities like Berlin and Dresden. From Prague, fast trains head southeast to Brno, with excellent onward service to points in Austria, Slovakia and Hungary, or to Olomouc, with onward service to destinations in Poland and further east. České dráhy has a handy local train timetable on its website. The **German Rail** (www.bahn.de) website has a comprehensive international train timetable.

In addition to ČD, two private railways operate in the Czech Republic and service international destinations:

LEO Express (☎220 311 700; www.le.cz; Wilsonova 8, Praha hlavní nádraží; ⊙ticket office 7.15am-9.30pm; Ⓜ Hlavní Nádraží) Train service to select destinations in the Czech Republic, with onward coach service to destinations in Poland, Slovakia and Ukraine.

RegioJet (☎841 101 101; www.regiojet.cz; Wilsonova 8, Praha Hlavní Nádraží; ⊙5.15am-8pm Mon-Wed, to 8.45pm Thu-Sat, 7.15am-8.45pm Sun; Ⓜ Hlavní nádraží) Train service to select destinations in the Czech Republic, with onward service to Slovakia.

Praha Hlavní Nádraží (Main Station)

Prague's main station, **Praha hlavní nádraží** (Prague Main Train Station; ☎840 112 113; www.cd.cz; Wilsonova 8, Nové Město; ⊙3.30am-12.30am; Ⓜ Hlavní nádraží), is conveniently located in the centre of the city and a short walk away from busy Wenceslas Square. It's also served by metro line C (red) at stop Hlavní Nádraží, and several tram lines (5, 9, 15 and 26).

TYPICAL DRIVING TIMES

Prague lies at the nexus of several European four-lane highways and is a relatively easy drive from many major regional cities, including:

Munich four hours

Berlin four hours

Nuremberg three hours

Vienna four hours

Budapest five hours

➡ On arrival, go downstairs from the train platforms to the busy main concourse, where you'll find shops, restaurants and ATMs, as well as a left-luggage office and luggage lockers (per bag 80Kč, take 10Kč and 20Kč coins only).

➡ Public-transport tickets are available at ticketing machines (have coins ready) or at newspaper kiosks in the station. There are taxi ranks at both ends of the concourse.

➡ Try not to arrive late at night – the station closes from about 12.30am to 3.30am, and the surrounding area can be sketchy at night.

TIPS FOR BUYING TICKETS

Although some staff at rail-station ticket counters can speak some English, many do not and will greet a request for 'a round-trip ticket to Brno', say, with a look of sheer bewilderment.

In order to speed up the process of buying a ticket and to avoid misunderstandings, it's often easier to write down what you want on a piece of paper and hand it to the clerk when you approach the window (this works for bus tickets too). Write it down like this:

z departure station, eg PRAHA

do destination station, eg BRNO

čas departure time, use the 24-hour clock

datum date, eg for 2.30pm on 20 May, write '14.30h. 20.05'. Or just *dnes* (today).

osoby number of passengers

jednosměrný (one way) or **zpáteční** (return)

If you're making a reservation on an EC (international) or IC (domestic) train, you may also want to specify *1. třídá* or *2. třídá* (1st or 2nd class), and whether you want an *okno* (window) or *chodba* (aisle) seat.

BUYING TRAIN TICKETS IN PRAGUE

ČD Centrum (☎840 112 113; www.cd.cz; Wilsonova 8, Praha Hlavní Nádraží; ⏰3am-midnight; Ⓜ Hlavní nádraží), the main ticketing office, is located on the lower level of Praha hlavní nádraží (Prague's main station). Sales counters are divided into *vnitrostátní jízdenky* (domestic tickets) and *mezínárodní jizdenky* (international tickets), so make sure you're standing in the right line. The windows also sell seat reservations. Credit cards are accepted.

Just to the left of the ticket windows, you'll find the **ČD Travel** (☎972 241 861; www.cdtravel.cz; Wilsonova 8, Praha Hlavní Nádraží; ⏰9am-5pm Mon-Fri; Ⓜ Hlavní nádraží) agency, which specialises in international connections. You can also buy tickets online through the **České dráhy** (ČD, Czech Rail; ☎221 111 122; www.cd.cz) website.

GETTING AROUND

Transport in the Czech Republic is reasonably priced, quick and efficient. For timetables throughout the country, head online to **IDOS** (http://jizdnirady.idnes.cz).

The main means for getting around include bus, car and train, with each having its own advantages and disadvantages. Buses cover nearly the entire country and, on some routes, can be as quick and convenient as trains. Trains are generally affordable and relatively fast between major cities, though the rail network does not cover every destination. Cars and motorcycles are useful for travelling at your own pace or for visiting regions with minimal public transport. Cars can be hired in every major city.

Air

Czech Airlines (www.czechairlines.cz) runs a handful of flights weekly from Prague to the eastern city of Ostrava, but the country is small enough that air travel is usually impractical. There are no flights between Prague and Brno.

Bicycle

Cycling is an increasingly popular weekend activity in nice weather, though its full potential has yet to be realised. Southern Moravia, especially along a marked wine trail that runs between vineyards, is ideal for cycling.

➡ Off the main highways, the country is criss-crossed by hundreds of kilometres of secondary roads that are relatively little trafficked and ideal for cycling.

➡ The cycling infrastructure, such as dedicated cycling trails and a network of bike-rental and repair shops, is slowly improving but still not adequate.

➡ A handful of large cities, including Prague, do have dedicated cycling lanes, but these are often half-hearted efforts and leave cyclists at the mercy of often ignorant and aggressive drivers.

➡ It's possible to hire or buy bicycles in many major towns, though not all. Rates average from 400Kč to 600Kč per day.

➡ A helpful website for getting started and planning a cyclist route in the Czech Republic is Cyclists Welcome (*Cyklisté vítáni;* www.cyklistevitani.cz).

BICYCLE HIRE IN PRAGUE

Several companies rent bikes and provide guided cycling tours:

AVE Bicycle Tours (Map p102; ☎251 091 118; www.bicycle-tours.cz; Pod Barvirkou 6, Smíchov; self-guided tour 600Kč, guided tour 1190Kč; ⏰Apr-Oct; 🚋7)

Biko Adventures Prague (Map p106; ☎733 750 990; www.bikoadventures.com; Vratislavova 3, Vyšehrad; standard rental per day 450Kč, group tours per person from 1250Kč; ⏰9am-6pm Apr-Oct; 🚋2, 3, 7, 17, 21)

City Bike (☎776 180 284; www.citybike-prague.com; Králodvorská 5, Staré Město; rental per day from 530Kč, tours per person 590-1050Kč; ⏰9am-7pm Apr-Oct; Ⓜ Náměstí Republiky)

Praha Bike (☎732 388 880; www.prahabike.cz; Dlouhá 24, Staré Město; rental per day 590Kč, tours per person starting at 590Kč; ⏰9am-8pm; Ⓜ Náměstí Republiky)

Boat

There's no regularly scheduled water transport along the Vltava River, though several companies operate pleasure cruises on the river.

Prague Boats (Evropská Vodní Doprava; Map p62; ☎224 810 032; www.prague-boats.cz; Čechův most; 1hr cruise adult/child 290/180Kč, 2hr cruise 450/290Kč; ⏰9am-10pm; 🚋17) Offers one-hour cruises year-round from Central Prague to outlying Vyšehrad.

Prague Steamboat Co (Pražská Paroplavební Společnost, PPS; Map p78; ☎224 931 013; www.praguesteamboats.com; Rašínovo nábřeží 2; ⏰Mar-Oct; Ⓜ Karlovo Náměstí) Runs various cruises from March to October from the centre to

ROAD RULES

- The minimum driving age is 18.
- Traffic moves on the right.
- The use of seat belts is compulsory for front- and rear-seat passengers.
- Children under 12 years or shorter than 1.5m (4ft 9in) are prohibited from sitting in the front seat and must use a child-safety seat.
- Headlights must be always on, even in daylight.
- The legal blood alcohol limit is zero; if the police pull you over for any reason, they are required to administer a breathalyser.
- In cities, trams have the right of way when making any signalled turn across your path. Drivers may overtake a tram only on the right, and only if it's in motion.
- You must stop behind any tram taking on or letting off passengers where there's no passenger island.
- In case of an accident, contact the police immediately if repairs are likely to exceed 20,000Kč or if there is an injury. Even if damage is slight, it's a good idea to report the accident to obtain a police statement for insurance purposes.
- For emergency breakdowns, the **ÚAMK** (Central Automobile & Motorcycle Club; ☎1230; www.uamk.cz) provides nationwide assistance 24 hours a day.

various points up and down the Vltava River.

Prague Venice (Map p62; ☎776 776 779; www.prague-venice.cz; Křižovnické náměstí 3; per person 290Kč; ⊙10.30am-10pm Jul & Aug, to 8pm Apr-Jun & Sep, to 6pm Oct-Mar; 🚊2, 17, 18) Runs entertaining 45-minute cruises in small boats under the hidden arches of Charles Bridge.

Bus

Long-haul and regional bus service is an important part of the transport system in the Czech Republic. Buses are often faster, cheaper and more convenient than trains, and are especially handy for accessing areas where train service is poor, such as Karlovy Vary and Český Krumlov.

Many bus routes have reduced frequency (or none) at weekends. Buses occasionally leave early, so get to the station at least 15 minutes before the official departure time.

Bus stations are usually (but not always) located near train stations to allow for easy transfer between the two. In Prague, the Florenc bus station is the main departure and arrival point, though some buses arrive at and depart from smaller stations along outlying metro lines.

Check the online timetable at **IDOS** (http://jizdnirady.idnes.cz) to make sure you have the right station.

Buy tickets at station ticket windows or directly from the driver. Be sure to have small bills handy, since drivers are rarely able to make change for large denominations.

Student Agency (www.studentagency.eu) is a popular, private bus company with regular service to a number of key destinations, including Prague, Brno, Karlovy Vary, Plzeň, České Budějovice and Český Krumlov. Buy tickets online or at station ticket windows.

Car & Motorcycle

Driving has compelling advantages. With your own wheels, you're free to explore off-the-beaten-track destinations and small towns. Additionally, you're no longer at the whim of capricious bus schedules and inconvenient, early-morning train departures. That said, driving in the Czech Republic is not ideal, and if you have the chance to use alternatives like the train and bus, these can be more relaxing options.

- Roads, including the most important highways, such as the D1 motorway between Prague and Brno, are in the midst of a long-term rebuilding process, and delays, traffic jams and long detours are more the norm than the exception.
- Most highways are two lanes, and can be choked with cars and trucks. It's white-knuckle driving made worse by aggressive motorists in fast cars trying to overtake on hills and blind curves. When calculating arrival times, figure on covering about 60km to 70km per hour.
- Western-style petrol stations are plentiful. A litre of unleaded 95 octane costs about 30Kč. Petrol stations invariably accept credit

cards, but you'll need to have a four-digit PIN to use them.

➡ Czech roads and highways are covered by most satellite-navigation systems like Garmin or TomTom. If you're going to be driving, download the most recent European maps and bring along your home sat-nav device.

Car Hire

International rental companies have offices in large cities and at Václav Havel Airport Prague in the capital. In addition, locally owned car-hire companies usually operate in large cities and can be cheaper. Book cars in advance via company websites to get the best rates. Drivers must normally be at least 21 years old, and the renter must hold a valid driving licence and credit card. Note, there may be restrictions on taking the car out of the Czech Republic, particularly to places like Romania, Bulgaria, Turkey, and countries of the former Soviet Union and Yugoslavia.

Speed Limits

Watch speed limits in towns and villages in spots where the legal limit drops quickly from 90km/h (56 mph) to 50km/h (30 mph). Highway speeds are often monitored by mounted surveillance cameras. On expressways the speed limit is 130km/h (78 mph).

Hitching

Hitching is a popular way of moving from town to town, where hitchers, often students, line up on the main road just beyond the town or city limits and display a sign with their destination to hail a ride. That said, hitching is never entirely safe, and we don't recommend it. Travellers who hitch should understand that they are taking a small but potentially serious risk.

Local Transport

Bus, Train & Tram

Czech cities generally have very good public transportation systems comprised of buses, trams, and, in some cases, trolleybuses. Prague is the only Czech city with an underground metro. The method for accessing the systems is broadly similar. Purchase bus or tram tickets at newsagents or street ticket machines before boarding, and validate the ticket once aboard. Tickets generally cost from 12Kc to 32Kc per ride, depending on the city and duration of the ticket.

Taxi

Taxis are a cheap and reliable supplement to the public transport systems. Drivers are required by law to post their rates, and honest cabs will always do this. The going rate varies from city to city, but as a rule of thumb count on 40Kč flag fall when you enter the vehicle plus 28Kč per kilometre and 6Kč per minute while waiting. Any driver demanding a higher fare is likely looking to rip off unsuspecting passengers.

When flagging a cab, look for a cab with its yellow roof lamp lit and raise your hand. Establish your destination and a likely fare before getting in, and make sure the meter is switched on. Only hail official, registered cabs – these are yellow, have a permanently installed roof lamp with the word 'TAXI' on it, and have the driver's name and licence number printed on both front doors.

Alternatively, call or ask someone to call a radio taxi, as they're better regulated and more responsible. Every city has a different cab company. In Prague, companies with honest drivers, 24-hour service and English-speaking operators include **AAA Radio Taxi** (☎14014, 222 333 222; www.aaataxi.cz), **ProfiTaxi** (☎14015; www.profitaxi.cz) and **City Taxi** (☎257 257 257; www.citytaxi.cz).

In addition to local taxi companies, various app-based ride-sharing services operate in large cities. The largest one of these, **Uber** (www.uber.com), is available in both Prague and Brno. A locally based alternative, **Liftago** (www.liftago.com), runs cars in Prague. To use these services, download the app to your smartphone.

Train

The Czech rail network is operated by **České dráhy** (www.cd.cz). Train travel is generally comfortable, reasonably priced and efficient. Trains are particularly useful for covering relatively long distances between major cities, such as between Prague and Brno, or Prague and Olomouc.

It's always safer to buy tickets in advance. Seat reservations are usually not necessary on smaller, regional trains, but are recommended if travelling on a Friday or over the weekend when trains tend to be more crowded. Bikes can be transported for a nominal fee (35Kč to 50Kč) on trains marked with a bicycle symbol on the timetable.

Two smaller private operators, **RegioJet** (www.regiojet.cz) and **LEO Express** (www.le.cz), operate daily high-speed trains from Prague to the Moravian cities of Olomouc and Ostrava, with the possibility to connect to onward coach service to Slovakia and Poland. Timetable information for all trains is available online at **IDOS** (http://jizdnirady.idnes.cz).

Train Categories

Several different categories of train run on Czech rails, differing mainly in speed and comfort.

➡ **EC** (EuroCity) Fast, comfortable, international trains, stopping at main stations only, with 1st- and 2nd-class coaches; supplementary charge of 60Kč; reservations recommended. Includes 1st-class-only SC Pendolino trains that run from Prague to Olomouc, Brno and Ostrava, with links to Vienna and Bratislava.

➡ **IC** (InterCity) Long-distance and international trains with 1st- and 2nd-class coaches; supplement of 40Kč; reservations recommended.

➡ **R** *(rychlík)* The main domestic network of fast trains with 1st- and 2nd-class coaches and sleeper services; no supplement except for sleepers; express and *rychlík* trains are usually marked in red on timetables.

➡ **Os** *(osobní)* Slow trains using older rolling stock that stop in every one-horse town; 2nd class only.

Walking

Walking is the best way to see the centres of most Czech cities. Indeed, the centres of many towns and cities across the country, including Prague, are closed to vehicular traffic, meaning walking is sometimes the only option for getting around.

In Prague, cars and vehicles are prohibited from crossing Charles Bridge and are banned from many streets in Staré Město (Old Town), Malá Strana and the area around Prague Castle.

Cobblestones and uneven pavements play havoc with heels, though. The best bet is to opt for comfortable walkers or sneakers.

Language

Czech (*Čeština* chesh·tyi·nuh) belongs to the western branch of the Slavic language family, with Slovak and Polish as its closest relatives. It has approximately 12 million speakers.

Most of the sounds in Czech are also found in English. If you read our coloured pronunciation guides as if they were English, you shouldn't have problems being understood. Note that ai is pronounced as in 'aisle', air as in 'hair' (without the 'r'), aw as in 'law', oh as the 'o' in 'note', ow as in 'how' and uh as the 'a' in 'ago'. An accent mark over a vowel in written Czech indicates it's pronounced as a long sound.

For the consonants, note that kh is pronounced like the *ch* in the Scottish *loch* (a throaty sound), zh is pronounced as the 's' in 'pleasure' and r is rolled. The apostrophe (') indicates a slight y sound. The sounds r, s and l can be used as quasi-vowels – this explains why some written Czech words or syllables appear to have no vowels, eg *krk* krk (neck), *osm* o·sm (eight), *vlk* vlk (wolf). If you find these clusters of consonants difficult, just try putting a tiny uh sound between them. Stress is always on the first syllable of a word – this is indicated with italics in our pronunciation guides. Masculine and feminine forms are indicated with (m/f) where needed.

BASICS

Hello.	*Ahoj.*	*uh*·hoy
Goodbye.	*Na shledanou.*	*nuh*·skhle·duh·noh
Excuse me.	*Promiňte.*	*pro*·min'·te
Sorry.	*Promiňte.*	*pro*·min'·te
Please.	*Prosím.*	*pro*·seem

WANT MORE?

For in-depth language information and handy phrases, check out Lonely Planet's *Czech phrasebook*. You'll find it at **shop.lonelyplanet.com**, or you can buy Lonely Planet's iPhone phrasebooks at the Apple App Store.

Thank you.	*Děkuji.*	*dye*·ku·yi
You're welcome.	*Prosím.*	*pro*·seem
Yes./No.	*Ano./Ne.*	*uh*·no/ne

How are you?
Jak se máte? — yuhk se *ma*·te

Fine. And you?
Dobře. A vy? — *dob*·rzhe a vi

What's your name?
Jak se jmenujete? — yuhk se *yme*·nu·ye·te

My name is ...
Jmenuji se ... — *yme*·nu·yi se ...

Do you speak English?
Mluvíte anglicky? — *mlu*·vee·te *uhn*·glits·ki

I don't understand.
Nerozumím. — *ne*·ro·zu·meem

One moment, please.
Počkejte chvíli. — *poch*·key·te *khvee*·li

ACCOMMODATION

Do you have a double room?
Máte pokoj s manželskou postelí? — *ma*·te *po*·koy s *muhn*·zhels·koh *pos*·te·lee

Do you have a single/twin room?
Máte jednolůžkový/dvoulůžkový pokoj? — *ma*·te *yed*·no·loozh·ko·vee/*dvoh*·loozh·ko·vee *po*·koy

How much is it per ...?	*Kolik to stojí ...?*	*ko*·lik to *sto*·yee ...
night	*na noc*	nuh nots
person	*za osobu*	zuh *o*·so·bu
week	*na týden*	nuh *tee*·den

campsite	*tábořiště*	*ta*·bo·rzhish·tye
guesthouse	*penzion*	*pen*·zi·on
hotel	*hotel*	*ho*·tel
youth hostel	*mládežnická ubytovna*	*mla*·dezh·nyits·ka *u*·bi·tov·nuh

DIRECTIONS

Where's the (market)?
Kde je (trh)? — gde ye (trh)

What's the address?
Jaká je adresa? — *yuh*·ka ye *uh*·dre·suh

Can you show me (on the map)?
Můžete mi to ukázat (na mapě)? — *moo*·zhe·te mi to *u*·ka·zuht (nuh *muh*·pye)

It's ...	*Je to ...*	ye to ...
behind ...	*za ...*	zuh ...
in front of ...	*před ...*	przhed ...
near	*blízko*	*bleez*·ko
next to ...	*vedle ...*	*ved*·le ...
on the corner	*na rohu*	nuh *ro*·hu
opposite ...	*naproti ...*	*nuh*·pro·tyi ...
straight ahead	*přímo*	*przhee*·mo

Turn ...	*Odbočte ...*	*od*·boch·te ...
at the corner	*za roh*	zuh rawh
at the traffic lights	*u semaforu*	u *se*·muh·fo·ru
left	*do leva*	do *le*·vuh
right	*do prava*	do *pruh*·vuh

EATING & DRINKING

What would you recommend?
Co byste doporučil/ doporučila? (m/f) — tso *bis*·te *do*·po·ru·chil/ *do*·po·ru·chi·luh

What's the local speciality?
Co je místní specialita? — tso ye *meest*·nyee *spe*·tsi·uh·li·tuh

Do you have vegetarian food?
Máte vegetariánská jídla? — *ma*·te *ve*·ge·tuh·ri·ans·ka *yeed*·luh

That was delicious!
To bylo lahodné! — to *bi*·lo *luh*·hod·nair

I'll have ...	*Dám si ...*	dam si ...
Cheers!	*Na zdraví!*	nuh *zdruh*·vee

I'd like the ..., please.	*Chtěl/Chtěla bych ..., prosím.* (m/f)	khtyel/*khtye*·luh bikh ... *pro*·seem
bill	*účet*	*oo*·chet
menu	*jídelníček*	*yee*·del·nyee·chek

KEY PATTERNS

To get by in Czech, mix and match these simple patterns with words of your choice:

When's (the next bus)?
V kolik jede (příští autobus)? — f *ko*·lik *ye*·de (*przhee*·shtyee *ow*·to·bus)

Where's (the station)?
Kde je (nádraží)? — gde ye (*na*·dra·zhee)

Where can I (buy a ticket)?
Kde (koupím jízdenku)? — gde (*koh*·peem *yeez*·den·ku)

How much is (a room)?
Kolik stojí (pokoj)? — *ko*·lik *sto*·yee (*po*·koy)

Is there (a toilet)?
Je tam (toaleta)? — ye tuhm (*to*·uh·le·tuh)

Do you have (a map)?
Máte (mapu)? — *ma*·te (*muh*·pu)

I'd like (to hire a car).
Chtěl/Chtěla bych (si půjčit auto). (m/f) — khtyel/*khtye*·luh bikh (si *pooy*·chit *ow*·to)

I need (a can opener).
Potřebuji (otvírák na konzervy). — *po*·trzhe·bu·yi (*ot*·vee·rak nuh *kon*·zer·vi)

Can I (camp here)?
Mohu (zde stanovat)? — *mo*·hu (zde *stuh*·no·vuht)

Could you please (help me)?
Můžete prosím (pomoci)? — *moo*·zhe·te *pro*·seem (*po*·mo·tsi)

Key Words

bar	*bar*	buhr
bottle	*láhev*	*la*·hef
bowl	*miska*	*mis*·kuh
breakfast	*snídaně*	*snee*·duh·nye
cafe	*kavárna*	*kuh*·var·nuh
children's menu	*dětský jídelníček*	*dyets*·kee *yee*·del·nyee·chek
cold	*chladný*	*khluhd*·nee
delicatessen	*lahůdky*	*luh*·hood·ki
dinner	*večeře*	*ve*·che·rzhe
dish	*pokrm*	*po*·krm
drink list	*nápojový lístek*	*na*·po·yo·vee *lees*·tek
food	*jídlo*	*yeed*·lo
fork	*vidlička*	*vid*·lich·kuh
glass	*sklenička*	*skle*·nyich·kuh
grocery store	*konzum*	*kon*·zum
highchair	*dětská stolička*	*dyet*·ska *sto*·lich·kuh
hot (warm)	*teplý*	*tep*·lee
knife	*nůž*	noozh

lunch	*oběd*	*o*·byed
market	*trh*	trh
plate	*talíř*	*tuh*·leerzh
restaurant	*restaurace*	*res*·tow·ruh·tse
spoon	*lžíce*	*lzhee*·tse
with	*s*	s
without	*bez*	bez

Meat & Fish

bacon	*slanina*	*sluh*·nyi·nuh
beef	*hovězí*	*ho*·vye·zee
chicken	*kuře*	*ku*·rzhe
duck	*kachna*	*kuhkh*·nuh
fish	*ryba*	*ri*·buh
ham	*šunka*	*shun*·kuh
herring	*sleď*	sled'
lamb	*jehněčí*	*yeh*·nye·chee
meat	*maso*	*muh*·so
mussel	*slávka jedlá*	*slaf*·kuh *yed*·la
pork	*vepřové*	*vep*·rzho·vair
pork sausage	*vuřt*	vurzht
prawn	*kreveta*	*kre*·ve·tuh
salami	*salám*	*suh*·lam
salmon	*losos*	*lo*·sos
steak (beef)	*biftek*	*bif*·tek
tuna	*tuňák*	*tu*·nyak
turkey	*krůta*	*kroo*·tuh
veal	*telecí*	*te*·le·tsee
oyster	*ústřice*	*oost*·rzhi·tse

Fruit & Vegetables

apple	*jablko*	*yuh*·bl·ko
apricot	*meruňka*	*me*·run'·kuh
banana	*banán*	*buh*·nan
bean	*fazole*	*fuh*·zo·le
broccoli	*brokolice*	*bro*·ko·li·tse
cabbage	*kapusta*	*kuh*·pus·tuh
capsicum	*paprika*	*puh*·pri·kuh
carrot	*mrkev*	*mr*·kef
cauliflower	*květák*	*kvye*·tak
cherry	*třešeň*	*trzhe*·shen'
corn	*kukuřice*	*ku*·ku·rzhi·tse
cucumber	*okurka*	*o*·kur·kuh
date	*datle*	*duht*·le
eggplant	*lilek*	*li*·lek
garlic	*česnek*	*ches*·nek
grapes	*hrozny*	*hroz*·ni
legume	*luštěnina*	*lush*·tye·nyi·nuh
lemon	*citron*	*tsi*·tron
lentil	*čočka*	*choch*·ka
lettuce	*hlávkový salát*	*hlaf*·ko·vee *suh*·lat
mushroom	*houba*	*hoh*·buh
nut	*ořech*	*o*·rzhekh
olive	*oliva*	*o*·li·vuh
onion	*cibule*	*tsi*·bu·le
orange	*pomeranč*	*po*·me·ruhnch
pea	*hrách*	hrakh
peach	*broskev*	*bros*·kef
pear	*hruška*	*hrush*·kuh
pepper (bell)	*paprika*	*puh*·pri·kuh
pineapple	*ananas*	*uh*·nuh·nuhs
plum	*švestka*	*shvest*·kuh
potato	*brambor*	*bruhm*·bor
pumpkin	*dýně*	*dee*·nye
radish	*ředkvička*	*rzhed*·kvich·kuh
raisin	*hrozinka*	*hro*·zin·kuh
raspberry	*malina*	*muh*·li·nuh
spinach	*špenát*	*shpe*·nat
strawberry	*jahoda*	*yuh*·ho·duh
tomato	*rajské jablko*	*rais*·kair *yuh*·bl·ko
zucchini	*cuketa*	*tsu*·ke·tuh

Signs

Vjezd	Entrance
Východ	Exit
Otevřeno	Open
Zavřeno	Closed
Zákazáno	Prohibited
Toalety/WC	Toilets
Páni/Muži	Men
Dámy/Ženy	Women

Other

bread	*chléb*	khlairb
butter	*máslo*	*mas*·lo
cheese	*sýr*	seer
chilli	*feferon*	*pfe*·fe·ron
egg	*vajíčko*	*vuh*·yeech·ko
honey	*med*	med
ice cream	*zmrzlina*	*zmrz*·li·nuh

jam	*džem*	dzhem
noodles	*nudle*	*nud*·le
pasta	*těstovina*	*tyes*·to·vi·nuh
pepper	*pepř*	*pe*·przh
rice	*rýže*	*ree*·zhe
salad	*salát*	*suh*·lat
salt	*sůl*	sool
sauce	*omáčka*	o·mach·kuh
soup	*polévka*	*po*·lairf·kuh
sugar	*cukr*	*tsu*·kr
vinegar	*ocet*	*o*·tset

Drinks

beer	*pivo*	*pi*·vo
coffee	*káva*	*ka*·vuh
lemonade	*limonáda*	*li*·mo·na·duh
milk	*mléko*	*mlair*·ko
orange juice	*pomerančový džus*	*po*·me·ruhn·cho·vee dzhus
red wine	*červeného víno*	*cher*·ve·nair·ho *vee*·no
soft drink	*nealkoholický nápoj*	*ne*·uhl·ko·ho·lits·kee *na*·poy
tea	*čaj*	chai
(mineral) water	*(minerální) voda*	(*mi*·ne·ral·nyee) *vo*·duh
white wine	*bílého víno*	*bee*·lair·ho *vee*·no

EMERGENCIES

Help!	*Pomoc!*	*po*·mots
Go away!	*Běžte pryč!*	*byezh*·te prich

Call ...!	*Zavolejte ...!*	*zuh*·vo·ley·te ...
a doctor	*lékaře*	*lair*·kuh·rzhe
the police	*policii*	*po*·li·tsi·yi

I'm lost.
Zabloudil/ Zabloudila jsem. (m/f) — *zuh*·bloh·dyil/ *zuh*·bloh·dyi·luh ysem

I'm ill.
Jsem nemocný/ nemocná. (m/f) — ysem *ne*·mots·nee/ *ne*·mots·na

Where are the toilets?
Kde jsou toalety? — gde ysoh *to*·uh·le·ti

SHOPPING & SERVICES

I'd like to buy ...
Chtěl/Chtěla bych koupit ... (m/f) — khtyel/*khtye*·la bikh *koh*·pit ...

Question Words

How?	*Jak?*	yuhk
What?	*Co?*	tso
When?	*Kdy?*	gdi
Where?	*Kde?*	gde
Who?	*Kdo?*	gdo
Why?	*Proč?*	proch

I'm just looking.
Jenom se dívám. — *ye*·nom se *dyee*·vam

Do you have any others?
Máte ještě jiné? — *ma*·te *yesh*·tye *yi*·nair

Can I look at it?
Mohu se na to podívat? — *mo*·hu se nuh to *po*·dyee·vuht

How much is it?
Kolik to stojí? — *ko*·lik to *sto*·yee

That's too expensive.
To je moc drahé. — to ye mots *druh*·hair

Can you lower the price?
Můžete mi snížit cenu? — *moo*·zhe·te mi *snyee*·zhit *tse*·nu

ATM	*bankomat*	*uhn*·ko·muht
internet cafe	*internetová kavárna*	*in*·ter·ne·to·va *kuh*·var·nuh
mobile phone	*mobil*	*mo*·bil
post office	*pošta*	*posh*·tuh
tourist office	*turistická informační kancelář*	*tu*·ris·tits·ka *in*·for·muhch·nyee *kuhn*·tse·larzh

TIME & DATES

What time is it?
Kolik je hodin? — *ko*·lik ye *ho*·dyin

It's (10) o'clock.
Je (deset) hodin. — ye (*de*·set) *ho*·dyin

Half past 10.
Půl jedenácté. (lit: half eleven) — pool *ye*·de·nats·tair

am (midnight–8am)
ráno — *ra*·no

am (8am–noon)
dopoledne — *do*·po·led·ne

pm (noon–7pm)
odpoledne — *ot*·po·led·ne

pm (7pm–midnight)
večer — *ve*·cher

yesterday	*včera*	*fche*·ruh
today	*dnes*	dnes
tomorrow	*zítra*	*zee*·truh

Numbers

1	*jeden*	*ye*·den
2	*dva*	dvuh
3	*tři*	trzhi
4	*čtyři*	*chti*·rzhi
5	*pět*	pyet
6	*šest*	shest
7	*sedm*	*se*·dm
8	*osm*	*o*·sm
9	*devět*	*de*·vyet
10	*deset*	*de*·set
20	*dvacet*	*dvuh*·tset
30	*třicet*	*trzhi*·tset
40	*čtyřicet*	*chti*·rzhi·tset
50	*padesát*	*puh*·de·sat
60	*šedesát*	*she*·de·sat
70	*sedmdesát*	*se*·dm·de·sat
80	*osmdesát*	*o*·sm·de·sat
90	*devadesát*	*de*·vuh·de·sat
100	*sto*	sto
1000	*tisíc*	*tyi*·seets

Monday	*pondělí*	*pon*·dye·lee
Tuesday	*úterý*	*oo*·te·ree
Wednesday	*středa*	*strzhe*·duh
Thursday	*čtvrtek*	*chtvr*·tek
Friday	*pátek*	*pa*·tek
Saturday	*sobota*	*so*·bo·tuh
Sunday	*neděle*	*ne*·dye·le

January	*leden*	*le*·den
February	*únor*	*oo*·nor
March	*březen*	*brzhe*·zen
April	*duben*	*du*·ben
May	*květen*	*kvye*·ten
June	*červen*	*cher*·ven
July	*červenec*	*cher*·ve·nets
August	*srpen*	*sr*·pen
September	*září*	*za*·rzhee
October	*říjen*	*rzhee*·yen
November	*listopad*	*li*·sto·puht
December	*prosinec*	*pro*·si·nets

TRANSPORT

What time does the bus/train leave?
V kolik hodin odjíždí autobus/vlak? — f *ko*·lik *ho*·dyin *od*·yeezh·dyee ow·to·bus/vluhk

Please tell me when we get to ...
Prosím vás řekněte mi kdy budeme v ... — *pro*·seem vas *rzhek*·nye·te mi kdi *bu*·de·me f ...

Does it stop at ...?
Staví v ...? — *sta*·vee v ...

What's the next stop?
Která je příští zastávka? — *kte*·ra ye *przheesh*·tyee *zuhs*·taf·kuh

Please stop here.
Prosím vás zastavte. — *pro*·seem vas *zuhs*·tuhf·te

Please take me to (this address).
Prosím odvezte mě na (tuto adresu). — *pro*·seem *od*·ves·te mye na (*tu*·to *uh*·dre·su)

One ... ticket to (Telč), please.	*... jízdenku do (Telče), prosim.*	... *yeez*·den·ku do (*tel*·che) *pro*·seem
one-way	*Jedno-směrnou*	*yed*·no·smyer·noh
return	*Zpátečni*	*zpa*·tech·nyee

first	*první*	*prv*·nyee
last	*poslední*	*po*·sled·nyee
next	*příští*	*przhee*·shtyee

bus	*autobus*	*ow*·to·bus
plane	*letadlo*	*le*·tuhd·lo
train	*vlak*	vluhk
tram	*tramvaj*	*truhm*·vai

I'd like to hire a ...	*Chtěl/Chtěla bych si půjčit ...* (m/f)	khtyel/*khtye*·luh bikh si *pooy*·chit ...
bicycle	*kolo*	*ko*·lo
car	*auto*	*ow*·to
motorbike	*motorku*	*mo*·tor·ku

Is this the road to ...?
Vede tato silnice do ...? — *ve*·de *tuh*·to *sil*·ni·tse do ...

Can I park here?
Mohu zde parkovat? — *mo*·hu zde *puhr*·ko·vuht

Where's a petrol station?
Kde je benzinová pumpa? — gde ye *ben*·zi·no·va *pum*·puh

I need a mechanic.
Potřebuji mechanika. — *pot*·rzhe·bu·yi *me*·khuh·ni·kuh

Do I need a helmet?
Potřebuji helmu? — *pot*·rzhe·bu·yi *hel*·mu

The car/motorbike won't start.
Auto/Motorka nechce nastartovat. — *ow*·to/*mo*·tor·kuh *nekh*·tse *nuhs*·tuhr·to·vuht

I have a puncture.
Mám defekt. — mam *de*·fekt

GLOSSARY

Becherovka – potent herb liqueur
čajovná – teahouse
ČD – Czech Railways
chrám/dóm – cathedral
ČSSD – Social Democratic Party
cukrárna – cake shop
dámy – sign on women's toilet
divadlo – theatre
doklad – receipt or document
dům – house or building
dům umění – house of art, for exhibitions and workshops
galérie – gallery, arcade
hlavní nádraží (hl nád) – main train station
hora – hill, mountain
hospoda or **hostinec** – pub
hrad – castle
hřbitov – cemetery
kaple – chapel
katedralá – cathedral
kavárna – café or coffee shop
Kč – koruna česká; Czech crown
kino – cinema
kostel – church
lékárna – pharmacy
město – town
most – bridge
muzeum – museum
muži – sign on men's toilet
nábřeží – embankment
nádraží – station
náměstí (nám) – square
národní – national
ostrov – island
palác – palace
páni – sign on men's toilet
pasáž – passage, shopping arcade
pekárna – bakery
penzión – guest house
pivnice – small beer hall
pivo – beer
pivovar – brewery
potok – stream
Praha – Prague
radnice – town hall
restaurace – restaurant
Roma – a tribe of people who migrated from India to Europe in the 10th century
rybník – fish pond
sady – garden, park, orchard
sgraffito – mural technique whereby the top layer of plaster is scraped away or incised to reveal the layer beneath
stanice – train stop or station
svatý – saint
tramvaj – tram
třída – avenue
ubytovna – dorm accommodation
ulice (ul) – street
ulička (ul) – lane
Velvet Divorce – separation of Czechoslovakia into fully independent Czech and Slovak republics in 1993
Velvet Revolution – bloodless overthrow of Czechoslovakia's communist regime in 1989
vinárna – wine bar/ restaurant
vlak – train
záchod – toilet
zahrada – gardens, park
zámek – chateau
ženy – sign on women's toilet
Zimmer frei – room free (for rent)

Behind the Scenes

SEND US YOUR FEEDBACK

We love to hear from travellers – your comments keep us on our toes and help make our books better. Our well-travelled team reads every word on what you loved or loathed about this book. Although we cannot reply individually to your submissions, we always guarantee that your feedback goes straight to the appropriate authors, in time for the next edition. Each person who sends us information is thanked in the next edition – the most useful submissions are rewarded with a selection of digital PDF chapters.

Visit **lonelyplanet.com/contact** to submit your updates and suggestions or to ask for help. Our award-winning website also features inspirational travel stories, news and discussions.

Note: We may edit, reproduce and incorporate your comments in Lonely Planet products such as guidebooks, websites and digital products, so let us know if you don't want your comments reproduced or your name acknowledged. For a copy of our privacy policy visit lonelyplanet.com/privacy.

OUR READERS

Many thanks to the travellers who used the last edition and wrote to us with helpful hints, useful advice and interesting anecdotes: Ahliddin Gaffar, Alessandra Furlan, George & Linda Moss, Martin Winter, Miguel Marcos, Rachel Backhouse

WRITER THANKS

Mark Baker

Thanks to my editors at Lonely Planet, my co-author Neil Wilson and lots of people on the ground in my adopted city of Prague. These include Kateřina Pavlitová at prague.eu, Irena Dudová, Zuzi & Jan Valenta at tasteofprague.com, Iva Roze Skochová, Petr Kučera, 'Karim' at pragulic.cz, and many more.

Neil Wilson

Many thanks go to Jan Valenta of Taste of Prague, and to Bogdan and Irina, Alena Volpakova, Kraig and Lisa, Carol and my co-researcher Mark Baker.

ACKNOWLEDGEMENTS

Climate map data adapted from Peel MC, Finlayson BL & McMahon TA (2007) 'Updated World Map of the Köppen-Geiger Climate Classification', Hydrology and Earth System Sciences, 11, 163344.

Cover photograph: Prague Castle and Charles Bridge, Kaito Baka/500px ©

THIS BOOK

This 12th edition of Lonely Planet's *Prague & the Czech Republic* guidebook was researched and written by Mark Baker and Neil Wilson. The previous four editions were also written by Mark and Neil. This guidebook was produced by the following:

Destination Editor Gemma Graham

Product Editors Genna Patterson, Anne Mason

Senior Cartographer David Kemp

Book Designer Gwen Cotter

Assisting Editors Gabrielle Innes, Anne Mulvaney, Victoria Harrison

Assisting Book Designer Ania Bartoszek

Cover Researcher Naomi Parker

Thanks to Ronan Abayawickrema, Claire Naylor, Karyn Noble, Sandie Kestell, Doug 'the human' Rimington, Kirsten Rawlings, Angela Tinson

Index

A
accommodation 290-2
  language 304
air travel 297-8, 300
amusement parks
  DinoPark 208
  Mořský Svět 100
  Výstaviště 99
Apple Museum 75
aquariums
  Moravian Museum 229
  Mořský Svět 100
  Výstaviště 99
Archbishop's Chateau 255
architecture 87, 249, 278-81
  art nouveau 279-80
  baroque 279
  communist 281
  cubist 280-1
  Dancing House 86
  functionalist 281
  Gothic 278
  Hotel International 101
  Lucerna Palace 81
  National Theatre 83
  neoclassical 279
  Renaissance 279
  Romanesque 278
  Rotunda of St Longinus 87
  Vila Tugendhat 230
  Zlín 249
area codes 295
art galleries, *see* museums and galleries
Art Gallery for Children 26
arts 273-7, *see also* literature, music
Astronomical Clock 68-9, **68**

B
Barborská 179
Baťa, Tomáš 249
beer 12, 19-20, 145, 286-8, **12**, **17**
  books 287
Bethlehem Chapel 76
Bezručovy sady 251
Black Tower 185
Blansko 232
boat travel 300-1
Bohemia 30, 173-224, **178**, **190-1**
  accommodation 173
  climate 173
  food 173
  highlights 174-8
  itineraries 182
  travel seasons 173
bone churches, *see* ossuaries
books 258, 282-4, 287
border crossings 298
breweries 286
  Budweiser Budvar Brewery 185, 287
  Chodovar Brewery 222
  Pilsner Urquell Brewery (Plzeň) 207, 287, **191**
  Regent Brewery 199-200
  Staropramen Brewery 111, 287
  Štramberk Municipal Brewery 254
Brownnosers (David Černý statue) 276
Brno 227-34, **228**
  accommodation 230-1
  drinking 233
  entertainment 233-4
  food 231-3
  nightlife 233
  sights 227-30
  travel to/from 234
Brno Observatory & Planetarium 230
Budvar (Budweiser) brewery, České Budějovice 185, 287
bus travel 298, 301, 302
business hours 294

C
Cabbage Market 227-9
camping 290
Capuchin Monastery 229
car travel 298-9, 301-2
  hire 302
Castle Spa 215
castles & chateaux 19
  Archbishop's Chateau 255
  Český Krumlov State Castle 10, 194, **10**
  Hluboka Chateau 189, **190**
  Hrad Loket 218
  Karlštejn Castle 11, 174-5, **11**, **174**
  Konopiště Chateau 176-7, **176**
  Lednice Chateau 244-6, **20**
  Mikulov Chateau 240
  Prague Castle 9, 18, 36, **40**, **9**, **36 39**, **138**
  Špilberk Castle 227
  Telč Chateau 235, **242**
  Třeboň Chateau 198-9
  Troja Chateau 101
  Valtice Chateau 244-6
  Znojmo Castle 246
cathedrals, *see* churches & cathedrals
caves 232, **226**
caving 232
cell phones 295
cemeteries
  Capuchin Monastery 229
  Jewish Cemetery (Mikulov) 238-9
  Jewish Cemetery (Třebíč) 237
  National Cemetery 183
  New Jewish Cemetery 91-2
  Old Jewish Cemetery 67, 71
  Olšany Cemetery 72, 91
  Vyšehrad Cemetery 101
Černín Palace 49
Černý, David 18, 59, 71, 143, 276
  installations 91, 101, 208
  MeetFactory 162
  sculptures 58, 60, 73, 77, 81, 83
České Budějovice 185-92, **186**
  accommodation 187
  drinking & nightlife 188-9
  entertainment 192
  food 188
  sights 185-7
  travel to/from 192
Český Krumlov 10, 192-8, **193**, **10**, **190**
  accommodation 195-6
  activities 195
  drinking 197
  entertainment 197-8
  food 196-7
  nightlife 197
  shopping 198
  sights 192-5
  travel to/from 198
Český Krumlov State Castle 194
Charles Bridge 9, 54-5, **8-9**, **54-5**, **136**
Charles Square 86-7
chateaux, *see* castles & chateaux
children, travel with 25-6, 230
churches & cathedrals
  Assumption of the Virgin Mary 245
  Bethlehem Chapel 76
  Cathedral of St Barbara 179
  Cathedral of Sts Peter & Paul 227, 229
  Chapel of St Jan Sarkander 249

Map Pages **000**
Photo Pages **000**

churches & cathedrals *continued*
Church of Mary Magdalene 214
Church of Our Lady Before Týn 61
Church of Our Lady of the Snows 82
Church of Our Lord's Transfiguration on Mt Tábor 203
Church of St James 70, 229, 235
Church of St Nicholas 247, **139**
Church of St Sebastian 240
Church of St Vitus 195
Church of Sts Peter & Paul 214
Church of the Ascension of the Cross 217
Church of the Assumption of the Virgin Mary 219-20
Church of the Holy Spirit 235
Church of the Most Sacred Heart of Our Lord 89
Church of the Virgin Mary & St Giles 200
Holy Hill 240
Loreta 47
Rotunda of Our Lady & St Catherine 246-7
Sedlec Ossuary 179, **10**
St Bartholomew Church 207
St Michael's Church 249
St Moritz Cathedral 248-9
St Nicholas Church 52-3, **139**
St Procopius' Basilica 237
St Vitus Cathedral 42-3, **2**, **42**
St Vladimír Church 221
St Wenceslas Cathedral 251
cinemas 159
climate 14, **14**, *see also* individual regions
climate change 297
Colloredo-Mansfeld Palace 71

Map Pages **000**
Photo Pages **000**

colonnades 214, 219, *see also* springs
consulates 292
Crematorium (Terezín) 184
Cubist Lamp Post 82
customs regulations 292
cycling 103, 171, 240, 300
Czech language 304-9 *see also* language

D

Daliborka 46-7
Dancing House 86
dangers, see safety
hitching 302
desserts 27, **27**
Diana Funicular Railway 211
Diana Lookout Tower 211
disabilities, travellers with 296
Divoká Šárka 109
dogs 271
Dolní náměstí 249
DOX Centre for Contemporary Art 96
drinking 286-8, *see also* individual locations
language 305-7, 307
drinks
beer 286-8
wine 240, 241, 245

E

economy 258-9
electricity 292
embassies 292
emergencies
language 307
Estates Theatre 75
etiquette 17, 170
events *see* festivals & events

F

festivals & events 21-2
Burning of the Witches (Pálení čarodějnic) 21
Český Krumlov International Music Festival 22
Dvořák Prague International Music Festival 22
Febiofest 21
Festival of Songs, Olomouc 22
International Music Festival 197
Karlovy Vary International Film Festival 216
Masopust 21, **2**
Prague Fringe Festival 22
Prague Spring 22, 108
Prázdniny v Telči Folk Music Festival 235
Three Kings' Day 21
Znojmo Wine Festival 247
film 159, 258, 284-5
fish ponds 200
food 19, 27-9, **27**, **29**
fish 200
language 305-7
oplatky 215
football 116
Forman, Miloš 284-5
fountains
Caesar Fountain 248
Hercules Fountain 248
Křižík's Fountain 99
Orion Fountain 248
Parnassus Fountain 228
Singing Fountain 219
Františkovy Lázně 217
Franz Kafka Monument 72
funicular railways
Petřín Funicular Railway 61

G

galleries, *see* museums & galleries
gardens, see parks & gardens
gay travellers 272, 292
Goat Hill 239-40
Graphite Mine 194

H

Hašek, Jaroslav 284
Havel, Václav 71, 83, 259, 268
health 293
Heydrich, Reinhard 82, 86, 94, 258, 265, 285
hiking 101-2, 240
Karlovy Vary 211
Mariánské Lázně 223
historic buildings
Colonnade 219
Estates Theatre (Prague) 75
Italian Court 180
Klementinum (Prague) 75
Mirror Maze 62
Municipal House (Prague) 72
New Town Hall (Prague) 87
Strahov Library 47
historic sites
Crematorium 184
Main Fortress 184
history 260-8
books 266
Celts 260
communism 267-8
Czech independence 265-6
Czech revival 265
Czechoslovakia, breakup of 268
Habsburg era 263-5
Holy Roman Empire 262
Hussite Wars 262-3
Moravian Empire 261-2
Nazi occupation 266-7
Slavs 260
Velvet Revolution 268
WWI 265-6
WWII 266-7
hitching 302
Hluboká Chateau 189, **190**
Hluboká nad Vltavou 189
Hodějov Pond 201
Holy Trinity Column 248, **243**
hostels 290
Hotel International 101
Hotel Jalta Nuclear Bunker 81
hotels 291
Hrabal, Bohumil 282-3
Hrad Loket 218
Hus, Jan 204
Hussites, the 203, 204

I

ice hockey 116, 270
insurance 293
internet access 293
internet resources 291
Italian Court 180
itineraries 23-4, **23**, **24**

J

Jan Palach Memorial 81
Jan Palach Square 72
Jan Žižka Statue 91
Jewish cemeteries 91, 94, 237, 238-9
Jewish history 20, 86, 264
Jindřišská Tower 85-6

Josefov 71-2
John Lennon Wall 59, **137**
Jubilee Synagogue 86

K

Kafka, Franz 41, 282-4, 264, 276, **285**
grave of 91,
monuments 72,
museums 58,
sculptures of 83,
Kampa 59
Karlštejn Castle 10, 174-5, **11**, **190-1**
Karlovy Vary 13, 211-19, **212-13**, **13**
accommodation 215-16
activities 215
drinking 217-18
entertainment 218-19
food 216-17
nightlife 217-8
sights 211-15
travel to/from 219
Karlštejn Castle 11, 174-5, **11**, **174**
K (David Černý Sculpture) 83
Kateřinská Cave 232
Kinský Palace 70
Klec 201
Klementinum 75-6
Konopiště Chateau 176-7, **176**
Křižík's Fountain 99-100
Klášterní pivovar Strahov 142, **17**
Kroměříž 254-6
Kun (David Černý statue) 276
Kundera, Milan 282-3, **282**
Kutná Hora 11, 179-81, **180**, **11**

L

language 17, 304-9, 305-9
Lednice Chateau 244-6, **20**
legal matters 293
Lego Museum 26
lesbian travellers 292
Lesser Fortress (Terezín) 182-3
literature *see also* books 282-4
Lobkowicz Palace 45-6
Loket 218
Loreta 47
Lucerna Palace 81

M

Main Fortress (Terezín) 184
Malostranské Náměstí 53
Maltese Square 60
Marian Plague Column 249
Mariánské Lázně 219-24, **220**
accommodation 222-3
activities 221
drinking 223-4
entertainment 224
food 223-4
sights 219-21
travel to/from 224
Masaryk, Tomáš 265-6
measures 291
Mělník Chateau 183
Memorial to the Victims of Communism 61
Mikulov 238-44, **239**
accommodation 240-1
drinking 241-4
food 241-4
sights 238-40
travel to/from 244
Mikulov Chateau 240
Miminka (David Černý art) 276
Mirror Maze 61
mobile phones 295
money 17, 292, 293-4
Moravia 30, 225-56, **226**, **242-3**
accommodation 225
climate 225
food 225
highlights 226
itineraries 231
travel seasons 225
Mořský Svět 100
motorcycle travel 298-9, 301-2
Municipal House 72
museums & galleries 19, 26
Archbishop's Palace 251
Archdiocesan Museum 250-1
Art Gallery for Children 26, 70-1
Bechyně Gate & Kotnov Tower 203
Bílek Villa 48
Brewery Museum 207
Castle Museum & Tower (Český Krumlov) 194
Charles Bridge Museum 76
Chemistry Gallery 96
City Museum 217
Convent of St Agnes 71
Czech Museum of Music 59-60
Czech Silver Museum 179
DEPO2015 208
Dox Centre for Contemporary Art 96
Dvořák Museum 87
Dvorak Sec Contemporary 71
Egon Schiele Art Centrum 194
Franz Kafka Museum 58
Fryderyk Chopin Memorial Museum 221
Futura Gallery 101
Gallery of Central Bohemia 179
Ghetto Museum 184
House at the Stone Bell 70
Hussite Museum 203
Jan Becher Museum 215
Kampa Museum 59
Karel Zeman Museum 53
Karlovy Vary Museum 215
KGB Museum 60
Kinský Palace 65
Kroměříž Museum 255
Lapidárium 100
Lego Museum 26, 77
Leica Gallery 81
Mánes Gallery 86
Marionette Museum 194
Mendel Museum 230
Miniature Museum 48
Moravian Museum 229
Moser Glass Museum 214-15
Mucha Museum 81
Municipal Museum 220-1
Musaion 61
Museum Fotoateliér Seidel 194
Museum Montanelli 56
Museum of Communism 82
Museum of Czech Cubism 75
Museum of Decorative Arts 71
Museum of Modern Art 249-50
Museum of Public Transport 100-1
Museum of Romani Culture 230
Museum of South Bohemia 185, 187
Museum of the Infant Jesus of Prague 59
Náprstek Museum 77
National Memorial to the Heroes of the Heydrich Terror 86
National Monument 90-1
National Museum 77, 80
National Museum New Building 80-1
National Technical Museum 94
Patton Memorial Pilsen 207
Prague City Museum 83-4
Prague Jewish Museum 13, 66-7, **13**, **66**
Puppet Museum 207
Regional History Museum 250
Regional Museum 194
Salm Palace 49
Schwarzenberg Palace 49
Smetana Museum 76
South Bohemian Aleš Gallery 189
South Bohemian Motorcycle Museum 185
St George Museum 176
Strahov Picture Gallery 47
Techmania Science Centre 208
Terezín Museum 184
Václav Havel Library 71
Veletržní Palác 11, 94, **11**
music 162, 273-5
classical music 273-4
jazz 274
rock 274-5
pop 274-5

N

Na Kopečku 201
Na Příkopě 81-2
Náměstí Přemysla Otakara II (České Budějovice) 185
Náměstí Republiky 249-50
Národní Třída 82-3
National Theatre 83
Nerudova 53-4
New Jewish Cemetery 91, 94
New Town Hall 87
Nový Svět Quarter 48

O

Ohřě River 218
Old Town Hall (Prague) 68-9, 68
Old Town Hall (Brno) 227
Old Town Square 10, 5, 10
Olomouc 12, 248-54, **250-1**, 12, 243
 accommodation 252
 drinking 253
 entertainment 253
 food 252-3
 nightlife 253
 sights 248-52
Olšany Cemetery 91
opening hours 294
oplatky 215
ossuaries
 Brno 229-30
 Sedlec Ossuary 10, 179, 10

P

painting 276-7
palaces, *see also* castle & chateaux
 Rosenburg Palace 46
Pařížská 72
parks & gardens
 Charles University Botanical Garden 88
 Children's Island 60
 Divoká Šárka 109
 Franciscan Garden 81
 Letná Gardens 94, 96
 Palace Gardens Beneath Prague Castle 56
 Riegrovy Sady 88-9
 Stromovka 98
 Vojan Gardens 58
 Wallenstein Garden 56
Parnassus Fountain 228
pensions 291
Petřín 60-1
phonecards 295
photography 277
Pilsner Urquell Brewery (Plzeň) 207, 287, 191
planning
 accommodation 16
 budgeting 15
 calendar of events 21-2
 children, travel with 25-6
 clothing 16
 Czech Republic basics 14-15
 Czech Republic's regions 30
 first-time visitors 16-17
 food 27-9
 internet resources 15
 itineraries 23-4
 Prague's neighbourhoods 34
 repeat visitors 18
Plzeň 205-11, **206**
 accommodation 208-9
 drinking 210
 entertainment 210
 food 209
 nightlife 210
 sights 207-8
 travel to/from 210-11
politics 258-9, 272
population 259, 269
post 170, 294
Powder Gate 75
Prague 9, 10, 30, 32-172, **34,** 5, 8-9, 10, 33, 34, 138
 accommodation 32
 Bubeneč 98-101, 120-1, 155-6, 168-9, **98-9**
 climate 32
 Dejvice 98-101, 120-1, 155-6, 168-9, **98-9**
 drinking 142-57
 entertainment 157-63
 events 108-9
 festivals & events 108-9
 food 32, 121-42
 highlights 33-8, 36-41, 42-3, 66, 68-9, 104-5
 Holešovice 94-7, 119-20, 134-5, 153-5, 161-2, 168 **96-7**
 Hradčany 44-5, 109, 111, 122, 142-3, 163, **44-5**
 internet resources 169
 itineraries 23, **23**
 Josefov 71-2
 Karlín 18, 89-94, 118-19, 133-5, 152-3, 162, 168, **92-3**
 Malá Strana 52-61, 111-12, 122-3, 143-4, 163, **50-1**, **57**
 Nové Město 77-88, 114-15, 128-30, 159-61, 147-9, 166-7, **78-9**, **84-5**
 nightlife 142-57
 Prague Castle area 163
 shopping 163-9
 sights 36-41, 42-3, 44-101
 sleeping 109-21
 Smíchov 101-3, 121, 141-2, 156-7, 162, 169, **102**, **106**
 Staré Město 61-77, 112-14, 125-8, 144-7, 157-9, 163-5, **62-3**
 tourist information 170-1
 tours 103, 106-108
 transport 171
 travel seasons 32
 travel to/from 297-300
 Vinohrady 88-9, 115-18, 130-3, 149-51, 161, 167-8, **88-9**
 Vršovice 88-9, 115-18, 130-3, 149-51, 161, 167-8, **88-9**
 Vyšehrad 101-3, 121, 141-2, 156-7, 162, 169, **102, 106**
 walks 57, 74, 95, 110, 123
 Žižkov 89-94, 118-19, 133-5, 152-3, 162, 168, **92-3**
Prague Castle 9, 18, 36, **40**, 9, 36, 39, 38
Prague Jewish Museum 13, 66-7, 13, 66
Prague Planetarium 100
Prague Zoo 97
Proudy (David Černý Sculpture) 58
public holidays 295
Punica Cave 232
puppets 26, 161, 162, 163, 164, 138
 museums 194, 207
 National Marionette Theatre 158

Q

Quo Vadis (David Černý Sculpture) 60

R

radio 291
religion 259, 269-70
road rules 301
Roma people 271-2
Rosenberg Palace 46
Rotunda of St Longinus 87-8
Royal Way 58
Rudolfinum 72
running 103

S

safety 302
Schwarzenberg Mausoleum 199
sculpture 277
Sedlec Ossuary 10, 179, 10
shopping
 language 307
Singing Fountain 219
Smítka 201
smoking 291
Špilberk Castle 227
springs
 Hot Spring Colonnade 211
 Mill Colonnade 211
 Park Colonnade 213
squares
 Charles Square (Prague) 86-7
 Dolní náměstí (Olomouc) 249
 Horní náměstí (Olomouc) 248
 Jan Palach Square (Prague) 72
 Malostranské Náměstí (Prague) 53
 Maltese Square (Prague) 60
 náměstí Zachariáše z Hradce (Telč) 235
 Žižkovo Náměstí (Tábor) 202
Staropramen Brewery 111, 287
Strahov Library 47
Strahov Monastery 47
Štramberk 254
streets
 Na Příkopě 81
 Národní Třída 82-3
 Nerudova 53
 Pařížská 72
St Nicholas Church 52-3, 139
St Vitus Cathedral 42-3, 2, 42
St Vitus Treasury 9
Šternberg Palace 48
 synagogues
 Great Synagogue 207
 High Synagogue 240
 Rear (New) Synagogue 237
 Synagogue (Český Krumlov) 195

T

Tábor 201-5, **202**
taxis 302
Telč 12, 235-7, **236**, 12, 242

Map Pages **000**
Photo Pages 000

Telč Chateau 235, **242**
telephone services 295
tennis 270
Terezín 182-5
time 295
  language 307-8
tipping 17, 291
toilets 295
tourist information 295-6
town halls
  New Town Hall (Prague) 87
  Old Town Hall (Brno) 227
  Old Town Hall (Prague) (68-9), 68
  Town Hall (Olomouc) 249
Toy Museum 46
train travel 299-300, 302-3
tram travel 302, **136**
transport
  language 308
travel to/from Czech Republic 297-300
travel within Czech Republic 300-3
Třebíč 237-8
Třeboň 198-201, **199**
Třeboň Chateau 198-9
Třeboňsko Protected Landscape 201
Troja Chateau 101
tunnels
  Cabbage Market 229
  Underground Passages 202-3
  Underground Plzeň 207
  Znojmo Underground 246
TV 291
TV Tower 91
Týn Courtyard 64-5

V

vacations 295
Václavské náměstí 250-1
Valtice Chateau 244-6
Valtice-Lednice 244-6
Veletržní Palác 11, 94, **11**
Velvet Revolution 268
Veselí nad Lužnicí 201
viewpoints
  Petřín Lookout Tower 61
  vineyards 86
visas 296
Viselec (David Černý Sculpture) 77
visual arts 275-7
Vltava River 195
volunteering 296
Vyšehrad Cemetery 101
Vyšehrad Citadel 104-5, **104**
Vyšehrad **106**
Výstaviště 99

W

walks 57, 74, 95, 110, 123
Wallenstein Palace 56
weather 14, **14**, *see also* individual regions
weights 291
Wenceslas Square 77, **136-7**
wine 19, 183, 240, 241, 245

Z

Žižka, Jan 203
Žižkovo Náměstí 202
Zlín 249
Znojmo 246-8
Znojmo Castle 246
zoos
  City Zoological Garden 230
  Zoo Plzeň 208

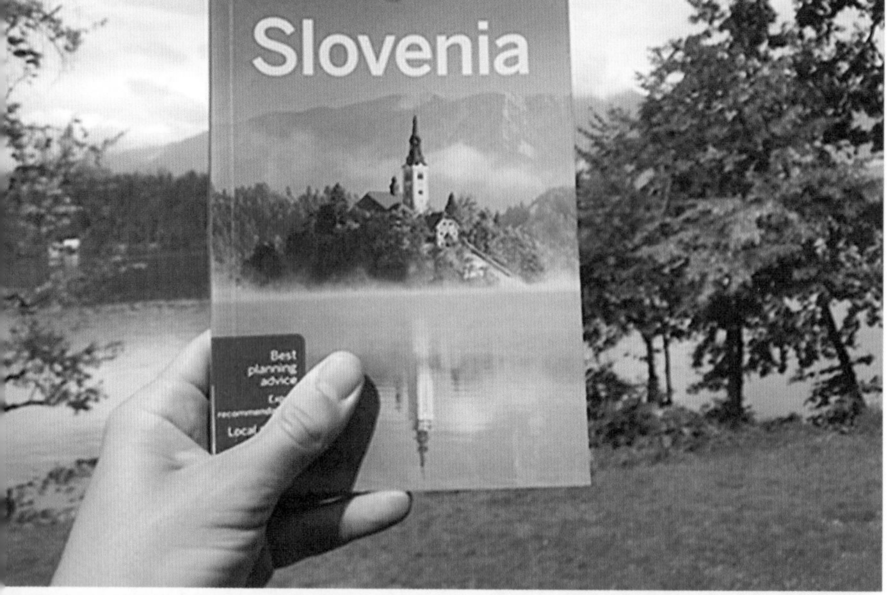

Map Legend

Sights
- Beach
- Bird Sanctuary
- Buddhist
- Castle/Palace
- Christian
- Confucian
- Hindu
- Islamic
- Jain
- Jewish
- Monument
- Museum/Gallery/Historic Building
- Ruin
- Shinto
- Sikh
- Taoist
- Winery/Vineyard
- Zoo/Wildlife Sanctuary
- Other Sight

Activities, Courses & Tours
- Bodysurfing
- Diving
- Canoeing/Kayaking
- Course/Tour
- Sento Hot Baths/Onsen
- Skiing
- Snorkelling
- Surfing
- Swimming/Pool
- Walking
- Windsurfing
- Other Activity

Sleeping
- Sleeping
- Camping

Eating
- Eating

Drinking & Nightlife
- Drinking & Nightlife
- Cafe

Entertainment
- Entertainment

Shopping
- Shopping

Information
- Bank
- Embassy/Consulate
- Hospital/Medical
- Internet
- Police
- Post Office
- Telephone
- Toilet
- Tourist Information
- Other Information

Geographic
- Beach
- Gate
- Hut/Shelter
- Lighthouse
- Lookout
- Mountain/Volcano
- Oasis
- Park
- Pass
- Picnic Area
- Waterfall

Population
- Capital (National)
- Capital (State/Province)
- City/Large Town
- Town/Village

Transport
- Airport
- Border crossing
- Bus
- Cable car/Funicular
- Cycling
- Ferry
- Metro station
- Monorail
- Parking
- Petrol station
- S-Bahn/Subway station
- Taxi
- T-bane/Tunnelbana station
- Train station/Railway
- Tram
- Tube station
- U-Bahn/Underground station
- Other Transport

Note: Not all symbols displayed above appear on the maps in this book

Routes
- Tollway
- Freeway
- Primary
- Secondary
- Tertiary
- Lane
- Unsealed road
- Road under construction
- Plaza/Mall
- Steps
- Tunnel
- Pedestrian overpass
- Walking Tour
- Walking Tour detour
- Path/Walking Trail

Boundaries
- International
- State/Province
- Disputed
- Regional/Suburb
- Marine Park
- Cliff
- Wall

Hydrography
- River, Creek
- Intermittent River
- Canal
- Water
- Dry/Salt/Intermittent Lake
- Reef

Areas
- Airport/Runway
- Beach/Desert
- Cemetery (Christian)
- Cemetery (Other)
- Glacier
- Mudflat
- Park/Forest
- Sight (Building)
- Sportsground
- Swamp/Mangrove

OUR STORY

A beat-up old car, a few dollars in the pocket and a sense of adventure. In 1972 that's all Tony and Maureen Wheeler needed for the trip of a lifetime – across Europe and Asia overland to Australia. It took several months, and at the end – broke but inspired – they sat at their kitchen table writing and stapling together their first travel guide, *Across Asia on the Cheap*. Within a week they'd sold 1500 copies. Lonely Planet was born.

Today, Lonely Planet has offices in Franklin, London, Melbourne, Oakland, Dublin, Beijing and Delhi, with more than 600 staff and writers. We share Tony's belief that 'a great guidebook should do three things: inform, educate and amuse'.

OUR WRITERS

Mark Baker

Curator, Prague, Moravia Mark is a freelance travel writer with a penchant for offbeat stories and forgotten places. He's originally from the United States, but now makes his home in the Czech capital, Prague.

He writes mainly travel guides on Eastern and Central Europe for Lonely Planet as well as several other leading travel publishers, but finds real satisfaction in digging up stories in places that are too remote or too quirky for the guides. He also contributes to publications like the *Wall Street Journal* and *National Geographic Traveler*. Prior to becoming an author, he worked as a journalist for the *Economist*, Bloomberg News and *Radio Free Europe*, among other organisations.

When he's not travelling, these days he's teaching Central European history and journalism at Anglo-American University in Prague or out riding his bike. He has a master's degree in International Affairs from Columbia University in New York.

Neil Wilson

Prague, Bohemia Neil was born in Scotland and has lived there most of his life. Based in Perthshire, he has been a full-time writer since 1988, working on more than 80 guidebooks for various publishers, including the Lonely Planet guides to Scotland, England, Ireland and Prague. An outdoors enthusiast since childhood, Neil is an active hill-walker, mountain-biker, sailor, snowboarder, fly-fisher and rock-climber, and has climbed and tramped in four continents, including ascents of Jebel Toubkal in Morocco, Mount Kinabalu in Borneo, the Old Man of Hoy in Scotland's Orkney Islands and the Northwest Face of Half Dome in California's Yosemite Valley.

Like most Lonely Planet authors, Neil fell into the guidebook-writing business by accident. Having fled the rat race of the oil industry soon after graduating as a geologist, he returned to university to do postgraduate research. But academia turned out to be just as dull as industry, so like any sane person he gave it all up to be a penniless writer. The penniless bit was easy. On the writing side, he began by producing articles for a Scottish magazine, but was soon off to photograph Corfu for a guidebook. Since then Neil has written and photographed dozens of guidebooks for several publishers.

Published by Lonely Planet Global Limited
CRN 554153
12th edition – November 2017
ISBN 978 1 7865 715 88

10 9 8 7 6 5 4 3 2 1
Printed in China